SOCIAL DEVELOPMENT
IN YOUNG CHILDREN

SOCIAL DEVELOPMENT IN YOUNG CHILDREN

SUSAN ISAACS

SCHOCKEN BOOKS · NEW YORK

First SCHOCKEN PAPERBACK edition 1972

First published 1933
Library of Congress Catalog Card No. 70-179484
Published by arrangement with Routledge & Kegan Paul Ltd
Manufactured in the United States of America

TO
JOAN RIVIERE

WHO HAS TAUGHT
ME TO UNDERSTAND
MY OWN CHILDHOOD

CONTENTS

	PAGE
PREFACE	xi
PART I. THE PSYCHOLOGICAL DATA	1
CHAPTER ONE: INTRODUCTION	3
CHAPTER TWO: RECORDS:	24
I. SOCIAL RELATIONS: LOVE AND HATE IN ACTION	30
A. PRIMARY EGOCENTRIC ATTITUDES	30
B. HOSTILITY AND AGGRESSION	35
1. Individual Hostility	35
a. The motive of possession	35
b. The motive of power	41
c. The motive of rivalry	48
d. Feelings of inferiority or superiority or general anxiety	64
2. Group Hostility	73
a. To strangers and new-comers	73
b. To adults	77
c. To younger or inferior children, or any temporary scapegoat	81
C. FRIENDLINESS AND CO-OPERATION	93
II. THE DEEPER SOURCES OF LOVE AND HATE	113
A. SEXUALITY	113
1. Oral erotism and sadism	113
2. Anal and urethral interests and aggression	121
3. Exhibitionism: a. Direct	135
b. Verbal	138
4. Sexual curiosity	140
5. Sexual play and aggression	143
6. Masturbation	147
7. Family play, and ideas about babies and marriage	155
8. Castration fears, threats and symbolism	163
9. "Cosy places"	167
B. GUILT AND SHAME	172
C. AN INDIVIDUAL CHILD: URSULA	188

CHAPTER THREE: THE THEORY OF DEVELOPMENT — 205

INTRODUCTION — 205

I. SOCIAL RELATIONS — 213

  A. PRIMARY EGOCENTRIC ATTITUDES — 213

  B. HOSTILITY AND AGGRESSION — 218

    1. Individual Hostility — 218
- a. The motive of possession — 221
- b. The motive of power — 226
- c. The motive of rivalry — 231
- d. Feelings of inferiority, superiority or general anxiety — 243

    2. Group Hostility — 247
- a. To strangers and new-comers — 255
- b. To adults — 256
- c. To younger or inferior children, or any temporary scapegoat — 264

  C. FRIENDLINESS AND CO-OPERATION — 266
- a. Friendliness to adults — 266
- b. Friendliness to other children — 272

II. THE DEEPER SOURCES OF LOVE AND HATE — 280

  A. SEXUALITY — 280

  Introduction — 280
1. Oral erotism and sadism — 321
2. Anal and urethral interests and aggression — 327
3. Exhibitionism (direct and verbal) — 335
4. Sexual curiosity — 339
5. Sexual play and aggression — 341
6. Masturbation — 345
7. Family play, and ideas about babies and marriage — 350
8. Castration fears, threats and symbolism — 354
9. "Cosy places" — 362

  B. GUILT AND SHAME — 366

  C. AN INDIVIDUAL CHILD: URSULA — 376

III. THE RELATION BETWEEN THE SOCIAL AND THE SEXUAL ASPECTS OF DEVELOPMENT	384
PART II. THE EDUCATIONAL PROBLEM	401
CHAPTER ONE: THE RELATION BETWEEN THE PROCESSES OF EDUCATION AND OF PSYCHO-ANALYSIS	403
CHAPTER TWO: SOME PROBLEMS AND CRISES OF EARLY SOCIAL DEVELOPMENT	414
APPENDIX I	457
APPENDIX II	458
APPENDIX III	462
BIBLIOGRAPHY	463
INDEX OF AUTHORS	469
INDEX OF SUBJECTS	470

PREFACE

THE bulk of the material which forms the basis of this study in the social and sexual development of children was gathered in my work at the Malting House School during the years 1924 to 1927. The first volume dealing with the records, *Intellectual Growth in Young Children*, appeared in 1930, and I had hoped that this second volume would follow at no longer interval than a year. Its preparation, however, has been much interrupted by other responsibilities, and I have only now been able to complete my theoretical survey of the material itself. This delay has yielded certain advantages. In the first place, I have been able in the interim to bring together a mass of other confirmatory material from various sources, which both support and further illumine the data gathered from the Malting House School itself. In the second place, certain other important publications have appeared in the interval, of which I have been able to make use in my final revision. One of these is Katherine Bridges' *Social and Emotional Development of the Pre-School Child*, upon the material of which I am glad to have been able to draw. I have not, however, found her theory of any particular use to my own understanding.

Of altogether greater significance have been the various papers by Melanie Klein and by M. N. Searl (see Bibliography) and the volume *The Psycho-Analysis of Children* published by the former just before my own book goes to press.

I am very deeply indebted to these two leaders in the psycho-analysis of children, not only for their published researches, but also for the personal teaching they have both given me in the work of child analysis. My theoretical interpretations of these observations of children's behaviour rest upon their fundamental and epoch-making researches into the psychology of infants and young children ; their work, in its turn, owes its foundations and its inspiration to the discoveries of Freud. My own personal study of young children has served only to increase my deep admiration and gratitude for the genius of Freud, in being able to penetrate so deeply and so surely to the actual mind of the little child, through the study of the minds of adults.

My acknowledgments are also due to the parents of the children whose observations I quote, and especially to those who have given me their friendly support and unqualified permission to use all the observations I made of their children. I wish to express my gratitude to them not only on my own behalf as author, but on the behalf of my fellow-psychologists, who may be able to use these records, and of other people's children who may benefit by them. Especial thanks are due to Ursula's mother, who with great patience and assiduity kept such full and detailed records of her daughter's sayings and doings, and allowed me to make use of even the more intimate passages, for the purpose of furthering the general understanding of children.

I have also to acknowledge the kindness of the friend who has allowed me to quote some relevant incidents from her notes upon the behaviour of the children in her own school; and of Dr. I. Schapera and Professor C. G. Seligman for letting me have the material of Appendix II.

I am indebted to Miss Hilda Lawrence for her patient care in preparing the index.

SUSAN ISAACS.

January, 1933.

PART I
THE PSYCHOLOGICAL DATA

CHAPTER ONE

INTRODUCTION

1. *Intention and Plan.* This book is addressed to the scientific public, and in particular to serious students of psychology and education. It is not intended as a popular exposition, whether of the psychological facts or of the relevant educational theory.

* * * * * * *

The main part of the material quoted and discussed was gathered in my school for young children, but in spite of this, I am offering it in the first instance (with the further material from other sources) as a contribution to psychology rather than to education. In order to keep this distinction as clear as I believe it should be, I have divided the book into two parts, the first devoted mainly to a survey of the actual facts of social behaviour in young children which I have had the opportunity of observing or collating, and the place of these facts in psychological theory; the second, to the bearing of the psychological facts upon the question of how the parent and teacher can best help the social development of their children. It seems likely that only by keeping these two realms of discussion apart in our minds can we bring ourselves, on the one hand, to face the facts dispassionately, or on the other, to see clearly what meaning, if any, they have for educational practice. Otherwise, we readily pre-judge the facts in the light of what we would have them be or feel they ought to be.

2. *The Value of Qualitative Records.* In my introductory chapter to *Intellectual Growth in Young Children*, I discussed

the value of purely qualitative records of children's behaviour, and the particular nature of the records offered there. The chapter was intended to introduce this present volume as well as *Intellectual Growth*, since the two together constitute a single study of the behaviour primarily of a particular group of children under particular conditions.

I there suggested that not only are such qualitative records an essential preliminary to fruitful experiment in genetic psychology, but that they may well remain an indispensable background and corrective, even when experimental technique is perfected. Without such a background of the total responses of children to whole situations, partial studies of this or that response to limited experimental problems may be no more than sterile and misleading artifacts.

The actual records of children's cognitive behaviour in *Intellectual Growth* established, I believe, the truth of this contention in the intellectual field. But the consideration holds good of social development even more profoundly. Experimental methods have in fact proved enormously fruitful in the study of intellectual growth, of learning and of language. But in the field of social development they are almost inapplicable. Most attempts to apply them have proved rather sterile. To study the moral development of children by asking for their judgments at different ages on a series of fables or of moral situations, for example, is to consider only one very limited aspect of the problem. To ask children what they think should be done in certain situations, or what they believe they themselves would do, is perhaps to learn something of their *ideas* of morality, but not of their *morality*. It is hardly even to study their ideas about it—but only such ideas as they dare to communicate. We can only study their effective morality in its spontaneous action in *real situations*.

The main development of technique in recent years among serious students of children's social life has been along the lines of *systematic observation*. Systematic observation has recently been defined by John E. Anderson, in his excellent discussion of *The Methods of Child Psychology*,[1] as " a technique . . . in which the observer selects beforehand from a mass of events which are occurring in the development of a child a particular event or series of events for observation, and develops a technique whereby

[1] *Handbook of Child Psychology*, 1931, pp. 1-27.

the observations are recorded regularly in accordance with a predetermined plan. Emphasis, however, should be placed upon the fact that the behaviour which is recorded is that which occurs naturally." Such observations are contrasted with *incidental observations*, made in a haphazard way under ordinary everyday conditions.

The records offered here from the Malting House School are systematic observations, not so much in the sense that particular series of events were selected out before they happened and then systematically recorded, but rather in the sense that something approximating to the total behaviour (in the large) of the children was noted down, and the whole chronological record then followed through for this and that systematic thread. Moreover, the life of the group was carried on under conditions controlled by a deliberate educational technique.[1]

A special type of systematic observation which is being more and more widely adopted, in the field of social behaviour as well as of general learning and language, is the *rating* method. In this, an attempt is made to arrive at a developmental scale for every sort of behaviour, in the relations of children with each other and with adults. Such a scale, of course, ultimately rests upon qualitative individual judgments, but it attempts by various devices to standardise these judgments and make them more objective and exact than ordinary impressions.

Much of Gesell's work is of this nature. In her important article on *The Social Behaviour of the Child*,[2] Charlotte Bühler has surveyed the yield of such studies to the time of her writing. One of the most interesting recent researches on these lines is that of Katherine Bridges, *Social and Emotional Development of the Pre-School Child* (1931). Professor Bridges holds that " the chief merit of the scales, both social and emotional, lies in the assistance they offer for the *qualitative* study and analysis of children's social and emotional development. With the help of the scales certain behaviour trends may be brought to light and subsequently given special educational treatment. Rough comparisons may also be made between children of the same group both with regard to general development and the persistence or changes of

[1] This technique is fully described in Chapter II of *Intellectual Growth in Young Children*.

[2] *Handbook of Child Psychology*, 1931, pp. 392-431.

certain specific trends. Further, parents, teachers and psychologists will find the scales particularly helpful as a means of training their own powers of observation. Consideration of results will also give them greater insight into the social and emotional significance of small aspects of children's behaviour which would ordinarily pass unnoticed " (pp. 36-7).

With these views I largely agree, and in due place I shall quote some of the valuable material which Professor Bridges has brought together in the course of her own study. And yet I feel that my own reservations with regard to the method of the rating scale are still justified, and may usefully be repeated here. " . . . It can never be allowed to take the place of a direct examination of the full concrete behaviour of children. The actual choice of items in the rating scale is again an act of qualitative perception, and systematic scrutiny of the actual events *from the psychological point of view* (not the ethical or educational) is an essential preliminary. It would be quite sterile to substitute premature quantitative treatment for detailed and concrete study of individual psychological events and their concrete inter-relations—especially if the rating scale were set up with an educational or moral bias, which apparently tends to be the case. The rate of change in children towards behaviour which is considered desirable is not more significant psychologically than the actual behaviour which they do show at any given stage. For instance, it is surely at least as important to investigate the concrete situations which give rise in particular children to aggressiveness or defiance as it is to estimate the degree of their social adaptiveness at a given age, on a conventional scale."[1]

This need for caution in entering upon extensive quantitative studies has, I think, been further reinforced by some of the actual researches recently carried out.

Briefly, the major error into which quantitative studies handling large masses of data readily fall is the oversimplification of the problem, and the treatment of very different situations as being essentially the same. This happens through the overlooking of qualifying differences—differences which most *un*academic persons used to observing children and their parents would know to be vital. A few examples may suffice.

[1] *Intellectual Growth in Young Children*, pp. 5-6.

One of the most significant, and indeed a classical example, is provided by Watson. In *Psychological Care of Infant and Child*, Watson advocates that mothers should " condition " their children not to reach out for things they are not intended to have, for example, utensils on the meal table, by rapping them over the knuckle with a pencil. He appears seriously to suggest that such a situation, in which *the mother* deliberately causes pain to the child (its slightness is irrelevant), is exactly parallel to the child's falling down and bumping his own knee on the floor. That is to say, if the mother makes her attitude impersonal and unemotional, she really becomes as neutral *to the child* as a piece of furniture is. Such a proposition surely needs only to be stated to be seen as false.

Moreover, as regards the innate fears of young children, the careful recent observations by C. W. Valentine,[1] largely repeating Watson's work, have shown that the stimuli to such fears are never simple. The setting is always all-important, and it is a *whole situation* which affects the child. The presence or absence of the mother, for instance, may make all the difference to the child's actual response.

This social factor of the child's response to particular adults has again been shown to be important in a recent study of children's day-time habits of sleep, in which it has been elaborately demonstrated that children will settle down to sleep more readily and sleep longer with one particular person in charge, than with another.[2] My own impression is that the behaviourists generally altogether under-estimate the significance of this type of social factor, because of their predilection for isolated mechanical situations. It is touched upon incidentally here and there, but little significant use is made of it.

The importance of the social factor is again emphasised by one extremely interesting result in Brainard's attempt to repeat Koehler's experiments on apes with his own young child.[3] The child's first response to her father's unusual behaviour in putting a proffered chocolate out of the window, in order to see whether she would understand how to get it,

[1] C. W. Valentine, " The Innate Bases of Fear ", *Journal of Genetic Psychology*, Vol. XXXVII.
[2] R. Staples, " Some Factors Influencing the Afternoon Sleep of Children ", *Journal of Genetic Psychology*, Vol. XLI.
[3] P. Brainard : " The Mentality of a Child Compared with that of Apes ", *Journal of Genetic Psychology*, Vol. XXXVII, p. 268.

was a social one, an exclamation of protest at her father doing such an unheard of thing—" Hi ! " she said ; and then a moment later, " Daddy get it ! " Only when she had got over the shock of her father's perverse behaviour was she able to deal with the cognitive problem itself.

Those investigators who are attempting to build up rating scales and schedules for social and emotional development do not always seem to me to provide sufficiently against the risk of over-simplification, for example, the neglect of the difference in the reactions of a child according to whether he is at home or in school. Most of us have had experience of how differently a child may behave in these two environments. A single illustration may suffice to show how striking the difference may be.

" My little girl, practically eight years old, is so difficult to manage as to be almost impossible, most of the time (at home). She does not always say ' No ' but either ignores and does not answer—or pretends she has not heard or seen. What worries us far more than that is her excessive cheek and answering back most rudely. She must always have the last word. If she cannot go on being as cheeky and rude as one can possibly be and answering back, she cries in a most babyish way, always making a dreadful noise. She is never spoken to except in a polite, kindly way—has never seen anything but kindness all around her, and we cannot understand where she gets it from. Her little brother, nearly five, adores her and would do anything for her, whereas she can be awfully unkind and cruel to him. She will often say she wished we had not got him—also that she does not love her Daddy or Mummy. Although she is so impossible at home, she behaves quite well at school. In desperation I have been twice to consult her head mistress, and have been told that never had she been punished or even had her name called for the least offence ; her teachers have nothing but praise for her and are most satisfied with her progress, behaviour and everything."

One could take point after point of those appearing on the various rating scales or developmental schedules, and show how far they are from being single trends which can be measured in themselves apart from specified total situations. For instance, rating scales sometimes attempt to quantify and grade the child in cleanliness and control of sphincters. But one finds children who are clean in one respect and very far from clean in another. I have had many cases of children who were perfectly clean and independent as regards the bowel from one and a half years, but difficult and dirty with regard to bladder control up to three or four years and even later. Cleanliness is by no means a single factor. Moreover, the child may be clean and responsible when in the hands of one adult, and not with another. I quote later on (p. 330) a little girl who was obstinately constipated, but volunteered to a new nurse, "I will do my 'duty' for *you*."

At various later points, I shall be able to bring out another set of facts of the greatest relevance to rating scales and developmental schedules, namely, the way in which children who have been " conditioned " to clean habits in the earliest weeks, and appear to have established such habits perfectly, may break down completely later on, and show a further period of months, or even years, in which they are extremely difficult and dirty. These facts are unintelligible on any quantitative approach, and can only be understood in terms of qualitative emotional experience.

In general, one can say with regard to development under five years, that *what a child does for one person under certain conditions is no reliable index of what he may do for another person in another situation.* The state of flux of the affective-conative trends in the mental life of young children is bound to influence their particular response in any given situation, and that in a way which cannot be predicted on the basis of simple inspection of previous reactions to previous situations, unless the inner aspects of these events in the psychic life of the child have been understood. Moreover, the hair trigger action of external events (for example, loss of the nurse or the mother, severe treatment for bed-wetting, forcible interference with thumb-sucking, unhappy experiences with other children, etc.) causing a profound redistribution of internal forces at any point of experience, may alter the course of the child's development in a way that could hardly be foreseen at an earlier age. There is great need for a new critique of rating scales and developmental schedules on the basis of the educated clinical judgment of investigators with a psycho-analytical training. In my third volume in this series I hope to present two parallel pictures of one child, as he was superficially observed in the school and as he was seen through the analytic technique; and this may help to make the point still clearer.

The need for such a critique with a proper perspective in regard to the psychological significance of details of behaviour is, I think, shown most clearly in the theory offered by Katherine Bridges, who groups together, under the term "mannerism," such various types of behaviour as thumb-sucking, nail-biting, nose-picking, twisting of the clothes, grimacing, rubbing of the eyes, scratching, etc., and masturbation, not, however, to show how these "mannerisms" may be a substitute for genital masturbation, occurring under the pressure of guilt, but (apparently) in order to suggest that masturbation itself is of no greater psychological significance than such "mannerisms" as grimacing and twisting. Moreover, the poverty of her interpretative theories actually makes it possible for her to suggest (apparently) that the specific emotions of fear and anger are not to be seen in the young infant, and are scarcely differentiated until two years of age. This seems again to me a case of eyes blinded by inadequate psychological theory.

This present study, like that of *Intellectual Growth in Young Children*, is based entirely upon the spontaneous behaviour of children in the real situations of their daily social life. Its primary aim is the direct qualitative study of the individual children's feelings and doings amongst their fellows, but many of the problems it raises (e.g. the question of normality) are linked up with quantitative issues, and may help to prepare the ground for these.

3. *The Subject-Matter of the Book.* I have called this volume *Social Development in Young Children*, but with regard to its subject-matter there are certain considerations which I feel it important to bring forward at once.

A. In the first place, it is entirely on the ground of practical convenience that I have dealt with the problems of social development separately from those of intellectual growth. In reality, these two aspects of children's life are bound together in the closest intimacy. Those who have read my first volume will remember how much of the children's *discovery, reasoning and thought* was the fruit of their common activities in play, and social in its very texture.

The great bulk of the material quoted in *Intellectual Growth* would thus illustrate the children's social development. It would do so in one sense, indeed, even more significantly than much of the material offered in the present volume, since it represents a large part of the children's positive, constructive social relations. Whereas a good deal of the behaviour to be quoted now represents either the pre-social matrix of individual feeling and phantasy out of which social relations are differentiated, or those disruptive forces which have to be transformed before positive social relations can be maintained. For a full or a just picture of social development in young children, therefore, the two volumes need to be read together.

B. In the second place, a glance at the table of contents of this volume will show that I have included in my present survey a great deal of behaviour which would not ordinarily be called " social " in the narrow meaning. In the strictest sense of organised group reciprocity, there is little truly social behaviour among children under seven or eight years. Piaget has expressed this fact by saying that it is not until seven or eight years that " the social instinct develops . . . in clear-cut forms ".[1] I do not myself feel that this is the best way of regarding the facts referred to, for reasons I hope to show in my theoretical chapter. But the facts themselves are fairly certain. Not until the middle years of childhood does one see that ability in the child to identify himself with his equals, and to maintain a positive attitude to them in spite of minor differences of individual interest, which underlies *stable* group relations. In the earlier years, the child is very largely a naïve egoist, and other children are to him mainly rivals for the love and approval of adults. With continuous support from adult justice and adult love, little children can carry on sustained co-operative pursuits, but their ability to do so seems to rest heavily upon this binding force of the love and approval of adults.

The more truly social ways of older children have their *beginnings* in early childhood, however. Their roots lie in the family itself. The child's relation with his mother can be called social from a very early age, in the sense that there is a mutual action and reaction of feeling and behaviour. And his complicated emotional attitudes towards the two parents together and separately from, say, six months onwards, are the key to many of his later responses to other children. The " social instincts " do not appear in the child unheralded.

[1] J. Piaget, *Judgment and Reasoning in the Child*, p. 209.

They have a pre-history which it is the task of genetic psychology to trace out.

That is what I have essayed to do in this volume. I have tried to unravel the pattern of the young child's behaviour so as to show the threads by which his pre-social feelings and phantasies are carried forward into the social relations of later life. When I came to the study of the records I was concerned, for example, with the problem of social *co-operation*, why it is so unstable in young children, and what the psychological changes are which make it more stable in later childhood. The material given here will suggest that the answer to these queries is by no means that a new set of *instincts* appear at a given age. It is rather that the young child's marked *ambivalence* of love and hate towards his fellows becomes gradually and effectively less. And it does so, partly because a wider experience enables him to project much of his hostility on to children outside his immediate circle of playmates, but partly also because his emotional conflicts tend to become less acute at the onset of the "latency period" of sexual development.[1]

I was interested, too, in the problem of the development of social *responsibility*, and the forms which the individual's conscience in relation to his fellows first assumes. And the study of these children's behaviour very quickly showed that their feelings of guilt were bound up with their sexual interests and aggression no less than with their more direct social relationships.

In these ways, I was led to deal with the emotional life of the children as a whole. It became clear that one could not be content to study only the developing superstructure of explicitly social relations, but needed also to penetrate to their underlying foundations in the child's more intimate personal and bodily responses to adults and to other children.

The spontaneous behaviour of these children fully confirms what the psycho-analytic study of individuals had already shown, viz. that it is to the family rather than to the herd that we must look for an understanding of human social life. And the study of the child's early emotional experiences in the family situation necessarily includes those bodily feelings and

---

[1] These brief and rather cryptic remarks will be found fully amplified in Chapter Three.

interests, and the wishes and phantasies arising out of them, which together constitute infantile sexuality.

The whole problem thus becomes one of tracing out the complicated interplay between all the different sides of the child's development—social co-operation, hostility, guilt and sexuality.

C. The material I am offering here thus of necessity includes records of those sorts of behaviour in young children (sexual interests, aggressive conduct and guilt feelings) which are usually slurred over, hidden away, or altogether denied by ordinary people and by many psychologists ; or, if admitted, then considered wholly exceptional and deeply abnormal. The evidence I give here will (I believe) go far towards establishing the view that such behaviour is neither abnormal nor very unusual. But since many readers may be disturbed by these particular records, I wish to state at the very outset what my reasons are for gathering and publishing them. I do so with a full sense of my responsibilities.

a. The first reason is that I myself happen to be interested in *everything* that little children do and feel. I am unable to accept the idea that anything that is true of children can be too shocking for adults to know. If a thing is true, we should surely be able to bear knowing it. If it is *said* to be true, or wears any air of truth, then all lovers of children must needs find out how far and in what way it is true. And I know that I am not alone (even apart from psycho analytic circles) in this willingness to discover the full truth about children. There are enough genuine lovers and dispassionate students of children to justify my offering all the facts.

b. The second is the great, the desperate need of children themselves to be *understood*.

I do not mean to suggest that it is necessary (or possible) for every parent and teacher to have a detailed understanding of the *deeper* psychological problems of their children, nor that they cannot be excellent educators without it. This is a question which I go into more fully in the second part of the book, where I discuss in detail the relation between psychoanalysis and education. Nevertheless, it is my hope that the publication of these records and their theoretical discussion will benefit ordinary parents and teachers and children indirectly in certain definite ways.

I believe it would be an advantage for all parents of young children to have the general knowledge that little children normally have sexual interests, since then they would be less likely to hurt their own children by excessive horror or severity if they met with any open expression of these interests. One hears now and then of mothers who have treated their children as pariahs for some openly sexual behaviour of a kind that needed little more than common-sense in handling.[1] The attitude of parents and nurses to such behaviour will, of course, always be largely determined by their personal reactions; but in part at least, it is affected by the general atmosphere of educated thought about such matters. In any particular case, the balance may be turned towards wisdom and understanding by the knowledge that the behaviour in question is not unheard-of in children who are normal and lovable and who grow up quite satisfactorily. The general sum of current knowledge does influence parental attitudes to some real extent, in this as in all other matters affecting early education.

Again, however, I may say here what I show more fully in later sections of the book—I do not mean to suggest that sexual or aggressive behaviour in young children should simply be *sanctioned* by their educators. There is no reason to doubt that children need our help against the internal anxiety which their sexual and aggressive wishes spontaneously engender. But the question of *how* we can best help the child is by no means so simple or so obvious as is often assumed. The one thing certain is that the common attitude of, on the one hand, denying that children have these wishes, and, on the other, treating the slightest outward expression of their existence with crushing severity (and, incidentally, always blaming other people's children), is *not* the most desirable. A great many people somehow manage to say almost in the same breath that such things do not happen, and that they ought not to be allowed to happen. But this automatic policy of hushing up the facts, either with or without harsh treatment of the children who do not easily learn to hide them, is very far from being the most helpful. To prevent children forcibly

[1] In a footnote to " The Mentally Unstable Child and its Needs ", *Studies in Mental Inefficiency*, January 15th, 1921, Dr. Robert Hughes says : " I was informed a short time ago of a case in which a child of five had been diagnosed as a moral imbecile solely on account of a certain sex habit."

from talking does not necessarily prevent them from feeling and wishing. To whip or scold them severely *may* do serious harm, and cannot do more good than to make the child hide his impulses and phantasies from grown-ups, even when it succeeds in doing this. Several of the children quoted here were scolded or whipped at home for rude remarks, but how little this treatment helped is seen by the way their phantasies broke out again into open expression on the first opportunity.

On the whole, it is probably true (as I shall amplify later) that the natural reaction of the more understanding and sympathetic parent towards such behaviour in children is sound. " It's better not to do those things—come and do these other things instead." Mild, sensible handling, that does not make the child feel himself to be a monster or an outcast, but nevertheless holds up firm standards of restraint and consideration for others, will carry most children safely through this early and most difficult phase of emotional development, as the methods of any good nursery school show.

If one could win parents generally to realise that occasional or mild masturbation, for example, or other open expression of sexuality, is a common happening belonging to a normal phase of development, and one best dealt with indirectly, then the real danger of too harsh treatment might be avoided. But, on the other hand, if one could get it widely understood that where masturbation is continuous or persistent, the child is in urgent need of skilled therapeutic help, *not* whippings or leg splints, then a great deal of serious mental disturbance in later life might be happily forestalled.

It would be an advantage, too, if parents and nurses had the general knowledge that the tempers and tantrums, the defiance and stubbornness, the phobias and night-terrors, the idiosyncrasies about food and difficulties as to training in cleanliness, which are liable to arise at any time in any ordinary nursery or nursery school, are themselves mainly the outcome of deep-seated mental conflict connected with the sexual life. It would be a great help to many parents if they understood that in minor degrees such difficulties *are* common and normal, and that the child will probably grow out of them with sensible handling ; but that where they are specially severe or prolonged, the help of a psycho-analyst should be sought.

Such difficulties, of more than a negligible degree of severity, are far commoner than is yet realised by parents generally, or even by many psychologists. I have recently[1] drawn attention to this fact, and to its theoretical significance, in a paper dealing with psychological material gathered from a group of personal letters from mothers and nurses. These letters describe in detail the behaviour of particular children, and ask for practical advice. Out of a total of six hundred and twelve letters, four hundred and twenty raise problems of *difficult* behaviour. I have drawn upon this material in the *Records* chapter, and give a classification of the specific problems dealt with.

In so far as it helps towards the understanding of such difficulties, then, I believe my book to be a contribution to the present general movement for mental hygiene.

There are, moreover, certain aspects of modern nursery technique, for example the growing practice of very early and rigid training in bowel and bladder routine, which I am not sure are soundly based. There are facts which suggest that this early and unremitting attempt to make the child " clean " may be at the best a waste of time, and at the possible worst, an influence tending towards guilt and unhappiness.

Certainly we cannot hope to discover the *best* technique for training the child in personal cleanliness and the connected social standards unless we have some understanding of what these things mean in the emotional life of the child himself. The question is one which calls for further research, and some of the material I offer in this book has a definite bearing upon it. In a later section I take it up again more fully. Here I adduce it only to point out one of the directions in which the facts quoted in this volume may be of indirect benefit to ordinary parents, by helping to modify the teaching that is now being given in infant welfare centres and in books on nursery training.

c. My third reason for publishing all this material is its scientific value. Whether or not the ordinary parent and teacher is better off for knowing all these facts, it is unquestionable that neither the academic psychologist nor the psychotherapist can afford to shut his eyes to them. The most

[1] " Some Notes on the Incidence of Neurotic Difficulties in Young Children." *British Journal of Educational Psychology*, Vol. II, Parts I and II.

fundamental questions of genetic theory are bound up with them, as I hope to show.

At the very time when I was gathering together most of the facts here presented, one of our leading Professors of Education found himself able to tell the public that " the dogma of infantile sexuality is now exploded ". To speak of the theory as a " dogma " obviously implies that it is an article of belief resting upon no actual evidence. The objective behaviouristic records offered here are, I think, enough to show that it is neither a dogma, nor " exploded ". Much of the ground covered is familiar everyday stuff to the psycho-analyst, whether of children or adults; but it is seen here in directly observed spontaneous behaviour, and not arrived at by any process of interpretation.

These observations of mine are not, however, by any means the only objective records now available. An experienced American child psychologist has recently stated, " After infancy he (Freud) says that the sexual life of the child manifests itself in the third and fourth year in some form accessible to observation. Nursery school experience with children of this age supports Freud's opinion. Three and four years is the age of curiosity about sex parts, male and female, and about the origin of babies. It is the period of continued playing and experimenting with parts of the body. It is also the period in which adult inhibitions come into play. The age period of three and four years, then, constitutes a stage in the development of sex."[1] The confirmatory evidence I am able to offer from a wide variety of first-hand sources will support this view further. It will be noted that none of the other authors quoted in the *Records* is a psycho-analyst.

It was with this sort of consideration in mind that I decided, whenever possible, to give the actual instances in detail of the behaviour in question, and not to content myself with such general statements as that " children do behave sexually from time to time ", or " I have definite evidence to show that they are interested in sexual organs and the relations between their parents " and so on and so forth. Such general statements are practically worthless as significant evidence, since nobody knows from them how often and in what

[1] Helen T. Woolley, " Eating, Sleeping and Elimination," *Handbook of Child Psychology*, 1931, p. 66.

particular way the phenomena referred to occur. It might be very rarely, it might (as far as such statements would show) be the greater part of the time. Moreover, such general statements would leave it open to controversialists to presume that I meant by " sexuality " something to which they would not accord the name. Only the actual instances of words and behaviour will enable readers to understand just what I do mean by my descriptive terms, and to know how often and in what circumstances the phenomenon occurs.

With regard to the material gathered in my own school, I have endeavoured to record, and am offering here, practically every instance of such behaviour which took place under my cognisance, and that of my assistants, during the period I was in charge of the school. Naturally I cannot claim that it is in fact a total record, since neither I nor any of my staff was always free to write down these (or any other) instances at the moment they occurred, or as soon after as made memory reliable. But I am content that it is not far short of complete, and enough so to suffice, whether for judgment of the behaviour of these particular children, or for theoretical purposes. With much of the material from other sources, too, it will be seen that I am able to give actual first-hand descriptions of the children's behaviour, or their actual sayings. Where the statements are generalised ones, they are nevertheless drawn from unimpeachable first-hand observations, and are nowhere mere opinions or theories.

D. With regard to the material from my own school, there are further important (and to some extent personal) considerations which I should like to make clear, since they may help to keep a proper psychological perspective.

a. In the first place, this was not a " psycho-analytic school ", as was sometimes said by other people. I do not know what a " psycho-analytic school " might be, nor, I imagine, did those who so spoke of it.

The basis for this notion in other people's minds was mainly that I was known to accept psycho-analytic theories of neurosis, and to be a member of the British Psycho-Analytical Society. But this does not *necessarily* affect one's educational practice. I was a trained teacher of young children and a student of Dewey's educational theories long before I knew anything about Freud, and by no means approached the work of the school solely or primarily as a psycho-analyst.[1]

My psycho-analytic experience did naturally lead me to be interested in *all* the behaviour of the children, and meant that I was not prepared to select from it, for recording and for active understanding, only such behaviour as pleased me or as fitted into the general convention as to what little children feel and talk about, or what they should feel and talk about. I was just as ready to *record* and to *study* the less attractive aspects of their behaviour as the more pleasing, whatever my aims and preferences as their *educator* might be.

On the educational side, I took up the work with the deliberate hope that a greater degree of freedom in the children's relations with each other than is usually allowed, and especially a greater freedom of verbal expression of their feelings and interests, would prove a benefit to them both in their intellectual and in their social development. But, as I have tried to make clear in Chapter II of *Intellectual Growth in Young Children*, the educational method of the school was by no means simply a crude "freedom". It followed a definite technique with clear positive aims, a technique which I yet kept open to modification in the light of any further understanding which the actual behaviour of the children might yield. My attitude was rather more tentative with regard to the sexual curiosity and excremental interests of the children than elsewhere, since I felt that a good deal more watching and learning was needed there, before anyone could be certain that the *best* educational technique had been reached. Above all, the first necessity was to ascertain the actual facts. (To this problem I return in full detail in Part II.)

When, however, particularly troublesome sorts of behaviour arose, such as spitting (among a few of the children), I saw no

---

[1] In this connection, I need to point out that the reference made by Bertrand Russell in *The Scientific Outlook* (p. 186) to my school and to my book *Intellectual Growth in Young Children* is somewhat misleading. On the intellectual side, the school could hardly be described as an "application of psycho-analytic theory to education". It was far more truly an application to the education of very young children of the educational philosophy of John Dewey. This was my active inspiration. The only point at which psycho-analytic theory is touched in *Intellectual Growth in Young Children* has reference to its confirmation of the view, long held by psychologists and educationists in general, of the great educational value of *play*.

reason for departing from my general educational methods in this particular instance, and treating such behaviour with harsh reproof or whipping. The deliberately milder methods I followed did in fact achieve their end, and (I believe) without the real disadvantages of more severe treatment; but they took longer to stop the trouble than sharper ways of reproof would have done. One or two of the less understanding parents were terribly shocked on hearing or seeing that spitting sometimes happened (as if these were the first children who had ever been known to spit—or perhaps, shall I say, as if I myself enjoyed it), and one child was withdrawn from the school on the ground that I refused to whip him for spitting.

So with regard to the children's verbal aggression by remarks about excretions. Here, too, I followed steadily the general methods of education which I had already reason to believe were more fruitful and more permanently satisfactory than mere prohibitions, and took up sharper lines of action (such as definite reproof or isolation) only when these seemed really necessary in the special circumstances. That the methods followed were in fact advantageous is, I believe, abundantly proved by the total records of the school.

The actual reward of free social co-operation, rich æsthetic achievement and bold intellectual inquiry among the children did not, of course, appear all at once. It did come in due time.

b. In the second place, some things may usefully be said about the particular children in the school. (I have often been asked about these details, when lecturing on the methods of the school, and thus have reason to think they may be of general interest.)

The round dozen of boys (between the ages of 2;8 and 4;11) whom I had in the school during the first term offered a variety of types and temperaments. They were children from professional families, but were brought to the school at what was then (1924) for middle-class people in England an unusually early age, for two quite different sorts of reason. Some of them were the children of parents who understood the value of early education and of opportunities for social life in these years. These parents were fully sympathetic to the aims and methods of the school, and more helpful than I can ever acknowledge in their continued understanding and support. Others of the children in this very beginning of the school were sent only because they had already proved themselves difficult to manage at home. The parents of two or three of these children turned out to be not in the least sympathetic to the actual methods of the school, nor understanding of the nature of the educational problem their children created. They appeared to expect me to bring about a radical change in behaviour and attitude by some sort of educational magic, and when I was not at once able to do this, they blamed me and the school for the unhappiness and difficult behaviour of the children, apparently forgetting their own previous problems altogether. Very naturally, these children were taken away from the school, some at the end of the first term, others during the course of the first year.[1] By this process of natural selection, we presently had a group of parents who understood and valued the work of the school and gave it continued support to the time when it had to close down for financial reasons.

What, then, happened to these difficult children ? I have elsewhere summed up the course of the first year's life in the school, and may perhaps quote that description here. " During the first and critical year the behaviour of the children went through a succession of well-marked phases. The first was one of brief quiet and subduement, due in part to the strangeness of a new place and new people ; and in part, at least as regards the difficult children, to the expectation of the same kind of punishment as they were used to at home. Then they began to wake up to the fact that over a large area of their desires and impulses the customary checks and penalties were removed. They found not only that they were free to run about, and to occupy themselves in any way they liked, either with real material or phantasy, but also that at the first hint of quarrelsomeness they were not forcibly separated or scolded or spanked. Then followed an outburst of disorder and boisterousness, in which the aggressiveness of eleven or twelve physically healthy young boys found vent. Throughout this period a considerable amount of constructive play went on, and there were many periods of happy co-operation and contentment, of friendliness and affection to grown-ups. But there were hours when the majority of the children

[1] I do not mean that all children who did not stay more than one year in the school were "difficult". There were one or two who left for other reasons.

were concerned merely to assert themselves over against the others, sometimes in direct aggression, provoked or unprovoked, sometimes in destroying the activities of others, and in open hostility to the adults present. Then gradually, and with occasional resurgences of mere wild disorder, the group began to take a definite social shape, and the behaviour of particular children changed in the most remarkable way, until by the end of the year, any typical day was occupied by constant free activity, with full give and take of friendly adaptation. The children showed an outstanding zest and pleasure in all their activities, and an unusual degree of free inventiveness, combined with a concrete appreciation of social realities. The change in some of the more difficult children was remarkable—a change from fear and peevishness and active hostility, to calm and friendliness and freedom in play and cumulative activity.[1] In some cases it was a dramatic change, leading to a sharp contrast between the school periods and holiday periods. For example, two children of different families who had suffered from insomnia and night-terrors from the earliest babyhood began to sleep regularly the whole night through soon after they came to school, continuing to do so the whole term, but losing this within a day or two of the beginning of a holiday."[2]

The most satisfactory testimony as to these changes came from one of the children themselves. Harold's remark (18.3.25, recorded in its place on p. 99) that " There's no hitting now ", whilst somewhat over-generous and optimistic, was a spontaneous comment from one of the more difficult children which was very gratifying to me at the time.

Even those children who were withdrawn at the end of the first term already showed a great improvement in their life within the school, enough so to make their removal a source of grief to me. And of those who remained with me, some of the more difficult were nevertheless among the most gifted and attractive of the children, and of great social and intellectual value to the group as a whole, on all other than their worst

[1] I was told about the end of the first year of the school that someone had said in Cambridge that I " had taken the ten most difficult children in Cambridge and turned them into ten lambs ! " This was no little exaggeration in both directions. Not more than five of the children were really difficult, and as the records plainly show, they were not turned into " lambs."

[2] V. " Contribution à la Psychologie Sociale des Jeunes Enfants ", *Journal de Psychologie*, XXVII, 5-6.

days. In my third volume dealing with *Individual Histories*,[1] I hope to offer a study of one or two of these, since the psychological problems they presented are of the greatest interest.

The rest of the group were quite " ordinary " children in every sense except their intellectual gifts, which were in every case of a high order. As I have stated in *Intellectual Growth in Young Children*, the mean mental ratio for the whole school was 131. I had nowhere the problem of stupidity to deal with, and even the most difficult of the children had the (to me) endearing quality of high intelligence.

I have already pointed out that if the behaviour recorded in this volume is to be properly valued, it needs to be read in conjunction with the records of the children's intellectual achievements offered in my first volume. In particular, it would be very unjust to the school and to the children concerned if those who read this book do not refer also to the chapters in *Intellectual Growth* giving the full background of the ordinary life of the school, viz., *Four Sample Weeks* and the *Summary of Activities*. Only there can it be seen how much of artistic and practical achievement and happy dramatic play, as well as of discovery, reasoning and thought, even the difficult children accomplished, and that even in their most difficult period.

A word may be said about the comments of visitors to the school. It was very striking to me, and an object-lesson in the difficulty of forming just judgments of the schools or institutions that I might myself visit, to notice how greatly the opinions of visitors varied, according to the particular happenings they saw on the particular days they came. (During the first year we had an observation gallery for visitors, but later we gave this up, as it was very disturbing to the children, since so few people could refrain from moving and talking in a way that showed the children they were being observed.) Many people saw the school on difficult days, and most of them took it for granted that the children never did anything but squabble and say disagreeable things. Others saw it on happier occasions, and then their comments sometimes were, " But of course *you* have such an easy problem—they are such delightful children ! "

---

[1] The third volume was never written.

CHAPTER TWO

THE RECORDS

INTRODUCTION

The whole of the material from my own school quoted here was written down on the days when it occurred, either at the moment or at the end of the school day. The actual records are simply a chronological and unclassified account of the happenings in the school. In my first volume, I selected from this chronological story the incidents which illustrated the children's *discovery, reasoning and thought*. For the present volume, I have brought together all those incidents which have to do with the children's social relationships and personal feelings.

The broad lines of classification adopted for the material arose mainly from my own initial interests in the problems of love and hate, and of the relation between sexuality and guilt. But the more detailed groupings under these four main headings were arrived at directly from a study of the material. In reading those incidents which could be grouped as *aggressive behaviour*, for instance, such queries naturally arose as: What sort of situations give rise to aggression? What specific motives can be seen at work? The grouping offered is a partial answer to these queries.

In gathering the confirmatory material from other sources, I had the classification of the school material already in hand, and the further instances available were allowed to fall into the scheme which was emerging. It seemed desirable for theoretical reasons to confirm certain of the sorts of behaviour shown by my own group of children, but it was obviously unnecessary to do this with all sections of my material. I did not need, for instance, to find further illustrations of *friendliness and co-operation*, since no one needs to have it proved that little children can be friendly and mutually helpful, and everyone working or playing with them can supply endless instances of his own.

The classification which has actually emerged is as follows :

I. SOCIAL RELATIONS : LOVE AND HATE IN ACTION
  A. Primary Egocentric Attitudes
  B. Hostility and Aggression :
     1. Individual Hostility
        a. The Motive of Possession
        b. The Motive of Power
        c. The Motive of Rivalry
        d. Feelings of Inferiority or Superiority or General Anxiety
     2. Group Hostility
        a. To Strangers and Newcomers
        b. To Adults
        c. To Younger or Inferior Children or Any Temporary Scapegoat
  C. Friendliness and Co-operation

II. THE DEEPER SOURCES OF LOVE AND HATE
  A. Sexuality
     1. Oral Erotism and Sadism
     2. Anal and Urethral Interests and Aggression
     3. Exhibitionism : 1. Direct
                         2. Verbal
     4. Sexual Curiosity
     5. Sexual Play and Aggression
     6. Masturbation
     7. Castration Fears, Threats and Symbolism
     8. Family Play, and Ideas About Babies and Marriage
     9. " Cosy Places "
  B. Guilt and Shame

One of the chief difficulties in sorting out the various incidents was that so many of them inevitably overlap and belong to more than one section of the grouping. Questions of personal rivalry and of possession, for instance, merge readily into each other, and it is far from easy to distinguish between aggressive behaviour springing from *rivalry* motives and that from a simpler love of *power*. Yet there seemed enough clear cases of each to justify separating out these groups. Nor is the margin between individual and group hostility always clear, since the latter is always evanescent, and commonly arises in the individual attitude of one of the more influential children. Then again, there were many incidents which began as *hostility* or *aggression* and ended up as *friendliness* and good humour, either as a result of the adults' handling, or by spontaneous changes in the children's feelings.

The same difficulties occurred within the large section of *sexuality*, and it will not seldom be felt of particular incidents that they might as well have been in one of the minor groups as in another. This will be particularly noticed with regard to *anal and urethral aggression, exhibitionism*, and *sexual play and aggression*. This is partly because at these ages so much even of the genital sexuality of little children is strongly tinged with anal and urethral colourings.

But not even the two larger sections are altogether exclusive. Many of the instances of *biting*, for example, have been put into *aggression*. Yet there is no doubt that they belong also to the oral stage of *libidinal* development. And much of the hostility arising from rivalry motives undoubtedly belongs to the theme of sexuality, some of the particular incidents showing this beyond cavil.

The most interesting aspect of this problem of overlap is, however, that of the common ground between *aggression* and *guilt*. There is little doubt that much of the children's hostility is due to *projected* guilt, as I hope to show in the theoretical chapter. Group hostility to younger or inferior children has probably little motive other than this and direct rivalry.

These overlaps are thus no accident. They are the key to our understanding of the deeper sources of love and hate, and to the whole genetic development of the child's inner life.

When faced with the problem of the overlap of classes of incident in *discovery, reasoning and thought*, I tried to deal with it by repeating those incidents which seemed to belong to more than one section, in each that they illustrated. One of the reviewers of *Intellectual Growth in Young Children*, and one or two private commentators, found this annoying, and apparently did not appreciate the reason for it. Since other readers may have felt the same, I have chosen here to enter a cross-reference only, giving the date of any incident in a second appropriate section if it has already appeared in one. In the theoretical survey, in Chapter Three, however, I have quoted again in full, either in the text or in a footnote, most of the incidents referred to, since I have reason to think that the majority of readers prefer this to having to turn over the pages to read the actual records again.

A certain amount of repetition, both of the data and of parts of my theoretical statement, inevitably arises from the method of presentation adopted. The advantages of keeping the actual material apart from its theoretical interpretation seem to me, however, to outweigh any disadvantage of minor repetition.

SOURCES OF MATERIAL

The records offered are drawn from the following sources :
My own material

α Systematic observations of the children in the Malting House School for three and a quarter years. (Thirty-one children in all.)

β Incidental observations of individual children in ordinary life.

γ1 Over 420 letters received from mothers and nurses, describing at firsthand the behaviour of their children in detail, and asking for practical advice in difficulties of nursery training. I have elsewhere described the general material gathered from these letters (themselves a selection from a larger number), and discussed its evidential value. The writers are ordinary mothers and nurses, untrained in scientific judgment, but free from psychological theory. They give the descriptive facts simply in order to ask for help.[1] The difficulties described fall into the following groups :

		Boys.	Girls.	Total.
1.	Children difficult mainly in relation to authority	41	29	70
2.	Fears, night-terrors and general anxiety	24	43	67
3.	Failures in cleanliness	32	11	43
4.	Thumb-sucking	13	14	27
5.	Feeding problems	19	14	33
6.	Bed-time and sleep problems	21	16	37
7.	Masturbation	12	17	29
8.	Speech problems	15	6	21
9.	Aggression	18	7	25
10.	Jealousy	13	8	21
11.	Temper	11	6	17
12.	Nail-biting	10	5	15
13.	Excitability	3	5	8

[1] "Some Notes on the Incidence of Neurotic Difficulties in Young Children", *British Journal of Educational Psychology*, Vol. II, Parts I and II.

			Boys.	Girls.	Total.
14.	Shyness	.. ..	4	3	7
15.	Destructiveness	.. .. ..	2	2	4
16.	Lying	.. ..	1	—	1
17.	Stealing	.. ..	1	—	1
18.	Cruelty	.. ..	—	1	1
19.	Tic	.. ..	1	—	1
20.	Hypochondria	.. .. ..	1	—	1
21.	Fixed phantasy	.. .. ..	—	1	1

Relevant examples from the actual letters are quoted in the text.

γ2 Ursula: An individual child.

Other authors: K. Bridges, J. B. Watson, C. Bühler, H. T. Woolley, V. Rasmussen.

INDEX TO SOURCES

α Malting House School material.
β My own incidental observations.
γ Letters from mothers and nurses.
δ Other authors.

AGES OF CHILDREN QUOTED IN MALTING HOUSE SCHOOL MATERIAL

(The ages of other children are given with the incidents quoted.)

Year 1924-5. Ages on 1.10.24.

Benjie	4;0	Laurie	4;6
Cecil	3;10	Martin	2;7
Christopher	4;0	Paul	3;6
Dan	3;4	Penelope	3;1
Duncan	6;5	Priscilla	5;1
Frank	4;11	Robert	4;6
George	4;1	Theobald	4;7
Harold	4;8	Tommy	2;7
James	2;6		

Year 1925-6. Ages on 1.10.25.
Quoted in addition to above children:

Alfred	3;6	Jessica	3;0
Conrad	4;9	Lena	2;9
Dexter	4;0	Phineas	2;7
Herbert	2;3		

Year 1926-7. Ages on 1.10.26.
Quoted in addition to above:

Alice	2;4	Gerry	4;9
Denis	2;10	Noel	7;11
Jane	10;5	Ivan	5;10
Joseph	3;6		

GENERAL NOTE *re* SCHOOL RECORDS

It might perhaps be useful for me to remind my readers here that the school records which follow are *not* records of an educational method. They say nothing, in the great majority of cases, as to how the adults in charge responded to the quoted behaviour, but give only the words and deeds of the children on the particular occasions. An account of the principles upon which we actually dealt with the various situations follows in Part II, with the general discussion of educational aims and methods.[1]

---

[1] My general views on the education of young children are also set out in my recent books *The Nursery Years* and *The Children We Teach*.

SOCIAL RELATIONS: LOVE AND HATE IN ACTION

A. Primary Egocentric Attitudes in Social Play

α

This type of behaviour includes a variety of instances, having a certain broad character in common. The child implicitly expects other people's behaviour to fall into the pattern of his own phantasies, and when it does not, he attempts to enforce his will upon them. The instances given in chronological order below could be grouped into a series of progressive psychological situations:

a. An arbitrary fixing of another person's part in the play, with a minimum regard either to the other person's wishes or to external realities. This represents, of course, the typical play of children between two to four years of age, and could have been multiplied here indefinitely. Every reader will be able to supply unlimited instances.

b. Claiming leadership or assigning inferior parts to others.

c. Refusing to reverse superior and inferior parts.

d. Egocentric threats, bribes and appeals, to maintain leadership, or to get one's own way.

14.11.24. Christopher asked for the " shopping " ; he made a " bed " in his shop and went to sleep. Mrs. I. was supposed to go to the shop, wait for some time, and waken him by knocking.

30.1.25. Frank made everyone go to sleep on the rug, while he went as Father Christmas and took them presents.

Dan and Frank had the box motor car again. Frank was sitting in the front; Dan said he also wanted to sit in the front. Frank said, " Oh no, two can't sit in the front ; *you* must sit in the back."

10.2.25. Dan and Frank moved all the tables and chairs to one side of the room and ran round the empty floor ; Frank took the lead and asked Dan and Mrs. I. to " hook on ". He ran in a spiral, saying, " First we will have a big ring, and then it will get smaller and smaller and smaller."

Frank and Dan played shop. Mrs. I. was asked to buy from the shop. Then Dan said to Frank, " Shall we make a shop house ? " He hid under the table, and Mrs. I. had to knock at the door when he said, " Come in, Sir."

12.2.25. Frank constructed a " Christmas Tree ", with presents piled all around. While he did this, Dan and Mrs. I. had to close their eyes, and then presently they opened their eyes while he took them presents, bundled up in rugs as " in their stockings ". Then they had to dance round the " Christmas Tree " and receive their gifts from it.

17.2.25. Frank was very constructive, but wished to lead all the time and would not join in when any of the other children led. He asked for " Grandmother Gray ", he himself being the Grandmother, and when Dan wished to take his turn at being a " Grandmother " Frank then would not play any more, but immediately started another game.

24.2.25. Tommy brought his mouth organ to school, and Dan suggested, " Shall all the boys take turns to use it ? Shall we be a band and *I'll* go first ? " He then tried to take the mouth organ from Tommy. " Oh, *give* it me," he said, " *I'm* going first, we're going to be a band ! "

26.2.25. Dan and Theobald ran round with Frank in the sleigh, Theobald helping to pull because he wanted to have " the next turn " in the sleigh. Frank, however, refused to pull the other boys when his turn was over.

6.3.25. The children became " giants " and climbed up a laurel bush, Harold sitting high up in the bush for some time, talking about the " bean stalk " and the " giants ". Tommy (the smallest child), climbed up, saying, " Here is another giant."

12.3.25. Martin filled a pail with sand and brought it to the top of the steps, and said, " Come and look at the cake I made, come and see it," and insisted on Mrs. I. pretending to eat some several times.

21.4.25. Harold found a toy revolver in the sand pit, and used it for some time. He said to Mrs. I., " I know a lovely game. You go along there and then I will say, ' A lady to shoot,' and then you must fall down." The others joined in too.

15.5.25. In the morning, when the other children were running as engines, Paul had taken a trowel and thrown it up into the air as a signal for the engines to start or stop, calling out to Mrs. I., " When this goes up, you must stop." He did this for a long time.

19.5.25. The children played a family game as " kittens ". Harold, Paul and Duncan lay asleep as " little kittens " on some chairs. Theobald, as the " father kitten ", presently went up with a book and began at first in fun and then in some seriousness to hit Duncan as a kitten because Duncan " opened his eyes ".

21.5.25. Dan brought his motor car to school. Harold got almost exclusive use of it by continual bargaining with Dan. " If you don't let me use it all the morning, you shan't use my grey car." Harold monopolised it for about two hours.

Whenever Dan said " Now *I* want it ", Harold made a bargain with him about " bringing you a toy " or " letting you ride in my grey car ".

10.6.25. The children often now use the threat to each other, " Then I shan't come to tea with you," as a means of getting their own way.

11.6.25. Duncan makes the other boys help him at anything he does, and is very dominant, either by force or cajolery.

15.6.25. Paul said to Dan several times when he wanted some favour, " I *am* your brother, aren't I ? Then do " so-and-so.

18.6.25. Dan said to Frank, " Shall we put our bathing suits on ? " Harold hearing this, and having been told by his mother that he must not do so, said, " I won't let you come to tea with me if you do." Dan said, "I *shall* put it on." Harold said, " But *are* you my brother, Dan ? " Dan replied, " Yes." Harold said, " Then don't put your bathing suit on."

24.6.25. In the family play Duncan was very domineering and managing, and the others were very meek and docile to him.

25.6.25. At lunch there was some argument which led Dan to say to Miss B., " Then I shan't come to tea with you." Then he asked her to invite him to tea again. " Say, ' Will you come to tea with me.' " She did so, and he at once said, " No, I won't."

26.6.25. Duncan and the others made a house with the rug and chairs, and fixed up a " wireless ". Duncan was again very dominant over the others. He refused, for example, to let Priscilla and Christopher come out of the house when they wanted to.

29.6.25. The children made " a motor bus " and " went to the garden party ". When one or two of them wanted to get back into the motor bus, Duncan very impatiently said, " The garden party lasts a *long* time, it's not over in a minute like that," and tried to prevent the others going, by force.

10.7.25. At lunch it was Duncan's turn to serve, and as usual he tended to be domineering over the other children, and to use the fact that he was serving to enforce his own wishes. He said he would not serve Frank and Dan if they sat on certain chairs. This led to a momentary but sharp quarrel between Frank and Duncan, in which they pulled each other's hair. It passed over in a moment, however, and Duncan then served Frank first and very courteously.

5.2.26. Priscilla wanted to play a family game, and insisted on Dan joining her. When he said he wanted to look at the engine books, she said, " All right, then, I shan't marry you." He then did what she wanted.

16.2.26. Priscilla suggested a game. All the children sat round on the platform, she bowed to each in turn, and then took them to a row of chairs which she had arranged, and told them to do certain things—to put their toes on the floor and their heads back, and clasp their hands. She washed them then, told them to open their mouths, and so on ; put them to bed and " took their temperature ". She is " the nurse " and Christopher is to be " the doctor ". They have " a temperature of 103 ". Frank and Dan were the patients in bed. When they grew tired of the game, and of having everything determined by her, Priscilla kept them in bed by the continual threat, " Well, then, I won't *marry* you ! " Frank in the end said, " I don't care if you don't," and went to his own pursuits.

12.3.26. Priscilla again bullied Dan to do what she wanted, for example, to finish his sewing, by saying, " I shan't marry you." This morning she wanted him to sew, and he asked, " Can I mend the floor ? " She replied, with a lofty air, as if disowning responsibility, " If you like." He said quickly, " But then you won't marry me ! " and so continued his sewing.

3.6.26. Priscilla wanted Jessica to join in their family play, and tried to cajole her away from the other younger children, but she did not want to go. They then tried to bully her, but Mrs. I. intervened. Priscilla called from the stairs, " Jessica, will you come up here ? " in a rather threatening tone, but Mrs. I. said to Jessica, " Go, if you want to, Jessica, but not if you don't want to " ; and Jessica stayed near her. Then Priscilla called out, " Jessica, I'll bring you something tomorrow if you'll come." Jessica replied, " Well, I will," and joined in Priscilla's play.

4.6.26. To-day Jessica and Dan were Priscilla's " puppies ". After a time they rebelled against this. Jessica said, " I *won't* be a puppy, Priscilla, I'll be your girl." Priscilla said, " I won't bring you anything then." Dan was shut in the tool-house as part of the puppy game, and evidently finding this very dull, he too protested against the game, presently beginning to cry a little.

10.6.26. To-day Alfred wanted to make Herbert his " puppy ", and Herbert refused, after agreeing for a short time. Alfred kept trying, " Herbert, you *must* be my puppy ", but Herbert kept to his refusal.

22.11.26. Jane and Priscilla had a " hospital " ; Dan was " ill in bed ", Jessica and Lena also for part of the time. When Lena got tired of it, she got up and did other things for a time, and then went back to the game. Jessica, too, got tired of being a docile patient, and insisted on carrying her own pursuits on while sitting on the bed, and would not lie down and " be bandaged " as the others wished her to. They tried to put her out (she resisted very determinedly), and were a little rough. But seeing Mrs. I. watching, they said, " All right, then, we'll let her stay in, but we won't take any notice of her." When Lena finally left the group to do her sewing, Jessica returned to it as a docile patient once more.

March 1927. Dan wanted to use the potter's wheel, and asked Gerry to turn the handle for him. He said to Gerry, " You turn this handle, will you ? And when *your* arm gets tired—I'll get someone else to turn it ! "

B. HOSTILITY AND AGGRESSION

1. INDIVIDUAL HOSTILITY

a. *The Motive of Possession*

α

17.10.24. The children plucked the withered hollyhock stalks and used them to march round the garden in " Follow my Leader ". There was a good deal of squabbling amongst the children as to whose were the longest of the sticks, everyone wanting these. Cecil was standing in the sand-pit with his own stick in his hand, and saw another child with one exactly similar in shape and size. Immediately, quite unaware of the stick he was holding, he shouted out, " That's *mine*," and tried to take it—looking surprised when we pointed out that he already had his.

22.10.24. The children again marched round the garden with hollyhock sticks, and again they squabbled as to who should have the longest of the sticks. Cecil and Dan were in the garden gathering leaves. There was a good deal of quarrelling for the use of the wheelbarrow; but after a time they settled down to sharing it.

14.11.24. Frank was making a " bed " with chairs when Harold took one of the chairs. Frank threw a cylinder at Harold, which Harold caught and threw back at Frank. Frank was going to throw it again, when Mrs. I. intervened. He protested, saying, " It didn't hit him ! " as if that gave him the right to throw it again.

14.1.25. Dan and Frank tended to quarrel about the bricks, Dan standing up to Frank (a good deal bigger) very well. Frank shows more hostility to Dan than to Tommy.

22.1.25. Frank kept taking away a wooden egg which Theobald had brought.

11.2.25. Miss B. had given Dan a pair of scissors to use, and when he had put them down and left them for a time, she took them up to use them. He saw this and immediately screamed, " Those are *my* scissors, I want them, *now*," and it took some time to quieten him and make him willing to let her use them.

12.2.25. While Dan was occupied with something else, he saw Harold take one of his engine books, which he had left on the shelf, to read. Harold put it down on the table and remarked that he was going to read it " all the morning ". Dan immediately said, " *I* want it," and tried to take it from Harold, and screamed and cried. He took it away in the end.

16.2.25. Theobald had brought his scooter with him and all the children wanted to take turns in using it. Frank and Dan squabbled about it, Dan being very insistent. Mrs. I. suggested that Dan should get his own scooter, and then all the boys could take turns with the two scooters. Dan agreed and asked Miss B. to get it out for him; but when he got it, he would not share it with anyone.

17.2.25. Dan had had a piece of rope to pull his cylinder train, and after he had finished with it, Harold took it. Dan immediately wanted to have it back and for some time would not agree to let Harold have it.

19.2.25. Frank and Christopher took some post cards which Tommy had brought with him, Christopher saying, " Let's take them." Tommy ran after them laughing, and presently asked Mrs. I. to run after them with him. She did so, and there was much laughter, but Frank squashed up one of the cards.

Dan refusing to pass Christopher any plasticine to use, Christopher took some for himself. There was a struggle, but Christopher kept what he had taken.

11.3.25. When the children were putting on their outdoor garments for the garden, Tommy saw Martin's red slippers, and took them away to hide them. This distressed Martin very much and a little struggle ensued, Tommy laughing and for some time refusing to give up the slippers.

26.3.25. Harold and Paul often say to the other children, " You are *not* to talk about ' Humpty Dumpty '—you are not to talk about " so-and-so, referring to rhymes or stories they have in their books at home or on their own gramophone. They seem to look upon these as their own special possessions, like toys, and often forbid the other children to talk about them or sing them. They say, " It's in *my* book at home."

30.4.25. Paul brought a top to school for Dan. Frank span it once or twice, the children enjoying this very much. Then Frank (obviously envious of Paul) threw it across the room two or three times, and broke it, which seemed to amuse the other children as much as the spinning. But Paul protested, angrily, " I shan't bring any more, if that's broken."

2.6.25. James came as a visitor. He had a toy engine and ran about with it. Tommy took away the engine, saying, " You shan't have it."

3.7.25. Priscilla and Christopher had a struggle for the rake, in which Christopher won.

Frank took one of the rugs which Duncan had been using on the swing earlier in the morning, and Duncan tried to get it from Frank, saying, "It's *my* rug." There was a struggle.

Mrs. I. intervened, pointing out that the rugs were for " all the boys " to use, and that if Frank was using it now, Duncan could not do so, but would perhaps get another ; after a time he accepted this, but then seeing that Dan had in the meantime taken the second rug, he tried to get that from Dan and Mrs. I. had to intervene again. Then Mrs. I. said, " There is another rug, will you find that and use it ? " He said, " No," in a very sullen voice, " there's *not* another." Mrs. I. said, " There is, will you come with me and look for it ? " He went with her, but repeated all the time, " There's *not* another." They found the third one and took it back to the swings. By this time Dan and Frank were both on the two low swings and Dan was on the one that Duncan particularly regarded as his own. He tried to pull Dan off and gave his hair a very severe tugging. When Mrs. I. interfered, he protested violently, " But it's *my* swing—he's got *my* swing." She said, " Will you have another? " pointing to the third one. He said, " No, I don't want that, *this* is mine ". Mrs. I. said, " The swings are for all the boys to use." He said, " No, they're *not*. It's mine, the swing is *mine*." She again said, " The swing is for all the boys to use. Sometimes you use it, sometimes Dan uses it, sometimes so-and-so uses it," mentioning each of the boys in turn. He then replied, " But it was *I* who thought of making the swings ! " And repeated this several times, clearly feeling that that gave him the proprietary right to the swing when made. Mrs. I. replied, " But you did not make it. It was Miss B. who made it, you thought of it, Miss B. made it, and it was made with the wire that is in the garden for all the boys to use. You use it now and another boy uses it another time." He kept on making hostile remarks, very disturbed, and trying to push a chair over on to Mrs. I., saying, " I'll tell my aunt of you," and, " I don't like you," and so on, but gradually he calmed down and appeared to accept the facts fairly well and went away to do something else. Later he was entirely friendly and calm. This outbreak seemed to be the culminating point of a period of difficulty with him. Afterwards he was more even in temper and much less defiant.

6.11.25. Christopher, Tommy and Penelope were rather quarrelsome about toys and gardening tools towards the end of the morning.

17.11.25. Frank had brought some confetti in a silver bag, and when he was showing it to the other children, Tommy snatched at it, spilt it on the floor and ran off with some. The others were all angry at this, and there was some squabbling with Tommy. He stood up to them, and then again snatched at the confetti. Later on, Dan said, " Tommy is *silly*."

8.3.26. Christopher was making a ditch in the sand, and Jessica wanted to join in this. He did not want her, but she insisted on it. Presently Christopher said, " I *hate* you, Jessica. Did you know ? " " Yes." " How did you know ? " " Well——," said Jessica. This was said in the most matter of fact tones.

11.3.26. The children made " shops " with the various things on the shelves. There was some squabbling, as each child wanted to have the largest share and the favourite articles. When Mrs. I. remarked that " everybody seems to be wanting everything ", they laughed heartily and became more amicable about sharing.

15.3.26. Jessica accidentally tore a card which had been sent by Miss C. to all the children. Dan said he would " get a policeman to put her in prison ", and " I'll kill her, because I hate her."

27.4.26. The younger children's use of the pulleys led to some social difficulty, as the older children, although they had clearly been told yesterday that the pulleys were " for all the children ", felt that they had established a proprietary right to them by fixing them up, and were very angry when the younger ones played with them. Mrs. I. told them again, " They are for all the children to use—sometimes you can use them, and sometimes Phineas and Tommy and the others " ; but Dan and Priscilla found it hard to accept this, and told the others several times, " You're *not* to do that, it's *my* pulley ! " Dan was very cross and determined about it, and even at the end of the morning, he and the elder ones showed little sign of accepting the idea of common ownership.

7.6.26. Dan spoke of the tricycle which Tommy had lent him. Dan said, " Tommy lent it to me while he was ill—I wish he was dead then I could have it always."

15.6.26. Alfred and Jessica had a quarrel about a " boat " they were making with chairs. Jessica had contributed one of the tables that was being used, and felt that this gave her a share in the boat, but when it was finished, Alfred and Herbert did not want her to join in. When they tried to push her out, Jessica hit Alfred. Alfred cried and told everyone about it, as he usually does. Dan advised him to " push Jessica down and then run away ". Alfred tried to do this, but could not. Then he tried to cajole Jessica, saying, " You hold my hand and come with me, and I won't *do* anything." After some persuasion, Jessica agreed and went with him. He took her over to the hen-house, persuaded her to go inside, and then

SOCIAL RELATIONS

shut and locked the door on her. She screamed, and when Mrs. I. went to them, he told her he had shut her in " because I don't want her in the boat ".

19.10.26. Lena always wants to have any object which another child happens to be enjoying, e.g. the tricycle or engine, and tries to get it forcibly.

20.10.26. Lena and Dan had a struggle for the use of the bicycle, and Lena said, " I *mentioned* for it first."

21.10.26. Lena and Dan had two or three struggles during the morning for the bicycle, trumpet, etc., Lena being very determined and tenacious. She scratched Dan.

26.10.26. Lena and Jessica had several struggles for the tricycle, in which they seemed to be very evenly matched. The elder children kept an even justice, taking either of the two off when they thought she had had " her turn ".

27.10.26. Lena came in from the garden and told Mrs. I., " Jessica wants to have the tricycle all the morning and won't give it to me ". Mrs. I. asked, " Well, what are you going to do ? " Lena said, " Well, I *want* it." Mrs. I. suggested that she should ask Jessica to have it " perhaps four more times round the garden and then let Lena have it ". She said she would do that. Mrs. I. then said, " And perhaps, after you've had it four times round, then you'll let Jessica have it again ? " " Oh, no—I shall have it *many* more than four times—I shall have it as many times as she has had it altogether, not just four—that wouldn't be fair, would it ? " She then ran out and tried to get Jessica to agree, but Mrs. I. could hear that they were quarrelling. When she went out, she found them both hanging on with grim determination to the tricycle, both crying very loudly. They were equally matched in power and will, and neither would give way. They were so absorbed in the struggle and in their cries that for a time Mrs. I. could not get their attention. After they had struggled, neither giving way the least fraction, for about a quarter of an hour, Mrs. I. asked them, " Well, what can we do about it ? " They replied together and with equal emphasis, " Well, *I* want it." Mrs. I. suggested their sharing, but they repudiated this. Mrs. I. then said, " Well, then, if you won't share, there's nothing *I* can do, is there ? " and walked away. Lena at once shouted after her, Jessica joining with a little less eagerness, " Oh, come back, Mrs. I., come *back*, we will share, we *will* share ! " Mrs. I. went back and said, " Well, how shall we arrange it ? Suppose Lena (who was actually on the saddle) has it once round the garden and then lets Jessica have it once, and then Lena again, and so on ? " This renewed the quarrel, as each wanted the " sharing " to be a mere excuse for getting it into her own hands for as long as possible. After a time, however, and with Mrs. I.'s renewed suggestion, they agreed to this, and kept up the arrangement amicably all the rest of the morning. (This was the last occasion of any such extreme greed and obstinacy about the tricycle ; after this they showed a greater readiness to find some sensible compromise for their conflicting desires.)

May 1927. Conrad constituted himself " the gramophone man ", and bullied the younger children into letting him take charge of it, choose the records and decide everything !

γ

1. " You gave me considerable help about my little boy M., aged four, last year, but one of the problems I mentioned does not seem to show any sign of being solved. He has a brother one year younger, and takes everything from him that he can get, sometimes there's a fight, but as a rule the younger one being good tempered and for the sake of peace, gives in. The eldest one always asks, ' Is mine bigger ? ' and if we say ' Yes ', all is well. But should he discover that C. has for instance a piece of string an inch or so longer than his, then he works himself up into a passionate frenzy, sobbing the whole time and saying, ' C.'s string shouldn't be bigger than mine, it should be shorter, he's smaller than I am and should have the smaller piece,' and to him it appears to be a passionate matter of justice. If we try to reason with him he says, ' I don't care, I *want* to be selfish.' He seems to want things in a passionate sort of way, and the younger child doesn't seem to want things in that passionate way at all. So that for the younger one to give up things does not necessarily mean he is less selfish, but more indifferent."

2. "We would very much like to have your opinion on a problem of our own nursery. It concerns my eldest little boy of six years old. In disposition C. is highly sensitive and a keenly affectionate child. He will weep over a dead mouse and if he sees a brother in pain will suffer almost as much in sympathy. Usually gentle in his ways he is perfectly sweet with his baby brothers whom he protects and adores. In one respect, however, he is ungenerous with the other children and here lies my difficulty. If a new toy appears in the nursery C. at once wants to have it. Even though it belongs to the smallest boy, he will have no hesitation in appropriating it. Should the owner refuse to surrender the coveted object on request, C. will not usually employ force to secure it, but will await his opportunity. Quite skilfully he will endeavour to divert his victim's

attention into some other channel and, the moment this ruse succeeds, and the toy is cast aside, he will take possession. Unfortunately the others make this easy as they quickly tire of their playthings and forget them. But C. has endless patience and resourcefulness in acquiring booty. He is also a great ' keeper ' and generally has a store of treasures in some corner or old box. But I do not worry about this as I think it is quite common among little boys. C.'s sense of property (if one may so describe it) leads him to be very careful with his things whereas the others are most destructive. But what I do *not* like is the selfishness behind these tendencies. If we explain that the other children have superior rights to any toy he replies invariably that he *wants* it, and nothing else seems to matter. He has rather a way of collecting knick-knacks at home from drawers and cupboards of grown-ups. But he makes no effort to hide these."

δ

BRIDGES, *op. cit.*, p. 46.[1] " It is well known that young children claim or hold on to everything that appeals to their interest of the moment. When children first come to the nursery school they claim one toy after another whether a child is playing with it or not."

b. *The Motive of Power*

    a. Real aggression

α

16.10.24. Robert wanted to smash a plant pot, and when prevented by Mrs. I., he bit her wrist severely.

27.10.24. The elder boys wanted to shut some of the younger ones into a hut as a " prison " ; Frank, Harold and Paul often suggest, and sometimes do this.

10.11.24. The glass of the garden door having been broken by accident, Cecil and one or two others went on to break it further deliberately, shouting with glee. (They watched the plumber mend it on the following day ; and Cecil and these others often again suggested breaking it, during the next week or two.)

28.11.24. When Mrs. I. was kneeling to help the children put on their shoes, Benjie several times ran up behind, jumped on her back and clasped his hands very tightly round her neck. (Clearly a mixture of affection and hostility, but it felt more hostile than affectionate !)

[1] All further references to Bridges are from the same source, *The Social and Emotional Development of the Pre-School Child.*

22.1.25. Yesterday Frank and Dan had each drawn an engine on the blackboard. This morning, before the others came, Dan had " hooked them together ", by drawing a coupling hook, and later there was a lot of squabbling about which engine was pulling which. Each wanted his own to pull the other.

26.1.25. Frank said, " George *mustn't* scribble, or I'll tear the paper " ; but later on he said, " He *can* scribble if it's for smoke "—i.e. smoke from the engine he was drawing.

2.2.25. When running round, Frank insisted that *he* was to be " in front ", and when Dan went in front, he bit Dan. Later he deliberately bumped Theobald with the cylinders.

11.2.25. While Dan and Theobald were sitting on the floor looking at the engine book, Frank became " a fairy climbing on the roof "—a fairy that threatened and interfered with the other children !

19.2.25. Paul had been very friendly to Dan in the early part of the morning, but later on he threatened to knock Dan's bricks down and persisted in harassing him, and teased Tommy.

24.2.25. George and Dan had some difference and Dan leant across and squashed George's truck, then as George came round the table to retaliate, Dan scattered all the plasticine on the floor.

27.2.25. Harold was sitting at a table making a kite with Miss B., Dan sitting near him. Harold began to tease Dan. He shouted at him in his ear very loudly, and talked about " getting robbers to steal Dan's toys from his room ". Frank then joined in with this. Dan was very distressed and cried and went to Miss B., whereupon they teased him still further.

5.3.25. When Paul was resting in the afternoon he wanted to go downstairs, but Mrs. I. said, " No, will you rest a little longer, please." Paul said, angrily, " I don't think you are *really* kind, Mrs. I.," and, " I'll send you away, and cut you up and eat you."

27.3.25. Mrs. I. promised Harold she would go out in the garden and find him a stick to make a windmill, as the wind was too cold for him to go out. He was very impatient to have it, and Mrs. I. was, for the moment, occupied with something else. She said she would go " presently ". He said, " Go and get them *at once*." Then, " If you don't, I'll kill you and throw you on the roof."

21.4.25. Harold and Paul brought Mrs. I. some shells which they had gathered at the seaside. They did not like the other boys having them. Mrs. I. said she would leave them for " all the boys " to look at. Later on Harold said, " You must give me lots of money for them—a million pounds—or I shall smack your face." . . . This was said in a half joking manner.

24.4.25. Mrs. I. was singing Nursery Rhymes to the children, and Harold stood by, saying, " Silly Mrs. I., *silly* tune," because the tunes were different from those which he had on his gramophone at home.

4.5.25. Harold was painting pictures, and presently said, " Will you pass me another piece of paper ? " As Mrs. I. was engaged at the moment, she said, " Perhaps *you* will get it." He said, " You horrid Mrs. I. ! " and stopped painting. He said he would "throw the painting water out of the window", and did throw it out of the door.

18.6.25. Frank overturned Dan's motor car, and in doing so, broke the steering wheel. He shouted with glee to the others.

24.6.25. It began to rain when the children were in the garden, and they and Mrs. I. took shelter under an overhanging creeper. They stayed there some time watching the rain and listening to it. Mrs. I. asked the children if they could hear it. One or two of them said, " Yes." Duncan said, " *I* can't," and when the other children said, " We can," he said, " No, you can't," and tried to enforce his opinion by hitting them. This happens with all the children sometimes, but Duncan is very dogmatic, and often tries to enforce his views by shouting and hitting.

29.6.25. When Mrs. I. would not do something Harold wanted, he said, " I shan't have you to tea now, Mrs. I. I shall shut you out when you come." (He had previously invited her to tea on the following day.)

27.10.25. Priscilla and Dan were making a "mulberry bush ", and asked Mrs. I. not to look at it until it was finished. Presently Priscilla called Mrs. I. to look, but Dan said, " No, it's not enough," and when Priscilla persisted, he shrieked out, " No, it's *not* enough," and pushed her. She hit him, and he then bit her severely, leaving a deep mark. She cried bitterly and came to Mrs. I. for comfort. He stood beside her looking very miserable ; and, looking at the mark, said, " That doesn't hurt."

19.1.26. The children had made a " boat " with the upturned garden seat, Christopher being the driver. When he got down for a moment, Jessica at once took his place and refused to give it up again. Christopher said, " I'll push you off." Jessica shouted emphatically, " No, you must not, you must *not*, Christopher," but would not give way.

17.3.26. Priscilla bullied Jessica to-day, and tried to bully Christopher, too. She said to him, when she wanted him to follow her whim, " Choose which you'll do. Will you be my baby, or shall we make you cry ? " Later on, when her behaviour had led him to call her " a beast ", she wanted to make him retract this, and said, " Will you either be my baby, or say I'm not a beast ? Say it *quickly*." Christopher replied, " I'm not going to do *both* " (i.e. " either "). He went home very early because of this squabble ; but came back in the afternoon bringing Priscilla a present of a boat.

9.5.26. Alfred annoyed Dan when the latter had a towel in his hand, and he flipped Alfred with the towel. Mrs. I. asked him not to do this, and he struck at her with it. She took the towel away, and he was very angry. His mother happened to come into the school at that moment, and he ran to her, told her (quite accurately) what had happened, with bitter tears, and said, " I *hate* her—she's a beast." Then to Mrs. I., " I shan't come in a punt-boat with you next time you ask me." But after a moment's reflection, he added, "At least I shan't sit next to you—bang fool beast of an I. ! "

10.5.26. Dan just now tends to hit out at the other children if they refuse his wishes or interfere with him in the least, or even if he wants to show his disapproval of what they are doing. To-day when playing " Nuts in May ", he and Jessica were pulling at each other, and because Jessica pulled harder and got him over to her side, he was angry and hit her. When standing near the door to watch one of the others go, he slipped and hurt his head on the door. Mrs. I. was standing just behind and reached forward to save him, but he said that she had pushed him, and was very angry with her.

11.5.26. Because Jessica took her coat off when Dan thought she should not, he hit her with a towel he was using. When Mrs. I. took the towel from him, he said, " Well, she was going to take her coat off, and she shouldn't."

1.12.26. Phineas was hammering nails into the door, and Conrad opened the door from outside, thereby pushing it against Phineas. The latter hit Conrad with his hammer, and when Mrs. I. took the hammer away, said, " But he opened the door and I didn't want him to."

β

At 4;6, Y. went to school in charge of a neighbour's two boys aged 7 and 9. For a few days all went well, and then every day Y. brought home complaints about the elder boy. Y.'s mother asked this boy, L., some questions, and decided that Y.'s complaints were some romance of his own. Then Y. started getting home very late from school, and told his mother he was coming home with P., a girl friend. His mother was very cross about this, and told him he was to come with L., the boy, and if he did not, she would spank him, as he was to be home in good time. The next day he came home again very late, and was found sobbing and saying, " I walked home with P." The mother whipped him, the first time since he was eighteen months old. Then from another neighbour the mother found that the boy had *not* come home with P. on any of these days, and further inquiries from another friend who had actually seen Y. with the elder boy, L., revealed the fact that L. had been regularly tormenting Y. He had knocked his hat off, pushed him off the curb into the road, and thrown stones at his ankles, and when Y., only half the size, lost his temper and tried to punch the big boy, L. burst into laughter and called Y. "Cry-baby, *cry*-baby ", and then ran off and left him alone in the road. The neighbour commented that she was sure that " Y. would rather do anything or say anything than come home with L."

δ

BRIDGES, p. 51. " Destruction of another child's work is a particular kind of interference. It may be the result of mere interest in the material and a desire to use it ; it may also be just an accident. But more often it is a sudden expression of anger, self-assertion and envy. The child may be annoyed at not being able to use the coveted material, so he expresses his wrath by knocking down the bricks or scattering the material. The other child may be older and may be making some block construction, drawing, or plasticine model more elaborate than the younger child could make. Since the youngster cannot match the other's construction, drawing, or model, he asserts himself effectively by knocking down the blocks, scribbling on the drawing, or hitting the model."

BRIDGES, p. 56. " It is interesting to note that violent hugging is often substituted for the pushing or hitting of the first social contacts which have met with rebuke. The child is not reproved for hugging another child, so he works off his assertiveness by hugging violently, even to knocking the other child over at times. This hugging may also be partly determined by a certain amount of affection for a fellow humanbeing of about the same age and size. It is often manifested by ' only children ' or those who get little opportunity to play with children of the same age."

BRIDGES, p. 61. "Children usually enjoy their first experience of disturbing another child. They laugh if they accidentally knock over a child's bricks, or trip him up, or hit him while wielding a spade. Very soon their sympathy and understanding grows to the extent of making them refrain from laughing at the discomfiture they have accidentally caused. They stand and stare in silence, looking somewhat perturbed themselves. Some children have reached this stage by the time they enter school. Later they may express their sympathy and perhaps regret by putting an arm around the child they have hurt, or by trying to comfort in some other way. When language is sufficiently developed a child will sometimes apologise for hurting or disturbing another. Any remark such as ' I'm sorry, I didn't mean to ' scores on this item."

BRIDGES, p. 61. " Some of the bigger children find it irresistible to knock about and fight the smaller ones. It gives them such a delightful sense of power. With the help of reproof and suggestions from the teacher this feeling of power comes to find ample satisfaction in protecting and helping the smaller children instead of bullying them."

BRIDGES, p. 66. " It is a good sign when a child, who has previously been acquiescent and passive in the hands of adults, refuses to put away his toys the moment he is asked, whether he has finished his little game or not."

BRIDGES, pp. 77-8. " Occasionally a child may be heard calling an adult bad names, scolding loudly, or making other abusive remarks. This usually occurs in a fit of anger when the adult has thwarted the child in some way, insisting that he do something he does not want to do, or preventing him from fulfilling his desires. Such behaviour shows antagonism, self-assertion, and a failure to accept the necessary authority of the adult. The following are abusive remarks made by a child when asked to take out of his mouth a pin that he was sucking : ' You good-for-nothing you. You mutt you. . . . I'll tell my mummy. I'll bring a stick and beat you.' "

b. Make-believe aggression

22.10.24. Frank and Dan were resting alone upstairs. Mrs. I. heard Dan crying, and on going up, found that Frank had said to him, " I'll bite you." Dan had taken this seriously, but Frank protested to Mrs. I., " I only meant to tease."

24.11.24. Christopher took bricks away from George, saying, " I am the stealer."

20.1.25. Harold invented a game. He built a large tower with bricks, asked Mrs. I. to sit on the table at one end of the room, and all the children under his direction ran round the room, saying as they passed her, " We are going to blow it up," and she was instructed to say, "No, no," every time they passed.

Theobald took the long sticks and said, "Let us fight with these sticks"; they were used as guns.

21.1.25. Frank made a model of a crocodile, showing the spine and the skin markings, the open mouth, and the teeth, quite plainly. When asked, he said he had seen only a picture of one " on the stairs at home ". " We have two pictures and one is biting a man's leg off."

22.1.25. Frank drew a crocodile. Dan at once made a plasticine crocodile " to bite Mrs. I.".

3.2.25. The children drew crocodiles on the floor and the blackboard. Then, starting with Frank, the children were " crocodiles " in turn, each chasing the others and pretending to bite.

9.2.25. Christoper drew a crocodile with a large mouth. Later Theobald drew a crocodile with a large mouth, which he said " would bite Dan's legs off ".

10.2.25. Paul, for a time, had a long stick as a gun and was " shooting people ". Tommy drew a battleship on paper and said to Dan, " I have got a battleship to shoot you with "; Dan replied, " Yes, I have one, too, and shall shoot *you* with it," and with quite good humour they " shot " at each other, bumping into each other and laughing.

11.2.25. Christopher and George made a " train " by putting several tables together. Presently Tommy got into their train, and said, " This is a monkey." Christopher and Tommy sat side by side, and squealed, and jumped about and crawled as " monkeys " for some time. Christopher in this way got rather excited, and flushed, and began to do roguish things to tease Mrs. I.—running off with a pencil and notebook from her shelf. There was no malice in this, and when she asked him to replace them, he did so.

19.2.25. Miss B. being out of the room, Harold asked for her and ran to the bottom of the steps to wait for her, saying, " I shall see her boots and I shall pull them off."

Some of the children used the long sticks as guns and " shot " with them. Seeing a visitor in the gallery, who sat with the curtains apart, they " shot " her also.

20.2.25. Frank, Tommy, Theobald, Christopher and Dan ran round as " lions "—" big lions coming to bite you ".

25.2.25. When Miss B., Mrs. I., Tommy, Paul and Dan went out, the others stood in the door, so as to keep them in. Frank said to Dan, " Say ' please '." Dan did so, whereupon he " opened the gate ". He and Harold then made a " wall " in the door, to keep them out, of bricks and the cylinder sets, etc. Presently Dan came in and joined the others in building the wall at the door. Harold and Frank and Dan enjoyed this game very much.

20.5.25. The children found a piece of sheep's jawbone with some teeth. Frank ran into the schoolroom with the teeth in his hand. He said, " They're tiger's teeth, and they're going to bite you."

19.1.26. Frank teased Jessica by saying he would bite her.

22.3.26. After lunch, when Mrs. I. was helping the children to wash the plates, Christopher and Dan kept smacking her in fun, with hearty laughter, but very persistently. When she asked them not to do so, Dan would have stopped, but Christopher would not—until she said that if they went on, she should leave them to wash their own plates. They then desisted, with amused comments, " Oh, if we smack her, she won't wash up ! "

c. The Motive of Rivalry

α

16.10.24. When the other boys ran into the garden, George went to Mrs. I. and said, " *We* won't play with the other boys, will we ? " He stayed half an hour with her.

31.10.24. Cecil was building with bricks. Benjie came near and was going to kick them over. Cecil at first protested and then invited him to do so, which Benjie did.

3.11.24. Benjie was heard saying to Dan, " I'll shoot you dead."

12.11.24. Benjie and others had been melting modelling wax on the hot water pipes with much interest and excitement. Dan ran to see it, but Benjie said to him, " No, *you* shan't see it," and pushed him down.

21.11.24. Dan, George and Frank were running round to music, Frank much enjoying it as usual, when Mr. X. came into the room, and on Mrs. I.'s suggestion also joined in the dance. Frank at once withdrew, went and stood by Mrs. I. and said, " I don't want to dance." This was the first time he had ever refused to dance.

26.11.24. Benjie always wishes to exclude Dan and Christopher and Tommy. He says, " No, he shan't see, he *shan't* see."

9.12.24. Speaking to Dan, Mrs. I. called him " darling ". Benjie at once said, " Why don't you call *me* that ? " Mrs. I. replied, " But I often do." Benjie then said to Cecil, " I don't like you, Cecil. I'll get a gun and shoot you dead."

15.1.25. When sitting down to model, George and Frank both wanted to sit by Miss B. Frank was there first; George sobbed bitterly, but presently he agreed to let Frank sit there for a short time and that he should do so later.

Frank drew a crocodile on the floor and said it would " bite the other children's legs off ".

20.1.25. Harold said that to-morrow he would " bring a pin and stick it into Theobald ". Frank said, " To-morrow, when you come, I shall ask you if you *have* brought a pin, and if you have, tell you to stick it into Theobald."

28.1.25. Dan insisted on sitting *next* to Miss B. on the rug, both Tommy and Frank being already there, one at each side. There were many bitter tears, and for a long time Dan could not resign himself to the fact that they were there and would not get up for him. " I want to, I want to *now*," he kept saying, but presently he settled down to the idea that he would sit beside her later.

2.2.25. Theobald made a pointed thing with plasticine, and said he would " kill Dan with it ", and that he *had* " killed Dan with it ".

6.2.25. When modelling, Theobald first of all made a pointed thing " to kill Dan with ".

9.2.25. Theobald drew a crocodile with a large mouth, which he said would " bite Dan's legs off ". He usually directs this playful hostility to Dan.

Frank shows more hostility to Dan when the others are present, and this seems to be increased by the return of Harold and Paul.

Paul also shows a little hostility to Dan, saying, " You shan't come in *this* house," although Dan had helped to make it.

10.2.25. When sitting down to plasticine, Dan had been offered a chair beside Miss B. He, in a contrary mood, would not take it. Presently Frank came and took it; Dan wanted it at once and screamed and cried, " *I* want it." Presently Frank gave it up and got another, but put it nearer to Miss B. Dan then stormed and screamed again; he wanted to sit next to Miss B. He tried to push Frank off and hit him with a brick. Frank, though determined, was fairly restrained. He said, " Shall I have it for a short time and you later ? " Dan replied, " I want it *now*." And Frank said, " Oh, *please*, Dan, *do* let me do plasticine." Dan would not. After a time, Mrs. I. lifted Dan up on to the first chair and talked the matter over with him. He was quite unresisting, and a little sullen, but quietened down. After a time he slowly thawed and joined in the modelling. Later, Frank leaving his chair,

Dan then took it and said to Mrs. I., "*You* can't sit beside Miss B." Mrs. I. (knowing he wanted to work it out dramatically) said with a smile, " I *want* to," and the following playful dialogue then went on :
Dan : "You can't sit beside Miss B." Mrs. I. : "But I *want* to." " But you can't." " Perhaps I can after a short time." " No, not at all." " Perhaps I can after a *long* time." " No, *never*, you can't *ever* sit beside her." " Perhaps I can after a *very* long time." " No," he replied, " Never, never, *never !* " Then he asked Mrs. I. to say it all again. He said, "Say you want to sit beside Miss B." and the whole dialogue was repeated eight or ten times, at his request.

12.2.25. George, seeing Miss B. sit down to the table with bricks, left his modelling and went at once to sit beside her. Dan and Frank also went and a squabble ensued as to who should sit next to Miss B. As none of them was willing to give way, Miss B. got up and went back to the modelling table. Dan did not notice this and went on building, but George and Frank saw it at once and left the bricks, and went back to the modelling table to sit one each side of her. When, presently, Dan realised what had happened he came again and cried and screamed to sit beside her.

20.2.25. When Frank arrived in the morning, he saw Dan with his mother, and at once called out, " Naughty Dan," although he had not said this for a long time previously.

26.2.25. Dan's mother had come into the schoolroom with him ; when she was in the gallery, going, he called out, "Would you like to kiss me ? " She replied, " Yes." He said, " Come down and kiss me then." Frank was in the cloakroom and heard this. Turning to Mrs. I., he said at once, " Naughty Mrs. I.; *dirty* Mrs. I." several times, and " We'll spit in your face " ; he banged the piano and said, " Shall we tear it ? "

2.3.25. When Theobald and Frank were making aeroplanes with the long rods and plasticine, Dan joined in the making of Theobald's, and told Mrs. I., " We're making an aeroplane." But when it was completed, Theobald would not let him share it.

Theobald did not want to let Dan look at his painting.

12.3.25. Dan bit Paul, in a quarrel this morning.

13.3.25. Frank brought his father and grandfather to look at the pictures, and as soon as they went, he turned round and kicked Dan.

17.3.25. Miss B. reported that the day before, having tea in a café, Dan had seen a pleasant-faced young woman there, sitting opposite to him, and had presently said, " I would like to go and live with that woman. She seems nice to me."

He said this several times, so presently Miss B. said, "Well, will you go?" He said, "Yes—no, I will wait until I am as big as my daddy, and then I will go and live with her." In the evening he told his mother all about it—that he was going to live with this other woman, and then said, "She will have a little boy then, and *you* won't have any."

18.3.25. Martin told Mrs. I. he had made a "lovely railway track"; he had made it with the colour tablets put in a long line. He would not let Tommy look at it and several times tried to push him away, saying, "*You* must not look, you must not do that; it is not nice, it is *rude*."

Martin was inclined to be rather aggressive, particularly to Tommy, whom he hit several times.

23.3.25. Martin, while modelling, was sitting opposite to Tommy and said several times, "Naughty Tommy, naughty Tommy." He seems to feel a definite enmity to him.

March 1925. Penelope came to tea with Mrs. I. There were several women there, all friendly and sympathetic to children. But Penelope gave all her interest to the one man present, making him play various games with her, caressing him and sitting on his knee, monopolising his attention all the time and not readily allowing him to take any notice of anyone else.

7.5.25. Mr. X. came to lunch at Dan's request. On sitting down to the table Frank at once became perverse, and refused to eat any of the first course, being quarrelsome with Dan, and moodily pushing his spoons into a crack in the table.

14.5.25. Frank and Priscilla became rather hostile to Dan. Priscilla decided she would not "do" Dan until later (i.e. wash his legs after being in the sand-pit). Dan replied that he "*must* be done first" as he was going out to tea, and made a long speech about this. Priscilla and Frank laughed, and said, "You don't know what you're talking about," and Dan said, stamping his foot, "Yes, I do," and put a muddy finger on Frank's legs. Priscilla then said, "Now I shan't wash your legs," and she did not. Dan said, "But I will tell you who does *not* know what he is talking about—Christopher does not know." The other two replied, "Oh, yes, he does." Dan then said, "You know what this is for, this is to put on the path, so that when Christopher runs he will slip," and he left a pile of mud there, saying, "Now he will slip." Frank and Priscilla told Dan that he "told lies" and called him "naughty". He stamped his foot and said, "I'm *not* naughty, and if you say that, I shan't ask the X.'s to lunch" (Jessica and her mother).

18.5.25. When Frank had finished his dinner he went to Laurie and pulled away his chair from under him. Dan said, " Oh, here's another—I'll give you another chair," to Laurie. Frank said, " Oh, I'll take that one, too," and started to do so, Dan saying, " Oh don't; oh, *don't*." Duncan then said, " No, *I* won't let you," and went to Frank and pulled him away, putting his arms behind him and marching him off to the lawn, and put him there. A struggle ensued, Frank saying to Duncan, " I'll bite you." He did bite, leaving marks on Duncan's hand. Frank called to Priscilla to help him, but Duncan said, " I can manage both of you," and put his arms round both their heads.

19.5.25. When modelling, Frank and Priscilla said, " We shan't tell Dan what we're making," and Dan retaliated by whispering the same thing to Mrs. I. but in rather a loud whisper, so that the others could hear it.

24.6.25. There was some talk between Duncan and Harold about who was the taller ; they were very dogmatic and in the end squabbled about it, until Mrs. I. suggested that they should measure.

8.7.25. Theobald joined Paul in making a motor bus, etc., and they talked to each other freely. Theobald said, " *Christopher* shan't come in, shall he ? " Paul replied, " Yes." Theobald said, " No, he is too nasty." Paul replied, " I like him."

9.7.25. Priscilla and Dan had agreed to take their tea out on the fens. Frank evidently felt a little out of· it and began to talk about his going " on a roundabout ". Dan said that he and Priscilla would also. Frank said, " Oh, but mine is bigger." After some discussion of this kind, Frank said he would " put Dan in prison ". For a moment or two Priscilla joined with Frank against Dan and there were some mutual threats and recriminations. Then Dan said, " Oh, but we won't talk about that—won't it be lovely, Priscilla, when we take tea out ? " Presently Frank returned to the subject and Dan again made the same sort of protest, and said, " We won't talk about *that*—it will be so *lovely* when we take tea out, won't it, Priscilla ? "

12.10.25. Frank brought a bow and arrow to school, and showed those who were present (i.e. the women and girls—at first there were no boys there) how it worked. He shot quite successfully with it several times, and had no difficulty in managing it. Then another boy, Christopher, came on the scene, and after that Frank did not seem able to use it at all, made several unsuccessful attempts, and then gave it up in disgust, and asked Mrs. I. to put the bow and arrow away on her shelf.

29.10.25. Dan was happily making something with plasticine, but when he saw Priscilla sit down with Miss C. to use the insets with her, he ran across the room and said, " No, *I* want to ! " Miss C. said, " Will you do it later, after Priscilla ? " He was very angry and cried bitterly, throwing the insets on the floor and pulling Priscilla's hair. He went on crying in a desultory way for some time, but gradually grew more cheerful, and in the end helped to pick up the things he had thrown down.

20.11.25. Frank had been very amiable all the morning, but when Dan's father and Conrad's mother came into the schoolroom he (as before on similar occasions) at once became hostile to Dan and Conrad. He came running up behind Mrs. I. and jumped on her, half affectionately, half aggressively.

1925. Some quarrel arising in their play, James bit Dan very suddenly and savagely, leaving the marks of his teeth on Dan's skin even through his woollen jersey. He tried two or three times to do it again, until Dan was very frightened, and the two had to be kept apart. Biting was James's natural mode of aggression at this time, and he had to be watched very closely.

28.1.26. There has for some time been rivalry between Dan and Frank for the favour of Priscilla, and to-day this broke out acutely. Priscilla pinched and hit Dan because he would not get out of the swing when Frank wanted it, and Dan replied by biting Priscilla's arms. There were many tears and recriminations. After a time they settled things amicably and returned to the swing, but Priscilla remained quite excited for some time.

24.3.26. Just now, Priscilla and Christopher are allied against Dan. They shout " *What ?* " when he speaks to them, refusing to answer, or repeating his question and saying they are " deaf ". He takes it in good part, and it remains a game, but he looks very tired of it sometimes. They ran off with his tools, and he chased them until he was tired out. He confided to Mrs. I. that it was " a horrid game ", and said once or twice that he wouldn't play it any more ; but ran after them cheerfully if they came near to tease him. This " teasing game " was kept up for two or three days.

28.4.26. Jessica and some of the others asked Mrs. I. to lift them up so that they could swarm down the high pillar under the gallery (a favourite game). Priscilla came running to do this, too, and wanted to be lifted up just as Mrs. I. had begun to help Tommy. When she was asked to wait for her turn, she was very angry and said to Mrs. I., " I shan't talk to you." When offered her turn in due course, she refused it at first; but came back soon afterwards when Mrs. I. was again engaged. As she could not then have it, she became hostile and contrary again; but presently grew more friendly, and when, much later, Mrs. I. offered to help her up the pillar, she accepted pleasantly and happily.

29.4.26. At lunch-time, Christopher and Priscilla had a violent quarrel about a chair which Priscilla wanted Miss B. to have. Priscilla cried, and in the end Christopher gave way to her courteously.

28.6.26. When Penelope had been told that on her return to England (the family were abroad) she would be able to come to the school again, she had said at once, " Oh, shan't I have some larks with Mrs. I.," and other affectionate anticipatory remarks. But at the first moment of actual greeting, she said, " I shall push you over." Her mother said, " Oh, you were going to give Mrs. I. a big hug." She then did this, and was very affectionate and friendly.

7.7.26. Mr. X. came to lunch, and Penelope was very affectionate with him, turning away from Mrs. I., although ordinarily very attached to her. She was standing in the garden holding his hand, after having asked him to play with her, when she caught sight of Mrs. I. looking through the window. She immediately made a hostile gesture, and called to her, " I hate *you*."

16.7.26. To-day, as for a few days now, Priscilla is rather hostile to Christopher, and favours Dan.

19.10.26. Tommy pinched Lena several times. When Mrs. I. held his arm to stop him, he was very angry and struck her in a way he had never previously done; but soon forgot his passion and became friendly again.

14.11.26. Dan said to Jane, " Priscilla doesn't like you as much as me." Jane replied, " Does she like Conrad at all ? " " No." (Conrad was there.)

17.11.26. Dan and Jane were very friendly to Jessica; asked her to sit between them at tea, and told her they didn't like Conrad (who was there too). They asked her if she did, and of course she said, "No." Jane then asked her, "Do you like Lena ? " " No, not a little bit." Jane then asked Dan which he liked best, Jessica or herself. He replied hesitatingly, " I don't know quite." Jane : " We don't like Conrad, do we Dan ? We call him ' piggy '." Conrad said, " No, you *don't!* Nasty Dan—faeces. Horrible Dan—anus." Jane : " Isn't he *rude ?* " Dan showed more hostility to Conrad than ever before. They were all inclined to be cross this afternoon. In the games, later, Jane would not let Conrad play.

SOCIAL RELATIONS

21.11.26. For some days now Jane has been very hostile to Conrad, teasing him and openly expressing her dislike. When asked why she did so, she said, " I don't like him—he's so selfish." Mrs. I. suggested to her that he was not very happy, and not very used to playing with other children, and that perhaps if she did not tease him and say she disliked him, he might be happier and therefore more friendly ; she responded to this to some extent, but chiefly when Mrs. I. was present.

28.11.26. Jane asked Dan, " Do you like Priscilla better than Christopher ? " " No." " Do you like her better than me ? " " No—I like you both the same." " Do you like Christopher better than me ? " " Yes, a little."

29.11.26. Conrad was playing happily with Jane and Dan, and said to Jane, " When Lena makes anything and says, ' Isn't this nice ? ' I say, ' No, it's horrid,' because I don't like Lena. I hate Lena, don't you ? " Jane : " Yes."

In the evening, Conrad kicked the door, and said, " That's to keep the ghosts out. There aren't any ghosts, are there, Jane ? " Jane replied, " No, of course not. Have you ever seen a ghost, Miss D. ? " " No, Jane, I haven't." Conrad then said, " I expect *Lena* would have said, ' Yes, I have.' " Later, when they were using Meccano and talking, Dan said, " I know someone I don't like," and told the story of a girl who had pushed him in the street. Jane said, " I know who I don't like. It's a girl." Presently, Conrad : " I know who you don't like, Jane, it's Priscilla." Jane replied, " Shan't tell you." " You used not to like her." " Well, I might have changed my mind."

22.12.26. Jane and Dan went to the Zoo together. Jane asked Dan, " Do you like Conrad ? " " No." (There is every reason to think this false.) Jane : " Neither do I."

31.1.27. Lena brought to school a pen with a cap fitting over the nib as in a fountain pen, and showed it to the others with great pride. When Jessica saw it, she said, " I'm going to *buy* one—I'm going to buy one as big as Mummie's."

8.3.27. The children were eating apples, and each of those present had one. One was being kept for Lena and Phineas to share, and Dan did not want them to have it. He suggested various other people to Priscilla, who had charge of it. When he said, " Well, then let Jane have it," Priscilla replied, " No, not Jane, don't let's give it to her—we hate her." Just after this, Priscilla was rather rough with the little ones, until she was firmly stopped by Mrs. I., upon which she cried unhappily.

11.3.27. This afternoon, Jane had won Dan over to her side against Priscilla, who was looking rather forlorn.

29.4.27. Lena and Joseph (Joseph's first term) were playing in the sand-pit when Phineas arrived. As soon as Phineas approached, Joseph stiffened aggressively and clenched his fists. They both eyed each other up and down hostilely for several seconds, then Joseph relaxed, Phineas moved away,— and each went on with his own pursuit. No word was spoken.

23.5.27. Lately there has been keen rivalry between Herbert and Alfred, on most points. To-day, Mrs. I. opened the gramophone when Alfred was standing near. He took no particular notice of it until Herbert began to use it, when he at once wanted it, too, and began to criticise and interfere. After a good deal of struggling and scratching, Alfred agreed to the suggestion to let Herbert complete his turn and then have his own. After this they used it alternately in a friendly way.

23.5.27. There was a slight squabble between the children playing in the sand-pit, and Lena threw sand at one of the children who had " spoiled her castle ". Joseph told Mrs. I. about this. Mrs. I. reminded Lena that she wouldn't be allowed to stay in the pit if she threw sand, and when she did it again, Mrs. I. lifted her out. Joseph got very excited about this, and said, " Now *I'll* throw sand at her." When Mrs. I. asked him not to do so, he replied, " Put her out of school." Mrs. I. said, " No, I won't do that." " Well, she threw sand at us—throw her over there " (pointing to the garden wall), " so she can't come into school." Presently he began to throw sand himself. Mrs. I. told him, " If you do that, Joseph, I shan't let you go into the sandpit." He replied, defiantly and amusedly, " Oh, you can't stop me ! " When presently she lifted him out, he seemed very amused.

25.5.27. All the children were taken on the river for a picnic with some grown-up friends. Penelope attached herself to Mr. X., particularly on the walk back from the river. She made some remark about Dan's mother and Mr. X. " belonging to each other ", and then invited Mr. X. to " come to the school-house ". When he replied that there was no room for him, she said, " But you can have Dan's room." He said, " Perhaps Dan will be there—then what should I do ? " " But you can sleep with me !—I should like to have three, you and me and my dolly." The next morning she was particularly affectionate and clinging to Mrs. I., and when Mr. X. came in, she greeted him with " Silly old John." This is another instance of Penelope's high ambivalence to men and women friends—she swings about between the two affections and finds it unusually difficult to hold them together.

May 1927. Joseph and Tommy have been the storm-centres this month (Tommy having returned to school after a long illness). During the first three weeks, Tommy showed considerable malice towards the younger children. Without frowning or appearing angry, he would push them or take their things without any provocation. E.g., he snatched away a basket which Alice was carrying with flowers in it, and the other children were very indignant at this. On several occasions he pushed children into the sand-pit. During the fourth week this happened much less often, and he became more friendly and sociable.

Joseph during the first three weeks showed increasing malice towards the younger children, never joining in their pursuits, and always seeking to have an adult exclusively to himself—clinging to one and following one about all the time. When the other children were in the garden, he begged one to go inside with him; when they were in the schoolroom, he invited one to go out. This culminated towards the end of the third week, when on one morning he pushed two or three children down. The next morning he was very unhappy, clinging to Mrs. I. convulsively all the morning. During the fourth week, however, he became much more friendly, and less frightened and quarrelsome; and began to join in the various games, and be less dependent on adults. A certain amount of dislike and criticism of Joseph by the older children very naturally developed, but this was never expressed in any dramatic way, nor very marked.

Joseph was sitting on a table in the cloakroom one lunch-time, swinging his legs, when Mrs. Z., who had come to take one of the other children home, asked him affably, " And do you like coming to this school ? " " Oh, yes," said Joseph. " And what do you like doing ? " " Oh, I pinch all the children," he replied, swinging his legs more vigorously. This was liable to be only too true.

Priscilla was quite happy this term, having been accepted back into the group by Jane and therefore by the other children. After her timidity on the first day, a happy relation was established. Jane was overheard to say in the fourth week, " I don't like Priscilla—she tries to take Dan away from me."

Phineas often expressed dislike of the other children—very emphatically: " I *hate* Lena," " I *hate* Joseph."

One morning, Lena had a quarrel with Dan, who pushed her down, so that she got up sandy and muddy. She came running to Mrs. I. to tell her. " I don't like Dan. He pushed me down—I hate him." All this was said with a frowning face of anger. Then, suddenly, lifting her face up, with a most ingratiating smile, she said, " And I hope *you* do, too." She seemed very disappointed when Mrs. I. said, " No, I don't."

11.10.27. As soon as any adult visitors appeared, Joseph would take their hands and lead them to admire his private garden plot. When alone with Mrs. I., he said confidingly, " It's *better* for me when there aren't any other children about, isn't it ? "

β

1. N., when 5;6, was staying at the seaside with her mother and two brothers. She developed a great fear that her *mother* would get caught by the tide under the cliffs and be drowned. When they walked round the beach under the cliffs she hurried on in front, weeping in fear, not for herself but for her mother, and knelt down and prayed God to " save mother ".

2. On a visit to the home of Phoebe, she and her girl companion (aged 2;6 and 3;6) spent two or three hours in the drawing-room with three women and one man guest. The younger child (whose mother was present) stayed rather closely beside her mother and took no special notice of anyone. But the elder girl made love to the man friend most charmingly, fetching her plasticine to make little gifts for him. At the end of an hour he had a whole row of little plasticine offerings—figures of various sorts, baskets, a nest with eggs in it, etc., etc., on the arm of his chair. She took practically no notice of the women friends, and made no gifts for them.

γ

1. "The main causes of his (aged 3;6) bad temper are annoyance with his little sister of 17 months, who has now reached the stage of playing with his toys and unintentionally spoiling castles he is building, knocking down his toy animals, etc., and generally getting in his way."

2. " I wonder if you could advise me on the subject of my son (aged two and a quarter). My trouble is his acute shyness— it is a real phobia. He is a fine healthy child and has never had a day's illness and his cheery little face absolutely belies his true nature, except at home where he is perfectly happy. He will not allow anyone in the house without howling unmercifully. It is impossible to ignore him because he drowns our voices, and he will not be coaxed. He is somewhat backward in talking, although perfectly intelligent, so I can't reason with him. He will not go into the back garden to play if the next door neighbour is in her back garden. When

anyone comes through the back gate he commences to scream and if they should attempt to cross the threshold he doubles his effort. I cannot sufficiently stress the lengths he will go to to display his obvious terror of apparently everyone but his parents and the maid, who has been with me since he was seven months old. Also, he will not go into a shop or anyone else's house without similar disturbances. The worst of it is, he doesn't get over it but just screams until the caller goes. I am almost distracted for I assure you I have underrated rather than exaggerated my troubles."

3. " She is possessed of a violent temper and lately seems to have become worse. She is normally a most winning child, very affectionate, high spirited and very quick and full of boundless energy, on the go from morning till night, big for her age but thin and wiry, but she is dreadfully jealous of the others, except Baby whom she adores. When she flies into a temper she will kick or strike any of us, or roll on the floor or get into a corner and refuse to move. If you go near her her shouts can be heard in the next road. I have tried to explain as fully as possible, as it is almost frightening to see Jean worked up in one of her rages and I feel the example is so bad to the others. She is usually repentant after but will not speak about it or answer any questions, always turns the conversation. The jealousy was very acute when Baby arrived, but I got her to love the baby and now I think she only feels jealous over her father or me if we do anything for the others or take them out and not her."

4. " But it is his attitude to his little sister that worries me most. I cannot make him remember he is older or instil the smallest bit of the protective attitude into him. He wants to be treated exactly as she is and to have everything she has, and takes anything from her, often hitting her or knocking her over until I am really scared to leave them together. I may say she sticks up for herself well, but there is three and a half years' difference. When talked to he is all affection and promises at once never to do it again, but not five minutes elapse before he is as bad as ever."

5. " I must write and tell you of my experience with this ' jealous hostility '. I took your advice and a month ago two little two-year-olds came to live with us as companions for my son of the same age. They looked so sweet together—all red-cheeked, curly-haired, adored only children but, unfortunately, *they hated each other*. I was in despair. I'd no idea babies could be so horrid to each other. We daren't leave them alone for a moment—such shrieks and yells would come from the nursery. They would pull each other's hair out by

the handful—scratch, bite, push each other down—tread on each other. It was heart-breaking. I've seen chickens persecuting a lame fowl—almost pecking it to death. These babies were just little animals. If one fell and cried because of the bump, the other two rushed over to pull his hair and increase the yells. ' Pip ' loved to bang the others on the head with a brick."

6. " He (aged 3;0) whines at nothing, hangs about me and if I get anyone into the house he won't go near them. My wee girl was born last January and he is very jealous of her, even to-day, hits her—molests her in general."

7. "My other difficulty is about the unkindness of the two elder ones (girl aged 6;6 and boy aged 5;6) to the child of three and a half. They have always resented her existence I know, though I tried to avoid making them jealous. They are devoted to each other and are quite kind to the baby, but Cecilia's life is really hardly worth living because they are so nasty to her. They tease her constantly by running off with her doll's blankets or knocking over her tea-cups or just by pushing her away (she is learning to tease, too) and also in more subtle ways by making her say foolish things and then jeering at her. She, poor thing, never remembers how she's been caught before, and constantly gets caught again, and she is old enough now to mind considerably."

8. " My little girl, aged one year ten months, has become very difficult to manage owing, I expect, to jealousy, as she has a little brother of five months. At first she would hit him and start whining whenever I picked him up. I have not taken any notice of these fits, and never asked her to do anything for him, as I realised it only made her more angry. I am pleased to say this has been very effective, as she now asks to tuck him in, and mind him for me. She also offers him her toys, although she does not like parting with them. The real trouble now is that she absolutely refuses to have anything to do with strangers. If anyone says, ' Good morning ' or speaks to her at all, her reply is nearly always a very definite ' No, don't ' or ' No, won't '. She screams if they touch her or try to pick her up."

9. " He is a big boy for his age (3;3) and seems very healthy. He is very excitable. To give you an example : He was given a sink full of water and some corks to float. He rushed in full of fun to tell me about it and seeing the baby on my lap smacked her three times across the face. After the first smack I said, ' how very unkind ', and asked him why he did it. Without replying he did it twice more before I could ward him off. He will also hit her when I am not in the room."

10. "My little boy is one year ten months, and his sister is nine months old. He was very unhappy at her arrival and used to try and pull her off my lap. Now he is on the whole very good—tries to protect her from 'bumps', shares things with her, etc. But if he is tired or hurts himself at once he wants my exclusive attention. As I am often quite alone this is sometimes difficult, and now he has a funny new trick. If anything goes wrong or at the slightest word of censure he flops down and *crawls*. He has walked since he was ten months old, and is particularly active and sure-footed —can climb and run like a three-year-old."

11. "When the baby brother arrived and she (aged 3;0) saw him she said, 'Oh, what a nice baba.' She was amongst a number of aunts and uncles who adored her and perhaps she didn't realise the baby was mine. Then I had a very trying voyage, often having to neglect her, and she became jealous and almost ill. She developed all sorts of fears and when we joined my husband in a bungalow in a wood she would not let me out of her sight. I was very careful with her and when we came here she seemed happier, but she would often lie awake for hours after being put to bed, talking to herself, etc. She always slept alone. The baby was restless, too. Then I thought I'd put the baby in with her and that worked miracles. She slept far better, although there was the chance of being disturbed during the night by the boy. I argued that probably when she was alone she always suspected that I was with the baby, whereas when he was in the room with her, she knew I could not be nursing him."

12. "Occasionally when friends have brought small children in, my boy (aged nearly three) smacks and pushes the little ones the whole of the time, and will not let them share the toys but will sit down and cry or do anything to be unpleasant, even when out walking he will try and get near enough to push another little boy that we frequently meet."

13. "Peter, nineteen months, is a very lovable chap. Isabelle simply will not play with him and snatches all his playthings from him. He has been very good about this, looking round for another toy only to have that snatched away from him also. It is only recently he has begun to protest. He loves Isabelle in spite of all this, but when he hugs her, or wants to kiss her, she frowningly pushes him away, pinches him or gives him such a violent push so that he falls."

14. "I wonder if you can advise me how to treat my little boy of three years when he persistently ill-treats his sister, aged three months? When they are in the same room it

seems as though he simply cannot resist the temptation to poke her eyes, smack her face, or do something else to make her cry. He does not seem to be jealous for he often strokes her and says ' nice girl ' and laughs at her funny little noises and generally takes an interest in her. But I simply dare not leave them together for a minute, for as soon as my back is turned he will be up to some mischief. I have carefully explained time and time again how he must hurt Sheila and sometimes he will stroke her and say ' sorry '. I have also smacked him, but that made no impression at all, he just howled at the top of his very loud voice, which frightened poor baby all the more. He is very backward in talking but understands everything we say to him, and has a good memory."

δ

BRIDGES, p. 43. " New-comers in the nursery school will often speak more readily to an adult than to a child, especially if they have not played much with other children."

BRIDGES, pp. 43-44. " Apparently, aggressive behaviour on the part of a new-comer to a group of pre-school children is really a definite stage in social development, and is usually followed by obviously sociable behaviour. The child who does not make such active and bodily contacts on coming into a group may be more socially advanced, but in all probability he is still unsocial, egoistic and indifferent to the group, and may be slow in social development. A child who reacts to the social situation in any of the active ways mentioned in the previous paragraph, such as by hitting, pushing, or stroking, scores a point on this item. Pulling a child's hair, hugging him or knocking him over may also be manifestations of the same thing, and should likewise score a point."

BRIDGES, p. 46. " Children will ask an adult for help long before they will ask another child."

BRIDGES, p. 52. " Some children are gentle with one another from the moment they enter the school, probably a result of training and experience at home, and possibly because they have less assertiveness and anger in their make-up. Other children make a few exploratory attempts at pushing or pulling others, but give up after the first week or two. Still others continue to knock their little playmates about for months after they are admitted to school. They are usually aggressive, active children who have been a trouble to their parents and who have built up some defiance against authority, perhaps through lack of skilful management. Size is not necessarily a causal factor, as quite small children are often as aggressive as bigger ones."

BRIDGES, p. 56. "There are many ways other than those already mentioned in which a child may assert himself to the annoyance of others. Amongst the most common seen in the nursery school are throwing sand at a child, taking away or hiding his toys, tipping him out of his chair, or hugging him roughly."

BRIDGES, pp. 61-2. "A child who has been rather a tiresome bully in a group may find great delight in taking care of some small child, helping him to undress, teaching him how to use materials, or defending him against the interference of others. At the same time his sympathy develops and he refrains from punching the smaller children or handling them roughly. Any of the older children who have refrained from fighting or pushing smaller ones gain a point on this item."

BRIDGES, p. 62. "A child who is constantly ordering others about, telling them to do this and not to do that, placing smaller children in chairs or on the floor to suit his own convenience, may perhaps be showing leadership, but this quality is not being expressed in a socially desirable way. Such a child would ordinarily be called bossy or domineering."

BRIDGES, p. 63. "Just as correcting others may become a social nuisance when pressed too far, so helpfulness may defeat its own end if not expressed wisely. The older children in the group may be so anxious to help the younger ones in undressing, feeding, or use of materials that they hamper the little ones' movements and interfere with their self-expression. The wise and considerate child will see from the little one's protests or other reactions whether the help is required and appreciated or not, and will continue or desist accordingly. The child who is a little too much dominated by a sense of superiority and the desire for power will continue to press services on the smaller child, even when they are no longer required, and bring protests from the little one. Such a child would fail to score on this item."

BRIDGES, p. 83. "One of the first reactions of a new-comer to a group, when he becomes interested in the other children about him, is to hit out and watch the effect. This kind of behaviour is not so much characteristic of a particular age as it is an indication of the length of time a child has played with a group of children. New children as old as three and a half or four years may behave in this explorative way, if they have never played much with other children. Such behaviour is, however, more common among children under three. The new child may explore in a gentle way by patting or stroking another child, or he may hit him violently, push him, or throw sand at him. In time he discovers that the more violent behaviour causes trouble and distress both to himself and to others. His interest in various activities develops and he learns to get his thrills and to cause impressive effects in other more desirable ways."

BRIDGES, p. 85. " Some of the bigger children find such intense delight in their sense of power and superior ability that they bully or bother the little ones unduly. They order them about, scold them and try to correct them or press unwanted services upon them. In time they learn to be more considerate and heed the protests of the little ones. They help only when help is needed and show greater gentleness and kindness in their actions."

d. *Feelings of Inferiority or Superiority or General Anxiety*

α

6.10.24. Cecil hit Robert with a broom, deliberately, with a sullen air. There seemed to be no reason for this.

14.10.24. Cecil was very aggressive and defiant; he turned the tables over, took the soda crystals out of the box, and threw them on the floor, refusing at first to pick them up.

23.10.24. At the end of his first day in school, Benjie's mother came to bring him home. He was in the sand-pit digging, and when he saw her, he looked up with a frowning face and said with hostile emphasis, " *You go back where you came from !* "[1]

12.11.24. Frank came into school saying, " Kill Miss B., kill Miss B., kill Miss B.", and kept saying it every now and then during the day. After one of these moments of unprovoked and moody hostility, Frank suddenly burst into tears, and when asked what was the matter could only sob, " I don't know, I don't know." This was one of his specially unhappy days.

21.11.24. This morning was the most difficult period of the whole term. It was wet and the children could not go into the garden; they were all in very high spirits and a very aggressive mood, particularly Harold, Frank, Cecil and Benjie. They did not readily settle to any occupation and were not responsive to music, but rushed about aimlessly and very aggressively for some time, with much shouting.

2.12.24. Benjie and Paul were building together with bricks in a very friendly way for a long time; then Benjie suddenly

---

[1] It is worth noting that Benjie's mother told me that he had frequently bitten her breast when being suckled as a baby, and that she had always smacked him for doing so, as she " believed that you couldn't begin to train them too early " ! At four years of age, he was one of the most hostile and unhappy children I have ever seen.

said, "I don't like *you*, Paul." Paul was very distressed, gathered up his own bricks and started to go to another table; in doing so, he accidentally (!) knocked over Benjie's building. Benjie was angry, and hit Paul. Harold came to defend Paul and hit Benjie. After some squabbling Paul said, "But Benjie said, ' I don't like you ' "; then Benjie replied, "But I do, I *do* like him."

12.1.25. At the modelling table Frank was quarrelsome, particularly with Dan. " I won't speak to you, you mustn't speak to me," and so on.

14.1.25. Theobald showed some hostility to the other children when running round with engines; and Frank a good deal—hitting out as they ran past, without any provocation.

15.1.25. Frank began rather quarrelsomely, but later settled down.

16.1.25. Frank again began very quarrelsomely. He drew the "crocodile" on the floor, and when the others did the same he rubbed theirs out. In modelling, he spoilt the other children's models of a garden, crushing his own *first*, so as to avoid retaliation !

26.1.25. Frank said that Dan's pencil was "dirty", and the engine he had drawn was "dirty".

January 1925. During the first week of the second term, Frank had had a cup to get a drink, and going into the schoolroom Mrs. I. found him standing by the piano, just about to bang the cup down on the piano or on the floor with a stormy gesture, and his face full of distress and anger, saying, "I'll break it." Then he broke into tears and sobs. Mrs. I. said, "Please don't break it, what is the matter, Frank?" And he said, "I don't know," and cried and turned to Mrs. I. for comfort. After a moment or two he was quite calm again.

9.2.25. Frank greeted Miss B. with "Dirty Miss B."; the first time he had said this for a week. He tended to interfere with the other children, throughout the morning. He had been digging with a large hoe; and presently held this in a threatening attitude towards other children. When Mrs. I took it away, he tried to bite her. He put sand down Tommy's neck.

13.2.25. When all the children were playing trains, Harold and Frank were restless and rather inclined to interfere with the younger children. Tommy was pushed by Harold, and pushed him back, and for some time they pushed each other with much laughter, Harold being quite considerate with Tommy.

16.2.25. Harold and Paul were much less wild this morning, but still tended to interfere to some extent with what the others were doing, to cut the string of other people's engines, and so on.

24.2.25. Theobald said to one of the other children, who had drawn a train, " That's a *silly* train."

25.2.25. Harold drew a large ship on the blackboard. Dan said, " It's not a nice ship ", Harold and Frank having said this to him earlier, about a cracker which he had made.

27.2.25. Harold shouted " Funny face " to Tommy, when he cried after falling and hurting himself.

Harold said to Mrs. I. in the cloakroom, with no apparent stimulus, " You are the nastiest, wickedest Mrs. I. I have ever seen." And when she was playing the piano, he went to her and said the same thing, and, " I'll have you killed "—again without any apparent provocation.

2.3.25. Frank noticed some visitors in the gallery, and shouted hostile things to them: " You dirty creature."

He and Paul were speaking of " killing giants ", and said, " You dirty old giant."

4.3.25. When the children were modelling, Christopher made a long thing, which he wagged about, and said, " Ding ding." Theobald laughed scornfully at this, and said, "*That's* not like a bell, it hasn't got anything inside."

5.3.25. Frank had brought to school a large piece of thick brown paper, and asked Mrs. I. to make it into " a Red Indian's dress " for him. They did it together, cutting out the head-dress and cloak. The others then wanted the same, all except Harold and Paul, who said " It's *silly* to be dressed in paper ".

6.3.25. Frank refused to let Paul have any plasticine. Paul told Mrs. I. about it and said, in the tone of a disapproving grown-up, " I am *very* disappointed with him. I am very *angry* with him."

Frank, seeing the letters which the children and Mrs. I. had sorted out spread on the shelves, muddled up one of the shelves of letters.

When, before going to rest, Mrs. I. was helping Paul to button his trousers, he said, without any apparent context, " It is a pity I have such a nasty teacher as all that."

9.3.25. Jessica came to lunch. Before she came, Mrs. I. told the boys she was coming, and that Mrs. Z. was coming with her. Harold at once said, " What a silly name," repeating the surname, and laughed about it several times.

Theobald, as usual, took a long time to put on his out-door things, and to several of Mrs. I.'s suggestions, he said, " Shan't."

11.3.25. Paul ran round for some time, saying, "Wretched little Tommy, wretched little Martin," although nothing had happened to provoke this.

17.3.25. Tommy, seeing the counting sticks and boxes on one of the tables, deliberately scattered them on to the floor, looking at Mrs. I., as if expecting a protest.

19.3.25. Paul said he did not like Mrs. I.'s " silly crêpe soles ".

25.3.25. Martin walked round the garden with sticks, saying, " I am a man—I am a *man*." He had one or two altercations with Tommy, and seeing Theobald use the big broom he went up and tried to take it away, saying, " It's *my* broom, it's my broom."

23.4.25. Frank throughout the day was in a spiteful and interfering mood, showing this as soon as he arrived by attempting to bite, and making hostile remarks to Mrs. I. and Miss B. He attempted to take Dan's torch from him when Dan and Norman were running round as engines.

24.4.25. Frank was again in a difficult and hostile mood, spitting, saying " dirty ", and biting. When the children were running round he took away a penny of Dan's and put it down a crack in the floor.

4.5.25. When Mrs. I. and the children sang " Dickory Dickory Dock ", Harold called that a " silly tune ", and said there were " too many ' Dickories ' in it ". He said it should only be " Dickory Dickory Dock " and that Mrs. I. sang it too many times.

8.5.25. Theobald is hypercritical both of himself and of others; he criticised Christopher's drawing, saying, " That's a silly one." He often says this with regard to other children's models and drawings.

15.5.25. Running in, Priscilla and Dan pushed each other and this led to a quarrel which lasted ten minutes, each of them saying, " *You* pushed me " and going on pushing, stopping for brief intervals, but going on again because neither would give way; each showed the greatest persistence and tenacity about it.

27.5.25. Towards the end of the morning, Theobald, without a word to anyone, and with a very determined air, went round the room taking off all the labels which the others had written and pinned on the various things in the room, and crumpled them up and threw them out of the window.

May 1925. Laurie was standing near a short ladder on which Priscilla had climbed, and suddenly gave it a malicious push so that she fell off. Although she had only been two or three rungs from the ground, she happened to fall in such a way that her collar-bone was injured. Laurie was a visitor to the school for a few weeks only. He had been teased by the other boys (saying "Pop" to him) and had been too frightened to stand up to them. (His mother had meanwhile been urging him that he ought to fight them, and that he was a coward, and so on.)

9.6.25. Laurie had been using the shears on the lawn. He went to Mrs. I. and said, "I'll cut your head off," and, "I'll cut your arm," and made a furtive attempt to do so.

24 6.25. When Frank came, his first action was to upset the box of shells which Mrs. I. had given Priscilla to use for number work.

6.7.25. Theobald modelled a "punt with a hood", and talked to Mrs. I. very freely and eagerly about it. She said she would make "a barge with a cabin". He said, "You won't be able to make it as well as mine." She said, "No, perhaps not." He repeated this several times.

8.7.25. Duncan was finishing the letter he had begun to his mother, and this led Dan also to write "letters" to his mother. Duncan was very scornful about this and said, "Dan doesn't know *how* to write."

10.7.25. The children were a little distracted and excited by a new supply of plasticine. They all talked together very eagerly, Duncan speaking very loudly and shrilly, but telling the others in a loud voice "*not* to make such a noise".

13.7.25. Priscilla asked Mrs. I. to get her an apple from a tree. Mrs. I. said, "Perhaps you could get it yourself?" Priscilla evidently felt this to be a rebuff, and presently when Mrs. I. suggested to her that she should help her put the straw from the rabbit hutch on the bonfire, she said to Dan, "No, we *won't*, will we? You nasty old thing."

15.7.25. Duncan said, "Shall we tie it (the kitten) in a knot?" Dan said, "No, shall I tie *you* in a knot?" Duncan said loftily, "Oh, I'm stronger than you!"

21.10.25. To-day Tommy was very hostile, particularly to Penelope and Mrs. I., and inclined to be solitary. He was often occupied, but usually alone. (This hostility to Penelope may link up with their family play, in which she usually makes him into "the baby" with herself as "mammy", and is very domineering.)

27.10.25. Tommy was again markedly hostile to Penelope.

30.10.25. Frank to-day was rather hostile and domineering; he hit Jessica and one or two of the others.

11.11.25. After a long period of steady and concentrated work, Frank passed into a restless mood. He tied a bundle of green raffia under his chin, and ran about the room calling himself " the tiger queen ", and frightening the other children. He deliberately knocked over the bricks Mrs. I. had built with Penelope. Mrs. I. therefore took away the raffia. Penelope and Tommy then tied raffia on and rushed about as " tigers ". Frank remained in a contrary and destructive mood, and when he and Priscilla were doing plasticine with Mrs. I., they suddenly spoiled her work, pointing out that she " couldn't spoil " theirs as " we haven't made anything yet ". Mrs. I. took away the raffia mats they had been working on, and this made them very angry. Priscilla said she would " tell her grandmother ", and would " serve you last at dinner " or " not give you any dinner ".

16.11.25. On arriving, Frank greeted Mrs. I. very charmingly; but on seeing Jessica he said he would bite her. This was purely verbal, however, and in behaviour he remained very friendly all the morning.

18.11.25. Dan once or twice laughed at Tommy for his indistinct speech.

3.12.25. The children had made coloured paper hats for themselves, and there was some talk, as they looked in the mirror, as to which was " the most babyish ". Frank said that Christopher's was, and snatched at it and tore it.

22.1.26. Frank was again difficult for a time to-day, would not join with the others unless they obeyed his wishes, and said he hated the grown-ups.

30.4.26. Dexter has made two or three sudden attacks on the other children when he has found an opportunity, and this, coupled with his excessive fear of their teasing, defeats his general desire to be friendly with them.

27.5.26. When the elder group were painting the long table, Dan was scornful about Dexter's work, although in fact it was as good as his own.

28.10.26. Dan began the day in a quarrelsome mood, trying to intimidate the others, to break up Phineas's modelling, and so on. He threatened to strike Phineas with a heavy engine in his hand, and when Mrs. I. took this away, he said she was " horrid ", and, " I'm not coming to this school any more." In this mood, for a part of the time, he pretended to be " an engine that ran over people ".

1.12.26. Phineas was hammering nails into the door, and Conrad opened the door from outside, thereby pushing it against Phineas. The latter hit Conrad with his hammer. Conrad cried because this hurt, and when the other children came to see what had happened, he shouted angrily to them, " *Don't look* ". They laughed at this, and he became very angry, and rushed at Dan as he was passing, and bumped him against the stairs.

13.12.26. When cleaning his teeth, Conrad broke his tooth-glass by knocking it against the tap. He at once said to Miss D., " It doesn't matter—it's mine." But then he burst into tears, and said, " It's *your* fault, you made me break it, you horrid thing," although Miss D. was not near him, and not even speaking at the time.

2.2.27. Conrad went to his room alone. When Miss C. went in, he had a khaki hat and sword on, plunging up and down playing at "soldiers". He was talking quietly to himself, and was for several seconds quite unaware of Miss C.'s presence. He seemed to be acting out some phantasy of bravery. When he saw Miss C. he stopped and said, " I *hate* the others, they're beastly."

In the evening, the others were chasing each other about and romping, and Conrad joined in with them. He ran at Jane quite valiantly. She was surprised and taken at a disadvantage, and called out that he had kicked her. This rallied Dan and Norman to her side, and Conrad was frightened and ran away to his room, calling out, " I hate you all."

May 1927. Joseph was verbally threatening to " kill " some woman who had been talking to him, and he was asked, " What do you mean when you say that—what do you feel like ? " " Oh, I feel *big*."

October 1927. Joseph had refused to join in the Eurhythmics class with the other children, choosing to come and sit with the grown-up staff in the gallery who were watching the class. Presently, sweeping a lofty glance over the dancing children, and the female staff sitting near him, he turned to Mr. S., who was also in the gallery, and said, as from one man to another, " *Aren't* they *silly ?* "

γ

1. " He was the most perfect baby till about a year old but during the last few months and especially the last few weeks he has become very cross and bad-tempered and also shows signs of cruelty which alarm me. When he does not get his own way, he smacks me or looks round for something naughty to do, smacks his own face or throws himself on the floor. His tempers don't last long but are frequent. He only has tempers with my husband and myself, sometimes with his grandmother, and he is very sweet with strangers."

2. " She is an only child, aged 3;6, fully developed, of normal and regular habits. The trouble at present is that she takes fits of crying without any obvious reason, accompanied

by stamping of feet, and very often disobedience at these times. E.g. at lunch the other day, she was asked whether she would have an apple or an orange; she chose the orange and then immediately changed her mind and wanted an apple; which when handed to her, she refused, and commenced crying and stamping her feet. Another example: she was playing in the garden with her doll's pram, while I was cutting the grass—suddenly she started crying—on being questioned as to what was wrong—had she fallen, or had anything frightened her—she refused to answer and continued to cry and scream for about an hour. Some time later on being questioned as to what was wrong, she told me she could not manage her pram on to the lawn. I tried to explain to her, that if only she had asked I would have helped her—but she evaded my reasoning."

3. "Almost the first little definite action was to throw out her hands and scratch or tear at anyone nearest her. Now at the age of twelve and a half months she is worse than ever. If anyone happens to touch a toy in her possession she immediately flings out to claw at them and if she cannot reach will scratch at her own face. Scolding does no good but produces a scene of screaming and kicking. This is not only done when her temper is aroused, sometimes while happily loving someone and stroking their face she will suddenly pinch and claw them in a most spiteful way. I am always afraid of holding her too near another child, for fear of his being hurt."

4. "Although she (aged 2;6) is very sweet-tempered and loving, she has lately developed the habit of smacking people —sometimes for no reason at all, or if only mildly annoyed. Or she will even smack her own head or try to twist her hand off, saying, 'Pulling hand off.' Even her beloved 'Teddy' and 'Golly' do not escape. They have lately been squeezed or pressed on the floor unmercifully, the accompanying remark being 'Break Golly. Poor Golly!' These curious actions are not as a rule done very violently, nor is her voice malicious —though she sometimes grinds her teeth together."

5. "He (aged 20 months) now cries when anything he wants very much is offered him and rolls on the floor in a paroxysm of rage. It is most extraordinary as he has never been teased or repressed in any way."

6. "My little charge, aged four and a quarter, is a highly strung, nervous child. I find fault as little as possible, but when she has to be corrected she has a most puzzling way of behaving; for instance—if I tell her in a very serious voice I am very displeased, she will come to me a few minutes

afterwards and say, ' It is not nice of you to speak to me like that, now *I* am very displeased and shall not smile or talk to you, you see you have made me displeased and I am looking very cross ! ' "

7. " Occasionally at meal times she (aged 1;6) starts to scream for apparently no reason, and perhaps gradually works herself up, until it is impossible to continue with her food. Often she has a spasm of getting up when ' seated ', and when put back again, she obeys quietly enough, but screams and screams at the same time."

δ

BRIDGES, p. 55. "Hitting or pinching for fun, through sheer self-assertion and love of power, may be distinguished from hitting in anger by the lack of a provoking cause. A child hits in anger because he has been interfered with or provoked usually by the child he tries to hit. This kind of behaviour is scored on the emotional scale. But when a child hits another for fun, he is not annoyed by anything in particular. In fact it is usually the passive non-interfering child whom he is bold enough to hit or push."

BRIDGES, pp. 73-4. "Deliberate destruction of materials at the pre-school age, when the child is able to control such actions, is often done to annoy adults. It is then an act of excessive self-assertion, a defiance of authority or an expression of anger. Destruction of materials may also be a result of failure to respond to adult training and indifference to adult disapproval. It may occur sporadically due to excitement, or when a child is in a rebellious and irritable mood. In any case it is anti-social behaviour."

BRIDGES, p. 88. "In brief, children between the ages of two and five years progress through three roughly defined stages of development in their social relations with adults. In the first or dependent stage the child is somewhat passive and relies upon the adult for assistance and attention. The second stage which reaches its height between two and a half and three years is one of resistance against adult influence and striving for power and independence. The behaviour of the child then gradually changes from being resistive or obstinate to being co-operative and friendly. The desire to win approval and avoid disapproval grows. Conversation develops, and topics change from protests and wishes to descriptions of events or actions of mutual interest between child and adult. Thus the third stage, reached usually between the fourth and fifth year, is one in which the child shows self-reliance, trust-worthiness, and friendly co-operation with adults.

"There are, of course, individual variations in actual behaviour, and each child relapses at times to earlier modes of reaction. The conditions under which a child's social behaviour often falls noticeably below his usual standard are, when he is tired, when he is incubating a disease, when recovering from an illness, and after an emotional disturbance."

BRIDGES, p. 137. "A youngster who finds a task difficult or who fails to accomplish it may react to the situation by destroying *another's* work. Since he cannot show-off and assert himself by his own constructive efforts, his infuriated ego finds vent for itself in an act of derogation and destruction. An illustration, already referred to in connection with social development, may be found in the situation where two children of unequal abilities are building blocks together. The less clever child desires to emulate the more skilful one, and on failure to do so he may knock down the other child's block construction. In the mental examining room it is fairly common for a child to knock down the examiner's model after failure to copy it."

2. GROUP HOSTILITY

a. *To Strangers and New-comers*

α

21.11.24. A visitor was in the gallery and the children got a glimpse of her; they rushed up the stairs to stare through the curtain and watch her, and shouted out, "Old lady, old lady."

3.3.25. Christopher had been away for some time, and all were hostile to him on his return. Paul said, "Wretched Christopher." Harold would not let Christopher look at his painting, shouting vigorously, "No, you shan't." Later, all the older ones, running round the room, said, "Horrid Christopher, horrid Christopher," as they ran. Christopher wanted to go into Harold's aeroplane, but Harold would not let him, and had Dan in.

9.3.25. A visitor had come into the schoolroom during the morning, and Harold led the other children in clustering round her and saying with laughter, "Silly lady, silly lady." This appears to be his reaction to anything new and strange, as he and the other boys often say it about anything new in Mrs. I.'s dress or shoes. The boys were all very interested in Jessica, another visitor. At first sight they expressed various hostile intentions such as smacking her, kicking her, etc., but this very soon passed off, and she was very happy amongst them.

10.3.25. Emily came to lunch, when the boys were washing their hands. Their immediate reaction was one of hostility. Several of them said, " We'll smack her." Dan put a towel on her head, but as she made no response except to smile, this very soon passed off. Paul said once or twice she was " a wretched little thing ".

12.3.25. Frank and Harold brought a small snowball in and threatened to throw it at Martin, who came for the first time yesterday.

17.3.25. During the morning Mrs. I. told Harold and Frank that Priscilla was coming to lunch. They asked what her name was, and laughed at it very much. They at once spoke of " smacking her " and " throwing things at her ". When Priscilla came, Dan, sitting opposite to her, said several times, " Shall we shout in her ear ? " and, " Shall we hit her ? " Mrs. I. said to him, " Would you like it if we shouted in *your* ear and hit *you* ? " He at once replied, " No, I don't like to be hitted." Mrs. I. said, " And perhaps Priscilla does not like to be, either ". He replied, " No."

After lunch, when they went into the garden, the boys stood round her at first in an affectionate way, but later in a rather hostile manner. They said they would " squeeze her ". Dan stood with his arms open, saying, " Let's squeeze her." She replied, " If you squeeze me, I shall squeeze you " ; but later she found the boys rather overwhelming, and began to cry for her mother.

18.3.25. Martin came dressed in a sailor suit with long trousers, which interested the others greatly ; they laughed at him. Tommy said he was " a sailor " ; the others said he was a " silly sailor ", and they showed some hostility for a little time, Dan and Frank saying, " Shall we hit him ? " He had brought a woollen model of a dog, which one or two of the other children tried to take, until presently Martin took it to Mrs. I. to be taken care of.

Dan had brought several spare biscuits for lunch, including one specially for Theobald, but as he was not there, he gave it to another boy. He gave one to each of the boys, except Martin, and said there " was not one for Martin ".

Frank was trying to hurt Martin, and when Mrs. I. interfered, Harold, looking on, said, " *You'll* be killed soon, Mrs. I."

27.4.25. Priscilla came again to school. The boys showed at once a good deal of hostility to her. Dan referred to her as " he ", and they talked about " cutting her head off ", went into the garden and brought a saw and some shears, and approached her in very threatening attitudes. This lasted for twenty minutes or half an hour, but even from the beginning it was clearly mixed up with affection. Harold and Dan spoke of her former visit when they " made her cry ". Dan said they had " whipped her with a long pole " (a phantasy). Harold, Dan and Paul saw the scavengers sweeping the street, and spoke of them as " sweep men ". Paul said, " Hasn't he got an ugly face ? "

28.4.25. Laurie came at about 10.30 (as a visitor). The other boys were hostile at once, and when Frank insisted on saying " pop " to him, he cried bitterly. He worked in the garden sowing seeds, and was very interested in the hen. Frank kept coming and saying, " I shall say ' pop '. "

1.5.25. When Priscilla was leaving with her mother, Dan said to her mother, " We made her cry again." Mrs. I. replied, " Perhaps Priscilla might make you cry." He said, very heartily, " Oh, *I* should not cry. *I* shan't cry." They had " squeezed her hard " and made her cry, he said.

8.5.25. In the middle of the morning Laurie and his young brother came again. Frank at once began saying, " I will say ' pop'. " All the boys showed hostility to them, for a short time, Harold and Frank talking of " kicking him in the face ", but this very quickly wore off.

Theobald showed the most persistent, although not the most active hostility to the newcomers, as he had done to Christopher, too, a day or two earlier.

18.5.25. In the morning Dan, Frank and Priscilla had baited Duncan (a new-comer) a good deal. Priscilla said, " Shall we hit him ? " The three of them had torn up a painting which he had done. He had defied them in good humour. At one time, sitting on the stairs, they and Harold had said they would " pull him down ", and he had said, " Oh, you can't," and held on tight while they tried. When modelling, Dan took a large piece of plasticine and put a number of sticks into it. Priscilla laughed at this and said he was " silly ". She said several times to Frank and Dan, " We don't like Duncan, do we ? " She laughed at Dan when he spoke of candles, saying that he said " canles ".

19.5.25. Laurie wanted to join in the game that the others were playing, but Frank refused to allow him. He said, " *You* shan't come up."

22.6.25. A visitor spent the day in the school. She sat quietly on a seat. The children soon noticed her. A few of them spoke of her as " that old lady ", one or two of them called her " Dirty lady ". Later, when she was sitting near the water tap, Harold and Frank talked of " pouring water on her feet " and did pour water on the ground near her, but it was in a playful way, and they soon stopped doing it. She had lunch with the children, and Frank made only one hostile remark about it, saying she was "*not* going to have lunch with us". After that he was quite friendly.

19.1.26. When an old lady came to take Tommy home, Frank called her "a beast". This still seems to be his spontaneous reaction to any stranger.

28.1.26. Frank tried to get the others to say hostile things to Phineas, the new arrival. They all ran about rather excitedly, and Priscilla and Dan crawled towards Phineas, waving their arms about in a threatening way. Frank spoke of "pretending to shoot Phineas" with his toy gun, but Mrs. I. did not allow the game, as he would have been really frightened. Later on, Dan whispered to Priscilla that they should go and kiss Phineas's mother, and both ran to do so in turns. They did it several times, and the other children joined in. Then they began to do it to Phineas himself, who liked it and responded.

30.4.26. Dexter had been absent for a day or two, and when he returned to-day Dan and Priscilla said he was "beastly"; but they did not tease him further. They still, however, repulsed his overtures to friendliness.

14.6.26. A small boy came as visitor with his mother, and Priscilla and Dan greeted them roughly, threatening to "tie up" the boy.

10.2.27. Phineas and Lena were digging happily together in the sandpit. Lena began making her "pie" into a "castle". She made a little hole in the side with her finger and said, "There's a pussy in there." Phineas, looking in: "Where? Can you see it?" Lena: "It doesn't like you." Phineas: "Why?" "*Because it hasn't seen you before!*" Phineas, after a pause: "Does it like me now?"

δ

BRIDGES, pp. 54-5. "A group of children quite often behave like a flock of hens when a stranger is within their midst. Just as hens peck and chase a strange bird, so children may strike and tease a new child in the group. If a very young child is introduced to the group some of the children, especially 'only children', will be sufficiently interested to want to play with the baby and will follow him about and be gentle with him. Others will watch at a distance, or ignore him. If the new-comer is older than the members of the group, the children will stare apprehensively at first and later make friendly conversation. A child of the same age as the group may not fare so well.

"A new child who is aggressive and who interferes with

other children's activity may be treated very roughly. He may be punched and knocked about and scolded loudly, especially by the younger children in the school. The older ones will be more forbearing. If the new-comer is very tearful or obstinate he may be taunted, laughed at or scolded, and even pushed away from joining some small group. Even if the new child is just quiet and retiring he may be teased by scoffing remarks from the others and left out of group play."

BRIDGES, p. 64. "Although popularity is a behaviour manifestation of others rather than of the child under consideration, in the nursery school it may be taken as a good indication of the social nature of the popular or unpopular child. If a child has been scolded and shunned or even chased by the group, it is almost as sure a sign of the social undesirability of his behaviour as any of his own behaviour manifestations. Children scold one another for what annoys them personally, or for what they know to be wrong. They avoid children who are in disgrace or who annoy them; and they may even unite and ' set on ' to the bully or the rough torment.

"It is true that some children attack or just avoid the new child who has not misbehaved in any way. But if the group as a whole scolds the new child and refuses to play with him or have anything to do with him, then the new child has probably behaved in some disapproved way. He may have taken their toys, knocked down their building constructions, hit them, thrown sand at them, cried frequently, destroyed materials, or done other things of which either children or adults would disapprove. Thus if a child has been scolded by most of the other children, left out of group play or generally ignored, it may be taken that his behaviour has failed to meet the social standards of the group, and he should not gain a point on the above item."

b. To Adults

α

20.10.24. Robert and Frank were digging in the garden, and found some worms. Mrs. I. was digging near them, and Frank said to Robert, " Shall we put a worm down her back, so that it will bite her ? "

4.11.24. Dan said to the others, " Hit Mrs. I."

10.12.24. Frank having told Benjie to hit Cecil, and Mrs. I. having intervened, Frank whispered to Paul, " Shall we not speak to Mrs. I. ? " Paul replied, " No, we won't, because we don't like her, do we." This was said several times by Benjie, Paul and Frank.

3.2.25. Frank asked first Dan and then Tommy to " make Mrs. I. blind ".

6.2.25. Theobald said he would " get a lion and a tiger to eat Miss B. up ".

9.2.25. Mrs. I. asked Frank and Dan to put away the bricks they had used. They agreed, but said they would not do it " tidily ", that is, they would not fit them correctly into the box, but only " just put them in ".

11.2.25. At lunch there were the usual jokes about " taking all the sugar ", and about " not giving Mrs. I. any ".

17.2.25. Frank and Harold knocked down the things Miss B. and Mrs. I. had built with bricks.

20.2.25. Frank, Tommy, Theobald, Christopher and Dan ran round as lions, " big lions coming to bite Mrs. I.".

4.3.25. During lunch Frank, Harold and Paul talked about " killing Mrs. I. and Miss B.", and Dan said, hesitatingly, " Yes, we don't mind being alone, do we ? "

5.3.25. When Mrs. I. was playing the piano, Harold said to the other children, " Shall we take the piano chair away and not let her have it back again ? "

6.3.25. Frank and Harold had a squabble and Frank hit Harold on the head with a cardboard clock. Mrs. I. took the clock away according to her rule. Frank protested violently against this and Harold took his part against Mrs. I. Paul then joined in, too, with the others against Mrs. I., saying, " *Here* is the beast, I'll pull her down ! "

16.3.25. When the children were making a house in the sand-pit, Paul said, " Miss B. won't go into the house, will she ? as she didn't help to make it." Frank said, " Oh, yes, Miss B. will come into the house, but we won't have Mrs. I. in." Paul said, " No, wretched Mrs. I." Theobald said, " Horrid Mrs. I., we'll smack her to death one day, won't we, Dan ? " All agreed that they would not have her in the sand-pit.

Later on Frank said to Dan, " Miss B. is naughty, isn't she ? " " No, she is not naughty," said Dan, " she is lovely." Frank said, " Well, Mrs. I. is naughty, isn't she ? " Dan said, " Yes, naughty Mrs. I."

17.3.25. Dan and Tommy were there first, and when Mrs. I. said " Good morning " to Tommy, Dan said, " No, we won't say ' Good morning ', will we, Tommy ? " and presently asked her (playfully) to say " Good morning ", to him, so as to have the pleasure of refusing to say it. She did so, and he laughed heartily.

19.3.25. Dan asked Frank to sit next to him when painting, saying, " Because I don't like Harold." Harold evidently felt this very much. He at once threatened to throw water over Dan. Mrs. I. asked him not to, saying that she would take the water away. Harold immediately invited Dan to help him throw Mrs. I. " head over heels out of the window ". He went to her and pretended to do it. She laughed at him and all passed off in a joke.

20.3.25. Mrs. I. asked the boys to help her put the canoe back into the canoe house; they did so but pretended to refuse with much laughter. " No, we shan't, shall we ? " they said ; but they all helped.

24.3.25. Harold and Paul ran in from the garden, and said to Mrs. I. that they were going " to take you out and burn you up on the bonfire ". They laughed, put their arms round her and pulled.

25.3.25. On their arrival Paul and Harold remarked on Mrs. I.'s dress, one they had not seen before ; they said, "It's a silly dress, a wretched dress." Paul said, "Wretched Mrs. I."

22.4.25. The carpenter came to repair the hen-house and put locks on. The children watched this for some time, but Harold and Paul made one or two hostile remarks to the carpenter.

27.4.25. When the bonfire was burning Harold told Mrs. I. that one day the cocoa had been on the gas fire at home in the pan, and it had boiled over and made a " sissing noise " when it went into the fire, and that his mother was very cross because he had not told her that it was boiling over. Harold said, " I won't tell her another time." Frank remarked, " No, don't be kind to your mother—be naughty to her." Harold replied, " Yes, I *will* be kind to her, but I won't tell her when the cocoa boils over."

9.7.25. Dan and Priscilla pretended to be sick in the sand-pit, very realistically. At first in no particular connection, but later, it was Mrs. I. who " made them sick ". To-day and for the next two days, they often said, " Oh, there's Mrs. I.—she makes me sick," with dramatic gestures and sounds.

24.11.25. This morning Tommy and Priscilla were hostile to each other, no ground for this being noticed. When Mrs. I. defended Tommy from Priscilla, Priscilla herself became angry with *her*, and tried to get the others to join with her against Mrs. I.

The children wanted to bring out all the (extra stored) chairs from the cloakroom, to put round them as they worked " to keep them warm ". As on the last occasion there had been difficulty about putting them away again, Mrs. I. refused to allow this to-day. They said, " You're a cross, nasty old thing." And when presently Dan wanted to keep the general box of plasticine on his own table, and dole the plasticine out as he wished, and Mrs. I. refused to let him, he was very angry, and he and Priscilla and Christopher rushed about wildly for a time, shouting defiance. When, however, Mrs. I. said she would put the plasticine away altogether if they were not going to use it, they settled down to steady work in a friendly way.

27.11.25. Priscilla pushed Tommy when he was carrying a jar of water, trying not to spill it. When Mrs. I. held her arm so that she could not push him, she became very angry, and all the other children took her part, saying, " Beastly Mrs. I.", etc. Christopher and Priscilla were going to throw beans at Mrs. I., but gave this up cheerfully when she reminded them what a long job it would be picking them up again.

2.2.26. Dan and Priscilla said they would " push Phineas to make him cry again ". When they were going to him again, Mrs. I. held them back and would not let them go near him, and in trying to run past Mrs. I., Christopher bumped his head on the door. The others thought Mrs. I. had done this to him, and were very angry, saying that she was " horrid " and " beastly ", and " we shan't come to tea with you any more ". Priscilla said, " Let's be rude to her," and made threatening faces at her. When presently they understood that she had not done it to Christopher, they calmed down and were friendly.

12.3.26. Priscilla instigated Christopher to join her in pushing Jessica against the iron pillar in the schoolroom. When Mrs. I. interfered and held Priscilla's arm very firmly, and said, " You shan't do those things to Jessica "—showing some anger—all the children, including Jessica herself, joined against *her*. They said, " You're a beast," and, " Now we *shan't* come to tea with you when you ask us ! "

29.3.26. Priscilla was hostile to Mrs. I. this afternoon, and led Dan and Christopher to be so also. She called her " a beast " and threatened to spit at her. They were eating oranges, and Mrs. I. told them that if they spat she would take the oranges away. Priscilla did spit, and Mrs. I. took her orange. She was not very upset. Christopher remarked, " That was a good spit, Priscilla." She asked Mrs. I. whether she would give the orange back later, but Mrs. I. said, " No." They accepted this without further comment, and presently settled down in a friendly way.

7.5.26. Priscilla and Dan took away the beans that Alfred and Herbert were using on the rug. When Mrs. I. asked them not to do so, they called her " a fool ", and they and Christopher kept trying to take the beans again, partly in fun, partly in earnest. When he saw that Mrs. I. was serious in not letting them take the beans, Dan spat at her and said angry things.

June 1926. Herbert had threatened to hit another child with his spade, and Mrs. I. took the spade away. He stormed and cried and hung on to it while Mrs. I. had hold of it and was asking him to let it go. Suddenly Phineas, standing behind Mrs. I., hit her a sharp blow with his hand. When she turned and said, " Please, Phineas, don't do that," he said emphatically, " I shall if you're unkind to Herbert."

15.12.26. Dan was away, and Jane and Conrad talked about him. Conrad said, " Dan loves his mummy—he adores her." Jane: " Yes, he thinks she's everybody." Conrad: " But she isn't everybody, is she ? She's only one person. Do you like her ? " " No, not much." Conrad: " Neither do I." (There is every reason to think this last remark was quite untrue, and was mere pandering to Jane.)

Autumn Term 1926. Miss D. joined the staff of the school half-way through this term. For two or three weeks a group of the children, including Jane, Dan, Conrad, Priscilla, were extremely hostile to her, frequently calling her " a beast "—" Oh, here comes that beast "—saying they did not want to be with her, and creating difficulties at meal times and bed times. After two or three weeks this wore off and she was promoted to one of their " best friends " and a favourite member of the staff.

Easter Term 1927. Miss C. joined the staff at the beginning of this term, and was subjected to the same group hostility as had been shown to Miss D. last term. The children involved were again Jane, Dan, Conrad, Priscilla, with Lena and Jessica. The hostile attitude gradually faded away as she established herself in their affections.

c. *To Younger or Inferior Children or any Temporary Scapegoat*

α

10.11.24. The children very often like to exclude one or two of the smaller ones from their group. They say, " Shall we bury so-and-so in the castle ? Shall we kill so-and-so ? Shut him out," or, " So-and-so cannot come into our shop," " There are no so-and-so's in our castle."

When they all ran in from the garden to-day, they shut Benjie out.

12.11.24. Harold and the other children were saying about someone (whose name Mrs. I. did not catch), " I don't like his face, it's so ugly." Benjie suggested that Harold should run off with Dan's shoe; but Harold did so with Benjie's own. He hid it in the " dark place " in the garden. When Mrs. I. insisted on his finding it, he took a plant pot and threw it on the ground to smash it, piece after piece. Presently, however, when Mrs. I. suggested helping him to find the shoe, he cheerfully joined in and found it and returned it.

In a long imaginative game in the garden with " the coopie house ", (the tool shed), and " Mr. Coop ", Paul and Harold and Frank would not let Dan and Benjie and Tommy join in.

21.11.24. In the garden Harold, Paul and Benjie shut Tommy into one of the wired-off hen-runs. Half an hour later when the same boys were inside the run for some game, Tommy ran up and shut them in and fastened it triumphantly.

25.11.24. Frank and Dan were using plasticine together when Benjie came in from the garden. Frank said several times to Benjie, " Hit Dan in the face," and "Take Dan's plasticine."

2.12.24. Frank told Cecil to knock over Harold's model. Benjie asked him not to. Cecil did it. Benjie then said, " *I* shall knock yours over." Cecil replied, " Well, Frank told me to." Harold threatened to hit Cecil for doing it, until Mrs. I. explained to him that Frank had told Cecil to do it.

9.12.24. Frank cannot bear the other children to exclude him from the group in their talk although he often does this himself to other children, saying, " We don't like so-and-so " ; or, " So-and-so shan't come in this boat," and so on.

2.2.25. Frank and Theobald sat behind the blackboard, calling it " our house ". Dan said, " Shall I come to tea and dinner ? " Frank replied, " No."

16.2.25. Harold and Frank made a " prison " of bricks, the large bricks, being careful to leave no holes. They said it was " for Dan ".

After lunch, Harold, Paul and Frank were very noisy; they said to Dan, " Get out of here—get out of this house."

24.2.25. When the children were in the gallery, the others shut Dan out. After asking for a few moments to go in, he turned away and said, " Well, I'll make a motor bike myself."

25.2.25. Harold, Frank, Theobald and Paul teased Dan a good deal this morning, poking him with the toy soldier's bayonet, and Harold shouting in his ear very loudly, Paul also doing this a little. Frank, Dan and Harold made a " wall " in the door. Theobald came and knocked the " wall " down. Dan and Frank ran after him, and came back, saying, " I hit him," with much glee. Frank danced as he told Mrs. I. Harold said, " Shall I go and hit him ? " They kept building up the wall and saying, " If they want to come in, they shan't."

27.2.25. Dan cried when the others spoke again about " robbers stealing his toys ". Harold and Frank then shouted " Funny face " to him. Later on Dan began to laugh at all this, and when Frank talked about making a man " to steal Dan's things " and made a model in clay, Dan was unconcerned, and took it all as a joke. Theobald said to Dan, " Why don't *you* make a man to steal Frank's things ? " When Harold talked further about " making Dan " and " putting him in somewhere ", Dan said, " Oh, it will only be a plasticine Dan ! "

4.3.25. Dan and Frank were drawing steamers all round the floor. Paul began to walk on these, although Dan objected. Frank said, "You won't walk on *mine*, will you, Paul ? " Paul said, " No." He walked on Theobald's picture.

At lunch Paul served, and when Mrs. I. said, " Now, will you serve Dan ? " he said, " No, I *won't* serve Dan. I won't give Dan any dinner, bad wretched little thing." He did so, however, when he had served the others.

Harold and Frank tried to keep Dan from using the see-saw.

5.3.25. The children wore " Red Indian " head-dresses which they had made. When running round, with these on, Frank said, " Would you like one, Harold ? " and then, " You'll tear Christopher's, won't you ? "

6.3.25. When the children were playing at giants in the laurel bush, Paul and Theobald said, " This giant is going to kill Dan "—but later they were friendly to him.

12.3.25. Frank and Harold were hostile to Dan this morning. Theobald spoke about " dragging Dan in a sack ".

When the children were modelling, Harold and Paul made guns, and pointing them at Dan shouted very loudly in his ear. Dan pushed Paul. A struggle ensued and Dan bit Paul. Paul said he would " tell his mother what Dan had done ". When his mother came in the afternoon, Frank reminded Paul to tell her what Dan had done. She at once asked, " What had *you* done ? " and Paul told her.

Frank was very threatening to the younger children this morning, and Theobald more so than usual.

17.3.25. Theobald and Dan teased Tommy a good deal while in the sand-pit, taking his sand and other things away. Harold and Frank carried sand to the far end of the garden and made a sand castle. Theobald wished to join in this. Frank did not want him to, and they had a considerable struggle, Theobald rushing at Frank, and although much smaller and lighter, coming off undoubtedly the victor.

Harold had brought Dan a present of a cardboard clock, and then said to Dan, " We'll hit Theobald, when he comes, won't we, Dan ? " Dan said, " Oh no, oh no."

23.3.25. Paul and Harold made hammers and swords, and said they would " cut off Tommy's head with them ". Tommy then made a hammer and pretended to cut off Mrs. I.'s head, with much laughter.

27.4.25. Some reference being made to Dan's electric torch, Frank went to the place where it was under one of the bushes in the garden, found it, showed it to Dan, Harold and Paul, and, in spite of Dan's protests and tears, threw it over the wall into the next garden. Frank two or three times talked about "taking a hammer and smashing all Dan's toys up" in his room.

30.4.25. Mrs. I. overheard Harold, Paul and Theobald talking in the sand-pit about Christopher, who is not present this week. They had evidently been discussing where he was, and one boy said, " Perhaps he is dead." Another boy said, " I hope he *is* dead."

4.5.25. Theobald was hostile to Christopher. He hit him once or twice, and said, " You dirty horrid beast." He and Harold laughed at Christopher's pronunciation of " blossom ".

15.6.25. Harold, Frank and Dan conspired to try to make Christopher drink a glass of what they called " lemonade ", which was muddy water, and tried to force him to do so. Frank said, " Pinch his nose and make him drink it," and tried to do so.

19.6.25. Frank brought a box of strawberries gathered in his home garden. He began to give them to the boys at once, except to Christopher, and said, " Christopher shan't have any, shall he ? "

15.7.25. When Tommy and George went about with " coffee " made of sand and water, saying, " Coffee for sale, coffee for sale," to each of the children, Tommy, as usual, left out the initial " s " in " sale " and the other children all laughed at him and imitated him.

27.10.25. Frank and Priscilla were being hostile to Penelope. They said, " She's dirty—she's a faeces girl—she's hateful."

9.11.25. Frank and Priscilla were hostile to Penelope, saying she was "dirty", "a faeces girl", and so on. Priscilla kept this up with more persistence and vindictiveness than Frank. All the children just now say they " don't like Penelope " ; it seems to be a social fashion.

1.12.25. Tommy painted his hands, and Christopher, Dan and Priscilla called him dirty, spat on his painted picture and spoilt it. Miss B. took away the things they had been making, and they then turned their hostility to her, calling her dirty, horrid, and so on.

7.12.25. Dan brought some new toy engines to school, and let some of the other children play with them. When Jessica wanted to do so, Dan and Christopher took them from her forcibly, and made her cry in doing so. Christopher remarked justly, " It was hard to make her cry."

8.12.25. Christopher was rather irritable this morning, and Priscilla and Dan were overbearing with Jessica. Priscilla shook her when she would not do what Priscilla wanted; she and Dan took away Dan's engine from Jessica when she was playing with it.

19.1.26. Frank said he would bite Jessica, and tried to make the others join in hurting her. Christopher and Dan went at her, and talked of twisting her arms, but soon gave this up when Mrs. I. interfered, as it was only half-hearted and done to please Frank.

22.1.26. Dan brought some sugar-sticks to school and told the other children to help themselves from the bag. When Jessica arrived, the children all said they would not give her any, and called her " nasty, beastly ".

26.1.26. The children took down the coloured paper streamers they had put up about the room before Christmas, and ran about with them. Tommy happened to get a long piece and trailed it about. Frank instigated Christopher to tread on this and take it away. It was a green piece, and Frank and Priscilla and Christopher tore it up for " leaves " to tread on while they had " a wedding ". Presently they asked Mrs. I. to get down for them the remaining pieces, and she said she would do so if they gave a piece of it to Tommy. Some of the pieces happened to be longer than others, and Tommy got one of these. The others protested, with much discussion. Dan said, " He's *not* to have more than me, because I want so much."

2.2.26. Phineas cried vehemently when his mother left him, and this made the other children scornful and hostile. Dan and Priscilla said they would " push him to make him cry again ".

2.3.26. Dan and Christopher tried to get a button from Tommy. They couldn't get it, so Dan then said, " All right, Tommy, let me have it, I won't do anything." Tommy replied, " All right, then ! " and gave him the button. Dan's face showed the most amusing mixture of surprise, contempt and glee, at getting it by this device. He and Christopher ran off with the button, and Tommy chased them both about, enjoying the game as much as they. After a good deal of running and laughter, Dan in the end gave it back to Tommy.

3.3.26. Tommy wrote letters with paint and brush, showing great delight in doing it. The others laughed at his letters, Dan saying, " Shall I scribble on them ? " Tommy let him do so, standing by and looking on. Christopher asked him, " Don't you mind ? " Tommy replied, " No." He then " played " the piano, and the others again made scornful remarks, but he went on serenely.

14.4.26. When the children were using plasticine, Dexter made a hammer with a lump of plasticine on a stick, and hammered the table with it. The others were annoyed by this, and his very shrill loud voice, and said they would " tease him if he made that noise ".

19.4.26. Priscilla and Dan began to tease Dexter, running off with his crayons, etc. He came to Mrs. I. in tears for help, and did not try to defend his things.

21.4.26. Dexter can read very well, and Priscilla and Dan are much behind him in this. They have made one or two envious and surprised comments, but do not say as much about this as about his faults and deficiencies. He is much clumsier than they in holding cards, for example, and they are very scornful about this. They often tell him they don't like him. To-day, when he dropped something, Priscilla said, " You're like my Frenchman—and now I *don't* like you."

23.4.26. Dexter accidentally pushed some sand down into the ditch which the others had been making, and this led to their teasing him for some time. Jessica joined in at Priscilla's invitation, and sprung up and clung on to his collar. Although she is half his size, she has so much more determination, and was so fierce, that he was terrified and rushed to Mrs. I. for help. Later on, Dexter was allowed to join in the others' games, and all ended quite happily.

30.4.26. Dexter had been absent for a day or two, and when he returned to-day Dan and Priscilla said he was " beastly " ; but they did not tease him further. They did, however, repulse his overtures to friendliness. Later in the morning, when several of the children were busy in the tool-shed, Dexter suddenly, without any provocation, shut and locked the door on them. They were very cross, and when Mrs. I. undid the door, they wanted to do the same to him. They tried to pull him into the shed, and although he was much the largest of the children, he was terrified, and clung to Mrs. I. in urgent appeal. He was in such neurotic terror, in spite of his strength and size, that Mrs. I. had to protect him. They readily stopped, but Dexter cried to go home, and would not leave Mrs. I. for the rest of the morning.

4.5.26. Dexter had brought several bundles of bus tickets to school with him, and Dan wanted to have some of them. Dexter would not even let him hold them for a time, as he asked, and Dan snatched at them. Christopher and Priscilla joined in this, and ran off with the lot. Dexter came to Mrs. I. for help, and she suggested that he should run after them. He did so, but half-heartedly, and could not catch them; he kept returning to Mrs. I. to complain. Later on when he was doing other things, the children kept coming to him and offering the tickets, but snatching them away again as he reached out for them. He often got hold of the tickets, but did not hold on with any grip, and gave up readily when they pulled at them. On the whole he remained fairly cheerful through all this, and tried to laugh with the others, but tears were never very far away. Later on Mrs. I. asked the others to return the tickets, and they did so. Dexter wanted to join in with their pursuits, but they would not have him.

18.5.26. Dan, Priscilla and Christopher were again unfriendly to Dexter, and there was a good deal of mutual hostility, calling each other a " beast ", etc. When Dexter called Priscilla a " beast ", she said, " But I'm not. I know I'm *not* and *you* are." At cocoa time, Christopher, Priscilla and Dan sat down on a rug, saving a place for Miss B., and saying that they would not let anyone else sit there. Phineas said to Mrs. I. that he wanted to sit on the rug, and walked towards it, but made no actual attempt to sit down. He evidently felt the exclusiveness of the group, and said repeatedly, " I'm going to sit on the rug, aren't I, Mrs. I. ? " but did not make any attempt.

28.5.26. Dexter had brought a toy to school to show the other children, and let each of them have it in turn, except Jessica. He said he wouldn't let her have it " because I don't like her ". A few days later, Jessica had a toy which she was lending out, and she refused to lend it to Dexter " because I don't like him ". He was very hurt at this, evidently quite forgetting his own refusal to her.

When the children were modelling, Dexter made great effort to construct a railway line. His work is much more clumsy than that of the others, and they were quick to point this out, with scornful comments. " Isn't it a silly train—isn't he *stupid ?* " He crumpled it all up and started again.

20.7.26. Priscilla played a family game with four of the younger children, and this led to rivalry between this group, and Dan and Christopher, who were modelling and showed that they felt left out. They invited her once or twice to join with them, and when she did not do so, there were some passages of hostility between the two groups. They called out to each other, " You're not nice." " Yes, we are. *You*'re not," and so on. This was kept up for some time, partly as a joke. At lunch-time, Priscilla, Noel and Dan made what they called " a silly game ", making foolish gestures and baby talk, and saying to Mrs. I., " You won't know what we're talking about if we talk silly." Their antics and queer gestures when eating led Alfred to say with scorn, " You don't eat properly." " Oh, yes, we do—it's *you* who don't." " Yes, I do." " You're contradicting—don't contradict." " No, we're not—you are." This was kept up for some time ; then Dan tried to smooth things over, by saying, " It seems to us that you contradict and don't eat properly. It seems to you that we don't. But we do." There was then some discussion as to what " contradict " meant.

18.10.26. The children were drawing and painting. Dan and Jessica expressed great scorn of Phineas's picture of an engine, sniggering at it behind their hands, and saying to him, " That's not a nice engine."

10.11.26. The younger children made two " ships "— Phineas and Jessica had one, Lena and Conrad another. There was rivalry between the two, each pair declaring that the other was " a silly ship ".

2.12.26. The others all laughed at Phineas because he said " sigernal " for " signal ".

23.1.27. Conrad went out to lunch with his parents, and Jane and Dan said several times that they were glad he was going, and they didn't like him.

24.1.27. When the elder children heard that Lena had arrived, they said as if at some concerted signal, " Oh, that dragon has come," and ran into the schoolroom shouting in a hostile and intimidating way, " Oh, there is the dragon." Lena was at the other end of the room with Miss S., and did not seem to realise what they were saying. They were going to run near her and repeat it, but Mrs. I. prevented this. During the next two or three days, they made occasional hostile remarks, but were on the whole quite friendly to her. It all appeared to be a phantasy game rather than real hostility to Lena ; a few days later they invited her into their special rooms for play together.

Conrad's mother was in the school, and she was writing with him. Jane and Dan were occupying themselves apart, and Jane said, " I hate Conrad." " So do I," replied Dan. This seemed to be provoked by the mother's presence.

SOCIAL RELATIONS

25.1.27. To-day the children turned the hostility game which they had played yesterday, on to Phineas, running towards him with scissors which they had been using in their hands. Phineas is more easily frightened, and cried.

28.1.27. To-day after lunch, before the table had been cleared, the children were enjoying a romping game, and Conrad was watching them. He was so absorbed in watching their play, that he leant too heavily on the table and tipped it up so that some crockery fell off and was broken. He flushed and looked ready to cry, but refused to help pick the things up. The other children were very scornful about this, called him " a beast " and said they " hated him " because one of their favourite red plates had been broken. During the next few days they reminded him of the incident more than once.

7.2.27. Lena picked up a stick, which she held out in front of her as a sword, and Phineas ran into it. It was entirely an accident, and Lena at once dropped her sword, but Phineas was angry and cried. All the others said, " Now, we won't fight Phineas, we'll only fight Lena." Lena ran and clung on to Miss C., really frightened, but soon they were friends again.

8.2.27. The elder children (Priscilla, etc.) had borrowed Jessica's table to take upstairs for their own purposes. To-day she wanted a table to do picture blocks, and used one of Priscilla's which was downstairs. Priscilla remarked on this, and Jessica said, " Can I use it ? " Priscilla: " Oh, yes, I'll let you because we've got your best table upstairs." Priscilla could see more quickly than Jessica how the picture ought to go, and began to interfere with her. Jessica called out, " No, no ! " Priscilla said, " Very well, you shan't work on my table." Jessica tried to resist for a moment, so Miss C. asked her, " Would you like to get your own from upstairs ? " Priscilla and Dan opposed this, because they said the typewriter was on it, and Jessica was " not allowed " to go upstairs. Miss C. and Jessica went up to get it, and Priscilla and Dan and Conrad tried to prevent her getting it, but soon accepted the situation.

Spring Term 1927. Jane led the boys, all younger than herself, in frequent expressions of hostility to Priscilla, shutting her out of their games and persuading them to say they did not like her. Priscilla, who had reigned supreme before Jane arrived, was really miserable most of the time because of this, and did not recover her spirits until Jane went away before she did, at the end of the term.

9.3.27. To-day there was hostile feeling and rivalry between Jane and Conrad on one side, and Priscilla and Dan on the other.

14.3.27. Priscilla was very pleasant and helpful with the younger children to-day, but evidently feeling her exclusion from the group of the older ones, which they still maintained.

Later in the day, Dan played with Priscilla, and left Jane and Conrad together.

17.3.27. To-day all the older children banded together against Priscilla, saying they would not " let her have her turn " at anything they were doing, calling her " silly " and " a cry-baby ", and threatening not to let her have any dinner. She was pale and miserable, and very subdued. Jane kept up an ostentatious talk with the boys, openly cutting Priscilla out ; and under her influence Dan pulled Priscilla's hair. Later on, Jane took an opportunity to pinch Priscilla, but said she " did not hurt her very much ".

At lunch-time, Dan was serving, and said he wouldn't serve Priscilla—or at any rate, would serve himself first, which he did. Priscilla cried and said she wanted to go home. But he gave her a second helping when she asked, and although he pretended he was not going to give her any fruit, he did so, a generous helping. After lunch, Jane and Conrad went into the garden, and Priscilla at once began to try to make Dan friends with her. He had a water pistol, and squirted a few drops of water on her stocking. Miss C. took it away, but Priscilla asked for it back, saying she " didn't mind ", and that she wanted to look at it—all this obviously to try and win Dan's goodwill. She was successful as long as the other two were outside, and began to cheer up ; but when they were together again, Jane and Conrad renewed hostilities.

In the morning, Priscilla was again very friendly and helpful with Lena and the other younger children.

22.3.27. To-day Priscilla would not make any attempt to win the friendliness of the others. She said on arrival, " I do feel bad in my tummy," and was persuaded to lie down on one of the beds in the rest-room. She stayed there all the morning, and cried to herself, complaining later of a headache. The others took almost no notice of her, but made occasional remarks, " Little cry-baby ! " " She wants to go home." She would not come down for lunch, but ate what Miss C. took up to her, and went home early in the afternoon. She did not come to school again for a few days. Mrs. I. was away ill, and Priscilla said she wouldn't come until Mrs. I. was back.

28.3.27. Priscilla came to-day, and told Miss C. that she had had a letter from Mrs. I. (who had been away ill) to say that she was returning this morning. One of the other children said to her, " Silly little thing," and she began to cry, saying,

" I don't like them." During the rest of the morning, things went more happily. In the afternoon, the elder children were going on the river in a punt, but Priscilla preferred to go home.

29.3.27. When Priscilla arrived, Conrad at once called out, " Oh, there's that silly little thing," and she cried again. She had brought a toy to show the others, and presently they became interested in it for a time, and friendly. Later on, Jane was more friendly, and Priscilla was allowed to take part in the general play. At one point Jane reminded Dan that he " didn't like Priscilla " and tried to prevent him being amicable with her; but as Priscilla did not this time react to it, the incident passed off. The children told Miss D. that Priscilla had cried yesterday and to-day, but Priscilla took no notice of this, and had a much happier and more successful morning than for some time.

31.3.27. The hostile attitude was still marked; no aggressive acts, but scornful remarks and the refusal to co-operate. Jane said, " Don't let's do anything to her, but just don't talk to her." Mrs. I. carried her work to a rug on the lawn, and Priscilla sat beside her. Presently Dan joined them, and was friendly to Priscilla. Later on Conrad, and then Jane, also took their work there, and all happily talked together.

1.4.27. To-day the other children went away early for the vacation, and Priscilla and Dan were left together. Dan had promised to go and see the others off at the station, and Miss C. asked whether there would be room in the taxi if she and Priscilla went also to see them off. Jane looked dubious for a few moments, and then said fairly cordially, " It would be nice if we all went together." This was the first occasion on which she had voluntarily included Priscilla, and after that there were no hostile remarks from the others. Priscilla was allowed to have one of the favourite " spring-up " seats in the taxi, and they were all friendly to her at the station.

On returning to the school after this, Priscilla began to get very excited, with the triumph of having Dan to herself. She talked in a very excited voice. She and Dan climbed into a big box, their " house ", and talked of " getting married ", how they would " take a flat and live together ", and so on. After Priscilla had also gone home, Dan spoke of her a good deal, saying that he would ask her to tea. He spoke of her the next day again several times, in the most friendly way.

26.4.27. After the vacation, Priscilla seemed rather lonely and timid. Jane showed no hostility to her, and left her with Dan. Once or twice she commented scornfully on Priscilla's method of cutting-out when she was making dolls' clothes.

δ

BRIDGES, pp. 47-8. "Part of social development is learning to distinguish between right and wrong conduct—that is, socially approved and disapproved behaviour. A child first learns what to do and what not to do himself, and as he begins to take more notice of the behaviour of other children he also learns to recognise their good and bad behaviour. Errors, mistakes, and bad conduct seem to be recognised first. It is much later that a child points to, or comments upon, another child's success or good behaviour."

BRIDGES, p. 48. "The remark may only be intended to show recognition of an error and to have it corrected with no thought of personal comparison, but it may imply also an element of smug self-satisfaction on the part of the righteous complainer."

BRIDGES, p. 62. "One way is to taunt other children in a provoking way when they have made some little mistake, when they have been reprimanded by an adult, or when they are otherwise in trouble. Typical jeering remarks from the nursery school are, ' You're a silly baby, you're a cry-baby, cry-baby, silly cry-baby,' or ' He won't eat his dinner, he won't eat his dinner ' made into a rhythmic song. The child is apparently conscious of his own virtue for not having made the mistake or done the silly thing, but he shows no sympathy for the other child in trouble. As he develops he learns to control this tendency to ' lord over ' unfortunate or younger children, and to show sympathetic feeling and helpfulness towards the other child."

BRIDGES, p. 84. "It is quite common for three- and four-year-old children to taunt others by repeating their short-comings in a little sing-song. The older ones soon desist when they find it causes distress."

C. Friendliness and Co-operation

¶ The happiest days with children, as the happiest women's lives, are those that have no history. Only the more explicit and dramatic instances of *friendliness and co-operation* are quoted here as separate events. There were countless minor incidents of mutual helpfulness and common activity which could not be recorded, and long stretches of quiet constructive work which do not show here. For the sense of some of these, the reader may turn again to *Intellectual Growth in Young Children*.

α

6.10.24. All the children helped to carry chairs and tables, crockery, etc., into the garden for lunch.

Dan saw Cecil hit Robert with the broom, and Robert cried. Dan said to Mrs. I., " He did hit him, and he cried." Then, to Cecil, " You won't do it next time ? " Cecil replied sullenly, " No." Dan told Robert, " He won't do it next time, he won't do it next time."

15.10.24. Jessica came to lunch, and Dan took charge of her. He told her where to sit, and what to do, squeezing her affectionately every now and then.

16.10.24. Cecil was very helpful in putting things away to-day.

17.10.24. George and Cecil were climbing on the window-sill together. Cecil said to George, " I love you." George replied, " And I love *you*." " Do you ? " said Cecil, " Why ? "

21.10.24. When Frank said he would " bite Mrs. I." because she did not go to him the moment he called, Dan said to him, " Please don't bite Mrs. I., please *don't*." And to her, " He won't bite you."

7.11.24. Frank had hurt Harold's leg in a quarrel, and Harold lay on the floor with his head buried in his hands. Presently Dan, who was modelling, went to Harold and asked, " Is it better now ? Will you come and do plasticine ? " Harold took no notice and did not reply. Soon Dan went to him again, and asked the same questions ; and after a time, he said again, "*Won't* you come now and do some plasticine ? " Harold then joined the others and became cheerful again.

12.11.24. The children were all modelling, very quietly, and Dan made a boat and gave it to Benjie. Benjie told the others, " He has made a boat for me." Dan remarked, " Yes, I like you very much, and I'm going to kiss you." He kissed Benjie's hand. Benjie told the others, " He likes me." Dan then said to Harold, " I like *you*, and I'm going to kiss you," and kissed Harold's hand. Harold said, " He's a dear little thing," and all the others agreed.

25.11.24. Dan's father came into the schoolroom, and sat down beside Dan and Benjie, who were modelling. Benjie asked him, " What have you come for, Mr. X. ? " " To talk to you and Mrs. I." Benjie made a basket with eggs in it, and gave it to Mr. X. Then he made a motor boat and gave that to him, and then another basket. All this was quite spontaneous and most friendly.

8.12.24. When Harold was leaving in the afternoon, he took Mrs. I.'s hand affectionately and kissed it.

9.12.24. Mark came to lunch and stayed for part of the afternoon. The children were very interested and friendly, and wanted to show him everything. He ate his dinner slowly, and had not finished when the others went into the garden. They kept running in and calling him, " Where's Mark ? When will he come ? We want to show him the swing," and so on. When he left, they took him to the door in the most charming way, saying, " Goodbye, goodbye."

10.12.24. Harold and Benjie were pushing the large table to the other side of the room, and accidentally bumped Paul with it. Paul flung himself on the floor crying (although not much hurt physically). Harold ran to get his own handkerchief for Paul, and sat down beside Paul with his hand on Paul's head, comforting him. He kissed him, and sat by him until Paul stopped crying and got up.

Paul kissed Frank when leaving in the afternoon.

11.12.24. Tommy said to Mrs. I., " I'm going to kiss you," and kissed her hand several times.

When Benjie went home, he kissed all the boys except Paul, who followed him and asked to be kissed.

12.1.25. The first day after the holidays. Dan was there first, and said, " When *are* the others coming ? " Then, as Christopher arrived, he shouted, " Oh, *here* is one of the boys."

The children were all eager to talk and tell the others about all they had been doing in the holiday, and there were many shouts of friendly greeting and pleasure at being back.

21.1.25. The children had been playing a long game of " shopping ", and when they saw Mrs. I. sit down to the modelling table, they all came to join in. When Mrs. I. said, " Oh, we haven't put away the shopping things, have we ?

Shall we do that first?" they responded at once and all helped cheerfully to put them away.

22.1.25. Frank invented a new game, in which all the others joined, following his instructions happily. They all had to sit on a rug, with their hands behind them, and one child went round unclasping their hands; then they all had to chase and catch him, the one who caught him being the next to go round behind. Later on, the children asked Mrs. I. and Miss B. to "make a bridge", while they ran round and under the bridge as a "train".

28.1.25. Dan and George said to Mrs. I., "Will you come and have tea in our house?"—the corner behind the blackboard. With Tommy, they all played "visiting" and having tea, for some time. At one moment, when Mrs. I. went into George's "house", he said to her, "I want to come and have tea with you in your real house, your *proper* house."

6.2.25. Dan and Frank made an "iced" cake by crayoning the paper all over in different colours. When Miss B. returned to the schoolroom after an interval, Frank at once said, "Ask me to give you a piece of my cake." She asked for a piece, and he cut one for her.

9.2.25. Frank and Dan made a ship of chairs. They made a door to the ship, which they could open, and invited Mrs. I. into the ship. They took it in turns to run round the room a certain number of times, and then knock at the door of the ship, the one inside saying, "Come in, Sir." Dan insisted on the "sir". They asked Mrs. I. to run round and knock at the door, and got her to run round three times. Then they both ran together, ten times, this number being Frank's choice, and Mrs. I. having to count as they ran.

13.2.25. During the morning Harold and Frank had taken a knife that Theobald had brought and had put it down one of the cracks in the floor, but when Theobald was going home, Frank showed him where it was and they helped to get it up.

All the children helped to put away the chairs they had had for "a train", Harold and Frank at first saying they would not help, but doing so all the same.

16.2.25. Paul ran in when he arrived, saying, "I'm going to buy a polar bear now for you boys. When I get home, I'll go right out and get a polar bear—a real one, not a toy one." Paul has been very friendly to everyone for some time now, and particularly to Dan.

Seeing Mrs. I. open the skylight window, Dan, George and Tommy went to do it. They took turns, but when Dan had had his turn, he insisted on holding the end of the rope while

Tommy was using it. Tommy asked him to let go, but at first Dan would not. Mrs. I. asked him, " If you were doing it, would you want Tommy to hold the rope ? " He replied, " No," and let it go.

17.2.25. Paul had been very angry with Mrs. I. during the morning, after she had prevented him from teasing Dan. But afterwards he was particularly friendly. At lunch-time, someone noticed that she had not a cup, and Paul at once ran to the shelves at the other end of the room and brought her one. He put it beside her, saying, " It's for you." Later in the afternoon, he went into the garden, gathered a bunch of crocuses and took them to Mrs. I. and said, " These are for you, Mrs. I." During the following days, he was most friendly and co-operative with the other children and with Mrs. I.

Theobald persuaded the others to sit opposite each other on the floor in pairs, with feet touching and hands clasped, moving backwards and forwards. He called it " racing ". They all joined in, and greatly enjoyed it.

Dan had brought a cake to school, and asked for a knife to cut it with, sharing it equally with all the others.

18.2.25. Frank found a very large plant pot, and said he wanted to fill it with sand and make a " Christmas tree ". The others helped him to carry it to the sand-pit, fill it with sand, and lift it out. Frank chose branches of laurel, etc., and stuck these into it. Harold then asked for help in making another in another pot, and the other children helped in this, too. They then said they wanted to have the two trees in the schoolroom, and all helped to carry them in. Tommy asked the others, " Don't go too *quickly*—so that I can help ! " They spread the rugs out and put Frank's tree in the middle of the floor, and Harold's on the platform. Harold suggested that they should sing, and they sang the " Mulberry Bush ", and danced round as " fairies ". Later on, they modelled various things to put on the Christmas trees—balls, flags, toys, Father Christmas and his sleigh, etc.

20.2.25. Harold and Paul started a " shop ", and invited Tommy and George to join in. They did so, and played at this very happily for half-an-hour, asking Mrs. I. to go and buy crackers, etc. Later on they went into the garden, and took turns at pulling and riding in the " sleigh " they had made out of an old broken canvas chair.

24.2.25. Several of the children made motor boats or buses or cars with chairs, etc. Paul came to Mrs. I. and said, " Your motor bus is going," and when presently she went into it, he stopped " driving " it and said, " This is your house." Later on Frank and Harold invited her into their " cars ".

At lunch, Dan saw there were three brown cups. He said with glee, " There are three brown cups, now you can have a brown cup, and you and you," saying this to five people.

2.3.25. Frank brought a toy airship, and Dan wanted to use it. Frank let him use it for a time until the other boys came, then he refused to let Dan have it. Later on, Dan again wanted to have it, but Frank would not give it to him. Presently Dan went to Frank and said, " Frank, I have a big motor bus, and you can use that." Frank said, " Have you ? Can I ? " Dan said, " Yes, and now will you let me use your airship ? " Frank let him. Frank whispered to Dan, " Shall we bring the motor bus into the schoolroom ? "

4.3.25. Frank arrived first and said to Mrs. I., " I have brought some sweets, one for me, one for Harold, one for Paul, but not one for Dan." Miss B. told Mrs. I. later that Frank had brought one for Paul and one for Dan yesterday.

Dan was alone with Miss B., and talking to her ; he said, " Cecil doesn't come any more, does he ? I wish Cecil *would* come—I like Cecil. He hit me—sometimes. How does Cecil talk ? "

Harold asked Frank and Dan, " Would you like a ride on the rug ? " and pulled them round the room on it in turns, until he fell and bumped himself.

6.3.25. The children became " giants ". During the play Paul said, " This giant is going to kill Dan." Theobald at first talked also about " killing Dan ", but then became friendly to Dan, and said, " Will *you* be a giant ? Shall I get you a piece ? " (of laurel bush) and plucked a piece for him.

Paul was in the garden, and wanting to come in when the door was shut, he called out to Mrs. I., " Open the door, my Princess dear, open the door, my Princess dear."

9.3.25. Some of the children made an aeroplane with the wheelbarrow, etc., and Tommy joined in with the older boys very freely. Harold was a little hostile occasionally to him, but Tommy did not seem to be disturbed.

Frank asked Mrs. I. for some string and made a train with one of the cylinder sets, and began to pull it. Jessica immediately wanted to have it to do the same ; at first Frank resisted, but then, quite pleasantly, on Mrs. I.'s suggestion, let her have it for a short time, taking it back later. (N.B. This friendliness followed on much *verbal* hostility.)

10.3.25. Harold wanted to run round the garden as an engine, and asked Mrs. I., " Will you be a coach and hook on behind ? " (This was for him a very definite advance in social feeling.)

The children all modelled together the " things for Miss B.'s birthday party "—cups and saucers, plates, the tea-pot, a cake with nineteen candles, etc. (It was her nineteenth birthday.)

Later on, they carried some planks to a stone pedestal in the garden, and arranged them to lead up to the top of a box and then on to the pedestal, taking turns at running up and balancing on this.

11.3.25. Herbert came to lunch, and the other children were very friendly and polite, showing things to him and explaining them, and inviting him to join their games, etc. They took him on to the planks on the pedestal, which he called " London Bridge ".

Martin fell down and hurt himself, and Paul said, " He is a brave boy ", because he did not cry.

12.3.25. Frank suggested they should be " fairies ", and said that he would be " Iolanthe at the bottom of a pond " and the other people were to " call him ". He made a pond with some chairs and a rug and lay down, and asked Mrs. I. to call him and wave a wand over him, and he then skipped about as a fairy. He then took turns with the other children in doing the same.

17.3.25. Dan was going to tea with Theobald, and sat beside him whenever possible, saying he liked him better than he liked Frank. Theobald had told him he was going to give him a steam-roller, and Dan said several times during the morning, " *Oh, thank* you, Theobald," and told Miss B. and Mrs. I. about it.

18.3.25. Harold arrived first, and asked for Dan at once, saying, " I've brought a present for him—it's a clock." When Dan arrived, Harold gave him the clock. It was a cardboard model, and in turning it round, Dan broke one of the hands off. Harold gummed it on again, with great care and patience. (N.B. This is to be related to Theobald's present to Dan the previous day ; for Harold then went on to say persuasively to Dan, " We'll hit Theobald when he comes, won't we, Dan ? " Dan replied, " Oh no, oh no." And later in the morning, when there was some slight difference between Dan and Harold, Harold said, " Well, I'll take your clock home." This was very slight and momentary, and Harold and Dan played and worked together all the morning in great good fellowship.)

Martin had hit Dan, and followed this up by saying twice, " May I kiss your hair ? " But Dan shook his head.

Martin had been a little aggressive, and Mrs. I. asked him not to hit—putting it concretely, " Please don't hit Dan, or

Harold, or George or any of the boys." Harold overheard this and said," *I* wasn't hitting." She replied, " Oh, no—I was asking Martin not to hit you." Harold said thoughtfully, " There isn't any hitting now, is there ? "

19.3.25. The children were digging below the main support of a trellis-work, and Mrs. I. asked them not to do this. When she interfered, Harold said, " I'll brush you down " (with a large brush); then that he would " throw dust " at her. She said to him, " Would you want me to throw dust at you ? " He said, " No." Mrs. I. said, " Then please don't throw it at me," and he smiled and gave up his hostility at once.

Harold painted a house and said he would not let Dan see it. Dan asked Harold to let him see it. Harold replied, " Not if you don't love me." Dan said at once, " I love you." Harold then showed him the picture.

Tommy and Martin were in the sand-pit, and talked to each other thus : Martin: " Do you love me ? " " Yes, I love you." Martin: " I love you—I'm not going to hit you again. *Shall* I hit you again ? No, I'm not going to hit you again." Martin repeated this two or three times.

George defends the smaller children if the older ones tease. Paul was shutting Martin in the " coopie house ", and for a moment George joined in this, but then held the door open and would not let Paul shut it until Martin had come out.

Seeing the picture of a house that Harold had made, Dan said to Frank, " That's our house, isn't it ? " Frank said, " No, not yours—mine and Harold's." Dan replied, " Well, when I paint a house, *you* shan't come in it." Frank: " Then it's yours." Dan: " And Harold's and yours." Frank said, " Yes." Dan shouted with laughter and jumped up and down —" It's lovely, isn't it ? *Our* house."

20.3.25. When Mrs. I. was standing in the garden, Paul voluntarily brought her a chair, saying, " Here's a chair for you, Mrs. I."

23.3.25. Dan cried at lunch-time because he had not been given a brown plate, and when Harold, who had a brown plate, had finished his pudding, he took his spoon off and passed it to Dan—" You can have my brown plate." He stroked his hand affectionately several times, and Dan said to him, " I love you, Harold, I love you."

Dan's mother had come to lunch, on receiving a written invitation from Frank, and Harold was very considerate for her, pouring out water for her, and passing her things.

Tommy had thrown some spoons and forks on the floor, Paul, seeing them, said, " Someone has put spoons on the floor ", and picked them up. Tommy also threw some pieces of plasticine on the floor. Harold told Mrs. I. someone had "thrown plasticine on the floor". She said, "Who has thrown it?" He said, "I don't know." She said, "Shall we pick them all up together?" and he at once helped to pick them up. Tommy then began to pick them up, too, with a fork.

24.3.25. Harold brought a gift for Dan, a single piece of rail. When told it was for him, Dan said, "I'll bring one for Harold then. I know what it will be—a big large engine."

25.3.25. Harold and Dan painted at the same table, Dan sharing Harold's paint-box; he had not asked Harold for this, but Harold let him do it.

22.4.25. Harold brought a small metal object, which, he said, "will bang", as a gift for Dan; and Paul brought him an electric torch and a postcard.

24.4.25. Harold asked Dan whether he could take home and keep the toy engine which Dan had brought to school that morning. At first Dan said, "No," but when Harold said, "Then I won't bring you anything again," Dan said, "Yes, you can take it." In the afternoon, Frank asked Dan to give him a wooden bath; Dan said, "Yes, you can have it." Frank asked Mrs. I. to write the following on it, "Dan gave this to Frank to take home. It's a bath with flowers painted on it, and two tin bands round it. It's not for Arnold to play with" (Arnold being Frank's younger brother).

28.4.25. Harold and Paul brought gifts for Dan, including a large wooden engine.

29.4.25. Harold brought a paper windmill for Dan and a cardboard clock for Frank.

30.4.25. Harold asked Dan to give him the large wooden motor bus "for keeps", and said, "If you do, I'll give you my motor bus." There was a long talk about this exchange, and Dan agreed to it.

Priscilla often helps the boys to wash and dry their feet and put their shoes on after paddling.

1.5.25. Harold and Paul had had a squabble, and Harold had hit Paul with a muddy hand. Paul ran in, crying vigorously, and Harold ran after him. Harold came to wash the mud off Paul's face, and they both went out again together. Frank asked Harold, "What did Mrs. I. say to you?" "Nothing," replied Harold. "What did she say to Paul?" "Nothing, I washed Paul's face myself." (There had been no need to say anything.)

4.5.25. Frank asked Mrs. I. to help him write a letter to Dan's mother inviting her to come to lunch again. She told him how to spell the words he wanted to write, and he printed them; and sent the letter off to Mrs. X.

12.5.25. Priscilla brought a cardboard box full of small gifts for the other children, including a small basket for Mrs. I. She gave Paul a flat cardboard model of a boy, and he was very pleased with this for some time, running about the garden carrying it. But presently he said to Mrs. I., "*You* can have this, if you like." And when she said, "Thank you," and took it, he said, "Can I have the basket?" She gave it to him.

When Priscilla, Frank and Dan were digging in the sand-pit, Priscilla carried many cans for water for the other two, distributing them with severe justice, and explaining at length whose turn it was next, etc. She then (as usually) washed her feet first " so as to be ready to do you ", as she puts it, washing and drying their hands and face and feet, then helping them to put on their shoes.

13.5.25. Mrs. I. asked the boys to bring her a chair, and Harold and Paul ran to get one, carrying it between them. Paul said, "We brought it together."

14.5.25. The children and Mrs. I. were running round the garden as engines, and Paul said to her, "Do you want a rest?" She replied, "Yes, I do." "Come and sit on the ' 10 ' seat," he said. He then got her to join him in the game of sitting on various seats and counting up to so many on each—the " 5 " seat, the " 8 " seat, and so on.

18.5.25. Paul brought Mrs. I. a gift—a cardboard box containing boracic powder, "in case you have spots", he said. (His mother told Mrs. I. that it was entirely his own idea—he had asked her for a box and some powder to put in it.)

19.5.25. Harold fell down and hurt his knee. Duncan said at once, "Shall I bathe it for you? because you bathed mine yesterday." They went in together, and spent some time bathing the wound.

Christopher and Paul were running round the garden together as an engine, and Dan called out, "Paul! Paul! Stop! I want to talk to you! Don't run too fast, or Christopher will fall again and hurt his nose." (Christopher had fallen and made his nose bleed a few days earlier.)

21.5.25. Dan, when running, fell and hurt his knee, and cried. Paul came at once to see what was the matter, and shouted out, "Who hurt Dan? Who hurt Dan?" very indignantly.

Priscilla looks after the order in which the boys use the motor car, saying to each in turn, "Wouldn't *you* like a turn now?"

26.5.25. Two visitors were in the school and as soon as Tommy saw them, he went up to them, shook hands, and brought a third chair beside them, and sat talking to them. Christopher had already given chairs to the visitors.

Josephine came to lunch, and Dan and Frank gave her great attention, competing for her interest and affection.

19.6.25. Frank brought a box of strawberries from his home garden, to share with the other children, distributing some to each.

Harold had taken off his glasses, and left them behind when he went. Frank was saying " goodbye " to Harold and Paul and their mother, standing at the door, and noticed that Harold had no glasses on. He ran back into the cloakroom for them, and then ran after Harold down the lane, looking very pleased that he had remembered them for him. "*Wasn't* it a good thing I remembered he had left them ? " he said several times.

23.6.25. Frank asked Mrs. I. for the new shears at a moment when she was looking for them to use herself. They looked together, and agreed that whoever found them should use them first, and then hand them to the other. Mrs. I. found them, and used them for ten minutes, Frank waiting very quietly and patiently until she handed them to him. When she gave them to him, he said, " Thank you "; she remarked, " Perhaps you will hand them back to me when you have finished with them." " Yes," he said ; " and perhaps you'll pass them to me again when *you've* finished with them."

24.6.25. Dan brought a packet of sweets for Priscilla, to redeem a promise he had made two days ago. When he gave them to her, he said several times, " Aren't I kind of you ? " and told the other boys about it, saying again, " Aren't I kind of you ? " Then he said to her, " Now will *you* bring the present you promised *me* ? " (It had been a mutual arrangement.)

6.7.25. Frank saw Mrs. I. going to fill the chicken fountain at the garden tap, and heard her ask Harold to move out of the way. He came up and said gently, " Harold, will you move ? Mrs. I. wants to fill that." He took it and filled it, and carried it back to the hen-house for her.

8.7.25. Theobald and Paul made a motor bus, and were talking freely together. Theobald said, " Christopher shan't come in, shall he ? " Paul said, " Yes." Theobald: " No, he's too nasty." Paul replied, " *I* like him." Paul later made a house and invited the others in, saying, " I allow three boys in our house."

10.7.25. A lady visitor was in the school, and three different children at different times went to her and asked, " Won't you stay to lunch with us ? " When she said she would, Dan jumped up and down with delight and shouted " Hooray, hooray ! "

14.7.25. Several of the boys had used the plasticine and run into the garden leaving it about. As soon as Mrs. I. said, " Will the boys who have had the plasticine please put it away ? " Frank said at once, " Did *I* ? " and ran in to put it away.

12.10.25. Dan had not seen Priscilla for some weeks, and when he heard that she was returning to the school to-day, he was very eager for her arrival. When Penelope and Tommy arrived, he said to them, " Oh, you should have been Priscilla." When she came he greeted her with great delight, and took possession of her. They walked about arm-in-arm, and said, " We'll talk to each other, won't we ? because we like each other."

16.11.25. Frank offered to share his garden with Priscilla, and they dug together for some time.

20.11.25. Conrad came as a visitor, but was too shy to come into the schoolroom. He sat up in the gallery peeping through at the children ; they ran up and talked to him in the friendliest way, inviting him down. Later on Tommy asked Mrs. I. to go up and persuade Conrad to come down ; she suggested that he should go, and he took her hand to go with him. But Conrad would not come. When the children had cocoa, they tried again to get Conrad to join them, and Tommy poured out a cup of cocoa for him. He now did come, reassured by their friendly invitations, and spent the rest of the morning joining in happily with the children's activities.

1.12.25. Jessica was in the garden, and Priscilla and Dan wanted her to come in and join their play of " school " ; they kept inviting her, and after a time she did so. Priscilla took off Jessica's outdoor things and washed her hands for her. Dan said to Jessica, " You've come in because you love us, haven't you ? "

2.12.25. Phineas was left in the school without his mother for the first time. He cried with distress, and climbed to the top of the stairs, and sat there rocking himself with grief and anger. The others were very interested in him, asked why he cried, and made friendly comments. They kept coming up and talking to him, and showed him things to play with. Presently they won his interest and friendliness, so that he came down and sat with Jessica on the rug, using the beans and wooden measures. He was so happy with them that he did not want to leave when his mother returned.

8.12.25. When Mrs. I. left to-day, Priscilla and Dan kissed her—" everything she has on ".

9.12.25. Christopher asked Mrs. I., "Please will you send me a message as soon as you come home from your holiday, and I'll come to tea the next day." Dan said, "Will you send me a message also—no, two!" Christopher: "Yes, two messages, both saying the same thing!"

15.12.25. Jessica made presents of her drawings to the other children.

16.12.25. Some trestles for a trestle table had come from the carpenter, and before they were set up the children were using them as "horses". Dan, Frank and Priscilla had one each, and Christopher sat looking longingly at them for a time. Presently Priscilla invited him to share her horse, and sit up behind her. Later on she also invited Jessica to share it.

18.1.26. Dan was there first, and greeted Mrs. I. very eagerly—"Good-morning, Mrs. I. Will you come to tea on my birthday?" (In May.) He said several times this morning (the first day after the vacation), "Oh, I love you, Mrs. I., and I love you, Miss B." At one moment he put his arms round both, saying he "loved them both".

21.1.26. Tommy had put a chair on to a table, trying to reach up to pull down one of the lights (on a pulley). He could not reach it, but Frank, seeing his efforts and being taller, volunteered to reach it for him.

22.1.26. Dan and Christopher were going to tea with Mrs. I., and said several times during the day, "Oh, we're *so* glad it's the day we're coming to tea—oh, we shall dance in the bus!"

25.1.26. Priscilla and Dan wrote letters to Mr. F. "Dear Mr. F., We love you. We can come to tea on Saturday." Dan continued, "I'll bring you a funny thing. Love from Dan." When he had finished his letter, he said, "I *have* done a lot, haven't I? Oh, I do love you, Mrs. I." He is full of affection just now.

At lunch the children were teasing Miss C., but agreed among themselves "not to tease Mr. F., because he's such a darling. He's so nice, and we love him so."

29.1.26. Phineas came again with his mother, and the children were all very friendly and considerate to him. Jessica, Tommy and Christopher played ball with him, to make him feel at home.

1.2.26. The children had a game of "hospital" in which Mrs. I. was "the patient". A bed was made for her with chairs, pillows and rugs, and they all became either doctors or nurses. Tommy was very tender, held Mrs. I.'s hand and stroked her face, and presently said, "This doctor must come into bed with you." He tried to get in, but Priscilla said, "You must not," and insisted on his getting out.

2.2.26. Jessica told her mother, " Mrs. I. is my *great* friend."

Priscilla and Jessica again played with Phineas to make him feel at home—he was at first shy and reluctant to come into the school. He rolled a tin about on the floor, and Christopher, Tommy and Priscilla took turns in getting it for him when it rolled beyond his reach.

4.2.26. Christopher asked Mrs. I. to help him make " a wall of sand ", and while they were doing it, he asked her if he could " come to tea next Sunday ", and said he would " like to come *every* Sunday ". Later on, Jessica heard Christopher and Dan talking about this, and presently whispered to Mrs. I., " *I'll* come to tea with you one day, too."

10.3.26. Mrs. I. heard Priscilla suggest bullying Tommy. She asked Christopher, " Shall we, Christopher ? " They all started to do so. When Mrs. I. walked near to them, they rushed away, as if they expected to be punished. Priscilla called her " a little fool ". Mrs. I. stood quietly by, and Priscilla then said, " Oh, she's smiling ! All right, we won't do it," and came to her and put her arms round her.

16.3.26. When the children were drawing in the afternoon, they arranged their tables very close to Mrs. I.'s, saying, " Lovely Mrs. I."

23.3.26. The tension between Christopher and Dan for Priscilla's favour has been rather acute lately, but to-day they solved it satisfactorily for the time. They were making " boats ", and at one moment Priscilla said she wanted " to be alone with Christopher ". This led to a little trouble, but then she spontaneously arranged both Christopher's and Dan's boats in a symmetrical relation to hers, which made them all happy.

15.4.26. Dan is very friendly to Jessica just now, calling her " my lovely Jessica ". This may have been because Jessica brought him some beads the first day after the holiday.

22.4.26. For several days now, Priscilla and Dan have asked Mrs. I. to " be their mummy " ; and have insisted that she shall not call them by their names, but always as " lovey ", " sweetheart ", " darling ", etc.

4.5.26. It had been arranged that the children should go on the river in the afternoon, and during the morning several of them brought Mrs. I. flowers, saying, " Because you're taking us in a punt-boat—we do love you because you're taking us in a punt-boat."

5.5.26. Dexter and the others were to-day very happy and friendly together. The children were digging in and near the sand-pit, with a game of "making a new road". Dexter voluntarily put his superior reading and writing at their service, and wrote a notice, " This road is up for repairs," and fastened it up where they were playing.

6.5.26. The " road-making " went on again to-day, and Dexter wrote another notice, " This road is up. Cambridge," and asked Mrs. I. to pin it up near the " repairs ". The others were pleased to have the notice but did not invite him to join their game to-day.

11.5.26. The children were writing and posting letters to their parents. Dan wrote, " Dear Daddy, I love you up to 16." Then he said, " I want to put ' *beauti*ful Daddy ' "—very expressively and emphatically ; and this was spelt for him.

Dexter again wrote a notice for the play of the other children, a " nursing home " play—" Nursing Home, Cambridge."

12.5.26. Dan told Dexter, very apologetically, that he had accidentally dropped Dexter's spade down a hole in the floor of the summer-house. He said, " I'm *very* sorry, and we're trying to get it up." Dan enlarged the hole with his hammer, until Mrs. I. could put her arm down and get the spade up. He then helped to mend the hole with new wood.

19.5.26. Phineas had turned all the cardboard letters out of the boxes on to the rug, and came to help Mrs. I. sort them out. He remarked on those which he recognised, with great eagerness, saying, " Nice letters, aren't they ? *Nice* W. I want more W's, more S's," and so on. He kept giving Mrs. I. one or two of each kind, " *You* can have those, can't you ? " and continued patiently until the three boxes were sorted out and put away.

Alfred and Herbert stayed to lunch, and the other children played host to them very charmingly. Dan got out various things for them in the afternoon, and sat down beside Alfred. " I do love Alfred. I love him best in the school."

2.6.26. Dexter has several times refused to lend things to Jessica, saying, " I don't like her." To-day he made " pictures " for her, and took them downstairs to give to her. Then he made other pictures for Priscilla, Christopher and Dan, taking them to each in turn. Phineas and Herbert were using the insets, and they brought some to Mrs. I., saying, " *You* can have these, can't you ? "

4.6.26. When Priscilla shut Dan up as a " puppy ", and he began to cry with boredom, Alfred said to him, " Don't cry, Dan—I'll be your nurse," and Priscilla agreed to this.

10.6.26. There was an argument between Christopher and Dan as to whether Christopher could take the tricycle outside and ride it. Dan said, " You must *not*," and Christopher replied, " If I don't have it, I shan't love you." Dan: " All right, then, you can."

18.6.26. Jessica was trying to build with bricks on the rug on the lawn, and they would not stand up. Priscilla then showed Jessica how to lay a table down flat and build on that.

24.6.26. The other children were very concerned for Herbert when he was frightened of a spider, and did their best to reassure him that it would not hurt him, and later that " Mrs. I. has taken it away."

28.6.26. Dan and Christopher knocked nails into the wooden floor of the summer-house. The boards were very springy, which made it difficult. Mrs. I. put her foot on a board to help, and Dan looked up and said, " Oh, *thank* you, Mrs. I., for standing on it—that makes it much better." Christopher said, " I'll get you a chair so that you can keep your feet down."

7.7.26. The carpenter came to make a see-saw, to the children's delight; and when he came the second time, they ran to greet him, " Oh, dear Mr. Jones—we love you, we love you."

20.7.26. Mrs. I. told the children that Dexter, who had been away from home for some weeks, had come back, and that she had seen his baby sister. They said they " wished he would come to school ", and used many affectionate expressions about him. They asked, " Will you invite him to come? " Mrs. I. replied, " Perhaps you'll do so? " Christopher, Dan and Priscilla at once sat down and each wrote a post card inviting him, and saying, " Will you bring the baby as well ? "

21.7.26. Mrs. I. was writing in the schoolroom, and most of the children were in the garden. Christopher came and asked her, " Won't you come and write outside ? " She said, " Perhaps the wind would blow my papers about." He replied, " We can put something on them to keep them down," and carried bricks to a table for her.

3.10.26. Conrad gathered a large box of pears, brought them in and suggested that they should cook some for lunch. He, Phineas, Lena, a visitor and Mrs. I. then together peeled and cooked some. This was Conrad's first voluntary share in the life of the school, and he did it with eagerness and pleasure.

8.10.26. The children were using the bells, and taking turns at this very amicably. Phineas found it difficult to await his " turn ", but did not express his impatience in any more forcible way than by saying, " It *is* a long time to wait ! "

11.10.26. Tommy had scattered the beans on the floor, and Jessica volunteered to help him pick them up, doing so very patiently.

27.10.26. Tommy gathered figs from the fig tree, cut them into halves and made presents of them to the other children. The older ones were very much occupied, and Noel said he didn't want the figs—with some impatience at being interrupted. Tommy asked, with a puzzled air, " *Why* doesn't he want them ? " He asked where Priscilla was, as he wanted to give her a present. She had gone home early, and he said he would send them to her. Mrs. I. asked, " How will you send them ? " " Well, if you'll give me an envelope, I'll put them in it." She gave him one, and he asked her to write the address on it, he dictating. He then said, " I'll post it if you'll give me a stamp," and did so, putting in the two halves of a fig.

28.10.26. Mrs. I. began to wind some skeins of wool into balls, and Jessica, Dan, Lena and Tommy offered to help, and did so for a long time, with great care.

Dan was particularly sociable at lunch, and through all the later part of the day—full of help and attention to other people, in striking contrast to his difficult mood of the early morning.

25.11.26. Priscilla was making a jumper and skirt for herself, and wanted to complete it in time for the Eurhythmics class. She finished the skirt entirely by herself, but asked Mrs. I. to help her with the jumper. Mrs. I. buttonholed the neck and sleeves ; Priscilla hugged her, saying, " Oh, I *do* love you. Do you know why ? It's because you've done my buttonholing so nicely ! "

29.11.26. When Miss D. invited the children to stay up to supper with her, Dan jumped up and down for joy, and said " Oh, I do like Miss D. She is my fourth nicest lady."

1.12.26. To-day Dan came to Miss D., put his arms round her, and said, " I do love you ! I love you next to my Daddy ! "

2.12.26. Priscilla had brought sheets of coloured paper to make streamers to decorate the schoolroom. She made rings and strung them together. The other children wanted to join in this, and she generously gave them each some paper, and showed them how to make the rings. The younger ones sat round her in a circle to learn. She gave particular help to Phineas, who was very anxious to do it, but rather inept. He struggled very hard to learn, and spent all the rest of the morning on it, in the end making a long string of rings. The other children commented on his achievement in admiring tones, standing round—" Fancy Phineas being able to do that ! Isn't it splendid ! "

3.12.26. Dan had spent several days making a bag. He asked Mrs. I. if she would buy it. As she had already bought as many as she wanted, she refused. He said, " Won't you buy it to give someone for a Christmas present ? " " No, thank you, I have enough for that purpose." With a most gracious air, he then said, " Oh, well, *you* can have it as a Christmas present."

9.12.26. Jane was teasing Conrad, and Dan took his part against her, saying, " I like him very much indeed—I *adore* him."

10.12.26. Dan's mother had tea with the children. Before she came, Dan arranged a place for her next to him, spreading jam on the bread. When she arrived, he showed her what he had done—" It's because I like you so much. I do love you so."

The children were making " ships " with the chairs, and wanted to use the chair on which Miss D. was sitting. She offered to sit on the table. Jane said, " Oh, isn't she nice ? " Dan : " Yes, very nice. She can come into my room without knocking."

12.12.26. When Miss D. arrived, Dan called out, " Here is my dear, here is my dear."

19.1.27. Jessica hurt her finger when moving one of the tables. Phineas at once went over to her and said, " Jessica, I'll rub it for you."

21.1.27. The children were using paste and paper, and Phineas put a little rag on to Jessica's tables, saying, " There's a little one to wipe your fingers when your fingers get pasty."

24.1.27. The children were making paper chains, and Phineas began to sing softly in a sort of chant, over and over again, " Look at the lovely one Lena is making."

25.1.27. Jane, Conrad and Dan were out for a walk with Miss D., and Conrad said to Dan, " I love you, Dan. Do you like me ? " " Yes."

26.1.27. Conrad dug a trench in the garden, and had been working quite hard at it, when Phineas came out, and also began to make a trench near by. Conrad called to him, " I'll come and help you soon, Phineas," and Phineas told Miss C., " Conrad's coming to help me." Lena helped both of them by bringing up the barrow to carry away their heaps.

31.1.27. Dan had brought a new and very large wooden engine to school, and one of the younger children got on to it. At first Dan protested sharply ; but when Mrs. I. asked him to put it away if he did not want the others to use it, he said cheerfully, " All right, they can use it. I'll leave it there for them."

4.2.27. The younger ones were playing a " hiding " game, and during this Phineas ran up to Lena, put his arms round her and said, " I'll love you, Lena."

Dan made an elaborate sand-castle for Jessica, " because I like her so much."

Phineas ate his orange so slowly that there was a half untouched when the others had finished theirs. Dan pointed to it and asked, " Can I have it ? " Phineas said, " Yes." Dan : " Oh, thanks ! I do love you."

Phineas made a sand-castle. He poked holes in the side with his fingers, and said, " Look at all my windows." Then he asked Lena, " Do you like my castle, Lena ? " " No." " Why ? " " I hate the windows." Phineas: " I'm going to cover the windows," and he smoothed them all out.

8.2.27. Dan and Priscilla had some sort of " secret ", and shut Jane out of this. She was drawing, and presently offered to " draw a picture for Priscilla and Dan ". They both said they liked her, after this.

9.2.27. Dan asked Priscilla if he could go home with her to tea in the afternoon. She replied, " Yes, I think you can. I think it will be all right. My mummy is going to have tea with me at home to-day." Dan said, " Oh, then I can come. Oh, I am pleased." And later, " Oh, I'm so pleased." And again, " Oh, I *shall* be pleased when half-past three comes." He was asked, " Aren't you pleased now ? " " Oh, yes, but I shall be more so when it's time to go."

11.2.27. Lena and Phineas were " building a wall " with bricks, using the sand as mortar. Lena said, " I'll be the putty-man and you be the one to stick the bricks." At one moment Phineas said, " Help me put this here, then I'll be glad." And again, " Help me do this, then I'll be very pleased." She did help him.

12.2.27. Phineas was digging quietly in the garden, when he turned to Miss C. and said, " I wish I lived here. I love being here. I love the Malting House."

21.3.27. A lady visitor had been in the school for some hours, and when she left, Phineas said to her, " Goodbye ! Come again some day—you are a nice lady."

29.3.27. The children had made a steamer, and had " gangways " of the small ladders. When Jessica was crossing one of these, the ladder slipped and she fell and hurt herself a little. Dan said he was " *Very* sorry " about it, " I *am* sorry, Jessica," because he had put the ladder up, and " should have put it firm ". He repeated how sorry he was, and invited her to share his " cabin ". As she had been wanting to get into his cabin for a long time, this made her very happy.

28.4.27. Alice took Mrs. I.'s hand and said, " Shall we pick some daisies ? " She led Mrs. I. to a patch of daisies at the far end of the lawn and picked some. After carrying them about for some time, she gave them to a man visitor. (She often made these gifts of flowers, throughout the term.)

Herbert was delighted with the experience of sawing with the two-handled saw. He called to several people, "See what I'm doing!" And said to Miss C., "After all, I'm only a little boy and *men* saw wood!"

7.5.27. Penelope said to her nurse, "I like James, he's a funny little boy—and so am I." She was asked, "You're a little boy?" "No, but I'm funny."

24.5.27. A number of children were standing rather crowded round the edge of the sand-pit, and when Phineas did not move out of Dan's way immediately on request, Dan pushed him. It was quite a slight push, but it happened that Phineas was standing precariously balanced, and that he fell in such a way as to hit his head sharply on the side of the wall. His head was cut, and the children were all very subdued when they saw the blood. Half a dozen of them followed into the cloakroom and stood around in silence while the wound was dealt with. Dan was very distressed at the result of his hasty action—"I didn't mean him to cut his head on the stone, and he wouldn't get out of the way when I asked him to." Presently he followed the others into the cloakroom to watch Phineas, and said, "I'm awfully sorry, I'm *very* sorry—I didn't mean to hurt him." Mrs. I. replied, "No—a thing like that is very quickly done, isn't it?" He told Phineas, "I'll give you a present, Phineas," and gave him a much-treasured book that he had made himself. Phineas was very little disturbed, and only cried a little. The children standing round remarked on this, and admired his courage.

27.5.27. Priscilla defended James against Tommy, who had pinched him and made him cry. She is at present extremely sociable, sensible, and apparently very happy among the others.

May 1927. The children all helped to carry into the garden enough chairs for each child to have one of his own. Each child sawed off a piece of the legs to make the chair the right height for himself, and then painted it a chosen colour. Mrs. I. suggested to the older group that they should do their sewing and painting in the afternoons only, as there were so many children present in the morning. Although they were very eager to get on with it, they agreed to this after a little mild protest.

June 1927. A man visitor, an old friend of James', had had tea with the children in the garden, and afterwards James went up to him, and said, "When are you going?" The visitor replied, "Oh, presently." James: "Will you go now?"

"Why?" "Well, after you've gone I'm going to play with Denis, but as long as you're here, I'd like to talk to you, so please will you go now?"

23.7.27. Denis spent the morning in the school in response to the children's invitations. They treated him in the most friendly and hearty way, Dan shaking hands with him when he arrived. He joined with all in a picnic up the river in the afternoon, on Priscilla's invitation.

II. THE DEEPER SOURCES OF LOVE AND HATE

A. INFANTILE SEXUALITY

1. ORAL EROTISM AND SADISM (Biting and Spitting)

α

16.10.24. Robert and George, when supposed to be resting in the schoolroom, made a loud screaming noise; they then took the rugs, put the end in their mouths and ran about. (Note also 16.10.24 under GUILT AND SHAME.)

22.10.24. George again put the rugs into his mouth when resting. He always puts his plasticine into his mouth.

At lunch, Robert said, " Shall we wee-wee on the table ? " and then suddenly, " Here's the wee-wee," and spat on his plate.

24.10.24. (See incident under CASTRATION FEARS, THREATS AND SYMBOLISM.)

28.10.24. Cecil spat at the other children, in anger. (This developed in him spontaneously and suddenly, before any of the other children had spat, and was a difficulty for some weeks.)

29.10.24. When drinking out of their cups, the children made bubbling noises with their mouths. Benjie and Harold began it, and the others followed.

4.11.24. There was again much spitting and bubbling at lunch, and the children showed each other the food protruding from their mouths.

5.11.24. Benjie very often spits in defiance.

14.11.24. Benjie spat several times to-day, at Dan and at Mrs. I.

28.1.25. George and Frank, having climbed up to the window overlooking the lane, to see a motor, began to spit on to the window; Dan joined in; they all spat vigorously, and said, " Look at it running down." George also spoke of " belly ", and Frank of " ah-ah lu-lu ", and " bim-bom ", both laughing.

12.2.25. George spent about two hours modelling. At first this was directed and constructive, but later on he began to fiddle with the plasticine, sitting vacantly with it and putting it into his mouth.

25.2.25. Harold had accidentally kicked Mrs. I.'s foot under the table, and this led him to say, " I'll undress you and take off your suspenders, and gobble you all up."

2.3.25. Frank spat at Dan, but wiped the saliva off.

23.3.25. Tommy pretended to eat plasticine, occasionally putting a small piece into his mouth. He brought spoons and forks from the shelf to use with the plasticine.

24.4.25. Frank was again in a difficult and hostile mood, spitting, saying " dirty ", and biting.

8.5.25. George and Christopher were sitting opposite each other at one table doing plasticine and somehow excited each other very much. They began throwing the plasticine at each other, putting it in their mouths and biting it and laughing in an excited, screaming way. This went on for some time, until Mrs. I. took the plasticine away.

20.5.25. (See also the incident with " tiger's teeth " in MAKE-BELIEVE AGGRESSION, on p. 46.)

17.6.25. Some of the children, who had been in " a hiding place ", came out, led by Duncan, who was carrying a stick as a weapon, looking very fierce. They came out looking for animals " to kill for meat " to take back to the house. Apparently Duncan was " the father ". When they saw Mrs. I. through the window of the schoolroom, they came in to her, saying, " There she is," looking very fierce, and said they would cut her up. All joined in the play and then ran off happily.

24.6.25. When Priscilla, Frank and Duncan were playing with the puppy, Priscilla said something about " sucking that ", obviously referring to the dog's penis. Duncan said, " Oh, you dirty thing." Frank laughed. Priscilla said, "and get milk ". Duncan: " You don't get milk from dogs ! " Someone asked where one did get milk. Duncan replied, " From cows and goats."

29.6.25. At lunch there was some talk of spitting, and Duncan said, " Here's the spit-jar "—referring to a glass jar he had there.

Summer 1925. During this first year, Frank was constantly putting something into his mouth to suck or bite—pencils, chalk, plasticine, bricks, a sponge, sticks, the handle of his spade, or anything else he was using ; and when not occupied, he sucked his finger vigorously and continuously. As a result, his mouth was always dirty. On two occasions during the first term, he bit a hole in Mrs. I.'s mackintosh hanging up in the cloakroom, and more than once suggested to Dan and Harold that they should tear the coats of other children in the cloakroom.

11.10.25. In the garden, Tommy ran after Mrs. I. and caught her. He said, " I'll kill you," and called Christopher and Penelope to " come and help me push her down and kill her—and make her into ice-cream!" Then to Mrs. I., "I like ice-cream! It will be pink ice-cream! I like ice!"

2.2.26. At lunch there was some talk about "cutting Mrs. I. up" and "having her for dinner". Priscilla said she would "have her head", Christopher "her finger", Dan "from her tummy to her bottom".

29.3.26. Priscilla was again very hostile this afternoon, and led the others to join with her in calling Mrs. I. a "beast", "filthy" and so on; and threatening to spit at her.

Autumn 1927. Denis, throughout the term, was very fond of biting the finger of any grown-up he passed near, and unless prevented would bite quite hard. This was not done in apparent temper; and when one refused to let him bite, he would sometimes say, "Then I'll kiss you," and kiss instead.

21.10.27. At the lunch table, Ivan had been annoying the other children by making "engine noises" continually with his mouth. One of them said in desperation, "I wish there was no such boy as Ivan." Dan said, "I wish he was a fish-cake, and then he would be eaten up." Some of the others pulled sour faces and said, "Oh, no, we wouldn't eat *him*." Presently Denis said, reflectively, "I wish he was *this* piece of fish-cake" (putting it into his mouth) "and then he would be eaten up!"

β

1. X., a girl, when about 9 years of age, was playing at "Postman's Knock" and called out of the room a boy "sweetheart" of the same age, to give him "a letter", i.e. a kiss. At the critical moment she was overcome with shyness and offered him "a bite of her apple" (which she was eating) instead. To her great chagrin, he took this instead of the kiss.

2. At 6 to 7 years X. often ate chalk and paper. Up to 8 or 9 years she tore the corners off the pages of any book she was reading and chewed them.

3. H., aged 2;6, was asked by a grown-up, "What does J. have for his tea?" (J. being a baby brother of 5 or 6 months). H. replied, "Bites Mammie."

4. C., about 5 years of age, was stroking a large collie dog, when it sniffed at his trousers in the genital region. "Oh", he said, "it wants to suck."

5. "At 4 years of age N. was found nearly choking, and purple in the face, swallowing something very large. As soon as she had got it safely down and could speak, she told her nurse, "It's B.'s whistle" (an ordinary sized whistle belonging to her elder brother, of which she had been very envious).

She said, " I didn't like the noise it made, and so I hid it in myself. "

6. A woman friend in charge of two children, a boy of 7 and a girl of 6, both charming, intelligent and quite healthy and normal children, told me that she overheard the boy ask the girl, when they were both resting in their room in an afternoon, to lick his penis. The girl said she did not want to, and the boy then said she " must do it " when he went to the lavatory. Later on, he tried to get her to go to the lavatory with him, but of course the governess prevented this.

γ

Problems with regard to food and feeding arising among young children (in my letters from mothers and nurses) include the following : Refusal to eat particular foods (e.g. jelly, milk, white of an egg, the meat course, etc.), this refusal being either habitual or of a sudden onset ; general unwillingness to eat unless coaxed or pressed or spoon-fed or talked to entertainingly ; taking a long time by dawdling or playing ; refusal to eat anything but soft food ; refusal to drink at all ; gobbling and cramming, with tears and temper if this is interfered with ; restlessness and fidgets at the meal, hysterical vomiting at particular foods (not necessarily the same foods every day) ; " parking " the food in the side of the mouth for an indefinite time and refusing to chew or swallow it ; " talking nonsense " as soon as the meal starts and showing disagreeable obstinacy if this is prohibited ; sudden screaming at the sight of the meal or in the middle of the meal ; rage and screaming even when the food offered is known to be liked, and rolling on the floor in rage at its being offered ; throwing plate or spoon on the floor as soon as the meal starts, etc., etc.

1. " She (aged sixteen months) is always ready for her food, and gets very excited when she hears it being brought up, but the minute I start feeding her she starts to cry. Sometimes it's only a sort of grizzle to start, but often ends in a very loud scream. She wants the food, but is crying the whole time she is eating."

2. " He (aged twenty months) now cries when anything he wants very much is offered him and rolls on the floor in a paroxysm of rage. It is most extraordinary as he has never been teased or repressed in any way."

3. " My boy is twenty-one months and is thoroughly healthy and normal physically. Sleeps fourteen hours or so, is extremely intelligent and vivacious, but inordinately strong

willed. We have had innumerable tussles with him of a more or less tempestuous nature but he has come smilingly through them all and has given in over every point except meals, and the latter are a nightmare. It started at fifteen months over tea time and has now spread to every meal. He would sooner go without rather than eat rusks, toast and bread and butter. About six weeks ago I tried starving him for twenty-four hours, after which for over a fortnight his meal times were a joy to us all and he put on twenty ounces. Since then he has relapsed again, first whined over his tea, messed it all up and had nothing, next, the same procedure over his breakfast and finally over his dinner. He loves his milk (one pint per day at most) and would eat porridge *ad lib.*, or cake, but I will not allow that, and if he refuses or throws his rusks about I take all his food away and leave him without. By the next meal time it is evident he is ravenous but has no intention of yielding and keeps himself going on a mug of milk. He will, on the other hand, eat a huge quantity if he goes out to tea, but he will not do so at home whether Nanny or Daddy or I give him his tea. He is equally bad with any of us."

4. "My little boy is two years old, and until now has been quite normal in his habits. He has taken his meals regularly and although not voracious has eaten normally. One day a fortnight ago he began playing with his dinner, a thing he never does, and when I began to feed him he protested and wanted his pudding first. I really thought he was just being stupid and went on with his dinner, but he then spat it out, scattering it all over his chair, so I took it away and got his pudding but he also refused that, so we made no more fuss, and I realised or thought that he had had an aversion to his dinner on that day, and that perhaps I was unreasonable in persisting. However, at tea all was well and also at breakfast next day, but every day since he has refused dinner. For two days I just took him his dinner and he said, ' No, no,' so not wanting to sicken him I immediately removed it and he had his nap and nothing to eat until tea-time, and he didn't want anything to eat I could see. To-day, I thought I would try dinner again but as soon as he saw it he screamed and nothing would induce him to touch it. What am I to do ? He isn't a bit spoilt."

5. "Directly any suggestion of food is mentioned or she (aged 2;3) sees the table being laid she whines and screams and declares she doesn't want any food. I have had the doctor in and he has given her tonics but they seem to have no effect. I have asked him to examine her throat as she usually seems to have trouble in swallowing, but he says there is nothing

wrong. We have played with her, telling her stories, etc., with no effect. She takes an hour over her meal and usually heaves two or three times and sometimes ends in being sick."

6. " My little boy of 2;8 is a normal healthy child and very intelligent but has a terrible habit of retching and bringing up at meals when he has anything he doesn't like especially. I try to give him things he likes but it is very difficult as he has so many dislikes and one day he likes a thing and the next time he has it he won't."

7. " I have great difficulty with him (aged nearly 5) at meal times—dinner being the worst meal of the day. He never seems eager for food and at dinner time often flatly refuses to touch his food and sits at the table drawing pictures on the cloth with the forks and spoons. For the sake of peace and quiet I usually have to spoon-feed him myself talking to him all the time and trying to distract his attention while I am doing this."

8. " A. (4;0) and J. (2;6). Meal time is an absolute purgatory. They will both put a spoonful in their mouths and hold it there sometimes for ten minutes, without attempting to swallow it, and then only if we are standing over them continually reminding them to *be quick*. They will often take one and a half hours over their tea."

9. " My little D. developed the habit of sucking wool, blankets, clothes or anything she could get, while only a few months old. Now she is 2;6 and still sucks wool, dolls' clothes, bits of yarn, and even bits of fluff and dust off the carpets. I thought it would pass off when she had all her teeth, but such is not the case, and it is affecting her in a troublesome way. The hairs are irritating the bowel and causing bladder irritation and making her wet her cot at night very badly after having been dry for many months. It has been a very great worry to me and nothing seems to help. She can get bits of fluff and wool in spite of our vigilance."

10. " Within the last month or two she has developed a habit of violently sucking any wool she can get hold of—chiefly in bed or in the pram—but also at other times. She stuffs her coat or the blanket into her mouth voraciously, and sucks and sucks until she goes to sleep. She seems to love the feel of wool, and laughs and chuckles if one plays with the blanket over her face, or if one tucks it under her chin. She will suck the front of her nightgown until it is wringing wet on her chest, and this together with the fact that she swallows little pieces of wool, makes me feel that we must stop it in some way."

11. " My baby girl, now 15 months old has, since she started cutting her double teeth at about 11 months, always

sucked the first two fingers of her right hand when put down to sleep. I have several times tried to break her of this habit (as it seems to me almost as bad as a dummy) but she has only screamed sometimes for three hours at a time and appeared so distressed and exhausted that I have given in."

12. "She is 5 years old next August and ever since she was about a year old she has gone to sleep sucking some part of her clothing or bed-clothes."

13. "I have resorted to smacking in order to show him how he (aged 3;6) hurts other people. But the only result is to make him wild with rage, and he has attempted to bite me once or twice."

14. "She (aged 2;6) plays in her cot for an hour in the afternoon, but whatever I give her to play with she now puts into her mouth. She'll eat up a whole book in an hour. She doesn't swallow the paper but chews it up and spits it out, and what she doesn't chew she'll wilfully tear up. So although she loves picture books I can't let her have them. She'll take her hair-ribbon off and chew that, or pull a button off her jumper and chew that."

15. "For the last three months my small son, aged four and a half, has been waking in the night—or rather, the early hours of the morning—crying out in an unhappy little voice that he 'sees nasty things'. Frequently, too, when he is just falling asleep at night he will say that he is 'afraid to close his eyes because he sees things'. He seems unable to describe them, except that they are 'very, *very* nasty' and sometimes he says 'they bite'. On being gently assured that there is nothing there that could hurt a little boy with Nannie or Mummie beside him and a big Daddy so near, he replies, 'Yes, I *know* that, but I *think* them.'"

16 "He (aged nearly three) used to go to sleep quite happily as soon as he was put to bed, but now, as soon as I leave him he calls me back ''Cos Goo-goo comes'. He calls me again and again to tell me about 'Goo-goo'. At first I told him there was no such person when he said, 'Goo-goo bites the windows all up, and bites the doors and bites everything,' but he *insists* that there is, so thinking he might get worse fears through repressing it I encourage him to talk about it. I suggested 'Goo-goo' was a little boy and little boys didn't bite windows, etc., only nice things like biscuits and apples. But that was no good. Then he called me in a more frightened voice, and when I told him to shut his eyes and go to sleep he said, 'No, if I shut my eyes Goo-goo will come and eat *me*.'"

17. "She (aged 2;8) suffers from nightmare—which must

be intensely vivid, as spasms recur during the day. She frequently wakes in the night frantic and screaming because she fancies there are animals about the room, and in her bed. All my efforts to reassure and pacify her are useless for a time—and when finally she ceases screaming, she keeps clutching at me, and will not go back in her bed. The trouble commenced about last August. She was sleeping in a cot in my bedroom. When I ran up to see what was wrong, she was trying to climb out and seemed terror-stricken. Nothing would induce her to go back in the cot—she said ' An animal bite her feet,' although she has always been very fond of cats and dogs and cannot pass one without wanting to love it, in fact she shows great interest in all animals."

18. " I should be so much obliged if you could give me any advice about the one peculiarity of my elder child. She is now two-and-three-quarters and a thoroughly healthy and happy small person. The whole trouble is nothing very vast. When she was a baby I stopped her sucking her thumb by pinning a light shawl round her shoulders and she soon stopped it. Later, though, she began to suck her tongue. I can't quite describe how she does it, sticks it out a bit and sucks it. The effect is not pretty ! And after that when she could walk she insisted on having one or two small coloured blankets with her and waving one about in front of her face while she sucked her tongue and now in any trouble she runs for it. She does not actually suck it—holds it near her face and sucks her tongue. I suppose I ought to be thankful she does not suck the wool ! She will not go to sleep without it, either for her morning rest or at night. Don't you think the beginning of it all was my being too fussy over thumb-sucking ? I feel inclined to let the baby suck hers to her heart's content—which I may say, she does ! And she is such a model baby in every other way it seems a pity to interfere with her."

19. " How can I deal with this problem ? My little boy of two-and-three-quarters has recently begun to spit and will spit in one's face without any warning or apparent reason. He did it once before about nine months ago and then I put him out of the room, but this time it usually happens when he gets into my bed in the morning and then I put him back into his bed, which seems to make an effect. He also does it with his nurse although he is perfectly happy with both of us. Otherwise he is a normal happy child, very helpful and useful in his nursery, hanging up his clothes, washing himself and so on. Do you think that we should take a firmer tone and smack him ? He calls it ' bubbles ' and incidentally is very fond of blowing bubbles."

δ

RASMUSSEN: *The Primary School Child*, p. 130. " R. has an absolute repugnance to fondling. S. said one day that she would like her mother to fetch her from the dance along with me, ' because I like them both the same '. R. said on this : ' Oh, if only there was a place where I could spit ! ' "

BRIDGES, *op. cit.* pp. 55-6. "A child who has asserted himself by biting or spitting at other children (more than once) fails to score on this item. Like hitting and pinching, the above forms of aggression are particularly undesirable, and are usually shown marked disapproval by adults."

2. ANAL AND URETHRAL INTERESTS AND AGGRESSION

α

21.9.24. Dan's mother reported that this afternoon, when she was carrying him on the return from a walk, he had asked her, " Shall I make water on you ? " She said, " Do you want to make water? I'll put you down." " No, on *you*, shall I ? "

27.10.24. Frank, seeing the cat, said, " I can see his ah-ah bottie " ; Benjie then joined in, and the two chanted it.

28.10.24. Tommy went to the lavatory with Miss B. George went to look in, and said, laughing, " I saw him in the lavatory."

October 1924. Miss X. and Mrs. I. went to talk to Dan in his bath at bedtime. He made love to Miss X. by offering her water cupped in his hands ; then suddenly said, " I'm going to pass faeces on the floor and on the towel."

October, 1924. (See incident re Penelope and Dan under GUILT AND SHAME.)

12.11.24. Harold put the soap down the lavatory pipe. (A few days later, he put both soap and sponge down.) He and Paul made water in the garden.

19.11.24. At lunch the children had a conversation as to what people were " made of ", and spoke of people being made of pudding, pie, potatoes, coal, etc., and of " bee-wee ", " try ", " do-do ", " ah-ah ", " bottie ".

24.11.24. Harold often speaks of " bogies " (the dirt out of his nose). At one moment this morning, he ran to the lavatory, saying, " I'm going to see if anyone is in the lavatory."

When washing their hands, Harold, Paul and Benjie put the wash bowls on the floor, and sat down in them, saying, " I'm trying, I'm trying on Paul, on Dan, etc."

Christopher took a bowl from Benjie. Harold said, " I'll hit you in the face if you take mine." Benjie: " I'll wee-wee in your face." Benjie and Harold said to Tommy, " We'll put bim-bom-bee-wee water in your face." When he is angry with Mrs. I., he sometimes says to the others, " Shall we pee-wee on someone ? "

The children were getting water to drink in cups, and Harold told the others that he had given Frank some " wee-wee water " to drink. He often says " there's wee-wee water in the bowl " in which he washes his hands. Later he said he had drunk " wee-wee water ", and that the water in the cups was that.

Frank said, " Shall we make Benjie drink bee-wee water ? " " Yes," Harold said, " and poison him." And another time, " and make spots come out all over him ".

26.11.24. When marching round, the children took the enamel bowls to use as drums ; then they put them on the floor and sat in them, first calling them " boats ", and then as lavatories, to " try " in ; Harold and Paul sat in them, saying, " I'm trying."

Paul told Mrs. I., " Do you know what I have to make me try ? . . . Grape fruit."

At lunch, Harold said to Mrs. I., " You are made of try." Frank . . . " You are made of water." Benjie . . . " of bee-wee ".

27.11.24. Playing house with chairs, Frank said, " I'm going to eat my bogies—I don't want any dinner." Harold then said the same. Paul told the others, " I tried on Mrs. I."

4.12.24. Harold said (as on several occasions), " Shall we eat bogies ? "

12.1.25. Paul poked a pencil into his nose, and then licked it.

26.1.25. Frank suggested putting a cup down the lavatory.

29.1.25. Dan said he did not like Tommy's hair. Frank said, " No, he's dirty ; he's a lu-lu spout."

Frank said to Dan in a low voice, " We want to make water, don't we, Dan ? " Dan laughed and said, " Make water in the other place, won't you ? " (Frank often asks Dan to go with him to the lavatory.)

10.2.25. Frank went to the lavatory, leaving the door open. Mrs. I. was playing the piano. Frank called to Dan to " tell her not to " ; Dan said, " *Don't* play—you wicked Mrs. I.," then ran back and shouted to Frank, " She won't stop—but she has done now." Afterwards they talked about " smacking " her, " hurting her eye ", " shooting her ", and their stock joke about " going up in an aeroplane ", and Mrs. I. " having to go up in a motor car ". And about making " it " (Mrs. I. could not catch what the " it " was) " as big as a cloud ", " as big as a house ", " as big as the school ", " as big as London ". Then Dan, " and we shall smack everyone, shan't we ? "

11.2.25. After lunch, Frank and Dan made a " house " with chairs. Frank said, " and we'll have a little lavatory, a little lav-lav ". Presently he went to the real lavatory, saying, " Shall we go to our little lavatory ? "

16.2.25. There was some talk of again putting the sponge down the lavatory.

27.2.25. Frank was in the lavatory, and called to Dan. Dan came back into the schoolroom to see what Mrs. I. was doing. She was painting, and Dan said, " What are you painting ? You shan't paint, you wicked Mrs. I.," and spat on her painting. She said, " Please don't do that, Dan." Frank called out, " Kick her." Dan said to her, going towards her, " I'm going to kick you," then ran back towards the lavatory shouting out to Frank, " I've kicked her " (but of course he had not) ; Frank shouted, " Did you kick her ? " Dan said, " Yes." Frank : " Kick her again " ; Dan ran towards her and shouted, " I have done."

2.3.25. Frank asked where Harold was resting, and when told, said, " In that end room ?" and then with laughter, " in the do-do room ? "

Frank said to one of the others, " You've got a silly old ah-ah-bottie."

6.3.25. Paul said to Mrs. I., " I hope you smell—you smell yourself." Dan went to the lavatory to make water. Frank was in the cloakroom, and was heard to say to him, " Dan, you are a ah-ah-ah-ah-ah-bottie—say that, Dan." Dan did so. Dan told Mrs. I. that Frank was " passing faeces ".

20.3.25. Frank and some others were looking at a picture, and Frank suddenly hit it, and said, " I smacked its bottie."

Harold told Mrs. I. that George " wee-wee'd " in the garden " always ".

25.3.25. The children spoke again of " bee-wee gnomes ".

Two or three of the children were using one of the moveable blackboards. Harold said, " Shall I try on it ? and make it black, make it dirty ? "

26.3.25. Dan asked, " How could we wipe our anuses if we had no paper ? "

24.4.25. Theobald poured water into the sand, and called it " bee-wee sand."

Frank was heard to say to another child, " Shall we put some faeces in a cake and give it to Dan's mummie—and then she won't know what she is eating ? " On another occasion, he was heard to tell Dan, " Pass all you have in your bottie."

Dan replied, " Then I shan't have any more to pass out."
Frank : " Then your bottie will be flat."

29.4.25. Harold brought water in the bucket with sand as " mortar ", but called the bucket a " try-pan ", and threw it into the sand pit.

1.5.25. Dan and Frank were interested when Priscilla went to the lavatory in the afternoon, and spoke of it to each other. They said, " Oh, she's passing faeces," and when she came out, they asked her, " What colour is it ? " After some hesitation (she did not know the term " faeces ", but evidently had a glimmer of the meaning), she replied that she did not know. They ran to look, and came back, saying, " Oh, it's white." She had, of course, pulled the plug before coming out.

4.5.25. The children were helping Mrs. I. to feed the rabbit and give him fresh straw ; they noticed his faeces in the box, and called it " the rabbit's lavatory ".

8.5.25. The children again cracked one egg each (from those the hen had been sitting on and had deserted) into a large tin. Presently they took the tins out on to the steps, and called them " lavatories ", and told Mrs. I. they each had " four lavatories ".

26.5.25. While a visitor who was sceptical was talking to Mrs. I. about the concept of " sublimations ", Mrs. I. had instanced the children's play with mud and water as an example ; just then Harold came out of the schoolroom to where the children were playing with water, carrying in one hand a can of water, and in the other the roll of toilet paper from the lavatory, which he put down in the mud, and poured water over it.

16.6.25. To-day they discovered for the first time that they could turn the main tap on in the yard, and there was tremendous excitement and interest at this. When they had their bathing suits on, they put their hands over the running tap and squirted it all over themselves and over the garden, Duncan saying several times, " Someone is ' bee-weeing ' on me."

18.6.25. Tommy and Christopher spent half-an-hour making what they called a " bee-wee pie " with sand and water.

In the sand-pit, in the morning, Paul and Harold, and later, Frank and Dan, had " made try "—mixing sand and water with their hands, " with salt ", they said. Frank piled it up on a brick in a loaf shape, and Paul called it a " loaf of try-bread ". Harold did the same, and said, " When someone wants to eat a try-loaf, we'll give them this." Paul and

Harold went on with this "try-bread" for some time, and said they were going to cook it. Harold later asked Mrs. I. if she would like a loaf, and took her some.

24.6.25. The puppy made water on the floor of the schoolroom, and there were shocked protests and laughter from all the children. Priscilla carried him to the lavatory.

When painting, Frank and Dan painted their hair and faces brown, and called it "faeces colour". Presently they washed it off.

30.6.25. Priscilla modelled a bath and the tray of soap with pieces of soap in it and herself and her mother in the bath. Duncan asked, "Where is her bim-bom thing?"

7.7.25. At lunch, Mrs. I. asked who had served the food yesterday, when she was not there. Frank told her that Miss Y. did. Duncan said, "Yes, she passed faeces and then served it to us."

8.7.25. In the lavatory, Harold undid the whole of the roll of toilet paper. He helped to roll it up again, when asked.

13.7.25. When dressing after bathing, Theobald and others chanted about a "bottle of brown bee-wee water". This happened on two or three days. They talked of "selling it".

(N.B. Theobald's talk re bee-wee has occurred coincidently with much social freedom, friendliness and generally greater interest and activity.)

13.10.25. Priscilla and Dan, when using paints, painted their hands all over. When Mrs. I. asked them not to do this, but to paint only on the paper, they insisted that they would do so. She made this a condition of their having the paints to use, and when they did it again, she then took the paints away. In defiance, they painted the tables with the brushes and water. When Mrs. I. removed these, they ran after her, shouting in defiance, and Dan spat at her, Priscilla imitating him, but with less vigour.

15.10.25. The children were having a "picnic" under the stairs, and Penelope whispered to Mrs. I., "Let's pretend there's a lavatory up there—only *pretend!*"

9.11.25. Frank and Priscilla were being hostile to Penelope. They said, "She's dirty—she's a faeces girl—she's hateful."

17.11.25. Dan went to get a drink, and afterwards said, "When I drink water, it makes me make water." In the afternoon, Mrs. I. went to the lavatory. Priscilla heard her, and told Dan, "She has gone to make water." When Mrs. I. came out, Dan asked her, "Did you make water?"

18.11.25. Watching the dog, the children saw him make water and pass faeces, and laughed and commented on it. Tommy said, "He passed faeces."

Frank and Priscilla and Dan always call a particular colour of paint, a yellow-brown, " faeces colour ", quite as a matter of course.

27.11.25. Priscilla pushed Tommy when he was carrying something very carefully ; when Mrs. I. held her arm so that she should not upset him, Priscilla was very angry, and the other children took her part against Mrs. I., all joining in saying, " Horrid Mrs. I.—she's a faeces woman—ah-ah, bottie ! " and so on.

1.12.25. When painting, Tommy painted his hands ; Christopher, Dan and Priscilla said he was " dirty ". He retorted, " No, I'm not." They spat on his picture and spoilt it. When Miss B. interfered, they said she was " dirty ", " a faeces person ", " horrid ", etc. Later on, when Tommy was pouring some peas into a wooden measure, he spilt some on the floor ; the other children spoke about this ; but presently, when Mrs. I. stood near before he had picked them up, Priscilla and Frank pretended that it was she who had " made water and passed faeces on the floor ". " Look what a lot she's done," they said, laughing. " We can see it—you'll have to brush it up," and so on.

In the afternoon, Dan and Priscilla were for a brief time rather hostile, and Priscilla said to Mrs. I., " Go away, you beast, you horrid Mrs. I.", several times. She then ran into the lavatory, and shouted out that she was " falling down in it ", calling to Mrs. I. to go and " pick her out ".

2.12.25. Christopher, Tommy and Dan made a " corridor train " with chairs. Dan showed the two passengers where " the lavatory " was, saying, " In case you want to make water." Tommy and N. (a visitor) then pretended to go to the lavatory, Dan saying, " Can you undo your trousers ? "

3.12.25. Priscilla this afternoon was feverish with a sudden cold, not fit to be at school ; she was sent home as soon as possible. She was very restless and destructive, and would not settle to any occupation, nor let the others do so happily. Mrs. I. was using number rods with one of the others and Priscilla came and tried to push them on to the floor. When Mrs. I. prevented this, Priscilla began, in her anger and defiance, to urinate on the floor ; but at once cried in distress, " Oh, no, Mrs. I.—oh, I want to make water," and ran off to the lavatory. After that she settled down to a period of quiet occupation.

11.12.25. One of the children brought to school a rubber mouse that could be used as a squirt. They said it " makes bee-wee out of its mouth ".

14.12.25. Frank, Priscilla and Christopher took away Tommy's cocoanut, and put it in the pan of the lavatory. They were angry when they found that it had been taken away.

21.1.26. Frank and Dan said that Mrs. I. " did faeces writing ".

5.2.26. In a moment of anger, Priscilla took her doll and said she would make it " pass faeces " on Mrs. I. ; she held the doll's legs towards her and said, " Bang."

8.2.26. Frank found some water held in a leaf in the garden, and called it " the fairies' lavatory ".

8.3.26. During the family play, Jessica was taken to the lavatory and made to pass water in reality.

11.6.26. After the rain-storm, Phineas suddenly wanted to " do ah-ah ", urgently.

8.12.26. The cat was rolling on the floor, and Conrad said, " Stick a stamp over his anus so that he can't pass faeces."

10.12.26. The children (Jane, Conrad, Dan) were playing " ship ", and each child had a waste-paper basket of his own as a " lavatory ". They pretended to be sick, to make water and to pass faeces, saying, " Mine's full." " Empty it in the sea," and so on.

11.12.26. They began playing the same game again to-day, but seemed to get bored with it and gave it up for modelling.

15.12.26. In the " ship " play to-day, the ships again contained " potties ", but these were used less to-day.

21.1.27. Jessica and Phineas asked Miss C. to " make a ship " with them, and arranged a " potty " in the seat of a wicker chair. Jessica asked Miss C., " We want you to sell us some paper to wipe ourselves." Phineas said, " I want another piece of paper." Miss C. took a piece of crumpled paper from the wicker chair, but Jessica shouted, " Oh, you can't have that ! I've just used it. I'm going on the potty again." Then to Miss C., " Not *real* potty—just 'tending." This was interspersed with other sorts of happenings in the " ship "—starting and stopping it at different places, carrying parcels, and so on. Phineas wrapped up a toy train in a piece of paper, tied it with string and asked Miss C. to " be the postman and deliver it ". Jessica: " I wonder what's in here." She cut the string: " Oh, it's a parcel from Father Christmas. She asked Mrs. I. to find some more parcels, and they both made parcels for her to deliver to them. Phineas said to himself, " Jessica must say, ' I wonder what it is ? ' "

24.1.27. In their play after lunch, Jane, Priscilla, Jessica and Dan played a family game which included sitting on " potties ", " passing faeces ", and falling off the pots (cushions) with laughter. They went on with this until Mrs. I. called them to come and do something else.

2.2.27. At bath-time, Conrad and Dan had an indiarubber man. There was a hole in its foot, through which they made water squirt. Conrad said, " This funny man has his penis in his foot—it must be a sort of toe, I suppose."

10.2.27. Jane took a glass vessel with a tube attached, and began to pour water into it through a funnel. Dan said, " I know what you're going to do—you're going to make water." Jane laughed and said, " Yes "; they all laughed in a tone which suggested that this had been so described before.

11.2.27. Jane, Priscilla, Conrad and Dan played " house " and had a dolls' tea-party. Jane arranged two " lavatories " in the house, " one for men and one for women ".

8.3.27. When playing in the garden, Conrad said to Jane, " You go into the lavatory. I'll say, ' I want to come in,' and you say, ' You can't—I want to do potty.' " Jane said, " All right "; but she did not go.

12.3.27. During the day, the children, especially Conrad, talked a good deal about " anus " and " flatus ". Jane did not join in, but giggled when the others did. They giggled about the words " business " and " buzz " and " long nose."

13.3.27. Again a good deal of giggling and talking about anus, penis, flatus, etc. A boy visitor joined in this, although he said it was " rude ". Jane said she " often talked like that " with her old school friends. (At her previous school, a well-known girls' school.)

Summer term 1927. In response to our suggestion that it was better not to talk so much about going to the lavatory, etc., they substituted " telephone " and " telephoning " for the direct description, and took every opportunity of talking about this, with the same giggles and sly looks.

May 1927. One of the children had been given a tent for a birthday present, and he brought it to school and had it set up on the lawn. To-day a group of children (including Jane, Dan, Conrad, Priscilla and Jessica, among others) were playing inside the tent. They seemed to think that because they could not be seen, they could not be heard, and were joking and laughing about " anus " and " big noises ", etc., in loud unconcerned voices and laughter. When one of the staff called to them to suggest some occupation outside the tent, they fell silent and came out with sheepish looks.

β

1. J., a healthy and well adapted girl of 3;6, who had long since established normal control over her excretions, was

left alone with her father at the sea-side for a day, which was a rare experience. On the way down to the beach she urinated in her knickers, her father having to take these off for her. He put on her bathing suit, and before they had gone much further she had defaecated into this—a quite unheard of occurrence in her life.

2. At 4 years of age, N. persistently drank her bath water, and would not yield to correction about this. On one occasion she was caught drinking the water in which tadpoles had lived and died.

3. J. and H., aged 1;6 and 3;6 respectively, were found comparing the amounts of faeces in the two chamber pots after they had defaecated. The elder boy told his mother, " I did *three* things, J. only did two."

4. In childhood, X. slept in a bed placed close along a wall. At 7 or 8 years she had the habit of depositing the dirt from her nose on the wall, and on one occasion put a fragment of faeces there, suffering great shame at the memory of this in later childhood. As a grown woman she had a great dislike of dark or patterned wall-papers.

5. K., 9 months. She was lying on her rug in the garden; several friendly adults were near, looking at her, talking to and about her. Her uncle went up to her, whereupon she began to smile and laugh and gurgle, and wriggle about, with an appearance of great pleasure. He thought these were signs of pleased recognition of himself, and friendliness to him. He laughed back, and repeated the little grunting noises—*er, er, er*, which she was making. After a few moments, the smile faded and the grunts and gurgles ceased, and she lay quiet. Her nannie, who was near, recognised the situation and took her up to change her—she had evacuated into her napkin.

6. An adult patient had a dream in which he and his analyst " were sitting at a fireside carrying on the analysis." He, the patient, "was playing with a poker in the coals on the hearth ". On the basis of many previous associations to coal and fire, the analyst suggested that this item in the dream represented either the infantile wish to play with urine and faeces, or the memory of having done so. The patient at once said, " That was what the baby visitor was doing yesterday "— a child of fifteen months, who had urinated on the floor, and before anyone could intervene, had stamped and splashed in it with her feet. The child's parents had told my patient that " she was always doing that."

γ

The following types of problem occur under this heading (in letters from mothers and nurses) : Bed-wetting; persistent refusal to use the pot either or both for urination and defaecation, this refusal ranging from constant failure to ask for attention in time, to absolute obstinacy to use the pot when presented, or absolute terror and screaming at the sight of it ; severe constipation ; refusal to urinate when held out at 10 p.m., or screaming and restlessness through the night if held out then ; wetting the floor or a particular piece of furniture in the night time ; and one case of complete adaptation to the pot *only*, so that the pot has to be taken about wherever the child goes. These cases vary in degree from mere lateness in acquisition of control to severe obstinacy and terror at a later age, the age range being ten and a half months to thirteen years, three children being six years and over.

The following are illustrative letters :

1. " Tony's (aged 3;6) other trouble is that if I have to correct him he has always an answer for me and threatens to ' cry all night ' or ' I'll wet my knickers ', and although I ignore him will keep his threat going for half an hour or longer, insisting that I shall hear him."

2. " My little boy, now three and a half, is naturally excitable. When he gets into these fits of excitement, he shouts out all sorts of ridiculous things. Some of them are just nonsense, but he has got into the habit of shouting a few really objectionable remarks, always with reference to his daily motion, or his ' botty '. It sounds quite horrible when he goes round shouting about these things, ' You're a dirty botty ', and ' I'll sniff your botty.' In common with, I believe, quite a number of little children, the whole subject has always fascinated him and in his own private conversations with his sister he frequently talks about these things in a very amused way, and he is always highly tickled by the way the dogs will sniff each other in the road (hence the second remark I quote). I am sure he has never heard any coarse remarks."

3. " She (aged sixteen months) was trained from birth to be a clean baby, but within the last two months she has persistently fought and screamed every time the chamber is produced. When she comes in from the garden she is immediately held out, but I can never get her to do anything— and she does nothing but pinch me and go perfectly stiff on my lap. Then after she has played around for a few minutes she will wet herself, and looks up at me as if she knows that she has been naughty."

4. "My baby boy, aged two, has suddenly, after having been practically perfectly clean in his habits since he was a year old, taken to wetting his trousers. Smacking has not helped—in fact he comes up to me and in my face, though with no defiance, he says, ' Mama, I'm wee-weeing.' When I say angrily, ' What will Mama do now ? ' he says, ' Give me a good smacking.' He gets it, but an hour later repeats the performance."

5. "My baby son, aged ten and a half months, was first put on the chamber when I weaned him at the age of eight and a half months and he responded splendidly for one month. This last month, however, whenever he is put near the chamber he screams violently and however long I hold him gives no reaction but soils his napkins instead—afterwards."

6. "My boy baby, aged thirteen months, is rather a difficult child. In the nursing home they used to say ruefully he was born grumbling—and I must say he never was the sunny nature the elder girl was. He progressed normally until about two months, when he began to develop boils and eczema. His nurse kept him on the wrong diet, so I changed, and the next nurse brought him on till he was an entirely different baby. He always was a screamer and possessed unusual vocal power—amazing in a baby. At first of course, it was the inadequate feeding and then the boils. But now he is exceedingly strong and big. And very healthy indeed. The trouble is that the moment he catches sight of the ' throne ' he simply begins to bawl and refuses completely to do what is required, even to the point of defying us for an hour together when we all know that he must want to be clean very badly indeed ; but he keeps it back and back—and there can be no trouble physically because immediately afterwards he presents us with a dirty nappy. All this is accompanied by shrieks of pure rage right from his stomach and I am afraid there is no question that it is pure defiance—with a bad temper. All other times he is fairly quiet and good. We have tried persuading him, coaxing, leaving him alone to do his ' duty ' (this last is best, though it is intermittent, and after fourteen days of peace we'll have a week of screams), suggestion, and every type of ' throne ' to meet with the situation. He has worn out three nurses who simply can't compete with the noise and temper, and we are dreadfully worried because we don't want to ' break ' his temper, yet one *must* cure his temper, which is really violent. He absolutely kicks and hammers on the ' throne ' table with anger and not a tear on his face. He started on the usual ' pot '. Then he could not be left by himself, even secured to a chair, as he kicked it from beneath

him. We therefore made him a wooden polished square seat to cover it. He then kicked the throne one way and the pot the other, levering himself by the bedpost. We then mounted it on a sort of platform which by his own weight was unable to be moved. He then moved sideways and covered himself with the contents of the pot. Finally we made arms and a back to it and moveable tray in front of him which, when fixed, prevents him from getting his hands inside. His fury when he beheld this was almost funny. He now puts the energy he exerted physically before into his roars."

7. " From four to ten and a half months I never had a soiled napkin, then at that age we took him on a holiday. From the first day he changed completely—refused to use a chamber, but stiffened and screamed every time he was held out. He waited till I had put a napkin on, then wet or soiled it, and has done so now for four and a half months, though I have always held him out as a matter of routine."

8. " My son, (aged three), is in every appearance strong and well, although rather excitable. Every night he wets the bed, and wets his trousers during the day and frequently makes a mess in them also. I have tried all your suggestions to other people and some of my own, but am still completely in the dark as to the cause or how to cure. I might say that this dirtiness during the day is quite a new thing, as he has been clean for many months now."

9. " I have just taken my first post as nurse, to a little girl of three years. I find her very difficult as regards her daily motion, she does not say, ' I can't go,' she simply says, ' I won't go,' or ' I don't want to go.' "

10. " Once or twice in the week for nearly three or four weeks he (aged 10;0) has wet his bed; but worse still, he has the habit of doing it on the floor, and on a certain piece of furniture. We have tried every possible thing we can do ; at last we have taken that piece of furniture away and for three nights he has been dry in the morning. His father asked him why he did not go to the W.C. and the boy replied that he didn't know he was doing it. He says he ' does it in his dreams '."

11. " I have a small son aged seventeen and a half months, and for the last two months or more he has simply refused to use his chamber. The moment he is put into his play pen or pram, everything happens in his trousers ! We've tried regular doses of fruit juice—putting him in the middle of the room, with nothing to distract his attention. He won't be left alone, or at least he won't stay on the article ! He has completely defeated myself and

Nanny—and I feel sure that it is only naughtiness. We've tried to make him indicate to us by sounds that he wishes to perform, but he always lets us know afterwards and *not* before."

12. " My sister's boy of twenty-one months has not used his chamber since he was a tiny baby though he is put on it regularly every day. He does not dislike it, but has decided that he likes better to do ' his business ' on the floor, and so sits for a little on the chamber and then gets up and does it on the floor a little later. She does not let him see how worried she is, but gently remonstrates with him. He does not seem to like it on the floor and even gets a cloth and tries to dry it up. He is a bright healthy child and clever for his age. He has never really used his chamber at all except merely by accident."

13. " I am very anxious about my baby boy of nineteen months. I have a nurse help to look after him but it seems that she cannot get him clean ; he refuses to sit down and it is quite a fight with him all the time. Could you make any suggestion ? I looked after my elder child myself and she was absolutely clean by the time she was a year and the thought of baby of nineteen months is too awful."

14. " I have been helped so often with your advice to other mothers, and now I wonder if you would be so good as to help me with my problem. My baby girl, aged one year and two weeks, will not do her duties when I hold her out. She either screams and twists about or just plays and wriggles. Then a few minutes later will dirty her nappies. I am always very gentle with her and a few weeks back I did manage to catch her sometimes, but now I can hold her for ten minutes without any success, and it really gets tiring holding her for a long time when she just cries and wriggles and pulls my hair, etc. When I used to lift her up at 10 p.m. I used to be able to make her do her duty after a little coaxing, but now she screams and sobs and gets so upset that I don't try for long and even when the light is out again she will stay awake crying and sitting up for quite a time. As she gets rather constipated and the doctor has advised me to give her special medicine each day, she never does her big duty in the proper place. In the morning when I put her out about 10.25 she is very wet when I bring her in about half an hour later, and it is useless to hold her out. Apart from this trouble she is a very happy little soul with a smile for everyone."

15. " I have a baby girl, aged fifteen months, an only child. She is a very healthy child, full of life and high spirits, and extremely bright and intelligent. She is a happy little soul,

very easy to manage, and has never been any trouble except in one respect. She seems to *hate* sitting on the chamber to do her little jobs! I have taken her to the doctor who says she is quite normal in every way, and she is never constipated. I have come to the conclusion that this is a psychological problem that faces us. Nurse and I have been very patient with her and have never scolded her when she has soiled her pants, but just taken her quietly to the bathroom and put clean ones on. We never show baby how much it distresses us when she has an accident, and as she has always had a lot of loving, I cannot think she does it just to get my attention. This morning, after her breakfast, Nurse sat with her for twenty minutes, trying to get her to use her chamber, but she just played with her fingers and sang, and refused to do anything. She was then put into her pen to play alone and when Nurse had finished her breakfast and went back to baby, she had soiled her pants. This happens nearly every morning. If she is left only five minutes, it is the same, and we come back to find an accident. We have tried leaving her alone to do it; we put her in the bathroom, sitting on the chamber, and when we go back in five minutes, we find that either she has done nothing or else has made a mess in the corner, on the linoleum floor. I have bought her a new chamber, thinking the old one might be uncomfortable or have hard edges, but it has made no difference. She has never been cut or hurt in any way when sitting on the chamber, and I simply cannot understand her aversion to it."

16. " Whole school seated at dinner. A visitor, the father of one of the boys, had been very critical of the school, the equipment, the staff, the lessons, and though the boys did not realise this fully, they evidently had some sense of it and they were a bit hostile. Mr. Q. was seen to be without a serviette. ' Run up and fetch Mr. Q. a serviette from the linen cupboard ' I asked the youngest boy who was quite friendly (apparently). He was away longer than was necessary but brought one. ' You have to look at the picture in the corner' said one of the others to Mr. Q. (Instead of using rings we have different designs on each serviette, that the boys may know their own.) Mr. Q. unfolded it and saw the word *lavatory* in red letters in the corner, and the next two minutes was spent in laughing."

δ

Woolley, *op. cit.*, p. 65. " The function of urination is more likely to be indulged in too frequently than to be restrained for erotic reasons. The passing of urine affords a mild stimulus to the sex organs of the infant. The child may adopt the habit of urinating with unnecessary frequency just because of the sex pleasure derived from it. In my treatment of cases of enuresis among somewhat older children, I have encountered eight-year-old girls who insisted that they kept on wetting the bed just because they enjoyed the sensation. Ordinary urination on a toilet could not assume the same sex quality as the secret performance of the function in an assumed attitude."

3. Exhibitionism

a. Direct

α

7.10.24. Robert and George were in the garden together. Robert pulled up his trousers and exposed his penis, saying, " Look at my wee-wee thing ! Where's your wee-wee thing ? " George did the same. Whenever these two were together in the garden, and thought themselves free from observation, they were liable to do this, Robert always initiating it, but George following readily. On one occasion, later than this, Mrs. I. went to join them in the sand-pit, after there had been a sing-song about " wee-wee things ", when George suddenly said to her, " Do you know where the wee-wee thing is ? Here it is," exposing his penis.

15.10.24. George said he was " going to wee-wee " ; Robert said, " I'll come and watch."

16.10.24. In the garden, Robert and George exposed themselves ; at any moment during the day they may do this, suddenly, and at the same time make a shrill, squealing noise.

29.10.24. As on several previous occasions, George asked Mrs. I. to go to the lavatory with him, as he wanted to make water, and when doing it, he throws his head back, looks at her and laughs, showing obvious pride. To-day she suggested that he could go alone. He needs no actual help, and asks none ; he only wants an audience.

4.11.24. George made water outside, as once or twice before. Harold was also going to, but Mrs. I. said, " Please don't " ; presently, when he thought he was not seen, he did it under the steps, into a pail, and told Mrs. I. afterwards.

14.11.24. While resting, Frank and George had taken their socks off. Frank said to George, " I can see your big toe," with a giggle ; whereupon George immediately pulled his penis out.

16.2.25. Frank made water in the garden. Dan saw him, and stood in an attitude as if doing so himself, although he did not. Later, Frank was going to make water on the steps.

When Mrs. I. asked him to do it in the lavatory he ran down the steps to the school entrance, opened the door, and was about to do it into the street, but was stopped.

25.2.25. Frank made water down the steps, and wet Paul's coat; Paul cried.

27.2.25. In the morning, Tommy went to the lavatory, and Harold ran "to see Tommy's tummy" and to get a drink and make water himself. Tommy had his knickers off and stood smiling with his jersey held up and his stomach protruded.

At lunch, Harold had said he would "take his jersey off" and "show his braces"; in the afternoon Frank did so, beginning apparently accidentally, meaning to undo his trousers for the lavatory. He pulled his arm out of the sleeve, put it in again, but then undid the neck and took the jersey off. He did all this behind the piano, then came out laughing and drew attention to what he had done.

In the lavatory, passing faeces, Dan talked of the amount of paper he used, and then showed Mrs. I. "much faeces" on the paper.

3.3.25. Dan again, in the lavatory, spoke of the amount of faeces on the paper.

4.3.25. In the lavatory, Dan wanting to make water, asked Mrs. I. (as he often asked) to hold his penis (as is commonly done with tiny boys); she refused. "Why don't you?" he said. He was some little time before actually passing water, and showed conflict or hesitation; he remarked, "First I did and then I didn't, and then I did, and then I didn't."

6.3.25. Frank made water on the bonfire.

19.3.25. Frank "wee-wee'd" on a table in the summer-house. Mrs. I. asked him to wipe it off. He denied having done it, and said, "Perhaps it is a little something." When Mrs. I. said, "Please get a cloth and wipe it off," he did so, but said, "I shan't do so next time."

25.3.25. In the garden, the children were calling to the maids through the windows, and Harold said, laughing, "I see the lavatory" (it was the scullery he saw). Frank at once said, "I'll bee-wee in the garden."

They spoke again of "bee-wee gnomes".

22.4.25. In the lavatory in the afternoon, Dan passed faeces, and on wiping his anus, showed Mrs. I. the paper, saying, "Oh! much faeces! Would you like it?" And when she said, "No, thank you," he offered to wipe it on her frock.

24.5.25. When Priscilla, Frank and Dan were washing after bathing, Priscilla insistently called the attention of the boys to the fact that she was " going to wash her tummy ", and did so, sticking it out, and laughing.

15.6.25. Several of the boys ran about the schoolroom naked after bathing, with great delight and laughter. Duncan, Frank and Dan ran on all fours as " doggies ". They soon came to dress when called.

7.7.25. In the morning, when in his bathing suit, Duncan called to everyone to look at him: " This is going to be bee-wee water." He poured a cup of water down inside his suit, so that it ran out at the legs; and repeated this, again calling the others' attention with eagerness and laughter.

10.3.26. Mrs. I. was ill, and had to leave two or three children with a maid for an hour in the afternoon. She reported that Priscilla took off many of her clothes, and Dan's, and wanted to take everything off.

16.3.26. Priscilla, Dan and Jessica wanted to take their clothes off. It was very cold, so Mrs. I. did not allow it. Jessica was very persistent, and Mrs. I. had to prevent her forcibly, although Priscilla had made the suggestion. After lunch Priscilla shut herself in the lavatory and then ran out naked.

10.5.26. Herbert and Alfred beg Mrs. I. to stay with them and " watch " when they go to the lavatory to urinate.

10.11.26. When bathing before bed, Dan said, " My penis is curved under "; and later, " I'm twisting my penis."

γ

" I am so very much upset and worried over my little boy of 5 years old, Z. He is a very bright, handsome and affectionate child—and everyone thinks him charming. He is an only boy, with two little sisters, one older and one younger than him. About a month ago I heard him say to his sister, ' I know a good game '—then I heard laughter—then, ' I'll do it again.' I looked in and to my horror saw him pull out his little penis and jump up beside his sister who was reading on the sofa. I sent him upstairs to bed, but next day when he was sent to the lavatory, I heard him call, ' Come with me, B., and see my " suckie " when I go to wee-wee.' I took him to his Daddy, who spanked him and threatened to send him away to a school for naughty rude boys. He wept bitterly and was most subdued for a day and I did so hope it was but a transitory thing, and to-day when I was getting their dinner ready and they were playing in the next room with the door ajar I heard him say, ' Here, aren't I pretty, would you like to look at this ? ' and saw him lift his pinafore and start to undo his knickers ! "

b. Verbal

α

8.10.24. Robert and George again half-chanted " wee-wee thing " and " do-do thing ", when running in the garden. With this they tended to get very excited, and to make a half-screaming, half-wailing noise.

16.10.24. In the garden, Robert and George spoke in a sing-song of " wee-wee " and " do-do ".

10.11.24. Frank, running in the garden, often chanted " lu-lu wee-wee ".

12.11.24. Frank and Benjie were heard chanting " put do-do in our mouths ", and " wee-wee on our dinner ".

Harold suggested " wee-wee-ing " into the wash-hand basin.

14.11.24. Overheard, Benjie in the garden speaking of someone who " cannot . . . (something or other) because he has put wee-wee water into his mouth ". George: " I put it in my botty." Harold: " . . . in my tummy ". George, with appropriate gesture: " Here is my botty." Benjie also.

19.11.24. Harold and Benjie chant about " bim-bom-bee-wee-thing ".

27.11.24. While doing plasticine, Harold chanted, " Long, long years ago, there was a bim-bom-bee-wee thing."

Benjie made a long snake-like thing with plasticine. Mrs. I. asked him what he called it. " A wee-wee thing." At lunch, Paul said, " I tried on Mrs. I." Harold repeated this, too.

11.12.24. When the children were running round to music, Harold began to strike his own stomach: " Shall we hit our tummies, shall we hit our bee-wee things ? "

11.2.25. During the morning, Harold said, " bim-bom-bee-wee thing ", but none of the others took any notice this time.

25.2.25. At lunch, Harold spoke of a " bee-wee gnome ", and said, " He is called that because he bee-wees ".

27.2.25. In the lavatory, Harold spoke with laughter of " bee-wee water ", and said, " I'll put it all over you," and, " I smell bee-wee water."

11.3.25. At lunch, and again in the afternoon, Harold spoke of " bim-bom-bee-wee ", and Paul also.

12.3.25. Paul said, " Goodbye, bim-bom," to his mother, several times.

24.3.25. While the others were modelling, for a time Paul, Frank and Harold had the rugs round them and first ran about as " fairy godmothers " ; and then crouched on the platform, each with a rug covering him right over, as " gramophones ", and sang songs, singing, " Hey diddle diddle ", " Humpty dumpty ", and " bim-bom ", " bee-wee " and " try-pan ".

21.4.25. The carpenter arrived to fasten up the trellis railing. Dan and Frank watched him with great interest. They watched him tar the wooden support, and wanted to touch it and to use the tar. When the carpenter said, " No, don't touch that, it will make you in a mess," they said, " Oh, we should like to be in a mess, we should like to be black."

22.4.25. Frank said " lu-lu " several times, and " dirty Mrs. I."

24.4.25. Yesterday, Dan spoke of " bee-wee water " at lunch.

6.5.25. Mrs. I. suggested to Christopher and Dan that they should water the seeds in the three boxes, which they had sown yesterday. They did so, but poured in too much water and the soil swam round in a puddle. This stimulated them to put their hands in, and presently all the children (except Priscilla, Christopher and Paul) put in their hands and feet and stood in the wet soil until they were black from finger to elbow and from toe to knee. With immense delight and enjoyment they described themselves as " Indians " and " dirty Indians ", and ran about the garden for half an hour. Theobald called himself " a clown ". Frank called himself " an Indian ", and Dan said he was a " dirty Indian ". They chased the three who did not join in and tried to put some soil on them. They enjoyed the process of cleaning up just as much.

15.7.25. Just before washing, at the end of the afternoon, Dan and Priscilla covered their arms and hands with mud and called themselves " Indians ".

12.10.25. In the sand-pit, Tommy put some sand up the leg of his trousers, and let it fall down again, saying, " See how it pours."

20.1.26. In putting armfuls of paper away, Priscilla stuffed some up her jersey, saying that she was " going to have a fat tummy ". Dan followed her in this, saying that his was " so big that he could poke with it ", suiting action to word.

9.2.27. Dan was going out to tea with a friend, and was very delighted and rather excited about it. He said at lunch-time, " Oh, I'm so pleased, I want to wriggle my penis." Then, to Priscilla, " Don't you, Priscilla ?—Oh, you can't, you haven't got one."

10.2.27. When Dan was painting, he admired a particular piece of his own work, saying, " You'd hardly think I'd done that, would you ? You'd think a grown-up had done it, wouldn't you ? It's so well done, isn't it ? You come and look, Jane and Mrs. I. ! "

25.2.27. Conrad often makes references to going to the lavatory. To-day he acted it when out of doors, pretending to sit down on a tuft of grass, and making noises with his mouth.

3.3.27. To-day, the children shouted:

> Ena dena dina do,
> Put a baby on the po,
> When it's done, wipe its bum (or—when it's done call its mum),
> Ena dena dina do.

Priscilla shouted the loudest and seemed the most excited. Jane said that she " knew that at my other school ".

4. Sexual Curiosity

α

21.9.24. Mrs. I. happened to be seated in a low chair. Dan knelt on the floor close to her feet and tried to see up under her skirts. She showed him some berries she had in her hand; he took them and put them in his pocket, but knelt down again at once. His mother then showed him some loose leaves in a rose bowl which he had previously played with, but he refused to be interested in them. Presently, Mrs. I. was standing up near the table. When Dan came near her she showed him a card she had in her hand. He took it, looked at it, put it down, and then bent down and looked under the table. Then he went round to the other side of the table, underneath it; played with the legs, shifting them (it was a gate-leg) on both sides until the leaf fell, then called out with glee, " Look there," showing his mother and Mrs. I. the exposed leg. Then he came to Mrs. I. again, and said to her, " You sit there,"pointing to the low chair, which gave him more chance of observation; but she said she was going out at the moment. Later in the same day, he repeated the attempt several times, particularly when Mrs. I. was sitting on a chair in the bathroom while he was undressing for his bath. At one moment, he suddenly turned her skirt up to the knee.

21.11.24. When Mrs. I. was in the lavatory, Harold went and tried to peer through the frosted glass, shouting, " I can see her in the lav. I can see her combinations "—with glee. Later, he tried to turn up her skirt, to see them.

24.11.24. Frank was standing at the bottom of the stairs when Mrs. I. came down, and threw his arms affectionately round her, his head being at the level of the pelvic region. At

SOURCES OF LOVE AND HATE

once he said, " Shall we see her wee-wee thing ? " And then tried to lift up Miss B.'s skirt.

4.12.24. Frank said, " Shall we look at Mrs. I.'s dress ? Shall we look at her petticoats ? And the big fat thing on her tummy ? " Harold . . . " Yes, shall we undress her ? "

2.2.25. In the afternoon, Mrs. I. was playing the piano, and Dan and Frank sat on the floor below her. At first, this was to watch the action of the pedals ; then they suddenly turned up the edge of her skirts, saying, " Shall we see her suspenders ? "—with laughter.

19.5.25. In the afternoon, Priscilla washed Dan and then Frank, and took Dan into the lavatory to make water ; she undid their trousers for them, and then said, " Now you have not wet your knickers," Laurie watching. On later occasions, she often asked a boy, " Do you want to make water ? " and took him into the lavatory to attend to him.

27.5.25. When Mrs. I. was stooping down to help Tommy with his shoes, he suddenly put his hand down, pulled the front of her frock forward, and tried to look at her breast, saying, " What is that ? " very affectionately.

24.6.25. When the children were playing a family game with the puppy as baby, Duncan said : " Undress him." Priscilla : " Yes." Duncan : " and then we can see his bim-bom " ; there was great laughter and excitement among the children and all repeated, " see his bim-bom ". Priscilla undid the rug in which he was wrapped and called others to look : " Come on, come on, look underneath." The puppy stood on its hind legs near Priscilla. Duncan : " Oh, he tried to get to your what-d'ye-call-it."

13.7.25. When at the picnic in the garden, Mrs. I. was sitting with the children on the floor ; Priscilla laughed and said to her, " Oh, look—I can see right up your legs."

Duncan saw Nora at the bathroom window, and said she was " in her night-dress ". Nora said, " No." He then asked her if she was having a bath : " Oh ! Undressed ! "

16.11.25. When drawing on the blackboard, Tommy's drawings had clearly a phallic meaning. He saw the dog in the garden to-day, and asked Mrs. I. whether it was " a man or a lady ", and whether " the brown dog next door " was " a man or a lady ".

18.11.25. Some of the children heard Mrs. I. go into the lavatory, and all ran to try to peep through the frosted glass, saying, " She's making water." When she came out, they said to her in a matter-of-fact way, " You made water ".

17.5.26. While sewing in the afternoon, Priscilla told us that she had " seen a bull " while on the way to school. Dan said, " A bull, what's a bull ? " Priscilla said, " A he-cow ". Dan said, " But isn't a cow a he ? " Priscilla and Mrs. I. said, " No." They spoke of " he " and " she " animals, and Mrs. I. gave them the names " male " and " female ". They instanced the male and female among the children in school, the mammies and daddies and other grown-ups they knew. Then Dan said, " What do you call it when there's a he-and-a-her, a she-and-a-him together ? " Mrs. I. was not quite sure what he referred to, but said, " Do you mean when they are together in the same room ? " He said, " When they are touching." She touched his hand, and said, " Do you mean like this ? We haven't one word to refer to this. We say ' he and she are touching '." He said, with a shy look and a little hesitation, " No, I mean when they are very close together, standing up." The conversation was broken off at that point by the interruption of a visitor.

13.12.26. While Jane, Conrad and Dan were drawing with crayons, Conrad asked Jane whether she had " seen Dan's mummie's penis "—but at once corrected himself and said, " No, she hasn't got one. Have you seen her overs ? " (ovaries? vulva ?) Jane replied, " No, I haven't, but I've seen my mummie's." Conrad: " So've I."

16.12.26. There were frequent references to " anus " and " penis " again in the talk between Jane and Conrad in the evening. Conrad referred to " Mrs. Z.'s penis " ; then they both exclaimed, " But she hasn't got a penis ! "

27.1.27. Jane and Conrad went with Mrs. I. to the ethnological museum to-day. When looking at a human figure made of bamboo, Conrad pointed out the prominent penis, giggling, and saying, " What is that funny thing, sticking out ? We know, don't we ? " They whispered and giggled about it.

10.2.27. Jane was cutting out and colouring paper costumes for her dolls, and a suggestion was made that she might make them for different countries—a Russian winter, or the heat of Africa. She replied, " Well, *then* she would hardly wear anything." Mrs. I. replied, " No, not much—perhaps a string of beads." Conrad, with a sly giggle, said, " and something *there* ", touching the genital region. Priscilla said, " Where ? " and Conrad repeated the remark and gesture with a giggle, and they all laughed.

16.3.27. When Jane went to the lavatory, several of the others ran to the door and stayed outside. They came away when we called them to do so, but presently Conrad ran quickly back and called out something about " little white knickers ". Jane called to him to go away, and he obeyed.

5. Sexual Play and Aggression

α

10.11.24. Harold and George " undressed " Paul in the sand-pit, and were " looking at his tummy " (they said), i.e., they had undone the front of his knickers and pulled down his vest. Later, they were running after Benjie to " undress " him.

25.11.24. Harold had made a plasticine aeroplane. Frank shouted when Harold was running round with it, " Shall we shoot it at Mrs. I.'s bee-wee thing ? "

28.11.24. When Mrs. I. was kneeling on the floor for some purpose, Harold suddenly put his hand down her back to " tickle " it.

16.1.25. While modelling, Frank said, apropos of a long piece of plasticine, " Somebody's climbing up the lady's ah-ah house."

19.1.25. Dan asked Mrs. I. to lie down so that he could " sit on her ". When she refused, he said, " Then I'll push you down."

26.1.25. Mrs. I. was in the lavatory with Dan, helping to fasten his braces and trousers. Frank came in. She was bent low, and he tried to put his hand down and to see down the front of her dress. Dan then did the same, with much laughter and excitement. " We shall see your comb's " they said.

9.2.25. Dan and Frank made a " house " on the top of the steps with the wire gate as a roof, taking out chairs and the rug, telling Mrs. I. " We can see you through the roof ". She was standing near and Frank squeezed her ankles hard with both hands ; Tommy did the same imitatively.

6.3.25. Christopher and Dan, standing near Mrs. I., became affectionate and embraced her. Christopher then put his head underneath the border of her jumper, with much laughter and amusement, saying " how nice and dark " it was inside.

Harold and Tommy were hitting each other. Harold said he would " tease Tommy, and cut him open, and pull his inside out ", and would do this to " all the boys except Frank and Paul ".

20.3.25. Harold, running round as an engine, bumped into Mrs. I. heavily at the piano and then began to hug her, and ended up by kissing her hand.

23.3.25. Dan's mother came to lunch, and the children were all very affectionate ; they hugged her and romped with her. After lunch, they ran round as " engines ". They asked Mrs. X. to be the buffers, kneeling on the floor ; but when she knelt, Harold jumped on her from behind and hugged her, and then tried to sit on her lap. The others all hugged her in a boisterous but affectionate way.

26.3.25. A pair of Mrs. I.'s shoes had been left in Dan's mother's room, and Dan saw them there. Later on, he told Miss B. that he had " made water in Mrs. I.'s shoe ", which was, of course, pure phantasy. Miss B. said, " Oh, but how would *you* like it if Mrs. I. did that to your shoe ? " " She can't—she hasn't got a penis."

8.5.25. When Mrs. I. was resting on the lawn to-day, talking to another adult, Dan, who had been playing near-by with other children, came to her, and quite suddenly turned up her skirt and flung himself across her leg, saying, " Will you be a motor-bike ? " He was angry when she refused and lifted him off.

His mother told Mrs. I. that once or twice lately when he has come into her bed in the mornings, he has got astride her leg, with an obvious erection, and tried to " ride " her.

13.5.25. In the garden, Mrs. I. was bending down at one moment, when Paul climbed on her back and put his arms round her neck.

16.5.25. Several children were playing in the garden with adult visitors. Dan asked Miss F. to " give him a ride " on her back. She did so, and he wanted to go on with it indefinitely, again showing that he was strongly stimulated by the position and movement. He was angry when Mrs. I. asked Miss F. not to go on with it, and he then tried to get other women to indulge him.

10.6.25. Again, when Mrs. I. happened to be sitting on a rug on the lawn, Dan suddenly sat down across her leg, and held himself there with great persistence, and clear signs of an erection. When she asked him to get up, he said he would " make water " on her, or " pass faeces ", and showed angry determination to get the pleasure he was denied. This was the last occasion when he attempted such an assault upon a grown-up, as he evidently came to realise quite clearly that it would not be allowed.

23.6.25. Tommy, very frequently, during these past few days, climbs on Mrs. I.'s back, saying, " I shall climb on your back," if she bends down, for example, to cut the grass. He is rather persistent in it, and laughs a good deal about it.

30.6.25. When in the garden, Tommy went on to Mrs. I.'s knee. He presently tried to put his hand down the front of her frock, smiling ; and pulling his bathing-suit forward, asked her to put her hand on his chest.

9.7.25. Priscilla, Frank and Dan went to rest ; Frank and Priscilla would share the same bed. Mrs. I. asked them to lie in separate ones ; when she came down, Dan presently called to her that they were again in the same bed. When she went up, they were covered up with a rug over their heads. Dan said to them, " I told." (Mrs. I. had heard him say that he " would tell.") When Priscilla was asked to lie on another bed, she whispered to Frank that when Mrs. I. had gone, she would return.

14.7.25. Harold spoke again of " eating bogies ", and in a moment of hostility threatened to " push things up your nose ".

17.11.25. When playing with Priscilla and Mrs. I., Dan pretended to be " something in the sea ", " a gangi ", which later on was " a tiger or a lion ", and became very sadistic, without any quarrel or provocation. He suddenly wanted to hurt Priscilla and Mrs. I., and picked up a piece of sewing and threw it at them. It had a needle in it, and when Dan saw this, he asked Priscilla, " Did it prick you ? " " No." " It would have been better if it had," he said.

When Mrs. I. was getting ready to leave, Priscilla and Dan made a fuss about her going, and insisted on kissing her " all over "—face and hair and dress and shoes. After this, Dan fidgeted about in a way that clearly indicated an erection, and asked her to " lie down and be a motor-bike ", assuring her that he " wouldn't hurt her ". (Of course she did not do so.) After Mrs. I. had said goodbye, she had occasion to return, and was standing on the bottom step of the stairs talking, when Dan bent down and kissed her ankle, then suddenly thrust his hand up her leg. Priscilla then tried to do the same, which, of course, she prevented.

8.12.25. Mrs. I. had occasion to take away Dan's spade, and Priscilla was angry on his behalf. She said, " I'll put sand on you " ; bent down, and said, " I'll put it up there," meaning up her skirt.

2.2.26. In the morning, Priscilla and Dan came into the cloakroom where Miss B. and Mrs. I. were doing various things, and asked them to go out. They said," Not just now ", as it was not convenient. The children begged them to do so, saying, " Well, if we tell you what we want to do, will you go ? " Mrs. I. said, " That depends on what it is." " We want to do a rude trick." " Do you ? " " Yes, we want to take our knickers off and wash our feet and legs." As their legs were not dirty Mrs. I. did not allow it.

5.2.26. In the afternoon, Priscilla talked of feeding her doll, and said, " I know how I shall feed her—not from the bottle, but a funny way—like Mammy used to feed me." Mrs. I. said, " How ? " She whispered to Dan, then said, " A funny way, but real people do it ". Presently she took her doll, and pushed it up her jersey in front, smiling ; Dan did also.

6.6.26. When the children were playing at a journey game, Priscilla became " a motor-bike " for a time, and lay on her face on the floor, with Dan " riding " her, making thrusting movements with his loins, and showing sexual excitement—until Mrs. I. intervened and suggested some other form of " motor-bike ".

At about this time, there were two or three occasions when this play was begun, and would have gone on if Mrs. I. had not interfered.

18.5.27. After lunch, the children bathed in the sand-pit. Three of them, when drying and dressing in the cloakroom, asked Miss D.: " Please go away and leave us alone." When she refused to do so, they were very angry and made violent protests ; and ended by saying that *she* was " rude ", as she insisted on staying with them when they were dressing ! And all wrapped towels round their middles, so that she could not see them—trying to dress under the towels—with an air of completely shocked and injured innocence !

β

Information from a woman acquaintance :

1. At 5 years of age, playing in a field with a neighbour's son of 8 or 9 years, the boy exposed his genital fully and tried to persuade the girl to allow him to " put it in ". She was shy and frightened and ran indoors.

2. At 8 years of age, after a picnic, she was left in a field with a boy of two years of age. She exposed the boy (still in petticoats) and tried to effect coitus. Her guilt about this incident was very great and remained even in adult life. She knew the boy and his parents at a later period of her own childhood, and could never see him or hear his name without feeling a pang of guilt and dread, lest she had done him some permanent harm. She always had the feeling that any illness the boy suffered from, or any difficulty with his parents, was her fault, and it was an immense relief to her when he grew up and she heard that he was doing well in business and in life generally.

γ

(See also behaviour of Z. quoted under EXHIBITIONISM.)

SOURCES OF LOVE AND HATE

δ

STERN: *Psychology of Early Childhood*, 2nd English Edition, p. 63. " Charlotte Bühler . . . believes that in the very middle of this period, that is then about 3;0, a change takes place of a violent and critical nature, resembling in a minor degree what takes place on a larger scale in the crisis of puberty. Manifestations of defiance, sudden increases in affection and other emotional disturbances are said to be the signs of this critical period. She even believes that a first suggestion of sexual development then takes place, ' a brief flicker of emotion which ebbs away again later on and does not recur again before puberty '."

6. MASTURBATION

α

26.10.25. For a few days round about this date, X. appeared to be masturbating at frequent intervals; he sat or stood about in a vacant, dreamy way, fidgeting with his genital, for half-an-hour at a time. On one occasion, Penelope saw him doing this, and said, with much contempt, " Silly little boy." X. was very angry, and replied, " If you say that again, I'll kill you ! "

γ

1. " Since she was eight months old she (aged 2;5) has indulged in bad habits. At first she simply rubbed her thighs by crossing her legs. I have taken her twice to a children's specialist. The first time, March 1931, he said we were to distract but not to scold her. We did distract her but with no success. Her Nurse was very patient. The second time, September 1931, he said she must be stopped at all costs and if everything else failed we would have to try apparatus. I had a trained hospital and maternity nurse with me. She and I never left the child and after a fortnight she was much better. Then she found other ways of rubbing (sitting with her heel under her, standing with one leg lifted, sitting with legs tightly together though not crossed) and since then she has been gradually getting worse again. She is unusually intelligent (this is not merely my opinion !)".

2. " C. is a strong healthy child (aged 3;6) and has a habit which I seem powerless to break. When I put him down to sleep at night he very often keeps himself awake for a very long time by laughing and shouting. This habit started at least a

year ago and has been gradually getting worse. The same thing happens if he wakes in the middle of the night. He sleeps in a room alone and often my husband and I have woken up to hear peals and shouts of laughter. Also he does this when he wakes in the morning, i.e. between 5 and 6 a.m. As I write this down it seems a trivial matter but I don't think it is. It does not seem a natural laughter, and apart from the actual laughing he makes queer growling noises. Once or twice I have asked him what he was laughing at and he says, ' I am laughing at ladies and babies,' and once I asked him why he laughed and he said, ' I can't help it—I must.' "

3. " As I have had my little girl of about four giggling in the night, I am wondering if in the other cases it arises from the same cause, that is the sensation caused by ' touching ' themselves in their private parts. My nurse had spoken of my little girl's laughing in her sleep, but as she is a very happy little person we thought it was dreams. While my nurse was away, however, she slept with me and I heard her do it, at the same time sucking her thumb. The sound seemed different from an ordinary laugh so I got out to inspect and found that was what it was—really half in her sleep."

4. " I came to her (aged 3;0) when she was eleven months, and the first morning I put her into her pram to sleep, I saw what was happening. For twelve months I took no notice of it, only in an indirect way—giving her an animal to hug, etc. This was alright for a night or two, then it was thrown overboard. She was very highly strung, excitable, irritable, very underweight, pale pinched face and very dark around the eyes. Wherever I went everyone said how ill the child looked. She also had no appetite and her nights were very bad. She would be awake for three or four hours night after night, practising this habit. She has never been scolded or punished for it. The trouble got worse and worse. At the end of the first year I put her into splints. There was a marked improvement in a very short time—her appetite improved, her weight went up, she was altogether happier, and everyone said what a change there was in the child. She slept the night through and with no wet bed. I kept them on for three months, then I left them off and everything went well for two months. Suddenly, I cannot think why, she started it again. I left her without taking any direct notice. Back she went at once to her old ways, you would not credit the difference in the child. I left the splints off for two months, and she looked just as ill as she did when I first saw her. She also lost weight both months. Again I returned to the splints, and she is still wearing them. She asks for her ' long legs ' as she calls

them—every night. She is now a picture of health, round, rosy, and as happy and busy as can be. She has gained two pounds in the last three months."

5. "My baby girl of 18 months has developed a funny habit: when she is in her bed or pram she shakes the bed, and, lying on her face, bumps herself up and down straight on for perhaps three minutes at a time. Then she sings and crows and off again with this peculiar bumping. It has suddenly dawned on me that this is a real 'bad habit'. I called in the doctor and he says we must divert her attention and prevent her from doing it. This is not easy as she generally does it after she is settled in the evening in her cot. Baby is inclined to 'play with herself' too when she has the chance."

6. "My eldest little girl, aged 3;6, has got into the wretched habit of masturbation, and I do so wonder what is the best way to deal with it. She started it over a year ago, but for the last six months she appeared to have forgotten it, but now this last week it has broken out again, worse than ever. When first put to bed is the worst time, but she will do it any time if left alone. One of us always sits with her at rest time, and she threads beads, etc. She knows it is 'naughty' but doesn't seem able to make the effort to overcome it."

7. "I am now going to ask your help in a problem of my little charge, aged 5, a girl. Ever since I have been with her (about eighteen months) I have noticed she has very bad habits which try how I might she does not give up, namely, nail biting, nose picking and eating, and lastly and most worrying, she is continually playing with herself—in bed especially, although I give her toys to cuddle. I have never scolded her for it, but have told her that nice little girls don't do those things, but I don't keep at her about it in case she is attracted too much to her faults. N.'s mummie says every little girl does it, but I had two little girls before I had N. and they did not."

8. "I should like to ask your advice with regard to my little girl (age 3;9) who has contracted the habit of masturbation. This condition began about two years ago—and for the last 9 months I resorted to splints for her legs at night. This treatment resulted in the habit occurring during the day —if she was left alone to play—while previously it had only been noticed at bed time and during her afternoon rest. A few weeks ago I took her to a psychologist and nerve specialist —who advised me to discontinue the splints and her afternoon rest. I stay with her at night until she's asleep. My Nannie is with her constantly during the day (but without appearing to watch her) only seeing that she is occupied or interested. The

trouble now arises early in the morning as the child wakes up and the habit is resumed without her disturbing me—for a time at least, although her cot has been moved into my room."

9. " I should be so very grateful if you would give me your advice about my small son, aged 1;6. When we put him to go to sleep we notice that he sucks and tugs his blanket and rubs his thighs together—and goes red in the face. I noticed this several months ago. He started at about nine months when he was weaned. Though I did not at first recognise it I can now only think that this habit is masturbation and I am, of course, most anxious to stop him as soon as possible."

10. " I should be very grateful for your advice with regard to the recurrence of the rather unusual behaviour of my little daughter of 2;5. When she goes to bed both for her afternoon nap and at night she invariably turns on to her tummy and putting her hands between her legs (she wears a sleeping suit and cannot actually touch her body) works herself about grunting, and appears to draw her knees up together and then to push them out. I have told her that it was not the nice way to go to sleep and consequently she waits until I have left the room and then begins. She had this habit about twelve months ago, but by sitting and watching her until she went off to sleep I thought I had cured her of the habit for she has gone to sleep quite naturally until recently. Now the habit has recurred again."

11. " I wonder if you can give me some advice about my little girl, about whom I am very worried. She was four years old last February and for about a month now I have noticed that she takes an excessively long time to get to sleep when put to bed at 6.30 p.m., and also gets unusually hot, although lately she has only had a sheet over her. I thought perhaps she might play some vigorous game when she was left, to account for the sleeplessness and heat, so I determined to find out, and one evening watched her, quite unseen by her. I found that instead of playing about as I thought she might, she was rolling about under the bedclothes and grunting and gasping in the most peculiar way, stopping every now and then to rest and to cool down and then continuing. This lasted for about an hour and a half, when I thought I had better put a stop to it, so went and sat by her bedside and asked with all interest what she was so busy about. She told me she was ' squeezing her legs together, and that it was lovely and a great treat ', and demonstrated to me in the most realistic way, using herself up in the process while she clung to the sheet with her hands."

12. " My little girl who is 5;6 has got into a bad habit of playing with herself. We noticed once or twice that she was very sore in that part and one day saw her doing it. We told her it was naughty—would make her ill but she still does it. Mostly I think when she is resting or if she does not go to sleep at once at night. She drops off when she has done it. I feel that the rest in a room by herself is so good for her and everyone else, but would it be better to give her something to do instead of leaving her idly ? "

13. " My little boy, aged 3;7, has developed a very nasty habit, and, as it has gone on for more than a month now I thought perhaps you would tell me if I am adopting the right course—for I have seen no improvement at all. When anything pleases him or he is excited his hand at once goes to his ' private part ' and clutches or fiddles with it. I usually try to find the hand something else to do as quickly as possible— or tell him gently to leave his knickers alone. Added to this, at times, e.g. bath time—he pulls it and examines it minutely. I have tried in this, too, to occupy the hands at once but it does not always answer and he continues to do it when opportunity occurs. I do not mean he is *always* doing it, but often it occurs once in a day."

14. " My little girl of 4 years old has developed the most terrible habit of lying about on the floor with her legs crossed or sitting on the edge of a chair and rubbing herself on the corner, or sitting with her hands, palms together, between her legs. She is a perfectly normal child but very highly strung and excitable."

15. " I should be very glad if you can give me advice, about my boy of 2;6 who has a habit of handling his genital organ whenever he settles to sleep. I heard a matron of long experience say that she almost invariably found that when children were deprived of thumb-sucking they took to this worse habit instead. My little boy does both, however ! He took to touching his ' tail ' in the day-time as well as at night a while ago."

16. " I am very worried about my daughter. She is just 7 years of age. When she was about 9 months old I used to notice she would lie on her back and rub her tummy until she went scarlet in the face and used to go to sleep. I mentioned this to the matron of the Nursing Home where she was born as I had no one whom I could ask for advice. Matron alarmed me by saying it was a form of self-abuse and she would eventually go out of her mind unless the habit was broken. She advised smacking very hard. I did not smack her but showed her that I was cross and until she was three years of age

I used to nurse her off to sleep and I believed that she had forgotten the habit. I then started putting her to sleep on her own but found that the trouble was worse. She still rubbed her tummy and at times lay on it and rocked the cot."

17. " How can I cure Vera (aged four) of pushing things up her nose, and how ought I to treat her when she has done this ? The first time was when she was about two. She pushed up some wild flowers and leaves. I took out what I could and then went to the doctor who could not find any more. I thought this was due to boredom, so thereafter always kept her occupied in the pram. The second time was when she was about three and a half when out here. She pushed up a eucalyptus seed (about the size of a pea and hard). I managed to extract this myself. The other day she and I were picking fruit in the garden and she came and told me she'd pushed a wild mulberry up her nose. The fruit is like a blackberry, but longer and thinner. I could not get it down so took her to the hospital, where the doctor put her on the operating table and removed it with tweezers. To-day she was making sand pies in the garden with nurse quite close to her. I heard her sneeze about six times and I asked her if she'd pushed anything up her nose and she said she'd filled her nose with sand. I never scold her, nor show the slightest alarm, as I do not want her to be too afraid to tell me what she has done. I so hoped that the visit to the hospital and the paraphernalia of the theatre, which she hated at the time, would have cured her. It has been far more frequent recently and it does not take place when she has nothing to do. Luckily nothing serious has happened so far, but the habit is fraught with danger, especially out in the tropics, where anything picked up off the ground may contain germs and should never be put in the mouth or up the nose."

18. " Group of boys in bath room, bathing, etc.

" Boy, twelve and a half, popular, confident, good looking, clever and happy, having just dried after a hot bath, standing playing with his penis a moment in full view of everyone else in the room. No one paid any attention or appeared to notice except the new boy (aged 11), who sniggered, looked round for someone to share the snigger, met my eyes, flushed guiltily, giggled again. 'What's the matter ? ' asked one of the boys. ' Have you been doing anything wicked again ? ' (He so often looked guilty that the boys teased him about the murders he had committed, etc.)"

19. " With a stick he (aged 7;9) will tap about at the floor or chairs if he has nothing better to do, *or* if he is talking to you. I have asked what he is thinking about, and it is usually

of what he is going to be when he grows up or of his grandfather's big game hunting, etc., that he would like to do. I imagine he has formed this jiggling habit this way—a year ago in the summer he was allowed to play with the garden hose, which delights every child, and was allowed to help clean the car, etc. Then when it was too cold he had the hose in the house and would pretend to hose by the hour. He was a very solitary little boy then, no children near—I think he got into the habit of shaking the hose and so shakes sticks or whips now. He is very sensible otherwise and sits still when occupied or read to."

20. " Went to say good-night to X. and while I was talking he was playing with himself under the bed clothes. *Do you often do that?* Sometimes he's lonely. *When is he lonely?* Oh, when I'm sad sometimes. He wants a little love. *Oh, well, you're not often sad.* Some mothers (went on X.) scold their little boys for that. H. (mentioning a day boy) thinks it makes you very ill. *Yes, a lot of mothers think it is bad for their children.* Is it? *No.* They think it's rude (wanting me of course to pronounce some sort of judgment). When you were a little girl did you? *I don't remember doing it but I remember being slapped for doing it, so I suppose I did.* Slapped? (said X. in rather a surprised way). Not your mother? (He knows my mother. I was very glad to be able to say): *No, one of my older step-sisters that you don't know.* (He turned to a book he had on the bed and started telling me about Robin Hood.)

δ

WOOLLEY, *op. cit.*, p. 66. " It is now generally conceded that infants and young children almost universally find out that pleasant sensations are aroused by manipulating the sex organs and frequently adopt the habit for a time. They wish to maintain and repeat the sensation. Even before it had scientific recognition, unscrupulous nurses knew that infants could be kept quiet by stroking and pressing the sex organs and practised the art. When the infant himself adopts the habit, it may be regarded as a preliminary stage of masturbation."

WOOLLEY, *ibid.*, p. 67. " The manipulation of the sex organs, or masturbation, is a habit which it is peculiarly difficult for parents to treat with any understanding or sympathy. The *Minnesota Handbook* says, ' No other childish habit is so misunderstood, or is the object of so much unreasoning emotional reaction ' (14, p. 98). The physiological harm done by the amount of masturbation which a normal well-regulated child does is negligible."

BRIDGES, p. 181. " An occasional child of any pre-school age may manipulate the genitalia when unoccupied or disinterested in an occupation. This is more frequent among boys than girls, perhaps due partly to difference in clothing. Thigh-rubbing may occur on occasion, and this along with genital manipulation may perform a similar function to thumb-sucking. These reactions are probably soothing and comforting in effect. They relieve tension and at the same time provide an easy and pleasant occupation in place of a disinteresting one or none at all. The children who behave in this way are the ones who have diffuse attention or scattered and indefinite interests, or those who have very few interests. Thus the restless children with much undirected energy, the disinterested and the lethargic children seem to be the ones who tend to masturbate. As children develop organised interests in different occupations, and as they take delight in developing their own skills and in rhythmic and other activity, these habits disappear."

J. B. WATSON: "What the Nursery Has to Say About Instincts," *Psychologies of 1925*, p. 19. " At what age tumescence becomes a conditioned response is not known. Masturbation (a better term with infants is manipulation of the penis or vagina respectively) can occur at almost any age. The earliest case I have personally observed was a girl around one year of age (it often begins much earlier). The infant was sitting up in the bath-tub and in reaching for the soap accidentally touched the external opening of the vagina with her finger. The search for the soap stopped, stroking of the vagina began and a smile overspread the face. Neither in the case of infant boys nor of infant girls have I seen masturbation carried to the point where the orgasm takes place (it must be remembered that the orgasm can occur without ejaculation in the male before the age of puberty is reached). Apparently a great many of the muscular responses later to be used in the sex act, such as pushing, climbing, stroking, are ready to function in the male at least at a very much earlier age than we are accustomed to think. In one observed case which came into the clinic, a boy of $3\frac{1}{2}$ years of age would mount his mother or nurse, whichever one happened to be sleeping with him. Erection would take place and he would manipulate and bite her breast ; then clasping and sex movements similar to those of adults would ensue. In this case the mother, who was separated from her husband, had deliberately attempted to build up this reaction in her child."

J. B. WATSON: *Psychological Care of Infant and Child*, p. 143. " Masturbation is not, however, a problem that begins in puberty. For the parent it is a problem which begins at birth. Children as young as six months begin it."

7. FAMILY PLAY, AND IDEAS ABOUT BABIES AND MARRIAGE

α

22.10.24. Robert and then George and later Frank pretended to have a baby in their arms and rocked about, saying, " Baby, baby, baby."

26.11.24. Frank and Benjie spoke of someone who was " crazy " ; she was " going to the police station, and getting married, and then we will kill her after that ".

29.1.25. George and Frank drew on the window with their fingers, the windows being a little steamy. George drew a picture of Frank, " When you were a baby," he said.

Miss B. reported that yesterday, during the rest hour, the children had talked about putting one's thumb in one's mouth. Dan said, " Henry " (his father) " does, when he goes to sleep." Frank said, " He's a naughty boy." Dan: " Oh no, I don't call him a naughty boy—he's a man." Frank: " Was he a boy when you were a little baby ? " Dan seemed puzzled and asked, " What did you say ? " Frank repeated the question, and Dan seemed to consider, and said, " I don't know."

3.2.25. Frank told everyone that when he was coming to school he saw " a carriage all dressed up with ribbons " ; he thought " someone was going to be married ". Christopher said, " Yes, someone is going to be married, aren't they ? " The children all joked and laughed about this for some time. Christopher said it was " Mrs. Laws ". They all laughed. Frank said, " When she is married we shall spit in her face, shan't we ? "

9.2.25. Frank plucked some laurel leaves and said, " It's a wedding." He ran round the garden with the leaves.

12.2.25. In the morning, when Christopher was modelling, he made a " duck ", the head and mouth of a duck, with the mouth wide open, and then talked of the " baby duck ". Then presently, while cutting a piece of plasticine up, he said, " Here is another mother duck being born."

13.2.25. Frank found some small cards with numbers printed on and called them " wedding cards " ; used them as confetti, running round the room and scattering them over all the other children. He kept talking of a " wedding ".

16.2.25. Frank cut long strips of paper to decorate everyone with, and called it " a wedding ".

27.2.25. When modelling, Paul said he would make " a rabbit like his own ". He made a " baby bunny ".

Frank wanted to have a wedding. He said to Mrs. I., " Will you be married, Mrs. I. ? " She was not attending fully at the moment and said to him, " What did you say, Frank ? " Whereupon he was overcome with shyness and would not say it again. Theobald said, " Mrs. I. is going to be married." Frank said he would have " the wedding place " in the cloak-room and we would have the schoolroom with the tree in it for a dance.

Later, after running round the room as fairies, Dan and Frank made a " wedding car ".

11.3.25. Frank saw a spray of pink blossom on a fruit tree, and asked Miss B. to pluck it for him, and then ran about the garden with it as an " Express Wedding Train ".

21.4.25. Harold and Paul brought Mrs. I. some shells which they had gathered at the seaside. Paul showed her one as " a little baby shell ".

7.5.25. Priscilla and Frank told Mrs. I., " We're going to be married," and asked her to " take our photographs when we're married ". Frank said that Dan would carry Priscilla's train.

8.5.25. Frank asked Mrs. I. to be " a wedding lady " and had her fasten on with pins the large red rug as a train, and she walked round the schoolroom, carrying a bunch of flowers, with five of them holding her train.

After a time Miss B. did the same, and Frank asked several of the children to do the same, but none of them would.

24.6.25. Dan, Duncan, Priscilla and Frank played " doctor " and " nurse ", " father " and " mother ", with the puppy as the baby, Duncan as the doctor, Frank as the nurse, with the rug wrapped round him.

25.6.25. Dan, Frank, Priscilla and Paul made a house in the wire enclosure and had the puppy in there as a baby, with a rug and chairs. Later, the children asked Mrs. I. to be " a doctor ".

29.6.25. Harold asked for Priscilla and looked about for her. " Where is Priscilla ? " he said. When he found her he said to her, " Will you go into the little house and I'll be the Daddy ? " She did not reply ; he repeated the question, and said, " I'll be the Daddy and go past in my motor-car." She refused.

In the afternoon the children made two houses, one in the old hen-coop and one some distance away on the lawn, with rugs and chairs. They modelled telephones in plasticine, quite excellent models, and joined up the two houses with real wire and telephoned from one to the other. They had the small rabbit as " the baby " in the family, and the two households visited each other with friendly conversation. The house on the lawn had two verandahs made of chairs. When Mrs. I. came out after a little time, they gave her the house in the hen-coop and from the other telephoned to her and asked her to come to tea. This was repeated twice. She went to tea, and they ate apples which they had brought down from the trees. This was a long quiet play.

3.7.25. Priscilla and Frank had a house together under the bushes beside the garden steps. Dan and Duncan had another, with rugs and chairs, and the two households visited each other. For a time Priscilla and Frank were " mice " going to " steal things " from the other house, pieces of bacon, paper, etc. Later they were visitors, and Duncan asked them whether they would have " polygon " cake or " round " cake. Presently Priscilla and Frank were Aunt and Uncle, and Duncan and Dan brought bricks to make something at the house of Priscilla and Frank. Duncan referred to Dan as " sonny " and " my boy ". Earlier, Dan had said in an inquiring tone of voice, " I *am* a man, aren't I ? "

8.7.25. While Frank, Priscilla and Dan were dressing after being in the garden in bathing suits there was a long conversation about " being married ". Priscilla said she could not marry Frank because she had already married Dan. Then Frank said, " Oh, but you promised to marry *me*," so Priscilla said to Dan, " I'm very sorry, but I promised Frank to marry him if he would do (something) for Duncan." Dan then said, " Well, I'll marry Duncan." The others laughed and Duncan said, " Oh, you can't, boys don't marry boys." Priscilla said, " I can marry any boy, can't I ? But not a grown-up." Duncan said, " Oh, yes, any boy, but you can't marry a girl."

While the other three were in the cloakroom Dan was with Mrs. I. in the schoolroom for part of the time. He was also listening to the conversation of the other three and joining in. Presently he said to Mrs. I., " I can't be married to a boy and Priscilla can't be married to a girl." And then, " Priscilla can't be married to you, but I can. Yes, because you are a lady." And then, after a pause, " No, boys can't be married to ladies," he said.

9.7.25. Dan, when Priscilla arrived, very charmingly invited her to tea. Later there was again some talk about her " marrying " him. He asked her to, saying, " Because I love you "; Priscilla said, " I'm sorry, but I promised Frank to marry him if he would give the beads to Duncan," so Dan said, " Then I shan't have you to tea." Priscilla did, however, stay to tea in the afternoon.

24.9.25. When using the counting rods, Dan for the first time used them imaginatively, calling the smallest one " the baby ", and the largest ones " daddy and mammy ". At first he called the longest of all " the mammy ", but said, " No, that's daddy. My daddy is bigger than my mammy."

11.11.25. Frank and Priscilla began to sew " egg-covers ", on Frank's suggestion ; they made several, small but well-shaped and well-sewn. While sewing they talked about being " mummie " and " daddy " and said, " We're making things for when we're grown-up—*really*, we are ! " Priscilla said, " We're going to be married and have some little babies." Penelope and Tommy were another " mummie and daddy ", in a rival game.

Later in the day, Frank asked Miss B., " When we buy babies, do we have to pay for them ? "

2.2.26. The children said they were " going to have a wedding ", and there was much talk as to whether Priscilla would marry Frank or Dan, who are the two rivals for her affection. To-day she seemed to favour Dan, and said she didn't like Frank. Frank said, " You *can't* marry Dan, because daddy must be bigger than mammy." They argued about this, and then appealed to Mrs. I. as to whether " daddies are always bigger than mammies ". She said, " Well, let's ask everyone about it," and asked each child in turn whether his mammy or his daddy was the bigger. Christopher reported quite accurately that his mammy was ; but Dan denied this of C.'s parents, and said, " No, they're the same." The others all agreed that " daddies *must* be bigger than mammies ! " Dan then said, stamping his foot, " Yes, you see, I *shall* be bigger than Priscilla," thus twisting Frank's argument to suit his own phantasy. Priscilla, however, agreed to " marry " Dan first, and then Frank later. Priscilla and Dan therefore had the first " wedding procession ". Miss B. was asked to be " the bridesmaid ", and Priscilla wore a flowing robe and veil, with a wreath and bouquet of jasmine flowers from the garden. Frank carried " a silver wand ", and they walked round. Then Miss B. was told to give Dan a ring, which he put on Priscilla's finger. It was then Frank's turn to be the bridegroom ; and later, they repeated the ceremony, with Frank as the " bride " and Priscilla as the groom. Tommy " played the organ " (piano) during the ritual.

12.3.26. Jessica talked of " marrying Priscilla ", which much amused the others.

15.3.26. Priscilla and Dan talked again of marrying each other. " We'll have a party when we're married. It will be in the garden if it's a fine day." Dan said, " I know—shall we live at Hunstanton ? Hooray ! "

19.3.26. For about three weeks previous to to-day, Priscilla has been in a very difficult and unhappy mood. She was hostile and defiant to adults, and cruel and tyrannical to the other children, mainly owing to home circumstances. Her mother was away for several weeks, and Priscilla was staying with her father at her grand-parents' house. This morning her mood had totally changed. Her mother had returned after the child was in bed the previous evening, and had brought Priscilla a large and life-like baby doll. She brought this to school, glowing with pride, and played in the tenderest maternal way with it ; she was friendly and affectionate and gentle with Mrs. I. and with all the other children. She let the others take turns at holding the doll and asked Mrs. I. to " be the auntie ". There was not one hostile word or action on her part to anyone all the day.

22.3.26. In the " family play " to-day, Priscilla was the " baby " and Dan the " mammy ", wheeling the baby about in the pram, with a long elaborate play. When later on Priscilla suggested changing roles, Dan refused, evidently enjoying the novel situation in which Priscilla was subordinate.

1.7.26. In the family game, Priscilla was the mother, Dan and Jessica her babies who had " fallen from the top of a taxi and been hurt ". They were in hospital, and Mrs. I. was asked to be the nurse. Presently they became " new babies, just born ". Then Priscilla asked, " *Where* are babies born— how do they come out ? " Dan at once replied, " They come out of the vulva—*here*," with the appropriate demonstrative gesture. Priscilla was clearly shy about it. Jessica and Christopher listened. Further conversation went on about this.

9.7.26. After the children had noticed the large abdomen of the mother mouse, Dan said to his mother, " You are going to have another baby." *Am I ? I didn't know I was.* " Yes, your tummy is fat, and when ladies have fat tummies, it means that they are going to have a baby."

20.7.26. Penelope's baby sister, a year old, was brought to school this afternoon, and the children all talked to her with great interest. They noticed her small hands and feet, put the rug down for her to crawl on, and laughed at her movements when she did so. They asked, " Can't she talk ? Why can't she ? "

25.1.27. Dan and Priscilla walked about with their arms round one another, and talked of " getting married ". Dan said, " But we haven't the ring." Priscilla: " What ring ? " Dan : " You know—what you wear on your finger." Priscilla replied, " Oh, I have one at home."

1.4.27. Priscilla and Dan spent the day together after the other children had left for the vacation. They climbed into a big box, their " house ", and talked of " getting married ", how they would " take a flat and live together ", discussed whether or not they would " have a servant ", and whom they would allow to come to the flat, etc.

23.5.27. Joseph looked down at Alice, who was sitting on a lower step, and said, " I'm bigger than you, arn't I ? " Penelope, who was standing near, said, " Yes, and you're older, aren't you ? Alice is only three." Joseph replied, " Oh, yes ! But I was three once, but one day I shall be bigger ; I shall be a grown-up man, and then I can marry Muriel." Mrs. I. asked, " Is Muriel a friend of yours ? " " Yes, she takes me out in the afternoon." (His nurse.)

8.6.27. Penelope invited Mr. Y. to come and stay at her house. Mr. Y. said, " Oh, you haven't a room for me." Penelope replied, " Oh, but you can sleep with me. I should like to have three, you and me and my dolly."

β

1. Told me by a woman acquaintance, with regard to theories about the origin of babies:

" My first memory is that I had accepted the ' brought by doctor ' story. From what I have been told since, I, at 3, was somewhat critical of doctors' methods, for they brought babies to ladies who were ill, or made them ill. My mother tells me that before one of my brothers was born (I am $3\frac{1}{2}$ years older than he) I accompanied her to the doctor, and he asked would I like him to bring us a baby, to which I replied, ' Yes, a *brother* please, and bring him when Mamma is well, not when she is ill ; you made the other lady very ill.' " (A neighbour.)

2. When X. was 6;6 years of age a man friend often petted her and told her he was " going to marry her." One day on the train, she being on her way to school, he said in her presence to a clergyman they both knew, " When are you going to marry us, Mr. B. ? " The child took this with complete seriousness, and on returning from school the same afternoon she went straight to the house of this man friend, instead of home. She told his housekeeper (he was unmarried), " I'm going to live here now. I'm going to marry Mr. B.," and refused to go home, even when her father and elder sister came

to fetch her. She stayed the night, sleeping in a nightdress of the housekeeper, but was persuaded to go home on the following afternoon by a practical joke of her father's, which made her realise that the remarks of the man friend had not been meant seriously. Her father sent a large parcel supposed to be her "clothes", but when she undid the parcel, it had nothing inside but newspapers. In adult life the memory of the intense grief and bitter chagrin she felt on opening the parcel remained very vivid.

3. Y. said to his mother, at 4;0 years, " Mummy, I'm growing a baby sister." *Oh no, Y., you can't do that.* Well, then, it's a baby brother. *Oh, no, you can't grow babies—only Mummies can do that.* Well, Mummy, there's *something* happening in my tummy ! "

4. Z., aged 5, asked her mother, " Is Auntie X. killed ? " Her mother said, " What do you mean ? " Z, "Is she dead?" M. " What do you mean by dead ? What do people do when they die ? " Z. "They go back into their Mummie's tummy." M. " But how could Auntie X. go back to her Mummie's tummy? You know her Mummie, and how small she is." Z. " Well, when Auntie X. dies, she becomes a teeny, weeny baby again and goes back to her Mummie's tummy."

γ

1. " I must say we live on a farm and from the time the children (twins, aged 5;6) could walk with a basket I have let them collect the eggs, visit the cows being milked, etc. Before they were three they astounded their grandmother by playing at ' laying ' their Easter eggs. They would put them behind them on their little armchairs and get up and expect us to be very surprised and pleased ; quite their own idea and it only lasted a day or two. I could see by this that they realised how the hens laid and when the boy asked where the calf came from I said ' where do eggs come from ? ' And the girl jumped to it at once, ' out of the cow of course.' The boy said, ' Where does it come out ? ' And the girl replied, ' behind of course.' This was before they were four. A short while after, the boy had forgotten again, and when they were five and a baby was born in the neighbourhood the girl had to tell him once more. I only just put in a word here and there. All the year from 4 to 5 it had thrilled the girl to talk of the time when she was inside me, and once she suddenly remarked, ' Who did Daddy come out of ? ' The boy found it very hard to realise that he was not his Daddy's and the girl mine (though he is far more devoted to me) because his father's father is alive and so is my mother. However, I think at 5;6 the idea of birth is clear

to them both, and the last month has cleared their ideas on marriage. I never bring up these subjects but as they crop up in daily life I hear their opinions on them and when asked for information give it, or correct any obvious mis-statement. A few weeks ago the boy mentioned to the district nurse that she was married, when asked ' who to ' he said the name of her landlady. Nearly two years ago the girl told me she would marry her aunt, but now she mentions a small boy friend, so realises that marriage takes place between the sexes."

2. " Mixed group of boys and girls, six and seven years.

' TERMAN,' dictated the owner of the name to me as I wrote a label for him to put on his work. ' All right,' I said, ' I think I know how to spell your name.' ' Yes,' he agreed, ' I'm sorry. My Auntie always spells it out, she never thinks I know it.' ' Grown-up people never think we have any sense,' said Mary. ' When I have some boys I shall not spell their names for them.' Terman looked curiously at Mary. ' I don't suppose you ever will, though,' he said in a final way. Mary flushed and sat up angrily. ' Why do you say that ? ' she demanded. ' You can't possibly know, no one can possibly know except God. Can they, Mrs. —— ? ' Terman was stammering, ' No, I don't . . . I didn't mean. Of course you might but it doesn't seem likely . . .' ' I don't see how you can know,' and she was nearly crying now. ' I *hope* I have some anyway.' ' Do you want a lot ? ' I asked. ' Well, not too many, because I couldn't look after them properly. Two girls and two boys.' ' Just a nice number,' I agreed, as if her wishes were most reasonable.

(N.B. Mary in a questionnaire on their plans for grown-up life had answered, ' I want to be just an ordinary mother.' She is very pretty, an only child, and plays with many dolls at home.)"

δ

RASMUSSEN: *Child Psychology*, Vol. 2, p. 43. " When four years and one month old, R. inquired: ' How are ladies made ? ' Her mother, startled at the question, inquired: ' Why (do you ask) ? ' But R. had her good reason, and said: ' Because there's meat (on ladies).' To make sure of her meaning, her mother demanded: ' Which ladies ? ' and received the answer: ' You and other ladies.' It being thus placed beyond all doubt that what R. desired was general information relating to the origin of ladies, she received the unsatisfactory answer, ' I don't know.' R. being thus thrown back on her own resources remarked: ' I think it's a " meat-man "; don't you ? ' It is rather obscure what she meant, but I assume that she possessed a vague notion that ladies—in whom 'meat' struck her as a salient characteristic—were manufactured by a person analogous to what she called a 'meat-man'."

RASMUSSEN: *ibid*, pp. 43-4. "S., when only three years and eight months old, asked: 'Mother, where did I come from?' and later: 'Where do they get all these children from?' R. for her part displayed interest at the age of four years and ten months with the inquiry: 'Where's the child (now) which the lady is going to have in the summer?' Her mother replied: 'In the stomach of the lady.' This evidently appeared to R. somewhat peculiar, for, after a pause for reflection, she asked: 'Has she eaten it, then?' Her mother answered: 'No'; but R. persisted: 'Does it come out of the mouth?' Her mother, realising that there was no escape, at last answered: 'No, it comes out of the tail.' This truthful explanation contented R., who, however, for her own satisfaction, carried the matter further, and said: 'Then she sits on the chamber, and then it comes, and then it gets wet and has to have its feet dried.'"

8. CASTRATION FEARS, THREATS AND SYMBOLISM

α

24.10.24. Just before bedtime, with his mother, father and Mrs. I., Dan was tired and very querulous. He pushed a corkscrew which he was holding into his mother's leg, to see if it hurt. When his mother said she was going to put his bath on, he said petulantly, "Oh Mummy, I want my supper *now*—I want it badly, here in the drawing-room." His mother said he could have it soon, but in his bedroom. He stood beside her, caressing her breast through her blouse and feeling as if for the nipple: "I want an egg for my supper."

Presently, sitting beside her upstairs, eating his supper (and still more querulous as a result of a slight accident and hurt fingers), he said, "I want to be mummy"; then asked her to hold his bread and butter and feed him—the first time he had asked for such a thing, since infancy. He insisted that the milk must be warm, and said twice, "It's not sweet enough."

October to December 1924. Frank is always very fond of wearing bead necklaces, ear-rings and bracelets, which he makes for himself, of fastening coloured ribbons or a hair slide on his hair, and in general, behaving rather more like a girl than a boy. His favourite occupations are sewing, crochet-work and knitting. On one occasion there was some talk amongst the children about which were girls and which were boys, and Frank insisted that he was a girl.

2.12.24. Benjie said to Cecil, " I'll cut off your ears, your eyes, your nose, your hippopotamus thing ! "

20.1.25. Frank spontaneously cut out in paper a jersey and a pair of knickers. Mrs. I. suggested he should cut out a boy to put them on ; he replied, " No, a *girl*—they are a girl's." He cut out the " girl " and sewed the jersey and the knickers on to the figure.

3.2.25. Frank and Tommy threaded beads, Frank finishing off a necklace which he wore fastened round his neck.

5.3.25. Frank had wanted Mrs. I. to make a Red Indian's dress for him, with a piece of thick brown paper he had brought. They did it together, cutting out the head-dress and cloak. Later, having now put on his Red Indian dress again, he said, " I am a *girl* Red Indian." And later, when Dan called out to him, " Hullo Father," Frank replied, " Red Indians are girls."

26.3.25. (See Dan's remark in incident under SEXUAL PLAY.)

14.4.25. Talking to his father when in bed, with the latter sitting beside him, Dan said, " Christopher got a big hole in his penis. I've got one also only not so big. It's where the water comes out of my penis—shall I show you ? " (Does so.) " Christopher got a very big hole in his penis."

Later in the conversation: " Have I got a vulva behind my penis ? I'll look." He made a desperate attempt to see. His father suggested that perhaps he meant the anus, but the boy made it clear that he was not thinking of the anus, as that was " between the bukkuks ".

30.4.25. In the afternoon Dan and Frank played in the sand-pit. They took off their shoes and stockings and dug their feet in, so that these could not be seen. Dan then called out to Mrs. I., " Tell Priscilla to ask us to come and love her." Mrs. I. did so. His reply was, with much laughter, " We can't, because our legs are cut off."

19.5.25. When Priscilla and the boys were dressing after bathing, Priscilla looked at Frank's penis and said, " Oh, look, what have you done, it's bleeding ! " (There was nothing wrong.)

Her mother reports that she asked her later on "When shall I grow in front like the boys ? "

15.6.25. Harold said he would " cut off Christopher's nose, and see the bogies ".

September 1925. Dan was staying with Mrs. I., as his mother was away. He was happy during the day, but often

SOURCES OF LOVE AND HATE

woke up in the evening crying for his mother or his nurse. One evening he dictated the following letter to his nurse: " Miss C. I love you. If I have lost some of my toys, will you send them on to me by post. Could you buy me a new pair of shoes, 'cos I've only about eight. What colour will the shoes be ?—oh, and then say what size they're going to be."

Another evening he woke up and talked to Mrs. I., the following being fragments of the conversation : " Where's Mr. I. ? " *In the study.* Is he writing ? *No.* Who does he write to when he writes ? *To his father.* Has he got a father ? *Yes.* Has he got a mummy ? *No.* Have you got a mummy ? *No.* Have you got a father ? *No.* Then do you share Mr. I.'s father ? How tall is Mr. I.'s father ? Has he got a father ? *Who ?* Mr. I.'s father ? *No.* Has he got a mummy ? *No.* Oh, my daddy *is* a long time away.—Interspersed with these questions were many stretches of phantasy. E.g., " Oh, I got run over by a roller at the station ; oh, it *was* nasty—oh, it *did* hurt ! Then I got on top of another train and rode along on it—then came to a station and got down. And there was a very tall man—taller than Mr. I.—oh, so tall. (*Your daddy is tall, isn't he ?*) Oh, yes, he's tall. But I'm growing every day—I'll soon be big. When my daddy comes home, he'll see how big I've got. My daddy's in Switzerland—and my mummy's away, too."

27.10.25. Dan and Priscilla quarrelled to-day ; Priscilla hit Dan, and he bit her finger severely. She cried bitterly ; he looked very miserable, and stood beside Mrs. I. looking at the mark on Priscilla's finger. He said, " *That* doesn't hurt ! " Mrs. I. reminded him that he didn't like it when James bit him. He replied, " No. And a big giant bit me once, and bit my finger right off, and it was bleeding." He said this again soon, showing Mrs. I. his fore-finger : " It was this finger, and he bit it right off, and it was bleeding."

8.11.25. Dan, sitting on the pot to urinate, said his penis had been " cut off ", and, " I haven't any penis."

For several previous nights, he had wakened up calling out and crying, and been found right under the bed clothes at the bottom of the bed. The first time he complained that he " couldn't find his way out " ; on later occasions, that he " couldn't get any further in ". About this time, there were several occasions of bed-wetting. This night-terror had first occurred after the following conversation with Priscilla and Mrs. I. (4.11.25) :

Priscilla, Dan and Mrs. I. were modelling together, and some point arising about ages, Mrs. I. referred to the time when she was " as old as Priscilla ". Priscilla asked her, " Where is your mother ? " *I haven't any.* " Why not ? Where is she ? " *She's dead.* " When did she die ? " *When I was about your age.* The two children then kept repeating while they were modelling, " Poor Mrs. I., poor Mrs. I." And presently asked her, " Do you hear what we're saying ? " *You're saying " poor Mrs. I."* " And d'ye know why ? It's because your mammy is dead." They then asked various details about it. " Did you cry ? What did you do ? How did she catch cold ? Was she in bed ? Did you see her ? Had she a nurse ? Where is she now ? " And then talked about brothers and sisters. Priscilla then said, " Oh, I should cry if *my* mammy died, wouldn't you, Dan ? " Dan replied, " No, I should go to my other mammy ! " *Have you another mammy, Dan ?* " Oh, yes, I've two or three." And then, later, " I've got fifteen mammies."

11.11.25. Penelope and Tommy were playing " mummy and daddy " and Tommy insisted on being the mummy.

14.12.25. Whenever anything is being cut—paper or sewing material or canvas—Priscilla is extremely anxious that no one should " have their finger or thumb cut off ". The fear is expressly " cut off ", not just " hurt " or " cut ".

5.3.26. Several of the children played a family game with Mrs. I. to-day. Dan wanted her to be the " mother ", with Jessica and Tommy as her " babies ". But Tommy would not have this—he said *he* was " the *mummy* " and Mrs. I. the " daddy ".

13.12.26/16.12.26. (See Jane's and Conrad's remarks under SEXUAL CURIOSITY.)

24.1.27. Dan and Priscilla were writing opposite to each other at a table, and Mrs. I. was near. Suddenly Dan began swaying his body about in a tense way, with lips pursed up. Priscilla looked at him and said, with a meaning smile, " I know who you are—you're Miss X." Dan laughed, and said, " She's always moving about, isn't she ? When she stands up she moves like this." Then, with laughter : " I expect it's because she wants to make water, and can't. I expect she's been to the hospital and they did something to her, and now she can't make water."

3.2.27. Lena, Phineas and Jessica were digging in the sand-pit. They were getting in each other's way and quarrelling a little about their " castles ". Lena said something which annoyed Phineas, and he replied, " If you do, I'll hit you." Lena said, " I'll cut your hands off." Jessica: " So will I." Lena: " I'll cut off one hand and you can cut off the other."

8.2.27. At bath-time, Conrad said to Dan, " Let's have fur over our penises." He held his sponge in front of him and said, " Now I'm a lady." (See also Y's remarks under Section 7, p. 160.)

9.2.27. (See Dan's remark re Priscilla, under VERBAL EXHIBITIONISM.)

9.2.27. In the music period to-day, Mrs. S. played and sang " Three Blind Mice ". Phineas suddenly said, " *Smack* the naughty lady ! " Mrs. S. asked, " Why ? For cutting off their tails ? " " *Yes*," said Phineas, with great emphasis.

β

At 5;6, N. was talking of the length of her hair. She had cut hers off without her mother's permission, and her mother was making some mild protest. The child replied, " If you would go away, Mama, then I could have my hair as I liked." A year and a half earlier she had persuaded her elder brother to cut her hair short, telling people, " *Now* I am a boy."

γ

1. " My little boy (aged 5;0) asked me the other day why his little sister of 3;0 has not a similar body to himself. They were both in the bath together and he was evidently comparing notes. He also asks why she has to sit down always in the lavatory whereas he can stand."

2. " Ages 8;0, 8;0, 10;0. Three boys bathing. All in bath together, getting out. X. sticking out his posterior at a boy and roaring with laughter. All three boys laughing. One of them sticking his front out slightly, and then all three laughing again. Looking to catch my eye, then laughing again. So infectious was their laughter that I could not look solemn. Then as they jumped out to dry themselves, I said, ' I really think boys are ruder than girls ! ' X., ' Well, they've got more to be rude about, haven't they ? ' The air of superiority, lord-of-creation and tolerance for the other sex with which he said this set us all laughing again. By the time they were dry and had their pyjamas on they were deep in a discussion as to how to make stilts, and what wood they would need, straps, etc., and the next day they made them."

9. " COSY PLACES "

α

8.12.24. George put two chairs together and sat alone in one on top of another for a long time, without joining in what the other children were doing. After a time Mrs. I. asked him what he had made. He said it was a " cubby hole ", and sat quietly there for a very long time.

11.12.24. The children made " ships " and " gun boats " with tables and chairs, Harold and Benjie and Frank and Paul in one, Tommy, Dan, Christopher and Mrs. I. in another. The children put rugs over their heads. Tommy said to Mrs. I., " I am going to kiss you," and kissed her hand several times.

October to December 1924. Frank is very fond of making " nests " for himself to sit in with cushions, or hay, or long grass.

13.1.25. Tommy went into a " house " made by the others beforehand with rugs and tables. He called George and Frank to join him.

2.2.25. Tommy covered himself up with the rug and sat for a long time under it.

3.2.25. The children had a house and later a train in the old hen-coop.

6.2.25. Dan and Frank made a house behind the blackboard. They asked Mrs. I. to tea. They then went to " her house " under the stairs. Christopher joined in, but later made his own house in the school entrance.

11.2.25. Frank and Paul had a " house " with a rug. Dan and Tommy had another. Frank said to Dan, " Shall we be friends and visit each other ? " and they did so.

In the afternoon Dan and Frank made a train with the rug and all the chairs round on the platform, " a train on which you could go to sleep ".

13.2.25. The children had made a long train with chairs and were playing on it. George did not go on it, although he looked as if he wanted to do so. He wandered about rather irresolutely, and presently went and sat behind the blackboard.

16.2.25. Theobald and George did not go into the garden, but played " house " behind the blackboard, making a gate with some chairs.

17.2.25. George was very pensive this morning, and he stood quietly behind the blackboard for an hour and a half until he sat down to model.

18.2.25. The children played in the " canoe house " (a cellar under the house with a door to the garden, where an old canoe was kept).

20.2.25. Theobald and Tommy made a house under the stairs with the chairs, and asked Mrs. I. to go and sit in the house.

26.2.25. Paul came in from the garden and stayed alone

for a long time. He said, " I am wanting to make a house," and presently, " What about the rugs ? " Mrs. I. suggested that he should use a small one. Then he said, " I am wanting this one," i.e., the larger, and he put both on the long table. He went underneath, then came out and said, " I want someone to be ' Father Christmas '." Mrs. I. offered to be. He replied, " What will you have for a bag ? Will you have the thing that is in the bathroom—the pinny ? " (meaning her overall that hangs in the cloakroom). She did this and took him some gifts. He lay under the table talking to himself and did not notice when Mrs. I. brought the gifts, and later on asked her to do it, as if she had not already done so.

2.3.25. After lunch, three of the children went into the gallery and Frank asked Mrs. I. to hang a rug over the gallery door, " so that nobody can look in."

3.3.25. Tommy rolled himself right up in a rug, and lay quiet for some time.

5.3.25. Dan wanted to make a " house " with rugs.

6.3.25. Paul and Dan played at house in the hen-coop— " coopie house." Paul invited Mrs. I. to go and live with them, very charmingly. Dan invited her to go and " have tea and dinner " with them.

19.3.25. The children played in the " coopie house " for a long time, digging in the dust.

23.3.25. Mrs. X. came to lunch. After lunch, Frank suggested they should make " nests " with the rugs and chairs, and they put chairs in a ring with the rugs over them. Harold, Paul and Frank had a rug each. Dan said he wanted one, but there was not another, so Mrs. I. and Mrs. X. suggested they should all make one big nest. They did this.

24.3.25. The children piled up a tower of chairs in the schoolroom, piling them very high, and were very delighted with this, hanging a rug round the tower, and getting inside underneath.

25.3.25. The children went into the canoe in the canoe house and later Frank came to Mrs. I. in another part of the garden and said, " Oh, Mrs. I., we are doing such a funny thing, do come and see." When she went to the canoe house she found that Harold and Paul and Theobald had gone through the small hole in the wall of the canoe house into the dark inner chamber and were shouting with delight. Dan and Frank also wanted to go in, but were shy of doing so until she went. Paul very heartily invited her in there. She managed to crawl through this hole and Dan and Christopher and Frank also went. Tommy stayed in the outer part of the canoe house and would not go through. They all ran about and said,

"Oh, isn't it *lovely* and dark?" and were thrilled to see the spiders' webs in the holes in the brick-work.

21.4.25. George suggested to the other children that they should go into "the dark place" and get the canoe out.

23.4.25. For a time, all the children, except George and Christopher went into "the dark place," shouting and peeping out and laughing.

1.5.25. Frank and Dan had had a tea-party, using the lunch-table with a rug on it for a cloth. Later, the table with the cloth became a house. Dan sat under it in the house, while Frank ran past as an engine.

14.5.25. Harold put a rug over the step-ladder and he and Frank sat underneath talking about who was climbing up their roof, as the other children climbed up and jumped off.

17.6.25. Duncan, Dan, Frank and Harold made a small place amongst the grass and Michaelmas daisies, and stood there talking for a quarter of an hour. Presently Christopher, going near them, was admitted in a very friendly way.

9.7.25. Duncan, Frank and Harold took the painting things to the "little house" in the garden.

14.7.25. Frank and Duncan went into the hen-house, to "talk secrets".

24.11.25. The children wanted to bring out all the extra stored chairs and arrange them round themselves "to keep them warm", as they have done on several previous days.

8.12.25. When the children were reading, they arranged chairs all round their tables "to keep them warm", and called them "a house". When Mrs. I. wanted to sit near them, and turned a chair round to sit on, Priscilla protested, but Dan said, "It's all right—you can be the door to keep us warm."

24.3.26. When drawing and crayoning to-day, Dan and Priscilla arranged chairs round themselves, "to keep out the fox".

5.5.26. The elder children arranged chairs and tables round themselves in the summer-house, while they were modelling, "to keep the tigers out". They asked Mrs. I. to "be a tiger and come"—and to "come from a distance, so that we can hear you growling".

6.5.26. Several of the children—Tommy, Hugh, Adrian, Jessica, Christopher, Florence, Dan and Priscilla—went into the canoe house again and crawled through the small hole into the inner dark chamber, with some excitement and great pleasure—finding spiders' webs, saying, "Isn't it dark, isn't it lovely and dark!"

23.11.26. Lena brought a chair and put it close beside Miss D.'s, saying to her, with a confidential air, " We're in a ship, aren't we—a cosy little ship."

November 1926. This term several of the older children have made what they call " secret places ", with an arrangement of tables and curtains, each beside his own cupboard. No one is allowed to go to these but the owner, save by invitation.

31.1.27. Jessica carried two chairs and put their backs to the sides of the chair she was sitting in. She climbed in and called out gleefully, " I'm in a cosy." Seeing Conrad hold up a stick as a gun, Jessica held her hands as if she had a gun. She bent down to Phineas who was sitting near and said, " I won't fight *you*, Phineas," but pretended to take aim at Conrad, and quivered all over with the intensity of her attitude. Presently she took her hands down, and began singing to herself, " It's dead and gone for now, for now."

October 1927. Conrad had nightmare, in which he called out while still asleep, " Oh mummy, mummy, give me a hole to put my finger in."

B. Guilt and Shame

α

8.10.24. The children were standing at the door, watching a heavy shower of rain. They heard the rustling noise of the rain on the leaves, and when something was said about this, George remarked, " Perhaps it's God saying He will punish us for doing things we shouldn't."

16.10.24. George, using the plasticine, made a snake and said, " I have a fat snake in my bed which might bite me."

27.10.24. The elder boys wanted to shut some of the younger ones into a hut as a " prison ". Frank, Harold and Paul often suggest, and sometimes do this.

October 1924. Penelope and Dan went to tea with Mrs. I. They played with a small statuette of a boy, as a doll baby. They wrapped him up and put him to bed. Suddenly Penelope uncovered him and said, in a shocked tone, " Oh, look what he's done—he's wet his bed, the naughty, naughty baby."

7.11.24. Benjie, after lunch, dropped the water-jug accidentally. He looked quickly at Mrs. I., laughed excitedly, then kicked it across the room ; he was about to kick it downstairs. Mrs. I. asked him not to do so, but before she could get near he had done so, and broken it. Then he was very defiant, shouting, " I'll hit you in the face ; I'll not come to school any more," and so on. This was clearly remorse that took the form of defiance.

10.11.24. When Benjie spat into the pudding dish, and Mrs. I. hastily said, " Now you can't have any pudding," he threw his plate on the floor and broke it. Then he cried very bitterly in anger and defiance.

21.11.24. In the afternoon, Paul, when running round, said, " Shall we call Benjie ' the breaker ' ? "

26.11.24. Harold had made a large house of plasticine bricks, and the children talked of " Naughty Mary " who lived in this house and " had not kept the fire in "

28.11.24. When the children were using scissors for cutting out, George applied them to his own finger and pressed sufficiently hard to make it bleed, Frank and Dan saying to him, " Harder, harder." Dan then took scissors and also tried, George saying to him, " Hard, harder," but Dan did not make his finger bleed.

November 1924. One day Frank ran towards the lavatory, then stood still and began to cry desperately, " Oh, I'm doing it in my trousers—oh, do look and see if I have done it in my trousers," with tears and sobs. Mrs. I. sponged him. "Oh, do wash it off," he said. He grew calmer, and when Mrs. I. sponged his trousers, he said, "Oh, *don't* make them wet, or mummy will think *I* have wetted them!"

12.1.25. Frank's first greeting of Mrs. I. was, "Naughty Mrs. I."

14.1.25. Frank said very frequently, "Dirty Mrs. I.—dirty Miss B.—dirty" so-and-so. Dan joined in this on one occasion. Dan playfully wanted to "put Mrs. I. in prison" by rolling her up in a rug.

19.1.25. Dan often said, "Naughty Mrs. I."

20.1.25. After the children had played Harold's game of running round the room, saying that they were "going to blow up" the tower of bricks which he had built, they presently asked Mrs. I. to say, "I'm going to tell the policeman"; and soon Frank begged her to "go and *pretend* to tell the policeman".

26.1.25. Dan said, "My name is Tickly Georgie," one of the boys having introduced this phrase a week or two before. Frank asked George whether he had "told 'Tickly Georgie' to his mother?" George replied, "No, it's rude." Frank said, "No, it's not rude, is it Mrs. I.?"

The children played the game invented a few days earlier by Harold, building a tower of bricks and then running round and saying, "We're going to blow it up," Mrs. I. having to say, "No, no."

Tommy wrote "a letter" and folded it and brought it to Mrs. I.; then later he took a bundle of raffia and "wiped" the letter, because, he said, "it had got dirty all over".

29.1.25. Miss B. reported that yesterday, during the rest hour, the children had talked about putting one's thumb in one's mouth. Dan said, "Henry does, when he goes to sleep." Frank said, "He's a *naughty* boy."

3.2.25. Frank and Dan told "a man" to "put Mrs. I. in prison", and then announced that he had done so.

6.2.25. There was a long conversation and play between Frank, Theobald and Christopher on the one side, Miss B., Dan and Tommy on the other, about putting each other in "prison". Theobald had suggested the prison when he was building with bricks.

In the afternoon, when Dan and Frank were building with bricks, they made "prisons" to put Mrs. I. and Miss B. in, putting in bricks to represent them.

9.2.25. Frank saw the new curtains at once. He said to Dan, "Those are silly curtains, Dan, aren't they?" Dan replied, "Yes, they are." Both then called out to the curtains,

"Silly curtains, silly curtains." Dan said to Frank, " There is a policeman over there. Go and tell him to put the curtains in prison," with laughter.

Frank greeted Miss B. with " Dirty Miss B." ; this was the first time he had used this term for a week. Then he said, " Miss B., she won't answer, will she ? " And both Dan and Frank said this several times, obviously as a joke : " Miss B., she won't answer."

Frank and Dan built with bricks and built prisons.

While putting their bricks away, Frank began to speak of " naughty children " who would not put them away, and of " putting them in prison," and then they called out to " a policeman " to " put Mrs. I. in prison ".

13.2.25. When running about, Frank asked Mrs. I. to be a " policeman " and to put them (Harold and Frank) into " the prison ", the " prison " being the cloakroom. She did this once and they much enjoyed it, and several times asked her to do it again.

16.2.25. Harold tried to break open the swing gates and tried to break the blackboard, Frank and Dan joining in this. Mrs. I. then said to Harold that she had asked him not to do that, and that very often he asked her to do things for him and she did so, and perhaps he would do that for her—give up breaking the blackboard when she asked him. He agreed. She then said the same to Frank, who also agreed. Dan, having heard her speak in this way to the other two, came and said, " *I* did it, too," wanting Mrs. I. to say the same things to him ; she did, and he also agreed.

In school Harold and Frank made a " prison " of bricks, the large bricks, being careful to leave no holes. They said it was for Dan. After Harold and Paul had gone home, Frank and Dan " put Mrs. I." into it, with much laughter.

17.2.25. Some of the children dramatised " Red Riding Hood." While Dan was sitting on the chair in the corner, with the rug over his head (as the Grandmother) Paul and some other boys began to tease Dan, pulling the rug over his head so that he could not see. Dan was screaming. Mrs. I. took hold of Paul's arm very firmly and said, " Don't do that." She had not spoken so firmly to Paul before. It was a great surprise to him and he was very hurt. He turned on her very angrily and said he would " tell his mother of her ", and he " would not come " if she did that, and started to hit her, obviously feeling that she had been unkind. She left him alone and he lay on the floor refusing to speak to anyone for an hour and a quarter. Mrs. I. went up to him several times and tried to get him to talk it over, but he would not listen and just

SOURCES OF LOVE AND HATE

rolled over. Harold went up several times. Presently Paul began to run about again and smile and be friendly, and Mrs. I. took an opportunity, when he was near her, to speak of what had happened. She said, " I would not have spoken to you so if you had not done that to Dan." He flushed again and looked angry, and then said in a very emphatic way, " I am *very* ashamed of you." She said, " Are you, Paul ? " Then she said again, " You were teasing Dan, and so I did that to you, but I would not have done so if you had not done that to Dan." Then he became friendly again, and through the rest of the day he was more friendly than he has ever been. (See 17.2.25. under FRIENDLINESS AND CO-OPERATION.)

20.2.25. Frank made a " prison " of plasticine. He pretended to put Mrs. I. in it, to " shut her up ", and said he would "never let her come out ", and that he would give her no food, and then " she will starve ". Then he asked Mrs. I. to " make my house " and " a policeman's house ". When the houses were finished he asked her to put the " policeman's house " up on the " iron rod ", i.e., one of the cross-beams of the schoolroom.

24.2.25. Dan and Frank asked Mrs. I. to " put them in prison " (behind some chairs) and then to " go away on your motor bike ". Later they put her " in prison ", saying, " Please don't come out until we tell you to," and they kept her there about five minutes.

When Paul came down from resting they were all looking at the engine books, and Paul said, over and over again, " Wicked Dan, wicked Dan ! I shall say that every time I come to school."

25.5.25. Frank and Dan were climbing on the window-sill. Frank said he would " push Dan's foot up ". Paul said, " Yes, he'll push Dan up to God." Frank said, " Yes, and perhaps He'll kill him."

Frank said " dirty creature " two or three times to-day.

26.2.25. Harold said Mrs. I. was " wicked ", and he would have her " searched and put in prison ".

27.2.25. Harold at lunch, in the middle of teasing Dan, remarked sententiously, " I don't like big boys to tease little ones."

2.3.25. Paul ran about saying in a dogmatic tone, " Silence at once ! silence at once ! " several times.

4.3.25. At lunch Paul served, and when Mrs. I. said, " Now will you serve Dan ? " he said, " No, I won't serve Dan. I won't give Dan any dinner, bad wretched little thing." He did so, however.

9.3.25. The children saw an aeroplane passing over the

garden and, as they often do, shouted to the man in the aeroplane, " Come down, come down, you naughty man."

Paul wanted to urinate, when washing his hands, and his hands being wet, could not get his buttons undone in time, and he wet his trousers ; bitter tears and sobs. " I'm *so* ashamed of myself, I'm *so* ashamed of myself," he said, and he could not be comforted for a long time.

12.3.25. When Martin came to school, he walked right into the schoolroom, stood on the platform and shouted, " Hullo." Dan said to him, " You must not make so much noise."

Tommy deliberately spilt some water on the mat and on the steps, and spoke of it as " a mess ", and said, " *Isn't* it a mess ! " Martin also went to the door and said, in an awed tone, " Isn't it a mess ! "   Tommy said this several times.

18.3.25. Martin told Mrs. I. that he had made a " lovely railway track ", and this was done with the colours put in a long line. He would not let Tommy look at this, and several times tried to push Tommy away, and said to him, " You must not look, you must not do that, it is not *nice*, it's *rude*."

20.3.25. Harold and Paul were talking during their rest hour, and said something about " But he won't go to prison, will he ? "

Harold told Mrs. I. that George " wee-wee'd " in the garden " always ".

23.3.25. Mrs. I. told Tommy that she wanted him to shut the door as the wind was cold. He said, " No, I won't let you shut the door. No, you shan't." Martin told Tommy he was " rude ".

Martin, while modelling, was sitting opposite to Tommy and said several times, " Naughty Tommy, *naughty* Tommy." He seems to feel a definite enmity to Tommy.

In the morning in the garden, Paul had been down the garden path by himself and had been using some planks that Harold and Frank had fixed up in a sort of tripod earlier. Mrs. I. saw him standing by them a long time, and then presently he began to cry very bitterly. She went to inquire what was the matter, the other children also running to know whether Paul had hurt himself. The trouble was that he had moved the planks and could not put them back as he found them. He said, " I can't mend it, I *can't* mend it," with bitter grief. When Mrs. I. showed him how they went he was quite satisfied.

Harold brought a present of a model railway truck to Frank, and gave it to him on arrival. His mother told Mrs. I. that Harold had said he had promised it to Frank "·if he would not do in the garden what he ought to do in the lavatory ".

SOURCES OF LOVE AND HATE

(N.B. In the first term Harold himself had several times made water in the garden.)

24.3.25. At ten o'clock Martin came in. The door was shut when he came to it, and he cried; when Mrs. I. opened it for him he said, " Naughty, naughty, *naughty* boys."

Martin used the colour tablets for some time, arranging them and building with them, and talking very volubly while he did so, a long monologue, partly about what he was doing, calling the holes in the thing he was building " naughty " and " good ", saying, " They are good because they do " (so-and-so) ; " naughty, naughty holes ".

Tommy was building with bricks and Martin was running round with a long stick as a gun, saying, " Bang, bang," and whether intentionally or accidentally, hit Tommy on the head with the stick. Tommy cried for a time. Martin looked very ashamed and ran and hid behind the piano. When Mrs. I. had comforted Tommy she went to Martin and talked to him about it, and said that " we can't have the sticks if we hit another boy with them ", and took it away.

25.3.25. In the garden, Harold heard Frank say, " I'll bee-wee in the garden." Harold reminded him that he gave the truck to him " not to do that—but to do it in the lavatory".

Paul again wet his trousers a little, and cried bitterly ; but refused to wear Dan's knickers and have his own dried, although he complained bitterly of their being wet and making his legs sore.

27.3.25. Mrs. I. and the children were singing songs, one of them being about " Dr. Faustus ", and the picture in the song-book showed the pedagogue with birch-rod and book and mortar-board, chasing the little children. Some of the older children already knew the words and spoke them, and asked Mrs. I. to sing it. It amused them very greatly, and they said, " Oh, let's *do* Dr. Faustus. You be Dr. Faustus and we will run away ; or Miss B. be Dr. Faustus and you play it." They gave her a mop as the birch-rod, and a book to hold, and asked her to run after them. They then asked her to put a hat on. For half an hour the children continued playing this, sitting in a row on the platform very quietly, and saying, " When we make a noise, you run after us and whip us," and then they gave a yell and ran away. Then Frank was Dr. Faustus for a time, and then Dan, but the older boys turned on Dan and whipped him. Presently, when modelling, they suggested that they should make Dr. Faustus in plasticine, and while Harold made bricks for Dr. Faustus' house, Frank made one of the children running away. Miss B.

modelled, under the children's direction, Dr. Faustus himself, putting a hat, the spectacles, the birch-rod and the book. They all enjoyed this very much.

23.4.25. Norman had brought an electric torch, and this made Dan want to take his into school. When he met Mrs. I. he asked anxiously, " Are you sure that I can take this into school ? " and when she replied, " Yes," he said, with a worried air, " Are you *sure* ? "

27.4.25. Harold went to Mrs. I. in the garden in some distress because his combinations showed below his trousers' legs, and whispered to her that " they show ", as if it were something very serious. This was repeated again later, until Mrs. I. had succeeded in folding them so that they would not come down.

30.4.25. Dan gave Harold a motor bus. Harold put it in the cloakroom, and when his mother came, she said it was not convenient to take it home that day. Harold was very angry at this, and hit his mother several times and said hostile things. She said she was very sorry, but she could not do it. The next day she told Mrs. I. how, all the way home, he kept hitting her and saying hostile things, and how a long time afterwards he asked her, " Do you still love me ? " and when she said " Yes ", he said, " What, after all that ? "

—.5.25. Harold and Paul began to beat the enamel washing-up bowls as drums. Harold took the hammer to beat his bowl with, and began to do it in earnest, with great energy, until he had hammered holes in the bottom. Theobald, seeing this, went out also, took another hammer and began to break up the old wooden engine. Harold, seeing him do this, said, " Oh, you *are* a destructive boy to break it to pieces, it's not your engine."

The children asked Mrs. I. to be a " policeman " and to run after them, and " put them in prison ". She did this for a time ; they had as their prison the square enclosed by the tables, and she had to lift each one up in turn and put him in, the others shouting with delight.

Presently they gave Mrs. I. a stick and asked her to " be Dr. Faustus and chase us ".

When playing Dr. Faustus, Paul, if Mrs. I. ran near him, tended to take it as a serious situation and to turn on her in retaliation.

7.5.25. When doing plasticine, Harold and Frank made " a wireless " with some sticks fastened up with plasticine and some raffia. They then asked Mrs. I. to join in the game of building up the wireless, they running round and saying, " We are going to blow it up," she having to shake her head and say, " No, no," as they ran past. They then " blew it up ", and asked her to put them in prison. She did this, putting each one in prison. Theobald, contrary to his custom, joined in this, and then wanted the others also to play " Cinderella and the two *wicked* sisters ".

19.5.25. Laurie rests in Dan's room and seems to spend most of the time in playing with Dan's toys, but jumps back into bed with a rather guilty air as soon as he hears anyone open the door.

17.6.25. Paul, seeing the others playing the game of " killing animals for meat ", said, " Here is the policeman, the police has come ", and ran out into the garden after the boys. Presently he returned and said to Mrs. I., " The policeman has been whipping them—it's quite right, isn't it ? "

19.6.25. James had bitten Dan, and Frank saw the marks of his teeth. Dan said, " Yes, wasn't he naughty ? Wasn't he silly ? " with emphasis. Frank said, " I shall bite *him* when he comes to school again." Dan said, " Yes, because he bit me."

29.6.25. Harold and Paul were washing their feet and putting on their shoes in the cloakroom, and Harold evidently having felt thwarted at not being allowed (by his mother) to wear his bathing suit, he jumped into the bowl of water and spilt a good deal of water on the cloakroom floor. He agreed to wipe it up fairly willingly. When he was in the middle of this he began splashing the wet floor cloth about and throwing it at Mrs. I. ; she showed some impatience at this, and he said, " I shan't have you to tea now, Mrs. I. I shall shut you out when you come," referring to the invitation that they had given her to go to tea the following day. She replied, " Will you ? " and went on talking in a friendly way and taking no further notice of his remarks, which he did not repeat and immediately resumed friendly relations.

June 1925. Dan was on the river with his father, and defaecated in his trousers. He burst into deep sobs of distress, and said, " Oh, what shall I do! oh Daddy, *Daddy*." Dan had never been scolded or even slightly reproached for such " accidents ", which were very rare.

7.7.25. Some of the children, Duncan, George, Dan, Frank and Priscilla, ran in from the garden in pretended terror of a large black cat which they had seen ; they ran and shut themselves in the lavatory, talking about " the cat ", " it's coming, it's coming—it can't get us ", and so on, with great excitement and tones of mystery. They came out half-way once or twice, and rushed back ; but presently became more interested in the music which was being enjoyed by the others.

The following morning they wanted to repeat this with an imaginary " bear ", but Mrs. I. did not allow this because they got too excited about it.

8.7.25. In the afternoon Frank showed Mrs. I. his trousers, wet, and said that Harold had wet them in the morning. It seemed more likely, from the place of the wet, that he had urinated in them, and Miss B. confirmed this ; it happened while he and Priscilla were resting upstairs.

15.7.25. Frank, Dan and Priscilla made a house in the rabbit-hutch and had " a policeman " there.

16.7.25. When Mrs. I. left early to-day, Frank quite spontaneously kissed her " good-bye " ; the first time he has done that. Yet his first greeting of her the next morning was " dirty old Mrs. I."

Tommy, in his bathing suit, had diarrhoea, and cried bitterly.

27.10.25. Christopher, Dan, Priscilla and Jessica played " house " with Jessica as the baby. Priscilla and Dan sat Jessica down on a chair, and said in the severest tones to her, " You're a naughty little girl." Priscilla domineered over her so much that Mrs. I. had to interfere.

10.11.25. Christopher and Priscilla were jumping over a rope in the schoolroom, and Mrs. I. was tidying a drawer. Because she did not take much notice of them, Priscilla said, " Oh, she's *cross*, she's cross." She ran up to Mrs. I. saying, " You're cross because we ran out " (a little earlier they had run out into the pouring rain without coats). When Mrs. I. laughed and said, " No, I'm not cross—I was thinking of something else," Priscilla replied, " Well, you *were* cross when we spoiled what Tommy had made ! " And went on, " You didn't know at first that *I* helped to spoil it—you thought it was only Frank." (This was true. Mrs. I. had taken Frank's clay away because he had wantonly spoilt Tommy's model ; Priscilla had then defiantly told her that she also had helped in the spoiling.)

1.12.25. When Tommy painted his hands, Christopher, Dan and Priscilla said he was " dirty ", although they have often done it themselves.

5.2.26. Priscilla, Dan and Frank were playing a family game with dolls, and left their babies at home while they played " hockey ". When they went back " home ", they said their babies were " naughty " and " did all sorts of horrid things ".

Later in the day, Priscilla was playing with her dolls, and told Mrs. I. that " hers had been a horrid little beast ", that it had " been fiddling about in the pram all the time ", and that she " would give her a good whipping ". She washed the doll, and said, " Say good-night to Mrs. I.", made it kiss her, and then told it, " Go straight to bed, and don't fiddle about and do such horrid things." Priscilla was in a mood of defiance herself just before this, saying that she would " tell her daddy not to give you any money ", although she " would come to school all the same " ; and threatening to spoil some number cards. Then this doll episode followed, after which she settled down and was more friendly and constructive.

8.2.26. Phineas spilled some cocoa on the table when drinking, and Priscilla said to Mrs. I., " Tell him he's naughty."

8.3.26. Tommy urinated in the garden to-day, alone, and told Mrs. I. to go away when she went near him.

9.3.26. Priscilla said she had told her daddy that they had " been running about doing naughty things ".

18.3.26. Priscilla was very hostile this morning, and made the others so. She was angry at one moment when Mrs. I. and Miss B. spoke to each other and laughed together at some point. She said, " You were laughing at *us*, you horrid things."

19.3.26. (See incident re Priscilla in FAMILY PLAY.)

13.4.26. While looking for some lost article, Priscilla and Dan walked into a bed of poppies and irises in Miss B.'s garden. Mrs. I. asked them not to walk there. Later they took a rug, spread it out on this bed, and lay down on it, crushing the plants. Mrs. I. asked them, " Would you like it if Miss B. did that to your gardens ? " They replied, " Oh, will you tell her ? Oh, we'll do it to our own "—and both pulled up a few plants in their own beds.

29.4.26. Tommy and Herbert put some dried peas down a hole in the floor. Alfred, seeing this, called out, " You mustn't do that—it's naughty, it's naughty." When Mrs. I. said that they might if they wanted to, he joined them, and did it with greater eagerness and insistence than any of the others.

10.5.26. Mrs. I. gave each of the older children a pen and ink bottle. Dexter refused the pen, saying, " I'm not allowed to use ink " ; although Mrs. I. replied that in school all the children were allowed to use ink, he insisted that he was not and refused the pen. She therefore passed it on to Christopher as his was old and poor. Later on Dexter asked for it, and Mrs. I. said she would get him one for the next day. He was insistent about having it at once, saying, " If you don't give me a pen, I shan't come to this school."

17.5.26. Priscilla had sprained her ankle a few days ago, and had to be kept off her feet. This led to her sitting in the pram in the afternoon, and being pushed about as the " baby ", with Dan as the " mummy ", talking in baby language. She pretended to be "a naughty baby", screaming when she couldn't get her way, snatching at the flowers and crying in temper if she couldn't reach them, and so on.

When looking at the map of Cambridge with Mrs. I. this morning, Dexter had noted the signs for " public lavatories " among other things, and had asked what they were. She explained. Towards the end of the morning, he suddenly urinated in his trousers, with great distress and guilt. His mother reported that it was a very long time since this had happened.

4.6.26. Phineas accidentally spoiled a plasticine model which he and Alfred had been making together. Alfred drew the attention of the others to this, and Priscilla scolded Phineas severely, " You naughty little thing, you fool—you are horrid," and so on.

9.6.26. Alfred and Herbert were watching the mice, and making them run up and down the stairs in the mouse-box. When they couldn't make them do this, they called them " naughty mice "—" Aren't they naughty mice ? " Mrs. I. said, " Are they ? " and they replied, " They won't do what we want, so aren't they *naughty* ? "

14.6.26. Phineas wanted to urinate, and on the way from the garden to the lavatory, he kept asking, with obvious anxiety, " I want to do ah-ah—I'm *not* wet, am I ?—we'll soon be dry, won't we ?—you're not wet, are you ? " and so on, repeated all the way. (He was a little wet.)

15.6.26. The children had begun " to make stuff ", i.e., weave on small cardboard looms, quite on their own initiative. They had asked Mrs. I. " how stuff was made ", and she had prepared a loom to show them, and was using it, when they came and asked to do it also. After working quietly and steadily, and with much enthusiasm and interested talk, for about an hour and a half, they got up and ran about. Then Priscilla said, " Oh, you *do* make us do it when we don't want to ! " Mrs. I. laughed and said, " Do I ? " " Oh, yes. You say, ' You *must* do that work.' " They laughed at this joke a good deal.

29.6.26. After school yesterday, Christopher and Dan had been hammering with large hammers which Dan had bought himself, and the prong end of Christopher's hammer had come down on Dan's finger, injuring it. Christopher was obviously suffering under a heavy feeling of guilt for this. He had run away when the adults had approached him after the accident, and then had said, " They won't blame me, will they ? " All to-day, he tended to go off by himself, into the far part of the garden, staying alone there on his cycle. He told Mrs. I.

" not to go near Dan's room, as Dan would not want us to ". Actually, however, when we had occasion to pass the room, he went in to talk to Dan. They were both quite friendly during the day. During the afternoon, Christopher became very bored and restless, saying, " What is there to do ? What can I do ? " Mrs. I. suggested playing dominoes, but he soon got bored again with these. The following day he was again rather bored and restless, not accepting friendly suggestions as to what to do. This boredom is so uncharacteristic of Christopher that it is only explicable as a result of anxiety and guilt.

7.10.26. Christopher and Priscilla were practising writing ; when they heard Mrs. I. coming into the room, they hid under the table, laughing rather excitedly and foolishly. Priscilla then said, " Oh, she'll smack our heads if we don't write this." Mrs. I. laughed and said, " Shall I ? " " Oh, yes—oh, will you ? " They played the game for a short time. Christopher then scribbled in his book and began to get excited, and threw his pencil across the room. When Mrs. I. suggested that if he wanted to throw, he might throw a ball in the garden and keep the pencil for writing, he said, " All right, I'll write with it ", and settled down to quiet work.

14.10.26. Phineas accidentally broke his cup when drinking cocoa a few days ago. He at once said, " Now I can't have any cocoa " ; and since then he has steadily refused to have any, although he has been repeatedly offered it in another cup.

7.12.26. At bed-time, Jane asked Miss D. whether she "liked Priscilla". Miss D. said, " Yes, very much." Jane : " I don't, I hate her, because she's so selfish. She always tries to get the best things for herself." Miss D. said she thought a good many people did that. Jane agreed, but said, " Priscilla's worse than most. And she's cross and rather sly."

2.2.27. A workman was putting in new glass in one of the windows. Jessica and the others were watching, and Jessica scribbled on the white paint of the window-sill. Miss C. gave her a piece of paper and suggested she should use that, saying it was " a pity to mark the white paint ". She was immediately very much confused and ashamed ; she didn't want Miss C. or anyone to see the marks she had made, and covered them up with the paper, scribbling on the paper very hard. Presently she had to move her hands in order to let the man put the glass in, but was very unwilling to have the paper removed and the marks seen. Miss C. tried to reassure her that the marks would come off, and rubbed most of them away with a rag ; but Jessica remained very ill at ease for some time.

10.3.27. Lena and Phineas were poking a stick into a hole in the plaster of the wall. The stick came out covered with dust and cobwebs. They said in awed tones, " Isn't it a naughty wall ? " Mrs. I. asked, " How is it a naughty wall ? " "Look at the dirt on the stick." Mrs. I. said, " Yes, what is it ? " (having in mind that they might see that it was cobwebs). Lena replied, gravely, " *Muck*—isn't it a *naughty* wall ! "

1.5.27. James had lunch with Mrs. I. the day before term began. He said to her, challengingly, " Dirty Mrs. I.," repeating this two or three times ; then suddenly he took his own table-napkin, dipped a corner of it into his glass of orange squash, and sucked it. " I like it," he said—but at once put it away from him with a gesture of disgust.

2.5.27. Miss C. was up in the gallery, and James, down below, called out shyly to ask where the lavatory was. Before Miss C. could get down to show him, he lost control and wet his trousers. He cried and was ashamed. Conrad saw it, and called to the others to " come and see ", in scornful tones. He made two or three scornful remarks about it to the others during the afternoon, but they did not take it up.

18.5.27. (See incident in SEXUAL PLAY.)

24.5.27. Noel's mother reports that he complains at home that he doesn't " have enough hard work to do in school ", and that he wishes they would give him " some hard sums or writing to do ". His actual behaviour in the school is quite contrary to this ; he looks entirely happy, both in the garden and when weighing and experimenting in the laboratory. Miss D. reports that when she has followed the hints given as to his wishes by his mother, and asked him to do a set task in arithmetic, or writing, or spelling, his face always changes and he seems to resent the suggestion very strongly. He is always keenly absorbed and interested when measuring, weighing, etc. This week he has devised an apparatus for forcing water through a glass vessel into a vertical tube, and has been quite ingenious in his attempts to make the vessel air- and water-tight.

June 1927. Joseph (aged 4;0) prefers "lessons" to any sort of playing or handicraft. He asked for lessons in reading this morning, and told Mrs. I. " I'm a *studious* boy."

June 1927. Tommy asked recently to be taught to read and write, and insisted on writing as his first lesson, " Tommy is a naughty boy." He wrote this in large letters on a large sheet of paper, and fixed it up on the wall of the schoolroom with pride. He laughed with amusement when he drew the attention of the others to it, and when they asked, " Who wrote that about Tommy ? " he replied proudly, " *I* did."

October 1927. Conrad, while at home in the summer, drew on the wall above his bed a picture of " a gallows with a man hanging ".

October 1927. Denis's semi-affectionate greeting is "dirty Mrs. I.". His father reports that that is often his first greeting of him on waking up in the morning, half-playfully, " dirty old Daddy ".

October 1927. Denis had stayed in the " quiet room " by himself, when all the others were in the garden. Mrs. I., going in, found him sitting on the floor with a glum, red face. He looked at her surlily and said, " Go away." She left him there, but going back in a few minutes, found him still sitting there, very still, and again he told her to go away. When, guessing that he had wet his trousers and was overcome with shame, she asked him to come to the lavatory and be dried, he refused with great guilt and distress, and would not move for a long time. He had defaecated into his trousers, and was too frightened and unhappy to move at all.

β

May 1926. Miss B. told me of a girl of three and a half years who asked her mother what would happen if she were naughty at school. Her mother said, " Well what would? " The child, after a pause, said, " I know—God would drown the world."

γ

1. " I should be glad of your advice in regard to handling my boy of two years nine months. He has never been smacked for any reason, but through contact with a small girl, whose mother *does* resort to smacking, he has just learnt to connect disapproval or even consciousness of having done something naughty, with smacking. The other day I found he had thrown several toys out of the window, and told him not to do it again as they might get broken and added that they would be confiscated next time. When I had finished he said, ' Mummie cross, have to smack Bill.' I didn't reply, whereupon he threw another toy out and said, ' *Now* Mummie smack Bill.' I felt I must answer this challenge so I told him to come to me and said, ' What did Mummie say she would do ? ' at which he burst into tears and said, ' Mummie not do it.' From his face I could see he was torn between curiosity and fear. I left him to pull himself together because frankly I didn't know what to do. Just now I told him not to open a parcel. He stopped and talked to himself thus: ' You mustn't undo it 'cos Mummie have to smack if you do,' etc.

This, of course, I ignored but obviously the whole question is worrying him and I feel he will go on trying to make me smack him till I do. Naturally I don't want to, but I can't see a way out as he is too young, I think, to understand any explanation of why he is not smacked as the little girl is. Incidentally the children are neighbours, the same age and very friendly, so it's obviously not practical to prevent their association. I might add I have just changed nurses so at the moment he is leaning to me very much for everything."

2. " Will you help me with my small charge? He is fifteen months, perfectly healthy and normally developed, usually very happy and contented, but he has occasions when he gets impatient, or when he can't just manage to do what he wants, such as open the door or climb on the chair, he will then start to bump his head against anything that is near. Soft or hard, it makes no difference, and just lately he has started to do it when either his mother or father leave the nursery. He will just throw himself on the floor and bump his poor head unmercifully. I am so afraid he will really injure himself. I try to attract his attention to something else and interest him in it. If left to go on he just bumps and bumps until he hurts himself. Then he cries and all is over until next time, but leaving him to hurt himself has not cured him."

3. " My little boy is one year nine months old. He is very healthy and full of life, but if crossed in any way, such as not allowed to go out when anyone comes to the door, if his engine turns over or if checked for doing wrong, he gets down on his knees and bangs his forehead on the floor several times as hard as possible, or against the wall. He must hurt himself, as he cries."

δ

BRIDGES, p. 112. " One of the major interests which children develop early is interest in good conduct. They wish to be approved, to do the things which bring pleasing results. They develop a love of power and set high standards or ambitions for their own achievement. Some children, when they fail to achieve the standards they emulate, when they are afraid of losing adult approval or meeting disapproval, become depressed or annoyed and cry in disappointment. Their assertive tendency or drive for power is thwarted, their love of display is unsatisfied and their self-confidence is shaken. If adults are too harsh in their discipline when a child is already depressed and miserable over his own failure, the little one may develop an emotional attitude of shame towards his conduct. This shame, this fear of failure and disapproval will grow with repeated experiences of like kind until later it may drive the child into more serious delinquencies in order to cover up a deep but inappropriate sense of guilt. Lying, truancy and even stealing may be numbered among his offences. Thus a child who was previously socially sensitive and over-anxious to do the right thing may become a real delinquent.

" The little conduct failures such as children may cry over in the nursery school are, failure to eat or pour milk without making ' spills ', failure to carry out instructions or complete tasks correctly, and failure to control urination in the playroom or at nap-time."

BRIDGES, p. 113. " . . . an illustrative example of distress over failure to achieve a desired standard of conduct. The child had wet her clothes on coming into the warm school after outdoor play in the cold. Although the incident was regarded as an accident by adults and no remarks were made, the child herself was distressed and despondent for some time after the incident."

C. An Individual Child: Ursula

γ

The following records of Ursula's sayings and doings over a critical period of her life illustrate several different sections of the main classification of material. I have, however, kept them together as an individual study because of the supreme interest of watching the movement of a particular child's mind as she passes through events of such central importance for her emotional life.

At the beginning of the period covered by these records, Ursula was an only child. A sister was born half-way through the period, and her mother endeavoured to prepare Ursula for this event by telling her of it beforehand, and by being entirely candid in reply to all the child's questions, whatever they might be.

Ursula is highly intelligent (see her part in the Appendix to *Intellectual Growth in Young Children*); and she is a healthy, normal and most attractive and delightful child. She is happy with her friends and socially successful at school. She quickly took up a maternal rôle to the new baby, and remains on the whole a happy and devoted elder sister. There is a photograph of her holding the baby in her arms, with a blissfully maternal expression and pose.

Certain well-marked general phases of emotional attitude occurred during the period recorded, which perhaps do not come out so distinctly in the detailed records as they showed in reality.

a. Towards the end of her mother's pregnancy, she evinced a good deal of occasional anxiety and querulousness, together with excessive demonstrations of love for her mother, and reluctance to part with her, e.g. to go to school. b. After her mother's return home (the birth took place in a nursing-home, and the mother was ill for many weeks there, the baby sister going home with a nurse some time before the mother), there was a period of some fretfulness and contrariness, the maternal attitude to the child being disturbed now and then by open jealousies. This fretfulness gradually died away, and Ursula became ordinarily cheerful and amenable again. After some months, during which the exploratory and masturbatory interest in her own genitals developed, she began to display a series of minor phobias and anxieties. At the time of writing, her mother reports : " She will not go upstairs alone, or to the lavatory, and dislikes staying in a room alone. At the same time, she has occasionally made a distinct effort to do so but has drawn back, obviously finding it impossible. Otherwise she is very happy, at home and at school, eager and greedy to learn, keeping herself amused and finding herself occupations and being delightful and sweet."

(Aged 3;2) Ursula admired a little baby in a 'bus. Ursula : " I would like a little baby like that. Will you get me one ? " Mother: *Where shall I get it?* You can buy it in a shop. *What sort of shop sells babies ?* A shop like that where Daddy took my dolly to be mended. *Do you mean a real baby or a toy baby ? Does the shop sell real babies do you think ?* It sells real babies and dollies and toy babies.

(3;5) Apropos of a story of how her mother went to Belgium as a child, the question again arose as to where *she* was then, leading to other questions again : " *How* did you make me ? " " How did I come out ? "

(3;5) To her father during his bath: " Your underneaths shake, Daddy. Mine don't shake."

To her mother later with glee: " My underneaths are shaking now, Mummy ! "

(3;5) Carrying her doll: " She keeps falling down. She's as heavy for me as I am . . ." (Presumably to complete, " for you ".)

(3;5) Examining her person : " Are your underneaths like my underneaths, Mummy ? " Pointing to one part of herself: " What's that for ? "

U.: " How did you eat when I was in your tummy, Mummy ? "

(3;5) U.: rather querulously, " Mummy, *why* was I in your tummy ? " " How did Daddy plant the seed in your tummy ? "

(3;6) A dream. " About a doggie and he did a-a on the stairs, like a pudding, like a jelly, and everybody had to jump over it. Wasn't it a funny dream ? "

(3;6) After a visit to the lavatory: " Our underneaths don't shake, Daddy's do."

(3;6) Molly came for the day. After lunch they both went with B. to the " weeny park ". At tea-time U. came rushing up to her mother angry and tearful: " Molly got home first. *I* wanted to be first." Passionately angry: " I don't want her to come again."

(3;9) Her mother had once about a month ago asked U. whether she would like a little brother or sister. She had answered, " Both, a brother *and* a sister." Her mother had said, " I don't think I can promise you both. It would have to be one or the other." She generally said she would prefer a girl but on one occasion said (after her mother had told her she thought she could only make one at a time), "Well, *you* can make the brother and *I'll* make the sister." Her mother asked how she'd do it. She said, " Like you do ! I'd plant a seed." Her mother said that little children couldn't do that. She said, " I mean when I'm big." She has often since talked familiarly of this future " brother-or-sister ".

(3;9) U. was with her mother while she was bathing. Her mother said, *U., do you know what's in here ?* " No, what ? " *Your little brother or sister.* She went very red and said in a weepy voice, " *Why*, Mummy ? I don't want one while I'm little. I don't want one till I'm big." This was repeated several times. Then followed various questions and comments : " Why do you have it there ? " *To keep it warm till it's ready to come out.* When will it come out ? To-morrow ? *No, not for a long time, not till the summer.* Why not ? *It's not strong enough or big enough yet.* How big is it ? *So big, I should think.* Where will it come out ? *There.* How will it get out ? *When it's big enough and strong enough it'll push and I'll help it until it gets out.* How will you push ? *Like this.* How did you make it ? Did Daddy plant a seed? *Yes.* When did he ? Last night ? *No, not then.* When we were on our holiday ? *Perhaps.* Was I there ? *No, I don't think so.* Was I asleep ? *Perhaps.* Why did you make it ? *Because I thought you would like a brother or sister to play with.* I like sisters best. How will you feed it ? There ? *Yes.* You could make a brother and a sister. *Could I ?* One could feed that side and one could feed that side. Only they mustn't do a-a. *On me, do you mean ?* In your lap. *I expect they will sometimes. They won't know when they're tiny.* We'll have to teach them.

" Mummy, what does my brother or sister do when you do a-a ? " *Oh, it's all right. It's quite comfy. It just stays there.* How big is it now ? So big—or so big ? Let me feel. I think it's a little bigger, about so big I should think.

(3;9) U. (monologue): " Hullo, my precious, my darling. Don't cry. Mummy's coming soon." (To M.): " That's what I'll say to my brother or sister, won't I, Mummy ? "

" Hullo, my precious ! " U. addresses her mother's person and says, " Let me feel " and does so, and then says with great glee, " I've felt my little brother and sister, haven't I." (The infant is sometimes addressed as though it is a hermaphrodite!)

(Somewhere about this time.)

U.: " Granny, when my little sister comes you will have two grand-daughters."

" Mummy, you will be busy when my brother or sister comes out. You will have another boy or girlie to look after. When did I come out ? In winter ? In summer ? " etc.

U.: " Mary and John were talking about a-a." M.: *What did they say ?* I didn't hear them. Miss Jones heard them. *What did she say ?* " Talk about something else," and Mary said, " I'll talk about animals ! " Miss Jones said, " That's better."

A reference to the little sister (or brother !) : " She doesn't know you've got *me*, does she ? "

(3;10) " Mummy, look, I nearly reach my swing. Shall I when I'm six ? " *I think so.* And my little brother or sister will. *Not when you're six.* When will it ? *When you're about ten.* Then when it's ten, it's brother and sister will and when it's ten *it's* brother and sister will. *I don't know if I shall make so many.* After this one, you can make another one and after that one you can make another one and after that one you can make another one. That'll be like the old woman who lived in the shoe.

(3;10) " Mummy, how did Daddy plant a seed in you ? " *It's hard to explain, U. I must think of some way to explain so that you will understand it.* Tell me now, Mummy, how did he ? *I promise to tell you later on. I can't until I think of a way to tell you.* I'll ask Daddy. He'll know. *Yes, perhaps he'll be able to explain.* He ought to know. He did it.

(3;10) A dream. " There was to-day a little U., but not me, and that little U. went with her Mummy shopping and she had a handbag like mine with a tassel and she left it behind and then when the boy from the shop came and brought the chimney brush they bought, she remembered, so the boy went back and when he came again with the meat they bought, he brought it. I would like such a handbag, will you buy me one ? " (The bag with a tassel was one her mother lent her when she went shopping one day with the maid.)

U.: " When shall we get my brother or sister's cot ? What does a baby have in its cot ? I would like to buy it to-day."

" Why doesn't F. have a baby ? " *I suppose her Mummy and Daddy don't want to make one. She has a brother, hasn't* she? She might want to wheel my brother or sister in its pram. *She might.* I won't let her.

M.: *W. is going to have a brother or sister. It is nearly ready and will come soon.* I want mine to come out soon, before summer. Why can't it? Why isn't it ready? I want it to come out before W.'s.

U.: " What does my brother or sister eat? " She gave her mother some bread in her mouth: "That's for my brother or sister." " Does it know what it eats? "

U.: " What will my sister or brother say when it comes out? Let me feel it."

" Is baby lying down or sitting up? "

" Sweet, they are, aren't they? " " Sweeter than a dolly."

(3;10) In her cot at night, with great yearning in her voice: " Oh, Mummy darling, I do love you so much."

(3;10) To her father, after her mother had left her for the night: " I do love Mummy so much."

An unfortunate incident in a 'bus: There were two little girls there and as they got out, U. said, " That one's the sister of that one, isn't she? Yes, she must be. I wish I had a little sister. Does my little sister like tomato sauce? " (Which U. loves inordinately!) Someone sitting opposite: "How old is she? " M.: *Nearly four.* Opposite: " Then she ought to have one. *I'll* give you one, duckie. But you must be a good girl. Mind you're good or else you won't get it." Her mother managed to whisper to U., " She's a silly old thing and doesn't know," and they got out. U.'s face had clouded over and as they got out, tears gathered in her eyes and she said, " But she doesn't know, does she? I *will* have one, won't I? " *Of course you will.* And I don't need to be good. I'll have one just the same, won't I? *She didn't know, darling. She didn't know I had one already in my tummy, did she? How could she give you one. You know Daddy and I have made one because we've told you. And you know it's here, because you've felt it. And it hasn't anything to do with good and naughty, and anyway you're good and I love you and Daddy loves you,* etc. The next day U. said as they got in the same bus, " I thought we might see that silly old woman again," and appeared quite unperturbed.

(3;10) As U. and her mother walked home in a thick fog: " Does my little sister like the fog? " *I don't think she knows anything about it. She's very warm and comfortable inside.*

Before her mother left her for the night: " Oh, Mummy, my underneaths hurt." *Would you like me to put some ointment on?* My brother or sister can't have any ointment on, can he?

(3;10) U.: "Will those be flowers in the summer?" *Yes. What flowers? Wallflowers.* What colours will they be? *Brown and red and yellow.* Brown's a *funny* colour for flowers!

After discussing the Liberty bodices worn by a little girl at school: "Is my little brother or sister warm?"

(3;10) U.: "What shall I do when my little brother or sister comes and sleeps in my room and cries and 'sturbs me?"

(3;10) M.: *Look, U., here are some things for you to cut out for your scrap-book, little boys in pyjamas and little girls and babies.* U.: I want the girls but I don't want the boys. I don't like boys. They're not nice. They're not as nice as girls, are they? *It depends on the boys, I think.* I like my Daddy 'cos he's a gentleman.

Before going to sleep. U.: "I want Daddy." Her mother repeated what she thought she heard her say: *You want one Daddy. One Daddy and one girl. One Daddy and one girl. Soon there will be one Daddy and two children. And then there will be one Daddy and three and . . . I don't know whether I shall make three.* Daddy could. *Yes, Daddy could, but I should have to help him.* Why? *Well, I'd have to keep the baby in my tummy.* How does Daddy plant the seed, Mummy? *Oh, U., I must think of a way to explain it. It's a hard thing to explain.* Yes, but *how*, Mummy, *how*? *Where does he keep the seed? In his underneaths.* Why? *Oh, it's a good place to keep it.* How does he plant it? *He just puts it in.* Where? *In my underneaths.* How does he? *He just pushes it in. And then I keep it in my tummy, and when it's ready it comes out and it's a baby and then it grows into a boy or girl and then into a man or woman.* And then *they* have babies! And that's how it goes on! (in a jolly voice as though reciting the end of "The house that Jack built").

(3;11) At breakfast-time, U. was eating and watching her mother to see whose mouth was empty first. Hers was. She said, "Mine's gone." Her mother pinched her tummy and said, "There!" She said, "What's in my tummy, only food?" "What's in yours? Mixed? Baby and food?" "I wish . . . How is the seed planted? You did tell me. But how is it made?" *It grows inside Daddy.* Why does it? *Well it has to start somewhere.* Well, it could grow in the garden. *In the garden seeds of plants grow, not seeds of babies.* Well, it could, with others, and then you could pick out the seed of baby and plant it. (The suggestion was, her mother thought, "in its usual human surroundings".)

U.: "My little brother or sister might come in March or April, mightn't it? *We can't be sure. Or perhaps in summer.* I would like it in summer."

To her father who was telling her of some past happening: " Where was I, Daddy, was it when I was in Mummy's tum-tum ? "

To her father: " And this baby will have a baby and this baby will have a baby and that baby will have a baby."

(3;11) U. constantly refers to the baby now as " My baby ". E.g., " When my baby calls me I shall have to go to it. It will want me." She also repeatedly refers to the possibility of a succession of babies. " When this baby will be three and a half it will have a party." *Yes. Then we shall have two parties every year.* And when that baby has a baby we shall have three parties, etc.

(4;0) U.: " I had a nasty dream last night, about a maid and a chimney and she sat on the chimney and smoke came up and made her apron dirty and there was a chimney sweep . . ." (Her mother forgot the rest—not much more. Reminiscent of Captain Hook in " Peter Pan.")

(4;0) U. has for some time past been talking of the baby as " my baby " and her mother was not quite certain as to how she regarded it. To-day, in the course of a talk, she was very distressed that her mother and not she was to be the baby's mother. She wept bitterly: " But *I* want to be its mother." " But why can't I ? " etc.

(4;0) This was quite a jolly talk.

U.: " I *shall* be baby's Mummy." M.: *How will you be her Mummy?* I'll put her in her pram and give her milk. *How will you give her milk?* I'll give her milk and milk. *And you'll go to school* (laughingly). *And what will they call me in school?* Mrs. B. *Oh, won't that be funny, for " Mrs. B." to be one of the children!* *And what will Miss Y. call me?* Ursula. *And will Molly let me play with her? And will X. let me play with her?* etc. (The answers to these questions were always given laughingly but her mother did not know whether they were " Yes " or " No ".) *Do you think we can both be her Mummy?* Well, I may grow up into a Mummy very quickly. But I can't take care of her very often 'cos Granny said she'd buy me a puppy. Daddy knows a shop. *And will you be the puppy's Mummy?* Yes. Then you can take care of her.

(4;0) M.: *You're going to school on Monday.* That's the day after to-morrow. I'm not glad. I don't want to go. *Why not?* I want to be with you. *But you will be with me ever such a lot.* I want to be with you *all the time.*

(4;1) U.: " I don't want you to go out, Mummy. I want to come with you. I want to be with you *all the time.* . . . But I don't want you to go. I love you so much I want to be with you always." Much weeping because her mother *had* to go.

U.: " I love you, Daddy, and I love Else and I love Mary and I love Mummy. I love you very much but I love Mummy most of all."

(4;1) U.: " I love you so much, Mummy, fifty thousand. I love you more than I can tell you."

(4;1) U.: " When will baby come out, Mummy? I would like her to be a girl."

(4;1) Patting her mother several times: " Oh, isn't baby getting big? " And another time: " Isn't baby growing? "

(4;1) Her mother shared her cream at dinner and said, " Oh, U., this will make me a fat Mummy! " U.: " Oh, don't be! I don't like fat Mummies." *Why not?* They look so silly. *Who has a fat Mummy?* W. has.

(4;2) U., very insistent and in worrying and worried tone: " When will baby come out? How long will it be before baby comes out? . . . How long will it take before baby comes out? " M.: *Oh, later on in summer. Not yet.* " Yes, but, when, when? " Relapsing into half weeping, almost in the same breath: " I have to go to school the day after Monday, but I don't want to go. I want to stay at home with you." *Oh, well, baby's not coming out for some time.* When, after May?

(4;2) Her mother was again in bed for a few days. U.: " My darling, sweet Mummy. This might make you feel better," giving her one of her sweets.

(4;2) U.: " My sweet Mummy! Nearly everybody will be out. If I were here I would take care of you and do everything for you." This was accompanied by some very tender caresses, stroking of her mother's face and rubbing her cheek against her mother's. Her actual behaviour lags far behind her good intentions, for when her mother is indisposed she makes the most diabolical fuss about any change of her usual routine, and her mother is given very little peace.

(4;2) U. had her arms round her mother, who must have been leaning rather heavily against her. She pushed her mother away and said, " Oh, this baby is heavy."

She asks her mother very often at night when she will sleep with her. This night, as her mother was saying " Good-night," she said, " Oh, Mummy, when will you sleep with me? " M.: *Some time, later on, after baby's born.* I'm not happy with Else. *Why not?* Because I want you to sleep with me. *Well, later on, Daddy will be going away for a time and then sometimes I shall come in here and sleep with my two children.* Rather put out: " But baby might cry in the night and wake me up. What shall I do ? " *I shall put her in another room. But we might hear her through the doors. Then what shall we do ? I shall have to go to her and see what's the matter and I shall have to teach her not to cry at night.*

(4;2) F came for the afternoon. When she left, U.'s mother kissed her. U. gave her a violent push so that she fell over, saying, " Don't kiss her."

(4;3) U.: " When baby comes, Mummy, I can show her to A., can't I ? " *Yes, of course you can.* " I shall show her every day." Then the following monologue occurred, half to her mother, while she was dressing her doll. : " The first day I shall say, ' A., would you like to see our new baby ?' ' Oh, yes, certainly,' she will say. ' Look, here she is. Do you like her ? ' ' Oh, very much. I wish I had one.' ' Why don't you have one, too ? ' " (or some similar question). " ' Where ' (or how) ' do you get them ? ' ' My Mummy made this in her tummy.' " (Looking at her mother): " Don't laugh, Mummy ! " M.: *I'm not laughing at you, darling, I'm only smiling because I feel pleased. You're smiling, too.* But don't laugh at me. *I'm not even smiling now, see.*

(In this interval, the baby sister was born.)

(4;3) U.'s father wanted Nurse to bath R. in U.'s night-nursery, but U. refused. On being coaxed, she mentioned a few days of the week (and which) when she would allow it. A day or two later, she said she would like R. to sleep in her room. Her father said that she couldn't yet as she hadn't learned to sleep all night without crying and would disturb her. He suggested that she might perhaps bath in her room at present and sleep with her a little later on. She agreed readily to this.

(4;3) U., on being asked what R. was like after her first visit : " She's only sweet ! " Another comment: " She's just what I wanted ! "

(4;4) There was some mention of R. U.: " I'm so glad she's in the house, Mummy." M. : *Is it nice to have a sister ? It's just what you wanted, isn't it ?* Yes, I guessed it would be a sister. Do you remember, Mummy ? You said you didn't know whether it would be a boy or a girl and I guessed it would be a girl. Do you remember ?

(4;5) At the end of a morning visit to her mother, just before leaving : " And the second daughter's coming at 4 ! "

(4;5) Whenever people speak of " a little girl " in U.'s presence, meaning her, she always now says, " You mean R."

(4;5) R. was on her mother's lap. U. leant over her and whispered, " R., soon we shall be going away to the seaside and shall have to leave you, I think you will be sorry." After a minute, to her mother, very gleefully, " She might be two when we come back, mightn't she ? Then she could play with me." *She would have to live many months before she's one and she'll have to be one before she's two.* One, two, three. She could play with me when she's three. That won't be *very* long, will it ?

Looking out of her mother's bedroom window in the morning, perched on the arm of a chair, U.: " I'm bigger than anybody." Then, " The sky's bigger than anybody, and higher."

U. (watching something R. did): " Isn't she clever. Cleverer than any other baby—as clever as me ! "

Nurse (asking U. not to claim her mother's attention because she wanted her to do something for R.): *Only a minute, U., and then I'll take R. away and you can have Mummy to yourself.* U.: But I want her to stay.

(4;7) With some self-reproach after a very tender and exaggerated and protracted " Good-night ", U.: " I love you more than R." The same evening she said, " Mummy, I don't have nice dreams." M.: *When do you have them, in the day or in the night ?* At night. *What do you dream about ?* They're not nice. *Tell me one.* I don't remember.

(4;7) U.: " A little girl I played with in school said a silly thing. Wasn't she silly ? She said, ' If you don't tell me your name, I'll hit you.' But people don't say those things to other people, do they ? " M.: *What did you say ?* I said, ' Don't do that.'

(4;8) Examining her person after a bath, U.: " My underneath's got a tongue. Why has it ? " M.: *It isn't really a tongue. It's a piece of flesh that looks like it.*

(4;8) In bed. U.: " Don't go away from me. You mustn't go away ever in your life, not till I'm a baby again." M.: *When will you be a baby again ?* U. (not answering), " I shall stay forty-eight. Will I be a lady when I'm forty-eight ? I'll be ninety. Will I be a lady when I'm ninety ? *You'll be an old lady when you're ninety.* I don't want to be old.

(4;9) " A nasty dream." " Nurse came in with R. and I hit her on the head " (several times ?) " And then there was something *very* nasty ! I *can't* tell you that . . ."

(4;9) U., telling her mother something about a little girl in a story, apparently an orphan: " She hadn't a mummy. Well, she must 'ov had the mummy who borned her and then she must 'ov died and then she went to live with an Auntie. I 'spect that's what happened."

(4;10) U. did somersaults on her bed for some time, then while her mother was feeding R. she went up and gave her mother two punches. M.: *Hullo! What's that for?* Spitting on R.'s head. *Stop that, U.* I'll spit on her food! *Then I won't have you in here while I'm feeding her. It's a pity because I like having you.* I'll do it all the same! I'll . . . (something or other). *Can't you think of anything else to do that I wouldn't like?* Yes, lots of things! *What?* Throwing over the chairs and throwing everything about! *And if you do that, d'you think I'll be pleased?* No. *And if I'm not pleased, how will you feel?* I'll be unhappy. *Look here, U., if you turn more somersaults, I can watch you even if I'm feeding R. She'll soon be finished and then I'll give her to nurse to put in her cot and help you to turn a back somersault.*

U. wasn't in a very happy mood and later when her mother went in to kiss her good-night she was lying on her face on her bed and crying. M.: *What's the matter, U.?* (Her mother had visitors coming.) U.: I wish I had visitors coming to see me like you. *But you do have your friends coming to see you.* I want visitors like you, *now*. *Well, your friends are all in bed now and my visitors haven't come yet. The only visitor here now is R. Would you like her to come up to see you?* No. I want visitors like you and friends. *But you've got lots of friends. And Mummy loves you very much, isn't that as good?* No! I liked my party better. *Well, you're having another party soon.* U. (cheering up): When? *In about four weeks' time it's your birthday. Five weeks to be exact.* (This was the turning point and after this U. became more cheerful.)

(4;10) U. wanted a third tangerine for her supper. Her mother thought she was doing this only to drag out the time, and her own supper was waiting, so she said she couldn't spare another, she was keeping the others for U.'s waking-up fruit. U. did her best to get her mother to change her mind by weeping, coaxing, etc. Then said, " I'll go away from you." *What, now?* Yes. *You can't now.* I will! . . . U., again, in a small, weepy voice: " I'll go away from you." (Pause.) " And you won't like it." (Pause.) In a still smaller and more pathetic voice: " And *I* won't like it ! "

Playing with R., tender, delighted, amused: "I *do* think she's a sweet thing ! "

(4;10) U. was holding R. and found her heavy to manage. Nurse: *You remember she was much littler when you used to hold her.* Well, as she grows, I grow too, so I'll be able to hold her even when she's fourteen.

(4;11) U.: " I think it's nice to have a little sister . . . It's a good thing, because if a friend had a sister and she came to stay with us, we wouldn't know how to treat her."

U.: " I shan't marry. I want to stay with you always."
More reflectively : "Well, I'll see how I feel about it when I'm grown up."

(4;11) Nurse was out. U. and her mother were having tea together. Her mother was reading to her. R. was asleep outside. Her mother thought she heard her voice and said, *I think I heard R. We'll have to have her in.* U.: When Nurse's out, I don't like it when R. comes in to tea. *You want me all to yourself ?* (R. screeches and interrupts a good deal.) Yes. *Well, she's my daughter, too, so you have to share me, don't you ? Perhaps R. will keep quiet till tea is over.* She did, and her mother read to U. who then said voluntarily : " R. can come in now."

(4;11) U. (of R.): " Isn't she sweet ? Isn't it nice to have a sister ? It's a good thing I wanted one. I hope I have one when I'm grown up." M.: *You mean when you have children ?* Yes. Well, if my first is a boy, I hope the second will be a girl.

(4;11) U.: I had a nasty dream. I didn't like it at all. I don't remember the beginning. Barbara (the kitten) grew big. She didn't exactly grow up. She stood on her feet and put her arms round my neck. Then she flew downstairs and up again before I could get to (call) you. *How did she do that ?* Oh, it was only a dream. *How did she fly ?* I mean she ran quickly.

(5;0) U.: " Sometimes when I want to do 'weeny' it wants to come out and can't. Something stops it. I suppose it's its Mummy or Daddy." *What do you mean ?* I mean " big ". " Big's " its friend, isn't it ?

U. was talking of boys and girls and said, " I'm glad you're a girl." M.: *Are you, why ?* Because I love you. *What would I be if I weren't a girl ?* My Daddy, of course. But I like you and I mightn't if you were different.

(5;0) U.: " I wonder who nurse will marry. I wonder who I'll marry." M.: *I hope it'll be someone very nice.* So do I. Someone like Daddy. Well, I shan't marry if I don't find someone I like. . . . I think I shall look a nice bride. . . . With fair hair ! (very confidentially). Shall I have a new party dress ?

U.'s mother had taken her to the lavatory. Her mother had wanted her to go alone but she had said she needed her mother and was going to do a " big ". She said she was ready and her mother reminded her that she hadn't done her " big ". U. (doing it and speaking her thought aloud): " Oh, that's a good idea. (Whispering to her mother): When you don't want to take me, I'll say I want to do a " big " and then you

hy did you whisper that? U. (persuasively): Oh, ⹁ps you'll forget by then.

⹁: *I think I should like to marry Daddy.* Well, I'll ⹁ou'll see how you feel about it when you're grown up?

(5;0) U.: "I had a long dream this morning, about you and Daddy and me and R. R. was in the room in her high chair and she called us and you went in only I stayed outside. And then she walked on hands and feet and said, 'Will you help my friend?' and I didn't want to but I did and she grew up very quickly and there were two trains and one train was her friend and one train went into the other—and there was lots more but I can't tell you now. (She was tired.) It was a very long dream and went on until I woke up."

(5;1) U. had a new game from which she derived a mysterious pleasure. Nurse cleared the cupboard of her wardrobe. U. sat huddled inside with only a crack open with a magazine on her knees and her electric torch in her hand. She came down to tea after about twenty minutes or half an hour, delighted, with flushed cheeks, and said she had been "reading" and "telling herself a story". It was about a princess but was too long to tell her mother.

(5;1) U.: "I love you very much, Mummy. I love you as much or perhaps a *little* more than R."

R. now sleeps in U.'s room. That means U. being very quiet when she goes to bed. She was crying and was very obstreperous. Her mother asked her to be quiet because she would wake R. U. (violently): "I can do what I like with her because she's my sister." M.: *Oh, no. She's my daughter. I won't let you wake her. I wouldn't let her disturb you if she were old enough to understand.* It's *my* room and it isn't R.'s room and it isn't nurse's room.

(5;1) U. (to M.): "I love you very much. I love you so much that I sometimes cry because I don't want anybody else, only you. That shows how much I love you, doesn't it?" M.: *Does it?* Yes. *Well, I love you very much.* Well, I can't show how much you love me but I can show how much I love you.

(5;1) Something U. wanted her mother to do that she didn't want to do. U.: "You *must*, Mummy, you *must!*" *Must I?* Yes, that's what Mummies are for, to do what their children want them to. *Is it?* Yes. And to look after them. *And what are children for?* To play, of course.

(5;1) U. was climbing on R.'s cot when her mother had laid R. in it for the night. Her mother asked her to come off. She was mischievously persisting. Her mother made a move to lift her. Spontaneously and from the heart she said, " It would be *nice* to have a Mummy who couldn't lift you ! "

(5;2) U. and R. were rolling over their mother like a pair of puppies one morning when the mother was in bed. R. burrowed into her mother. U.: " Look at R. ! I think she's trying to suck those things she used to suck when she was a baby, don't you ? She remembers."

(5;2) U. : " How can a baby come out of your underneaths ? " *Well, it has to stretch to make room for it to come out.* Does it hurt much ? *Well, yes.* Well, I won't have one if it hurts. *It hurts some people more than others and it's nice to have a baby.*

(5;3) U. had a friend to tea, and her mother overheard part of the following game. U. took S. upstairs when she arrived, to her room, where they undressed and re-dressed in some of U.'s clothes. Then they went into the garden and after a bit took off some of their garments. U.: " Oh, ooky (a favourite exclamation), I want to go to the lav. Oh, I can't be bothered to go upstairs. I know, I'll bring the chamber down here and do it here." (She rushed upstairs, brought it down, put it on the garden path, sat on it and "did it" there.) U., " Now you, S." (S. calmly and comfortably did.) U., " We'll keep it here." M. (from the kitchen window, anxious for the susceptibility of her neighbours): *I don't think you'd better have it there. You put it behind the bushes* (a secluded place behind the dining room). U.: " *Good !* We'll play schools and that'll be the lavatory." (She rushed up again and brought down toilet paper. They got umbrellas and hung them on a branch of a creeper, near the " lavatory ", presumably for a cloakroom. They had out U.'s desk and the game went on peacefully for hours.)

(5;3) U.: " Does age go on till a hundred ? " M.: *Sometimes, but not often.* U. (with the beginning of a whimper) : Oh, it's horrid ! *What is ?* How old will you be when I'm forty ? *About seventy.* U. (whimpering): Then you'll die and I shall miss you. It's horrid !

There was a discussion on surnames and U. said she would be " Mrs. B." when she grew up and her mother said only if she happened to marry a " Mr. B."

U. (on the swing) : " I hope I have a girl." *When you grow up, you mean ?* Yes. I won't want one if it isn't a girl. I'll tell my husband. *Well, you can't make whatever you like, can you ?* U. (half to herself, working it out) : Well, if there were pink and white seeds for girls and yellow and black seeds for boys and I would tell my husband. (Some questions from her mother): *Do you think he could arrange to have the kind you want ?*

You generally don't see it. It goes straight in. Well, he could take it out and have a look and if it was the right kind . . .

(5;3) U. (to S., who came to play with her): " Wasn't that a lovely game upstairs in the bed? " M.: *What was it?* U. (to S.): It's a secret, isn't it? She mustn't know, may she? We did make the bed in a muddle ! (At night when U. was getting into bed her mother said very confidentially: *What was that game you played with S. ? I would like to know.* U. (carelessly): Oh, just mothers and fathers, of course. M.: *Who was the mother and who the father ?* We were both mothers. *And who were the babies ?* The dollies, of course.

U. (to Eileen, at teatime, provocatively): " Can you see my botty ? " (showing her bottom quickly and quickly pulling up her knickers). Eileen giggled. U. (continuing the game): " You can't see my underneaths ! " (Showing " them " more obviously): " Now you can. Touch them." (E. tentatively touches.) U.: " Not there, right inside." E., " I don't want to."

Another time. U.: " Shall we play botties? " (This game consists of pulling down one's knickers very quickly and pulling them up again, quickly saying, " You can't see my botty," and attempting to get a glimpse of the other person's in the brief opportunity allowed. She sometimes pulls up her mother's skirt and says, " I can see your botty ! " as though catching her mother out, looking gleeful and as though conscious of doing something forbidden. One of these occasions developed into an amusing and amused talk in the course of which her mother said U. had a very nice bottom. She said she didn't like it, and when her mother asked why, replied, " Because it doesn't like to do ' big '.")

U. (to Nurse, and later told by U. to her mother, in the bathroom): " Look, Nurse, I'm doing such a lovely thing. I'm putting the soap on my underneaths. It's lovely, so cool, shall I do it to R. ? " Nurse: *No, she might not like it as you do.* When U. told her mother what a " lovely thing " she'd done, her mother said, *On your underneaths ?* U. said, " No, inside. It was so nice." *Why ?* So cool.

(5;4) U.'s mother was giving R. her mid-day meal and U. wanted her to take her to the lavatory (she won't go alone). Her mother refused to interrupt R.'s meal. U.: " You're not nice to me. You're much nicer to R. than to me." *No, I'm not, U., but you* can *go alone and it's hard on R. to have one person begin her meal and another finish giving it to her. It spoils her feed and I don't like doing that.* (The argument continued, with repetitions of U.'s complaint.) Later U. said, " R. has much more of you than I do." (The contrary is true !) Later in the day, U. and her mother were out together and her mother said, *You know, U., I was thinking of what you said about R. having much more of me than you. It seems to me that when you were R.'s age, you had much more of me than she does now.* Did I? Yes. *You see I had only one little girl then and you had all my time and attention, whereas R. has to share it with you.* (Apart from this U. is consistently charming to R.)

U. (one night, tearfully): " I shall grow up before R." M.: *Don't you want to?* No. I don't want to be grown up.

(5;5) U. has lately shown many unaccountable and unreasonable fears and anxieties. She says she feels " nervous ", does not like being left alone at bedtime, thinks of " nasty animals ", of a story if it is not entirely innocuous, of the picture of the kangaroo in " The Sing-Song of old man Kangaroo ", will not go to the lavatory alone. Yet she will go up the road alone to post a letter or to a paper shop to get her paper or chocolate, etc. The other day she and her mother were paddling in clear water and her mother called, *Oh, here's a crab.* U. rushed away, frightened, and refused to paddle any more. On another occasion she fussed dreadfully lest their shoes, lunch, etc., should be carried away by the tide which was more than an hour's distance away, a thing she could know from her daily experience. She is very interested in her " underneaths ", likes to exhibit " them " to her mother with an air of doing something amusingly forbidden. Tries to catch her mother out in the same way.

(5;6) U. has been showing all sorts of unreasonable fears lately. She was in bed and wanted her mother to stay with her and her mother wanted to go out of the room for a few minutes. U.: " The trouble is, if I were not a girl like I am it would be all right." *What do you mean?* Well, if I wasn't afraid of things. But I am afraid. If I were like T. or P. *Aren't they afraid? Why are you? You used not to be.* When I was younger, I wasn't. Now I'm older I am. That's funny, isn't it?

(5;6) U.: " The older I get the frightender I get. And the younger I am, the less frightened I am ! "

(5;6) (U. had asked her mother some time previously how one could tell whether a baby was a boy or girl.) U.: " You can tell whether a baby's a boy or girl by looking at its underneaths, can't you? Does a baby boy have a weeny penis? " *Yes.* Did you look at my underneaths when I was born? *The doctor and nurse did.* Did you look at R.'s?

(5;6) U.: (beginning to cry): " I don't want Barbara to bathe me. She'll see my botty."

(5;6) U. has taken to doing " weeny " in her bath and telling her mother with great glee and conscious " naughtiness ", sometimes only telling her mother when the bath is over. She says V. does it and initiated her into the habit and that they both did it when they had a bath together. Her mother suggested that she wouldn't like to wash in the " weeny " of a dog or cat for instance. She said, " Oh, I don't mind *my* weeny." One evening, when her father and mother were both in the bathroom, she sat across the bath over the water and ostentatiously did it into the bath, saying, " Look, I'm doing ' weeny ' in my bath ! " Her father, who had been going to tell her a story, walked out of the room. A few seconds later she said, " Where's Daddy, I want him to tell me the story." M.: *He's gone to the lavatory.* U. (quickly) : " No, he's gone downstairs because he didn't like me doing weeny in my bath." Just then her father came out of the lavatory and she said, " Oh, yes. He's coming out ! "

Apropos of her masturbatory exercises, once or twice she has shown her mother her " underneaths " and pulled herself in a rather painful-looking way, and her mother has said, *Oh, don't, U. I'm afraid you'll make yourself sore if you do that.*

(5;6) U.'s father was telling her a story and patted her thigh. She interrupted : " I like that, Daddy. Do that again."

CHAPTER THREE

THE THEORY OF DEVELOPMENT

INTRODUCTION

1. *The behaviour seen.* My readers have now followed a group of intelligent, vigorous and healthy young children through the vicissitudes of their feelings and doings with each other over a space of three years' group life. We have watched their behaviour and heard their conversation, and been able to compare many details of the life of this particular group with the sayings and doings of other groups and other individual children, recorded elsewhere.

We have seen these children playing out their private phantasies and trying to impose them upon their companions. We have heard them quarrelling for the possession of a coveted tool or toy, revelling in the sense of power over others and furious when occasion denied them this pleasure. We have seen their miseries and hatreds when rivals claimed a place in the love or attention of playmates or grown-ups, and their unscrupulous efforts to turn such rivals out of favour. We have noticed the moody disaffection of some of the children, and how little any of them could ever bear to be inferior to others in skill or virtue. We have seen how naturally they show suspicion and dislike of new-comers, how severe their strictures upon weaker brethren can be and how even the adults, just judges and defenders of the weak, may incur the united displeasure of the group when fellow-feeling is strong.

We have seen, too, the charm of their friendly ways to their playmates and to grown-ups, their generous appreciation of each other and unstinted warmth of love. And we have watched their eager interest in making and inventing, their pleasure in song and dance and miming, in exploring the world of things and arguing about the world of people.

We have also seen how the younger children will bite or spit in playfulness or in anger. We have heard them chant about excretory products of the body, and threaten attacks with these. We have watched them display their bodily parts for admiration and seen their curiosity as to the parts and processes of others. We have noted unmistakable signs of sexual desire and excitement, and had glimpses of the dread of sexual injury and loss. We have watched their play of being fathers and mothers and babies, and heard some of their quaint notions of marriage and birth. We have seen some of the boys seek to play a feminine rôle, and watched the common delight of all these little children in making " nests " and " cosy places " to take refuge in. And, finally, we have remarked the first signs of guilt and shame, and seen how absolute and unrelenting the moral judgments of such young children can be.

2. *The need for a genetic theory.* How are all these different forms of behaviour linked together? What is their meaning in the present life of the children and in the total process of social development? Such are the general questions which arise as we read. But many detailed problems crowd upon us, too. Why did Frank come to school on many days so unhappy and ready to quarrel? Why did Benjie want to shut Dan out from so many pleasures, and wonder so wistfully why he, too, was not called " darling", when he was addressed like this as often as any other child? Why did Roger sometimes expose his genital and giggle about it? What made George suddenly show his penis when Frank said, " I can see your big toe "? What led Frank to choose to be a girl? And why did he say, " When she is married, we'll spit in her face "? Why do the children love to make "cosy places" " to keep the tigers out "? What led Tommy to choose to write about himself, " Tommy is a naughty boy "? What is it in the children which makes them so hard upon others who are more clumsy or foolish? And why, in general, were children who came from such good homes so often defiant, rude and contrary?

At this point, then, the need arises to pass from description to understanding. The facts observed must be linked genetically with each other, and with those coming before and after in the growth of the children. What relation do these sorts of behaviour bear to the earlier feelings and experiences, and to the later development of these children? How are they connected with the behaviour of ordinary adults in ordinary social life? What light do they throw upon the social characteristics or private difficulties of normal and abnormal adults?

It is, however, very difficult on any merely descriptive approach to understand all the behaviour of children recorded here (including that to be quoted incidentally in the text later on). Taken as it stands, much of this descriptive material is unintelligible and carries no hint of its genetic significance. It raises many problems which call for further evidence from other sources for their solution.

Such further evidence, and an interpretative theory which suffices to bring order and meaning into our data, is offered us by psycho-analytic studies of the *unconscious* mental life of children and adults.

That theory, which serves to make these records intelligible both in detail and as a whole, is the fruit of Freud's epoch-making researches into the technique of studying the human mind.

Since Freud himself first opened our eyes to the reality of unconscious mental processes and the whole inner world of the psychic life, he and an increasing number of technically trained analysts have carried out a vast amount of research into the psychology of individuals of all types, normal, neurotic and psychotic. In the microscopic study of individual histories which psycho-analysis makes possible, every detail of the personal and social relations at each phase of development in the history of the individual is worked out from the inside. The particular distributions of mental energy in relation to instinctual trends, and the characteristic mechanisms for dealing with mental conflict, are in each case traced and evaluated.

The way in which, for example, the child's relation to his first teachers is intimately influenced by the special colouring of his previous relation with his parents; the way his attitudes to playmates at school, and friends in later life, reflect his earliest conflicts about possible rivals in the home; the way his feelings and phantasies about father and mother are taken up into his adult sentiments about home and country and government; the cross-currents of his later relations to men and women, to his own children or his parents' parents; the way in which his earliest play interests become elaborated or deflected into the sustained pursuits of adult life ; his inner attitudes to work and recreation alike—every aspect of his later social responses is brought into relation with his deep phantasy life, on the one hand, and his earlier real experiences, on the other. The psycho-analyst is thus in a specially privileged position for the study of the genesis and history of social relations as such.

Of recent years psycho-analytic theory has been strengthened, confirmed and further elaborated by the direct application of its technique in a special form to little children from the age of two years and onwards. Melanie Klein has been the pioneer in this work of child analysis, and M. N. Searl has helped to carry the method into new psychological territories, as well as to make many of its features intelligible to non-analysts. My own experience, both in my personal analysis and in working with adult and child patients, has given me a sense of the profound illumination which psycho-analytic theory and practice is able to throw upon the outward behaviour of young children. The theory gives us a more solid ground of understanding of the open anxieties and difficulties, as well as of the ordinary interests and activities of the child, than any merely classificatory description or quantitative study has done or could do.

Approached with the ordered knowledge of the unconscious mental life of the child which the psycho-analytic technique has given us, the incidents of children's sayings and doings recorded here fall into place as partial indications of deep, unconscious mental processes which link them together into a dynamic and intelligible whole. They would not, in themselves, completely suffice to establish the truth of psycho-analytic theory ; but, on the one hand, they present problems which require that theory for their solution, and on the other, they provide additional behaviouristic evidence of its soundness and adequacy.

Whilst I believe that the main structure of my ensuing theoretical argument is in accordance with general analytic theory, I alone am responsible for the detailed interpretations offered of particular incidents. These do not necessarily represent the exact views of my colleagues in the analytic field, although they are certainly in general accordance.

In discussing the data of overt social relations I shall use certain psycho-analytic concepts, the meaning of which

INTRODUCTION

will, I think, be sufficiently clear from the context. I shall, however, offer a more systematic account of the theory as a whole, before taking up the theoretical study of the sexual data.

It is, however, to be remembered in reading the theoretical commentaries which ensue, that these are the same children about whom I wrote in *Intellectual Growth in Young Children*, and who there demonstrated what a wealth of active curiosity, delight in understanding and disinterested pursuit of knowledge, even such young children could display in favourable circumstances. Here I am going to write about them from a different point of view, but the other facts remain, and must be held in view at the same time for any complete picture, even of the child's phantasy life. This is especially to be remembered wherever I am discussing the interpretation of symbolic activities and unconscious phantasy. Here I shall be interpreting the children's behaviour at the unconscious level. I shall, for example, be evaluating their interest in engines as representing the children's phantasy about parents and the sexual intercourse of parents. I shall not be considering it, as I was in *Intellectual Growth in Young Children*, for its value in relation to knowledge of real engines, and the general development of the child's understanding of the external world. I shall be examining it as an expression of unconscious phantasy, in relation to the child's deepest and most central emotional problems.

In *Intellectual Growth in Young Children*, I considered both imaginative and manipulative play as the starting point which leads to the child's discovery, reasoning and thought. " What imaginative play does, in the first place, is to create practical situations which may often then be pursued for their own sake, and thus lead on to actual discovery, or to verbal judgment and reasoning. . . . Imaginative play builds a bridge by which the child can pass from the symbolic values of things to active inquiry into their real construction and real way of working. . . . In his imaginative play the child re-creates selectively those elements in past situations which can embody his emotional or intellectual need of the present, and he adapts the details moment by moment to the present situation. . . . And in his make-believe play he takes the first steps towards that emancipation of meanings from the *here* and *now* of a concrete situation, which makes possible hypothesis and the ' as if ' consciousness."

But I referred there, too, to the ground of the present study. " Much of the child's earliest interest in physical objects is certainly *derivative*, and draws its impetus from early infantile wishes and fears in relation to his parents . . . the *first* value which the physical world has for the child is as a canvas upon which to project his personal wishes and anxieties, and his first form of interest in it is one of dramatic representation. The psycho-analysis of young children by Klein's play technique has shown that engines and motors and fires and lights and water and mud and animals have a profoundly symbolic meaning for them, rooted in infantile phantasy. Their ability to concern themselves with real objects and real happenings is a *relative* matter. It exists, in a very effective sense, and can be used for intellectual growth, as I have shown. But its *deepest* sources lie in the first ' symbol-formation ' of infantile mental life ; and it will continue to renew its vitality from the repressed wishes and fears and phantasies of that period.

" Psycho-analytic studies of little children, moreover, have also shown that in their free dramatic play, children work out their inner conflicts in an external field, thus lessening the pressure of the conflict, and diminishing guilt and anxiety. Such a lessening of inner tension through dramatic representation makes it easier for the child to control his real behaviour, and to accept the limitations of the real world. In other words, it furthers the development of the ego, and of the sense of reality. It helps to free the child from his first personal schemas, and to enhance his readiness to understand the objective physical world for its own sake."

Thus, whilst in *Intellectual Growth in Young Children* I was concerned to show what use the child can make in the real world, and for cognitive purposes, of those impulses which take their starting point in unconscious phantasy and are shown in make-believe play, my task in this present volume is to study and interpret those actual conflicts and the deepest sources of the child's intellectual impulses and emotional development, for their own sake. I will ask my readers to remember, however, that wherever in the passages to follow I take an activity at its *symbolic* value, I am never suggesting that this is the *sole* meaning of the activity for the child, nor have I lost sight of its cognitive significance in a real world. Both the imaginative meaning and the cognitive value are there in every activity of the child. As with the adult, any single piece of behaviour has both its unconscious meaning and its significance in the stream of conscious thought and activity. One of these aspects is relevant for a given purpose of study, another for a different purpose.

There is of course also a differentiation in the relative emphasis on the phantasy value or the cognitive value of any activity, according to the age of the child, the particular circumstance of the moment, and, in general, the degree of neurosis present. When, for example, a child of, say, fourteen to eighteen months, spends a large part of his waking time fitting things together, a lid on to a box, a stick into a hole, and so on, there can be no doubt that the cognitive activity, although present, is at a minimum.[1] Such a stereotyped action is best understood as a mode of discharging the anxiety raised by certain fundamental phantasies, connected in the first instance with unsatisfied oral longings. In his phantasy, the child is concerned with the relation between bodies and the primary phantasy is that of fitting his mother's nipple into his own mouth. From this aspect, the action may be an alternative to thumb-sucking. The same child fitting the Montessori cylinders into the block six months later is less completely under the domination of unconscious phantasy, and more concerned with the problem of space relations and skill

---

[1] " Would you give me your opinion of the following characteristic of my small son, aged fourteen months. Although this is not a problem of management or upbringing, I feel certain it has some definite psychological significance. Since he has been able to use his hands sensibly, he has shown a very marked tendency to fit things together, and put his finger or a stick into any hole which comes into his vision. This last is quite irresistible—in fact, for an example, we are staying in a house with a dog, and the boy has no interest in the dog except to try and put his finger into the animal's nostrils. When left to play alone this is almost the only form of play which he uses. Toy animals, or a ball, have no joy for him, and a cigarette packet, and a small stick give him most amusement. He is very patient and persevering in his efforts to get things to fit. If he has a ring, he puts a drum stick through it, and a ball of crochet cotton is stuck, with great pains, on the end of a stick and waved aloft. He puts two mugs one inside the other, and so on. He is a very healthy, happy and good-natured baby altogether, and has been very easy to manage so far. "

which the cylinders represent. At six years of age, when he uses the Tinker Toy or Meccano to build an engine or a bridge, his behaviour will still undoubtedly have a similar unconscious meaning, but its chief significance for his development then lies in the various problems it presents for skill and understanding.

3. *Classification and theory.* I have here, as in *Intellectual Growth in Young Children*, and for the same reasons, tried to keep the actual records of the children's behaviour apart from my own theoretical interpretations. This cannot, of course, be done quite literally and completely, since the mere classification along any lines whatever would involve *some* implicit theory. But I have tried to keep this indispensable element of theory in the arrangement of the records down to the minimum, and the offering of the records *en masse* will enable readers to see plainly its nature and influence.

In the first main section of *Love and Hate in Action*, I think it will be agreed that the theory implied is as slight as it could possibly be. In the second main division, however, the mere description of the children's behaviour as " sexuality" will seem to many people to be pure theory from the outset, and unwarranted theory at that. But in fact a scrutiny of the material itself will show that such a position could not be maintained with regard to many of the incidents quoted. No small part of the children's behaviour in these sections is as clearly and simply to be called " sexual " as any behaviour of adults ever could be. To deny the term to these incidents is both to shut one's eyes to plain facts, and at the same time to empty an ordinary term deliberately of its ordinary meaning, for the *sake* of a theory—the favoured theory that young children do not and cannot have sexual feelings. I can leave the behaviour of children to establish this point for itself. He that hath ears to hear, let him hear.

Others of the incidents included under sexuality would not at first sight be so included by most people. Nor would mere inspection of this material alone make one feel them to be so. But in the light of the larger study of the sexual life in general, and of psycho-analytic discoveries among adults and children in particular, there is every good ground for including them under this genetic heading, as I hope to make clear presently.

I. A THEORETICAL SURVEY OF SOCIAL RELATIONS

A. PRIMARY EGOCENTRIC ATTITUDES

The incidents quoted under this heading illustrate briefly what might perhaps be called the *primary situation* found in a group of very young children. When a number of such young children are brought together in a given space, but left free to play and move about as they wish, they do not at first constitute a *group* in the psychological sense. They behave simply as a number of independent persons, each mainly concerned with his own immediate ends, whether or not these ends cut across or chime in with the pursuits of others. The direct attitude of any given child to any or all of the others may be friendly or hostile; but even when he is friendly, he will not look upon the other children as ends in themselves, but always as a means to serve or an obstacle to hinder his own particular interests.

This primary situation is related to Piaget's *egocentrism* more closely than any other of the behaviour described in this book. It illustrates this concept in its least equivocal sense, and as actually seen in the spontaneous play of the children with each other.

The extent to which the attitude *dominates* the behaviour of any given child in the group will depend partly upon his age—it is the typical attitude of children under, say, four years; partly upon his previous social experience—many children of five or six may show it if they have not had much to do with other children, or if their temperaments are naturally less adaptable; and partly upon the day and the mood and the particular setting—under the stress of a strong desire or a vividly conceived purpose, any young child may fall into this attitude on occasion.

In itself, it seems to constitute the primary matrix of social feeling, out of which all others are developed by experience of one sort and another.

Its margin is not well defined. On the far side, it passes over into general make-believe play of a more varied and developed structure, which in its turn leads to miming and drama; and it merges into more developed and reciprocal social relationships, with a settled organisation (as in games and sports). On the near side, it is not always distinguishable from the purely solitary playing out of phantasies which literally ignores the presence of other people, as when Tommy would sit on a high stone pedestal, " being " an engine and making " engine noises ", quite withdrawn from the rest of the group; or when Martin made a " lovely railway train " of the colour tablets by himself in a corner. Such purely solitary play characterises chiefly the very young children— two and three years of age; but was rarely seen among the older ones if other children were about, although of course it would occur if only adults were present with, say, a four-year-old. A great deal of the children's behaviour was naturally of a marginal kind, showing strands of true egocentrism interwoven with a limited but genuine appreciation of the point of view of playmates, and with the recognition of independent but complementary rôles in co-operative play.

The essence of the true egocentric attitude (as I understand it) is that it involves a recognition of the *presence* of other children, but not of their personalities or independent purposes. The one child needs and uses the other for his own satisfaction. Two main characteristics can be seen to mark these egocentric situations: (*a*) Domination by pure phantasy of the form and aim of the joint play; and (*b*) the limitation of the other person's part to a minimal role. The other person is, indeed, nothing more than a pivot upon which the active player's phantasy can turn.

This is clearly seen in the first incident quoted. " Christopher asked for the ' shopping '; he made a ' bed ' in his shop and went to sleep. Mrs. I. was supposed to go to the shop, wait for some time, and waken him by knocking."

" Shopping " was a favourite game with many of the children, and took various forms. On many occasions, it would by no means deserve to be called egocentric, since it was a truly co-operative game with well-defined rôles of shopman and buyer, each active and complementary; and much real counting and reckoning of prices and change, and wrapping and delivering of parcels. That is to say, there was a considerable element of reality in the play, even though it was make-believe; and there was a real differentiation of equally important parts among the players (with, of course, always a prejudice in favour of being the seller rather than the buyer). But in this particular example of the shopping game, both these elements—reciprocity of rôle and admixture of real activity—were at a minimum. "Mrs. I.'s" part was to be merely instrumental to Christopher's private phantasy of being asleep in the shop and keeping someone waiting. The same thing is seen with Harold and his toy gun on 21.4.25. "Harold found a toy revolver in the sand-pit, and used it for some time. He said to Mrs. I., ' I know a lovely game. You go along there and then I will say, " A lady to shoot," and then you must fall down.' The others joined in too." And with Martin and his "cake" on 12.3.25: "Martin filled a pail with sand and brought it to the top of the steps, and said, ' Come and look at the cake I made, come and see it,' and insisted on Mrs. I. pretending to eat some several times." Paul's magical gestures with the trowel on 15.5.25 may be noted. "In the morning when the other children were running as engines, Paul had taken a trowel and thrown it up into the air as a signal for the engines to start or stop, calling out to Mrs. I., ' When this goes up, you must stop.' He did this for a long time." This is an instance of one child exploiting the independent activity of the others to satisfy a phantasy of power of his own. The other children in fact took no notice of Paul's commands, and as far as real effect went he had to be content with Mrs. I.'s obedience to his will. But as he kept the action up for so long, he was probably not looking for real satisfaction.

Typically, then, in this primary phase, the play of a number of young children is little more than a congeries of individual phantasies. When these phantasies happen to overlap, they give rise to common activity, and may for the time being weld the players together into a group. As the children get to know each other, and build up a common history, the mutual adaptation of phantasy occurs more and more often. They gain the experience of doing things together in some way and some sense, and discover the benefits and delights of mutual support, both in imaginative play and in real achievement.

But the misfits of these individual phantasies are perhaps even more educative. It is when his purposes happen to clash with those of others that the child is stirred to a vivid, if momentary, realisation of the reality of other people as persons. Several of the incidents quoted illustrate the typical first reaction of a child to such signs of independent life in the pawns of his phantasy. In the beginning, it is implicitly *assumed* that others will accept the assigned rôle. When this assumption is rudely shaken, the children try to enforce their wishes by threats or actual attack, or by bribes and appeals of one sort or another. As when Dan tries to take the mouth organ from Tommy on 24.2.25, or several of the children threaten " not to come to tea with you " or " not to marry you " " if you don't do " just what they want. The reality of these sanctions to the children themselves is shown by Dan's meekness to Priscilla's control in view of her threat " not to marry " him (12.3.26). " Priscilla again bullied Dan to do what she wanted, for example, to finish his sewing, by saying, ' I shan't marry you.' This morning she wanted him to sew, and he asked, ' Can I mend the floor ?' She replied, with a lofty air, as if disowning responsibility, ' If you like.' He said quickly, ' But then you won't marry me ! ' and so continued his sewing."

A specially interesting instance is that of Harold's and Paul's exploitation of the relationship of brotherhood to gain their will over Dan. On 18.6.25. " Dan said to Frank, ' Shall we put our bathing suits on ? ' Harold hearing this, and having been told by his mother that he must not do so, said, ' I won't let you come to tea with me if you do.' Dan said, ' I *shall* put it on.' Harold said, ' But *are* you my brother, Dan ? ' Dan replied, ' Yes.' Harold said, ' Then don't put your bathing suit on.' " Neither Harold nor Paul was really Dan's " brother ". The word has to be taken in some moral sense, as a way of behaviour—being loving or peaceful or considerate. And it suggests, of course, that Paul and Harold had themselves been told to " behave like little brothers ", or " you mustn't speak so to your brother "— or some similar exploitation of the relationship by an adult.

The situations where one child will play happily and considerately with the others so long as he is the recognised leader, or has the superior part, would seem to be less egocentric than the naive subordination of others to the position of mere pawns in one's private game, or the attempt to cow or cajole them into accepting this rôle. Frank, for example, could not be said to be merely exploiting the other children when he acted as the leader in a dramatic game. He taught them and led them most satisfactorily and charmingly, and gave them all real functions. But he could not bear to take part in any communal play in which he was not the acknowledged leader. (This should, of course, be linked up with the striking examples of rivalry to adults which he provided, as seen in a later section of the records.)

The most delicious example of the real exploitation of another person is that of Dan with Gerry and the potter's wheel, March 1927. " Dan wanted to use the potter's wheel, and asked Gerry to turn the handle for him. He said to Gerry, ' You turn this handle, will you ? And when *your* arm gets tired—I'll get someone else to turn it ! ' "

The rebellion of the players in the child's own game, then, and the enforced reality of *their* phantasies and their wishes, bring the first shocks to his egocentric assumptions and provide his first effective social education. This education is carried further by the experience of real *togetherness* on those occasions when phantasies do happen to harmonise and feelings and activities are shared in more mutually adapted play.

The crude desire to be a leader, moreover, and even the more naively egocentric imposition of his phantasy by one child on several of the group, is often a real benefit to those who are pressed into his service. They are by this drawn into playing actively *with* others, even though the momentary rôle be of a subordinate or passive nature in itself. To be someone else's " puppy " or " baby " may not be as glorious as being the kennel master or the parent, but it does mean active co-operation in the game, and often gives opportunities for minor inventions of one's own. The leader does in fact create a group, even though it be for his own ends. Even for the followers, it means a step forward in social experience. And few of the children accept a passive rôle all the time, or in relation to all playmates. The " baby " of one group may become the " captain " of another ; and some even of the eldest members of the group will occasionally agree to change rôles and be relatively subordinate for a time at least.

Here, then, we see the first great value to the little child of free play among fellows and equals. The child whose only companions are adults is not seldom left entirely alone to his solitary phantasies, apart from the times when he is being washed and dressed and taught conventional manners. And when the grown-ups do take notice of his play, they commonly fall into one of the two extremes, either fitting obligingly and passively into the child's phantasy and doing exactly as he wishes, or dominating him almost completely and telling him what he is to do with his own toys. He is thus deprived of the beneficent education of the *real* clash of wills among equals, and the *real* experience of mutual activity.

There are children, however, and there were one or two in this particular group (Theobald and Dexter to some extent, Joseph especially) who are hardly able to enjoy free play with others, because their feelings of rivalry are too acute and too fraught with anxiety. They have not the qualities which make leaders, and are unable to tolerate being followers. They despise their playing fellows and call them " silly ", and even at four years of age, they prefer themselves to be " studious ". It is these children, already circumscribed in feeling and poor in social response, who offer the educator her really serious problem—rather than children who, like Frank, may be often openly " naughty ", moody and perverse, but who are full of warm feeling and vivid social gifts.

One of the first general questions for the educator of little children arises from this psychological fact of their egocentric demands in play. What should the part of the grown-up be with regard to the clashes of interest among the children, or to the older children's naive assigning of passive parts to the younger members of the group ?

B. HOSTILITY AND AGGRESSION

1. INDIVIDUAL HOSTILITY[1]

Probably the first thing that struck readers about this part of the material was the sheer amount of spontaneous aggression in such small children coming from good homes, where most of them had of course been taught from an early age to be " kind " and polite. A few of the boys were familiar with aggression from adults in the form of more or

[1] It will be seen that for the purpose of the main classification, I am using " aggression " in its widest sense to cover all forms of aggressive behaviour, whether or not this arises from the need for *defence*— not just that narrower meaning which is implied in the appellative *aggressor*. It will be found in fact that most of the aggressive behaviour of small children has a considerable element of *defence* in it.

less severe whippings; but many of them had had the mildest up-bringing, and some of them had quite certainly never been whipped or even scolded. It is on the whole true that the more crudely aggressive of the children were the ones who were whipped at home, but there were one or two exceptions to this in both directions. George, for instance, was not seldom whipped at home by his father, yet he was the gentlest and least quarrelsome of all the children. On him the whippings had had a subduing effect. He was usually quiet and pensive, and showed a marked strain of masochism. (Note, for example, the way he tried to cut his own fingers with scissors on p. 172.) And his hostility to the other children usually took an indirect form, as is seen in the first incident quoted under the head of *Rivalry*. " When the other boys ran into the garden, George went to Mrs. I and said, ' *We* won't play with the other boys, will we ? ' He stayed half an hour with her." Whereas Dan, who had had a fanatically free and untrammelled early life, and was not amongst the most aggressive of the group, was yet at times markedly so.

But every one of the children was hostile to the others in some degree and some form, at one time or another.

The main surface motives which could be seen at work in these hostile impulses were, as I have shown, (a) possession, (b) power, (c) rivalry, and (d) general moodiness (with feelings of inferiority or superiority). These four situations are not mutually exclusive, but sufficiently distinct to deserve separate study.

Aggressive behaviour and hostile feelings arising from the motive of ownership—whether a child's possession of an object be challenged, or he covets something possessed by another—is perhaps on the surface the simplest of all these motives. The sense of ownership was undoubtedly very strong with these children, and the evidence here definitely supports the view that this is one of the spontaneous and innate trends in human nature—no matter whether we call it an " instinct," a " drive," an " urge," or what-not. As soon, however, as one asks *why* it should be so strong, or looks at the actual instances of it in these particular records, one sees that the picture is not quite so simple and self-sufficient as might at first appear. When, for example, one sees Cecil so overcome by the sight of Dan holding one of the treasured hollyhock stalks that he becomes blind to his own which he has in his hand at the moment, and cries " That's *mine*," then it seems clear that we have left the field of simple ownership and strayed into those of power and rivalry.

The motive of *power* still keeps us on fairly familiar psychological ground. The hostilities of these children when they were interfered with by a grown-up or another child is in direct line with Watson's work on rage in infants, and with the general academic view that anger and the fighting impulse are stimulated by the thwarting of any wish or interference with any activity.

Aggressive behaviour from the motive of rivalry, however, bulks more largely in the records than either power or possession; and my impression when watching the children was that it gave rise to more acute tension of feeling and was more difficult to deal with.

We should all feel it to be natural to respond with anger and hostility to any of these three sorts of situation. But the aggressive behaviour of the fourth group sprang up without any of these more ordinary provocations, and these incidents have been brought together for that reason. Very often there was no apparent stimulus at all; sometimes the child seemed to have been thrown into moody anger by home events, before he came to school. On other occasions, certain children were so sensitive to possible attack from others that the mere approach of another child was enough to call out defensive aggression. And sometimes a child's hostility appeared to spring from the intolerableness of any hint of any sort of inferiority.

The various *forms* in which aggressive impulses found vent are themselves of great interest: biting, spitting, hitting and kicking, scratching, throwing things, snatching and spoiling the work or possessions of others, verbal expressions of hate and contempt, and verbal threats of attack with excretory products (themselves thought of as highly dangerous), " teasing " in various ways, boycotting and exclusion from pleasures, winning the hostility of others to one's own enemy.

Biting occurs chiefly among the younger children, although two five-year-olds had recourse to it at times of stress. It is recorded of seven different children in the group, all boys. Spitting happened with a larger number of children (eleven), although in many cases there was only one occasion of it, and it was troublesome only with three of the children, and in the early days of the school. It may occur even in the older ones who have long given up biting. It is found among girls as well as boys, although (interestingly enough) there were in this group no instances of *playful* spitting among the girls, only of using it as an attack. The verbal threats of attack with excretory products again occur mainly in the earlier years. Few children who were not definitely abnormal would feel the necessity to use such expressions after, say, five years, and most would have abandoned them before this. The other modes of aggression remain normal, in so far as open aggression is itself " normal ", throughout the years of childhood.

a. *The Motive of Possession*

The instances quoted bear witness to the strength and urgency of the common wish of little children to have exclusive possession or at least the biggest share or main use of whatever properties are the centre of interest at the moment. The satisfaction of having things all one's own is deep, the chagrin at others' having more than oneself very bitter. As I have suggested, the spontaneity of these reactions and their toughness under training make it clear that they are unlearned modes of response to certain types of situation in human beings, although children may differ in the openness and the intensity of response.

The forms of the possessive impulse shown in this material are worth noting. (*a*) The first is the direct wish to own an actual object, or to have exclusive use of it (which makes it " mine " for all intents and purposes). Any situation in which there is only one thing of a kind, an insufficient number of things for the group, or an assortment of things of varying sizes, will give rise to immediate tension as to who shall have " it " or " the biggest "—until training supervenes. And with the very young children, it is often the mere size of the thing that counts, rather than its appropriateness. It is always the smallest children who insist on having the largest-sized tools, although they cannot manage them, and would get on much better with a medium-sized. The older and more experienced child will more commonly choose the more appropriate tool, and defend his right to that with equal tenacity. Nearly all the children under five went through a phase when, for example, they liked to dig with "a spade like Daddy uses", and only when this phantasy was satisfied were they able to appreciate the greater real pleasure of wielding a spade of more manageable size. Herbert's delight in finding himself able to manage with another small boy a two-handled saw of the sort " that *men* use " is to be remembered.

(*b*) Ownership is felt, however, in things other than actual objects. Harold and Paul felt a keen sense of property in the nursery rhymes and songs they had heard at home, or in gramophone records of a kind they had there. No one else had the right to sing or hear these things without their permission. All the children felt that any thing was " theirs " if they had used it first, or had made it, even with material that itself belonged to all. Duncan and others felt a thing was " theirs " if they had " thought " of it, or " mentioned for it first ", and so on. (One is reminded of controversies among scientific men as to the parentage of ideas, discoveries or inventions.)

(*c*) Many of the children took it upon themselves now and then to act as dispensers of the public property and materials—the plasticine, the gramophone, etc., etc. Here they were quite well aware that the property in question was not "theirs", but they got a sense of great power from deciding who should use it and who not, how much they should have, and so on, trying to favour friends and exclude enemies. And when controversy arose about this, the child who had constituted himself the master of ceremonies might easily begin to assert that the plasticine, etc. *was* his, perhaps glossing this assertion by the reason that *he* was " using it ".

(*d*) One of the commonest situations in which the property impulse was aroused was when a number of children wanted to use one of the larger pieces of school apparatus at the same time—the swing, the see-saw, the tricycle, the climbing pillar, the sand-pit. " Taking turns " is one of the hardest lessons for children under five years to learn. As the vivid quarrel between Lena and Jessica on 27.10.26 (p. 39) shows, the young child cannot without much experience believe that " his turn " really will come in due time. All that he knows is that the others " have got it " and he hasn't.

A few minutes is an eternity when one is eagerly waiting for a prized pleasure such as riding on a tricycle or a see-saw. Nor does one believe in the good-will of the others who are enjoying their turns first—one knows only too well how readily one would exclude *them* if one were allowed! Only the proved evenness of justice of the controlling adult will make a transition possible from the impetuous assertion of " I want it *now* " to that trust in the future which makes " taking turns " possible. In the *Friendliness* section there are many examples of the way in which even the most importunate of the children did learn to " take turns ". And the response of the group to Mrs. I.'s statement of the humorous side of the situation on 11.3.26 was noteworthy. " The children made ' shops ' with the various things on the shelves. There was some squabbling, as each child wanted to have the largest share and the favourite articles. When Mrs. I. remarked that ' everybody seems to be wanting everything', they laughed heartily and became more amicable about sharing."

Two interesting points may be noted as to the quarrel between Lena and Jessica about the use of the tricycle. One is that neither child was willing to accept arbitration until she had proved conclusively her inability to gain her will over the other by her own efforts. But once this lesson was fully learnt, sweet reasonableness entered in, and the incident was a turning point in the social development of both children. Here, however, the two children *could* teach each other that lesson, because they were so equally matched in power and persistence. It is when one child is bigger or more fierce than the other, and the question of real bullying arises, that the adult is compelled to take a hand at an earlier stage of the dispute.

The other point is the origin of the " sense of justice ". " Oh no, I shall have it as many times as *she* has had it altogether, not just four—that wouldn't be *fair*, would it ? " argues Lena. If my enjoyment has to suffer limitations for someone else's pleasure, then I must have at the least as much as he. If *I* cannot be supreme, we must all be equal. *My* wish for exclusive possession is tamed by my fear of *his* encroachments and the hope that if I admit him to equal rights he will take no more. But I cannot concede more. Equality is the least common multiple to these conflicting wishes and fears. If all are equal, no one has any advantage. And so " justice " is born.

Much of the material under *Group Hostility* bears out this picture, and it is seen in the psycho-analysis of every adult.

(*e*) From time to time a child would take away the property of other children, apparently for the mere sake of the taking, as a *teasing* act, rather than because the thing itself was specially desired. " Frank kept taking away a wooden egg which Theobald had brought." " Frank and Christopher took a postcard which Tommy had brought with him, Christopher saying, ' Let's take them.' " " Frank had brought some confetti in a silver bag . . . and Tommy snatched at it . . . and ran off with some." " Christopher took bricks away from George, saying, ' I am the stealer.' " Doubtless the objects in question were coveted and their possession envied, but the pleasure seemed to lie rather in the *act of taking* itself than in the resulting possession. This is probably a much more complex motive than the direct wish for actual possession. It is more sadistic and contains more *arrière pensée* of revenge. It has in it less of love of the object and more of hate of the other person. It matters more, here, to deprive the other person of what he has than to have it oneself.

But when we look more closely even at the simpler instances of the direct wish to own, and ask what gives the coveted objects their value as possessions, it is plain that the relation to the other *person* is a very important element there too. Neither the pleasure of ownership nor the chagrin of envy bears much relation to the intrinsic value of the things owned or coveted. Few objects, indeed, other than food when hungry, have an absolute and intrinsic value to little children, operating at all times and in all circumstances, and independently of what other children are having and wanting. As many of the quoted incidents show, what is so desperately desired may be wanted simply because some-one else has it or desires it. A thing that has long been treated with indifference or contempt by the owner may suddenly assume great value in his eyes, if another person begins to take an interest in it. Or an ordinary object in the common environment (such as the hollyhock stalks), which has had no attention from the children, may suddenly become the centre of an intense struggle for ownership, if one of the children (especially the older ones), or an adult, shows that it now has value for him.

These considerations suggest that the motive of possession is not to be regarded as an atomic psychological unit, one of the irreducible "instincts" of original human nature. To think of it so is to miss its most significant aspects, viz. its intimate relation with the motives of power and of rivalry. It is essentially a *social* response, not a mere direct reaction to the physical objects which may serve individual purposes.

Even in the least complicated situation, where the value of the thing owned is intrinsic, as the means of satisfying some (primary or derived) personal need, the actual wish to *own* it can only be understood in terms of power—or, rather, of *powerlessness*. I want to own it because if I do not it may not be there when I need it, and my need will go unsatisfied. If another has it, he may keep it for ever. If I am at the mercy of another's will for the satisfaction of my need, I am helpless before it. Only by having the means of satisfaction of my need as *mine*, mine to have and to hold, can I feel safe.

The ultimate situation from which the wish to own arises is, of course, that of the infant at the breast, whose satisfactions are indeed at the mercy of another's will. It is to the infant's sense of helplessness before the urgency of his own desires for love and nourishment, and the equally helpless rage stirred by the denial of immediate satisfaction for his desires, that we have to look for an understanding of the imperious wish of the child to *own*. If the source of pleasure is *his*, he is safe against both outer and inner dangers—the danger of frustration, and the danger of helpless desire and rage. Mere *having* thus becomes an end in itself for the child just beyond the distresses of infancy.

It is this early prototypic situation that gives the key to the ultimate meaning of ownership. In the last resort, one's possessions are felt to be extensions of *the self*, as William James long ago pointed out. What is mine becomes (in my feeling) a part of *ME*. The truth of this is obvious to anyone who reflects upon his own feelings and the behaviour of other people. The degree to which (among adults) one's belongings are felt as a part of oneself varies with their nature and one's own—to one person, her clothes, to another, his tools, to a third, his money, to a fourth, books or garden. The psycho-analytic study of children and adults shows that things possessed are (in phantasy) identified with one's actual bodily self, with the body as a whole, or with its particular parts and products. And the behaviour of these little children when any belonging was attacked, or any possession challenged, fully bears this out. Their response could often hardly have been more intense had it been in truth a part of their bodily selves which was in danger.

In the case of the infant at the breast, *to have* is literally and simply to take into oneself, into one's mouth. The nipple is only *here* at all when it is in my mouth, when it is (in feeling) a part of *me*. And to bite and swallow a thing is for long the only sure way of retaining it. (The incident of N's swallowing the whistle is very clear in this connection, p. 115.) This is the ultimate form of ownership, from which all others are derived. And this is what underlies the feeling that what is *mine* is *me*.

All this holds true even of the relatively simple situation where what is owned or coveted has intrinsic value. Even here, there is a reference to other people, as potential frustrators, challengers or rivals.

But, as we have seen, a great part of the value of this, that or the other of the things which little children want to own is far from intrinsic. It arises directly from the fact that others have or want the object. And thus we enter the open field of *rivalry*. Not to have what others have, or to have less than they, is to feel small and weak and helpless. Not to be given what others have been given, or as much as they, is to feel shut out from the love and regard of the person giving. It is, indeed, to be treated as not loveworthy. This much can be seen directly from the material of the *Rivalry* section. But from the psycho-analysis of children and adults, we can go further and say that the child who is not given what others receive (whether from playmate or adult) feels this exclusion to be not merely a denial of gifts and of love, but a judgment upon him, a punishment. That is its chief bitterness, and the main source of the intensity of desire, as I hope to make clear at later points.

b. *The Motive of Power*

Instances of real aggression have been separated from those where the intention was playful; but the one sort of behaviour very readily passed over into the other. We always had to keep an eye on those manly games of " shooting " or " fighting ", especially if the smaller children were taking part with the bigger ones, lest the play should suddenly become at least half-earnest, and the little ones suffer. If the contestants were equally matched, it was safer to leave them alone. On the other hand, it was very often possible to turn at any rate a half-quarrel into a joke, and laughter was always the best solvent for hatred.

It is interesting to see how large the playful threat of *biting* looms in the make-believe aggression. That is to say, it lasts as a mode of pretending to be hostile, of " teasing," long after it is given up as a characteristic form of real behaviour. (Note Frank, for instance, on p. 46, " I only meant to tease.")

Make-believe aggression does sometimes happen to be used as a first response to a real stimulus, if the provocation is not very great. One child might threaten to do something to another, half-jokingly, and perhaps keep his manner playful as long as the watchful eye of an adult was on him—but pass over into a real attack if he thought himself unobserved, or if the playful threat did not immediately gain his end.

A good deal of teasing is included under *real* aggression, since it was felt to be real enough by the sufferer, even though the aggressor could truly say, " I wasn't *doing* anything to him—I was only saying ' pop '." Little children do not believe that " hard words break no bones ". They are quite well aware of the hostile intention behind the mere words, and react to that with true understanding. The attitude of the teasing child frightens them, since they know how easily it slips over into hostile action, and have little reason to trust the other child not to *behave* so if he *feels* so.

A more exact classification would thus have to do its work twice over—once from the point of view of the teaser, and once from that of the sufferer. And the dates of the incidents placed in the latter group would be much later than those of the former. A child can say, " I only *meant* to tease " long before he can believe that the other child " is only teasing ", or can show the delicious sense of Dan when he replied to the others' threats about " making Dan " and " putting him in " somewhere where " robbers will steal his things ": "Oh, it will only be a plasticine Dan ! " (P. 83.)

But all these children knew well enough how often teasing would have passed over into real cruelty but for the restraining presence of Mrs. I. or Miss B. One hears now and then from other sources how cruel children can be to their smaller playmates, when they have the chance. (Note, for example, the incident on p. 44.)

A great deal of the make-believe aggression, however, was true play, and independent of any real situation. These games of " shooting " and " playing battleships " are fore-runners of the older boys' " Red Indians " and " English and Germans," as well as of the more conventional competitive games. In them the phantasy of power finds an admirable outlet.

An interesting point about Harold's invented game of running round the room and threatening " to blow up " the tower he had built (20.1.25) is the part he assigns to Mrs. I. She was asked to sit near and say protestingly each time he passed, " No, *no* ! " That is to say, whilst he might play out his phantasy of omnipotent aggression, she was to represent the restraining influences within his mind, his conscience (super-ego).[1] And in the play, he did not in fact try to carry out his threat—her protests were allowed to be effective. In

---

[1] A word may be said here about the term *super-ego*, by means of which we are enabled to refer to those psychic trends of guilt and anxiety which represent, at varying levels of the mental life, the familiar fact of " conscience". Many psychologists object strongly to the use of entities of this kind, and feel happier when mental processes are expressed in purely transitive terms, i.e. as events. I myself share this feeling, and have indeed a strong prejudice against personifications in general. But whilst I have little doubt that the processes to which we refer by the term *super-ego* could in fact be expressed transitively as a series of events, there are certain reasons why I am content to accept and use this term, as well as to refer to the undifferentiated instinctual trends as a whole as the *id*, and to distinguish both from the *ego*.

These reasons are two : (a) Not only are these terms an extremely convenient shorthand for the processes in question, but (b) their actual substantivity represents a very significant psychological truth, namely, the experience of *the divided self*, the actual phenomenological experience of one " part " of the self pulling against another " part". Critics have often said that psycho-analytic theory uses far too many dramatic concepts. Mental life, however, *is* dramatic—it is indeed the source of all drama. No one who has, with any degree of self-awareness, struggled with his wishes as against his notions of what he ought to do, can doubt the reality of this drama. Moreover, the primitive mechanisms of introjection and projection, and scarcely less so that of repression, often operate with such large areas of the total personality that one is justified, for the purpose of understanding, in treating these three subdivisions of the total psyche, the *super-ego*, the *id* and the *ego*, as relatively distinct parts. As far as conscious life is concerned, it is, e.g., possible at any one time for the whole of the wish-self to be

this way, internal equilibrium was preserved, and he could go on with his phantasy play undisturbed by terror of his own omnipotent success. Here is a point which will link up with the later study of *Guilt*.

The element of *power* in these various forms of aggression is very clear. Sometimes the aggression is a direct response to interference, as when Paul says to Mrs. I., " I'll cut you up and eat you " because she will not let him go downstairs the moment he wishes. (Here we see that *eating* is not merely the surest form of ownership, but also the most effective means of getting rid of one's enemy !) Or when a grown-up does not immediately do what a child requests, as on several occasions with Harold. Sometimes a child seizes an opportunity for power that happens to present itself, as when Benjie jumps on Mrs. I.'s back while she is kneeling. Or there may be a sudden assumption of the parental rôle, as when Frank says, " George *mustn't* scribble—well, he *can* if it's for smoke," and so on. Duncan's annoyance when the other children said they could hear the rain, after he had pronounced that it *wasn't* raining (since *he* couldn't hear it) seems to be the typical parental attitude, of laying down, not merely the law, but the truth And Dan was playing a pseudo-parental rôle in deciding when and how Jessica was to take her coat off.

We cannot doubt that in most of these situations of power, the child is doing to others what he feels has so often been done to him—either in reality or in phantasy. In Frank's playing the part of the fairy " on the roof ", we have a typical dream-situation of many adults, as well as a real position that all little children like to assume whenever opportunity offers—getting " on top " of things, and being " bigger than you ", in a position of supreme control. It is the phantasy of

---

projected on to some other person, and at another, the whole of the *super-ego*.

Pseudo-scientific behaviouristic descriptions, which attempt to leave out the dramatic element in human experience, usually leave out everything that has psychological significance at the same time. I have myself seen no statement of intrapsychical conflict in terms which expressly avoid these substantives which does not lose far more significant psychological truth than it gains. The psychical truth of *feeling* is expressed in such substantives. It does feel like that ; and for the purpose of understanding the young child, these feelings seem to me far more significant than any pseudo-scientific ideology.

Nevertheless, I would deprecate any tendency to multiply the number of such substantives, and I do not think any others are needed.

displacing the parents, and being in omnipotent control of them —as they are felt by the child to be of him, in actual experience.

One of the favourite childhood games of an adult patient of my own was to stand high on top of his mother's washing-machine, pretending it was a tram, with the bell from his father's desk under his foot as the tram gong. Thus he was supreme over the possessions of both parents, and, in phantasy, over the parents themselves. He could make them start and stop as and when and where he liked. And only thus could he be either safe or good. To be a child was (for him) to be *defenceless* against untold dangers; and it was to be *bad*, since it meant being full of fear and rage and envy and forbidden wishes.

The reasons why children want to be " grown up " and powerful are thus highly complex, and some of these reasons I hope to make clearer later on.

Two reactions of Dan's are worth special mention. When Frank draws a crocodile on the floor, Dan immediately draws one too—" to bite Mrs. I." He did not dare to tell Frank it was to bite *him*, although Frank's action was the stimulus. But he knew it was safe to say it to Mrs. I., and so shifted his hostility on to her. It is pretty certain that he was playing for Frank's good-will, too, by seeking to turn *Frank's* aggression on to Mrs. I. (as is seen in so many of the incidents under *Group Hostility*).

And in the incident on 10.5.26, when Dan fell and hurt his head on the door during an angry struggle with Jessica, he at once blamed Mrs. I. for the injury, saying that she had pushed him! We can only understand this by seeing it as an expression of *guilt*. The accidental hurt became a punishment for his own hostility to Jessica. Here we have an illustration of what psycho-analysis has shown to be one of the most profound tendencies in the deepest levels of the human mind. In those levels there are no "accidents", no chances, no impersonal happenings—only frustrations and punishments by parents, or by the parental representative within the mind, the super-ego. It was, however, easier for Dan to *project* his guilt on to Mrs. I., and blame her for the hurt, than to suffer the guilt within himself. A similar projection of guilt occurred in the incident on 2.2.26, under *Group Hostility*, as well as in some of the incidents under *Anal aggression*.

c. *The Motive of Rivalry*

The main situations of open rivalry occurring at one time or another in the school records can be seen to fall into two broad lines: *rivalry with other children*, older or younger, for the love and approval of adults or of the social leaders of the group, or for the homage of the younger members; and *rivalry with an adult* for the love and possession of another adult.

1. To consider the first of these general situations: Frank, George, Benjie, Theobald, Dan, Harold, Paul, Priscilla, Jane, Conrad, Alfred, Tommy, Martin, Dexter and Joseph all show this jealousy of other children at different times and in different degrees. The further material gives many other instances of it.

It can indeed be said, taking all our evidence together, that, in the earliest years, all children (with an intensity varying according to inner conditions and outer circumstances) feel other children to be actual or potential rivals. For there is a general fact to consider, in addition to the more specific examples of obvious rivalry, viz.: that an attitude of hostility to all the other children seems to be the primary active response of any young child on entering a group. As Bridges points out, aggressive behaviour to other children appears to be so normal as to represent a definite stage in social development. Bridges regards the child who does not act in this way as " unsocial, egoistic . . . and slow in social development". Pushing or hitting or pinching the other children means at any rate a definite recognition of their existence and presence, and a definite attitude towards them. It is a step in advance on the very first and passive reaction. " When children first come to school they merely watch others passively and go their own way " (p. 44).

I found this passive (but highly defensive) watching the most common immediate response on entering the group, with the two- and three-year-olds, or those four-year-olds who had hitherto lived solitary lives, or who (like Joseph) had some negativistic traits. With most of them it was first replaced by some form of actively hostile behaviour (which in its turn typically gave way to more friendly and co-operative play, punctuated by aggression for one or other specific reason). To be able to express the felt hostility in this or that form of definite attack is undoubtedly a social advance on hostile *watching*. It means a greater freedom of feeling and of action. It shows that the child has a little less need to be ready always to defend himself, and is less inhibited by anxiety. In spite of the practical difficulties it creates for the grown-up in charge, and the disorderly air it wears to the casual visitor, this aggressive behaviour is yet the most promising first response from a young child who has not already had plenty of social experience among his fellows. It presages an active and vigorous social life in the not distant future—under careful handling. (It is another matter, of course, when this attitude persists indefinitely, or remains the main response to the overtures of other children.)

So much for mere description. But why should it happen so ? Why should little children from happy homes feel so immediately hostile on entering a group of other children ? We can hardly rest content with simply noting the fact.

It has sometimes been suggested to me that this initially hostile behaviour of young children to each other might be regarded as a form of *experimental play*—an attempt to find out what the other animals are like, with perhaps an insurance against risks by assuming that they are dangerous until proved otherwise. This seems to me true as far as it goes ; but it does not go nearly far enough. It might perhaps account for such a piece of behaviour as that of Joseph and Phineas on 29.4.27. " Lena and Joseph (Joseph's first term) were playing in the sand-pit when Phineas arrived. As soon as Phineas approached, Joseph stiffened aggressively and clenched his fists. They both eyed each other up and down hostilely for several seconds, then Joseph relaxed, Phineas moved away, and they each went on with his own pursuit. No word was spoken." But in itself it would hardly account for the real fights and mutual injuries of the three two-year-olds, for example (p. 59), or for the earnestness and frequency of attack found among the children in these school records. Deeper and more permanent motives need to be looked for, linking up this behaviour with what comes before it in the child's life, and what follows after it.

The key is surely to be found in the family situation. The immediate hostility of a young child to others is only to be understood in terms of the motive of *rivalry* for the love of adults, and primarily, of course, of the parents. It is the young child's utter dependence upon the love and care of adults, his absolute need to possess them and their love, that makes the mere presence of another child seem to him a threat to his life and love. (I have quoted these particular passages from Bridges' material under my own *Rivalry* section because I believe this is the key to them.)

As again Bridges remarks, and my own experience endorses, a small child will speak to any strange *adult* and ask for help or protection, far more readily than to a strange child. The quoted behaviour of Gerald, Martin, Joseph, is a striking illustration here; but Tommy and all the other two- and three-year-olds clung very closely to the skirts of the grown-ups when they first came. (There were a few children of this age who came towards the end of the period covered by the records, and are not quoted.) At this stage other children are *presumed* to be enemies, but adults are presumed to be lovers and protectors—at any rate, as against other children. (In the middle years of childhood, of course, say eight to twelve, the very reverse is true.)

In infancy and the first year or two after it, the child is undoubtedly orientated mainly to adults (parents). They are the sources of his joy and his safety. Other children, more especially younger ones, are at first felt to be mere intruders, whose presence stirs hostile wishes because of the dread of exclusion and of the loss of love. Friendly feelings are more readily shown towards older children.

I have elsewhere recorded a striking instance of how even the bodily weight and health of a child may be affected by the intense jealousy and anxiety aroused by the coming of a strange child to share the home.[1] In *Intellectual Growth in Young Children* I described the temporary disturbance of the mental life of Alice and of Phineas in the school when a new baby was born in their respective homes. Phineas had also a phase of great difficulty at home about this time, particularly with regard to food and feeding. He would not eat at all for a long time unless he was fed on the lap like the baby. And the story of Ursula shows how strongly the rivalry may be felt from time to time even in a child who enjoys exceptionally careful handling and who is a loving and tender child, able for the most part to feel warmly maternal and protective to the new-comer.

As regards the behaviour of the children in the Malting House School, the two youngest and smallest children at the beginning of the school were Dan and Tommy, and it will

[1] *Health and Education in the Nursery*, pp. 239-240.

be seen (in several parts of the records) how much of the hostility of the others was centred upon them. It was especially acute towards Dan, since it happened that his father took a particular interest in the school, and came in to see it more often than any other parent.

Martin's enmity to Tommy is very interesting. Tommy was the only child of Martin's own age and size, at the time. He himself showed very little hostility to Martin, and gave him hardly any cause for jealousy other than his mere presence. I have no doubt that Martin was extremely jealous of all the other children, and disliked the older and stronger ones as well because of their having teased him a little. He would never play with any of them, and never took any active notice of them, but tried always to keep one of the adults exclusively to himself. He seldom dared show open hostility to the older children, however. But as Tommy was then the smallest and most peaceable, Martin ventured to pour out some of his general hostility on to Tommy's innocent head.

Benjie's response at the time when he heard Mrs. I. call Dan " darling " is worth attention (9.12.24). " Speaking to Dan, Mrs. I. called him ' darling '. Benjie at once said, ' Why don't you call *me* that ? ' Mrs. I. replied, ' But I often do.' Benjie then said to Cecil, ' I don't like you, Cecil. I'll get a gun and shoot you dead.' " He thus turned his anger on to another and irrelevant child who happened to be near, although it must really have been Dan towards whom he felt hostile at the moment. But presumably he imagined Dan to be in Mrs. I.'s special favour just then, and so dared not attack him with her standing near. But he had to have some vent for feeling.

This incident, and Martin's enmity to Tommy, both illustrate very simply the general mental mechanism of *displacement*—the displacement of a feeling-impulse from its immediate object on to another (less dangerous) one. I hope to show that this mechanism is of the greatest general importance in the social development of young children.

These are children who show little if any open hostility to the new baby in their own family—and much less than the average to other children generally. When one studies the total behaviour of such a child, one finds a variety of reasons for this, such as home circumstances, earlier experiences (particularly during the first year), the psychological constitution of the child, and the particular mental mechanisms (identification, displacement, repression, etc.) to which he has recourse. It may be, for example, that from the beginning he succeeds in deflecting the hostility stirred by the new baby on to other objects (as in the various phobias); or in turning it on to himself in various forms of self-punishment—in either case achieving a social standard at great cost to himself. Or it may be that his aggressive impulses are constitutionally less intense, or that he has suffered less privation of one sort or another in his earliest relations with his mother; his capacity for love and his trust in the love of the parents is thus greater and more secure. As a rule, such children very early succeed in adopting a tender parental attitude to the helpless rival. The more aggressive child may also use this mechanism of identification with the parent as a mode of dealing with his fear and hatred of the intruder, but in his case the element of power and triumph will show very plainly through the cover of protection and care for the younger child. He will be a highly tyrannical parent, ordering and controlling, not allowing the other to have a soul of his own. The less aggressive child will be a less interfering and more truly helpful parent to the young brother or sister.

Bridges found, too, that the first bullying impulses of the older and bigger child to the younger and smaller usually change into a protective care, under the influence and example of the grown-ups. This is the normal course of events. But the parental attitude will not as a rule become altogether stable and reliable until much later in childhood. It will naturally break down under any special stress. The majority of ordinary children under adolescence will show both attitudes, now bullying, now protective, to the younger children, from occasion to occasion, with of course individual variations in emphasis. And very naturally, they will be the more tender and protective when under the watching eye of an adult, and in a stable environment such as a good nursery school, and the more readily teasing or tyrannical when left alone with the little ones, or when in a less satisfactory general environment.

But this identification of himself with the parent on the part of the older child is itself one of the more subtle grounds for the rivalry *among* the older children for the affection and homage of the younger members of the group. The (unconscious) logic of the situation might be expressed thus: " If the little ones love *me* better than they love you, that is a proof that I am better than you, i.e. less jealous of them, less hostile to them, less hostile to my parents for having them, more loving and loveworthy." *Or* (with the more aggressive nature—but to some extent even with the more loving) " a proof that I am more *powerful*, less open to attack from them and/or my parents". " But if they love and obey *you* more than they love and obey me, that is a proof not only of my helplessness against them, but of my badness, and of my helplessness against you and my avenging parents."

It is from this sort of source that the tussle between the children for social prestige in the group draws its intensity. Success and failure alike go deep into the unconscious life of the child, into his own needs and anxieties with regard to his parents.

In passing, it may be said that the actual experience of the child among his fellows does a great deal to help in the transformation of his first hostile impulses into protection and care, or into friendly co-operation. The initial hostility itself largely springs from unconscious *phantasy*—the phantasy of danger and exclusion and loss of love. But actual experience (with loving parents or a wise teacher) gradually lessens the hold of this phantasy over the child's feelings. He discovers that the grown-ups do still in reality love and value and cherish him, and that the other child is not such a dangerous enemy as he feared. And he discovers also that the other child may even become an *ally* against the parents themselves, those terribly powerful arbiters of life and love. And so he begins to seek and enjoy the pleasures of companionship and *togetherness* with other children.

The value of real experience among other children (when it is good and not bad) is seen very clearly with such a child as Joseph, at four and five years of age so unfriendly and suspicious of other children. In spite of this early negative attitude, Joseph did become more companionable and freer in his social relations. And he is reported as being much easier and happier, in the preparatory school where he now is, with understanding adults and an active social life.

Here, then, we glimpse another point which bears upon early education.

2. The survey of the rivalry felt towards other children thus leads us to the primary relation of the child to his parents, and opens up the second type of rivalry situation, that felt *towards one adult* (or older child functioning as an adult) for the love and possession of another. But this is a situation which for its full understanding needs consideration in the sexual as well as the social field, and I shall be able to deal with it more justly after surveying the material classified under *Sexuality*. For the moment I will glance only briefly at its more general significances.

Frank, Dan and Penelope all offer us the most striking examples of this sense of rivalry with an adult (usually of the same sex). The degree of Frank's sensitiveness to the presence of adult rivals was most striking. Whenever Dan's father entered the school, for instance, Frank changed in a moment from active gaiety to sulky destructiveness. Penelope, too, seemed rarely able to be loving both to a man friend and a woman friend at the same time. Nor did Dan, throughout the first year of the school, find himself able to love both Mrs. I. and her assistant at once. If he was loving to the one, he was hostile to the other. It was felt to be a great step forward in development when he could be friendly to both together. Many of the children quoted from other sources demonstrate this type of rivalry unmistakably, too. N.'s anxiety for the safety of her mother is hardly to be understood save in terms of an unconscious hostile wish for her mother's death, a wish that was expressed in many half-veiled forms. " If you would go away, I could cut my hair as I liked." (N. was at this time specially defiant and hostile with her mother.) Ursula also gives us many glimpses of her wish to replace her mother in her father's affections, and to be herself the mother of the new baby, in spite of her real personal devotion to her mother. At other times she seemed to want to exclude her father from the realm of her mother's attention.

Leaving on one side for the moment the question of sexual preference, it can be said of little children in general that they tend to be jealous and afraid of the relationship between their parents—or indeed between any *significant* adults. And when one young child is present with the two parents (or parent-figures) he will very often try to part them in feeling, and to win one of them over to himself, against the other.

It seems (using our psycho-analytic evidence to illuminate observed behaviour) to be not merely that the child wants to reign supreme himself in the heart of one or other of the parents, not merely that he feels that if they love each other they cannot love him as *fully* as he would like, but sometimes also that their love for each other is an actual *menace* to him. It does not seem to him merely that they are not showing their love for him, not attending to him for the moment. It very often seems as if they are *withdrawing* their love from him. He feels literally left out in the cold; the life-giving love he needs is actually taken from him. For to the very young child love is not first and foremost a state of mind, nor is it even a way of behaviour—it is something much more concrete than these. It consists of concrete physical experiences and even of actual bodily substances. It is (first and ultimately) the breast and the mother's milk—the smell and taste and warmth, the firm clasp of arms and contact of surfaces, the filling up of a cold void by the warm firm nipple and stream of milk. And this cannot be *shared*—it is either given or withheld. This is what love means for the child in his first actual experience, and what it remains in the deepest levels of unconscious phantasies. And these phantasies dominate much of his behaviour in the years we are now studying.

There are many further complications of feeling arising from the repercussion upon the child of his own rage and envy, with its consequent guilt and anxiety. To these I shall return later. But considering only the simplest and most direct aspect of the child's situation when he fears the mutual love of the parents, it should be possible for us to see how natural it is that he should feel jealous of the love of father for mother, of mother for father, of any two adults upon whom he depends for love and care—if we try to feel the situation as it comes to him in actual sensory experience at the earliest levels of mental development. It should be possible for us to understand why he so often seeks to attach the one or the other entirely to himself.

In my notes of recent years, I have gathered a great many instances of the way in which children who are friendly and amenable when with one grown-up only will become fractious and perverse as soon as another enters on the scene. A child may be happy and obedient with either the mother or the father, but disagreeable when both are there. He may contentedly obey the nurse when she has him alone, and be difficult when the mother comes into the nursery. He may be good with either mother or nurse separately, and contrary with the two together. It seems indeed a universal tendency of little children to become more difficult when two or more grown-ups are present than when with one alone.

A young child does not of course mind more than one adult being present *provided* they all centre their interest upon *him*. There is indeed nothing that a child under five or six enjoys more than having a group of adults pliant to his will, doing what he suggests and admiring what he says and does. And tiny children very commonly are given this delight from time to time, when, for instance, a group of admiring aunts and visitors gather round him at bath-time! It is always the adults who tire of this situation, never the child. The occasions when he has this pleasure of being the centre of attention, however, are normally few and far between. And the trouble for the child begins when the grown-ups withdraw their interest from him, begin to talk or smile or laugh with each other, do things together or appear in any way to shut him out from their love and regard. (Priscilla's suspicion of Mrs. I. and Miss B. when they shared some joke together shows how ready a child may be to fear that the grown-ups are joined together to laugh at her.) The commonest circumstance for troublesome behaviour arising from this jealousy is of course provided by the family meal-table. I have a great many records of special contrariness and defiance in small children at the general meal-table.

When a little child begins to whine and be contrary the very moment a second adult appears on the scene, although up to that moment he has been happy and docile with one, this is usually because he already knows very well that they will not subdue themselves to his wishes or direct their interest entirely to him. They are more likely to talk *about* him, or to unite in deciding what he is to do. At any rate he feels uneasy when both are present, and has recourse to querulousness and contrariness.

What the child very often tries to do in these circumstances is to *part* the grown-ups, to create dissension and strife between them. And it is astonishing how subtly clever even quite small children can be in bringing about tensions between parents, or between mother and nurse, causing one to criticise the other and to side with the child against the other. I have watched the actual process many times with certain children, and marked how acutely they seem to appreciate the weak places in the mutual relation of the particular grown-ups.

Psycho-analytic studies have shown moreover that this wish to separate the parents, to get in between them and win one of them to oneself, is always found in the deeper and unconscious levels of every individual mind. " He that is not with us is against us " is the child's universal cry. And when it seems that the two parents *together* are not-with-us-but-against-us, the way is opened to our ultimate terrors of loss and privation and destruction. At all costs they must be parted, and made aware of *our* needs and our demand for love.

There is another and very important factor in this attitude of the child to the presence of more than one grown-up, however, which must at least be mentioned at this point, viz. the child's *ambivalence* of feeling towards every adult, and towards both the parents singly. Even his loved mother is not only loved. She is feared and hated as well. The child inevitably feels hostile to her in part, since he early suffers inescapable denials and thwartings at her hands (as we shall see in discussing *Sexuality*). And this loving and hating of the same so important person is itself a source of great tension in his mind. But the presence of the two parents or two women brings him momentary relief from this tension—if he can part them—by enabling him to turn most of his hostility on to the one, and so have the delight of loving the other more whole-heartedly. (This was undoubtedly the chief key to Dan's behaviour, for example, when both Miss B. and Mrs. I. were in close relation with him.) This ambivalence of feeling is of the greatest significance in children's social development, and I shall have to say a good deal more about it presently.

The degree of tension arising in this fundamental situation of one child with two grown-ups will naturally depend upon a number of factors. It will show itself in quieter tones with older children and with less intimate and important grown-ups than it does with the very young child and his parents.

And even in the home it will be affected by the attitude and behaviour of the parents as well as by the particular psychology of the child. Many children and many parents are able to deal with the difficulties of this rivalry in mutual consideration and understanding. Some of them are able to cover it up or transmute it altogether; but no psycho-analytic theory is needed to show us the frequent instances of serious failure. Another general problem of early education thus obviously arises here.

In the nursery school, one does not usually see such rivalries anything like so plainly and acutely as in the home, partly because the presence of the many other children prevents the triangular situation arising between two adults and one child, partly because there is not as a rule any special relationship between any one child and any one member of the staff. Nor does the behaviour of the adults in charge lend itself so readily as that of the mother or the nurse at home to highly charged emotions; and interest is much more widely diffused.

Those instances in the Malting House School records where the feeling of rivalry with an adult was so marked each arose from a specific set of circumstances. Dan's feelings about Miss B. and myself, for example, were so acute largely because Miss B. had been Dan's governess before the school began. This special claim of Dan on Miss B. in its turn heightened Frank's hostility to her, itself so vivid in the early days of the school, although of course it died down later on as Miss B.'s disinterested relation with him and all the other children was built up. Frank's hostility to Dan's father (and to me when Dan's mother was openly affectionate to Dan in the presence of the other children) was again heightened by the special relationship of the adult in question.

3. In addition to the two main lines of rivalry we have now considered there was throughout almost the whole history of the school a special situation of acute rivalry between certain of the most influential of the children, a situation which did not fall into either of these two main patterns. It approximated much more closely to the sexual rivalries among *equals* in grown-up life. We were in fact after the first two terms never without a " triangle " of

two boys and one girl, or two girls and one boy (or more as a group), in deadly rivalry. The first of the three triangular situations was between Frank, Dan and Priscilla; the second, Christopher, Dan and Priscilla; and the third, a struggle between Priscilla and Jane, for the love and homage of Dan (in particular). Dan was a good deal the youngest child in each case, but his unusually vivid personality, coupled with his intimate friendship with Priscilla out of school, discounted the difference in age and made him a sufficiently formidable rival to the others. The various incidents described show how intense the rivalry was in each case, how far the successful rival would go in triumph over the excluded one, and how bitterly that exclusion was felt.

The third of these triangular situations was rather more complicated than the others. Jane's superiority in age to all the other children not only gave her prestige over the whole group, but emphasised the element of *power* rather than of love in her struggle with Priscilla. Dan was the main point of that struggle, although all the other younger children who had any interest at all for Jane were drawn into the arena as well. But it appeared as if Jane was more concerned to show her power over Priscilla than she was to enjoy the affection of Dan and the other small boys. Priscilla had now for the first time to suffer defeat, after having hitherto been in the ineffable position of the one sought after and contested for. It was in fact a very severe experience for her, unfortunately made more so by the accident that it largely coincided with a long absence of Mrs. I.'s from the school through illness, and the fact that Jane was far less amenable to the control or critical opinion of other members of the staff. (Much of this material will be found under *Group Hostility to Younger Children*, since Jane succeeded in welding most of the other children together into a group against Priscilla. But Jane was the mainspring of the machinery, and the whole situation was really a personal and sexual rivalry between the two girls.)

An interesting cross-current is shown in Dan's remark to Jane on 14.11.26, " Priscilla doesn't like you as much as me." Dan here felt Jane to be a rival with him for Priscilla's regard, and probably feared that Priscilla and Jane might band *together* against him, although he had in truth little reason to imagine such a possibility. And Jane's response,

" Does she like Conrad *at all* ? " gives another instance of the device so common among the children of soliciting the favour of one person by being ready to be hostile to another. Conrad himself has recourse to the same dodge when on 29.11.26 he seeks to curry favour with Jane by expressing his hostility to Lena. The implication clearly is " It is *she* I hate and *you* I love."

d. *Feelings of Inferiority, Superiority or General Anxiety*

The main descriptive character which the majority of these incidents have in common is that the hostility shown had no immediate or obvious stimuli. Frank and Cecil, for instance, on many days displayed a hostile and aggressive mood from the moment they entered the schoolroom. Both these boys, as well as Benjie, Conrad, Dexter, Joseph and to a less extent Harold and Theobald, were liable to become spiteful and perverse at any moment, without *apparent* provocation. (This characteristic grew less in every case with experience in school. It was very noticeably less in Frank during his second year.)

In the quotation from Bridges included under the present heading, she speaks of children sometimes " hitting or pinching for fun ", behaviour which is distinguished from " hitting in anger " by " the lack of a provoking cause ". Now hitting " for fun " did occur with my children too. It is naturally recognisable by the child's manner and facial expression. But the instances of unprovoked aggression quoted here were not "for fun". The children showed, by gesture, tone of voice or facial expression (even when the attack was merely verbal) that they were much in earnest, and were feeling a definite emotion of fear or anger or hatred or contempt at the time.

It is true that those instances where one might use the description " hitting for fun " are not *sharply* divided off from aggression of the moody type illustrated here. The two types merge at their boundaries. And this I believe is true just because there are deeper aspects of the " hitting for fun " than that too simple and superficial description suggests. The " fun " element, the laughter or air of amused inquiry accompanying the more playful attack, is certainly in part a direct expression of the sadistic *pleasure* of attacking ; but it also has the function of disarming the person attacked, persuading him that " there's no harm in it", turning aside his retaliation. And thus it expresses the fear of retaliation. But the very need to "hit in fun" is itself the need to prove that it is *safe* to do so, the need to test out deep sadistic phantasies in real experience.

This view of the "hitting for fun" as a testing out in real behaviour of unconscious phantasies is not based only on general psycho-analytic findings. It rests also on the direct psycho-analytic study of one of the very children in my own group who showed less real and more *make-believe* aggression than any other of the children. Christopher very rarely indeed hit or attacked any of the other children with serious intent, and was altogether a companionable and lovable child. But he had a roguish delight in *pretending* to attack, and no one could take offence when his brown eyes sparkled with laughter as he did it. It was he who ran off with another boy's bricks, laughing and saying, "I am the stealer." And two of the instances under *Make-believe Aggression* show the same hearty fun in playful attack. (22.3.26) "After lunch, when Mrs. I. was helping the children to wash the plates, Christopher and Dan kept smacking her in fun, with hearty laughter, but very persistently. When she asked them not to do so, Dan would have stopped but Christopher would not—until she said that if they went on, she would leave them to wash their own plates. They then stopped, with amused comments—'Oh, if we smack her, she won't wash up!'" 11.2.25: "Christopher and George made a 'train' by putting several tables together. Presently Tommy got into their train, and said, 'This is a monkey'; Christopher and Tommy sat side by side, and squealed, and jumped about and crawled as 'monkeys' for some time. Christopher in this way got rather excited and flushed, and began to do roguish things to tease Mrs. I.—running off with a pencil and notebook from her shelf. There was no malice in this, and when she asked him to replace them, he did so." Now for various reasons Christopher was analysed during his second year in the school by one of the leading child analysts. This was arranged by the parents and of course was quite independent of the school. But the analyst, Miss M. N. Searl, has told me since that it became very apparent during the course of this treatment how overwhelming was Christopher's *unconscious* aggression, and how enormous the anxieties to which it gave rise. His playful attacks were a safety-valve for this unconscious aggression, the only one he could allow himself, and at the same time an attempt to allay the associated anxiety.[1]

Even "hitting for fun" may thus take us deep into the child's internal psychic problems.

But to return to the behaviour included under the present heading. These outbreaks of moody hostility in certain children (and most of the children showed them, although in widely varying degree) were too sporadic and covered too long a period of time to fall into the class of *initial* hostility shown to other children as potential rivals. A feeling of rivalry probably does enter into this moodiness (as the behaviour of Benjie and Martin, for instance, suggests): but the moodiness is not aroused by any immediate or specific behaviour of other children. It is either a postponed response to earlier stimuli, or the effect of the general situation of rivalry acting indirectly and chronically.

Now and again we could catch a glimpse of a definite although more remote stimulus, as for example when Frank sometimes inadvertently called Dan by the name of his own younger brother. His hostility thus showed itself largely displaced from the direct rivalry with his brother at home. (Frank was reported to be even more difficult at home than in school.)

Moreover, the element of rivalry in this moody hostility was with certain of the children very clearly bound up with a general sense of their own relative helplessness or ineffectiveness. Cecil was a particularly clear example of this. He was a large but loose-jointed and clumsy child, who could do nothing skilfully. Everything he tried to build fell down, to his own distress and chagrin. He could not even wash his own hands when he first came to school at four years of age, having been trained to no sort of independence at home. It was very noticeable how his aggressiveness became less as his skill and self-confidence grew greater.

Among the inner stimuli responsible for unprovoked hostility to other children, thus, feelings of *inferiority* are clearly significant. But these feelings of inferiority very often express themselves in an aggressive assertion of

[1] In my third volume, *Individual Histories*, I hope to be able to include alongside the picture he presented in the school records an account of Christopher from the side of the analysis, by M. N. Searl. The third volume was never written.

superiority, as many of the instances quoted show. Conrad and Joseph both give us striking examples, and it needs no psycho-analyst to see the sense of inferiority behind their bombast. Theobald's contempt for other people's drawings, and his curiously deliberate destruction of the labels the other children had written for the schoolroom, very probably arose from an acute sense of his own relative ineffectiveness. Laurie's unfortunate attack on the unoffending Priscilla must have arisen in the same way. The push he gave the ladder on which she stood must have expressed all the bitter exasperation he felt against the boys who had tormented him by saying " pop ", and against his mother who had taunted him with being cowardly and helpless. (Their saying " pop " in his ear was the worst he had suffered from them, and he was the equal in size of any of them, and amongst the oldest.)

The incident when Martin walked about saying, " I am a *man* " and " That's *my* broom " is included here rather than under *Motive of Possession*, since his manner suggested that his momentary claim on the broom was a part of his self-aggrandisement. It was not so much a wish for the broom to be really his, but a phantasy that it *was* his, part of his phantasy of " being a man ".

I have included here a few incidents that actually had some sort of immediate stimulus, because the response of the child at the time was one which hinted at feelings of inferiority, and an attempt to deal with these by pretending to be grown-up or superior. Paul's comments to Frank's refusing to let him have any plasticine is a case in point (6.3.25). " Paul told Mrs. I. and said in the tone of a disapproving grown-up, ' I am *very* disappointed with him. I am very angry with him.' " This is a more subtle response than direct anger, and has a priggish note.

Priscilla's attitude when Mrs. I. had not obeyed her behest to get her an apple from the tree again suggested some more subtle feeling than anger. She seemed to feel Mrs. I.'s refusal as an insult, not merely as a denial ; and again we have a link with feelings of inferiority.

Duncan, again, seemed to be insulted at Dan's suggestion that he *could* do anything to anyone so strong as Duncan ; and Conrad could not bear the other children to have any glimpse of his distress at being physically hurt. (Conrad was especially sensitive in this respect.)

For the same reason I have included here Benjie's breaking of his plate when Mrs. I. told him he could not have any pudding after he had spat into the pudding dish. His manner did not suggest simple fury at being denied something or interfered with. It wore an air of guilt and distress at being treated as deserving such reproof.

Again, in the quarrel between Priscilla and Dan (p. 67), the striking thing was not so much the aggression each child showed, as the way each treated the other as blameworthy, "It was you pushed me." "No, it wasn't, you pushed me," each feeling that this fault of the other was a sufficient justification of his own annoyance.

It is clear that in its aspect of inferiority, this moody hostility is not far removed from the simpler motive of seeking power. But the power longed for is on the whole more subtle and indirect. The child is sensitive about social and moral rather than physical prestige.

This type of behaviour thus readily carries us over into the field of *guilt and shame*. There is, indeed, a considerable overlap between the material illustrating these feelings of inferiority and moody hostility, and that of *guilt and shame*, many examples being quite ambiguous. At a later point I shall in fact suggest that the major source of this unprovoked and moody aggression lies in unconscious guilt and anxiety. It will, however, be easier to deal with this point after examining the material of *Group Hostility*, *Sexuality* and *Guilt*.

2. GROUP HOSTILITY

It will have been clear to readers that no sharp boundary can be drawn between individual and group hostility. With such young children, the group has no permanence or organisation. It comes to momentary life at the behest of one of the older or more influential children. This is true enough even of children of later years, and of some forms of spontaneous group behaviour in adults, as all popular movements demonstrate. But with very young children, it is unqualifiedly true. The most lasting and cohesive group feeling shown in all these records was probably the hostility to Priscilla fostered by Jane, and this was a function of the fact that she was the oldest and most socially powerful of all the children who came to the school at any period. The group she created depended entirely upon her presence and prestige. It did not exist when she was not there to keep it alive. In a lesser degree, in the earlier days of the school, the leadership of Frank was potent in creating a group feeling of hostility either towards one of the younger children whom he did not favour, or towards one of the grown-ups—as in his happier moods, it was equally effective in engendering friendliness and co-operation.

Since, then, group hostility in little children is the fruit of individual influence, the fundamental motives at work will be found much the same as in individual hostility. The motives of possession, of power, of rivalry and of the sense of inferiority can all be seen operating in the various incidents detailed. I grouped the material of this section, however, rather with a view to bringing out some of those characteristics of group feeling which do differentiate it from individual emotions. The *object* of hostility, rather than the subjective ground, is the basis of classification here; but it will be seen that this offers a clue to the underlying motive in each case.

To consider now some of the broad general differences between individual and group hostility:

(1) The actual number of occasions of *group* hostility is less than those of individual aggression among the members of the group, for such reasons as have already been touched upon. (*a*) Children of these years are emotionally dependent upon *adults*, and see a more direct relation with them than with each other. The two- and three-year-olds cannot yet experience even that degree of fellow-feeling which makes a *common* dislike of another child possible; they are still too closely orientated to adults, and bound up in egocentric attitudes. With the older children of course, this becomes progressively less true; and it is with, say, the four- and five-year-olds that genuine group phenomena begin to occur. (*b*) The "group" (in the sense of two or more children welded together by a common purpose or a common feeling) even then has but a momentary existence, and is quite unorganised. It comes and goes, whilst the individual stays.

(2) Yet, once that level of social development is reached which makes possible a common emotion among two, three or more children, hostility is found to be more vividly shown in the group than in most children acting individually. It

is quite certain that none of these children acting singly would have felt able to express their hostility, whether annoyance with adult interference or dislike of other children, so openly and unreservedly as they do in some of these group episodes. This has some application even to many of the incidents listed under *Individual Hostility*. Even when the group was not acting as a whole, the presence of other familiar children clearly brought a stout heart to many an angry child. All children (of, say, four years or more) will go further in open expressions of hostility when " egged on " by the words or even the mere presence of their fellows. And there are many children who would never dare to express open hostility to an older or bigger child or to an adult, save when other children are about and perhaps joining in.

Thus, whilst group feeling in little children is evanescent, it may be warm and vivid whilst it lasts; and it may reach levels of dramatic intensity which at any rate very many of the individual members of the group would rarely if ever attain by themselves. (In this respect, the behaviour of young children is but another illustration of the familiar facts of " crowd psychology ".)

(3) I have already drawn attention to the device common among these little children of soliciting the favour of one by evincing or by trying to incite hostility to another. This, as has been seen, occurs as a feature of individual hostility, and of rivalry among three children. It is in fact one of the essential mechanisms by which the child begins to pass out of his egocentric attitudes into true social feeling. It gives us a fundamental key to the beginnings of group relations.

Through the operation of this mechanism, even two persons may be welded into a primitive group. When, of three individuals, one succeeds in getting another to join with him in antagonism to the third, the relation between the two joined together in common emotion is quite different from their direct mutual relation as two separate individuals. A sense of *togetherness* is born between them, fostered and heightened by the enmity to the third. *We* are together against him, the outsider.

The mechanism is clearer to our eyes when it operates with more than three persons, when we have what would ordinarily and descriptively be called a " group " of several children, playing together and showing pleasure in each other's company. Such groups tend of course to be very small, in children of these years. If there were, say, a dozen children playing in the garden or schoolroom, not more than three or four, or occasionally five, would be taking any friendly notice of each other, or playing "together". The rest of the dozen would, as far as the first (or any one particular group) was concerned, be treated either as non-existent, or as a *rival* group. That is to say, the "inter-tribal" relation would practically always be either complete indifference or active hostility. In children under six or thereabouts, the *area* which can be covered by actively friendly feeling seems to be strictly limited. These very small groups of three to five members thus form a definite transition between the primary egocentric attitude of the first three years and the more inclusive social entities which become possible later on. The groups to which any warm regard can be attached remain, of course, closely limited until the period of adolescence; but in the middle years of childhood, they are larger than in these first beginnings.

Even, however, when there are only four or five children present together in the garden or playroom, not more than might readily form one of the small groups possible in these ages, it still tends to happen that this small number is split into at least two groups—perhaps three children in one and two in the other, or four in a group and one shut outside. Sometimes, of course, there would be no *group* at all, but just four or five individuals playing separately. But whenever two or three or more of these young children draw together in feeling or aim sufficiently to create a group, they *tend* in their very drawing together, to find an enemy to the group, an outsider, one shut out and hated. It would seem that the existence of such an outsider is in the beginning an essential condition of any warmth of *togetherness* within the group.

The frequency and automaticity of this phenomenon was very striking. So was the vividness and intensity of hostility frequently expressed towards the group enemy.

We have here, in fact, one of the chief mechanisms by which the problem of *ambivalence of feeling* (mentioned in passing at an earlier point) is dealt with by the child. It is one of his main solutions for the psychological tension arising from the fact that he both loves and hates his fellows. (I shall come presently to the question of the child's ambivalence towards adults ; it simplifies discussion to take these situations separately in the first instance. And I shall discuss the deeper sources of ambivalence of feeling when discussing *sexuality*.)

At this point, we can throw the problem into relief by bringing together a number of facts already noted. We have seen, for instance, the initial hostility of very young children towards each other, and the marked aggression which even one- and two-year-olds may show towards rivals. We have noted the many forms and occasions of individual hostility occurring between individual children even when they have played familiarly together. We have seen, too, how warm and vivid their feelings of mutual love and admiration can be. The striking thing about the emotional life of young children is indeed the readiness with which attitudes change. The child who is at this moment saying, " Oh, I do, *do* love you ! " may at the next moment be saying, "You beast ! I hate you !" Even towards his best friends a child may burst out in furious anger on any stimulus—or sometimes, in the case of some children at least, without any " good " or immediate reason in the other's behaviour. And then soon again he may be admiring and loving his friend and obeying his behest. From laughter to tears, from admiration to contempt, from love to hatred, is but a moment's step in these early years. And each emotion in turn is experienced fully and intensely. There is no balanced feeling, no stable attitude.

When we do see the beginning of a more stable relation, a more steady attitude of friendliness in one child for another, we commonly find at work the mechanism we are now considering—that of *hating someone else instead*. In other words, the child is able to love one of his fellows more wholeheartedly, more faithfully, more steadily, *because he has turned his hostility on to another*.

Our understanding of this mechanism was not arrived at by direct observation, although we can in direct observation of very little children see it plainly at work. It was gained through psycho-analytic studies.

Every adult and every child, whether neurotic or normal, whose inner life has been penetrated by the psycho-analytic technique has been shown to have a much greater ambivalence of feeling than he is consciously aware of. Even towards those whom he loves much and with whom he maintains a satisfactory relation, there is found *unconscious* hostility. How far this unconscious hostility affects adversely his day-to-day intercourse with the loved person will depend on a number of different factors, which it is not relevant to discuss at this point. (Among other things, the original intensity of his hostility and sadism towards his first love-objects, his parents; the mechanisms he employs for dispersing, shifting or hiding it—and his psychological history in detail.) The neurotic is relatively unsuccessful in these aims, but the difference between the neurotic and the normal lies only in the final outcome of these various forces and mechanisms.

The particular mechanism of *displacement*, the shifting of a feeling-impulse from its true object on to a substitute, is one of the more significant ways by which adults as well as children purify their feelings towards those whom they desire to love or are afraid to hate. It is seen in every analysis how the patient turns his unconscious grudges and aggressive wishes from wife or parent or child on to some third person, towards whom he can indulge some measure of open expression, and disguise the true object from himself. It is seen how the patient vents the anger, the contempt, the complaints, the fears felt towards the analyst himself, in open expression about someone else. But the mechanism can always be laid bare, and the true object of feeling traced, since the patient usually gives plenty of indirect signs as to where his emotions really belong.

The reciprocal relation between loving one's friends and hating one's enemies can be plainly seen in many sides of ordinary social life among adults, too. The most impressive example is patriotism in war time. The flame of national devotion burns far brighter when men's hearts are drained of hatred and aggression towards their own countrymen by the common enemy. It was this that made possible the exaltation of self-sacrifice felt by so many patriots in every belligerent country during the early days of the Great War.

It can be clearly seen in class warfare, in the struggles of political parties, and in racial conflict, wherever one looks. The local loyalties of town and country make use of it to sustain civic pride. And it serves the minor as well as the more heroic affairs of men. It is always at work in the rivalries of sport. It is the key to the proverbial " back-biting " of women (or of men!) when they indulge in personal small talk. The friends of the moment glow with a sisterly warmth towards each other as they join in " pulling to pieces " the looks or the reputation of one not present, who is sacrificed as a common enemy. In every direction, it seems far easier to love "my neighbour as myself" when we share a common foe.[1]

To return to the behaviour of our children : it should now be clear that group *hostility* is closely bound up with the first dawnings of group *togetherness*. Through this turning outward of hostility from my fellows within the group to those who are not my fellows, who are outsiders, foreigners, enemies, I am able to love my friends and fellow-members more cordially, more purely and more steadfastly. The enemy is a foil and an assurance to the friend.

At a later point, I shall have to make clear that my account of group hostility as it stands here is too simple. When I come to the discussion of *Guilt and Shame*, I shall try to show that more than a mere *displacement* of one's hostile feelings from friend to enemy is involved. The mechanism of *projection* is also at work. The hated enemy is not only a substitute for the friend ; he is a scapegoat too, a representative of *my* bad self. *It is he hates my friend, not I.* I hate and condemn *him* for his hate to my friend, and feel justified in doing so by my own loyalty.

To this aspect of group hostility I shall return. Let us now look at the function of this splitting of love and hate in the social development of little children.

The casting forth of hatred and aggression on to outsiders not only brings to those within the group a warm sense of togetherness. It makes possible the active experience of *doing* things together. Egocentric isolation is broken down in action as well as feeling. The members of the group are enabled to follow a common aim. Common habits, common standards of judgment and behaviour slowly set their seal upon individual wishes and opinions, and a common history is built up. In this way, the group gradually gains some ascendancy over its individual members, slowly assumes an organisation and wins a measure of permanence.

---

[1] The more profound bearing on the problems of civilisation of these facts of ambivalence of feeling and the need for the displacement of hostility has recently been discussed by Freud in his *Civilization and its Discontents*, Hogarth Press, 1930.

In the years of childhood under study, the stability of group relations is still very tentative, and closely dependent upon the leadership of adults. I am examining tendencies and conditions rather than achievements.

It is not only positive relations within the group that come to enjoy some degree of permanence and organisation. The external rivalry, too, undergoes elaboration in social forms. For example, every form of competitive group game, in these years or later, builds up this rivalry, and serves to legitimise and honour it. It is implicit in all the loyalties of team or club and school or village. As educators, we have long made use of these group rivalries to break down the isolation of the individual and to foster group consciousness and pride of achievement. But we commonly turn our gaze from the negative to the positive side, preferring to dwell upon devotion to *this* group rather than on the correlative enmity to *that*. Yet the one largely implies and rests upon the other.

The function of these group rivalries is of course a continuous one. It is not only in its initiation that group loyalty rests upon the mechanism of displacement, but throughout its history. There is a continual drainage of the hostility aroused by the inevitable minor clashes of interest between the individuals forming the group, outward to the rival group. When this fails, or the tension of civil strife is so increased by events that the mechanism can no longer cope with it, the group breaks up.

The main direction of change in the social contacts of young children is thus that their loves and their hates alike become slowly stabilised. The fluid and fleeting attitudes of the earliest years settle down by means of experience and of history into the more organised and socially honoured group loyalties and rivalries. And the naive, spontaneous group fellowships and animosities so clearly shown in the years of these records form the bridge which carries each child over from his early egocentric attitudes to recognisably social modes of feeling, thinking and doing.

But the process is gradual. There is no sudden metamorphosis of the egoist into the socialist, at any given age. The change goes on at different rates in different children, and is in all of them subject to moods and occasions. In a moment of internal stress or external strain, any and every young child may break loose from his social bonds. Yet the process of growth continues, until the comparatively stable social relations of the middle years of childhood are achieved.

To look now at the different directions of group hostility which the school material illustrates:

a. To strangers and new-comers.

There is little now needing to be said about this specific type of group hostility. It obviously bears an intimate relation to the individual motive of rivalry, and repeats in a more developed form the very young child's first response to all strange children. But this is heightened in intensity and in toughness by group feeling. It is harder to win a group to be friendly to a new-comer than it is a single child—at any rate after the first four years. If the leader sets the desired fashion, the rest will tend to follow; if he remains hostile, the others of his group will be so too—as long as he is near them. Fortunately, the grown-up in charge is in the long run more influential than even the most effective leader among children of these ages, so that it is not difficult to change the mood of the group towards the new child, at any rate after the first spontaneous expression of suspicion and dislike.

It is very interesting to find so early and so clearly expressed that attitude of hostility towards new-comers with which we are long familiar in older children and in young adults in school or college—or in any close-knit social group. It would thus appear to be not merely a social convention, but a spontaneous and integral mode of human reaction.

In the incident on 10.2.27, Lena voiced unmistakably the child's naive assumption that people "don't like you—because they haven't seen you before".

I quote only to differ from it, Bridges' view that "if a child has been scolded and shunned or even chased by the group, it is almost as sure a sign of the social undesirability of his behaviour as any of his own behaviour manifestations", which she applies even to the new child. The hostile reaction of a group of young children to new-comers at least seems to me quite undiscriminating. As several of my instances show, it may be felt and expressed even before the child has actually appeared, on mere hearing that he is to come. It does not therefore depend in the first instance upon the real qualities of the new-comer. But its *disappearance* may depend on his actual behaviour. If he is persistently disagreeable and aggressive, or frightened and foolish, the dislike of the other children and their pleasure in tormenting him will be more likely to endure. If he is affable, confident and courageous, they will the sooner admit him to their ranks. But it is not necessarily on such qualities as the adults would judge favourably that a child gains the approval of the group. It may be that he has some personal prestige or quality of likableness that catches their fancy at once; but it may well be merely that he possesses some toy that the others covet, and hope to be allowed to use if they show love to him. *In the long run*, it is probably true that a child who is shunned or teased by the majority of the other children is himself unlovable in one way or another. But it is not necessarily so in the short run. As these records show, the judgments no less than the feelings of little children are too changeable and subjective to be trusted in appraisement of one of their number.

b. To adults

Here we touch upon very significant facts, which will carry us further in the understanding of social development.

In discussing the *Rivalry* section of the records, I drew attention to the way in which so many little children turn more querulous and defiant when a second grown-up appears on the scene. I suggested that this behaviour was to be understood partly as the need of the child to part the two parents, because of his fear of their being united against him; and partly as the splitting of the love and hate he feels towards each parent singly. It is this second aspect which I must take up again here. For the moment I shall start from the simple fact of observation that the child does feel both affection and hostility to both father and mother, and shall postpone the discussion of the deeper genetic sources of this ambivalence until *Sexuality*. The fact itself can be observed, quite apart from any theory of its genesis. It can be seen in ordinary life any day, as well as in these records. Every young infant and little child will show anger and defiance to either parent—although most of them display more open hostility to the one or the other. The degree of this ambivalence and the intensity of hostile feeling varies much from one child to another; but there is never a child who does not show it at some period, in some situations, and in some measure. And the individual study by the psycho-analytic method of children of two years of age and onwards has demonstrated that *unconscious* hostility, and the anxiety aroused by it, are always very much more intense than ordinary observation shows—alike in the more openly aggressive and " difficult " children and in the more docile.

As will be seen from the passage I quote on p. 72, Bridges takes the view that the open expression of defiance towards an adult again represents a definite advance in the child at a certain stage. It hints at greater confidence in facing the world, and must in part be an expression of dawning self-awareness. This observational view is fully confirmed by psycho-analytic studies. It is the children whose anxiety about aggressive wishes is so great that they can tolerate no expression of it in behaviour, who suffer the severest inhibitions of the emotional and intellectual life.

One of the general impressions I have formed from my correspondence with mothers and nurses, as well as from my own observations, is that every healthily-developing child goes through a phase—it may be at any age from nine or ten months—of defiant self-assertion against the world in general and his parents in particular. In happily placed children of normal development, the cruder and more destructive forms of this defiance gradually give way to the more constructive, as social independence and bodily skills are won. In those whose development is held up, whether because of an unfavourable environment or because internal difficulties are too great, it settles down into persistent defiance and destructiveness.

One of the *more* unfavourable situations for the child in this phase is to be constantly shut up to the society of one adult only—whether mother or nurse. There are many reasons why this is to be regarded as an unhealthy situation, but prominent among them is the fact that it gives at any rate the severely inhibited child no opportunity to find relief from his inevitable hostility towards the grown-up by outward expression. Since he is utterly dependent for love and safety on the one person, he dare not show his aggressive wishes to her; and so they remain untempered by experience.

But when there are two or more adults (leaving on one side now the question of other children) he does get some of the relief which he so much needs, by the splitting of love and hate, and the displacement of hostility on to the less important, the less feared or less loved adult.

This is the main key, for example, to Dan's early attitude of hostility to me when Miss B. was present, as well as to those everyday instances of difficulty in the nursery when both mother and nurse are there.

When two grown-ups are with the child, one of them may be won over to his side, and much of his hostility can then be expended on the other. These two aims, of parting the grown-ups, and of finding relief to the tension of ambivalent feeling by expressing love and hate towards different objects, thus dovetail into and reinforce each other. Dan's remark (4.3.25) when the other children talked about " killing Mrs. I. *and* Miss B.", " Yes, we don't mind being alone, do we ? " revealed the need to reassure himself against that very fear—he would have given a far readier and more cheerful assent to " killing " only *one* of us, and preferably " Mrs. I."

The active hostility shown to Miss D. and Miss C. in turn when they first joined the school staff reveals a choice of object determined simply by the fact that these grown-ups were strangers and new-comers. The children took advantage of their every piece of unawareness of the school customs or appurtenances to tease Miss D. or Miss C., and to attain a greater liberty than they would have enjoyed with the staff who knew where things were and what standards of conduct were normally expected.

The cruder and more direct expressions of the child's ambivalence towards people in his immediate environment naturally tend to become modified and tempered as he grows older, and as his feelings have the chance to diffuse themselves over a wider circle of persons outside the home. The hostility comes to take less often the form of real defiance, and more readily a playful expression of some sort, such as the giving of nicknames or the imitation of mannerisms.

We can see the mechanism at work with older children, however, in veiled forms. Most schools have, for example, at least one member of the staff who is disliked or despised, to a greater or lesser extent, and at least comparatively. The weak teacher in a school usually has to suffer all the mischievous pranks or open rebelliousness that the children dare not display to those whom they fear more, or love more. He pays the penalty of far more than his own faults. Yet there will of course be greater justice and a keener sense of reality in such reactions among older children, than there is in the like situation with little children in the home or the nursery school. The hated or despised teacher may be getting more than his deserts, but the children's attitude will as a rule not be altogether without reason. With very young children, the process may be entirely subjective. Many an excellent nurse suffers under it, with a querulous child and an indulgent mother.

After the sixth year or so, however, the child's attitudes towards adults become slowly more stabilised, in the same way as his feelings towards other children. And as his most acute unconscious conflicts towards his parents die down, with the onset of the latency period of sexual development, his actual ambivalence grows less intense, and it becomes easier for him to enjoy a more moderate range of feelings towards most of the adults with whom he comes in contact.

Much of the foregoing applies primarily to *individual* ambivalence of feeling towards adults, although it holds good of the group phenomenon too. But there is another thread of development which is specifically expressed in *group* hostility to adults, and of the greatest possible significance, viz. the fact that the children learn to band together as *allies* against the power and prestige of the grown-ups.

This fact is again one of common observation, known to every school teacher and student of children's behaviour. The feature of these particular records is the early age at which the process is seen occurring, and the consequent naïvety and vividness of its manifestations.

But although the fact is a familiar and well-established one, it is again the psycho-analysts from whom we receive understanding of its meaning and value to the children themselves. Freud's own studies of the emotional attitudes of individuals towards parents and brothers and sisters first gave us light upon this banding together of the children against the adult. The more recent analysis of very young children has made it still clearer.

Even the happy and loved child suffers the sense of his own weakness and inferiority as against his parents and the grown-up world, and fears (in unconscious phantasy) that they will revenge themselves on him for his own hostilities to them. He tries to quell the anxiety aroused by his helplessness by weaving those phantasies of omnipotence, often hinted at in his play, of being "on top of", "higher than" his parents and in control of them, as well as by trying to part them and win one of them over to his side against the other. But once (and in so far as) he has overcome his first dread of other children as rivals, and discovered the delights of *togetherness* with them, he finds that they can feel and act with him against the grown-ups too, no less than against other rival groups of children. The fellow-members of his group not only support him against other children outside his group—they give him courage and power to face adults. He and they can join forces, to defy the dreaded parent openly (" We shan't come to tea with you any more "—" horrid Mrs. I."—" We shan't say ' Good morning,' " and so on) ; or to plot and scheme against them in private (" Let's put a worm down her back to bite her ").

Now in a well-ordered environment and apart from specially difficult children, incidents of open and concerted defiance against the adults in charge on the part of *little* children are on the whole rare and transitory. Playful defiance will naturally be more frequent than real aggression. But open shows of hostility to the grown-ups, whether serious or playful, are but indications of an adjustment that is going on in the deeper levels of the child's mind, and that reveals itself also in many other and more commonly approved ways. The greater freedom of spirit, the greater openness and confidence of disposition shown individually as well as co-operatively by children who play freely among their fellows, as compared with solitary children, rests upon the greater security which this discovery of other children as allies makes possible. The benefits which the nursery school (or large family) confers upon its children are bound up with the ease and relief from unconscious (as well as conscious) fear of the parents which the companionship of other children brings to each.

Here, then, we touch upon a phase of his emotional growth which is of the utmost importance to all the future social history of the child. The banding together shown in these incidents of actual hostility is itself a fundamental step forward in social development, underlying all possibility of reciprocal action and feeling among equals. The mutual support which the children give each other in this common action towards grown-ups is (in spite of an appearance of mere disorderliness to the casual outside observer) itself part and parcel of their growth towards co-operation and love within the social group. It is an immense step forward on the attitude of the child dependent for love and approval upon the parents only, and feeling nothing but fear and rivalry towards his fellows.

It is not, of course, a single step taken once for all. It is a gradual change in attitude, with many dramatic moments, but slow in consolidation. Not until after six or seven years of age does it become stable. In the middle years of childhood, however, the child is characteristically far less dependent upon the approval or disapproval of adults than upon the praise or contempt of his companions. Loyalty to his fellows becomes his chief virtue, and the grown-up is largely shut out of the intimate circle of his feelings and values. Every group of boon companions of ten to twelve years of age will have its " secrets " (and very often a secret " language ") jealously guarded from the prying eyes of adults. Their morality is largely a morality of equals—but of equals banded together against the tyrant adults. These may be tolerated and respected, and may, if they are sensible and "decent", even be raised to the pedestal of heroes. But they will rarely be admitted to the inner fellowship of the children.

The occasional banding together of the children, in these records, to challenge the power and authority of the grown-ups, is thus the first hint of an essential and normal thread of development which goes on throughout the later years of childhood.

It is to be seen, however, that the psychological mechanisms of *displacement* and *projection* are at work in this group hostility against adults, also, just as essentially as in the hostility to rival groups. It is not merely that the children derive strength from the unity of numbers. It is also that the hostility and aggression of each child member of the group is turned outward on to the enemy—in this case, the grown-up. For the moment, they hate Mrs. I. or Miss D., not each other. They are able to love each other the more because they have a tyrant to defy, and are joined together against her.

The most striking and interesting incidents of the records are those occasions when Mrs. I. or one of the other grown-ups had reason to interfere on behalf of one child with others in the group—and the defended child then joined with the group in attacking Mrs. I. The brotherly feeling between Frank and Harold, for example, (6.3.25) was so strong that when Mrs. I. deprived Frank of the clock he had used to hit Harold, Harold joined with Frank in expressing anger to her. Jessica behaved in the same way when Mrs. I. protected her against Priscilla and Christopher (12.3.26). The reasons for this are, I think, quite complicated. In part it must be that the smaller child in question fears the other (bigger) children more than she fears the grown-up (with very good reason, of course—there is a sense of reality at work here). She is beginning to seek the love and approval of her bigger companions even more than that of (this particular) adult. Moreover, the luxury of being able to show hostility to an adult, and the sense of solidarity with the other children, momentarily overcome the earlier attitude of clinging to the adult for protection. It is, of course, further evidence of the quick-changing feelings and unstable attitudes of little children.

Only certain children showed this readiness to swing over into joint defiance of the adult who protected them. The children who instanced it were children always hypersensitive to interference from an adult, and it would seem that once they were safe from the immediate danger of bullying by the older child, the interference of the grown-up *on their behalf* became to them, too, mere *interference*—the interference of an adult with a child. It was then resented as such—and the favour of the older child won and assured for the future by this alliance against the tyrant.

But, again, even this is too simple an account. The *projection* of the child's own hostility to other children on to the interfering adult must be present, too. Some of the incidents show it very clearly. Take, for example, the incident on 2.2.26. " Dan and Priscilla said they would ' push Phineas to make him cry again.' When they were going to him again, Mrs. I. held them back and would not let them go near him, and in trying to run past Mrs. I.,

Christopher bumped his head on the door. The others thought Mrs. I. had done this to him, and were very angry, saying that she was 'horrid' and 'beastly', and 'we shan't come to tea with you any more'. Priscilla said 'Let's be rude to her,' and made threatening faces at her. When presently they understood that she had not done it to Christopher, they calmed down and were friendly." Here Dan and Priscilla had been actively hostile to a younger child, and Mrs. I., had interfered. Christopher then bumps his own head—and immediately Dan and Priscilla charge Mrs. I. with having bumped him, and are overcome with righteous indignation about it. This would be less surprising had the correctional methods of the school been more severe—had Mrs. I. been accustomed to whipping the children, for instance. But since she had never done so (although it is true she held them firmly enough when preventing them from attacking Phineas) the accusation can only be understood as a projection of their own hostility and guilt. Mrs. I. became the cruel, unkind one to little children, they the cherishers and defenders. Thus they felt justified (as their tones and gestures demonstrated) in calling her " beastly " and threatening that they would never "come to tea with you any more". Here again we touch upon the problem of projected *guilt* as a factor in aggression.

One further point must be made with regard to group hostility to adults. Once the values of an alliance with other children against adults have been established in the child's mind (and of course they may be momentarily felt even by younger children who have playmates or brothers and sisters), it is not necessary for the parents or other adults to be actually present for the children to feel themselves joined against the grown-ups. They may enjoy the feeling of oneness and the delights of conspiracy with other children against a *remembered* or imagined grown-up enemy. It is the emotions that bind, and they may be activated by phantasy. Indeed, phantasy as well as reality is always involved. And even the child who has never played with others, never entered into real alliance with them, will have his *phantasies* of alliance and conspiracy. But they will not advance his development, so long as they are not translated into real living. Only the actual experience of fellowship with other children, whether for positive or for negative aims, will carry him through and out of the cruder and less fruitful forms of the alliance of children against adults, and further his social development by means of it.

c. To younger or inferior children (or any temporary scapegoat)

The incidents brought together under this heading illustrate still further the direct rivalry of children in general with younger members of the family. On this theme little more need be said for the moment. But this primary rivalry with the new baby for the love and care of the parents is reinforced in the group by circumstantial reasons. It is naturally easier and safer to attack the smaller and younger children than the older and bigger—not only because there is less danger of effective counter-attack, but also because there is less to be gained by friendliness to them. The older or socially more effective members of the group are the natural leaders, and, after the adults, the natural arbiters of justice in the group. They attack or defend property, and dispense favours and prestige. Hence it behoves the bulk of children in the group to admire and follow them, and to hide or displace hostility. But the mundane advantages to be gained from the affection of the *younger* children are fewer and less certain. The motives for inhibiting any aggression that arises are weaker. Instances of open hostility to younger or inferior children thus occur more frequently than any other form of group hostility.

Sometimes the hostility of the majority of the children to a particular child is able to justify itself to some extent even in adult eyes. The child who is never able to co-operate, or who spoils group games or handiwork either by aggression or "silliness", is understandably not loved by the others. But such solid grounds for dislike and disapproval are far from sufficing on every occasion for the amount of hostility shown by a group, or for the particular choice of object among those children who are not strong enough to retaliate, or who have no favours they can withdraw in revenge.

We have to look for deeper motives if we are to understand all the instances adequately. The children themselves offer us plenty of hints as to the mental processes which on most occasions lead to hostility to younger or inferior children.

SOCIAL RELATIONS

When Harold says, " I don't like his face—it's so ugly," Paul calls Dan "bad, wretched little thing", Theobald says Christopher is a "dirty, horrid beast", Frank and Priscilla say Penelope is "dirty—a faeces girl—hateful", several of the group say Priscilla is " a cry-baby " and " silly " and Dexter is "stupid", or chant " He won't eat his dinner, he won't eat his dinner," it becomes clear once again that the mechanism of *projection* is at work. The younger or inferior child is being scorned because he represents not only his own weakness and inferiority, but the " bad self " of the hostile one too. The children blame these others for their own most sensitive faults, not yet surely overcome. " You don't eat properly." " Oh, yes, we do—it's *you* who don't." " Yes, I do." " You're contradicting—don't contradict." " No, we're not—*you* are." Here we have the situation crystal clear. Each feels the other to be bad, silly, stupid, rude, or dirty—and himself and his friends to be good, sensible, clever, modest and clean. He really *feels* that, as can be seen from face and voice and gesture. It is not a mere "excuse". All the bad things in himself are for the moment seen embodied in the other—and properly frowned upon.

Under cover of this projection of one's own evil on to the other, little children will go far in real unkindness or even cruelty, to the moral victim of the moment. They but exemplify, however, the profound moral aggression of human society as a whole. Human history sets forth an unending tale of burning, maiming, killing, torturing, imprisonment, and all the resources of human ingenuity in devising cruel revenge, under the pressure of this mechanism.

With little children enjoying a mild rule and having sensible standards set for them (as in the best nursery schools), the urgent need to hate others openly because of the faults in oneself is but transitory and occasional. With their growth in skill and social confidence, and the gradual lessening of internal conflict, the tender, protective impulses of children towards the younger and inferior ones begin to gain some ascendancy.

To these more beneficent attitudes, and to the general growth of friendliness and co-operation, we may now turn, leaving the further discussion of the element of projected guilt in group hostility until a later point.

C. Friendliness and Co-operation

From the nature of the case, the material under this heading gives a less representative surface picture of its theme than that of any other section does. Hostility and friendliness are alike states of feeling which issue in behaviour; but hostility tends to translate itself more readily into *dramatic* action. Quarrels and hostile remarks are definite emotional events. Friendliness is very often shown in almost uneventful hours of co-operative play directed to objective ends, with a relatively quiet emotional tone and few overt expressions of feeling.

Hostility too, of course, can be shown in continuous attitudes—refusal to play at all, solitary suspicious watching, and the like. This, however, tends to be characteristic of certain children only. With the majority of children of normal capacity for love, after the first fears of rivals are allayed, it is their friendly feelings which make the broad general background, sustaining many periods of happy unconcerned play. Every now and then affection may surge up into warm expressions—" I *do* love you "; but in the main it is shown in the actual *playing* together, rather than in specific and emotionally toned words or deeds. It is hostility which provides the drama in the lives of little children, as in that of adults.

For these reasons, a quantitative method of recording, such as the measurement of the actual time spent in quarrelling and in co-operating respectively, would have done more justice to the children's feelings of friendliness than my descriptive method can do. But I am more concerned in this study to show the deeper sources and the underlying mechanisms of social development in little children than to set forth an exact and balanced picture of its superficies.

The events and conversations quoted will at least enable us to see some of the more important general trends in the broad movement of the little child's mind towards friendliness and co-operation with adults and with his fellows.

a. Friendliness to adults

Let us look first at the attitude of the children towards the grown-ups. In the preceding section, we saw how they sometimes combined against an adult, feeling her to be unkind and tyrannical, and seeking to depose her from power. Here the opposite picture is revealed, one that represents the common and normal situation of this or any other group of young children in a favourable setting. For a large part of the time, the children implicitly accept the grown-up as the natural leader of the group. They offer her trust and affection, and look to her for protection, love and approval. Even the unhappy Benjie makes little plasticine offerings to Mr. X. when he comes into the schoolroom, and wistfully longs to be called "darling", although he finds it hard to believe that anyone can love him as well as Dan. The children like to show the grown-ups all that they have made— " Come and look at my *lovely* aeroplane "—and seek to please them by gifts or activities. Paul may sometimes feel that Mrs. I. is " the nastiest, wickedest teacher", but at other and more typical moments he calls to her, " Open the door, my Princess dear," and brings her the most thoughtful of all possible presents, a box of boracic powder " in case you have spots ". They all join in modelling "things for Miss B.'s birthday party", and honour her festivity as generously as one of their own. They welcome grown-up visitors, offering them chairs and inviting them to lunch. Even the carpenter who came to fix the see-saw is greeted as " *Dear* Mr. Jones—we love you so." The grown-ups are invited to join their games, to " have tea " in their "houses", or a " drive in the motor car ". The children speak of one grown-up as "my great friend", of another as " my dear " and " the fourth nicest lady ".

They seek to help the grown-up in charge at the moment maintain the order of the schoolroom, and offer loving appreciation of her services. They find tranquillity in obeying her behests, and follow happily what suggestions she may make for composing their differences or furthering their practical aims. Under her influence as leader, the whole group draws together in mutual tolerance, and often in active mutual helpfulness. Her prestige may indeed create and sustain a larger group than the purely spontaneous movement of the children would itself make possible. Even ten or twelve children may be brought together into group feeling, for short periods and for specific purposes such as a game, a song or rhythmic dance, a meal-time talk, or a practical schoolroom task. A group of this size will not last long with children so young, even at the instance of a loved grown-up, but it can be given momentary life for definite ends. (It is easy enough to maintain the *appearance* of a single group with a still larger number of children, if the grown-up enforces a rigid routine, or draws upon fear to inhibit the spontaneous expression of feeling. In under-staffed nursery schools, this often has to be done. But it is important to recognise that such a situation is quite different psychologically from the true group feeling possible to a smaller number of children—and is barren of the educational fruit yielded by the latter.)

The children will often defend a grown-up against aggression or exclusion, as they would one of themselves. Dan, for instance, intervened with Frank on behalf of Mrs. I., and assured the latter, " He won't bite you." The incidents quoted under *Group Hostility* of the children's shutting Mrs. I. out of their game, but agreeing to have Miss B. in, are examples of friendliness to the one no less than of hostility to the other. And in the later parts of the *Records* it can be seen how the degree of ambivalence of feeling towards adults gradually lessened, even in those children who had shown it most strongly in the earlier days. Thus Dan, after four terms of school life, and moved by the joy of returning after a vacation, exclaims, " Oh, I love you, Mrs. I., and I love *you*, Miss B.", putting his arms round both, and saying, " I love you *both*."

Bridges' summary of the successive phases of social relations to adults observed among her group of children may be quoted here. " In brief, children between the ages of two and five years progress through three roughly defined stages of development in their social relations with adults. In the first or dependent stage the child is somewhat passive and relies upon the adult for assistance and attention. The second stage which reaches its height between two and a half and three years is one of resistance against adult influence and striving for power and independence. The behaviour of the child then gradually changes from being resistive or obstinate to being co-operative and friendly. The desire to win approval and avoid disapproval grows. Conversation develops, and topics change from protests and wishes to description of events or actions of mutual interest between child and adult. Thus the third stage, reached usually between the fourth and fifth year, is one in which the child shows self-reliance, trustworthiness, and friendly co-operation with adults " (p. 88).

My own general experience with individual children, and my observations of the children in the Malting House School, hardly support quite so definite a scheme of development, with changes occurring at such clearly marked ages. Considerable differences between one child and another are found, and environmental influences are always potent. But it may be agreed that the general and normal outline of *tendencies* during this broad period of growth is very much as Bridges sees it. Under favourable conditions, the majority of children between four and five years do show themselves able to enjoy a friendly and co-operative relation with at least those adults who in their turn can show some understanding and restraint.

No one who has watched a group of young children playing contentedly together under the quiet and unobtrusive guidance of any sympathetic grown-up can doubt that such situations yield the happiest moments of their lives. It is easy to see that the children gain a sense of security from the leadership of an adult—provided she is one who understands their needs and whose rulings or suggestions follow the true lines of their social growth. They are (not all the time, but a large part of it) content to be led and guided for constructive ends.

Now this is an old and familiar fact. The great educators of little children have always known it. The sensible parent, the gifted practical teacher in the infants' or nursery school, always acts upon it. But once again it is Freud who has shown us its deeper meanings. It is not only that the little child naturally looks to the grown-up for love and protection and guidance, in a simple and direct sense, as being stronger and wiser than himself against external dangers and difficulties. It is also that the guiding adult eases the *inner* tension of the child's mind, by acting as the check upon his own disruptive tendencies, and relieving him of that necessity.

We have had many glimpses of the strength and urgency of those disruptive forces in the child—of his intense underlying hostility to other children and to rival grown-ups. We have had hints (and shall see much more presently) of the guilt and anxiety to which such hostile impulses give rise. It is clear that the task with which the child is faced, of hiding or transforming his aggressive wishes, in order to feel safe in the world and to keep the love of those upon whom his life depends, is very great and very pressing. Now when the adult establishes herself in firm but loving and understanding authority over one child, or as the accepted leader of a group of children, she gives the children essential aid, both against their aggressive wishes and against the anxiety which issues from them. She does this by taking over the function of the *super-ego* in the mind of the children individually.

I have already referred here and there to the problem of the super-ego in mental life, and shall deal with it more fully under *Guilt and Shame*. But it will be useful briefly to anticipate the fuller discussion at this point, so as to throw light upon the present material.

Our understanding of the super-ego was gained in the first instance by the psycho-analytic study of the unconscious guilt displayed so clearly by the obsessional neurotic and the melancholic patient, but confirmed by the further study of normal men and women. It is that organisation of forces within the total psyche which is very early differentiated off in development, after the pattern of the controlling parents, to do their work when they are absent. It is the forerunner of the adult conscience. Conscience is indeed but the conscious representative of this far deeper, more primitive and earlier formed super-ego in the unconscious levels of the mind. It is as if the child, at a certain (very early) stage of development, actually took the parents themselves into his mind. A part of himself begins to act towards the rest as (he feels) the parents act (or may act) towards his person as a whole. It becomes the *parents-in-him*, and in his phantasies is indeed the parents in him. The feeling of guilt is the dread of this part of oneself that *is* the parents, that (in phantasy) judges and condemns and reproaches and punishes; and in punishment does to oneself all that one wanted to do to others. A great part of the feeling of guilt is thus unconscious, inaccessible to one's ordinary self-awareness. And for reasons which will be clearer after examination of later sections of the material, the phantasied punishments from the super-ego are often greatly dangerous and destructive, even in children whose parents are in reality mild and loving.

Now when a group of little children are contentedly accepting the leadership of the adult in charge, she is functioning towards them as and in the place of the super-ego in the mind of each child. Just as they occasionally project all their aggressive impulses, their dirtiness or rudeness on to her, accusing her of these faults, so that she is felt for the moment to be the " bad self " of each, so in these happier and more general times, they project on to her that controlling, judging part of themselves, the super-ego. They feel it there in her—and are thus relieved from its inner pressure in themselves. It is by virtue of this function that she has so much power and prestige over them, and that they are (often) so content to be led and controlled by her. If they find her mild and loving as well as authoritative and reliable, then they feel themselves to be in far safer hands than when at the mercy of their own self-punishments, from the super-ego within them.

There is, however, one special function which the adult must serve *as* super-ego, if and when she is to bring her children into the haven of true friendliness and co-operation. She has to *help them to be good*, and to make good again those whom they wished to destroy in their moments of rage and hostility. The stern parent who rules only by fear and prohibition, and does not offer the children the positive means of making good, cannot give them this happiness or further their social development, even though she checks their open hostilities. Unless she provides the materials for their making and creating, and encourages active social skill in them, thus showing her faith in their wish to make good, she will not be able to create an expanding social world in and for her children. It is when she is helping them to be good and to make good that they love her most, and follow her most contentedly. That they do not always see her thus may be due at one time to the shifting stresses and strains of the children's own psychic life, at another to her mistakes and imperfections. But she is a true educator only when and in so far as she becomes the parent who offers the means and the encouragement to make good ; that is to say, when her super-ego function works unobtrusively towards active and constructive ends in the group of children.

She, thus, does not represent the vengeful super-ego of the most primitive mental levels (which in ordinary times may lie quiescent); but rather a controlling " ideal " ego, helpful not only by virtue of her control, but also of her power to aid real satisfactions.

And it is her proved mildness, reliability and love which enable the children to pass from the defiant, obstinate phase of growth to this of friendly trust and free co-operation.

What the meaning of " being good " and " making good " is for the children themselves will be seen more clearly after study of later parts of the material.

b. *Friendliness to other children*

To look now at the different forms and occasions of friendliness shown to playmates :

One of the commonest and naïvest grounds for feeling friendly to other children (or for that matter to adults) is gratitude for gifts received. " Dan was going to tea with Theobald, and sat beside him whenever possible, saying he liked him better than he liked Frank. Theobald had told him he was going to give him a steam-roller, and Dan said several times during the morning, ' Oh, *thank* you, Theobald,' and told Miss B. and Mrs. I. about it."

Here we have a universal motive, one that everyone understands. Nevertheless, it is a motive not seldom disparaged by adults even in young children. It is frowned upon as unworthy, "mere cupboard love". But such an attitude is hardly possible once we have a glimpse of the real meaning of gifts to the very young child. It is true that to love others simply for what they give is an entirely egoistic motive, involving no disinterested concern with the giver as a person or as an end in himself. But it is not true that this frank and open-hearted affection of little children for those who make gifts or perform services is simple greed in the adult sense. They do not so much love *for* the gift, as feel that the gift *is* love. They love for the giving, even more than for the gift. Both giving and gift are to them love itself.

The making and receiving of gifts remains the clearest, most unequivocal *sign* of love even in the conscious values of older children, and of very many adults. But to understand the full meaning of gifts to younger children, we have to look at unconscious values also, and to draw upon the deepest and earliest levels of the child's experience. In his earliest days, the child's life and love hang upon his mother's gift of the breast (or its cold substitute, the bottle). He has no other means of knowing her, nor can her love be experienced in any other way. And in the analysis of adults, we find that this first significance of love as the gift of the breast (a magic talisman of love and safety, without which all needs go unsatisfied) persists unchanged in the unconscious levels of the mind. In a thousand ways, every patient shows that the deepest layer of meaning of " being loved " is still receiving a gift ; and the primal meaning of being hated is being deprived, being robbed, since to the infant this means being destroyed.

In children beyond the first year of life, however, there is more at work than the direct desire for what is given. There is more than the wish to receive a gift as a sign of love. The child to whom a gift is offered (as I suggested earlier) feels *loveworthy ;* and he who is denied feels that he has been denied *because* he is bad, because he is or has been hostile to the giver. This it is which brings poignancy to the child's gratitude for gifts, and bitterness to his sense of loss when he is left out of the giving. The gift is not only a sign that the giver loves and does not hate ; it is also a sign that the recipient is believed to be loving, not hating and hateful. It thus brings him reassurance against his own sense of guilt and the pressure of his super-ego. The giver becomes a good helper (parent or ally) against the bad inside him. Whereas when he withholds, he abandons the child not only to his need, but to the rages and jealousies which that need and the sight of others' satisfactions arouse in him.

The obverse of all this is seen from the side of the child who makes gifts to those whom he loves. " Dan cried at lunch-time because he had not been given a brown plate, and when Harold, who had one, had finished his pudding, he took his spoon off and passed it to Dan—' You can have my brown plate.' He stroked Dan's hands several times affectionately." " Paul ran in when he arrived, saying, ' I'm going to buy a polar bear now for you boys—a *real* one, not a toy one.' Paul has been very friendly to everyone for some time now." " Frank offered to share his garden with Priscilla, and they dug together for some time."

The wish to be potent in giving is clear in Paul's phantasy about the polar bear, and still clearer in Dan's response to Harold's gift of a single toy rail. When Harold said it was for Dan, the latter replied, " I'll bring one for Harold then. I know what it will be—a *big large* engine." Dan was thus giving a much more magnificent present than he was receiving. But if one has " big large engines " to give away, one is indeed both safe and good. One is no longer the helpless puling infant, dependent upon the gifts of others, and driven by helpless anxieties to rage and jealousy. One is now the omnipotent parent, full of good things, safe from unsatisfied desire, and all-powerful to help others (viz. one's children). It is more blessed to give than to receive, because to be able to give is *not to need*. It is (in unconscious meaning) to be omnipotently safe and good.

But the giving is not only of material things. It is of services, too. Frank's sharing of his garden with Priscilla is something between the two. A clearer instance of rendering a service is : " Harold fell down and hurt his knee. Duncan said at once, ' Shall I bathe it for you ? because you bathed mine yesterday.' They went in together, and spent some time bathing the wound." Other incidents show how warmly the children appreciated services done them, whether by a grown-up or a playfellow. And Frank shows us how keen the child's pleasure in rendering a service to another can be, like potency in giving. When, for instance, he noticed that Harold had left his glasses behind, and ran after him with them, " he looked very pleased, and said several times, ' *Wasn't* it a good thing I remembered he had left them ? ' " Tommy, too, calls out to the children who are jointly carrying a large plant pot, " *Don't* go too quickly, so that I can help ! " We have the same situation when Harold generously offers to pull the others round the room on the blanket-boat (4.3.25). He obviously got great pleasure from being able (i.e. powerful enough) to be unselfish, to pull the rug with the others on it. In doing so, he became the omnipotent and loving father, they the children made good by the good father's gifts. He became the sort of father to them that he would have his own father be to him.

The child's real growth, not only in friendliness and generosity, but also in personal responsibility and social skill, depends very largely upon his assured belief in the good parent, and in the possibility of himself becoming a good parent. The translation of the phantasy, the make-believe play, into real behaviour and character traits, will largely depend upon the nature of his real experiences.

Another mechanism leading to friendly behaviour is the child's *identification* of himself with another, feeling what happens to the other as happening to himself. This is obviously at work in Dan's concern at Cecil's hitting Robert with the broom. Dan (then 3;5) told Mrs. I., " He did hit him and he cried," and said to Cecil, " You won't do it next time ? " then comforted Robert by telling him " He won't do it next time, he won't do it next time." Dan showed the same sympathetic concern for Harold when Frank had hurt his leg, asking him, " Is it better now? Will you come and do plasticine ? " and once again, " *Won't* you come and do some plasticine ? "

One of the striking things, in view of the age of the children, is the readiness with which they respond to the adult's appeal to this mechanism of identification. A quiet statement by the adult of things as they appear to the other children was often the surest way of settling any dispute. Without the enlarged vision which the grown-up can bring them, such young children rarely achieve this reciprocal imagination ; but when she lends them her eyes, they respond to the new point of view surprisingly often. Dan again gives us a ready instance of this, when the children were taking turns at opening and shutting the skylight window with a rope. "When Dan had had his turn, he insisted on holding the end of the rope while Tommy was using it. Tommy asked him to let go, but at first Dan would not. Mrs. I. asked him, ' If you were doing it, would you want Tommy to hold the rope ? ' He replied ' No,' and let it go." Harold responded to the same sort of appeal, when he was angrily threatening to " throw dust " at Mrs. I. because she had interfered with what he was doing. " Mrs. I. said to him, ' Would you want me to throw dust at you ? ' He said ' No.' ' Then please don't throw it at me.' Harold smiled and gave up his hostility at once."

Another pathway from egoism to social feeling starts in what appears to be a purely selfish reaction—the bargaining which so often takes place between two children for the exchange of gifts or services. When, for instance, Frank would not let anyone else use his toy airship, " Dan said to him, ' Frank, I have a big motor bus, and you can use that.' 'Have you ? Can I ? ' said Frank. ' Yes,' said Dan, ' and now will you let me use your airship ? ' Frank let him." Paul did the same thing with Mrs. I. when he coveted the basket that she had had from Priscilla, offering Mrs. I. the cardboard model Priscilla had given to him, before preferring his request for the basket. And in the incident on p. 99, one sees very clearly how this originally crude bargaining may yet lead to the sense of *ourness*. The actual exchange of services, privileges, or mere things, itself gives birth to the feeling of reciprocal action. " Seeing the picture of a house that Harold had made, Dan said to Frank, ' That's *our* house, isn't it ? ' Frank said, ' No, not yours—mine and Harold's.' Dan replied ,' Well, when I paint a house, *you* shan't come in it.' Frank: ' Then it's yours.' Dan: ' And Harold's and yours.' Frank said, ' Yes.' Dan shouted with laughter and jumped up and down: ' It's lovely, isn't it ? *Our* house.' " (19.3.25.)

Again, we get glimpses every now and then of the way in which joining in any common activity, but especially a disinterested one, enables this sense of reciprocity to replace the monadic outlook. For example, soon after the children had co-operated in modelling " the things for Miss B.'s birthday-party", and in playing out the party itself, "they carried some planks to a stone pedestal in the garden, and arranged them to lead up to the top of a box and then on to the pedestal, ' taking turns ' at running up and balancing on this." The possibility of "taking turns" equably rests upon this slowly growing sense of reciprocity—itself jointly the fruit of experienced "togetherness", and of the deeper mechanism of identification. The pleasure and pride which " togetherness " in loving services may bring is shown when Harold and Paul carry a chair for Mrs. I. to sit on, and Paul says proudly, " We brought it together."

One sort of behaviour which presently issues from all these threads of development is *remorse* at having, for instance, really hurt another, and a wish to make amends. Such remorse is rarely seen in children under four. A younger child will show guilt if he hurts another, and a defensive fear of retaliation, but he will not (as a rule) be able yet to show true remorse. Remorse eventually arises from his primitive ambivalence of love and hate, which, as we have already seen, the young child feels towards both playmates and grown-ups. In some of the quoted incidents, we can almost watch the first beginnings of integration of these opposed impulses. Martin, for instance, often showed his contrary feelings of love and aggression towards the same person in a very open way. His request, after he had hit Dan, " May I kiss your hair ? " seemed (to the observer) to express the primitive ambivalence itself rather than sorrow for having hit.

And in the incident with Tommy on the following day, it is plain that the love has hardly yet qualified or restrained the aggression in Martin's impulses. He is not yet able to give up the luxury of hitting, *because* he also loves. Nevertheless, his soliloquy does offer a foreshadowing of this renunciation, and of remorse for having hit one who is also loved. " Tommy and Martin were in the sand-pit, and talked to each other thus : Martin—' Do you love me ? ' ' Yes, I love you.' Martin—' I love you—I'm not going to hit you again. *Shall* I hit you again ? No, I'm not going to hit you again.' Martin repeated this two or three times." (19.3.25.)

In other incidents with the older children, we see the active desire to make real amends. For instance, " Frank and Harold had taken a knife that Theobald had brought, and had put it down one of the cracks in the floor, but when Theobald was going home, Frank showed him where it was, and they helped to get it up." A similar case is Harold's washing the mud from Paul's face after he had hit Paul with a muddy hand. Frank asked Harold, " What did Mrs. I. say to you ? " " Nothing. I washed Paul's face myself." And in Dan's behaviour after he had pushed Phineas into the sand-pit, we get the full flavour of remorse, and the wish to comfort and to make good again those whom he has injured—with at any rate some acceptance of responsibility for the injury shown in the spontaneous words, " I'm *very* sorry." The same growing sense of responsibility in Dan for the results of his own actions is shown in the incident with Jessica, on p. 110, although here there had been no active hostility to her.

The very young child cannot make amends. He has neither the skill nor the knowledge to do so. He can thus get little relief from the pressure of his own guilt by restitutive action in the real world. But growing knowledge and increasing skill gradually make it possible for the older child to make real amends. He can at the very least make amends in *words*, if not yet in deeds. If he cannot yet bind up a bodily wound, he can at any rate offer his favourite toy to assuage the spiritual hurt. The possibility of true remorse for hostile acts is bound up both with the development of the ego through real experience, and with the lessening of inner phantasies of retaliation and punishment from the super-ego.

Another important development in the children's behaviour, made possible by greater maturity as well as by experience and the influence of adults, is the growth of the wish to cherish and protect the younger children or the new-comers to the school. There are many instances of this. The underlying mechanism here, as in serving others generally, is that of identification with the good parent. The child who admires what the younger ones do—" Fancy Phineas being able to do that ! Isn't it splendid ! "—who cherishes them and is tender towards their needs, is being to them the parent that he would have his own parents be to him. In this, he is allaying his own anxieties connected with helplessness, need and aggression. And yet, at the same time, he is satisfying, indirectly and for a good end, the very aggression itself, since even in the helping and protecting, it is the younger child who is made out weak and helpless. In an earlier section, it was seen (and confirmed by other authors) how easily at this age the very helping becomes a too forcible controlling and even an actual bullying. It is only with the passage of years that the child's wish to behave as a good parent is proof against the uprush of the more primitive feeling of rivalry with the younger ones.

A few of the instances quoted in this section were noteworthy, not so much because of their intrinsic or general interest, but because they marked definite advances in social feeling in those particular children. It was, for instance, quite an event when Harold (towards the end of his second term, during part of which he had, however, been away ill) came to Mrs. I. in a friendly way, and asked her to " be a coach and hook on behind". This was not only friendly to Mrs. I.—it was so to the other children too, since it meant giving up the pleasure of scorning them and joining willingly in the general game of "engines". It showed a considerable lessening of anxiety about his rivalry with the other children, and some ease from the pressure of his super-ego, which tended to drive him towards behaving like a grown-up, rather than like a child. (The adult patient whom I quoted on p. 230, as seeking in his boyhood play always to be an omnipotent parent, told me how at a certain age, perhaps nine or ten, he suddenly gave up running altogether when out with his parents, feeling it to be "undignified", and thereafter felt he must always walk along quite soberly "like his parents".)

Theobald's demonstration of his " racing " game is quoted for the same reason. Theobald could rarely if ever learn from other children, or even just do as they were all doing. He mostly sat moodily watching, with a look of quiet scorn and a touch of suspicion, when they were freely and with loud happiness running round as " horses " or "engines". But on this day, he did at least become an *active* and friendly superior person, showing them something they enjoyed, and enjoying their enjoyment of it. Such rare moments of relaxation and companionableness must have a valuable effect on the emotional and social development of those, like Theobald, whose anxieties so often cut them off from the common life of the group.

II—THE DEEPER SOURCES OF LOVE AND HATE

A. SEXUALITY

INTRODUCTION

We have now surveyed the overt social relations of this group of young children, and tried to understand the significance of their behaviour to the children themselves. It remains to consider the deeper sources of love and hate and anxiety in their individual minds, by examining the records of their sexual development, and attempting to use those occasional signs and hints of deeper unconscious mental processes which every now and then the children offer us in their words and deeds.

I imagine that the reaction of most of my readers to the classification of incidents under the heading of *Sexuality* will have been one of two opposite kinds.

By far the larger group will have been a good deal puzzled by my inclusion of some of these incidents, e.g. " cosy places ", and perhaps even the anal and urethral interests, under such a heading, even though they may be willing to agree that many other of the incidents recorded are openly and unequivocally sexual in the ordinary sense. Much of the theoretical discussion which follows will, I hope, make clearer the grounds for this inclusion. But I shall not be able to set forth in full the case for regarding all this behaviour as sexual. I can only do so in a summary way. For the full statement it is necessary to turn to the classic literature of psycho-analysis.

The other, very much smaller group of readers, however, those who are already familiar with Freud's theory of libidinal development and the work of the child analysts, will have remarked that the topics actually covered by this material are distinctly fragmentary. Certain aspects of the child's sexual development are well documented, but others are omitted or barely touched upon. These school records, even as supplemented by the material from other sources, would thus not afford us the ground for a systematic survey of infantile sexuality as a whole.

The reasons for the relatively casual and partial nature of

this illustrative material are themselves psychologically important.

To begin with, the gathering of this evidence was naturally subordinated throughout to the proper work of a nursery school. The education of the children came always first; the keeping of psychological records second.

But a far more significant consideration is that the sexual interests of the children were themselves subjected to the same educational purposes and methods as their more open social relations and their emotional development as a whole. The children were *comparatively* free to show us their feelings and phantasies, but they were not left guideless. When necessary, actual prohibition was brought to bear upon speech as well as action, and at all times there was a positive aim of social control. We could, therefore, gain no more than hints of the children's deeper wishes and phantasies from their open sayings and doings, even under these relatively " free " conditions.

But apart from deliberate educational technique and the pressure of adult example and teaching upon the children's behaviour, it is quite certain that the *internal*, largely unconscious, psychic forces tending towards inhibition and modification of the young child's sexual impulses are so strong that we could not hope to arrive at a full understanding of the latter on the basis of even the most honest and exhaustive records of overt behaviour, under *any* conditions of ordinary life. . For that study, the specific setting provided by the child analyst, and the uncovering of unconscious wish and phantasy by the psycho-analytic technique are required.

Moreover, the behaviour of the children shown in these school records was further affected by *group* life. Group conditions act selectively upon the sexual impulses of children. They tend, for example, to pull the child away from solitary auto-erotic phantasy, and instances of masturbation are thus much rarer in the nursery school than in the home. Only one sporadic case of this occurred in the school records, and one might on this basis have been tempted to conclude that masturbation is rare in young children. Some of the material from other sources, however, serves to redress the balance of evidence in this and other respects, and helps to build up a more adequate total picture of the emotional life of the child.

The accidental circumstance that throughout the period of the Malting House School covered by these records there was a much larger number of boys than of girls further accounts for a certain disproportion in the illustrative material. The relatively scanty data as to the sexual phantasies of girls, and the preponderance of open sexual aggression in the records, are both due to this accidental factor.

Our material will thus not serve as a groundwork for a full systematic survey of sexual development in children. Nor is it my aim to offer this.[1] What I am concerned to do is, first, to show the developmental meaning of such sexual behaviour as does from time to time come to open expression in the ordinary life of young children, whether in the home or the nursery school, and to link this up with social development in the broader sense; and, later on, to consider the practical problems of education which arise from these facts. As these records demonstrate, far more such openly sexual behaviour occurs among small children than is usually admitted, and quite enough to bear witness to the truth of the psycho-analytic view of the child's emotional development.

To return now to the first question, that of the justification for bringing together all these different sorts of behaviour under the general heading of "sexuality"; my reasons for doing so are essentially *genetic* reasons. That is to say, psycho-analysis has revealed an intimate nexus of specific genetic connections between the sorts of fact which are included here, and through these we are able to arrive at a general understanding not otherwise available of the total development of the child, both as a whole and in its various and detailed aspects. We have come to see how all the different threads of social, emotional (and, in the last resort, even intellectual) development hang together, tracing them back to their earliest and simplest roots, and following them forward into their more complex later phases.

To particularise: if we take, for instance, the incidents grouped under *anal and urethral interests*, and ask, as one or two friends who read my records in typescript did ask, why the children's "natural" interest in the processes of

[1] The reader who seeks for such a survey should turn to *The Psycho-Analysis of Children;* by Melanie Klein, Hogarth Press, 1932.

excretion, or their pleasure in chanting " bim-bom-bee-wee " etc., should be called " sexual ", the answer could be roughly and very briefly summarised as follows :

1. Many adults retain sufficiently clear *memories* of their own secret games in childhood, say, from five to seven years and later, to be quite sure that, for example, the widespread " doctor " games (taking other children to the lavatory to urinate and defaecate, examining each other's genitals and buttocks, talking about these processes and so on and so forth) had exactly the same sexual quality, in feeling and sensation, as masturbation and other later sexual phantasies and experiences.

2. Close observation of the *behaviour of young infants* at certain stages of growth—round about, say, four to eight months and later—shows unmistakable signs of erotic pleasure during evacuation. (See note on p. 129. I have other records of a similar kind.) And observation of the behaviour of children of, say, four to six years, when they talk about excretory processes or are found trying to share these experiences, with mutual exhibition, etc., shows the same flushed excitement, the same tendency to furtiveness, and the same guilt and defiance as if the children are found in actual masturbation, in play with each other's genitals, or in talks about " what mothers and fathers do ", etc. Many of the details recorded here show the sexual meaning of these things to the children themselves very clearly, as will be brought out presently.

3. The psycho-analytic study of the *phantasies* of children (as well as of adults) shows that urination and defaecation have a profoundly erotic value, as well as an aggressive significance. Young children normally believe that the sexual act between their parents actually consists in some such process as urination.

4. The intensive study of the *sexual life of adults*, including the intimate practices of many normal people, sexual perversions (for example, male homo-sexuality), and such sexual disabilities as impotence and frigidity, makes it impossible to escape the view that the excretory processes have erotic value at certain stages of development, and retain this value in the unconscious levels of the mind even when they have lost it altogether in the conscious.

5. The study of the *neuroses and psychoses* of adult life first became fruitful under the influence of Freud's hypothesis of libidinal development, a development passing through oral, anal and phallic phases to the full genital stage of the mature sexual organisation. (Neurotic and psychotic individuals never in fact pass beyond these earlier phases to the extent to which the more normal person does, but remain more or less fixated at one or other of these earlier levels of sexual development.) More recently, the many serious difficulties of behaviour and neuroses occurring in childhood itself have been illuminated by further analytic research originating in this now well-established hypothesis.

6. Freud's discovery of the successive phases of sexual development not only gave us a true understanding of the relation between illness and health, but made possible for the first time a radical *therapy* for the neuroses, psychoses and perversions.

Through this understanding, then, we are enabled to build up an ordered and intelligible view of the whole emotional development through childhood to adult life, a view which serves to systematise the difficulties and anomalies as well as normal history, and provides us with a basis for an effective therapeutic technique in cases of disturbance.

These, briefly, are the more significant reasons which led me to group all the diverse sorts of behaviour in this general section under the one heading of " sexuality ". They will, I hope, be made clearer in detail by the course of my further commentary.

It should be remembered that the sub-headings of this general section were not arrived at by a systematic quartering of the theoretical ground, but by a direct survey of what the material itself happened to offer.

It will, however, be advantageous if, at this point, before taking up my detailed commentary on the actual material, I state in brief outline certain broad essentials of psycho-analytic theory which these data require for their understanding. Otherwise many of my detailed comments on particular incidents or particular sections of the material may be rather unintelligible. I have already used a number of psycho-analytic concepts in my interpretation of the children's social relations; and will gather these up into the broad theory.

In attempting to give a brief summary of psycho-analytic theory as it now stands, and as I have used it for the interpretation of my data, I will begin not from the psychological situation of the adult, or the chronological sequence of psycho-analytic discoveries, but directly from the infant's experience as we now understand it. This view of the infant's situation is based partly on direct observations, partly on inferences and reconstructions justified by the direct analytic study of children of all ages, and adults.

The Psychological Situation of the Infant

I may begin by quoting an illuminating passage from a recent important paper by M. N. Searl,[1] in which the fundamental psychic situation of the very young human child is set out more clearly than has elsewhere been done:

"We start, then, with a fact too familiar to us all to need further demonstration from either poetry or science: the fact that there can exist in a child a world of feeling, or emotion, completely inaccessible to reason: that there can be an apparently unbridgeable gap between emotion and reality. This fact seems to me the kernel of all difficulties of development. It is of far more frequent and universal occurrence than we are inclined to believe. To approach it with some understanding we need to take a brief survey of the child's early years from this angle.

"An infant normally has few and simple, but urgent and imperative, desires connected with strong feelings. He has, however, no power to satisfy these more urgent desires without the help of mother or nurse. He has no power to know anything of the whys and wherefores of any lack of satisfaction. When he has what he wants he has the feeling 'good'. When he has not what he wants he has the feeling 'bad'. Similarly the person or object from whom he gets what he wants feels to him 'good'; the person or object from whom he does not get what he wants feels to him 'bad'.[2]

[1] M. N. Searl, "Some Contrasted Aspects of Psycho-Analysis and Education," *B. J. of Educational Psychology*, Vol. II.

[2] This distinction between what is "good" and what is "bad", based in the first instance upon the experience of satisfaction or frustration of fundamental wishes, runs all through the child's *unconscious* mental life even in later development. Everything, in the concrete thought of early childhood, falls into this pattern—not only his parents, and the parent-self within him may become "good"

That is, any dawning perception of people and of situations is to a very large extent indeed in terms of his own feelings. In technical language, the libidinal life of the young child is very strong; his ego, that part of him which links with external reality, is very weak. Never again, in any even approximately normal life, will that individual tend to be so frequently, so easily, and so completely overwhelmed by his own feelings. To him, his wishes, desires, or urges, call them what we will, together with their outcome in emotions, are the one reality. With these he is familiar; these he knows. With such a weak sense of any other reality, his external world, as soon as knowledge of it begins to awaken, is understood very largely in terms of that with which he is already familiar—himself and his own feelings. As I have said, people, things, who do not *do* what he wants, are, for him, 'bad', in the same way and at the same time that he himself has the feeling, 'bad', when he does not *get* what he wants. No explanation, no reason is possible. Means of communication lag behind the strength of his desires. Peace can be restored by some type of immediate satisfaction only. For the fulfilling of the baby's self-preservative needs, the mother is, in the majority of cases, adequate. She acts as complement to the undeveloped ego of the child. As a complement to the ego in the direction of his wish-feelings, as contrasted with his needs, she is not and cannot always be adequate. There must inevitably be times when the child's wishes are not satisfied; there is no possibility of giving understanding of the reason; for the child it remains an autocratic denial. When, for whatever reason, the little child has to endure lack of satisfaction of very urgent wishes, when he wants very intensely and does not get what he wants, he tries to fight for his satisfaction; the feeble ego, driven by the unsatisfied wishes, struggles and screams. If this is still ineffective, the fight may become one of hate for the unsatisfying, therefore 'bad' mother. He would if he could,

---

or " bad ", but his real or his phantasied objects—e.g., his mother's babies, and those he wishes to have himself, and the substances and processes within his own body—whether food, faeces, urine or penis. The " good " object, whether external or internal, is always satisfying, altogether desired, and safe both for himself and other people; the " bad ", always hostile, terrifying, and dangerous for himself and others. This is the fundamental key to his anxieties when the deeper levels of his mental life are functioning predominantly. (S.I.)

scratch, bite, devour her. Let us again remember that he only can understand other people in terms of himself—with a difference, certainly, but with the difference disappearing under the drive of strong emotion. So that this 'bad' mother is understood in terms of his own present feeling of 'badness'. *He* wants to hurt, bite, scratch, devour *her* when *she* will not do what he wants, i.e., when she is 'bad'. Therefore *she* must be wanting to scratch, bite, devour *him* when *he* is 'bad'. We know how the calmest physical restraint of a fighting, struggling child in a fury of rage does obviously feel to him the most intense danger at the time; as if you could only prove yourself not the monster of his temporary feelings if you allowed yourself to be hurt without a single movement of self-defence. *You* feel to *him* what *he* is wanting to be at the time—an invincible agent of destruction. And if, as must often happen, signs of anger or impatience escape, the child is confirmed in his feeling of an antagonist's ruthless wishes. *That* he understands; any sign of feeling he understands, *as feeling*. What he does not understand are the ego forces in control of the feeling, particularly when he himself is compact of feeling, and his small ego overwhelmed thereby. Aggressive feeling of any sort he is lightning-quick to recognise, although, as I have said, he is unable to understand the ego forces in control of it. Hence the resultant true-untrue picture. A little girl of three was avidly collecting as many Christmas-cracker toys as possible. A grown-up gave her what she could. Suddenly the child stopped, looked wonderingly at her friend, and in a voice of bewilderment and incredulity asked, ' Don't *you* want lots ? ' That was at three years old, and an advanced three-years-old. There was comprehension only of an aggressive wanting; none of a state of mind different from her own, even though there was an intelligent awareness of the difference.

" To complicate the picture of the aggressive wishes we have a situation in human infancy unparalleled in the rest of the animal world. The nursing mother is not absorbed in the care of her offspring; her interests are really divided, and the quite small baby knows that others, bigger perhaps, and certainly biggest, share her love, her attentions, her body. Here is a setting in which the little child, from, say, the latter part of the first year to the fourth or fifth, very responsive to the emotions and physical sensations which make up so much the biggest part of his own world, is well aware of the emotional and physical ties of others, and reacts very early with jealousy, rage, emulation, defiance ; all the gamut of emotions which add themselves on to his desire for possession of the mother's body, that first desired source of satisfaction ; that gamut of emotions which makes up the ' Œdipus ' situation."

In this description, Miss Searl gives us an essential key to the young child's problem, namely, that he brings to his experience in the real world enormous intensities of feeling and desire, along with an almost equal degree of actual helplessness to effect such changes in the outer world as will lead to satisfaction of his desires. He is biologically and psychologically dependent upon his parents ; and in the first days, upon his mother. There is nothing the infant can do directly to effect his needed satisfactions. He can only act upon the real persons who must bring about the satisfaction of his desires for him. In the very beginning he is thus not in touch with an objective world of indifferent reality, but with persons. His own feelings are intensely personal, and he apprehends real experience only in personal terms. Thus, whilst the instinctual longings of the child for food and love are enormously strong, his ego is barely existent, and long remains weak and immature. It is his ego, that part of the total psyche which becomes organised round real experience, penetrated through by space and time and causal relations, which later on enables him to temper his own impulses and adapt them to the external world. In the early days of infancy this is, however, hardly developed at all.

It is the child's first experience of instinctual frustration, of unsatisfied longing for food and love in the intervals between satisfaction, which provides the first stimulus to his appreciation of the external world. When he wants the breast and it is not there, he cries out for it and eventually it comes to him. When he wants warmth and comfort and sheltering arms, he can obtain these by his cries directed to those who will bring him what he wants. But some gap between desire and satisfaction there must inevitably be, and since it is persons who bring the child relief, he apprehends his dissatisfactions in personal terms.

SOURCES OF LOVE AND HATE

There can thus be for him no mere indifference, no accidental deprivation, no mere loss of satisfaction. That is to say, loss is always felt by him as due to a personal action on the part of his mother. If he is not satisfied, it is she who fails to satisfy him, who is indeed felt to be actively hostile. He is being actively frustrated by persons, just as at other times he gains comfort and satisfaction from persons. This primitive personalising of all experiences and events has been summed up by Ernest Jones and Joan Riviere as: *Privation is equivalent to frustration.* Privation is always felt as frustration, in the earliest and deepest mental levels.

The sense of complete helplessness which the infant feels before the stress of urgent unsatisfiable need is in the phantasy life of adults and children alike the ultimate psychic disaster. The feeling of being kept in a state of helpless tension by the intense wish for love and food, together with the resulting impulses of rage, is something that cannot be tolerated. It means suffering psychic death, and in phantasy every person will inflict death upon others rather than endure this himself. Our knowledge of this psychic experience is arrived at not only by observation of actual infants but by the study of the phantasies of children and adults under analysis.

Freud has come to believe that the one actual experience in which this situation of absolute helplessness is most completely realised by the child is that of birth, which thus becomes the prototype of all helplessness. Later situations of helplessness before the onset of unsatisfiable wish (and undischargeable rage) are apprehended as foreshadowings of a state of absolute helplessness similar to that of birth. The approach of such a state before the surge of unsatisfied needs is experienced by the ego as *anxiety*, and the normal result of this feeling of anxiety is that the ego does whatever is possible, either to reduce or to satisfy desire.

And just as the infant will do his utmost, by cries of increasing intensity, to act upon the parents who alone can give him satisfaction, so, if his cries do not bring this result, he will use every desperate psychic means within his power to lessen the actual tension of desire.

If, when the child cries for comfort, his parents bring it to him within a limited time, well and good. The child's ego has achieved its end. If, however, the parents do not come, but keep him keyed up to the full tension of unsatisfied desire, his rage at being thwarted will grow more and more unbearable. If this situation continues, then the child's feelings grow so intense that his weak sense of reality is put out of action altogether, and the sense of frustration by cruel, hostile parents assumes the place of reality. Such intolerable tension is thereafter forestalled by the child's becoming a *controlling* parent to himself, damping down, shutting off, restraining, the over-strong instincts which lay him open to the pain of extreme frustration.

Out of this situation of helplessness, thus, there are for the child two main roads ; the first, which the normal child will attempt when desire is still not too overwhelming, namely the action of the ego by real adjustment to the outer world, in the first instance by cries to the mother, later on by speech and gesture, and presently by actual movements of the body in the ordered world of space and time along the lines of advancing skill and knowledge, which eventually make the child independent of his mother for gratification. The second, which takes its rise in moments of overwhelming deprivation and frustration when the real persons do not come to the aid of the child, but leave him to deal with his own internal problem, is the building up within the psyche of the parent representative, the super-ego,[1] which then in different ways serves to restrain the primitive wish-self of the child by phantasied punishments.

One of the first, and the most significant, of all ways by which the child attempts to control his primitive impulses of desire and rage is thus through the development of the *super-ego*. The child comes to feel a part of himself acting within his total self as the restraining influence of his actual parents. He himself, or part of himself, must *be* a parent, in order to control and restrain the primitive surging wishes, and so temper them to make a greater adaptation to external reality actually possible. The child feels, for example, that

[1] In the account which I offer in this and other passages of the earliest formation of the super-ego, it should be remembered that we are here dealing with one of the most difficult problems in psycho-analytic theory, about which there is still a good deal to be discovered. It is the point as to which we can know least by direct observation and have to rely most upon inference and reconstruction. The theory as I actually offer it seems to me convincing and well based; but in any of its details it is to be taken as still to some extent fluid and tentative.

if he bites, a part of himself within himself then threatens, *as* his mother, to bite the biting self. These early phantasies and feelings have very little relation to the real parents, but are intensely vivid and real to the child's mind. Before very long they become shut off, through the mechanism of repression, from the rest of the developing ego and the conscious mind.

What are these intense wishes which fill the child's mind in his earliest days and give rise to phantasies of retribution? The suggested answers to this question may at first sight seem very strange to many of my readers, since it is extremely hard for adults to think away all the ordered knowledge of the external world, and all their organised and tempered control of impulses, and to feel themselves back to the states of mind of the infant when mental life is entirely dominated by crude wishes, and by phantasies built upon actual sensory experiences. Under the conditions of analysis, phantasy states do occur which must approximate to the state of mind of the infant,[1] although of course this can never be recovered in its simple and primitive form. When one remembers, however, that in those early days the outward-turning senses, and particularly those which have to do with ordered relations in time and space, muscular control, touch and vision, are scarcely educated at all, and the outer world thus does not exist at all in ordered form for the infant, it becomes easier to understand that the child's physiological experiences in the narrowest sense, and the feelings and impulses connected with these, must make up the world for him to an extent which never again occurs. First one and then another *locus* of bodily sensation and impulse provides a nucleus for the mental life, with its own colouring and its own special structure. And this we can in part recapture through all the phantasies of the neurotic and psychotic, correlating them with the observable behaviour of children.

[1] For example, very recently a friend of my own, who is undergoing analysis, suddenly startled herself from a half-dozing state one early morning by a jump and a sharp cry which brought with it the feeling of a biting, attacking movement, a cry that was itself like a bite, and a feeling of being lifted rather roughly and inconsiderately, with a general tone of cold and guilt. Taking all these images and feelings together with relevant associations, they strongly suggested a fragmentary revival of the situation of being lifted up from the bed as an infant and found dirty.

The first nucleus of the developing life is found in the libidinal wishes belonging to the oral zone, which dominate the child's activity in the beginning. In his earliest days the infant is a suckling, and his relation with the outer world in the person of his mother is dominated by this need to suck. His love life, no less than his nutritional need, is expressed in this relation to the mother's breast. After the first two or three months, however, his oral attitude begins to change, as the biting impulses develop. This new phase may precede the actual onset of teething, with a biting action of jaw and throat and gums, but it becomes more acute as the teeth begin to pierce the gum.

The oral zone dominates the child's feelings and activities even in the third quarter of his first year, when he is characteristically a grasper and will reach out to touch anything that comes within his range of vision. He grasps primarily to satisfy his mouth impulses, everything he can lay hold of being put into his mouth and sucked or bitten. The relative dominance of this zone lasts, indeed, well beyond this first year, and even to the time when the child can move about in the world, when the development of musculature and nervous co-ordinations has brought the ability to walk, and some skill with fingers and limbs. The extent to which his oral desires and their satisfaction or frustration affect his emotional life is seen in the very marked response of the infant to the weaning situation, and the extent to which problems of feeding occupy the attention of the nursery even during the following years.

Well before the zenith of the oral period, however, a second part of the body begins to assume significance in the mental life of the child, viz. the sensitive membrane of the lower part of the rectum and anus, and the experiences connected with the relaxation and contraction of the muscles there. The anal zone probably comes into the mental field at the time when the rectal muscles gain a certain amount of tonicity, and the faeces some degree of solidity, and there is thus a greater active tension in the process of evacuation. The anal phase has two sub-phases, the earlier being that in which the optimal pleasure is obtained from expulsion of the faeces, and the later, in which it is gained from retaining, moulding and mastering the faeces.

Very presently the genital regions also begin to assume

a psychical significance, erections often being found and masturbation occurring well within the first year. The genital phase begins even at the time when the mental life is mainly under the sway of oral and anal impulses, but does not reach its peak, or impose its own characteristic colouring upon activities and phantasies, until very much later in development.

The dominance of the various zones is a relative matter; it is always the *child* who responds to the breast, or to the situation of evacuation or genital excitement. This can of course be seen by ordinary observation, and it is found to be true in the inner world of phantasy. What one means by " the oral phase " or " the anal phase " is that, in turn, each of these zones provides a nucleus around which a distinctive body of experiences becomes grouped, which lend their predominant character for the time, both to actual responses to the outer world and to inner phantasies. And these nuclei of instinct and resulting experience are to some real extent separate and independent, in the earliest days, although later they become more firmly organised into a stable whole.

In the oral phase, the child not only wants to suck more than anything else in the world, but his mother, in so far as she satisfies this wish, is to him an all-loving and all-beneficent nipple. In such moments of satisfaction, he feels completely identified with her. She and he are one. In the biting phase, the child wants not only more than anything else in the world to bite with his gums upon the breast, chew it up and take it into himself, or destroy it in his teeth with anger when it does not satisfy him, but he also feels that his mother will do this to him. And that part of his mind which has come to represent his mother, which *is* in effect his mother inside himself, his super-ego, will bite and chew up and destroy *him*, if he indulges his own biting impulses. In the same way the anal and, later on, the genital phase dominate in their turn activity and phantasy alike.

If development be normal and satisfactory, the genital zone becomes in the end stably dominant over other zones, so that, for example, oral sexual pleasures appear only as one of the normal and minor fore-pleasures of the full sexual act, not as a substitute for it. Development is, however, not always satisfactory or normal, and then one or other of these pre-genital zones may lend the chief colour to the sexual life as a whole, and to the attributes of the ego.

After the very earliest days, when once the super-ego has become established within the psyche, the child's mental life thus always presents a complex psychic situation, involving the interplay of three *relatively* independent factors, (*a*) the wish-self of the child (or *id*) ; (*b*) the super-ego, or parent-self within the child, restraining his wishes and returning upon him those primitive impulses of aggression which the wish-self seeks to expend upon the external world, and in as crude and primitive and phantastic a form ; and (*c*) the ego, which is the representative within the psyche of the real external world in its relational form. In normal development this factor grows in strength and endurance and embracingness. The wish-self remains the same, the super-ego is barely altered in type or intensity, but neither of these two latter factors has ever again the same dominance over the child's mental life, since the ego is an expanding function all through the years of development to maturity (unless of course its growth be inhibited and arrested by some special cause).

Now the work of the child analysts in recent years has revealed to us the great variety of quite concrete phantasies, most of them unconscious, which the child experiences in his inner life, about his relations to his parents and to other adults and children : what he might do to them and they might do to him. These phantasies, which on first hearing seem so extraordinarily phantastic that it is hard to believe they can be present in the mind of a little child, become much more intelligible if one relates them to the child's actual sensory experiences, and remembers always that these primitive sensory experiences must fill his world. As an example, I might take the wish of the little child, which has been shown over and over again in the analysis of young children as well as the phantasies of adults, to suck and scoop out, first the mother's breast and then later the inside of her body. These oral sadistic phantasies are of " a quite definite character, seeming to form a link between the oral-sucking and oral-biting stages."[1] Now at first sight it might seem an impossible notion, that a little child should wish to get possession of the contents of his mother's breast and body

[1] Melanie Klein, *The Psycho-Analysis of Children*, p. 185.

by sucking and scooping out. But if one observes the nature and intensity of his actual behaviour when he is denied the breast, the way he seeks it with mouth and hands, and his voracious nuzzling when he finds it, one can see how it is possible that such phantasies will arise from actual impulses and experiences. Mrs. Klein quotes and corroborates a suggestion from Dr. Edward Glover which makes the situation more intelligible. She says[1]: "Edward Glover suggested that the feeling of emptiness in its body which the small child experiences as a result of lack of oral gratification might be a point of departure for phantasies of assault on its mother's body, since it might give rise to phantasies of the mother's body being full of all the desired nourishment. Going over my data once more, I find that his suggestion is completely borne out. It seems to me to throw fresh light upon the steps by which the transition is effected from sucking out and devouring the mother's breast to attacking the inside of her body."[2]

In the same way, things "inside" himself literally mean to the child inside *his body*. And when the child takes the parents into himself to act as a controlling agent, it seems to him that they are thereafter inside his actual body. They become identified with internal bodily processes such as intestinal movements, stomach pains, breathing, and so on; and even with the actual bodily substances, for example, faeces and urine. These latter substances are universally identified by children, either (or both) with their own bad wishes and thoughts, the bad wish-self, or with the bad, attacking, internalised parent. The actual process of, e.g. defaecation, may then take on the meaning of getting rid, either of the bad wish-self or of the bad attacking parent.

The reasons why such phantasies, recovered through analysis, seem at first sight so immensely strange and incredible to us are : (*a*) in ourselves, these phantasies have, in the normal course of development, actually undergone a severe and well-nigh complete repression. (In hysterics and obsessional neurotics, however, repression has been less successful and such wishes and corresponding fears often appear in a disguised form, as one symptom or another.) (*b*) These

[1] *Ibid.*, p. 185.
[2] M. N. Searl suggests to me that the infant's actual experiences with real hollow objects containing food (cups, bowls, spoons, etc.) must further help to determine the form of his phantasies about his mother's body as the container and source of all good.

primitive libidinal wishes, and the phantasies of retribution to which they give rise, having been repressed, the great part of the conscious psychic field has then been occupied by the expanding ego, with its ordered relation to reality, and its cumulative experiences.

Owing to these two influences, one negative, one positive, our minds thus move so far away from the simple concrete images and experiences of early childhood that it becomes extremely difficult for us to recapture them. As my material shows, however, if we listen with open ears to the free conversation of quite little children, we are able to recognise signs of such phantasies ; and when we explore the phantasy life of adult or child by the psycho-analytic technique we do recover them in almost unqualified and unadulterated form.

The extent to which these primitive phantasies belonging to the earliest level of development continue to affect the structure of later mental development depends to a very considerable extent upon the actual experiences which the child undergoes. It is possible for a real situation to approximate so closely to a primitive phantasy as to confirm the child in his belief that the world really is like that. In such cases primitive anxieties are so enormously strengthened as to lead to quite serious mental disturbance.[1] Normally, however, these primitive phantasies are worked over and tested out

---

[1] One of the most striking examples of the way in which it is possible for experience to confirm phantasy is that occurring in the early life of a woman patient, who came for treatment on the ground of severe hysteria, but soon revealed a marked hypochondriacal condition, and what amounted to a psychotic inability to distinguish between real events in the external world and phantasied events in the inside of her own body. In the " hysterical " attacks, she had violent screaming fits which were her only way out of the most terrible state of internal tension connected with the feeling that she was only half alive, that she was " cold right in her soul ", that she might " fly out of herself " at any moment, " fly out from the inside of her body ", that she had " a fearful hole in her middle ", or an " awful blank in her brain ", and so on. In the course of the analysis, we touched on various points of real experience which threw light upon one or other of these symptoms. But presently we came to an early and central real situation, which had been so vivid and corresponded so closely to primitive early phantasies as to stamp its phantastic structure upon the world of reality, and arrest her further mental development. She had attained a thin coating of adaptation to the ordinary real world, but this only served to cover the true phantasy-reality which filled almost the whole field of her inner mental life. This central situation was as follows : After a difficult early childhood the child in her fourth year travelled with her parents, an older brother and sister, a governess and an eight months' baby, to the interior of a South American State. After the long voyage on board

against ordinary reality in an endless variety of ways, so that they gradually cease to dominate the child's appreciation of the real world, and his ego development.

Another facet of the real situation of the young human infant must now be noted, one of vital significance, without

---

ship, during which she " nearly drove her mother mad " by difficult and tantalising behaviour, there followed several days in the train, and then a week's journey in a covered mule wagon, through country infested by mountain lions and other real dangers. The whole family were confined for a week to this small enclosed space of the covered mule wagon, and all the family relations went on inside this space. During long moonlight nights the child lay awake, watching the father lie out on the tail-board of the wagon with a rifle cocked ready to defend the family and the fourteen mules from predatory animals and possible hostile natives, the moonlight shining on the father's bald head and the dark rifle. The child lay for hours in a state of tremendous tension, expecting the explosion of the rifle. It has not yet become clear in the analysis whether this actually happened, but it seems probable that it did. The terrors of such a situation can be well imagined, and the various hypochondriacal fears link up with these very plainly. Two identifications seem to have resulted from this situation : (a) The patient seems to have identified her own body with the mule wagon so that in phantasy she contains inside herself the father and the mother and the other children with all their mutual relations and antagonisms. This identification must have arisen through the long sustained moving and swaying of her own body in unison with the moving and swaying of the wagon, coupled with the intense emotional situation of her real relation to the rest of the family in this small enclosed space. (b) An identification of herself with her father's rifle. In her " panic " states she lies on her right-hand side with every muscle tensed up to rigidity, suffering the terror that if she moves she will fly out of herself. The patient's fear of " flying out of herself ", when she lies rigid and taut before she screams, undoubtedly repeats her long tension and terror of the dangerous fire which she expected to fly out of her father's rifle. Actually it is her own hatred and aggression towards her parents and rival brothers and sisters and husband that she fears will " fly out," and in so doing, kill her and everyone else. On at least one occasion, moreover, when camp had been struck, and the native attendants had built a camp fire that made a warm glowing circle of light surrounded by outer darkness and the bitter cold of night at a high altitude, the child had had a violent desire to defaecate, and had had to leave the safe circle of the camp fire, where there was a delicious smell of a cooking meal, and everything was warm and bright, to go out into the outer circle of dark and cold with unknown dangers ready to spring. It is this situation which links up with the feeling of cold in her soul and other terrors which later on centred round defaecatory processes.

A real experience at a still earlier age, which had a far-reaching psychic effect, may be quoted from M. N. Searl. " A patient with very severe agoraphobia was when a few months old discovered in a very seriously distressed condition—' black in the face '—as a result of her frantic efforts to satisfy herself by sucking at an empty bottle. I have no doubt that this incident provided a memory basis for a feeling of ego weakness whenever it was a question of battling alone with id wishes of particular intensity . . . " (Danger Situations of the Immature Ego, *I. J. of Psycho-Analysis*, X, p. 425.)

understanding which we cannot understand either the nature or the intensity of his mental conflict. As M. N. Searl pointed out, " The nursing mother is not absorbed in the care of her offspring, her interests are really divided, and the quite small baby knows that others, bigger perhaps, and certainly biggest, share her love, her attention, her body."

This central situation in which, at the time when the child is utterly dependent upon his mother for all his satisfactions, he is nevertheless obliged to realise that she gives herself and her love to his father, is almost, if not quite unique, in the mammalian world. It arises from two characteristically human phenomena, viz.: (a) Loss of sexual periodicity, the sexual life of the parents being a continuous one, and the child thus never enjoying the *exclusive* love and care of the mother ; (b) The much greater helplessness and much greater length of dependence of the human child upon its parents.

These two phenomena together create the specifically human family relation. Human society rests upon the long plasticity of childhood, coupled with the permanent relation of the child's parents in the sexual and parental functions. The particular tensions of jealous rivalry, the love and longing and hatred, to which the human child is exposed from a very early age take their rise in this family situation. And from these influences and conflicts are ultimately derived all the varied characteristics of later social life. From at any rate the end of the first year, if not before, the human infant has to deal with a vortex of conflicting emotions and desires, loves and hates, towards his parents and brothers and sisters. The way in which he learns to deal with these is the ultimate foundation for his later character and settled social responses. The troubles and difficulties of human life and human psychological development, as well as all the delights and values of permanent social relations, thus take their origin in this central psychic situation.

Psycho-analytic studies of the early phantasies and sexual behaviour of young children, as seen both directly and indirectly, have, thus, compelled a conclusion which seems a very hard scientific doctrine to those who have not met the evidence at first-hand in the actual work of analysis, viz., that at a very early age, certainly by the end of the first year, children not only are jealous of the father's relation with the mother and the mother's with the father, but have some intuitive awareness of its nature. They are perfectly aware that it is an intimate bodily relation of some kind. In the very beginning they undoubtedly think of it as on the lines of their own experiences and their phantasies, as father and mother giving each other good things to eat, or, as in the anal phase, father and mother putting excremental products into each other. The children's own genital excitements, which occur quite early in infancy, bring to them some sort of awareness that the genitals play a special part in this relation. The nature of the boy's organ as an instrument for penetration, with its corresponding impulses, leads him to seek the appropriate organ for satisfaction and to be intuitively aware that such organs exist. On the other hand, the girl's vaginal impulses influence her phantasy life directly, and give her an intuitive awareness of the appropriate organ of penetration. These intuitions and phantasies are nevertheless highly coloured by actual experiences, and by the physiological processes of eating, urinating and defaecating. Since his own experience of the genital is as a urinating organ, the child inevitably thinks of his parents' sexual relations also mainly in these terms.

In her paper, " Danger Situations of the Immature Ego,"[1] M. N. Searl has further elaborated certain fundamental aspects of the psychological situation of the child faced with this central emotional problem:

" The chief object of this paper is to show the importance of the relation between the ego and the id, a relation in which for safety the forces of the ego must predominate. It is scarcely necessary to say that this relation, to be in any way satisfactory, must be achieved by the strengthening of the ego, and not by the weakening of the id.[2] So that it is certain that for safety the complementary help must be what we may call ' ego ' help. To put it in its simplest form, the mother does not suckle her child *for the sake of* the baby's libidinal pleasure, or her own libidinal pleasure, great as both will be in happy motherhood, but because of the baby's alimentary needs. That is, in all situations of importance, the ego attitude must predominate in the mother, and in lesser situations must be immediately ready to reassert itself on

[1] *International Journal of Psycho-Analysis*, Vol. X, 4, 1929.
[2] A convenient term used to designate the primary undifferentiated instinct-self, as a whole.

any sign of anxiety. This assured ego attitude alone makes safe all the directly libidinal positions, contacts, caresses, etc. We can on this basis make out a kind of series of relations between parent and child from safety to danger, starting with what I will call (a) the 'ego' parent, supplying a full complement to the immature ego in satisfying or restraining in accordance with both realities, external and psychic, not stimulating beyond possibilities of satisfaction—a purely ideal parent, of course, because apart from the inevitable personal complications, who is able in all circumstances to understand or to be able to satisfy the psychic needs of the infant ? This I call the tragedy of human infancy, that the mother's understanding and help with regard to the baby's physical needs is so enormously in advance of similar possibilities with regard to its psychical needs.

" Then through various grades (b), (c), etc., of these relationships we reach, say (g), the parent who satisfies, stimulates and restrains the child with strong admixture of non-ego, of id and super-ego attitude, from dictates unregulated by reality—the average parent who shows all varieties in the proportion of non-ego to ego attitude. Then comes the situation mentioned earlier (s), in which the infant is left alone with strong wish tensions, unable either to satisfy them or summon help, leaving the ego weakened by physical and psychic exhaustion, with a memory trace corresponding roughly to the feeling, ' It may be dangerous to want something you cannot have.' Lastly, we reach (v—z) situations in which the parents are present, but stimulate the child's libido without either satisfying or restraining, disregarding the child in their mutual loves and angers ; ' libido ' parents with whom anything may happen. The child's ego-support fails, its own ego is weakened as in the last, the ' left alone ' situation, but its libido is stimulated and unsatisfied at the same time ; therefore the balance in favour of the ego is at its lowest possible ebb. Of such situations the prototype and the most extreme is (z) the primal scene.[1] Out of such scenes is built up the feeling ' it is very dangerous to want or feel too much; it must not happen'. The explanation of the immediate answer of libido to libido in these scenes, i.e., of the child's awareness of them, remains as far as I know an unsolved riddle, but at least it is clear that it is on a par

[1] i.e., parental intercourse.

with, or rather identical with, the problem of sexual attraction generally. The facts are undoubted. The *Zeitschrift für Psychoanalytische Pädagogik*, III, 1, quotes some instances supplied by Abraham, and these can be multiplied by everyone in touch with parents of sufficient frankness and by every child-analyst. Guided by the extraordinarily transparent ' primal scene' play of little children, let us try to understand the effect on the child of such libidinal situations. They are, of course, in their lesser degrees inevitable, but we can best understand the lesser by taking the most extreme, the primal scene, as the classical example and placing it well within the first year.

" The child becomes aware that something is happening in the parents' bed, a something so utterly unfamiliar, so foreign to its experience of its parents that it cannot by any means grasp the meaning of it. Try as it may to understand in terms of its own libidinal experience it feels despairingly that it does not and cannot. It cannot grapple with the problem. . . . Yet neither can the child remain untouched by the problem as with many other events in its small life beyond its power to grasp. For here it is drawn into the magic circle, it is directly involved ; it is aware of a very tense and direct erotic stimulation which has remarkably little to do with the extent of direct observation, whatever the importance of this for the child's phantasies. There are hints that in this direct answer of libido to libido we have a stimulation of genital sensation to a degree unbearable to the little being. And yet at this moment when the undeveloped ego has to cope with a highly stimulated libido, it is in a state of the most complete deprivation. Not only does the mother not come to give it any satisfaction, not only is it clear that she is absorbed in giving this satisfaction to a rival and a big one at that, but the parents themselves are completely changed—they are no longer ego parents, but at the very moment when the undeveloped ego is feeling the intolerable strain of libido at its highest tensions, they themselves, the essential supports, are 'libido'. Far from helping the baby's ego, they continue to stimulate the enemy libido, and therefore have become doubly enemies themselves. Something approaching this is, I am convinced, the feeling of the child in such and kindred scenes. It reaches, perhaps, its greatest intensity when the scene coincides with some oral deprivation, early morning hunger, weaning, etc. Intense rage, the longing to be able to jump from cot to bed, to stop the queer intolerable happening there, to wreak vengeance on these disturbers of the peace, these faithless ones, and this at a time when the child is not able to move out of bed alone, when it is a prey to the feeling of the most complete helplessness—this rage and longing with the stimulated eroticism produce a tangled flurry of emotions and sensations with small possibility of directing them in the desired quarter. Excretory activities or loud crying or both are in the majority of cases the only outlets for this psychic storm."

The sexual relation of the parents, then, creates a crucial emotional problem for the human child, and gives rise to fundamental anxieties which every child has to try to deal with in one way or another. This is the apex of all his mental conflict, and it comes to him at a time when he is at his most primitive levels of love, and has little hold upon external reality and little stability of ego development. It may be asked, " Does this problem only arise for children who actually share their parents' bedroom during their first or second years of life ? " The answer is that, in its broad structure, it arises within the psyche of every human child. The jealousies and rivalries connected with the child's relation to his mother on the oral and anal levels already hold the germ of this central situation, and the acute phase is probably reached in every child with the first incipient organisation of his libido under genital primacy, round about the end of the first year, whether or not he is actually present at the primal scene. His own development leads him to this situation, phylogenetic factors being involved as well as those of individual experience. But it seems clear that it becomes more traumatic to the child when it is one of real experience, and especially when, as M. N. Searl suggests, the child's presence in the room with the parents in intercourse happens to coincide with some other crisis of his own development, such as teething or weaning.

For the next few years the child's development is very largely a problem of mastering this deep conflict. By one means or another he has to deal with the stimulated instincts and the resulting anxiety, so as to leave his ego free for the possibility of real development—in skill and understanding, and stable social relations.

From all that has been said it will be apparent that the child's relation to his two parents at any phase of his development is very complicated. The broad pattern, whether for boy or girl, is laid down by hetero-sexual preferences. As a normal and major phase in development, the boy seeks his mother as his primary sexual object and feels his father to be a rival for her love, whilst at the same time wishing to be like the father in his power and potency—that is to say, identifying himself with his father. Similarly, the girl normally takes her father for her primary sexual object. Her wishes are towards him, and her mother is primarily a rival for the father's love, although she identifies herself with her mother and wishes to be like her in receiving the father's love and gift of children.

This broad, simple statement has, however, to be qualified in many details according to the age of the child and individual modes of dealing with the anxieties arising from this nuclear situation. Into those detailed phases, and the differences of development in boys and girls, I cannot enter, since they constitute a highly technical problem, and one that lies outside the main scope of this book, save in so far as particular aspects of it are illustrated in the actual data brought together. (I shall, for instance, draw attention to one special aspect, viz. the boy's feminine attitude towards his father at a certain phase of growth, because there happens to be clear illustrative material in the school data. And Ursula exemplifies in some of her behaviour a corresponding phase, when she tries to solve the problem of her rivalry with her mother by identifying herself with her father—a not uncommon solution among women to-day.)

Since the major problem of this book is the broad relation between the sexual and the social aspects of development, rather than the details of sexual development itself, I must leave readers who are further interested in the latter question to pursue it in the technical literature referred to in my bibliography.

I must now briefly survey some of the more important and general of the various psychological mechanisms by which the child attempts to control his impulses and allay anxiety.

Mechanisms

Every individual mind has its own special and characteristic modes of damping down instinctual tension, so as to make possible an adaptation to the external world and thus attain some measure of real satisfaction. In the work of analysis one of the main tasks of the analyst is to learn to appreciate these individual devices for dealing with psychic tension, and it is only by means of this understanding that the content of the neurotic symptom or the lines of character development, and the relation of these two to real experiences, can be unravelled. There are, however, certain broad and general psychic mechanisms which function to a greater or a lesser extent in every mind, some of which are well illustrated in the material of this book.

I shall not be able to give an exhaustive or systematic account even of the more important mechanisms, but will select those illustrated in the available material.[1]

The first and most fundamental mechanism is that already referred to in describing the differentiation of the super-ego within the child's mind, namely *introjection*. This is simply the mental function which is built upon the pattern of actual bodily experiences in the oral phase of development, namely, taking the outer world, and primarily, of course, the parents, into the internal mental life. Descriptively one could say, as I have already shown, that the child comes to behave towards himself as if he were a parent.

In his own phantasy the child does literally take not only the mother's nipple and breast, but the mother herself, and the father, into himself. He loves and dreads them there within him. They are now a part of his own psyche, and yet not himself, not, at any rate, his primitive wish-self. They, or that part of him which is identified with the parents, remain *parents* even though they be within him. In endless variation of detail, such unconscious phantasies of the parents incorporated within oneself appear in every deep analysis of children and adults, whether normal or neurotic. In psychotic individuals these phantasies come out unchecked into the open, since with the psychotic the mental life has

---

[1] Some very significant mechanisms will be omitted altogether, such as the mechanism of *undoing*, characteristically found in obsessional neurosis, but also playing some general part in ordinary development.

remained largely dominated by these early introjections, to the detriment of the ego.

This is the most primitive and the earliest mental mechanism, corresponding to the earliest stages of relation to the world. In itself it is perfectly normal and fundamental. It occurs again in a less dramatic form at later levels of the mental life, as for example, when one elderly partner in marriage loses the other by death and begins to feel and think in an extraordinarily similar manner to the lost real person, as if she were, not herself, but him. This mechanism also underlies the everyday imitative play of little children. When the child plays at being father and mother, bus conductor, soldier, or doctor, he is for the moment identifying himself completely with the person whom he imitates. In the normal course of his development he moves easily from one identification to another. The younger he is, the more complete is the introjection, the more he *is* for the time being the person whose activity he plays out. On the older, later levels, there is a less complete identification of his own personality, which has now become in itself more stably organised. He can be the father, the mother, the Red Indian, the Robin Hood, the fairy, and yet at the same time remain himself, in the characteristic mode of the actor.

The second fundamental mechanism of the mind for dealing with the stress of instinctual tension and anxiety is that of *projection*: perceiving that part of oneself which gives rise to internal tension, not as in oneself, but as out in the external world. It is, indeed, in the most primitive levels, more than merely seeing a part of oneself in another person, perceiving the other person, e.g., to be angry, and thus being blind to one's own rage; it is something more literal than that, it really is a *projection*, a throwing out. It *feels* as if oneself were no longer angry, greedy, lustful, whatever it may be, and the other person was so. The other person is invested with the whole significance of this projected desire, rage, or critical condemning attitude.

I have already drawn attention to many quite clear instances of projection, in discussing the data of children's social relations, and to the fact that projection may occur not only with one's wishes, as when the children say " Isn't he greedy! " " Isn't he dirty! " but also with the super-ego, as when the children expect an adult to smack or punish them. As we have seen, the super-ego results from introjection of the primitively conceived parents, parents who will bite and scratch and drown and burn one, in the way corresponding to the infant's primitive wishes. This introjected primitive parent in phantasy attacks one from the inside. The phantasies of some psychotics are extremely clear. They do literally feel that they are being cut in two, or burnt, or blasted to pieces, *from the inside*. Relief is gained from the worst terrors of this attack, or indeed from the less primitive, more developed feeling of guilt belonging to later levels of development, by projecting the super-ego again on to real persons outside ; who are then either accused of being cruel and condemnatory or actually expected to behave in such a way.

In the analysis of every adult, normal or neurotic, the projection mechanisms play an enormous part. The analyst does really at times appear to the patient as ready to attack him, to eat him up, to rob him of all his money, all his livelihood ; or to be critical and condemning in a less primitive but no less certain way. In certain types of psychosis, for example paranoia, this mechanism is the chief characteristic of the mental life. The patient genuinely believes that other people are conspiring, e.g. to poison or rob him, or take away his reputation. As a general mental mechanism on the early levels of development, however, projection is perfectly normal, in fact the little child is only enabled to adapt to reality and secure a solid development of the ego by real experience, in so far as he is given the opportunity of projecting his super-ego again on to adults who are fit to receive it, that is to say, who will use this power over the child for satisfactory purposes. I was able to bring this out in discussing the development of *Friendliness and Co-operation*.[1]

---

[1] It will be noted that at various points, I speak of the child's *dread of his super-ego*. This may seem strange in view of the fact that the super-ego itself is held to arise from the need to escape the overwhelming pain of frustration. Both are true, however. In the first instance the child becomes a parent to himself in order to control those instincts which if given their head expose him to the pain of frustration, that is (to him) to an attack by the cruel, hostile parents in the external world. The function of the internalised parent is to save him from retribution from the external parents. But since the internalised parent, or super-ego, is itself built upon the most primitive aggressive tendencies, it becomes also a source of scarcely less dread and internal danger. The cure is, thus, very little better than the disease.

The child then seeks to get rid of this internal danger by all the other mechanisms at his resource, and in the first instance, by *projection* of

Projection plays a large part in the common *phobias* of early childhood—some of which I have instanced. Little children very readily develop such phobias, which are sometimes quite slight and evanescent, disappearing with the gradual strengthening of the ego ; but in other cases, very

the super-ego itself. In the early phases of development his mind moves constantly back and forth between these two mechanisms of introjection and projection, according to the external situation. Moreover, both processes continue at work throughout the whole of his development. The child gains relief as a result of the projection of his most primitive super-ego on to the *real* parents, since they do not in fact fulfil his most primitive phantasies, and he can re-introject these real people again and again, with an increasing tincture of reality, as his perceptions of them develop and his experience is built up. There are thus many different layers to the super-ego, and it is the most primitive from which the greatest anxieties arise.

A further complication with regard to the super-ego is that the child not only introjects different sorts of parents coloured by differing degrees of reality, at different phases of his development, but that in the very beginning he builds up within himself two entirely different pictures of the parents according to typical but different emotional situations. In his moments of complete satisfaction at the breast, in the oral-sucking period, his mother can be to him only a wish-fulfilling parent, altogether good and beneficent. She is the prototype of the " good " parent, the fairy godmother who fulfils every wish in the moment of its dawning. The opposite picture arises from moments of intolerable frustration, that of the " bad " mother, cruel, hostile, revengeful. In an average infancy, neither of these absolute pictures bears much relation to the real behaviour of the real mother, but they represent all that the child is liable to *feel* about her in the earliest days ; and it is the " bad " mother who becomes the restraining, punishing, internal power.

If development proceeds normally, however, a certain amount of mutual interpenetration and fusion occurs between these two imagos. One very important picture soon built up in the mind of the child who is developing satisfactorily is that of the " *good-strict* " parent (whether external or internal), that is to say the parent who is (1) strict enough to control the child's impulses or help him to control them and so save him from the worst dangers of injuring his real mother and being injured by her, but who is (2) also good, because she gives some real measure of wish fulfilment, enough to avoid the dangers of complete frustration. It is this *good strict* mother who is represented by the skilful real mother, nurse or nursery school teacher, as we saw in discussing the material of *Friendliness and Co-operation*. The relative emphasis on wish fulfilment or control will of course vary enormously with different children, and at different periods of their growth, but such an imago seems to be an essential condition for the child's satisfactory emotional development.

The course of the child's development should lead him to approximate these pictures he forms of the real parents more and more to reality. Where this does not happen and the child remains dominated by the more primitive and phantastic imagos, we have one or other of the more severe difficulties of childhood, phobias, night terrors, tantrums, excessive defiance and stubbornness, etc., according to individual mechanisms.

intense and enduring, and not to be relieved except by radical treatment. In such phobias, the child shows a distressing fear of some animal or other external object, often without any or a sufficient "real" cause. The real source of the child's anxiety is his own aggressive wishes. It is largely allayed by his projecting the troublesome aggressive wishes on to an external object and so being afraid of *it*. The fear of this object is bad enough, but it is not so overwhelming as the internal anxiety and guilt it replaces. The dreaded animal or person can be avoided or kept out; appeal can be made against it to the loving real parents. And above all, *it* is the guilty one, not the child himself, and so he can hope to be loved and protected by the real parents.

Another general mechanism is *repression*, of which in recent years vague ideas have become familiar in popular psychology. Repression is a mechanism probably occurring rather later in mental development than the two just described, but nevertheless quite early. It is essentially a mental flight from internal phenomena, a shutting of one's eyes to a part of oneself, exactly parallel to bodily flight from external phenomena that are dangerous or unpleasant. It is a turning away, a denial, a refusal to allow instinctual trends or punishment phantasies to gain any representation in the conscious life. As far as awareness of the self is concerned, these things are not.

Like other mechanisms mentioned, repression can occur at different levels of mental development, the more primitive and the later; that is to say, early phantasies of being eaten up or drowned by avenging parents, early wishes to do this to the parents in anger, as well as actual memories of real experiences, can undergo repression. The popular idea of repression refers more to the later type, the repression of unpleasant war experiences, for example, or of memories of sexual experiences or of occasions of real fright in childhood or adolescence. In the work of analysis, repressions are slowly undone, both with regard to real memories and to early wishes and phantasies, thus making a more solid integration of the whole personality possible.[1]

---

[1] The work of repression is not, however, necessarily undone in a simple inverse chronological order, working back steadily through the years towards the earliest phantasies. Sometimes later experiences, for example, those of five or six years or even later still, can only be recovered after a great deal of work has been done on the most primitive and early levels of phantasy life.

In the social data reviewed there were a few clear instances of another fundamental mechanism: that of *displacement*. Displacement has many forms. In its essence it is the shifting of psychic accent, meaning or value, from the object or the organ to which it really belongs, to another for the moment less disturbing. If, e.g., one is angry with a certain person, but too frightened of him to dare to express such anger, one may turn that feeling on to another and innocent person. Or, if the impulses belonging to one part or organ of the body raise too much anxiety to allow real expression, they may find discharge through the activity of another part or organ, as we shall see in dealing with the sexual material.

This mechanism, too, is part of the normal mode of mental development. It makes possible the normal widening of the child's interests and activities from his primary wishes towards his parents out to a circle of other children and adults in the home and the school or in later social life; and finally to abstract entities, such as moral ideals. It serves to lessen the intensity of instinctual tension by diffusion, and thus to widen the scope of the emotional life. I have shown its working in discussing some of the material under SOCIAL RELATIONS.

A special type of displacement in which, however, repression also plays an essential part, is that described by the now familiar term *sublimation*. In the process of sublimation, the original primitive wishes and phantasies undergo not only a wide and varied displacement from their original objects, but a profound change in another respect, namely that the original sensuous aim of the activity in question becomes entirely repressed, and the activity thus desexualised. The activity itself, however, remains free to operate in the real world, towards aims that are socialised in character, and compatible with the ego development of the individual, on the one hand, and with the standards of social life on the other. Most of our adult pursuits in art and science and economic activities provide instances of sublimation. Sublimation is the most satisfactory mechanism for dealing with repressed sexual trends, since it leaves the energy belonging to these trends available for social and personal achievement. Mere repression impoverishes the personal life; sublimation fulfils and enriches it.

Another mechanism, one which plays a great part in the behaviour of children between the first or second years of infancy and later life, is that of *testing* inner phantasy by real activity aimed at attaining some proof that one's phantasies are not true. It is this mechanism which makes many a child of three and four years of age stubborn and defiant. He has to be naughty in order to see whether his parents will really injure or destroy him. It will readily be understood that a child only has recourse to this mechanism in any marked degree when his punishment phantasies are very acute, and he does really fear that his parents will burn or drown or eat him up for his aggressive wishes. But in a milder way it is a normal mode of psychic development with all children, and it is especially characteristic of the latency period of sexual development, that is, the period which ensues after the first deep emotional conflict with regard to the parents has undergone a greater or lesser degree of repression—from about four or five years onwards to puberty.

One aspect of this testing of reality by acting out the aggressive wishes, the results of which are so feared, is the child's wish to be in *control* of the situation. He feels he must learn how far instinct can be expressed, how much one can be angry, greedy or lustful without utter disaster; and, moreover, how much actual punishment one can endure without being destroyed. And he feels he must control both wish and retribution.

A striking example of this reality-testing occurred recently with a little girl patient of nine years of age, who had been under treatment with me for very severe anxiety attacks and phobias. The analysis had reached a phase in which her very deep fears of the bad introjected parents who would poison and attack her[1] were in the foreground. These anxieties had taken a special form connected with (*a*) the child's intellectual ambition in school work, that is, her wish that the contents of her head should be good, (*b*) the voice of the analyst, which often seemed to the child to be attacking her through her ear, and (*c*) her own bad thoughts and bad knowledge (obscene terms) which she had got into her head through her ear. These various anxieties were concentrated on the inside of the head, and resulted in a slight but persistent

[1] See p. 285, n.

discharge from the ear, which was known to have no organic basis. These anxieties were then enormously reinforced by two real and traumatic experiences. An uncle with whom she was in close touch was killed by a collision on his motor bicycle, dying from a fractured skull. Secondly, her younger brother, the one of whose birth she had been terribly jealous when she was between three and four years of age, developed blood poisoning through the septic condition of a wound in his leg caused by his being pushed down. These events produced the greatest degree of anxiety in the child, and in the analysis she played out every possible device for restoring the dead uncle to life, and making the ill brother well again. Both events linked up directly in her mind with her own special anxiety of being attacked inside her head by " bad " stuff. After several days' work had been done in the analysis and the worst of the child's anxiety relieved, she then engineered for herself a similar attack on her skull from the outside, by letting herself be run into from behind by a bigger girl in a way which was obviously her own fault, and having her head bumped so as to produce a severe headache and some slight bleeding. This was the playing out of a punishment phantasy, but it was not a simple self-punishment or atonement. It was much more in the nature of (*a*) a testing of reality by seeing whether it was possible to receive a real blow on the head from behind without being killed, (*b*) a projection on to the girl who bumped her of the dangerous super-ego (guilt for hostile wishes to father and brother) inside her own head, and (*c*) a demonstration of her power to control the whole event, to have it in her own mastery. Analysis of this event brought still greater relief of anxiety, as was presently shown in a new ability to express straightforward wishes. Up to this point, the child had never dared in any connection whatever to say simply and straightforwardly " I want " ; it had been far too dangerous internally to *want* anything. Now, however, she became able to say this, and even dared to stay away from the analysis just because she " wanted " to do her sums at school. Previously, whenever she had stayed away, she had felt it necessary to justify this to the analyst by saying, "My teacher said I'd better ", or " My mother said I was to ", and other similar defences against her dread of the analyst, as representing her projected super-ego.

There are two other broad general modes of dealing with the anxiety connected with real aggressive impulses, which are of universal significance in the normal development of children, namely, (a) the "flight to phantasy", and (b) the "flight to reality".

In the first of these, the child attempts to withdraw from contact with real people and real situations, these having for one reason or another become too difficult and dangerous. He takes refuge in a more or less complete and more or less temporary flight into the realm of imagination, usually some type of wish-fulfilment. Such a flight occurs to some extent in every neurosis, as well as in ordinary day-dreaming. It is found in a more general, more massive and more cumulative form in certain psychoses, notably schizophrenia.

In the "flight to reality", the child actively seeks real experience with people and events outside himself, as a reassurance against his inner phantastic dreads, reality having been found (as it normally is) to be safer and better than his worst imaginings. He limits his thinking as far as possible to the terms of real experience, and tries to exclude imagination and imaginative pursuits.

All children show these two mechanisms on various occasions and in various directions. Which of the two is characteristically and more permanently adopted will depend to a very large extent upon the course of actual experience in the early days of infancy and childhood.[1]

Both mechanisms, and the effect of an actual experience upon the child's choice between them, happen to be illustrated in a special degree by the behaviour of one little girl described to me by her mother. The mother wrote to me because she was troubled by the abnormal extent to which her little girl withdrew not only into phantasy in general, but into one fixed phantasy in particular. She wrote as follows:

"About six months ago she (aged 3;0) commenced pretending to be someone else, as I believe is common to most children, and I always joined in the game. To begin with, the pretences lasted only a few minutes at a time—she would be 'Teddy's little mother', then a 'Dadda', then the 'postman', and so on. Finally she was 'Dinkie', who in real life is a neighbour's black cat and who often visits us. She has

[1] See M. N. Searl, "The Flight to Reality," *International Journal of Psycho-Analysis*, Vol. X, 1929.

been 'Dinkie' now for about three months, and latterly will not answer to any other name. She curls up in a chair pretending to sleep, crawls on all fours, and comes to me to be stroked. The 'last straw' came this morning when she sat on the hearthrug licking her knees and said, 'Look at Dinkie cleaning himself.' I, by the way, have been named 'Tim', who is another cat we see sometimes! I used to welcome the real Dinkie's visits, showing her how to stroke him and treat him kindly. Latterly, however, I have been colder towards him, remarking that I 'don't care for cats about the house', but this had no effect on the obsession. Do you think this is being carried to excess, and if so what can I do to alter things, please? She is very good at amusing herself with her tea-set, building bricks, etc., but I notice that it is always the same idea—'Dinkie is going to give Tim a cup of tea,' 'See what a nice house Dinkie has made.' Till I almost wish I'd never heard the name. She gets annoyed at being called anything else, too."[1]

Nearly two years later the mother wrote again as follows:

"After I had written to you, my little girl got definitely worse—she was just three years old then—she left off playing with her toys, etc., and would spend quite a lot of time curled up in a chair or on the floor, and even took to 'licking her paws and washing her face with them'. But the cat itself cured her—it scratched her one day and she ceased to be Dinkie any more. She had this phantasy for about three months, gradually adding to it day by day. I often wonder now how far it would have gone had the real Dinkie been more complacent! After that nothing happened for about two months, when an imaginary person called 'Bisseker' (origin unknown) appeared. He used to run beside the pram and was variously a man, a little boy or a little girl. We still have him with us and a whole history has been evolved about him. He is now definitely a boy, age thirteen, and has a sister and a crowd of friends. But for nearly a year now Eleanor has said that 'of course he is only pretend'. When we go on holidays he sometimes doesn't come for a day or so, then she will remark 'Bisseker is coming to-day—he

---

[1] My reply to the mother was to advise her to observe the child quietly, and if within the next year or so the child showed no greater power of tolerating real life, on the one hand, and no greater mobility of phantasy on the other, she should seek expert psychological help.

is coming in his motor car', and thereafter we have him pointed out in the trams or buses, or in the sea. She has a vivid imagination—this is the sort of thing: She was tossing her ball up to the ceiling in the hall and all at once exclaimed, 'Come down, you naughty girl!' I said, 'Who is it?' 'Oh!' she replied, 'it's Olly. She jumped right up to the ceiling after my ball, and now she is swinging on a cobweb and I'm *so* afraid she will fall.' (Olly is one of Bisseker's friends, age two.) She *does* however, know the difference between 'real' or 'pretend'. She learnt this word when staying with a small cousin a few months older, a year ago. A small brother was here when she came home again, but of course she was expecting him. I told her months before that we hoped to have a little baby of our own, and she took great interest in the baby clothes, cot, etc. And when the baby arrived I wrote her a letter and told her the news, and that Dada would soon come for her. She was, and is still, delighted with him, and they are the best of friends. She was a consistent 'bed-wetter' till the baby came—in spite of belladonna, Radio Malt, a new chamber, etc., but we have had about five accidents since last Christmas, and none for three months now. I don't even lift her at 10 p.m. now, and she gets out by herself during the night if necessary. I usually hear her about 6 a.m. and then she goes asleep again till it is time to get up. She is a good child—no trouble at all. She can wash her face and hands, change her frock and knickers and do her hair, and be really quite presentable. She is tidy at meals, and has a fair appetite. She is *very* well in every way and always doing something. I wondered if Bisseker would fade when the baby came, but we still have him, although she told me one day she wouldn't have him when she was a big girl. She enjoys naughtiness by proxy—as follows: 'When Teddy was a little boy (this is the Teddy Bear) he put the marmalade all over his face and hands and all over the tablecloth and all over everything. His mother *was* angry with him.' 'When Teddy was a little boy he put a lot of paper on the fire and burnt *all* the things in his house.' I have been teaching her various things, but we have no set time for lessons. She learnt the figures from my inchtape, and often when I am sewing she will measure things, and so gets to know words like 'width', 'length', and 'height'. She is very good at drawing and modelling, also sewing, cutting out, etc. She has used scissors since she was two."

This little girl, thus, first solved her problem of how to deal with aggressive impulses of various kinds, which from her later phantasies we can see were, among others, being dirty, burning things and wetting, by a complete flight to one particular phantasy. It was not safe to be a little girl and to be aggressive. If one feels so aggressive the only thing to do is to be a cat. Cats are allowed to have claws and to be greedy and to eat off the floor. They are not hurt or destroyed for being so. Cats can even clean themselves in a way that for a human child would be considered dirty, that is, by licking with saliva. This sudden complete identification with an animal is a frequent device of little children in actual analysis, if there should be a sudden uprush of aggressive impulses. But it does not remain fixed in the manner in which this little girl's cat phantasy did. What is so specially interesting about this case, however, is not merely this unusual crystallisation of a definite animal identification, but the sudden change to the opposite type of mechanism following on the real experience of being actually scratched by the real cat. This event evidently broke the magic circle of phantasy for the child, by showing her that one could get real injury even if one was a cat. It is possible that she had thought that cats were never really aggressive, although they had claws. Now she discovered that it was unsafe to be one cat with another. Thereafter her chief mental drive is towards ego development, learning to eat tidily, to be neat and clean, to control her urine perfectly, to read and write, to sew and model. Fortunately phantasy is not completely repressed, and in her imaginary friends and the naughty things they do, she is able to gain some vicarious satisfaction for her own impulses. "Olly's" danger when she jumps up to the ceiling after the real child's ball, and swings on a cobweb, is a hint of the dangers which the child apprehended for herself—only a cobweb between her and destruction, if she was greedy and naughty. The Teddy Bear who "puts marmalade over everything", and burns "all the things in the house", is another clear sign of the child's own aggressive wishes. Another very interesting point in this little girl's development is the way in which her real behaviour actually improved after the new baby came—another instance of the "flight to reality", away from the worst terrors of phantasy. The dangers feared from the coming of the new baby (such as loss of the mother's love), are all of them allayed by the real presence of the baby, and the real behaviour of the mother in this situation.

It will readily be seen that these two modes of allaying anxiety, the "flight to phantasy" and the "flight to reality", both normally play a considerable part in the normal development of children—their make-believe play, on the one hand, and their normal development in skill and understanding on the other.

Another general mechanism for dealing with deep anxieties, not unrelated to the "flight to reality", is that of "making good", restoring, giving back, re-creating, what has in phantasy been taken from the parents or rivals. These tendencies are often collectively referred to in analytic work as *tendencies to restitution*. They are of the utmost importance in the normal development of ordinary children, who do succeed in learning to adapt to the real world, and becoming co-operative and helpful in social life.

In origin they are highly complex. They are largely a reaction to those primary wishes *to take*, connected with the biting phase of oral sexuality which themselves are inevitable in early mental life. The child has to take (food and love and his mother's time and labour) in order to live. Later on, the primary wish becomes extended into a desire to get for oneself everything that is good in the mother, her breast, her body, her love, her babies, the love the father gives to her. And if circumstances should stir defiance and aggression in connection with this wish, it will then give rise to the utmost anxiety of having everything taken from oneself, and thus being utterly destroyed. Not only so, it will then carry with it the dread of destroying the source of good by the act of taking—eating up, exhausting, the mother from whom all good comes (or later on the father, when he too becomes a source of good).

Many children meet this situation by building up the hope of giving back, of making better, returning to the mother (or the father) what has been taken, so as to make her better again, and thus make oneself better again. The sexual expression of this is a normal constituent in the later development of the boy, and a normal element in the sexuality of the adult male, the giving of love and power, of semen and children. Since he has this power of real sexual restitution, the destructive impulses themselves do not in the male undergo such complete repression, but commonly find fairly direct channels of expression in the real world through sublimatory activities of one sort or another. In the girl, the anxieties connected with the biting and aggressive impulses towards the mother's body are more profound and further-reaching than in the boy, primarily because they give rise to fear of her being destroyed in her own body, against which she cannot get the reassurance which the boy does from his real external penis. The girl, on the contrary, has no means of satisfying herself that her body has not, as she imagines, been injured in the inside. Indeed, what evidence she has seems to support this idea—the actual absence of the penis. Hence, tendencies to restitution are normally stronger in her. The drive towards giving back to the mother, restoring, making better, is necessarily stronger, and her fear of destructive impulses is greater and more persistent. This is probably one of the essential keys to the greater inhibition of curiosity which undoubtedly occurs in most girls, as compared with boys, and especially that inhibition of the mechanical interests, and taking things to pieces, which are so characteristic of the boy. The girl's need is to cherish and save life. Her typical lack of desire to take things to pieces, in order to see how they are made, springs from this deep emotional situation. With some girls the need to restore to the mother becomes so persistent and so acute that all their lives are spent in serving other women and children.

In the analysis of little girls, one finds this situation exemplified with great clarity and vividness. When a piece of real or phantasied aggression has been brought to light by the analysis, the anxiety raised is very often dealt with at once by some sort of real proof of the power to make good, to make things better again. The child will undertake some piece of real construction, drawing or sewing, or modelling, or cleaning the room, whatever activity happens to be closely relevant to the particular phantasy of the moment, in order to prove that things *can* be made better again—since only by making the mother better again can the child herself get good or be good.

This wish of the boy or the girl to make restitution always

involves a very deep identification with the injured person, one which rests upon the earliest phase of love, the sucking phase. As we saw, the moments of full satisfaction in the oral sucking period must carry with them a profound identification with the "good" mother, antedating the introjection of the "bad" mother in the oral sadistic phase which succeeds. And when the mother is "good", the child feels "good" and can be good. When she becomes "bad" as an outcome of his own "bad" impulses, then he cannot become "good" again either. This feeling that his own "goodness" and "badness" are inescapably bound up with those of his mother, and hers with his, is very profound in the depths of the little child's mind. To make her "better" by real or magical means is to make himself "better"; and conversely, to save himself, or make himself "good" again, is to do the same for her at one and the same time.

It will be apparent that this deep identification, and the tendencies to restitution which are its outcome, must be intimately bound up with later social development and the possibility of sympathising with or acting for the benefit of other people in the real world.

The consideration of these tendencies to restitution emphasises what is one of the central sources of difficulties and inner tragedies in early childhood, namely that at the period of development when the child's phantasies are most vivid and his anxieties at their most acute, he is so little able to make good in reality. Destruction is so much easier than construction in the early years. It is so much easier to scream and bite and kick, to wet and dirty, than it is to make things clean and good, to exercise patient control, to give loving service in real behaviour. This is of course because the child's development in phantasy and intense personal feelings inevitably goes so swiftly ahead of his development in real skill and knowledge. The little girl, for example, may wish to help her mother, may have a genuine desire to restore, but her real power to do so is very limited. In most cases the "giving back" of bodily substances (urine and faeces) in the way that pleases the mother, or the saying "I'm sorry" and trying to please, is enough to bring internal ease to the child. But if special circumstances or special inner stress increases the need to give back, the tendency may become compulsive and insatiable.

SOURCES OF LOVE AND HATE

Should these anxieties become very intense, a solution often adopted is the solution of despair, denying that one cares, being all the more dirty and difficult, in order to prove that it is safe to be so, and that if one cannot make one's mother good, one can at least fend off her attacks by being still more destructive. It is this feeling of real helplessness which in the years two to four makes many children dirty and destructive in reality. That is why those mothers and nurses or nursery school teachers who have the gift of showing children *how* to be clean, as well as of showing that they believe that the child can soon become clean, even if he cannot be so now, often save the child from the worst despairs. Many a girl child, however, who has long become skilful and stable and full of good works in her real character, retains in the depth of her heart a nucleus of feeling of deep unworthiness which is quite untouched by later realities, since it developed at the time when she could in reality do so little to make better those persons or things she had injured by being destructive and dirty.

A further mechanism which, as I have shown in the discussion of the social data, is of great importance in social development, is that of the *splitting* of ambivalent feelings, such as love and hate (which in the first instance are felt together towards each parent), thus making possible their separate expression towards different people. Since this was so clearly illustrated in the social material, and I shall be saying more about it at a later point, I need not consider it further here.

I have detailed these various mechanisms almost as if they were quite independent processes. They are not necessarily alternative, however, but often combined and amalgamated in many different ways, and variously resorted to according to the external stimulus or the internal stress of the moment.

*   *   *   *   *

We have now reviewed the broad essentials of the child's emotional development over the period of most acute conflict, from the first year of infancy to the sixth or seventh. It is this period which is characterised by all those signs of deep emotional conflict we have noted—open anxieties, night terrors, phobias, screaming fits, tantrums, idiosyncrasies as regards food, obstinate refusal to be clean, thumb-sucking, masturbation, and so on and so forth. These are but the open indications of that intense turmoil of wishes and rages and fears, loves and hates, guilt and remorse, which goes on within the child's mind, and chiefly in the unconscious levels. After this period, however, the child's conflict becomes less intense, and he enters upon what Freud has called the *latency period*, in which overt sexual interests become less apparent, and the whole personality wears a rather more settled air.

It is not suggested that sexual interests die away altogether in the latency period. No one who has any intimate knowledge of children between the years from five to twelve could imagine that this was true. But they become relatively subdued. The differences between this period and the earlier phase may be roughly summarised as follows : (*a*) The child's sexual wishes towards his *parents* have undergone repression, so that he himself is no longer aware of their existence in relation to his parents. (*b*) What sexual excitement he experiences is felt towards other children ; and even there the intensity of the emotions is damped down. Sexual play tends to be furtive and secret, since children are now fully aware that adults will not condone it. (*c*) The child has entered upon a serious and more or less successful struggle against masturbation, which he usually manages to hide, if not to control altogether. (*d*) The phantasy life as a whole gradually tends to become repressed, and the child begins to concern himself much more with what is real and true. The typical attitude of the latency period is the " flight to reality "—a point which I shall have to elaborate further in succeeding discussions.

* * * * *

After this brief general survey of the central psychological situation of the young child, the phases of libidinal and ego development, the chief sources of intra-psychical conflict and the chief mechanisms for solution of that conflict, I will now pass to a more detailed commentary on the actual material of *Sexuality*.

1. ORAL EROTISM AND SADISM

The incidents I have been able to bring together offer a clear if fragmentary illustration of the general theme of oral erotism and aggression.

The children's direct pleasure in the more primitive activities of the mouth, whether sucking fingers or other objects, spitting, or making bubbling noises when drinking, is very plain. How great this pleasure is can be observed in every young infant and most children under three or four years. There are few who do not show some reluctance to give it up, and, for instance, to conform to accepted modes of eating and drinking. Thumb or finger sucking is of course the most frequent mode of persistent oral pleasure in children, and so widespread and familiar that I need say nothing more about its occurrence. It forms one of the commonest " problems " of early training, as is seen in my table of difficulties on p. 27. (Of the children in the Malting House School, Frank would obviously be accounted one of the " difficult " children in this regard.)

What is the nature of the pleasure which the child gains from thumb-sucking or his bubbling noises with a cup of water? The answer to this is not a simple one.

In the first place, I have already spoken sufficiently of the grounds for regarding it as essentially sexual in character. In some respects this is clear to ordinary observation, since at least some of the oral elements in the sexual life commonly escape repression. The mutual approximation of oral zones which we call kissing, for example, remains (with a large part of the human race) an integral part of the normal and permitted sexual approach. It is true that kissing is also a recognised mode of showing affection in those relationships which as far as consciousness is concerned are not felt to be sexual. Psycho-analytic studies, however, have shown that these tender disinterested loves are genetically continuous in individual mental history with the early sensual affections of the infant, the sexual aim having become inhibited and the sexual feeling deeply repressed into the unconscious levels of the mind.

The earliest and prototypic pleasure of the mouth is of course satisfaction at the mother's breast. The breast brings to the child deep sensory satisfaction and the comfort of love as well as the stilling of hunger. It is this sense of completeness and safety yielded by the mouth-nipple situation which the infant seeks again in the sucking of his thumb. In the sucking of fingers and thumb, of pencils or other objects by *older* children, as seen in these records, the phantasied reinstatement of primary satisfaction at the breast is, however, the outcome of more complicated mental processes, and chiefly, the anxieties connected with the need for reassurance against the *biting* impulses.

In the children's bubbling noises at the meal-table, it was plainly to be seen that more was at work than simple pleasure in mouth-activities for their own sake. These noises were clearly made *at* other persons, whether playmates or adults. They had a definitely social intention, and were enjoyed as a means of power and aggression as well as of direct auto-erotic pleasure. From analytic work with children it can, moreover, be said that these " rude noises " made with the mouth are in the children's minds largely a substitute for the more reprehensible " rude noises " made with intestinal gas. In this sense they are secondary phenomena, due to *displacement* from one organ to another.

This displacement of erotic and aggressive significance from one part of the body to another is made crystal clear in the incident on p. 113 (22.10.24) when Robert tells us in plain words, " ' Shall we wee-wee on the table ? ' and then suddenly, ' Here's the wee-wee,' and spat on his plate."

His action was mainly erotic as far as his feeling towards his companions was concerned, but aggressive towards the grown-ups. In effect, he said, " Let us children join together in forbidden pleasures and so defy and annoy Mrs. I." But fear of external authority and the inner restraints due to the super-ego joined to inhibit direct *urinary* activity, and to substitute this less dangerous and less reprehensible behaviour. Spitting was in general of unmistakably aggressive intention, but certain of the incidents show plainly also the erotic value of the activity itself. For example, on 28.1.25,"George and Frank, having climbed up to the window overlooking the lane, to see a motor, began to spit on to the window ; Dan joined in ; they all spat vigorously and said, ' Look at it running down.' George also spoke of ' belly ', and Frank of ' ah-ah lu-lu ', and ' bim-bom ', both laughing." Its pleasure was of a sadistic type, derived from the phantasy of hurting with the saliva.

It is, however, in the various biting incidents that oral aggression and sadism is most plainly shown. I have already drawn attention to the fact that many of the biting incidents listed under the heading of aggression could properly have been included here also. For example (20.10.24), " Robert and Frank were digging in the garden, and found some worms. Mrs. I. was digging near them, and Frank said to Robert, ' Shall we put a worm down her back, so that it will bite her ? ' " It is probable that this was an erotic phantasy, not merely hostile. Those quoted here, however, show the erotic element beyond cavil. (11.10.25) " In the garden Tommy ran after Mrs. I. and caught her. He said, ' I'll kill you,' and called Christopher and Penelope to ' come and help me push her down and kill her—and make her into ice-cream '. Then to Mrs. I, ' I like ice-cream ! It will be pink ice-cream ! I like ice ! ' " (2.2.26) " At lunch there was some talk about ' cutting Mrs. I. up ', and ' having her for dinner '. Priscilla said she would ' have her head ', Christopher, ' her finger ', Dan, ' from her tummy to her bottom '." (P. 115) " X., a girl, when about nine years of age, was playing at ' Postman's Knock ', and called out of the room a boy ' sweetheart ' of the same age, to give him ' a letter ', i.e. a kiss. At the critical moment, she was overcome with shyness and offered him ' a bite of her apple ' (which she was eating) ' instead '. To her great chagrin, he took this instead of the kiss." (Autumn 1927) : " Denis throughout the term was very fond of biting the finger of any grown-up he passed near, and unless prevented would bite quite hard. This was not done in apparent temper ; and when one refused to let him bite, he would sometimes say, ' Then I'll kiss you,' and kiss instead." With Denis biting was distinctly a love habit and there was little evidence of pure aggression. What was so striking in his case was the plain transition from biting to kissing, when he was denied the more primitive sadistic indulgence.

The study of unconscious phantasy in normal and abnormal patients alike (as well as of certain perversions) shows that the infant's biting of the breast, appearing in the second quarter of his first year, is actually a primitive mode of love as well as of aggression. Every young infant shows at a certain stage the impulse to bite those persons and things in which he is interested. It cannot be doubted that N.'s swallowing of the whistle (p. 115) was quite as much because she *wanted* the whistle for herself as because she "didn't like the noise it made". We can be sure that she "didn't like it" not merely for aesthetic reasons, but because of the envy and greed it aroused in her.

Some of the children's remarks bring out very clearly the cannibalistic love phantasies which characterise the oral phase of libidinal development, the wish to eat up and incorporate the loved person entirely : " I love you so much I could eat you." For example, the incidents on 11.10.25 and 2.2.26, just quoted, as well as the following: (25.2.25) " Harold had accidentally kicked Mrs. I.'s foot under the table, and this led him to say, ' I'll undress you and take off your suspenders, and gobble you all up.' " (17.6.25.) " Some of the children, who had been in 'a hiding place', came out, led by Duncan, who was carrying a stick as a weapon, looking very fierce. They came out looking for animals ' to kill for meat ' to take back to the house. Apparently Duncan was 'the father'. When they saw Mrs. I. through the window of the schoolroom they came in to her, saying, ' There she is,' and said they would 'cut her up'. All joined in the play and then ran off happily." These are but playful expressions of phantasies which do in truth dominate the deeper unconscious levels of the young child's mind, and which are the source of his greatest anxieties. He dreads the injury and ruin which the fulfilment of his wishes would mean to the loved persons, and he dreads their attacks on him in kind. The play helps to allay these anxieties and ease the inner tension arising from them. But the anxieties themselves are plainly seen in some of the quoted cases of *phobia* (p. 119). Here the child's own biting and eating impulses are projected on to a real or imagined outer object, e.g. "Goo-goo", whose attacks on the child himself are then feared. The dreaded animal represents at one and the same time the child's primitive biting self, and the bitten and vengeful parents or rivals, who will in his phantasies do to him what he has wished to do to them. The actual phobia is an attempt to deal with the anxiety connected with the phantasies, by being able to feel, on the one hand, " It is not *I* who wishes to bite my mother or the new baby—it is Goo-goo " ; and, on the other, being able to gain the real sympathy and special care of parent or nurse by means of the phobia, and so prove constantly to himself that they are not in reality cruel and dangerous as he dreams.

Not all children develop these phobias in any marked way, but most young children show them in at least a mild and temporary form. The phobia is indeed one of the characteristic and normal phenomena of early childhood; and its deepest source is the child's own oral sadism and aggression. How far the phobias become severe and unmanageable in any child, as in some of the cases here quoted, will depend upon many factors, some of which will of course be the child's real experiences and actual environment. The verbal and dramatic expression of biting phantasies in *play* is in itself at once a sign and a safeguard of healthy development.

The not uncommon feeding difficulties of early childhood, occurring especially in the post-weaning period, are also to be understood in terms of the child's problem of oral aggression. The child who will not take hard food, who cannot bring himself to chew and swallow any solid food, the child who can scarcely be persuaded to eat at all—all these are suffering from excessive anxiety about the phantasies connected with biting and chewing and oral aggression in general. This has been clearly demonstrated recently,[1] in the actual analysis of children of two years and under, who were brought to a children's hospital because they could never be got to eat enough. In some cases this difficulty dated practically from birth; in others from weaning; in some it is definitely due to faulty handling, in others it would appear to be inborn. In each case the prime psychological factor (whether this was itself caused by internal or external forces) was the child's anxiety about oral aggression in sucking or biting the mother's breast, with unconscious phantasies of the irreparable injury this would do to the mother (eating up, exhausting and destroying the breast, which would then no longer be there for the child), and of the equally terrifying revenge which the mother would inflict upon the child. In extreme cases, even sucking is felt by the child to be sadistic, and one is then driven to postulate an abnormally strong constitutional sadism as the ultimate factor. But the unconscious

[1] By Dr Melitta Schmideberg, working at the London Clinic of Psycho-Analysis.

cannibalistic phantasy as such, with its accompanying anxiety, is normal and general. It can be dealt with by the ordinary child in the occasional development of minor and momentary phobias, by playful bitings (as in Denis), or games of the kinds here described, or by the ordinary channels of permitted sadism, in biting bone rings, hard food, etc.; and in the explosive sounds of speech.[1] In all these latter directions, the child's oral phantasies are put to the test of reality, and his impulses find an outlet that is free from guilt and danger, and aids his further growth.

Another significant psychological process is adumbrated in some of these instances. For example: (24.6.25) " When Priscilla, Frank and Duncan were playing with the puppy, Priscilla said something about ' sucking that ', obviously referring to the dog's penis. Duncan said, ' Oh, you dirty thing.' Frank laughed. Priscilla said, 'and get milk'. Duncan : ' You don't get milk from dogs ! ' Someone asked where one did get milk. Duncan replied, ' From cows, and goats.' " (P. 115) " C., about five years of age, was stroking a large collie dog, when it sniffed at his trousers in the genital region. ' Oh,' he said, ' it wants to suck.' " Here we see what appears on the surface to be a simple confusion between the penis and the nipple. That there often is such a confusion in children's minds with regard to the cow's udder is widely known ; but deeper study has shown that it is not merely an accidental fault of observation, but is prepared for in the child's mind by his own unconscious phantasies. In the development of his own sexual wishes the impulses and feelings and phantasies connected in the first instance with the oral zone do not remain isolated. The later genital phase does not start up entirely *de novo* and unrelated to the earlier libidinal experiences, such as the child's relation to the breast. It takes over many of the impulses and feelings belonging to the oral zone. In the very beginning the mother was a protruding nipple, and to love her was to take the nipple into one's mouth and receive the love gift of milk. In the later genital situations the boy wishes to give the penis to his mother, and of course later on to his mate, just as he himself received her nipple as a first experience of love. In the unconscious phantasies of child and adult alike the vagina-

---

[1] Anxiety with regard to oral sadism plays a great part in speech defects such as stammering.

SOURCES OF LOVE AND HATE

penis situation is linked up with and is psychologically a development from the mouth-nipple situation. The child's confusion with regard to penis and udder in the cow is thus itself a sign of this transition of sexuality from the oral to the genital zone. The same psychological process is clearly shown us in the incident on p. 137 when the boy naïvely refers to his own organ as his " suckie ", that is, as a nipple. Where this transition is incomplete and the sexual impulses remain more or less fixated at the oral level, one of the oral types of perversion in sexual desire or a certain type of sexual inhibition may be the outcome. Here, however, I am concerned only to show the ordinariness of these phantasies in ordinary children, and the general fact of transition from oral to genital experiences and impulses, in normal sexual development.

The experiences and impulses of the nipple are, as we have seen, of the utmost significance not only for libidinal development, but also for the development of the ego. I shall leave any further discussion of this, however, until I come to deal with the incidents grouped under the heading of *Guilt and Shame*.

2. ANAL AND URETHRAL INTERESTS AND AGGRESSION

The material gathered under this heading is of great significance in helping us to understand the child's point of view with regard to excretory processes, the regularisation of which constitutes one of the central problems of nursery education. Some of the phantasies which develop in the child's mind in connection with these bodily processes are clearly shown, together with the mechanisms which characterise the anal phase of libido development.

If we look first at the notes I am able to offer of the observed behaviour of quite young infants, along with certain of the incidents occurring with the younger children in the school, we see the earliest attitude of the child to his own excretory products: (P. 129, K., 9 months) " She was lying on her rug in the garden; several friendly adults were near, looking at her, talking to and about her. Her uncle went up to her, whereupon she began to smile and laugh and gurgle, and wriggle about, with an appearance of great pleasure. He thought these were signs of pleased recognition of himself, and friendliness to him. He laughed back, and repeated the little grunting noises—*er, er, er,* which she was making. After a few moments, the smile faded and the grunts and gurgles ceased, and she lay quiet. Her nannie, who was near, recognised the situation and took her up to change her—she had evacuated into her napkin." (P. 121, 21.9.24) " Dan's mother reported that this afternoon, when she was carrying him on the return from a walk, he had asked her, ' Shall I make water on you ? ' She said, ' Do you want to make water? I'll put you down.' ' No, on *you*, shall I ? ' " (P. 121, Oct. 1924) " Miss X. and Mrs. I. went to talk to Dan in his bath at bedtime. He made love to Miss X. by offering her water cupped in his hands ; then suddenly said, ' I'm going to pass faeces on the floor and on the towel.' "

In this phase (in normal children) faeces and urine are not yet objects of disgust and shame. The child takes a direct pleasure both in the act and the product, and will offer them as gifts to those whom he loves. (28.10.26) "Tommy made a present of some of the rabbits' faeces to a lady visitor to the school." The feeling that the *act* of voiding is a good thing, and a gift to loved persons, will of course persist after the faeces and urine themselves have become more or less " bad " things, and is a great aid to the educator in training regular habits of cleanliness.

His study of adults by the psycho-analytic method had long ago shown Freud that this attitude towards excremental products, so different from our ordinary adult feelings of disgust and shame, persists in the unconscious mental life of both neurotics and normal people, although deeply repressed in most. It finds many indirect and sublimated forms of expression in the ordinary activities of everyday life, although rarely coming to light among civilised peoples in a direct and naïve form. Among primitive people and peasants, as is well known, excremental products are often used as medicines, and not only for black magic. This notion of their curative value rests in the last resort upon the psychological attitude here illustrated by the naive behaviour of infants and very young children.

In this phase of development, when the child still feels faeces to be a good, pleasure-giving product, he will not uncommonly play actively with his faeces if he has a chance, and even smear them over his fingers and face and put them into his mouth. That this occurs in phantasy has long been known to psycho-analysts. I am able to quote some actual instances which came to my notice recently : " I should be so grateful if you could help me with my little girl, aged sixteen months. When she is left on her pot to do her morning duty she does it, and then proceeds to put her hands in and play with it. She does this if nurse is in the room and once or twice nurse has been outside and when she has come back has found Baby covered all over, with it smeared all over her hair, and sometimes eating and enjoying it. She also sucks her wet nappies. (She wears nappies when resting in her cot in the afternoon.) She is perfectly normal in other ways, very forward in walking. She walked at eleven months and is very tall for her age. I do not like to ask other mothers about this disgusting habit, as I feel quite ashamed to possess such a child. Baby has an enormous appetite and sleeps well, and is always happy and very independent. I enclose a snapshot of her with her sister, so you can see how well she looks." The father of a baby girl of just one year old told me of how, if a soiled napkin were not removed at once when she had defaecated early in the morning, she would wriggle about until she could get to the faeces and would then smear it over her fingers and face and put her smeared fingers into her mouth. She did this on half a dozen occasions until her mother learnt to remove the opportunity. Mrs. Y. and Mrs. Z., both mothers of boys, the first boy nine months of age, the second twelve months, both reported to me exactly the same behaviour. Mrs. Y.'s boy, for example, lay unusually quiet one morning before his parents got up instead of his usual moving about and gurgling in his cot. When his mother went to see what was happening, he had smeared his faeces over his hands and face and put it into his mouth.

The positive pleasure in the act and the product of evacuation does not, however, long remain uncomplicated in the child. The opposite feeling of the " badness " of excrement and urine begins to appear in varying strength in the overt behaviour of most children of eighteen months and over, and sometimes even earlier. Some of the incidents quoted here show this feeling plainly. For example : (p. 122, 24.11.24) " Frank said, ' Shall we make Benjie drink bee-wee water ? ' ' Yes,' Harold said, 'and poison him '. And another time, ' and make spots come out all over him '." (P. 123, 25.3.25)

" Two or three of the children were using one of the movable blackboards. Harold said, ' Shall I try on it ? and make it black, make it dirty ? ' " (P. 125, 9.11.25) "Frank and Priscilla were being hostile to Penelope. They said, ' She's dirty—she's a faeces girl—she's hateful.' "

The remarks quoted from these children hint at what we already know from, for example, the obsessional neurotic, that in unconscious phantasy the " badness " of faeces and urine goes far beyond their real (hygienic or physiological) harmfulness. It has for the child, indeed, little or nothing to do with this objective reality, although the teachings of adults may be woven into the texture of the child's phantasies. The content of the " badness " derives rather from the child's actual experiences in the anal situation, and his own hostile tendencies towards other persons.

These latter may take a variety of forms, the two main types being, firstly, obstinate withholding and retaining of faeces (as a means of pleasure to *oneself*), and refusing to part with it except at one's own wish. This obstinate refusal to give to others brings the fear of retribution in kind (denial of food, etc.) from others. The faeces become bad because they have made one behave in a bad way, and thus exposed one to danger. Moreover, this obstinate retention leads to an intensification of the endo-psychic experiences deriving from the action of the rectal muscles—forcing, cutting, expelling the faeces ; and the forcing, cutting feel of the (hard) faeces themselves within the bowel. In phantasy, the hard lump of faeces becomes a dangerous foreign object, sometimes identified with angry parents, sometimes with the child's own bad self.

I was recently told by a mother of a girl of three and a half, very obstinate in refusing to defaecate, sometimes for as long as four or five days, that the child took a great fancy to a new nurse, and her first expression of her liking was, within ten minutes of the nurse's arrival, voluntarily to fetch her chamber pot and say, " I'll do my ' duty ' for *you*." The child thus clearly shows us how love and a wish to please may reinstate the earlier attitude of making a gift of the act of voiding, even in a case where fear and hatred have led to serious and chronic difficulty.

The second form of active anal hostility is that of forcibly and defiantly expelling excrement and flatus (if one *has* to part with it) in an undesired time and place. This is commonly seen in obstinate children in their second and third years. The full content of the connected phantasy, occasionally expressed in actual behaviour, is that of putting the bad stuff on to or into the person who compels one to part with it, and generally using it as a magical means of attack. (P. 121, 24.11.24.) " Harold, Paul and Benjie put the wash-bowls on the floor, and sat in them, saying, ' I'm trying, I'm trying on Paul, on Dan, etc.' Christopher took a bowl from Benjie. Harold said, ' I'll hit you in the face if you take mine.' Benjie: ' I'll wee-wee in your face.' Benjie and Harold said to Tommy, ' We'll put bim-bom-bee-wee water in your face.' When he is angry with Mrs. I., he sometimes says to the others, ' Shall we pee-wee on someone ? ' "

The children were getting water to drink in cups, and Harold told the others that he had given Frank some " wee-wee water " to drink. He often says " there's wee-wee water in the bowl " in which he washes his hands. Later he said he had drunk " wee-wee water ", and that the water in the cups was that. (P. 123, 24.4.25) " Theobald poured water into the sand, and called it ' bee-wee sand '. Frank was heard to say to another child, ' Shall we put some faeces in a cake and give it to Sallie—and then she won't know what she is eating ? ' " (P. 127, 5.2.26) " In a moment of anger, Priscilla took her doll and said she would make it ' pass faeces ' on Mrs. I. ; she held the doll's legs towards her and said, ' Bang '."

Another phantasy of tiny children, one that is readily understandable in view of their limited knowledge and experience, is that there is nothing in one's inside but either good food or bad faeces (and urine). (P. 121, 19.11.24) " At lunch the children had a conversation as to what people were made of, and spoke of people being made of pudding, pie, potatoes, coal, etc., and then of ' bee-wee ', ' try ', ' do-do ', ' ah-ah ', ' bottie '." In Frank's remark (24.4.25) we see the notion that the buttocks, for example, are full of excrement, and will be " flat " if it is all passed out. One of the ever-present fears in the unconscious mental life of children is that there will be nothing but bad stuff, bad and dangerous inside one ; or that, as a result of their own hostile wishes and phantasied attacks, mother or nurse will come to have nothing inside but bad excrement and urine—

no good milk or food or love. These two things indeed go together—if mother is made of bad stuff, the child cannot possibly be good ; and if the child is bad, the mother will be made so, too.

These anxieties are here shown in a projected form of accusation : " *You* are made of try ",, etc. (P. 122, 26.11.24) " At lunch, Harold said to Mrs. I., ' You are made of try.' Frank . . . ' You are made of water.' Benjie . . . ' of bee-wee '." (P. 126, 1.12.25) " When painting, Tommy painted his hands ; Christopher, Dan and Priscilla said he was ' dirty '. He retorted, ' No, I'm not.' They spat on his picture and spoilt it. When Miss B. interfered, they said *she* was ' dirty ', ' a faeces person ', ' horrid ', etc. Later on, when Tommy was pouring some peas into a wooden measure, he spilt some on the floor ; the other children spoke about this ; but presently, when Mrs. I. stood near before he had picked them up, Priscilla and Frank pretended that it was she who had ' made water and passed faeces on the floor'. ' Look what a lot she's done,' they said, laughing. ' We can see it—you'll have to brush it up,' and so on."

Such accusations on the part of the child are partly true projections, meaning " You *are*, and I am *not* " ; and partly reassurances to his own self-love, on the ground that " You are *as well* as I." Some of the child's curiosity about the adult's going to the lavatory, etc., arises from the need to prove to himself that it is not only children who have this bad stuff, these bad selves, inside them, but adults too. On the other hand, the child who is suffering from an exaggerated anxiety about his own anal sadism and badness cannot derive much reassurance from the fact that mothers also have to defaecate—this is too frightening a fact for those to whom faeces and the act of voiding have become almost entirely bad. It confirms their dread that mother is no better than they, and therefore has nothing good to give them, just as they have none to give her. It is only when the earlier phase of goodness has not (from one cause or another) been altogether overwhelmed by the later one of active hostility that it means " I am no worse than she, and therefore I can receive good."

When the child's own unconscious wishes to attack with faeces and urine have been very strong (e.g. 24.4.25), there often develops a dread of being given bad food (in phantasy, faeces and urine themselves), a dread which may lie behind a poor appetite, a refusal to try new foods, or a reluctance to accept food from certain people. (In an adult patient of my own, generally healthy but with a very poor appetite throughout childhood, these phantasies of being given bad food from his mother turned out to have been very strong indeed, mainly as a result of his own wish to attack his mother's breast by means of his urine, a wish in its turn arising from disappointed desire.)

In many children beyond the first year, the observable obstinacy with regard to the use of a vessel, or to defaecation itself, is by no means due to a simple wish to retain the faeces and please himself about parting with it. This simple attitude is probably not found after the first year, if even so late. Later than this, refusal to defaecate or difficulty in doing so into a vessel, is rather the outcome of actual dread of the bad faeces, of putting it into a clean pot, and even the feeling that one ought not to have such bad stuff inside one at all. The act of bringing it out is a confession that it is there (as well as an act of trust in the adult of which the child does not always feel capable). It seems better to try to deny that one has any bad stuff at all. Not seeing is not believing. And so the circle goes on—a painful condition of faeces, greater fear of them, more difficulty in voiding them, and so on—especially if the child is punished or heavily reproached and so made more guilty. He then becomes still more afraid, and so more hostile and unwilling.

It is thus clear that any marked or exaggerated development of dread or shame about excrement or the act of voiding, whether engendered by clumsy treatment or by spontaneous endo-psychic processes, sets up one of the biggest obstacles to training and to bodily hygiene in young children.

I do not, of course, suggest that all cases of constipation in little children or adults are due solely to these psychic mechanisms. But there are very many cases observable where every known physiological factor can be ruled out as a primary cause, and where yet the difficulty is very troublesome and unyielding. Moreover, the psycho-analysis of normal and neurotic adults has shown that these psychological attitudes occur in everyone, with of course very varying degrees and varying psychical context.

The intensity which these special anxieties can attain in young children is clearly shown in some of the quoted letters from mothers and nurses. The naïve remarks of the children in the school records afford us a glimpse of the actual content of the anxieties, although none of these particular children happened to show any special difficulties of the type illustrated in the letters.

It will have been noticed, in the School records of this theme, that whilst a certain proportion of the children's references to excretory affairs are made in a hostile mood, and are expressions of hatred and defiance, quite a number are purely playful dramatisations, corresponding in mood and general significance to any other theme of their talk or dramatic play: (P. 124, 18.6.25) "Tommy and Christopher spent half an hour making what they called a 'bee-wee pie' with sand and water. In the sand-pit, in the morning, Paul and Harold, and later Frank and Dan, had 'made try'—mixing sand and water with their hands, 'with salt', they said. Frank piled it up on a brick in a loaf shape, and Paul called it a 'loaf of try-bread'. Harold did the same, and said, 'When someone wants to eat a try-loaf, we'll give them this.' Paul and Harold went on with this 'try-bread' for some time, and said they were going to cook it. Harold later asked Mrs. I. if she would like a loaf, and took her some." (P. 126, 2.12.25) "Christopher, Tommy and Dan made a 'corridor train' with chairs. Dan showed the two passengers where 'the lavatory' was, saying, 'in case you want to make water'. Tommy and N. (a visitor) then pretended to go to the lavatory, Dan saying, 'Can you undo your trousers?'" (P. 125, 13.7.25) "When dressing after bathing, Theobald and others chanted about a 'bottle of brown bee-wee water'. This happened on two or three days. They talked of 'selling' it. Theobald's talk re bee-wee has occurred coincidentally with much greater social freedom, friendliness and generally greater interest and activity." (P. 127, 10.12.26) "The children (Jane, Conrad, Dan) were playing 'ship', and each child had a waste-paper basket of his own as a 'lavatory'. They pretended to be sick, to make water and to pass faeces, saying, 'Mine's full.' 'Empty it in the sea,' and so on." To small children, it appears the natural thing to include a lavatory in their make-believe ship or train or house, and to play out lavatory situations like any other.

SOURCES OF LOVE AND HATE

The function of this play, or of such playful remarks as Conrad's on 8.12.26, p. 127 ("The cat was rolling on the floor, and Conrad said, 'Stick a stamp over his anus so that he can't pass faeces.'"), is to bring a measure of relief to the deep anxiety attaching to these psychic realities. Sometimes the freedom to include in their group play such direct representation of these recurring anal experiences will bring great emotional relief to a child who has been rather inhibited all round. (See note *re* Theobald, 13.7.25.)

It is not only through such *direct* dramatic representations that the child eases his conflict about excremental situations, however. Relief from tension comes to him also through the less direct process of sublimation. One or two of these children's naïve remarks point to the links which will carry anal interests over into the social and aesthetic activities of later life. In his painting and modelling (of which these children did a great deal and did it well—see *Intellectual Growth in Young Children*) the child not only obtains indirect satisfactions for primary anal pleasures, but also the continual and irrefutable proof that faecal-like stuff may be good and not bad, and that with it he can become a creator, not a destroyer.

3. Exhibitionism (Direct and Verbal)

There is naturally a good deal of overlap with the last section in the type of incident included here, especially in verbal exhibitionism. Even the genital phantasies of little children have so much anal and urethral colouring that their verbal references to sexual matters are frequently in terms of anal and urethral functions.

There are not many examples here of the socially forbidden forms of exhibitionism, such as actual genital display, since in most children these impulses very readily yield to direct or indirect training and social suggestion. Those cases which occurred were in the very early days of the school, and among two or three of the most difficult children. I have, however, included here all those specific incidents which can be described as definitely exhibitionistic in the widest sense, even when they were comparatively socialised and non-sexual in aim, as for example, Dan's delight in his own painting. (P. 139, 10.2.27) "When Dan was painting, he admired a particular piece of his own work, saying, ' You'd hardly think I'd done that, would you? You'd think a grown-up had done it, wouldn't you? It's so well done, isn't it? You come and look, Jane and Mrs. I.!'"

Two main aspects of the child's tendency to display himself with sexual intent, whether in words or deeds, are illustrated here.

(a) In the first place, the wish to display oneself is one of the component trends in the normal sexual impulse of both sexes, in children and adults alike. In adults, if not altogether repressed, it has become more or less confined to the specifically sexual situation, although, of course, it enters into ordinary social display (e.g. dress and manners, particularly of women) as a preliminary advance towards the sexual situation. Apart from this, however, the tendency to exhibit oneself is in the normal adult more or less disguised, appearing only in indirect and sublimated forms (sport, dancing, acting, etc.).

The naïve pleasure in being looked at and admired in the nude state shows itself quite strongly throughout the period of infancy. It normally meets with a certain amount of satisfaction from adults (e.g. at bath time), and only later comes under ban or discouragement. As one or two of the quoted incidents show (e.g. 29.10.24, p. 135), the quite small boy may show a natural and naïve pride in his penis and his urinary potency when he is attended in the lavatory by an adult: " As on several previous occasions, George asked Mrs. I. to go to the lavatory with him, as he wanted to make water, and when doing it, he throws his head back, looks at her and laughs, showing obvious pride. To-day she suggested that he could go alone. He needs no actual help, and asks none; he only wants an audience." Later on, the open showing of the genitals normally becomes inhibited, although pleasure in the display of the body as a whole remains very strong throughout early childhood. When, however, the display of the nude body for direct admiration, with a sexual tone, is no longer socially permitted, the child takes delight in " showing off " his clothed body, his dress, voice, gestures or achievements; and this type of pleasure persists throughout childhood and adolescence, up to adult life. Nevertheless, most small children, whenever they have a chance of doing it in secrecy away from adult eyes, will display the genital parts to each other in various types of play—family games, doctor games, lavatory games, and so on—these often continuing up to six and seven years of age.

(b) After the earliest years, however, the desire to show oneself for admiration, whether in a direct genital form, with regard to the body as a whole, or in various sublimated modes, is by no means a simple and uncomplicated impulse. As with so many of our primary sexual wishes, the exhibitionistic impulse adds certain secondary functions to its first primordial purpose. These secondary functions are scarcely less important than the primary ones. In discussing the last section of the material, we saw how strong the fear can be, and is even in normal children, of the badness of the inside of the body—badness due to the hostile thoughts and wishes connected with anal and urethral functions, as well as to the faeces and urine themselves. The need to display one's body, one's genital, or even one's achievements may arise from the anxiety connected with these phantasies. It may be either (1) the need to gain reassurance that one is not bad or dirty or destructive, but good, clean and lovable; or (2) the need to assert defiantly that one can with safety be bad, dirty or destructive, and not be attacked or destroyed for being so.

Some of the direct, and most of the verbal exhibitionism quoted here shows this secondary function, and many of the incidents illustrate the defiant mode of gaining reassurance, that is, not by winning love and admiration, but by daring to show the bad, and proving that bad things can safely be done. For example: (p. 135, 16.2.25) " Frank made water in the garden. Dan saw him, and stood in an attitude as if doing so himself, although he did not. Later, Frank was going to make water on the steps. When Mrs. I. asked him to do it in the lavatory he ran down the steps to the school entrance, opened the door, and was about to do it into the street, but was stopped." (P. 137, 7.7.25) " In the morning, when in his bathing suit, Duncan called to everyone to look at him : ' This is going to be bee-wee water'. He poured a cup of water down inside his suit, so that it ran out at the legs ; and repeated this, again calling the others ' attention with eagerness and laughter." (P. 138, 12.11.24) " Frank and Benjie were heard chanting ' put do-do in our mouths', and 'wee-wee on our dinner'. Harold suggested 'wee-wee-ing' into the wash-hand basin." (P. 139, 21.4.25) "The carpenter arrived to fasten up the trellis railing. Dan and Frank watched him with great interest. They watched him tar the wooden support, and wanted to touch it and to use the tar. When the carpenter said, 'No, don't touch that, it will make you in a mess,' they said, 'Oh, we should like to be in a mess, we should *like* to be black.'"

The compulsive type of exhibitionism occurring in perverse adults derives from these secondary functions, and chiefly the second mode. A less compulsive form of exhibitionism arises from a desire to have the genital, or the body as a whole (or less directly, the personality and social gifts), proved good by its power to give pleasure to others. If not too pronounced, this is, of course, a normal element in every love relation and every socially permitted type of self-display. In the strong wish of the little boy quoted on p. 137, to have his genital admired, the controlling factor must have been his overwhelming need to have his genital found good in the eyes of his sisters. Only the fear of its being bad and destructive could have led to this urgent and repeated exposure after severe correction, and the boy was undoubtedly in need of psychological help.[1]

There is one special point of interest to be noted in the *Records* (p. 135, 14.11.24.): "While resting, Frank and George had taken their socks off. Frank said to George, 'I can see your big toe,' with a giggle ; whereupon George immediately pulled his penis out." Frank's challenge about seeing George's toe thus immediately stimulates George to display his genital. George intuitively apprehended Frank's deeper intention and unconscious reference to the genital,

[1] "I am so very much upset and worried over my little boy of five years old, Z. He is a very bright, handsome and affectionate child and everyone thinks him charming. He is an only boy, with two little sisters, one older and one younger than him. About a month ago I heard him say to his sister, 'I know a good game'—then I heard laughter—then, 'I'll do it again.' I looked in and to my horror saw him pull out his little penis and jump up beside his sister who was reading on the sofa. I sent him upstairs to bed, but next day when he was sent to the lavatory, I heard him call, 'Come with me, Mary, and see my "suckie" when I go to wee-wee.' I took him to his Daddy who spanked him and threatened to send him away to a school for naughty rude boys. He wept bitterly and was most subdued for a day and I did so hope it was but a transitory thing, and to-day when I was getting their dinner ready and they were playing in the next room with the door ajar I heard him say 'here aren't I pretty, would you like to look at this' and saw him lift his pinafore and start to undo his knickers !"

and he responded to this subtle invitation by open display. He thus gives us a spontaneous interpretation of a symbol, and illustrates the fact so frequently seen in psycho-analytic work, of the displacement of psychic accent for the purposes of the conscious mind from the genital to another part or organ of the body.

Another minor detail is shown us in the incident on 27.2.25, p. 136: "At lunch Harold had said he would 'take his jersey off' and 'show his braces'; in the afternoon Frank did so, beginning apparently accidentally, meaning to undo his trousers for the lavatory. He pulled his arm out of the sleeve, put it in again, but then undid the neck and took the jersey off. He did all this behind the piano, then came out laughing and drew attention to what he had done." Here the showing of braces and suspenders (whose function is in fact to help hide the body) is itself felt to be a daring and defiant act—a subtle shift of meaning quite familiar in type to psycho-analysts. "If I draw attention to (or look at) what serves to hide the genital, I draw attention to the genital itself."

4. Sexual Curiosity

This section of the material deals, like the last, with genital sexuality. Very little comment is needed upon the incidents recorded. They show clearly the intense desire of small children—boys showing this more openly and boldly than girls—to see what the genitals of adults are like. Some of these incidents show the persistence with which children will pursue this desire, or the sudden way in which they will sometimes make an attempt upon an adult or another child in order to get a sight of the genitals. That it is more than idle curiosity, more even than the primary sexual wish to see for the pleasure of seeing, is readily understood from the material of previous sections, showing the child's anxiety about excretory functions. One of the things the child wants to know about his parents is whether or not their genitals, so closely associated for him with the excretory functions, are good or bad, clean or dirty, dangerous or helpful. Again, his very wish to expose the adult's sexual organs leads him to fear that all sorts of dangers may lie in wait for him, should he succeed.

There is no reason to doubt that all small children have this sexual curiosity about the genitals of parents and of other children. I have observed it very many times in children (without taking notes sufficiently exact to quote) from the time they can walk about—e.g. the wish to go into the bathroom or lavatory when the grown-ups are there, or attempts to crawl under a chair occupied by an adult, and to peep up at them—or, later on, more veiled and sidelong looks if an opportunity should seem to occur. The psycho-analysis of all types of adults and children shows this to have been a universal desire in early childhood, even in those in whom sexual curiosity has later been almost completely repressed.

One particular and important phantasy of small children is hinted at in the incident on 4.12.24 (p. 141), when Frank speaks of " the big fat thing on her tummy ". From this incident alone we should hardly know what it was he imagined to be there, but from psycho-analytic studies we do know that one or both of two things would be in Frank's mind. Either he was attributing the possession of a phallus to the grown woman, or he was referring to the idea that she had babies inside her (Frank's own mother had been pregnant not so very long previously). Little children do think of their mothers' bodies as containing a large number of children not yet born; they are there hidden away inside, as children, not as mere ova, about which of course they know nothing. This is another unconscious motive for their curiosity, to see how many children there are, and, indeed, to get at them and damage them as rivals who are feared and hated.

In the incident with Dan on 21.9.24 (p. 140), a significant detail is the shifting of attention from the woman in whom he was really interested to the table legs and underside of the table. In his play with the table, he was magically achieving the success which he was denied in reality; but as this did not satisfy, he returned at every opportunity to the real attack.

The incident on 19.5.25 (p. 141) is an interesting one, because it shows a piece of behaviour with many complex motives behind it : " In the afternoon, Priscilla washed Dan and then Frank, and took Dan into the lavatory to make water ; she undid their trousers for them, and then said, ' Now you have not wet your knickers'; Laurie watching." Priscilla was pretending to be a careful mother to the small boys when she took them into the lavatory to attend to their buttonings and unbuttonings, and she justified her attention by saying, "Now you have not wet your knickers", as though they certainly would have done so without her help. But her manner showed that her chief motive was, in fact, to get an opportunity of seeing the genitals of the boys, as well as to subdue the boys to dependence upon her, and so gain some alleviation of her own castration phantasies.

In the incident quoted on p. 141, 17.5.26,[1] we see the children occupied in their thought not only with the question of what makes the difference between male and female, but with the question of parental intercourse. There is no doubt that Dan's inquiry, " What do you call it when there's a he-and-a-her, a she-and-a-him together ? " may be taken as a question about what parents do in sexual intercourse, and this is confirmed by his shyness and hesitation. From the analysis of children, we know that one of the things they want to know is whether parental intercourse is good or bad—that is, hurtful or helpful to each other and to the children inside the mother.

5. Sexual Play and Aggression

The incidents under this heading are closely related to the last group, but differentiated from them by greater activity. Some of the behaviour recorded shows the marked sadistic element in the sexual wishes of very small children towards adults, and in their phantasies of the nature of sexual intercourse between parents. Although these direct wishes and phantasies belong to the genital level of libidinal development, they nevertheless retain many of the characteristics of the

---

[1] " While sewing in the afternoon, Priscilla told us that she had ' seen a bull ' while on the way to school. Dan said, ' a bull, what's a bull ? ' Priscilla said, ' a he-cow'. Dan said, ' But isn't a cow a he ? ' Priscilla and Mrs. I. said, ' No.' They spoke of ' he ' and ' she ' animals, and Mrs. I. gave them the names ' male ' and ' female '. They instanced the male and female among the children in school, the mummies and daddies and other grown-ups they knew. Then Dan said, ' What do you call it when there's a he-and-a-her, a she-and-a-him together ? ' Mrs. I. was not quite sure what he referred to, but said, ' Do you mean when they are together in the same room ? ' He said, ' When they are touching.' She touched his hand, and said, ' Do you mean like this ?— We haven't one word to refer to this. We say " he and she are touching ".' He said, with a shy look and a little hesitation, ' No, I mean when they are very close together, standing up.' The conversation was broken off at that point by the interruption of a visitor."

earlier, pre-genital levels (oral, anal and urethral), and it is from these sources that the sadistic element is drawn.

An example is the incident on 17.11.25.[1] Here we see very plainly a sexual phantasy of hurting—a phantasy ultimately based upon the child's own desire to bite his mother's breast, to penetrate it with his teeth, in the intensity of his wish to get it for himself. The anxiety which ensued in Dan from this active piece of sadism towards Priscilla and Mrs. I. then led him, first, to compensate for the attack by fussy kissing (i.e. in phantasy, sucking rather than biting) ; then to make the open request that Mrs. I. would submit to his sexual intent—the motive of this undoubtedly being to prove that he could get his pleasure *without* hurting her. When the opportunity for this was denied, he suddenly made his sadistic attack in an open, non-symbolic form.

The same aggressive intent, with a sexual colouring, is shown in Harold's threat (6.3.25) to " tease Tommy, and cut him open and pull his inside out ". There was no quarrel here, but a play situation between Harold and Tommy ; so that again we are not dealing with simple aggression. Harold's bumping of Mrs. I. with his engine (20.3.25), and then immediately going on to hug her again, showed the same colouring, as this, too (like Denis's biting, p. 115), was done in love, not in anger. So with the children's boisterous hugging of Sallie on 23.3.25.

Psycho-analytic studies have shown that all children have these sadistic notions of sexual intercourse in unconscious

---

[1] " When playing with Priscilla and Mrs. I. Dan pretended to be ' something in the sea ', ' a gangi ', which later on was ' a tiger or a lion ', and became very sadistic, without any quarrel or provocation. He suddenly wanted to hurt Priscilla and Mrs. I., and picked up a piece of sewing and threw it at them. It had a needle in it, and when Dan saw this, he asked Priscilla, ' Did it prick you ? ' ' No.' ' It would have been better if it had,' he said."

(It must be noted that there had been no provocation to this nor any quarrelling ; the situation was not one of ordinary aggression, but definitely sexual as immediately appears.) " When Mrs. I. was leaving, Priscilla and Dan made a fuss about her going, and insisted on kissing her ' all over '—face and hair and dress and shoes. After this, Dan fidgeted about in a way that clearly indicated an erection, and asked her to ' lie down and be a motor bike ', assuring her that he ' wouldn't hurt her.' (Of course she did not do so.) After Mrs. I. had said goodbye, she had occasion to return, and was standing on the bottom step of the stairs talking, when Dan bent down and kissed her ankle, then suddenly thrust his hand up her leg. Priscilla then tried to do the same, which, of course, she prevented."

phantasy, although they are very much more powerful in some children than others. Their ultimate source lies in the child's own earlier biting impulses towards the breast. These fuse with the later experienced thrusting movements of anal sadism, and with the child's attacks, by screaming and biting, scratching and kicking, his intense desire to grasp and hold, to crush and squeeze, if he cannot get all the satisfaction he wants at his mother's breast. These are the primary sources of his sadistic notions of his father's sexual relation with his mother. Such phantasies are naturally much stronger in children who are constitutionally unable to tolerate oral privation, or in those who, from circumstance, have to suffer more than normal.

These phantasies are, moreover, closely linked with the children's feeling that the parents (who, far more often than is commonly realised, are glimpsed or overheard in the sexual situation) are quite different from the day-time parents—much more like dangerous and uncontrollable animals. The mother's position in the sexual relation seems, in addition, to be a helpless and perilous one—utterly different from the mother who supports and helps children; and the father seems to be hurting and attacking her.

Such phantasies have a great deal to do with the castration fears of both boy and girl, to be considered presently. Moreover, when they are much exaggerated, they lead to an inability to find normal sexual satisfaction—either impotence or a turning away from women altogether being the outcome.

Naturally, they become much intensified when the parents *do* quarrel, or the father is cruel to the mother in reality. It is mainly through the over-stimulation of these unconscious sexual phantasies that the real quarrelling and cruelty of the parent have an evil effect upon the child's emotional development.

In the majority of children, however, these sadistic phantasies become tempered by their actual experience of love; and where the child is not fixated at the oral level, but passes on normally to full genital development, the sadistic elements become far less significant in his wishes and phantasies. Through the later course of his sexual and ego development, he comes to believe that his father and mother give good to each other, not hurt, in sexual intercourse; and that he can give good, not hurt, to one whom he loves. It is in the early crisis of his sexual life, in the years before the latency period, whilst his experience and sense of reality are still weak and inadequate, that the pre-genital phantasies dominate the child's genital wishes.

A number of the incidents in this section show a definitely anal colouring. For instance (16.1.25): " While modelling, Frank said, apropos of a long piece of plasticine, ' Somebody's climbing up the lady's ah-ah house.' " Frank's modelling, again, represented parental intercourse. (Most of the children, and especially all the boys, when they began modelling, made long " snakes " more frequently than anything else.) But when Frank says, " somebody is climbing up the lady's ah-ah house ", he is not only showing us parental intercourse, but also his dread that the body of the mother, into which the father enters, is nothing but an " ah-ah house," a lavatory, where there is nothing but faeces and urine. That is to say, Frank's genital phantasies are deeply tinged with the anxieties belonging to earlier anal situations.

The very amusing incident on 18.5.27 gives us a specially clear example of the mechanism of *projection*: " After lunch the children bathed in the sand-pit. Three of them, when drying and dressing in the cloakroom, asked Miss D. to ' Please go away and leave us alone.' When she refused to do so, they were very angry and made violent protests; and ended by saying that *she* was 'rude', as she insisted on staying with them when they were dressing! And all wrapped towels round their middles, so that she could not see them—trying to dress under the towels—with an air of completely shocked and injured innocence! " When Miss D. would not acquiesce in the children's wish to be left alone naked, and a sense of guilt was thus evoked, they dealt with this guilt by complete projection of the guilty wishes. It was not they, but *she*, who was " rude ".

At the end of the material I quote an opinion of Charlotte Bühler's with regard to " a first suggestion of sexual development, a brief flicker of emotion " occurring in the years round about 3;0. I quote it here, in connection with this series of openly sexual incidents, because it is an indication that the eyes of non-analytic observers are gradually being opened to what, only a few years ago, would never have been seen, or, if seen, admitted, in the emotional life of little children. Even such an inadequate observation as this, such a grudging admission of the psychological facts which psycho-analysis has revealed, marks a very great advance in the scientific accuracy and dispassionateness of the academic text-books. This most significant chapter in the child's psychological history is now beginning to gain admittance to the previously closed pages of academic teaching on mental development.

6. MASTURBATION

Only one instance of masturbation is recorded as occurring in the school, and that for a quite short period. As I pointed out in my introductory chapter, this has no bearing upon the actual incidence of the practice in small children, but throws some light upon its psychology. When playing actively with other children under supervision, only those children who are at the moment under great mental stress are likely to have recourse to masturbation. I have on one occasion seen a little girl in a large class in an infants' school engaged in the act while seated at her desk ; but that is quite uncommon. It is this psychological fact which has led some observers (e.g. Katherine Bridges, quoted on p. 154) to underrate the frequency of masturbation in childhood, and to believe that it is commoner in boys than in girls. In so far as it does occur under group conditions, it would more readily occur with boys, for various reasons ; e.g. the boy's clothes make his genital more accessible, the boy's type of masturbation with the hand is more readily resorted to in ordinary postures than the girl's characteristic type, boys are in any case bolder, more aggressive and less secretive than girls. The general experience of psycho-analysts and psychiatrists is, however, that masturbation is actually more frequent and more commonly of a compulsive type in little girls than in little boys. The evidence gathered from parents and nurses which I am myself able to quote (see pp. 147-151) definitely confirms this.

I have used the single case occurring in the school as an occasion to quote rather fully from the many cases of masturbation I have had reported to me by mothers and nurses, because it seems very important that it should be widely realised that masturbation does frequently occur in early childhood amongst both boys and girls, and amongst children who nevertheless grow up quite happily and satisfactorily. It is important that this should be known, both because of its great theoretical significance, and because of the need of the children themselves to receive wise treatment from parents and educators. In the letter on p. 151, a responsible matron tells the mother of the masturbating child that the child "will go out of her mind if it is not stopped". It is a very serious state of affairs that such falsehoods can still to-day be used to terrify both parents and children, and often itself to create the very harm which is attributed to the masturbatory act.

It is quite untrue that masturbation in itself can cause such serious disturbances of mind or body as are here attributed to it. When it is associated with serious mental disturbance or bodily ill-health, as it is in some of the children quoted in these letters, the key lies in the *phantasies* which the act of masturbation expresses, and the excessive anxiety arising from these phantasies.

The public attitude towards masturbation in little children tends to take one of two directions. The first, which is by far the commonest and most traditional, is the view that masturbation is not only a harmful, but a wicked thing, and must be instantly stopped if moral and physical ruin is not to follow. Now this attitude, although completely exaggerated, and false in its exaggeration, does recognise the truth that masturbation has a psychological significance, and that its intention is anti-social. The second attitude, very modern, and found in far fewer people—those, mostly, who feel themselves emancipated from sexual prejudices— is that the act of masturbation has no significance at all and is a purely localised sensation reflex which need not be commented on by educators and will die away of itself as the child gets older. Now this view is a probably far safer attitude for parents to take, and it is descriptively true that the great majority of children, who are not severely punished or terrified out of their wits by threats of the harm that will ensue from masturbation, do grow out of it as their normal interests and activities develop. Nevertheless, this second view has as much *theoretical* falsehood in it as the first view. It is not true that the act is purely localised and without psychological significance. It has profound psychological significance, but of so general and normal a kind that under any ordinarily favourable environment, most children find their own normal solution to the mental conflict which at its most acute phase manifests itself in auto-erotic acts. Whilst, therefore, it is a good thing if people begin to pay somewhat less attention to the occurrence and to feel less distressed by it, it is nevertheless desirable that responsible educators and psychologists should realise not only that masturbation has psychological meaning, but what that meaning is—should, in fact, understand the real grounds for the educational policy they adopt.

For an understanding of the psychology of early masturbation we have to turn to the unconscious phantasies associated with it which are revealed in the psycho-analysis of both children and adults. The material I am able to quote here gives us very little hint of what these phantasies are. The boy mentioned on p. 147, who shouts and laughs in his bed and says, "I am laughing at ladies and babies", and " I can't help it, I must " is pretty certainly engaged in some sort of masturbatory activity, and gives us the barest hint of his sexual phantasies about ladies and babies.

In detail, masturbatory phantasies vary characteristically from individual to individual, but the essential content always has reference to the child's sexual longings for mother or father, as the case may be, and his aggressive intentions towards his rivals, the whole being worked out by the omnipotent magical act of achieving sexual satisfaction in his own person. In most cases, this self-induced satisfaction is sought largely as a reassurance against the fear of having the genital attacked and removed by vengeful parents, and against the dread of its being bad, dirty and destructive.[1] So long as the sensation of pleasure can be repeated and

[1] I might instance in this connection the dream of an adult man patient who had been, as a boy, a compulsive masturbator, and suffered severely under the open threats of castration by his father. During his analysis there were periods when the need to masturbate became very strong again. Associated with one of these periods was a dream, in which he found himself in the presence of a certain young woman, he himself wearing only an undervest. He raised the vest to show his genital, saying to her, " There is nothing the matter with it, is there ? " and she replied, " No, there is nothing the matter, except that it is too hot." From the whole context, and many earlier associations, it was clear the dream thus expressed not only the intense need for reassurance which is usually involved in the exposure of the genitals—as I indicated in the last section of the material—and which is also a strong factor in masturbation, but also the particular nature of one dread connected with the genital, namely, the dread that it is nothing but an instrument for the expulsion of hot, burning urine, and therefore dangerous and destructive.

voluntarily achieved, the child feels he can prove that he has not been deprived of the organ, or of the power of pleasure, and that his genital itself is " good ", not " bad ". And if it is good, not bad, it is capable of giving help and pleasure to others as well as himself. The masturbatory act normally expresses this hope of giving and receiving love, and of creative potency, as well as the needed reassurance against the fears of revenge and castration.

Since, however, it is a magical reassurance within the child's own mind, having no relation to the world of outer reality, it is not secure. It has to be sought again. And where the act means to the child very marked defiance and aggression against the parents—the secret stealing of pleasure rather than the actual giving of love to other people—the need for reassurance arises again almost immediately.

Where masturbation is persistent and compulsive, it is because these anxieties arising from the aggressive elements in the act, the secret attack upon the parents to get pleasure that they do not give, are overwhelmingly strong. Such anxieties occur in a greater or less degree in all children, and the great majority of children (probably all) do, at some time or other, in some form or other, and in some degree or other, find masturbatory comfort and satisfaction, masturbation being the genital equivalent of what thumb-sucking is on the oral level.

It is, however, only in those children in whom these anxieties become very marked that the compulsive and persistent reassurance of the auto-erotic act is needed. Such a state may come about either (*a*) from internal causes, e.g. in those children who by constitution are very intolerant of any denial of satisfaction, or whose original aggression is unusually strong ; or (*b*) from external factors, for example, an environment, (1) where the normal sublimations of primitive impulses are not possible, the child being denied normal satisfactions in tender love, in muscular play and the development of skill, in ordinary curiosity and external interests ; (2) where he actually suffers some sadistic sexual experience ; or (3) where, by their excessive reproaches or threats of severe punishment and castration, parents or educators have shown the child that they appreciate only the aggressive, destructive element in the masturbation, and have no sense of the element of love or reassurance, or attempt to re-create, that it also contains.

Occasionally, the child's guilt and dread about the masturbatory act and the phantasies which it expresses are so great that he cannot deal with it himself, and does need the help of real external control. On p. 148, I quote a case of this type. Not knowing the earlier history of this case, it is impossible to say whether the excessive anxiety arises from something in the child's constitution, or whether, in spite of the nurse's statement that the child has never been scolded or punished for the act, she nevertheless has been acted upon too strongly in some indirect way by those in her environment. One thing is certain about such a child, namely, that she is in desperate need of psycho-analytic treatment and that nothing short of this will effect a cure, since she has to lean so heavily upon outside control that cannot be continued in later life, from the nature of the case.

Bridges seems to suggest in the quoted passage (p. 154) that children play with their own genitals *because* they have diffuse attention, or indefinite or limited interests. Cause and effect, however, lie in great measure in the reverse direction. They have few or scattered interests largely because so much of their psychic energy is locked up in deep internal conflict, itself expressed in the masturbation.

She further points out that as the children's interest in the activities provided in the school and their play with other children develop, the masturbation disappears. This is happily true, whether in home or school, except in the case of children who are too severely embroiled in internal conflict. The good nursery school is able to wean the ordinary child from playing with his genitals not only through the material and opportunity for other forms of pleasurable activity in which the infantile sexual impulses can find an indirect outlet (play with sand and water and plasticine, the building of big towers, dramatic expression, etc.), but largely through the atmosphere of security and affection which the adult provides, and the permission which she, acting as a mild external super-ego, offers to the child to be active in directions which have for him these unconscious sexual significances. The personal relation of the child to the teacher, as well as to other children, and the discovery that safe and satisfactory outlets for both sexual and aggressive impulses are provided and encouraged, enable the child to face outwards in the life of the emotions instead of seeking satisfaction and power within himself. The material of this section thus has very significant bearings upon problems of early education.

7. FAMILY PLAY, AND IDEAS ABOUT BABIES AND MARRIAGE

The general preoccupation of small children with the different facets of the problem of family relationships—father, mother and child—and the corresponding aspects of their own internal psychic life, is shown by the constant way in which they will turn any sort of external objects into "daddies", "mummies" and "babies". Even the Montessori "long stair" will be turned into "daddy sticks", "mummy" and "baby sticks" by very young children, and any small object will be regarded as a " baby " so-and-so. The family situation provides a pattern for the whole world of experience with children under four years of age. Later on, when they have acquired not only relatively impersonal interests, but the ability to hide their deeper feelings, this central phantasy comes out less often into the open and does not so naïvely dominate such a wide field of their activity, although it will still appear in the special situation of free, imaginative play.

In these incidents we are shown not only the wishes of small children to have babies of their own, and their early ideas about what babies are made of, but also some of their early notions as to marriage and the intimate relation between fathers and mothers, together with an occasional glimpse of their deeper unconscious phantasies about parental intercourse.

In some of their conversations about who can marry whom (for example 8.7.25, when the children have been conversing about being married, Dan sums things up by saying, " I can't be married to a boy and Priscilla can't be married to a girl ") it is not merely their intellectual notions about sex and the relation of the sexes which we see the children attempting to work out. This intellectual uncertainty is largely an outcome of the deeper conflict between their identifications with the two parents respectively. Both boy and girl show this conflict, each normally developing an identification with both father and mother.

Several of these incidents show the wish to have and produce a baby occurring in little boys as well as girls. When two or three of the boys rocked about as if they were holding babies in their arms, they were unmistakably behaving as if they were mothers. This wish of the boy to have a baby is on the basis of his identification with his mother, and these incidents thus link up with the next section of the material.

It is not generally recognised that boys have this wish to give birth to children as girls have, partly because they do not, as a rule, show it quite so openly as girls, partly because we ourselves are prejudiced against recognising it. In the analysis of boys, however, it has become clearly established that this wish is always present in a certain phase of their psychological development.

The intense wish of the little girl to have a baby (that is, to be given a baby by her father) is clearly shown in some of these incidents. When Frank and Priscilla together sew " egg-covers " (" We're making things for when we're grown-up—*really*, we are ! " and " We're going to be married and have some little babies ") the wish has come out fully into the open. The intensity of the wish in the girl child, and her anxiety with regard to her hostility to her mother because of this wish, was clearly shown in Priscilla's behaviour whilst her mother was away from home. This appeared to the child a wish-fulfilment, i.e. her mother had (to her mind) gone away *because* the child had wanted to have her father to herself. The absence thus laid her open to all the dangers that come to the child who has no good mother, who has driven her good mother away. Her guilt and unhappiness about this apparent wish-fulfilment led her to be very difficult and hostile in school. The striking thing was the complete change of mood when her mother returned and brought her a gift of a large baby doll. This meant to Priscilla not only the return of the helpful mother, but the mother's permission to have a baby and be a mother herself. Her babies would thus be good ones, since her mother helped her to have them—not bad as they would have to be if she drove her mother away and stole the babies for herself. Now, then, she could be friendly with other grown-up women, and loving and careful with all the other children.

It will be noticed that the children play quite a good deal, not only at the complete family situation, but at " getting married ". The charming play of the children with laurel leaves and flowers, ribbons and confetti and bridal trains, photographs and wedding trains and parties, not only works over the real social situations connected with weddings in the real world, but also represents their notions of the good food, good children, the pleasure and help which the good father and mother give each other in their sexual relation—for in unconscious phantasy "getting married" represents parental intercourse. And in the midst of all this delightful happy play at weddings, there peep out here and there, the deeper and more terrifying phantasies of the child about the nature of "getting married". Although these brief hints of deeper phantasies occupy but little space and time in the open words and play behaviour of the children, it is worth our while to glance at them, since they are undoubtedly linked up with the less happy characteristics of the children who reveal them. Frank and Harold, for instance, in their play of "express wedding trains", are representing the potent father, and showing us their notions of what the potent father does. When Harold asks Priscilla to "go into the little house and I'll be the Daddy and go past in my motor car", he is again representing parental intercourse. But when Frank says of someone who is going to be married, "When she is married we shall spit in her face, shan't we?" he is allowing us to glimpse another of his ideas as to what fathers do to mothers. On the surface his remark is quite unintelligible, but in the light of what psycho-analytic studies have shown as to unconscious urinary phantasies of male potency and intercourse, we can understand it. Frank was expressing, in the only terms permissible in his conscious mind, his anxiety about his belief that his father urinated into his mother. It is of course a phantasy built upon projection—since the child has nothing but urine to give to mother, the father cannot have and shall not have anything better to give. But it operates as a real belief and gives rise to great terrors in the child, making it harder for him to believe in good parents, and so in the possibility of being good himself. The great dread that Frank and Benjie had about the sexual relation between the parents is shown in an unqualified way when they speak of "Someone who is crazy" and "She is going to the police station, and getting married, and then we will kill her after that." They are speaking of the night-time sexual parents, whom they do not understand, who seem to them to be "crazy", so utterly different from the day-time parents. In their saying "We will kill her after that", they are expressing both their own hostile intents to the mother, on the ground of direct rivalry with her in relation to the father, and their phantasy of what the father does to the mother. It is to be remembered that both Frank and Benjie were difficult children, Benjie being a quite unusually hostile and unhappy child. These highly sadistic phantasies do occur in more normal children, but are in them in much less need of open expression; the child can (for a variety of reasons) deal with them more effectively by his real knowledge and experience of love.

A further phantasy of little children illustrated here is their notion that babies are made from the general contents of the mother's body, namely, food and faeces. When Frank asks Miss B., " When we buy babies, do we have to pay for them ? " we are struck by the curious form of the question. In fact, we know from similar remarks in many other contexts, that Frank is expressing the anal notion of how babies are made—and, in especial, his anxiety that if he gets babies for himself from his mother, he will have to give back something in return from the inside of his own body. His wish is to get something for nothing, to get all the good that he can from his mother for himself, including the babies and his father's love; but his dread, connected with early experiences in the training of anal habits, is that his mother will demand retribution, and take away everything good from him in return.

Y.'s idea that he is growing a baby in his inside, quoted on p. 161 ("Mummy, I'm growing a baby sister." *Oh, no, Y., you can't do that.* Well, then, it's a baby brother. *Oh, no, you can't grow babies—only Mummies can do that.* Well, Mummy, there's *something* happening in my tummy!) follows upon the cat's giving birth to kittens the day before. He was obviously wishful himself to create in this way, on the basis of his love for his father and identification with his mother. When his mother denied him this possibility by saying that " only Mummies can do that " the baby that he believed he had inside him became a forbidden, therefore a stolen one, therefore a bad one, therefore one that would make him ill —and he was actually sick. (No physical cause was known.)

The boy and girl twins (p. 161) show us the same phantasy that both boy and girl can have children. A further detail of a universal phantasy about children is shown by these two, namely, the idea that the baby is born from the anus— the so-called cloacal theory of birth. This boy also believed that his daddy had given birth to him, and his mummy to the girl, evidently the notion being that his daddy must have given birth to him because he was like his daddy. One surmises some repercussion of castration anxiety and dread connected with the idea of having been born from the mother.

In the quoted passage from Rasmussen (p. 163), again we have the phantasy of babies being made of food and coming out of the anus. In this case, however, the phantasy was reinforced by the actual terms of explanation given by the mother. The same child's notion of the " meat-man " who manufactures ladies illustrates, in an obscure way, the food theory.

In the conversation between the little girl and boy in my last incident in this section (p. 162), the girl shows us her intense anxiety when the boy challenges her happy assumption that she will have boys of her own. She feels the unconscious hostility expressed in his saying, " I don't suppose you ever will, though " and cannot bear the fear of such a possibility which this stirs up in her. " To be just an ordinary mother " was Mary's solution to her inner conflict, but since it was yet so far removed from real attainment, she could not feel secure in the hope that it would come true, when challenged in this dogmatic way by a boy playmate. She must have felt that he was saying, " *I* would not give you any."

8. CASTRATION FEARS, THREATS AND SYMBOLISM

We have already noted hints of those anxieties in the child which, when fully developed with specific reference to the genital organs, are familiar as fears of castration. The incidents grouped under this section give us plain illustrations of such fears.

In the boy, this anxiety takes the form of dreading that his genital organ will be attacked, injured or removed altogether by parents or rivals. The ultimate dread is that of the loss of all capacity for sexual pleasure,[1] but it is most clearly seen in the specific form of fear of losing the genital itself. In the girl, castration fears are rather more complicated. On the one hand, the girl commonly believes that she has already been deprived of a penis. In unconscious logic, not giving is equivalent to taking away, and she phantasies that it has been actually removed. But, deeper than this actual envy of the penis and grudge because it has not been

[1] For which Dr Ernest Jones has suggested the term *aphanisis*.

SOURCES OF LOVE AND HATE

given her, lies a dread that her own internal organs of reproduction, indeed the whole of the inside of the body, will be injured and destroyed. The inside of the body is naturally more significant for the girl than for the boy. So long as the boy can reassure himself by the actual presence of his real penis, he can feel safe and content. The girl has not this reassurance, and it is less easy for her to secure herself against the anxieties attaching to the phantasy that the inside of her body may have been spoilt or injured, or altogether destroyed.

If one asks what these castration fears (using the term to cover all this complex of anxiety) spring from, the answer is manifold. They spring from a variety of sources in the mental life of the child, many of them inherent and inescapable. They undoubtedly rise quite spontaneously, although, of course, they are reinforced, and may be over-stimulated until they become pathogenic, by actual threats from adults or other children. These threats do in fact occur, even from responsible grown-ups, more often than many people realise. Many children are threatened with castration, or an equivalent disease, because of bed-wetting, masturbation, or exhibitionism, and this may happen either with little children or with adolescents. "A policeman will come and cut it off if you do that" is sometimes said to little children. An adult patient of mine was told by his father, when he was fourteen, that if he masturbated "it would be necessary to send for the doctor, and an operation would have to be performed which would prevent him from ever being able to have children of his own."

Such threats are obviously overwhelmingly terrifying to children of any age; but they are not essential stimuli to castration dread. This undoubtedly occurs in every child, and may become quite acute even in those children who have not experienced such open threats. They arise partly from the child's internal psychic processes, and partly from inevitable real experiences. As to the latter, every little child suffers minor real injuries of some sort or hurts to the projecting parts of the body—a cut on the finger or knee, the loss of a tooth, having his hair cut off, etc. Every child also feels an actual sense of loss in the anal situation. With a certain pressure of faeces on the rectal muscles, the child experiences actual pleasure, but when the faeces pass out, he loses this pleasure, and loses the faeces themselves, which have been a part of his body. His unwillingness to experience this loss is, as we have seen, one of the influences which make him recalcitrant to anal training. Moreover, every boy experiences actual erection of the penis at some time or other in early infancy and the first years of childhood. In erection it seems to the boy that he possesses a larger, more solid, upstanding organ. But this does not last—it is followed by flaccidity, when the organ appears very small, shrunken and soft. The child knows nothing of the physiology or mechanics of this phenomenon; he knows that sometimes he has what appears to him a large and effective penis, and sometimes he has not, and he has no guarantee that the desired condition will come back again when he wishes it. The dread of impotence is one form of the dread of castration: the impotent penis is as if not there at all.

Probably more important than these factors, however, are the child's own aggressive impulses in the biting phase of oral sexuality, when he actually has to bite off and eat up objects that seem good to him and are a source of pleasure, when he actually wishes, moreover, to bite off the breast—whether because he loves and wants to possess it inside himself, or because he is angry that it does not come to him, and wishes to attack it and spoil it in anger. I have already shown how the impulses of the oral situation link on to those of the genital, and there is no doubt that the boy's wish to bite off the mother's nipple is a very significant contributory element to his dread that his own penis will be cut off, that is, bitten off, either by his mother or rivals.[1]

[1] In an important paper recently published, M. N. Searl has suggested that the ultimate source of the dread of loss of pleasure, that is, psychic death, which finds a specific expression in the dread of loss of the genital, is to be found in the child's experience of actual exhaustion after a fit of screaming, in early infancy. Miss Searl looks upon the screaming fit—the scream of rage, when the child cannot get satisfaction for his instinctual desires of hunger or love—as the first *real* attack of the child upon his real parents. But this at the same time attacks the child himself, rasping his throat, choking him and bringing a general feeling of pain and misery. If carried to the point of exhaustion, when the screaming does not effect any satisfaction of wishes, it leads to a state of very extensive loss of capacity for pleasure; and this is the primary and most generalised form of castration dread. It is probably this situation which first leads the child to feel, " If I attack other people, I shall be attacked in return," since he actually experiences an attack on his own throat and chest and body, which he attributes to those whom he wished to attack. ("The Psychology of Screaming," by M. N. Searl, *I. J. of Psycho-Analysis*, *XIV*, Pt. 1. A further paper on " Play, Aggression and Reality " is to appear in the same journal shortly.)

All these are, however, only contributory factors. The main and immediate source of the boy's dread that his penis will be attacked and removed is his wish to attack and remove his father's penis, either as a rival for the possession of the mother, or as itself a source of love and power which the boy wants to possess in love, instead of the mother's possessing it. In this latter situation, the mother is the boy's rival. Both of these attitudes to the father stir up profound castration dread in the boy: what he wishes to do, whether in love or anger, will inevitably be done to him.

Correspondingly, the girl's dread of being injured in her internal organs is mainly derived from her own wish to attack her mother as a rival, and get the babies and all the good things from the mother's body for herself.

This extremely brief account of the meaning and origin of castration dread may perhaps suffice to make the actual material more intelligible. Recognisable manifestations of castration dread are not very many in the school records—one would naturally not expect them to be. But those that did occur were very striking.

In some of these incidents, castration fears appear quite direct and open. In others, the child makes use of various symbols to express his anxiety indirectly: e.g. other parts of the body (legs, fingers, nose, hand, tail or hair), or external objects (stilts, shoes or toys).

Sometimes the children are seen endeavouring to allay and annul their own castration anxiety by threatening a similar attack on other children, or working out their phantasies by *playing* at being castrated, for example, when Dan and Frank bury their feet in the sand and then say, " Tell Priscilla to ask us to come and love her ", going on to add, " We can't, because our legs are cut off."

In the last incident quoted,[1] when these boys have been

---

[1] " Three boys bathing. All in bath together, getting out. X sticking out his posterior at a boy and roaring with laughter. All three boys laughing. One of them sticking his front out slightly, and then all three laughing again. Looking to catch my eye, then laughing again. So infectious was their laughter that I could not look solemn. Then as they jumped out to dry themselves, I said, ' I really think boys are ruder than girls ! ' X. : ' Well—they've got more to be rude about, haven't they ? ' The air of superiority, lord-of-creation and tolerance for the other sex, with which he said this, set us all laughing again. By the time they were dry and had their pyjamas on they were deep in a discussion as to how to make stilts, and what wood they would need, straps, etc., and the next day they made them."

showing to a woman their arrogant pride in the possession of the penis, saying that they " have more to be rude about" than girls have, one might well expect an uprush of castration anxiety, a fear that she might in some way revenge herself upon them. And the course of the later conversation suggests that this did occur—but was successfully dealt with by the talk about making stilts. We can take it that this plan for making stilts was a further phantasy of potency, and meant also a magical way of getting so high above the woman that she could not castrate them.

In other incidents the girl's feeling that she has already been deprived of a penis is shown. When Priscilla says to Frank, " Oh, look what you have done, it's bleeding ! " she is obviously expressing, under cover of her concern for it, an envious wish to injure the boy's penis, the bleeding, of course, being quite imaginary.

The children's gibe at Miss X. and their interpretation of some small mannerism (which they magnified) to the effect that " she's been to the hospital and they did something to her, and now she can't make water " links up their castration phantasies with urinary potency. In this context, making water is felt by them to be both a defensive attack on outside enemies and a means of getting rid of the bad that is inside. What they fear is that if one is bad, one's organ of potency may be cut off, and then one has nothing with which to defend oneself against external enemies (by urinary attack), nor can one hope to get rid of the bad enemies (urine, thoughts, wishes) inside one. Dan's bed-wetting at an earlier period, when his castration anxieties had first acutely developed, must have been to him a reassurance against these particular terrifying phantasies.

This idea of the penis as an organ of urinary control is an important element in the girl's envy of the penis, a wish for it as a proof that she has not been injured (" split in two ", as one child described to me the female genital) and therefore has not done bad things to justify this injury. Boys take a corresponding pride in their possession. But their contempt for girls rests itself upon anxiety. They fear that what appears to have happened to girls may yet happen to them, if their secret hostilities to the father and their sexual wishes to the mother become known. And they attribute to the castrated female the desire to take (bite off) for herself the so essential organ which they have and she has not.

The acuteness of castration dread, whether in the boy's or the girl's form, will obviously depend upon the whole course of the previous sexual history, and not alone upon genital experience. If, for example, the child's experiences at the breast have been satisfactory (whether for internal or external reasons, or both), he is by so much less likely to develop over-severe castration anxiety later on. Where he remains unsatisfied, or is badly handled in the weaning situation, he is all the more likely to suffer acute castration dread in the genital phase. On the other hand, a genital threat, or other traumatic experience at the time when his genital wishes are most acute (say round about 2-4 years) may itself serve to re-awaken earlier oral anxieties.

In the incident on p. 167, the little girl N. expressed her determination to be a boy by cutting off her own hair. On the surface this might seem to contradict the idea of castration, but the intention is obviously to make herself more *like* a boy—things that are made equal in one respect may then prove equal in another respect. Besides, there is all the difference in the world between, on the one hand, actively cutting one's own hair off oneself and having the instrument to do it with, and having it *done to* one by someone else, and especially by the mother, who is treated as so much of a rival, and whose attacks are feared as a return for the child's own hostilities to her.

When considering the theme of family play, I pointed out the way in which, with certain boys, even their overt behaviour occasionally shows a strong identification with the mother. This identification was particularly marked with one or two of the children in the school, and especially Frank. The general description of Frank and several of the incidents included here will make this quite plain. Dan, too, in the early period of the school, showed this identification very strongly. In the cases of Tommy and Conrad, it was comparatively sporadic.

This attitude in the boy is by no means always apparent in ordinary life, at any rate after four years of age. Usually it is relatively hidden from observers and largely unconscious in the boy himself. The analysis of young boys has, however, shown it to be a universal and comparatively early phase.

In its primary form it rests upon the transition from oral wishes and experiences to the earliest genital phase and experiences. As Melanie Klein has shown, the boy transfers to his father's penis the significance and the impulses which he has hitherto found in the mother's breast, and the sucking desire towards it. He wishes to receive the penis into himself, to incorporate it as the father's love and power, in the way in which his mother receives it, or rather, in the way in which, owing to his own oral wishes, he phantasies that his mother receives it: that is, in the mouth. He wishes to create babies himself, as his mother does, and the various incidents of this type quoted in the section on *Family Play* illustrate this wish very plainly. Y.'s phantasy, for example (p. 167), that he had a baby brother or sister " in his tummy " followed immediately on having seen the cat have her kittens, and showed the intense rivalry with his mother which this stimulated. He really wishes to be his mother and to take her place with the father. This is a normal and general early attitude of the boy child, and a step in the ordinary course of his sexual development, from his primary oral attachment to the mother to the later phase of identification with his father on masculine lines.

This normal phase of feminine identification on the part of the boy is, however, sometimes re-awakened by regression at a later age, when the genital rivalry with the father for the love of the mother has been over-strongly stimulated by one situation or another. If the child feels his rivalry with the father too overwhelming, and the anxiety connected with the phantasies of revenge and punishment by the father is too great, he may return to this earlier attitude of being a woman to the father, renouncing the mother herself as a sexual object and over-compensating his hatred for the father as a rival, by a feminine love attitude towards him. This is a contributing factor to the genesis of passive male homosexuality, when it becomes a fixed and settled solution of the boy's conflict about his rivalry with his father. It seems likely that Frank's exaggerated and consistent feminine attitude, at his age, represented this later regressive phase, and should be linked up with his strong open hostility to Mrs. I. and the other women.

In the various incidents quoted from Dan, we see not only his acute and open castration phantasies, but his identification with his mother on the basis of these phantasies, as, for example, when he looks to see if he has a vulva behind his penis. This involves the phantasy of playing a passive feminine rôle with the father in the sexual situation (" Oh, I got run over by a roller at the station "). Dan's castration phantasies were strongly stimulated at this time, not only by the temporary absence of both parents, and the consequent sense of being altogether lost and deserted, but also by the conversation with Mrs. I., when the children learnt that she had neither father nor mother. Dan's reaction to the idea of *his* mother dying (" I've got fifteen mummies ") was a characteristically omnipotent mode of reassuring himself against anxieties of loss, whether loss of the mother's breast or of his own penis.

In an earlier incident (20.10.24) we can see the regression from a masculine attitude to a feminine one in process: "Just before bedtime, with his mother, father and Mrs. I. in the drawing room, Dan was tired and very querulous. He pushed a corkscrew which he was holding into his mother's leg, to see if it hurt. When his mother said she was going to put his bath on, he said petulantly, ' Oh Mummy, I want my supper *now*—I want it badly, here in the drawing room.' His mother said he could have it soon, but in his bedroom. He stood beside her, caressing her breast through her blouse and feeling as if for the nipple. ' I want an egg for my supper.' Presently, sitting beside her upstairs, eating his supper (and still more querulous as a result of a slight accident and hurt fingers), he said, ' I want to be mummy ' ; then asked her to hold his bread and butter and 'feed him—the first time he had asked for such a thing, since infancy. He insisted that the milk must be warm, and said twice, ' It's not sweet enough.' " On this occasion Dan (then 3;6) begins by behaving in a masculine way, with a strong sadistic tinge, to his mother, pushing into her leg a corkscrew which he was holding, and asking her " Does that hurt ? *Does* it hurt ? " His father was in the room at the time, and Mrs. I., watching, saw the boy cast many inquiring glances towards his father, obviously anxious to see what his father was feeling about it. When, presently, his mother said she was going to put him to bed and get his bath ready, he dropped at once into the attitude of the querulous baby waiting to be fed, and caressed her breast like a tiny infant feeling for the nipple, saying, "I want an egg for my supper." When, presently, he was upstairs with her and she went out of the room for a moment, he did what is only understandable in terms of an unconscious wish to be castrated, and thus prove her hostile and vengeful, that is to say, he got down on the floor close to the door and sat with his fingers in such a position that she could not open the door from the outside without hurting his fingers. This actually did happen. His mother came in, not knowing he had moved from his position in his chair, and his fingers were slightly hurt before she could stay the movement of the door. He was then able to cry pitifully in such a way as to draw his father's attention to the injury his mother had done him. That is to say, he was representing himself as entirely passive and helpless and his mother as the active vengeful person. He then became more infantile in his behaviour than he had shown himself for a long time, insisting on being fed and on having the milk warm and sweet. The regressive movement, therefore, from the identification with his father and rivalry with him in the masculine attitude towards his mother, to the early phase of identification with the mother, is very clearly shown; and together with that, his dread of the mother as a rival for his father's love, which led him to engineer that she should actually hurt him.

This attempted solution of the boy's problem of rivalry with his father is, however, far from satisfactory, since the identification with the mother itself reinforces the vast anxieties attaching to castration phantasies. The boy can only become his mother by being castrated.

9. "Cosy Places"

The love of making cosy places of one sort or another is quite general in small children, both boys and girls. I have been struck by the frequency with which it occurs. Whenever the younger children in the school had an opportunity, they would arrange the chairs and tables so as to make a "cosy place" with a defensive rampart. Occasionally it would be a solitary day-dreaming child who made a "cosy place" for himself. But commonly it was a co-operative affair between two or three children.

The defensive element comes out clearly here and there— " so that nobody can look in ", " to keep us warm ", " to keep the tigers out ", or "to keep out the foxes". Sometimes the children added to the intensity of their feeling of security by asking a grown-up to " be a tiger—and come from a distance, so that we can hear you growling ".

Even apart from the times when there were explicit enemies of this kind outside, it was quite clear that the children sought the feeling of being warm and safe inside these places. (The phrase " cosy place " was their own.) They were always very friendly and affectionate and helpful to those who shared the " cosy place " with them, whether children or grown-ups. The enemies were always outside. All the bad thoughts, all the bad wishes, were outside. The children thus not only made themselves warm and safe, but friendly and loving and good as well. The whole situation indeed represented a good mother with her good children inside her, all safe and all loving. Sometimes the picture was completed by having a good " Father Christmas " to come and bring a present, but more usually it represented the stage of life when (in the child's phantasy) there *is* no one there but mother and child. All the bad feelings and intentions are projected on to the father who is the enemy, the " tiger ", the " fox ", and kept outside. The child says in his behaviour, " It is my father who is jealous and aggressive—or at any rate, it is he who makes *me* jealous and aggressive ; and if he is not there, if I have my mother to myself, then everything is good and lovely." Moreover—" If I am inside my Mummy, I don't have to do anything bad to her to make her give me what I want. I only have to be there and everything is given to me."

In analytic work with little children, if strong aggressive wishes arise in the child, he becomes terrified of these wishes and afraid he may really hurt the grown-up who is playing with him, and that she will then really hurt him in return. A very common resort of the child in this anxiety is suddenly to become a "new-born baby", lying on the couch, perfectly still, quiet, happy and warm, not having to *do* anything to get food, comfort and love, hardly even having to suck, whilst the analyst has to become the good mother who does nothing and exists for nothing but to wait upon the baby and anticipate his wants, so that he does not have to be aggressive to get his wants satisfied. This wish " to return to the womb " was first remarked by Freud long ago. But (as he and the child analysts have shown us) the wish is not simply a wish for pleasure, but also a way of avoiding aggressive acts and all the dangers which ensue from aggressive feelings towards the parents.

Some of these incidents show the children's fear of the mother more plainly. When, for instance, it was not a question of a " cosy place " they had deliberately made for themselves, but a large unknown place, such as the dark cellar (the " canoe-house ") which they found, their anxiety about the dangers to be anticipated from mothers came out more into the open. The children were always thrilled to go into the "canoe-house", and made many remarks about " Oh, isn't it *lovely* and dark ? " but it was always quite clear that there was as much fear as pleasure, and, indeed, that the constant assertion of " how *lovely* and dark " it was, was mainly a way of denying the fears which they felt, and yet had to deny, by going in and proving it safe. It was the dangers anticipated from their own aggression against the mother, when primary wishes (for food and love) are unsatisfied, which they were annulling by this adventure into the dark canoe-house.

These phantasies of entering the mother's body to get everything that is good there, and so making *themselves* good and loving and friendly, and on the other hand, the fears of what will happen if they try to penetrate into mother's body in the way the father does, links up this theme of " cosy places " with infantile sexuality. The understanding gained through the analysis of small children has shown that it is their sexual aggression against the mother and the fears connected with it which the children are denying when they delight in making these cosy places. They are proving to themselves that it is safe, indeed the only safe place, to be inside Mummy, and that all bad things are outside in the tigers and foxes and fathers.

In Jessica's behaviour (31.1.27) we see very plainly this projection, the putting of all bad wishes on to the bad enemies outside the cosy place. She comforts Phineas, who was inside or very close to her cosy place, by saying " I won't fight *you*, Phineas " ; but she pretends to shoot Conrad, the enemy : the bad person (whether her father or her own bad, aggressive self) who would attack her and her Mummy. And then she can sing, " It's dead and gone for now, for now." All the bad enemies and bad wishes were dead and gone. (" Jessica carried two chairs and put their backs to the sides of the chair she was sitting in. She climbed in and called out gleefully, ' I'm in a cosy.' Seeing Conrad hold up a stick as a gun, Jessica held her hands as if she had a gun. She bent down to Phineas who was sitting near and said, ' I won't fight *you*, Phineas,' but pretended to take aim at Conrad, and quivered all over with the intensity of her attitude. Presently she took her hands down, and began singing to herself, ' It's dead and gone for now, for now.' ")

In Conrad's nightmare the original sexual wish for his mother comes out in scarcely disguised form, with a simple displacement from his penis to his finger, on the basis of old oral satisfactions of sucking his own finger.

B. GUILT AND SHAME

In this section of the material I have gathered together the bulk of those incidents which illustrate the notions of young children about punishment for wrong-doing, and their actual feelings of guilt and shame.

These feelings are shown in three main modes: (*a*) in *direct expression*, such as, for example, when Frank cries bitterly because he has wet his trousers: " Oh, *do* wash it off ", he says, or when Paul in the same situation cries with bitter tears and sobs, " I'm *so* ashamed of myself, *I'm so ashamed* of myself " ; (*b*) when the children express their guilt in various forms of *play*, for example, the game of Dr. Faustus, or being put in prison by Mrs. I., or saying in a joking way, " Isn't it a mess, *isn't* it a mess " ; and (*c*) the *projected form* of guilt, when they call other people " dirty " or " horrid ", when, for example, Harold says sententiously, " I don't like big boys to tease little ones ", or Paul tells Mrs. I. he " is very ashamed of her ", because she has been cross with him when he teased Dan. He was himself really very guilty about having teased Dan.

This projected guilt is one of the biggest factors in the children's active hostility to each other. Very often they scold or push, or try to punish in some other way one of the other children, or try to be rude or defiant to the adults, through the pressure of guilt for their own " bad " impulses and unconscious phantasies. It is here that this section of the material links up so closely with both group and individual hostility. The children see their own faults in each other and attack each other as bad, whether by active aggression or by moral superiority and scorn.

These illustrations of guilt and shame in young children may be further discussed from three main points of view : (1) the type of situation which stirs up feelings of guilt and shame ; (2) the content of the feelings, that is, the nature of the punishment feared, or felt to be deserved ; (3) the question of how far these feelings are the result of either specific teaching or the general attitude of adults, and how far they are spontaneous in the child ; and, if the latter, the nature of the psychic processes which give them birth.

(1) The first hint as to the things that deserve punishment is given us by Penelope, when she says that her doll has wet his bed, " Naughty, naughty baby." Frank, too, shows his unhappiness when he wets his trousers ; and in general the children's frequent remarks about being " dirty " show that this question of dirtiness is an extremely important part of the content of naughtiness. This is shown in the clearest way by Lena and Phineas : " Lena and Phineas were poking a stick into a hole in the plaster of the wall. The stick came out covered with dust and cobwebs. They said in awed tones, ' Isn't it a naughty wall ? ' Mrs. I. asked, ' How is it a naughty wall ? ' ' Look at the dirt on the stick.' Mrs. I. said, ' Yes, what is it ? ' (having in mind that they might see that it was cobwebs). Lena replied, gravely, ' *Muck—isn't it a naughty* wall ! ' " (p. 184). We can, however, be sure that we are also dealing here with *projected* badness—Lena felt that *she* was naughty for poking and breaking the wall and pulling the cobwebs out, and so called the *wall* naughty for being spoilt and dirty.

Jessica shows a guilt reaction to having scribbled on the white paint and dirtying it.

Again, Frank shows us that people who will not put their bricks away are naughty, that is to say, children who make the place messy ; and thus obviously connects with dirtying.

Paul, who says, " Shall we call Benjie ' the breaker ' ? ", and so shows us that breaking and spoiling objects is a bad thing to do, shows us also the extent of his own anxiety when he cannot *mend* something that he has spoilt ; when, for example, he cannot replace the arrangement of some planks, he cries bitterly and says, " I can't mend it, I *can't* mend it."

The teasing of other children is felt by all to be reprehensible, and making a noise is also bad.

Harold, too, speaks of " Naughty Mary who had not kept the fire in ", that is to say, a maid (a mother) who had not kept the children warm and comfortable, and therefore good.

Looking at things that one is not permitted to is described as " rude " by Martin (18.3.25) : " Martin told Mrs. I. that he had made a ' lovely railway track ', and this was done with the colours put in a long line. He would not let Tommy look at this, and several times tried to push Tommy away, and said to him, ' You must not look, you must not do that, it is not *nice*, it's *rude*.'" Martin must have been scolding Tommy for the times when *he* himself had tried to look at really forbidden things (ultimately, parental intercourse).

Harold displays an exaggerated sense of shame when he is distressed because his combinations show below his trouser legs. And he, again, in his invented game of " blowing up " a building and then being put in prison, shows us his anxiety about his destructive wishes to buildings (i.e. mother). He is surprised that his mother can still love him after he has in reality been actively aggressive to her.

Laurie, too, behaves in a guilty way when he has been playing with another boy's toys without permission; and Dan and Frank consider James very naughty for biting.

Frank also tells us that " Henry is a naughty boy " because he puts his thumb in his mouth. We already know from a previous section of the material that thumb-sucking and, indeed, the sucking of all sorts of objects, is a greatly pleasurable thing to Frank, and here we see that it is also a very guilty thing.

In Priscilla's game with her doll, when she tells Mrs. I. that " her's had been a horrid little beast " and that " it had been fiddling about in the pram all the time " we cannot doubt that the doll is supposed to have been masturbating: " Don't fiddle about and do such horrid things."

Alfred gives us a glimpse of another content of naughtiness when he says Frank and Herbert are " naughty " for putting some dried peas down a hole in the floor. It happened that a year later I heard from Alfred's mother that he sometimes indulged in anal masturbation when in bed. With this further information, there can be no doubt that putting these dried peas down the hole meant anal masturbation, with phantasies of anal attacks upon his mother. That is why it was at first " naughty ", and then joined in with such eagerness, when permitted.

Priscilla, when she plays the part of the naughty baby, shows us that screaming when one cannot get what one wants, and snatching at things, are bad behaviour. Alfred and Herbert, again, call the mice " naughty " when " they won't do what we want, so aren't they naughty? "—the familiar childhood crime of disobedience.

James gives us a very complex piece of behaviour when first of all he accuses Mrs. I. of being " dirty ", and then immediately performs the action which he obviously wished to do, but felt to be guilty, viz. putting his table-napkin into his orange squash and sucking it. The inner meaning of this incident is, however, not given by such a simple statement. He ends up by turning away in disgust from the nipple which he has made with the napkin. His own guilt has been projected on to Mrs. I., and so she (in the last resort, his mother) seems to him to be so dirty and dangerous that he has to turn away from her.

Jane gives us a content for her (projected) guilt which approximates more to adult standards (Jane was a good deal older than the other children). She expresses her opinion of Priscilla as someone who is " selfish, cross and sly, and always tries to get the best things for herself".

Thus, the occasions which provide these feelings of guilt and shame in young children can be summed up in two main groups, as (a) the various forms of open aggression—screaming, biting, wetting, defaecating, breaking things, being greedy, being unable or unwilling to mend or tidy things ; and (b) certain forms of libidinal satisfaction, such as thumb-sucking and both anal and genital masturbation. The psychoanalysis of children and adults has, however, shown that in these latter situations it is not the libidinal wish-fulfilment pure and simple, which makes them also guilty and dangerous, but again the aggressive elements—the secret attack upon the parents, and secret stealing of sexual pleasure. As we saw when discussing masturbation, the actual pleasure is compulsively sought mainly as a reassurance against the terrors of punishment for the aggressive attack, to prove again that it is safe to do it.

It can therefore be seen that the child's feelings of guilt are closely related to his aggressive tendencies.

(2) The children's ideas as to the punishments they deserve and may receive for these guilty doings are various.

Benjie threatens to hit Mrs. I. in the face when he fears that she is going to punish him—so that is what he thought she would do to him. Paul says, " The policeman has been whipping the boys, it's quite right, isn't it ? " And a group of the children play the game of Dr. Faustus, when " Dr. Faustus " whips all the children.

Most of the children play from time to time at putting each other in prison or at being put in prison by Mrs. I. They will sometimes use this as a real threat, meant to be taken seriously, when they are angry. And this idea must enter into the way in which Paul and the other boys actually tease Dan when they pull the rug over his head so that he cannot see, trying to smother him.

Harold expects his mother not to love him any more when he has hit her and shouted at her.

Harold and Paul, too, when they are angry with Mrs. I., say they won't have her to tea, they will shut her out if she goes—that is to say, they will deprive her of food and shelter and love. Paul says he won't serve Dan with any dinner.

When Phineas breaks his cup, he says to himself, " Now I can't have any cocoa ", and carries out this self-inflicted punishment for some days.

When they play that " the cat " or " the bear " is coming, they dramatise their fears of being attacked and eaten up by the vengeful parent.

George imagines that the " fat snake " in his bed will bite him. And he attempts to punish himself by cutting his own finger off (castrating himself).

The children scold each other from time to time in various ways, calling each other foolish or horrid, naughty or dirty. They pretend that Mrs. I. makes them do hard tasks that they don't want to do. Conrad scorns James when he wets himself, and it was always clear in Conrad's behaviour that he feared scorn from the other children. But he feared more than scorn : he feared punishment by death, for he drew on the wall a picture of a gallows with a man hanging.

The little girl believes that if she is naughty in school, God will drown the world. George, too, believes that the rain is God flooding the world in punishment.

Thus, the children fear that what will happen to them if they are naughty are punishments ranging in severity from being given hard tasks, being scorned, laughed at and reproached, to being put into prison, whipped, shut out from the home and mother's love, deprived of food and starved, and done to death in various ways, for instance by drowning.

The significance of these greater terrors, which obviously have little or no relation to reality, will become clearer when we discuss their deeper sources in a moment.

(3) The third ground of discussion, namely, the question as to whether or not these fears of punishment and the sense of guilt proper develop spontaneously in the child's mind, or

are entirely due to teaching and adult prestige, is one which we have only been able to appraise and understand through the light which psycho-analysis has thrown on the earliest phases of development. In latter years, psycho-analytic studies have been largely directed to the problem of guilt and its relation to libidinal development. It has become definitely established—although this conclusion is so surprising to liberal educators—that the sense of guilt, or, more strictly, the deeper anxieties that represent the primitive forerunners of the sense of guilt, *do* develop spontaneously in the child's mind, whatever be the precise nature of his educational experiences. The environment can, of course, greatly foster and over-stimulate the sense of guilt by over-strict treatment, especially in the early days. It can, indeed, foster it so far as to cause serious mental illness. And milder methods of teaching and training undoubtedly help to lessen the grip of guilt upon the child's mind. But, in its essence, the sense of guilt is inherent in the fundamental interactions between human mental structure and inevitable early experiences.

From the descriptive point of view, it is quite clearly shown that a very strong sense of guilt may be developed by children who have certainly never been scolded or reproached or threatened. This was true, for instance, of one or two of the children in the school. Dan, for example, had had quite a fanatically non-didactic home, and had been most meticulously sheltered from outside influences of a kind that might directly stir up guilt. Several of the other children had very mild upbringings and gentle treatment, but nevertheless showed almost as strong a sense of guilt as some of the others who had been whipped or scolded. Noel, for example, who shows that he feels happier when he is being given some definite task, had never been whipped, and hardly punished, and had suffered only the mildest of rebukes and criticisms in his home.

We come, then, to the sources within the child's own psychic life of the sense of guilt and the dread of punishment—the problem of the super-ego. I have already discussed this at many points, and here need only bring it into further relation with the immediate material.

The psycho-analysts are, of course, not the first to appreciate and give voice to this feeling of the " divided self ", as St. Augustine called it. It is a familiar notion, and a familiar experience, that one part of one's total self acts against another : one part wishes and another attempts to deny, control, or punish. We are all familiar with this in consciousness, as the feeling of *oughtness*, the conscience set over against the wish feelings and temptations. But it is psychoanalysis that has shown us the far-reaching psychic truth of these experiences which religion and literature have dramatised, and the intense reality, at a very early age, of the internal conflict between the " strict self ", which represents the parents controlling and punishing, and the primitive " wish-self ".

We have come to see that the super-ego develops within the child's mind through this imaginative incorporation of his parents, based upon the real bodily experience of taking the mother's breast into the mouth, and the general domination of the child's mental life by oral impulses in the earliest months.

In an earlier footnote (p. 356), I referred to M. N. Searl's extremely illuminating view that the special situation in which this division of the child's personality into the wish-self and the parent-self, or super-ego, probably takes its most definitive form is the situation of the screaming fit. There are few children who do not scream on some occasion or other and to some degree or other, when their desires are not immediately satisfied. The age at which such screaming fits occur, and their severity, will vary greatly from child to child, and from circumstance to circumstance ; but there are none who do not experience it to a greater or less degree and on some occasion. No parent can or would attempt to satisfy all the child's desires at every moment when they arise—and to cry in rage is the child's normal way of attempting to compel the parents to satisfy his desires.

It is probable that with those children who are not left to scream to the point of absolute exhaustion the super-ego does not develop with the intensest severity. In those who suffer great oral frustration in the early days, so that they from the beginning cry fruitlessly and exhaustingly, the super-ego develops the utmost severity. The more frequently the child experiences such a situation, the more severe the effect will be upon his mental development. Resulting development will then take one of two opposite forms ; either the child will be obliged to project his super-ego entirely on to the external world, thus becoming a criminal or "moral imbecile"; or he will become quite unable to tolerate showing *any* open aggression of any kind, even in indirect forms, such as ordinary muscular activities or intellectual efforts.

The beginning of the development of the super-ego, as we have seen, occurs in the biting phase of oral sexuality, but it soon becomes linked with anal and urethral phantasies. And just as the child comes to use his excrement (partly in real dirtying, partly in phantasy) as a means of attack upon his parents, either in order to control them and bend them to his wishes, or in order to punish them for depriving him of satisfaction, so he dreads that they will do these things to him. Thus arise all those phantasies of poisoning with excrements, and in return being given only bad, poisonous food, which we noted in discussing *Anal Sadism*.

The greater terrors of the child, illustrated in these lethal punishments, belong to the deepest level of unconscious phantasy and are associated with the pre-genital phases of libidinal development. It is *because* the child himself wants to bite and eat up his parents (as he must at a certain age) that he dreads being attacked and destroyed, deprived of food or starved to death. Even his love for his mother, in so far as it takes an oral form, raises these terrors. If the " good " father and the " good " mother are eaten and destroyed, they are no longer there to be good and helpful; only the spoilt, " bad " ones are there, who will attack and destroy in their turn. So with the little girl who believes that " God will drown the world " if she is naughty. Such a belief is doubtless connected with Biblical stories of the Flood; but the idea that God will drown the whole world if *she* is naughty only becomes intelligible if her naughtiness attacks the whole world. And this we can only understand as attacking her parents, who naturally *are* the child's whole world in her earliest days. From analytic evidence, moreover, we can understand her phantasy still more clearly—her belief that God will drown the world springs from her awareness that her own secret " naughtiness " is a wish to flood her mother with a stream of urine, in anger when she cannot get all she wants, or hates her mother as a rival. This punishment phantasy thus links up with the child's early real problem of the control of urination.

And in the incident on 25.5.25 : " Frank and Dan were climbing on the window-sill. Frank said he would ' push Dan's foot up '. Paul said, ' Yes, he'll push Dan up to God.' Frank said, ' Yes, and perhaps He'll kill him,' " we may understand this curious remark as an expression of Frank's dread of his own real father, for his aggressive attacks on his younger brother, the dread that his father would really kill him because of his own real wish to attack his rival.

The milder punishments or reproaches only appear as a possibility when the child's love life has reached the genital level, where his phantasies have more relation to reality and his impulses are more tempered. Provided there has been no strong fixation on the impulses of the mouth and the anus, so that these are too strongly carried over into the genital level, the genital phantasies are of giving and not taking, of giving good and not bad, of creating and not destroying. The " good " penis is equated with the good breast giving milk, rather than with the biting teeth or the poisonous faeces.

The earliest phase of oral sexuality—sucking and receiving— is thus of great significance in the later development of both boy and girl. It is where this earliest phase has not been altogether lost or replaced by the biting phase, and the latter not too early and too strongly stimulated, that a satisfactory development is fully attained.

It is on the genital level of libidinal development that feelings of real moral responsibility can be sustained and acted upon. On the earlier levels, as we have seen, talion law of a primitive type rules. The super-ego in its earliest phases is a primitive avenger, to be evaded and escaped. The ordinary *conscience*, embodying some measure of moral perspective, belongs to the genital level of sexuality, where anxieties are not so great that they need to be altogether repudiated, and wishes have not to be altogether inhibited or projected. It is only on this level that the child can bear to feel that he *deserves* some reproach if he has done what he feels he ought not to do. He can more readily control and temper his wishes according to his conscience, since the content of what he " ought " to do has taken into itself a greater measure of objective reality.

It is on this level, too, that the wish to make good again when he has done wrong becomes stronger, and the belief in this possibility more assured. Obviously, such a belief in the possibility of restoring and making good what one has attacked and spoilt is bound up with the psychic development of the child as a whole and his growth in real skill and perception, that is, his total adjustment to the real external world But the possibility of this adjustment to the real external world is itself largely limited by the extent to which his earlier psychic life has been dominated by sadistic phantasies. In those cases where the super-ego develops very early and along very destructive lines, the development of the real ego and of skill and understanding in the real world are seriously inhibited. Within the last three or four years the leading child analysts have been working with children whose whole mental development has been held up in this way, and who have enormously improved in educability, in skill and speech and understanding, through the analysis of their anxieties connected with early aggression and the vengeful super-ego. It is through these studies that we have gained an understanding of the significance of these early forms of aggression, and the primitive layers of the super-ego.

C. An Individual Child : Ursula.

These particular records of Ursula's behaviour during two and a half years, covering critical situations in the home and a very critical period of development, illustrate a number of those themes which have already been discussed under separate headings with the material from the school and other sources.

It is to be remembered that the incidents presented here are highly selected. They do not represent the child's total behaviour, nor even her total relation to her parents and little sister. I have taken them out from their main context in order to illustrate these important psychological themes. Readers of *Intellectual Growth in Young Children* (Appendix C) will remember the observations and reflections of Ursula which were quoted there, and which pay high tribute to her sense and understanding and amenableness to reason. Those records should be taken in conjunction with the present ones, whether for the purpose of psychological theory or for the sake of getting a just picture of the individual child.

The main psychological situations which Ursula shows us here are (1) her rivalry with her mother for the possession of the father and her babies ; (2) her rivalry with the baby as a child to her mother ; (3) her castration anxiety ; (4) her identification with her father as a way of avoiding the rivalry with her mother ; (5) her theory of the origin of babies in food and faeces, and corresponding anxiety about anal attacks and the badness of her own genitals.

(1) The rivalry of the girl child with her mother is very plainly shown, whether in direct or indirect ways : " *I* would like a little baby like that. Will you get me one ? " " Mary got home first. *I* wanted to be first." After expressing her wish for both a brother and a sister : " Well, *you* can make the brother and *I* will make the sister." And again : " Ursula was very distressed that her mother and not she was to be the baby's mother. She wept bitterly, ' But *I* want to be its mother.' ' But why can't I ? ' etc." After her mother has told her that little children " can't do that ", she expresses her intense wish to grow big so that she can have a baby like her Mummy by saying, " Look Mummy, I nearly reach my swing. Shall I when I'm six ? " When she sits in the cupboard

telling herself a story about the princess, that is " too long " to tell her mother, we can be sure that the princess is herself, enjoying secret delights that she would not share with her mother—as her mother does not with her—intercourse and babies. She has become a princess, i.e. taken her mother's place. Again, the anxiety connected with her envy of the mother's pregnancy is shown by her impatience with the length of time before baby " comes out ", and her wish to stay at home instead of going to school. Later on her sexual wishes towards her father are more openly expressed: " I think I should like to marry Daddy. Well, I'll see." And in the dream which follows a day or two after this remark, Ursula expresses her phantasy of her own successful growing up, and so coming to enjoy intercourse: " She grew up very quickly and there were two trains and one train was her friend and one train went into the other." Ursula " stayed outside " with Daddy when her Mummie went in to help her little sister. Later on, when Ursula's father was telling her a story and patted her thigh, she interrupted, " I like that, Daddy. Do that again."

This is the first ground of Ursula's rivalry—her rivalry with her mother *as* a mother, for being given a baby by the father, and the father's love.

(2) The second ground is rivalry with the new baby as a child to the mother, i.e. rivalry for the mother's love. When she was told about the presence of the new baby inside her Mummie, " she said in a weepy voice, ' *Why*, Mummie ? I don't want one while I'm little. I don't want one till I'm big.' " " Mummie, you will be busy when my brother or sister comes out." That is to say, Ursula is afraid she won't get so much attention. " What shall I do when my little brother or sister comes and sleeps in my room and cries and 'sturbs me ? " She wants her mother to sleep with her: " Oh Mummie, when will you sleep with me ? . . . I am not happy with Else." Her jealousy is shown when her Mummie kisses a little girl visitor. Ursula gives the other child a violent push and says, " Don't kiss her." In a dream, " a nasty dream "—that is, a dream with open anxiety—her hostility to the little sister comes out very plainly: " Nurse came in with R., and I hit her on the head. And then there was something *very* nasty ! " And in the incident on p. 197 this hostility is shown in actual behaviour. She punches her

mother. When asked what for, she says for "spitting on R.'s head", as if it were her mother who had done this. Obviously it was she who had wanted to do it, since she goes on, "I'll spit on her food!" Later on, when Ursula has to be very quiet because R. sleeps in her room, she is very angry and says of R., "I can do what I *like* with her, because she's *my* sister." This can be understood as an indirect expression of the first wish, that R. was *her* baby. And on a later occasion she expressed her feeling that her mother is nicer to R. than to her: "R. has much more of you than I do", though, in fact, the contrary was true.

(3) Ursula shows us, too, some of the deep anxieties which arise from the intense wish to displace her mother in the father's love and have a baby of her own. These anxieties take various forms, the chief being the dread of being injured in her internal reproductive organs. A wish for a penis of her own also appears, largely as a reassurance against the deeper dreads. Envy of her father's penis gains importance, also, from her wish to play the father's part towards the mother, and so restore to her mother the penis and the babies which she has wished to take from her.

The penis envy and castration anxiety are shown when, for example, she dreams about the little Ursula that is "not her", who "goes shopping with her mummie" and leaves her handbag behind—the handbag with the tassel (a real bag of her mother's which had been lent to her, and which she wanted to have for her own). Here the loss of the bag with the tassel represents her fear of bodily loss and injury if she seeks to take the mother's placè. She asks her mother, "You can tell whether a baby is a boy or girl by looking at its underneaths, can't you? Does a baby boy have a weeny penis?" Again, she says to her Daddy, "Your underneaths shake, Daddy; mine don't shake"; and later on, to her mother, "Are your underneaths like my underneaths, Mummy?" And "What is that for?" Later still, she thinks she has a "tongue" in her genital (i.e. a penis).

This envy of the penis makes her fear the hostility of little boys and of her Daddy: "I don't like boys, they're not as nice as girls, are they? . . . I like my Daddy, because he is a gentleman"—a reassurance against her fears of her father on the ground of her wish to get his penis. She actually feels her "underneaths" hurt with the vividness of her fears:

" Oh, Mummy, my underneaths hurt ", and when her mother offers to put some healing ointment on she says, " My baby brother or sister " (not yet born) " can't have any ointment on, can he ? "

Another type of anxiety is that, even if her father gives her a baby, she will be injured in her own body by it. It will be a bad one. She asks, " How can a baby come out of your underneaths ? Does it hurt much ? " (a wish as well as a fear that it will hurt her mother). " Well, I won't have one if it hurts." When she is carrying her doll, she says, " She keeps falling down, she's as heavy for me as I am . . . " (for you). That is to say, because she is heavy and difficult to her mother, hostile to her mother, her own babies will be so for her, and she will not be able to carry a baby successfully.

In the minor phobias which develop when her little sister is about a year old, we see the extent of her anxiety of " nasty animals " and of " crabs " which may pinch and attack her (her mother attacking her with her father's penis). And in this later period she tries to deal with her fears of being injured, because of her bad wishes, by masturbation and a rather compulsive type of exhibitionism, showing her " underneaths " with obvious anxiety and a certain amount of defiance, to prove that it is safe to do this, and that they are not too bad to be shown.

(4) Another very striking element in Ursula's behaviour, however, is the tremendous effort she makes to deal with this hostility both to her mother and to her little sister. She over-compensates her hatred and resentment towards her mother by excessive attachment and expressions of love. She addresses the unborn baby, " Hullo, my precious ! " and often says " Isn't she sweet ? Isn't it nice to have a sister ? It's a good thing I wanted one." And to her mother, " I want to be with you *all the time*. . . . I don't want you to go out, Mummy. I love you so much I want to be with you always. " " I love you, Daddy . . . and I love Mummy. I love you very much but I love Mummy most of all." " I love you so much, Mummy, fifty thousand. I love you more than I can tell you." " My sweet Mummy ! " " I love you so much it makes me want to cry." It must be remorse for her hostility and jealousy that makes Ursula want to cry when she loves. Even when Ursula becomes " a princess " and tells " a 'citing story ", she only feels safe in

doing this when she is inside a " cosy place ", the dark cupboard in which she huddled. That is to say, when she is herself inside her mother as the baby sister had been, and is thus magically reassuring herself of her mother's love. She even goes so far as to say, " I shan't marry. I want to stay with you always." Here she adumbrates what with many women actually becomes a settled solution of their rivalry. They do not marry but devote themselves permanently to the mother, or to the love and service of other women. This devotion to the mother rests on an identification with the father. Such women attempt to play the part of a " good " father, and return to the mother in this masculine rôle the penis and the masculine service which they have in phantasy taken from her. This is the chief source of Ursula's wish to have a penis of her own. The electric torch which she holds on her knee in her " princess " phantasy in the cupboard illustrates this. The full meaning of this situation in the cupboard is doubtless the unconscious phantasy that she is, from the inside of her mother, controlling both her parents (the book and the torch) and making them do what she wants, omnipotently re-creating them.

(5) Ursula's infantile theories as to how babies are made come out very plainly in several incidents. When, for example, she feels that a part of her genital is like a " tongue ", she is obviously thinking of the whole organ as being like a mouth. And this goes along with her questions about what the baby feeds on, and her question about how her Mummy ate when she was " in her tummy ". Obviously the child's idea of the inside of her mother is of one large receptacle in which food and faeces and babies and " Daddy's underneaths " are all placed and mixed up together, and the child wonders how they are sorted out. For example, she says to her Mummy, " What's in my tummy, only food ? What's in yours ? Mixed ? Baby and food ? " " I wish . . . How is the seed planted ? You did tell me. But how is it made ? " When she feeds her mother and says, " That's for my brother or sister ", she is acting to her mother as she believes her father does. It is food or faeces that is the " seed " which Daddy puts into Mummy to make the baby.

The notion of the baby being made of faeces is expressed indirectly in her phantasy about flowers. " Brown's a funny colour for flowers " (flowers being a universal symbol for children). And the same notion is expressed in her idea that the seed could grow in the garden, and then " you could pick the seed of the baby and plant it." Her anal idea of intercourse is shown in the anxiety dream " about a maid and a chimney, and she sat on the chimney and smoke came up and made her apron dirty and there was a chimney sweep . . ." Here Ursula was expressing her fear of the penis as a dirty thing, but ends up with the reassuring notion that the organ that could make things dirty can perhaps make them clean. Her Daddy will be a " good daddy " and will sweep the " chimney " clean.

Her personification of the excretory processes, which is universal in little children but does not always come out so plainly, is shown when she says, " Sometimes when I want to do ' weeny ' it wants to come out and it can't. Something stops it. I suppose it's its Mummy or Daddy." *What do you mean?* " I mean Big. Big's its friend, isn't it ? " We get here a glimpse of the phantasy of the urine and faeces being separate entities, very often identified with the child's own bad self, and perhaps not less often with the angry and vengeful parents, attacking the child from the inside. When Ursula says " Big's its friend ", she is trying to reassure herself against her phantasies of being actually attacked by her faeces, a phantasy which is of the greatest importance in difficulties of training in cleanliness and in the development of neuroses.

A little later we get a conscious expression of the way in which her " big " can be used to exercise power over her mother and make her do what she wants : " When you don't want to take me (i.e. to the lavatory) I'll say I want to do ' big ', then you will." She actually whispered this to her mother, and when her mother said, " Why did you whisper it ? " she said persuasively, " Perhaps you will forget by then ", which suggests that she wanted to keep this notion of controlling her mother by her faeces a secret in her own mind. This idea of controlling the parents by the magical power of faeces is an extremely significant one, in, for example, obsessional neuroses, as well as in primitive magic. It is probably derived from the actual feeling of the sphincter muscles pressing and pulling, pushing or withholding and generally controlling the faeces itself, which are felt to be something that is foreign to the ego, although actually present inside the body. In her lavatory play with her little friend which developed not long after this period, Ursula must have been attempting to allay her anxiety about these hostile phantasies of attacking her mother with her own faeces, and the resulting dread that the faeces themselves would attack her. She brings the chamber pot out, and more or less defiantly performs her excretory functions in public, and exhibits her buttocks and genitals in order to prove that there is nothing to be afraid of ; probably also to provoke a reproof from her mother and thus prove that this could be borne and would not in fact injure and destroy her.

When presently she is speaking of her hopes to have a girl baby of her own she says, " Well, if there were pink and white seeds for girls and yellow and black seeds for boys . . . ", she shows that the yellow or black faeces are specially identified in her mind with males and her father's penis, and that when she feels the pressure of a large scybalum in her rectum, her phantasy is that it is Daddy doing to her what he does to Mummy. The anxiety about her nurse seeing her " botty " (her buttocks) comes out plainly later on, and again she tries to deal with these fears by a defiant type of exhibitionism, sitting on the bath and saying to her father and mother, " Look ! I am doing weeny in my bath." When she tells her mother she doesn't like her buttocks " because it doesn't like to do ' big ' ", she is expressing her anxiety about her open rebellion in refusing to defaecate when she should. But the difficulty in defaecation itself arises partly from the wish to retain the faeces in order to make babies with them and because they were identified with her Daddy's penis, as well as from anxiety about the faeces themselves as attacking and dangerous things, which ought not to be there at all.

At one point Ursula expresses with perfect clarity the child's philosophy of life and her view as to the proper relation between mothers and children. When she wants her mother to do a certain thing for her she says, " You must, Mummy, you *must* ! " Her mother asks, *Must I ?* " Yes," says Ursula, " that's what Mummies are for, to do what their children want them to." *Is it ?* " Yes. And to look after them." *And what are children for ?* " To play, of course." That is to say, Mummies must exist not for themselves or for Daddies or for anything else in the world but to take care of little children, serve them and feed them ; and little children have the natural privilege of being allowed to play and to enjoy unlimited pleasure.

. . . . .

At the time of going to press, Ursula's behaviour is happy and her development satisfactory, showing certain minor neurotic symptoms in the way the majority of children do, but with an unusual freedom and confidence in her mother and the world in general.

Doubtless many of my readers will be impressed by the unusual extent to which Ursula's mother and father gave her open information, and allowed her to talk out her questions and phantasies about their sexual life and the origin of babies. It may occur to some readers who are not sympathetic to this mode of education that Ursula's difficulties might be attributed to this rather unusual degree of knowledge. Such a view would, however, be quite unwarranted, as other portions of my material will plainly show. Emotional difficulties much greater than those of Ursula may arise in any child, and are even more likely to arise in those children who are not given honest information or are told lies and prevarications. It is not, however, the actual *information* that makes the difference, since Ursula obviously retains many of her infantile theories about parental intercourse, even though she has been told so much. It is rather the attitude of love and confidence which the parents show and are able to foster in the child that gives the special value of this method. Ursula will not have the cause for real distrust of her parents which so many children have ; and this open confidence is a great aid to a child in dealing with the anxieties arising from unconscious phantasies. Such a frank relation between parents and children will by no means solve all neurotic difficulties, nor will it altogether obviate them. But it does help to build up a solid and lasting friendliness and mutual respect between parent and child, which are of inestimable value in themselves ; and it does mean that the world of biological interests is kept open to the child's inquiries.

III. THE RELATION BETWEEN THE SOCIAL AND THE SEXUAL ASPECTS OF DEVELOPMENT

Having completed my survey of those data of children's sexual development brought together in this volume, I must now summarise the way in which the sexual aspect of children's development is linked up with the social. Before doing this, however, there is a qualification which needs to be made.

I have considered the material in so far as it illustrates the sexual impulses and phantasies shown, either directly or indirectly, in the behaviour of little children at different stages of their development, and the relation of these wishes and phantasies to the early anxieties and guilt. But such a presentation of sexual development is somewhat one-sided, since it lays more emphasis on the element of wish and phantasy than on the actual situations in real experience which have evoked those wishes and phantasies. The dynamic meaning of these latter, however, is always drawn from the child's total relation to external events at the moment, that is to say, to the real behaviour of other children and adults—apart, of course, from those situations of pure play which the child creates for himself by the spontaneous expression of phantasy. Even here, however, the expression of phantasy will have reference either to past real situations, or to hypothetical real situations. What we are dealing with in attempting to understand the child's behaviour at any given moment is always a situation of interplay between the child himself, and actual or possible events. And we cannot understand the actual course of his behaviour at any moment unless we take into account these external factors as fully as the internal.

I have, I think, made it sufficiently clear in a broad general way that I take this view, and I have detailed it here and there; but in this general exposition of the sexual development of children, I have tended to emphasise wish and phantasy more than external stimuli. This has come about partly for lack of space, but partly also because at the time when I was collecting this material in the years 1924-27, I was still so much an elementary student of children's sexual development that I concerned myself more fully with a naïve recording of the phantasy material than with a balanced appreciation of the total situation, including both the wish-phantasy and the real concrete stimuli. I should not fall into this error now, largely because of the experience I have since gained in the work of actual analysis, where it is no less vitally important to appreciate those immediate real events which call out the child's phantasies than to understand the phantasies themselves. At every point, whether in ordinary life or the analytic situation, there always is the most subtle interplay between the inner and the outer sets of factors.

It must suffice now to make this general point clear by reference to one or two of those detailed incidents, in which I have been able to bring out this interplay between the child and his environment. My readers will recall, for example, how a period of unusual difficulty with Priscilla in the school, when for three or four weeks she was hostile to adults, tyrannical to the children and generally peevish and unhappy, was actually the result of her mother's being away from home in order to nurse someone else's ill child, and Priscilla's being left alone with her father; and how when the mother returned, bringing Priscilla a surprise gift of a beautiful life-size baby doll, the child's behaviour in the school changed at once, and she became loving, co-operative and tender with the other children. In discussing this situation in the appropriate section (p. 351) I brought out some of the underlying phantasies which the mother's absence had stirred in the child. But it is clear that the real absence of the mother was no less significant than the child's unconscious phantasies and fears—chiefly because it seemed to confirm those phantasies and fears, which only the actual presence of the mother could counteract.

The behaviour of Cecil in the early days of the school presents us with another illustration of the same point. I have pointed out how helpless and unskilful Cecil was in every way when he first came to the school, chiefly owing to the fact that he had been given no training in independence at home. I have shown, too, how unusually aggressive to other children he was while this state of helplessness lasted. The aggression undoubtedly sprang from his fear of their attacking him, and the domination of his mind by unconscious phantasies of " bad " parents and dangerous rivals. He had little belief in the " good " parent or the child who might be a friend and not an enemy. But in the school, he presently discovered that there were grown-ups who would not only refrain from attacking him in turn by actual whippings when he was disagreeable and defiant, but would actually give him the means for putting his aggression to useful purposes, and show him how to develop real skill in jumping, climbing, washing his hands, building with bricks, etc. He discovered that spontaneous activity in building and climbing and jumping, which had to him the unconscious significance of rivalling his father, was here met with encouragement and help, and the anxieties attaching to such activities were therefore considerably lessened. He found people who believed in his power to be skilful and sensible, and in this situation he could make the attempt to become skilful and sensible. Cecil therefore illustrates for us the fact that the extent to which the child's phantasies of destruction and danger dominate his real activity very largely depends upon the real treatment he receives from those around him, and the real situation which his environment creates.

A third illustration can be drawn from the active hostility which many of the children showed to the grown-ups in the early days of the school. It will be remembered that many of these difficult children were used to being severely treated in their homes, and that when they came to the school, they found they were not scolded or punished for the very same behaviour which would have brought such results in their homes. In the records it is plain how puzzled they at first were by this situation, and how they felt the grown-ups to be bad and dirty and destructive, because they did not by scoldings and punishment serve as a direct check upon the children's own defiance and destructiveness. The unconscious punishment phantasies of the children led them to fear the utmost internal dangers, if they were not checked in their naughty behaviour by severe treatment from adults. And to these adults who did not scold or punish, their first response was, "He that is not with us is against us." The adults became in their eyes identified with the bad wish-self, destructive and dirty. The children's hostility was thus largely based upon the projection of the bad wish-self on to the adults, they themselves then playing the part of the destroying and attacking conscience. I need not describe how this situation was changed by the discovery that the adults did set real limits to the children's actual destruction, even though those limits were wider than the children had been accustomed to, and did offer them positive channels of activity. It is enough for the present purpose to bring out the fact that the children's excessive defiance and destructiveness in the first days of the school were largely an outcome of this real situation —that they were for the first time faced with adults who did not scold and whip them in the way to which they were accustomed. Their response was to feel that such adults must themselves be no better than bad destructive children.

At many points in the records of Ursula's development, too, it can be seen how closely her phantasies interact with the course of real events in her experience.

Perhaps these illustrations will serve to make clear the general point that for the full understanding of any particular child's behaviour at any given moment, we must take into consideration not only the phase of development he has reached, and the particular wishes and phantasies and anxieties characteristic of that phase, or of his individual personality but his real situation in the external world also.

* * * * *

It remains, then, to summarise the various ways in which these two aspects of the child's development, the sexual and the social, are linked together. I have touched upon this ground in many details during the general discussion of each, and need only recapitulate the various points in a rather more systematic manner.

(1) The material of this book will, I think, serve to make clear how little ground there is for holding that any new " social instincts " appear as such at any particular stage of development, whether at six or seven years, or any other. The bulk of the material quoted here is drawn from the behaviour of children under six or seven years, although it includes a certain amount from those ages. In these earlier years, however, there are plenty of hints of a growing ability for social behaviour and a social point of view, which link up,

on the one hand, with later forms of true social reciprocity, and on the other, with the child's early egocentric attitudes to parents and brothers and sisters. The threads of social development can be traced backwards and forwards, and whilst the total picture at the age of, say, six or seven years is in many respects very different from that presented at, say, two years, it is nowhere essentially new. There is nothing in the later phases which is not adumbrated in the earlier, and which cannot be traced through continuous processes of change and growth to the earlier.

(2) The study of the behaviour of little children in groups does not support that particular approach to social psychology which has had so much vogue in recent years, namely, the attempt to understand human social life by paralleling it with the herd life of certain other animals, such as the great herbivores. Certain superficial resemblances can, of course, be made out. Much of the behaviour of this group of small children could be described as "herd" behaviour; for instance, their joint hostility to a newcomer and their assumption that strangers are necessarily hostile. But this superficial parallel gives us no insight into the meaning of such behaviour for the individual children who make up the group, and is quite specious and misleading.

On the other hand, the behaviour of the children in the nursery school group can be vitally linked, point by point, with the family situation. Other adults are always in the first instance responded to as parents, and other children as brothers and sisters. We have seen this in detail with regard to individual and group hostilities, as well as friendly co-operation. Feelings of jealousy, rivalry, hostility, comradeship, etc., shown to school playmates can only be understood in terms of the child's previous responses to his family. It has become clear that this primary situation sets the fundamental pattern of his relation to the world as a whole, and all other social situations develop from it.

(3) We have seen, too, that the child's relation to his two parents at any phase is extremely complex. He is dependent upon them not only for the preservation of life and the satisfaction of nutritional needs, but for libidinal satisfactions as well. He has (or has had) real sexual desires towards them, varying in mode according to his phase of development and his individual way of dealing with anxiety.

His feelings, moreover, at any period after the oral-sucking phase, are highly ambivalent towards both his parents. Aggressive feelings and hate are stimulated by all the inevitable frustrations of his wishes, and these in their turn give rise to phantasies of retribution from his parents. This marked ambivalence of feeling, and a strongly sadistic tinge to sexuality itself, characterise all the early phases of libidinal development after the sucking phase. Only when and in so far as genital primacy is established does the sadistic element tend to lessen in intensity. Genital primacy is, however, not established to any extent until four or five years of age, and not finally stabilised, even in children who show the most satisfactory development, until after adolescence. All through the years of childhood, including the latency period, the child has to struggle in the deeper levels of his mind with anxieties arising from his own sadistic impulses towards those whom he loves, as well as with those projected phantasies of a sadistic sexual life in his parents, which themselves give rise to further terrors. Most of this struggle goes on far below the level of conscious understanding, and is to a considerable extent out of touch with real experience, although, of course, the outcome of the struggle is undoubtedly affected by the child's real experience and his growing knowledge of his real parents. It is, however, precisely with regard to their sexual life that he gains least knowledge of reality and has least chance of working over his phantasies by real experience.

(4) In considering the origins of later social development in the child's relation to his parents, we have to hold in mind not only his real external relations with the parents as he knows them in the later phases of his own development, and as they are in their real behaviour, but even more, his relations to them in terms of intra-psychical conflict. After his first year the child is always attempting to deal with internal tension between his own instinctual trends, whether libidinal or aggressive, on the one hand, and the *introjected* parents, his super-ego, on the other. His actual relation with his real parents in the second or third year onwards is largely affected by this internal situation, itself built upon the earliest and most primitive wishes and phantasies. We have noted in broad outline the various psychological mechanisms by which the anxieties arising from this intra-psychical conflict are allayed ; and we have seen these mechanisms

operate in various details of the children's actual social behaviour.

(5) It is thus clear that when a child enters a larger social group outside the home, the adults there will represent to him not only his real parents as he has come to know them in later stages of development, but also, in times of difficulty or stress, his primitive super-ego, the parent built up within the child's psyche at a primitive level of development, and now projected again. I have shown at various points what relief to inner tension comes to the child through this projection. It is from this function as projected super-ego[1] that the adult in charge gains his prestige, and his power to control the child and influence him for good or ill. The child will react in this way to any adult, by virtue of his being an adult, whether or not the latter seeks and wishes it. And upon the way in which the adult uses the prestige with which he is invested will depend much of the child's later success or failure in the world.

(6) The ambivalence of feeling which the child experiences towards his real parents in the earlier phases of development will tend to be felt again towards adults in the school and the larger world. In his first years in the nursery school the child of two and three will cling to the grown-ups for safety and for libidinal satisfactions with scarcely less intensity than he does to mother or nurse at home. He will show much the same anxieties when thwarted or denied—as must of course happen from time to time. Aggressive impulses will be stimulated by any frustration of his desires, as, for example, when the adults show themselves not existing solely for him, not preferring him to the exclusion of other children, but devoted to the service of others as well. The fact that they are devoted to the service of the group *as a whole* will not at first mean much to him. It will only seem to him that they devote themselves to his rivals. And when they have to thwart his particular wishes in any way, for instance, with regard to food, caresses, the possession of some object, or the desire to dominate over other children, he will at first feel almost as lost and deserted as he is in the nursery at home when the mother tends the new baby or his elder brothers and sisters.

(7) In the majority of cases, however, the child's responses

---

[1] Not so much the most primitive vengeful super-ego, as the 'good strict' parent-self, helpful by virtue of strictness.

to other adults outside the home, and other children in the nursery school group, are never quite so intense or so ambivalent as to the actual parents and brothers and sisters at home. It is indeed a not uncommon experience to find the contrast quite marked. There are some children who are much easier to handle by any other adult than by the actual mother, and it is an interesting psychological question as to why this should be so. The skill and experience of the trained nursery school teacher must, of course, count for a good deal, as against the mother of an only child who has had no other experience of handling children. But this cannot be the sole factor, since the contrast often occurs even with mothers who are wise and experienced, and as against an adult (e.g. an inexperienced aunt) who is not so skilful and wise as she. By no means all nursery school teachers are wiser than the children's mothers !

There must, therefore, in these cases have been something inherent in the child's relation to his mother which made things more difficult there than with another person. Two factors at least may well operate : (*a*) The child has been dependent upon his mother for essential physical satisfactions, and has suffered his first thwartings from her. She is the *fons et origo* of his first real anxieties, and this remains a permanent factor, even if repressed and unconscious, in his relation with her. If his primary ambivalence, expressed in actual behaviour towards his mother (screaming, biting, wetting, etc., with all the associated phantasies), has been very intense, there is at any later time a heritage of actual and specific memory which does not operate in relation to other adults. (The same will, of course, be true in a lesser degree of the child's real relation to his nurse.) With any newly met adult, these memories of real behaviour are not present, and he starts afresh at the level of development he has now reached. He has not bitten or dirtied or screamed at the nursery school teacher, and so he is less afraid of her. He may have no *real* reason to be afraid of his mother on these grounds, but his feelings are stronger than his knowledge of her real character. It is this psychological situation which accounts for some of those striking instances of children who behave so much better at school than in the home, as well as for the less marked differences shown by many ordinary children in their responses to adults other than the mother or nurse.

(b) Bound up with these elements in the child's relation with his mother, there must have been corresponding real elements on the mother's side. In some cases, the mother is more easily thrown into a state of anxiety about the child's behaviour than other adults are. She is more directly acted upon by his hostility, whatever form that may take. She feels herself far more closely involved in his behaviour than, for example, the nursery school teacher does; and this makes her own reactions to the child more intense. It is thus harder for her to maintain a just proportion in estimating the child's behaviour, and that quite as much because of her own emotional need that he should be a good child as because of her lack of experience.[1]

(8) Two other important mechanisms, (a) the splitting of the ambivalent feelings, and (b) displacement, contribute further to lessen the degree of emotional tension which the little child feels in relation to adults other than his own parents. I drew attention to these when discussing the material of social relations.

(a) We noted how often it happens that a child seems only to be able to love one adult when there is another to hate. Or, conversely, can only bear to show his hatred to one when there is another whom he can love and turn to for support. This way of dividing the *imagos* of the " good " and " bad " parents within his own mind, and projecting them on to two separate real persons, is a great help in the young child's relations with adults. It enables him to build up real

[1] I would not have readers jump to the conclusion from my statement of these facts that I think it is a desirable thing for children to be educated altogether by people other than their parents. It is a good thing for little children of over two years to be away from their homes in a nursery school for some part of each day. But the psychological evidence tells against a purely institutional education and in favour of the natural environment of the home. It is an essential part of the child's education that he should learn to deal with the central family situation, and be able to establish good relations with his own real parents and brothers and sisters. Many children, it is true, cannot learn to do this, usually because they or their parents are too neurotic. In such cases they are better and happier away from home with trained educators; but it does not follow that this is a normal and desirable thing for all children. There is no better educator for the child than a wise parent, although even the wisest of parents is not sufficient. The young child needs *both* a satisfactory home life and the opportunity for wider social contacts in a nursery school or kindergarten group.

SOCIAL AND SEXUAL DEVELOPMENT

situations of common activity and co-operation with the person towards whom he is feeling love and trust, whilst the possibility of expressing his hostility to another in safety gives him the chance of testing out his aggressive and retribution phantasies in reality, and thus lessening their hold upon him. It is the fact that he hates the very person whom he loves which is a nuclear source of difficulty, and any real situation which relieves this inner tension by separating these opposing tendencies and allowing them to find real expression towards separate people helps the growth of his power to deal with reality as well as his control of the impulses themselves.

(b) The mechanism of displacement is a constant element in the child's relations with all the adults whom he meets. All his varied emotions towards his parents, of whatever quality or degree of intensity, may be directed in turn or together on to other grown-ups, according to the situation of the moment. By this diffusion of feeling, the intensity of the child's emotions towards his parents themselves is gradually lessened. Just in so far as his world widens beyond them, so that they cease to fill it completely for him, his feelings towards them will become more manageable.

These two ways of lessening the intensity of his emotions towards his parents occur in the experience of most children in ordinary life, not only with those who go to a nursery school. Aunts and uncles, servants, nurses and governesses, and the ordinary friends of their parents, indeed even the people the child meets in the street or the shops, serve to deflect and diffuse the central emotions, thus enabling him to master and temper them.

(9) The same processes of displacement and the splitting of ambivalent feelings occur in the child's relation to other children, as we saw in considerable detail when discussing the appropriate data. The child's initial fear and hostility towards other children as potential rivals are lessened in intensity by the diffusion of his feelings over a larger number, so that he becomes less emotionally dependent upon any one playmate. And his primary aggression is turned outwards, away from his own immediate group of family or friends, to other groups, who can be openly and safely acknowledged as rivals. With the younger children, the particular " enemies " will vary from occasion to occasion, but these situations gradually

become stabilised in the organised rivalries of games, sports and social life.

Along with this deflection of hostility from friends to open foes of one sort or another goes the equally important development of allyship amongst friends. The compensating value of this rivalry of groups is that it brings to the children the active experience of mutual consideration and help within the group. They get the feel of working and playing *together*. They suffer the pressure of other children's wishes and contrary opinions which are yet not too different, not altogether contrary, since they come from friends. Each child's friendliness to his fellow-members of the group makes him more ready to give way, to try to see their point of view. It is possible to " give and take " with those whom he loves, although not with those whom he fears and dislikes. The quick-changing feelings of love and hostility which young children show for their playmates thus slowly settle down into the more stable friendships and personal rivalries in the work and the games of later childhood. And the spontaneous animosities of early group relations are gradually taken up into the approved and organised rivalries of a settled social life.

The child, moreover, discovers that other children can join with him, not only against other rival groups of children, but even more importantly against the grown-ups. This occurs even within the family, but more readily still in the larger groups of the school, or friends outside the home. This comradeship of other children, and the support which it gives against the child's deeper anxieties in relation to his parents, is an enormous help to him in developing confidence and security with the grown-ups. This support is felt not only against the real parents and other adults, but even more significantly against the internalised parents, the child's super-ego. What the group does together can be done safely. " If other children can do these things without punishment and danger, I can do them without punishment and danger." This sense of inner support which comes from the companionship of other children is not only a great relief to psychic tension, but a pre-condition of the development of a sense of reality in actual relations with adults.

It is under the shelter of this alliance with others of his own age that the child wins his first real independence of his parents and teachers, and begins to see them more nearly as they are. They cease to be the gods, the giants and ogres they were to his infantile imagination. He and his fellows together can now dare to look at the grown-ups with an appraising eye, and see whether they are indeed worthy of that respect which they demand. Children watch the behaviour of parents and teachers with quite as observant a glance as parents and teachers turn upon them, and often reflect upon what they see in a way that might disconcert most of us did we but know it.

Neither teacher nor parent can now maintain his prestige by mere virtue of being grown up. Authority has to be won and kept by the real tested qualities of sense and firmness. And the children will be continually trying out the power of the adult to keep their allegiance. They will be quick to sense and despise weakness, and quite merciless to exploit it—but as ready to yield respect to those adults who are at the same time tolerant, good-humoured, and sure of themselves.

In the years after six or seven, thus, the adult becomes to a far smaller extent than earlier the immediate arbiter of the child's happiness. The child no longer hangs upon the smiles and frowns of the adult as the three-year-old tends to do. He is much more sensitive now to the praise or contempt of his fellows. Children of the middle years can be excellent friends with adults, but will not take them into their inner confidence, as young children naturally do, and adolescent boys and girls will do again in their turn. They have less intimate need of adult friends, and far more of their fellows. In other words, a *morality of equals* now begins to take the place of a morality based on the parent-child relation.

(10) Another great development, one which has been going on in the little child from the time when he begins to walk and talk, but which gains an increasing momentum as the years pass, is the growth of his sublimations. In the development of bodily poise and skill and the use of his hands for making and doing, in the expression of his phantasy life in modelling, drawing, painting, story-telling, verse, dramatic play, in the satisfaction of his curiosities about the real world, he is not only developing real skill and gaining knowledge of the real world, but is at the same time finding indirect and satisfying expressions for his unconscious sexual wishes and aggressive impulses. These sublimatory activities, which

come to fill a larger and larger part in his life, contribute a very great deal to his *social* development, through the deflection and diffusion of anxiety which they make possible. It is a familiar fact to any experienced teacher of young children that children's emotional relations with each other improve as their actual skill in activity and expression grows, and this has been clearly shown in some of my quoted data.

(11) These modes of deflecting emotion and allaying anxiety, which free the mind of the child for real relations with adults or other children, thus further the development of his sense of reality in all directions. A greater sense of reality in his relations to people is one of those cumulative changes which become so substantial round about six to seven years that they make the attitude of the older child appear very different from what it is at the height of his emotional conflict.

This development of a social ego is not, however, only a function of the child's relations with other people. It has its beginnings in the very early days, from the child's first contact with the actual physical world. That there is this real contact with the physical world even in the early days of infancy cannot be doubted. As soon as the child's perceptions and movements gain any degree of organisation, he becomes aware of the physical world as such, which differs from the world of people precisely in that it cannot be affected or controlled by those cries and gestures and " magical " means which will affect and control human beings.

As I pointed out in *Intellectual Growth in Young Children*, " The child makes a partial discovery of the limits which the physical world sets to his activities surely almost as early as he comes to know other human beings as persons. The disappointments and sense of impotence which *things* force upon him are as much a part of his education as the denials and thwartings suffered at the hands of adults. The burnt child dreads the fire even in the stage of egocentrism. Only in the very earliest months can it be true that human relationships hold the stage completely. At least from the weaning period onwards, the physical world must have some part in the organisation of experience and in the fixing of cognitive patterns ; and increasingly so as development proceeds. . . .

" Whilst it is certainly true that the *first* value which the physical world has for the child is as a canvas upon which to project his personal wishes and anxieties, and that his first

SOCIAL AND SEXUAL DEVELOPMENT

form of interest in it is one of dramatic representation, yet . . . this does not prevent him from getting direct actual experience of physical processes. Physical events become, in fact, the test and measure of reality. There is no wheedling or cajoling or bullying or deceiving *them*. Their answer is *yes* or *no*, and remains the same to-day as yesterday. It is surely they that wean the child from personal schemas, and give content to ' objectivity ' "[1] (p. 79). This growing knowledge of the real physical world with its impersonality and stability must itself be a great aid to the child in attaining objectivity with regard to people also.

(12) The confluence of these various psychological processes, accumulating their effect from the first year of infancy to round about six, gradually changes the superficies of the child's behaviour so markedly that he does appear to enter upon a quite different psychological phase.

One of the chief characteristics of the child over six or seven is his wish to understand what is real and true. But this interest in reality itself rests upon another change which takes place on far deeper levels, namely, the *repression* of his central conflict with regard to his parents. Between the years (roughly) of four and six, the child's most intense sexual wishes and resulting aggression towards his parents undergo a very deep repression.[2] He thus turns away from his parents to other children for emotional satisfactions. Thereafter, as we have seen, he is (consciously) far more occupied with the feelings and opinions of other children towards himself than with the opinions and feelings of his parents. This is not, of course, a sudden change, but covers the space of a year or two, or even longer. But it does suffice to make

---

[1] The impersonal world indeed very often comes to have for the child so much and so precisely this significance of stability that in moments of great emotional stress he will, as it were, take a part of the physical world into himself, or attempt to model himself upon it, just *because* it is so unchanging and solid and unaffected by feelings. If one is, for example, a wall or a chair, one cannot be blamed for being stupid ; nor can one be hurt, because one is dead. If one is already dead then one cannot be killed ; so it is sometimes safer to *be* unfeeling, unchanging and dead like a physical object. (See M. N. Searl, " A Note on Depersonalization," *International Journal of Psycho-Analysis*, Vol. XIII, Part 3, 1932.)

[2] It is probable that at any rate to some extent this is phylogenetically determined, and not only an outcome of those various other processes and changes we have been examining.

the life of the child afterwards very different from what it was before.

This repression of the central emotional conflict itself contributes to the child's growing interest in and appreciation of reality.

(13) The typical attitude of the child in the middle years of the latency period (say eight to eleven) is, then, this testing of reality, not only in the shape of mechanical causality and the physical world, but of the human world also. He wants to understand the real behaviour of people, whether those immediately around him, or those of whom he hears and reads in the larger social world—in travel, adventure, exploration, science and history. We are all familiar with the way in which the general interests of the child characteristically become more matter-of-fact. His reading interests, his handicrafts and his dramatic play alike show this increasing emphasis on reality. Fairy tales and romance are gradually replaced by history and a concern with real people of the present day.

What this means from the point of view of his inner mental life is that the amount of anxiety arising from his deepest conflicts has been distinctly lessened, as an outcome of all the various influences we have been considering. It thus becomes more possible for him to deal with what remains by this working out in real experience. Since primitive phantasies about his parents and other children dominate his mind less fully, he is more free to look at them as they really are, to find out how they do in fact behave.

Underneath that comparatively easy reserve which at this period he shows towards adults, there is always a great deal of suspicion, always a watching to see whether grown-ups are honest or dishonest, reliable or untrustworthy, cruel and selfish or humane and considerate; to see whether or not they have the same secret hostilities and secret sexual indulgences and the same inconsistencies as the child knows within himself. It is this watching and testing attitude which makes it so much more difficult for an adult to win the full confidence of the child now. Both in ordinary life and in the analytic situation, the child will watch and thoroughly test the behaviour of any adult who seeks his confidence, before he is able to give it.

This ability to watch and observe the real behaviour of

other people, although it expresses such suspicion, is nevertheless a great advance upon the earlier attitude of the young child, for it means that the child has come to the point where he *dares* to look at what other people really are like. He dares now to note and to measure their real thoughts and real hostilities, because he has already had some degree of real proof that they are not altogether hostile. The importance of this is seen very clearly in those individuals who lack it, those who have never come to be able to gaze steadily at the real behaviour and real character of other people, but have had to construct romantic and idealised figures of parents and family and friends, as people who have no hostility, who are completely kind and beneficent. Such individuals always on the surface assume that other people act from the best possible motives. They dare not acknowledge the reality of greed or meanness or hate in others, because, for them, any signs of this at once open up the whole world of the child's phantasy of dangerous destructive parents or rivals. In such cases there have, of course, always been special historical reasons for their inability to learn what people are really like. They serve, however, to throw into relief this element in the normal development of the majority of children in the latency period, who do come to be able to look with more or less open eyes at the real behaviour and real characteristics of the people around them.

This thread in the child's development contributes greatly to that possibility of reciprocal social understanding and reciprocal behaviour which ripens in the latency period. It is only as and when the child becomes less afraid of other people, as and when he can bear to see them more as they really are, because his vision is less dominated by inner phantasy, that he can take their point of view as well as his own. He can become interested in their point of view when he has to some extent worked through his suspicions, and actually found other people in large part trustworthy ; that is to say, when his positive identifications with them have gained a certain measure of stability.

.   .   .   .

I cannot close this theoretical study without drawing attention to the fact that the account I have given, whether of the sexual or the social aspects of development or of the way in which these affect each other, is but partial and fragmentary.

A great deal more is positively known about the threads of sexual development and the mechanisms for dealing with anxiety than I have been able to make clear here. I have been able only to select certain of these, such as were illustrated in the material, or such as seem specially relevant to the problem of social development.

As regards the linkage of the social and sexual aspects of development, I do not imagine I have done more than suggest lines of investigation. Although my mode of presentation may at times have seemed very positive, I would not have readers assume that the views I offer are put forward dogmatically. They are intended to open up inquiry, not to close it. I shall be content if it is felt that I have been able to show, on the one hand, how fascinating a field of inquiry confronts us in this question of the relation between the sexual development of children as we have now come to understand it, and their social responses in every phase of their growth; and, on the other, how penetrating an instrument we have for this investigation in the psycho-analytic study of the individual.

PART II

THE EDUCATIONAL PROBLEM

CHAPTER ONE

THE RELATION BETWEEN THE PROCESSES OF EDUCATION AND PSYCHO-ANALYSIS

I have now to take up the question of the significance of this genetic psychology of individual children for everyday educational issues; and, first, whether it has any relevance at all. I do not, however, need to make out a general case for considering the direct bearing of children's overt behaviour, descriptively viewed, upon educational technique. Few people nowadays need to be convinced that an understanding of children's overt interests and normal activities is an indispensable part of the equipment of the educator, and all that one has to do is to show the specific bearing of this and that particular fact. The question of the relevance of the *unconscious* significance of the child's behaviour, and the facts as to his sexual development, is, however, quite another matter. How far, and in what way, can the knowledge of the child's unconscious mind at different phases of his growth have any bearing upon the work of the mother, the nurse, the teacher in the nursery or infants' school (or, for that matter, the teacher of older children)?

This is a question which has been variously considered by both educators and analysts, since the time when the work of Freud began to gain general public notice. In the early days, many practising analysts inclined to the view that the new discoveries as to the child's development would in the end completely revolutionise educational purposes and practice. The public pronouncements of some analysts, indeed, almost took the line that every educator should leave all other pursuits and attachments and devote himself to the study of analytic doctrine. Many educators, too, welcomed the new knowledge as giving them an altogether deeper insight into the children who are the subject of their work.

Those who held this view, of course, whether analyst or

educator, met with enormous opposition. Everyone will remember the shock and horror with which the public mind reacted to the idea that little children have sexual desires. As the evidence accumulated, and it was found that feelings of horror and disgust were not sufficient to overturn the solid truth which Freud's genius had discovered, the attitude of the general public, and particularly the attitude of the educational world, began to change. For some time now, there has been an eager concern on the part of many teachers and educational theorists to absorb all the so-called " new psychology", and apply it to their daily labour with children in the schools. Many popular expositors of psycho-analysis have arisen to meet this demand, the esoteric doctrine being thinned out and watered down in this way and that, according to the temperament of the writer or lecturer, to make it a little more palatable to the serious-minded but unanalysed inquirer. And two or three " experimental " schools have arisen which make the open claim to apply certain supposed psycho-analytic notions in a practical way to the education of children. These schools stand for extreme doctrines of " freedom", great play being made with, for example, the notion that " repression " is a bad thing in itself, and an avoidable thing. Certain parts of psycho-analytic theory, particularly the libidinal factors, have been avidly seized upon; but in most cases such reformers of education on supposed psycho-analytic lines have taken no account of the actual later course of psycho-analytic studies, and omit, for example, all reference to the guilt factors or the reality of those forces in the mind that lead to repression.

Meanwhile, however, parallel to the growth of this demand from the educational world for some sort of psycho-analytic information, there has been growing among technical analysts themselves a sense that knowledge of the unconscious, *as such*, has only a limited direct or usable value for the practical educator. In particular, the child analysts in England, working with the play technique of Melanie Klein, have been formulating their own notions of the relation of psycho-analysis to education, and have been deepening their sense of the essential difference between the two approaches to the child's mind.

These views of child analysts in England do not, it is true, represent the universal attitude of analysts, e.g. many of those practising in Germany and Austria. In those countries the original line of development, namely, the idea that psycho-analytic theory and practice had a close bearing upon educational theory and practice, that in fact educational work could only be made vital by being infused with psycho-analytic attitudes to the child, has remained in more favour. These views are specially associated with the names of Anna Freud, Aichhorn and Bernfeld.

The English group, however, have a different notion of the analysis of children itself from that of the school associated with Anna Freud. English readers have only to compare the latter's book, *Introduction to Psycho-Analysis for Teachers*, with Melanie Klein's recent publication on *The Psycho-Analysis of Children*, to appreciate the distinctive point of view of each. Anna Freud's analysis is itself largely didactic. It has deviated from the classical mode of analysis with adults on the supposed ground that the child had as yet no super-ego, and that this had to be put into him deliberately by outside influences. Melanie Klein's work has followed closely in the line of analytic technique with adults, except that it has adapted itself to the special needs of children by using the children's play as an expression of the unconscious, in place of verbal associations. Otherwise, it is in all essentials the same as the analysis of adults. That is to say, it is concerned primarily with the *understanding* of the child's anxieties and the unravelling of the intricate interplay of unconscious phantasies and real experiences, as these can be shown in the special situation created by the analytic technique. It aims at helping him to understand his own inner psychic life, leaving his educators proper to further his expressions of a modified super-ego and adapted wishes in the real world. Analysis, that is to say, aims at making the child more educable, but does not itself educate him in the narrower sense. It is true that in the actual work of analysis, the child is given many opportunities for forming a new " ego-ideal ", based on new identifications with the real patience, tolerance, mildness, honesty and sense of proportion of the analyst. But these are gained by experience, not by direct verbal teaching or a didactic attitude.

In 1929, a group of analysts, members of the British Psycho-Analytical Society, which included three members who had previously had considerable educational experiences with children of all ages, and two practising analysts of children, framed a memorandum to express their views on the relation of psycho-analysis to education. Extracts from this memorandum were quoted by M. N. Searl, in her paper, " Some Contrasted Aspects of Psycho-analysis and Education." I will not quote again from it, but attempt to set out, in my own words, the general conclusions which I share with my fellow members of that Sub-Committee.

The question of the relation between psycho-analysis and education falls into two quite distinct parts: (*a*) The relation between the actual *processes* of education and analysis : how, if at all, they are related ; what, if anything, they have in common and in what they are distinct. (*b*) The bearings upon educational aims and practice of the *facts* revealed by the psycho-analytic technique.

In this chapter I propose to deal briefly with the first of these questions. The second question will fall naturally into my next chapter.

The Processes of Psycho-analysis and Education

In the paper already mentioned, Miss Searl has brought out very clearly the essential distinction between these two processes. The analyst works with the child for a definite time each day in a very special environment, an environment designed to make possible the representation in play of every detail of the child's phantasy, down to the deepest level of the unconscious, free from the dangers of doing real harm in the real world. He has toys and material for his play, which adapt themselves to the expression of phantasy, and with these he is allowed to do everything that occurs to him. He is restrained from doing any real harm to the person of the analyst or his private possessions, or such damage to the room or permanent furniture of the room which cannot be made good again in the few moments at the disposal of the analyst between one patient and another. Even this restraint, however, is never allowed to take the form of " That is wrong, you must not do that ", but always " Show me that in another way." That is to say, the child is never prevented from revealing his feelings, his wishes, his phantasies and his fears of retribution. It is essential that all these aspects of his psychic life should be brought out to the full; but he is prevented from doing such real damage in the stress of his anxiety as would be a serious inconvenience to the analyst, or a danger to the child himself or other people.

Even in analysis, therefore, there is always a reference to reality; for this alone could give the child confidence that he may safely show what his wishes are. If he felt that he was being allowed to do real damage, he would no more dare to show his phantasies in the analytic room than in real life outside; if he felt that the analyst could not restrain him when he wishes to do real damage, he could not unlock the door of his inner life. Once, however, the analytic situation is set going, the child soon realises that here is a person and here is a setting whose sole purpose is to understand: he can then freely display his phantasies, whether wish or dreaded retribution, step by step, and show how these are evoked in him, moment by moment, by the real happenings of his outer life.

A small illustration may perhaps make clearer the child's own sense of the difference between the type of reality which the analytic situation represents, i.e. psychic reality, and the external reality of people and things. A seven-year-old boy patient of mine had been showing me many aspects of his wish to attack me (as representing his mother) and take away my babies (his rivals). He had also shown me the many ways in which he imagined himself making me better by being the " good father ", giving me back good babies and good love, how he believed that if he gave me love, he would get good milk in return, but that if he was angry, or screamed, or wet or dirtied his bed, he would either get no food at all, or bad food and poison. After some weeks of this type of play, I had a cold and was obliged to take two days away from his analysis. The day following my return the child showed not only the great anxiety which my real cold had caused him, as an apparent fulfilment of his destructive wishes against me, but also his appreciation of the fact that *real* injuries have to be made good, not by phantasied gifts, but by *real* gifts. For the first time, he gave me a slice of his real lunch apple. Many days previously he had eaten his apple under my eyes, in moments when his fear of me, as an attacking, avenging mother, had become too real and vivid to his mind and he needed real comfort himself. Now, as I seemed to have been made really ill by his bad wishes, then I must be given a piece of real apple, and a sign of real love, to make me really better. This was the only real amendment open to him, and a true sacrifice.

The child's analysis, like the adult's, proceeds by the gradual, step-by-step unfolding of the inner world of unconscious wish, phantasy and dread, all the intricate interplay of wish-self and parent-self and ego, as representing the world of reality, being shown from moment to moment, and played out in the most dramatic and vivid forms. Step by step the child's real judgment and knowledge of what he can in fact do, or would in the world of reality wish to do, and what other people would in the world of reality do again to him, come to work upon the actual imaginings and intense feelings, hitherto entirely shut off from the world of reality by repression. At times, when the unconscious wish to gain everything for himself or destroy what he cannot have for himself, the wish to bite and burn or cut or flood with water, comes near the surface, the anxiety of the child may mount up and take violent forms of defence by aggression, if it is not relieved by the analyst's immediate interpretation, showing that she understands, and does not fulfil the retributive phantasies, thus enabling the child himself to understand what it is he wishes and what it is he dreads.

Not only are the broad lines of psychic development, which the child shares with every other child, revealed step by step, but the intimate and individual details of each particular reaction to each particular situation of his early life, those individual responses which make him a personality, are brought into the light. They are thus either worked over, modified and changed, on the one hand, or consolidated and made more secure on the other, as the child's real ego has the opportunity to deal with them. The function of the analyst is, in essence, to act as the ego of the child in the moments of stress, when it feels to him that he *has* no ego, when he is all feeling, all wish, all terror. Through his interpretations the analyst not only tides the child over these moments of stress, but makes it possible for the child's own sense of reality to take over and master these immense charges of feeling, which hitherto he has been unable to deal with. In his work of interpretation, on the one hand, and the safeguarding of the child against doing or receiving real harm on the other, the analyst acts as the child's ego in the real world ; but at the same time he co-operatively responds to the play phantasies of the child, by accepting whatever rôle the child puts upon him in the play itself. This rôle is always initiated by the child, although accepted and responded to by the analyst. Now, the analyst may have to be a passenger in the motor car which the child drives ; now, a mother of babies, who receives a visit from " Uncle Tom "—that is, the " good " father ; now, a bad child at school who has done her sums wrong, or been talking when she should have been working, and is told by her " teacher " (the child) to stand in the corner as a penance ; now, a lady in a restaurant to be served by the child as waiter ; now, a maid herself, to clean the floor. The play function of the analyst changes from moment to moment, as the child externalises the various *dramatis personæ* of his own inner life. Sometimes the analyst represents the bad wish-self, sometimes the helpful real person, the real ego of the child or the real " good " parent ; sometimes the bad, attacking, phantasied super-ego or threatening judge, who will, if not herself annihilated, eat up and burn or destroy the child in instant retribution. But the analyst is all the time functioning also as an *ego*, since through all these dramatic situations she makes clear to the child at each point what he, the child, is doing and why he is assigning this or that part to the analyst ; and so assists the intelligence and judgment and sense of reality of the child himself to work upon the material of his own inner world. Through all this change of phantasy the child gradually builds up a sense of real trust and confidence in the analyst as a person to whom it is *safe* to show the inner world—apart, of course, from those moments of violent stress, when a new and deeper layer is being touched, and the analyst again, for the moment, becomes the bad, avenging parent, until the stress is again relieved by further interpretation.

This account of the analytic situation, though altogether inadequate to its complexity, may perhaps suffice to show what a completely different situation it is from that of the teacher and educator.

There are, thus, three main differences between the educational and the analytic situation : (1) The analyst has to uncover and accept and follow up not only the love of the child, but his hate. She must be able to tolerate the full expression of the child's *feeling* of hate and aggression (within the limits of action already described). If anything, this is even more important for the purpose of analysis than being willing to accept the love and trust, since it is primarily the forces of hatred and destruction which the child learns to hide from his real parents, and which give rise to the terrors of retribution. As we have seen earlier, the libidinal wishes of the early phases of sexuality become repressed mainly because of their association with the aggressive impulses.

The educator, on the other hand, cannot do her work well unless she attracts to herself mainly the forces of love. She must be a "good" parent to the child, even though she be a strict one. She must provide, it is true, generous opportunity for expression of the impulses of destruction in the real world, but in a very modified form (e.g. in the rivalry of games and sports, or in various forms of handicrafts). But she must not, by her real qualities, attract to herself the negative, explosive reactions of hatred and aggression. If she does, her work as an educator is made by so much the more difficult. Every good teacher, every good parent knows and acts upon this. She must behave in such a way that the child can love her, even though she uses the love solely for the child's governing and training; she must represent to the child the world of love and creation, and not become associated with that of hatred and destruction.[1]

(2) The second main difference is that the analyst can never rest content when she has reached a moment of *apparent* equilibrium and peace in the child's mind, until she knows that the full work of the analysis has been completed. She has always to look for signs of further anxiety, which would render that peace unstable. When the child is loving, she must look for any signs that he is not only loving, but also hiding his hatred; when he is making things better, she must show him not only the wish to make things better, but if it be there, the hidden and contrary wish to break and damage. The educator must not do this: it would be unwise if she tried to do it.

---

[1] I do not mean that educators have to be inhumanly perfect before they can educate at all. Children readily forgive occasional outbursts of anger and other real faults in an adult whose *general* attitude is reliable and friendly and understanding.

She must take the child's wish to make good, to create, as a factor in the development of his real skill and achievement. She must make use of it in the real world, and show him how to be effective with it in the real world. She has no direct concern in her work as an educator with the fact that the child's love and wish to make may be covering his fear and hate and wish to destroy. That is the analyst's concern, not the teacher's.

Where the child does *not* show a wish to learn, to make good, to be friendly in the real world, but only knows how to be defiant and to destroy and to hate, then, of course, it is the business of the teacher to understand that he needs special psychological help ; that is to say, when she has exhausted those general methods of patient encouragement and trust and teaching which will help most children out of their difficult moments, it becomes her business to understand the child's need of analysis. But the unconscious wishes as such are not, and cannot be within her competence—any more than the teaching and training of the child in skilful manipulation or understanding of the *external* world is within the competence of the analyst.

The educator, of course, makes use of the child's unconscious impulses, whether these be impulses of love or hate, of creation or destruction, since the child's unconscious wishes underlie every aspect of his conscious behaviour, and are its ultimate source. But the educator can only make use of unconscious trends in so far as they are available within the field of the conscious life, and in the form in which they are available in conscious life. She does not need to know that the child's interest in engines is ultimately linked with his phantasies of parental intercourse ; she does not need to know that the child's high tower of bricks represents, among many other things, his own or his father's phallus. If she be a psychologist as well as an educator, and interested in these things for their own sake, then there is no reason why she should not know ; but *qua educator*, she has no concern with the deep symbolism of the child's everyday activities. What she needs is to understand the normal conscious movement of the child's mind, as expressed in interests and activities and conscious pleasures or fears.

(3) The third chief difference between the function of the educator and that of the analyst is that whereas the

analyst, in his play with the child, allows himself to represent each and every aspect of the conflicting forces in the child's inner life, as the child himself takes on this or that complementary part in the played out drama, the educator's function is mainly that of super-ego. The analyst may sometimes play out the bad self of the child, sometimes the cruel phantasy parent, at other times the real good, or real strict parent, but the educator can only help the child by her willingness to act stably as a wise parent.[1] Not the more primitive parent of the deepest phantasies, but the mild, tolerant, friendly parent who is very close in his qualities to the world of reality, that is to say, whose *actual* values and judgments are measured and appropriate and well based. I shall develop this point in specific detail in the next chapter, and touch upon it here only for the purpose of contrasting the educator and analyst.

These three deep and essential contrasts having been drawn between the work of the educator and the analyst, it should be clear that no one person can combine the two functions to the same child, and that, moreover, it will be an unwise thing for a teacher or a mother or a person in a real relationship of authority to a child to attempt to undertake the work of an analyst, even by ever so little. An admixture of education and analysis tends to ruin both, and can do little for the child but confuse and bewilder him, and increase his conflicts.

One does, every now and then, meet people in ordinary social life who have read books about psycho-analysis, or even taken a little dose of the treatment, and who amuse themselves and others by lightning darts at the complexes of their acquaintances, adopting a superior air of knowing all about the motives, even the worst ones, of other people. Such a thing *may* be amusing in ordinary circumstances, and perhaps does no special harm. But in the relation of teacher and child, or parent and child, it does serious harm.

The point needs to be made because there are quasi-educators going about who do attempt to educate by a sort of analysis, as well as to analyse by a sort of education. I have myself seen a series of notes kept by one or two people

[1] Again, I do not mean that the educator has to be deliberately superior and constantly didactic. The best educators are indeed those who can wear their parental responsibilities lightly, without shirking them, and can talk and play with children on an equal human footing.

working in a school of this type, in which it seemed to me that real cruelty was being done upon the person of the child, through this undesirable complex-hunting in everyday life, and an attempt to educate in terms of misunderstood analytic notions. The serious risk when any person, with an active real relation to the child, makes attempts to get below the surface of the child's mind in the pursuit of his ordinary relation is that it is really impossible to know what the effect may be, what immense conflicts he may be stimulating, and what immense charges of feeling, positive and negative, he may be drawing to his own person, without ever being able to disperse these again by tracing them to their sources in the real experiences of infancy.

All this holds good not only of the educator of young children, but of all who deal with adolescents, too. The adolescent boy or girl stands in great need of real help and understanding on the part of older men and women. And this understanding can be very deep in its quality without touching the true unconscious. It should not attempt to touch the true unconscious, it should not attempt to explain conscious wishes and day-dreams and conflict in terms of unconscious motives and complexes. The explosive material of the unconscious can only safely be handled by trained analysts working in the proper technically controlled analytic environment.

All this refers to the actual *processes* of education and analysis, to the direct personal attempt to understand the immediate unconscious motives at work in any given piece of behaviour or conscious feeling. It is *not* to say that a general knowledge of analytic theory and the facts of the inner life which have been revealed by analytic technique are not, in a general way, of value to those who work with adolescents or those who educate young children. That is quite a different matter, and needs to be discussed for its own sake—the extent and the particular content of psycho-analytic knowledge which may be of use to the educator.

CHAPTER TWO

SOME PROBLEMS AND CRISES OF EARLY SOCIAL DEVELOPMENT

It remains now to consider the bearings of the *facts* of social and sexual development in young children upon educational problems.

In the first instance, I may remind readers that the general methods of training followed out in the Malting House School are described in Chapter II of *Intellectual Growth in Young Children*. I give there the broad lines of my educational technique, although I do not make specific reference to the issues raised in this volume. Moreover, the general methods which I advocate for early education have been set forth in my other recent books, *The Nursery Years, Health and Education in the Nursery*, and *The Children We Teach*. These methods have their ultimate basis in the psychological facts and theories set out here, although I do not in those volumes attempt to give the deeper picture of children's minds which is here presented. There I wrote for practical mothers, nurses and teachers, who have not the time, and may not have the interest, to consider underlying psychological principles.

In the present volume, however, I am writing for the scientific public, whether psychologists or educationists. And whilst it may not be necessary, or even possible, for practical teachers and parents to understand all the psychological facts upon which their practice depends, it is indispensable for educational theorists and trainers of teachers to be fully conversant with whatever is verifiably known of the minds of children, since this is the foundation stone upon which the science of education itself must ultimately rest.

I have no doubt that the deeper understanding of the emotional life of children which psycho-analysis has yielded will help to provide a more adequate psychological foundation for educational reform ; and this is likely to bring greater security and certainty in actual practice, as well as to confer immunity against mere changes of fashion.

Psychological fact, however, has to be translated into *usable* educational theory, and it remains in itself a technical problem as to how far and in what respects the deeper knowledge of the child's psychology can be made available to teachers in training and the parents of young children. This is very far from being a matter of telling them to read text-books on psycho-analysis, and by no means a question of mere popularisation. Not only is psycho-analytic literature difficult to understand without special training, but psycho-analytic doctrines in the raw are often very disturbing emotionally to those who come in contact with them for the first time. This is, of course, especially true of young teachers in training, who are themselves not yet out of the wood with regard to their own adolescent emotional conflicts. The more mature and stable person is more able to resist the disturbing effect of reading psycho-analytic literature. In one direction or another, he will accept or reject, as his own internal balance of forces determines; but at any rate his own particular equilibrium will remain more secure than that of young boys and girls of eighteen to twenty years of age can be.

I do not, therefore, think it is advisable to suggest that psycho-analytic theory as such has any claim to a place in the regular routine of lectures for teachers in training. Its place, if anywhere, is in courses of lectures for more mature and settled teachers, and for those who are to train teachers. Nevertheless, these facts as to children's minds cannot be kept entirely apart from the actual teaching of psychology given even to young students in the training colleges, and will inevitably affect that teaching in some way or other.

The question is, in what way should they be allowed to affect this teaching? What, of this body of psychological fact, can we safely and wisely and usably give to young students? I do not myself feel in a position to answer this question categorically, but I am sure that it needs a great deal of careful consideration by those responsible for the teaching of psychology in the training colleges.

My present task is, thus, to show in some detail the links between the facts of children's social and sexual growth which have been gathered together in this volume, and the practical advice which I am accustomed to offer to mothers and teachers, whether as to general lines of training or specific problems.

I may say at once, however, that I do not hold that any entirely new or innovatory educational principle emerges from this deeper understanding of the child's relation with his parents or fellows. Such is hardly to be expected, since wise mothers and gifted teachers have long known how to treat little children satisfactorily. Educational reform has not had to wait for psycho-analytic knowledge, although the latter has undoubtedly influenced educational thinkers of recent years in certain broad and indirect ways, such as by its emphasis upon the significance of the child's feelings, whatever these be, and of the imaginative life, whatever form this takes. Psycho-analysis has already contributed a great deal to the general re-valuation of the various aspects of mental life as a whole, in favour of feeling and activity as against an inactive mechanical learning or a crude intellectualism.

I hope to bring out in various specific details two main directions in which a deeper understanding of children's minds is likely to be of direct aid to educators : (1) in the reinforcement which it brings to certain already established educational principles ; and (2) in the correction and criticism which it offers of certain recent extreme tendencies among some educators of young children.

Let me first, however, bring into high relief those broad general facts of genetic psychology illustrated by this material, which appear to be relevant to the educational problem as a whole.

The first such fact, of the deepest significance and widest relevance, is the reality and power of the super-ego in the early years. We have seen that from at least the end of his first year, the child is by no means a creature of mere wish or impulse. He has already within his own psyche powerful controlling and inhibiting tendencies. He is already specifically human, in the sense that the characteristically human function of the super-ego is present in his psyche. This inhibiting force, moreover, is by no means entirely drawn from the teaching of parents, or other external influence : it is in essence intrinsic and spontaneous to the child's mind, although its later detailed history is intimately affected by actual experience.

The notion that we have to *put* controlling influences into the child, to *give* him a conscience or " ego ideal " is entirely false. Those cases of a-social children who appear altogether to lack inhibiting forces, the so-called " moral defectives " or " moral imbeciles ", have now proved under analysis to falsify this superficial picture completely. So far from suffering from a *lack* of conscience, they turn out to suffer from far too severe and overwhelming a conscience, but of the primitive sadistic type, belonging to the pre-genital levels of libidinal development. Their a-social behaviour and delinquency is an outcome of the need to ease the internal pressure of their sadistic super-ego, by proving that the *worst* does not in any case happen in reality, that it is *safe* to be bad : even the severest punishments stop short of death— but the child has to go on proving this over and over again. In such cases, educational methods are at a discount, and psycho-analysis is called for. I am not here concerning myself with such cases, however, except in so far as they serve to emphasise the significance of the early phases of super-ego development.

With those more normal children, whether amenable or difficult, with whom the educator can hope to achieve results, the primitive super-ego has been modified by the later phases of libidinal development and the growth of the sense of reality. It is nevertheless true that their difficulties, the ordinary difficulties of the ordinary child, which show every degree of seriousness, arise not from an absence of guilt, but from anxiety due to the more primitive and sadistic attacks of conscience. It is therefore important that difficult children should not be handled as if they were creatures of mere bad impulse, and that the idiosyncrasies arising from anxiety should not be dealt with by harsh threats and punishments, since this mode of treatment simply serves to increase the severity of the super-ego. What is required is the fostering of the child's belief in love and his sense of security in the real world. And this, provided his inner difficulties are not such as to make him unresponsive to training, is best fostered by a stable, ordered environment and the trust and consideration of the adults upon whom he leans. A real harshness, which approximates to the child's sadistic phantasies, simply confirms him in his inner dread and may tend to bring about a fixation at one of the more primitive levels of libidinal development.

To illustrate: If the child of six or seven months who begins to bite the breast sharply is met by sharp " biting " smacks, his fears of talion punishment receive strong confirmation, and the biting may become compulsive as a result. If he is left to scream indefinitely until he reaches the point of exhaustion, his idea of a terrible world in which he is deserted and lost and attacked, because he has wished to attack, becomes fixed and settled. If his bed-wetting at the age of two or three is dealt with by severe whippings and reprimands, a similar reinforcement of his phantastic dreads is brought about, and he will need to go on wetting all the more in order to prove that he can do so and live. Those mothers who have recourse to frequent whippings at an early age, on the plea that the child " does not understand anything else ", are building up within the child's mind a picture of themselves as really harsh, cruel mothers, corresponding to the child's worst phantasies.[1] The earlier the age, the more

---

[1] " I wonder if you would advise me with regard to my little girl of three years. For the last six months she has been most frightfully naughty and I am absolutely ashamed of the way she behaves. She smacks me and bites me. I smack her back because I want her to know what it is like for she does the same to other children—takes all the toys away from them and when they take anything she smacks them and pushes them down. She has a lot of little friends to tea, but I am stopping it as it makes me so miserable. She cries for nothing at all and won't play by herself at all and is most frightfully impatient. She has plenty of toys and goes for a walk every afternoon from 2.30 until 4.30. At times she is most affectionate and loving, but the grizzling is terrible."

" I should be so much obliged if you could tell me your reason for saying one should never smack a child. I have one small son aged thirteen months, and am most anxious to bring him up in the best possible way and to do what is right. However, I find excellent results from two short slaps, but am worried to see how against this you are. When D. will refuse to use his ' pot ' and I know by the time which has elapsed since he last did so that he must want it, I give him two slaps in the proper place and he stops kicking and screaming and at once obliges. Also, at times he will refuse to take his lunch, even though it may be one of which he is extremely fond. He turns round in his chair and looks over the back and the only way I can make him take it is by slapping his hand, and he will then sit round and eat it up with apparent relish. He very seldom cries when he is smacked and this will last a long time, and I have merely to say, ' David, do you want a smack ? ' and he eats properly. I don't see in what other way you can possibly teach so young a child. It's different when they are older and one can reason with them. In the same way, when he will throw

frequent the occasion, the more severe the treatment—the greater these effects will of course be. A whipping at a later age will not normally have the same far-reaching effect upon the child's mental life as even a milder but more sustained physical chastisement in the very early days. Nor will a whipping received from a person less close to the child than the real parent (e.g. the schoolmaster of a boy of ten or twelve) usually have such serious psychological reverberations as corporal punishment by the parents in the early years.[1]

These may serve as illustrations, for the purpose of the moment, of the general bearing of the fact that the child in any case spontaneously develops these phantasies of attacking parents, creating them out of the stuff of his own impulses, and that the task of the educator is not to reinforce but to dissipate such phantasies, in so far as real experience can affect them at all.

On the other hand, it will be clear that these facts as to the early development of the super-ego lend no colour to the theory that the little child needs and can make use of complete and absolute "freedom". This view has had a certain vogue in recent years, largely as a reaction to previous notions. There have been educational reformers, and to-day there are some schools for children, making a serious attempt to do away literally with every type of restraint or limitation upon the children's impulses.

The common sense of practical educators, whether mothers, nurses or teachers, has usually safeguarded them from excesses of this type, although it is true that a great many mothers to-day (not so often the nurses) do err on the side of lack of control, because of their own anxiety about the supposed evil effects of restraint and formal teaching. The view that

---

his toys into the fireplace a smack is the only thing that will stop him doing so. However, I am very anxious to hear in what way I am doing wrong by these methods and should be much obliged for your help and advice. He is a very strong-willed, determined child, but seems to bear me no grudge for the slap as he seems to realise he deserved it. I am so anxious that he shouldn't be spoiled, as he is a dear little chap, very happy and affectionate and I don't often have much trouble with him. I am sure there must be some very good reason why you always advise against a smack, and should so much like to know what it is, and what other methods I should employ."

[1] I do not say this to condone or justify whipping of older children, but only to show how false it is that the *young* child learns best by corporal punishments.

corporal punishment, and an automatic demand for obedience as such, is not desirable for young children, has rightly become widely influential, but as a result many mothers have become excessively nervous of interfering with their children at all, or taking any definite line of training. This is not yet the commonest fault; but it occurs very often—and especially in those who have thrown over the old automatic standards of good manners and obedience, to be enforced by immediate punishments and whippings, without having gained any ordered knowledge of children to put in their place.

The commonest situation of children to-day, especially in ordinary middle-class homes, is to suffer from an alternation of these two attitudes: a general lack of positive and informed guidance, relieved only by exasperated threats or bribings or actual whippings.[1]

What the child actually needs is that the parents and the

---

[1] " I wonder if you could give me any help as I am quite at sea as to the best way of managing my little boy of two and a half years. Everything is a struggle. He says ' No ' to everything and it is a fight to make him do what I want and not to give in to him. He screams, yells, sits down in the middle of the road. If he does not get his own way he whines and cries, and smacks and pinches those around him. He also bites. He really makes things very unhappy as life is a continual battle. At meals he will not sit still and eat properly, but bangs about with his spoon and stands up. He has to be strapped into his cot at night or he climbs out. He always wets his bed every night. If I shut him in the nursery to make him tidy his toys, he screams and wets the floor on purpose and bangs his head on the door. If I try to help him tidy the toys he throws them at me. Nothing I give him to do interests him for more than two minutes. He does not go to sleep at once when in bed, but throws everything out of the cot, and asks for his chamber, so that I have to take it, even though I know he does not need it. He snatches any food or sweets left in his way, and takes things from the larder if the door is left open. He turns on all the gas taps and electric lights. When out for walks he runs away and dashes into the road if I take my hand away from him. When in shops he pulls everything off shelves, etc. He does everything like this although we have done all we can to show him he must *not*, and to give him other occupations. My husband says the only thing left is severe beatings (he has had occasional smacks), but I feel smacking is wrong. I fear I have even *bribed* him now and then with promise of a prize if he behaves, but this I feel is worse than smacking. He is a great disappointment to me. He has been worse since his baby sister arrived three months ago, although I do my best to be very loving to him, in case he feels jealous. He was not even happy on the beach at the seaside, because he wanted to be in the water the whole time and screamed and bit when I had to take him out and dress him, and spent the rest of the morning trying to rush in in his clothes when my back was turned. I am quite worn out with trying to cope with him."

adults who make up his social world should represent to him a stable and ordered world of values, values closely related to the child's real abilities at any given age, and based upon an understanding of his psychological needs, but which are, nevertheless, firm and unwavering in themselves. Young children do need to feel that the adults around them are stronger than themselves and represent, not the forces of destruction, but those of ordered creation. There are times with every child when he needs to feel that he can be *made* to do things, that those whom he loves are not at the mercy of his own ungovernable instincts but are firmer and stronger and more reliable than he. If he is able to feel that he can do what he likes with them, he will suffer more acutely from the dread of *inner* retribution. It is to be remembered, again, that the phantastic super-ego which the child dreads within himself is built upon the earliest oral pattern, and that he finds relief from this dread of being attacked, bitten, eaten up, by discovering that the real parents can restrain and control him *without* eating him up. He finds relief from inner tension by being able to project his super-ego on to real adults who will exercise it for him. If that real external control is firm and secure, but mild and tempered, it enables the child to master his destructive impulses and to learn to order and adapt his wishes to the real world. If he neither finds fulfilment of his phantastic dreads in the outer world, nor is left at their mercy in his inner world by having no external support, but is slowly educated by a tempered, real control, mild and understanding, appropriate to each situation as it arises, he is led forward on the path of reality and towards all those indirect satisfactions in the real world, the sublimatory activities.

This, then, is the ultimate basis for the sensible practice of the trained educator, who provides a settled framework of control and routine, and definite help along social paths, yet with ample personal freedom, a practice which is fortunately to be found to-day in many a well-ordered nursery and nursery school. This, too, is the corrective for the idea that the child will never learn unless he is scolded or smacked, no less than for the notion that he need not learn, but need only bring out the good that is in him. The child can bring out the good that is in him, provided he is given support against his fears of the bad.

To make the point clearer by another illustration. The first crisis in my experience in the Malting House School which led me to give full appreciation to the guilt factors was with regard to the bullying of younger or smaller children by older and more powerful. In the first few days of the school, when I had ten or twelve very difficult and boisterous boys between two-and-a-half and five years, I was too passive in my treatment of situations of bullying and cruelty, in the hope that if the bullying elders were not interfered with, that is to say, received no " bullying " from me, the impulse would die a natural death. But I found this did not happen; and that, I felt sure, was not only because the aggressive children were still often aggressively treated in their own homes, but because the impulse is one that feeds upon itself rather than exhausts itself in fulfilment. It very quickly became clear to me, not merely that the younger children were meanwhile suffering, but that the older ones too were getting more difficult, more afraid of me, more anxious and miserable. What had happened is what always happens in such situations. If the adult in charge does not accept the function of the super-ego, she necessarily and automatically becomes to the child the representative of his own bad aggressive self.[1] Within a few weeks after the beginning of

[1] " And an adult who is there with the children cannot divest himself of his parental authority by an act of his own will, and create conditions so ' free ' that they rule out his prestige as an adult. It is not what we are to ourselves and in our own intention that matters; but what the children make of us. Our real behaviour to them and the actual conditions we create, are always *for them* set in the matrix of their own phantasies. And what they do make of us in the years from two onwards is in large part a function of the already highly complex interplay of infantile love and hate impulses, and anxiety reactions towards these. The intensive study of instinct and phantasy in individual children by the technique of psycho-analysis has shown that, even at this early age, guilt and anxiety and love invest any adult who has an active relation with the children with a prestige which he cannot escape. Whether he will or no, he is drawn into the ambit of the child's intra-psychical conflict. The child's world is a dramatic world, and the non-interference of the adult is interpreted in dramatic terms. The adult who does not interfere cannot be for the child himself a neutral observer —he is a passive *parent*. And if the parent is passive, one of two things happens; either the child believes that the grown-up *endorses* what he is doing, or he suffers internally from the tension of guilt which fails to find relief in his being told what he must *not* do, a tension which issues sooner or later in actions aimed at provoking anger and punishment. In my second volume, dealing with the social development of children, I shall bring forward evidence to support this view, and shall develop it in ample detail." *Intellectual Growth in Young Children*, pp. 8-9.

my experiment, therefore, I ceased to remain passive in such situations. I interfered to prevent actual bullying, and showed that I disapproved of it—but without strong moral reproaches and without, in my turn, being aggressive to the bullies, that is to say, without doing to them what they had wanted to do to the younger children, without fulfilling their phantasies of talion punishment. It was not only the younger children who were now saved from teasing or interference, and became more contented, but also the elder, stronger children, who now felt safeguarded against their own impulses.

Such an attitude is often uncovered in the analysis of certain types of adults, as, for example, with an obsessional neurotic patient of my own, with very marked aggressive impulses. When he was a young child, these sadistic impulses had undoubtedly had a certain amount of real expression, in the secret teasing of a helpless baby brother, as well as in the fact that his real mother had been over-indulgent and morally weak, so that he had been able to tyrannise over her by virtue of her love for him. It has been very striking how, in the course of the analysis, when these aggressive phantasies have been turned upon *me* (as the representative of his mother), they have aroused the greatest anxiety in his mind, on the ground of my being in reality much smaller and weaker than he, so that if he gave way to his aggressive impulses he could in reality do me physical damage. The idea of my *helplessness* before the drive of his aggressive impulses was extremely disturbing to him, and until it was itself brought into the light of day, made it impossible for him to reveal the aggressive phantasies themselves. This reinforces the view that it is essential for the child to feel that the adult who is responsible for him, who has the parental function towards him, should be really stronger than he, not only in the physical sense, but in the psychological sense also ; that the child should not be able to prostitute the mother's love by using it for his own purposes, for tormenting her and winning self-indulgence ; that he should not, in fact, be able to find more than a minimal amount of *direct* satisfaction for his aggressive impulses. Otherwise, her love becomes a much less valuable thing to him than it would be when associated with the power of real (though mild) control and firm (though liberal) training.

I referred earlier to the popular notion that " repression " is an evil thing and to be avoided at all costs. This notion is, however, by no means soundly based. Repression cannot be avoided in this massive sense, since it is one of the general mechanisms by which every ego deals, at a certain level of psycho-sexual development, with those impulses which cannot be satisfied in actual life, and the stress of which stirs up anxiety and guilt. Some degree of repression is thus essential to a balanced conscious life and adaptation to reality. Whether or not repression is harmful in its outcome is a matter of its degree and its particular incidence. And its amount and incidence are not directly within the control of the educator. Repression is an internal and unconscious mechanism, not to be confused with external restraint or inhibition. Whether, when and how deeply the child represses his own wishes (that is to say, turns away from them and treats them as if they did not exist) will always depend more upon the internal balance of forces than upon external events as such. The pressures we exert externally can increase the severity of repression, as, for instance, by demonstrating to the child that no sort of aggressive or sexual behaviour will be condoned ; but we cannot enact that no repression shall occur, nor can we determine, as educators, its amount and internal distribution. The values which the child's own phantasies lead him to give to our actual behaviour will determine the degree of anxiety he experiences in any particular situation ; and it is this anxiety which sets going the mechanism of repression. Naturally, our own deeper emotional attitudes will affect the child even more sensitively than our explicit teachings.

Moreover, the idea that if we leave the child entirely free to do what he likes we are thereby " avoiding repression " is a mistaken one, since, as I have already shown, this simply means leaving the child at the mercy of his own primitive super-ego, with all its accompanying phantasies of retribution. We do not, and cannot leave him free to the expression of simple, uninhibited wishes, as is sometimes imagined.

Nevertheless, it is clearly essential that the child should not be deprived by his environment of all satisfactions or indirect outlets for his unconscious wishes and phantasies. The environment can undoubtedly make a great difference to the psychic equilibrium of the child, as well as to his real gifts and achievements, by the opportunities it gives or withholds for his spontaneous activities. We come, thus, to the second general significance of the facts and theories here presented, namely, its bearing upon the educational value of play.

I have already, in *Intellectual Growth in Young Children*, elaborated at length the significance of play for the child's growth in manipulative skill, in imaginative art and in discovery, reasoning and thought. I have no need to go further into these, save to emphasise and link this general truth with the present material. Play is not only the means by which the child comes to discover the world; it is supremely the activity which brings him psychic equilibrium in the early years. In his play activities, the child externalises and works out to some measure of harmony all the different trends of his internal psychic life. In turn he gives external form and expression, now to the parent, now to the child within himself, and to each of the different aspects of his real parents, as he apprehends these at the different levels of his own development, through his own wishes and impulses. And gradually he learns to relate his deepest and most primitive phantasies to the ordered world of real relations.

Educators have long appreciated the vast significance of play, and many different aspects of its value have been brought out by different thinkers. It has remained for psycho-analysts, and in particular those working with young children, to show in the greatest detail how play is indeed the breath of life to the child, since it is through play activities that he finds mental ease, and can work upon his wishes, fears and phantasies, so as to integrate them into a living personality. The child does much for himself in his play, even without the help of an analyst, who is in any case but an auxiliary to the child's own integrative impulses.

The function of the educator with regard to play lies in the study of the normal interests and activities of the child at different ages, so that he may know how to supply those materials and opportunities and stimuli to play as shall give him the greatest fulfilment along all directions of his growth. It is here that the study of norms of development in the early years, with regard to skill or understanding, is of the greatest possible aid to the educator of little children. But not alone the study of the ordered play in which the child learns skill and knowledge. It is not less important that parents in the home and teachers in the nursery school should leave ample opportunity to the child for quite free, unhindered, unorganised, imaginative play, than that they should provide didactic apparatus and materials for development in physical skill. This passive work of the educator in leaving the child free to make-believe is as valuable a part of his function as his more active services—a point sometimes lost sight of in the modern nursery school.

The third general significance of the psycho-analytic study of young children, which links up with play activities, is that of the great importance of giving opportunities for the sublimations. Here, again, it is the function of the educator to be passive. He should not, for example, introduce a moral element into the teaching of art, as by over-valuing neatness, accuracy, or formal virtues of any kind. He needs to leave the child free with his painting or modelling materials, to develop his own skill of expression as his own inner needs dictate. As the wisest teachers have shown us, we cannot order or control the child's expression in art. We can but give him material and opportunity, and leave him free to his own creative spirit. This is now beginning to be understood in the realm of art; but it has a wider general application, too. Whatever line of real achievement we consider, that indirect expression of unconscious phantasy which we call sublimation can never appear at the behest of the super-ego, whether the primitive internal super-ego or the real external teacher. It is always the fruit of the child's own creative wishes. If we attempt to control and contain it, we simply make it lifeless and formal. It is not here that the active function of the educator as the super-ego should operate; here he must be passive and merely supporting. His active functions lie in maintaining the stable framework of ordered routine, and in the control of aggressive, destructive impulses in their crude forms.

The psycho-analytic study of young children, and especially of the early phantasies and anxieties, thus altogether re-emphasises the importance of respecting the child's individuality, even at an early age. The personality of the child, and of the adult that he is to be, rests in the last resort upon the inner flux of forces within his own mind, which it is beyond our power to affect and control by any deliberate act.

The way in which he will resolve his own anxieties, the particular channels he will find for indirect satisfaction of his early wishes, the lines upon which his ego will build up its control of primitive wishes, are largely out of our reach. They are determined by imponderable forces within the child's own psyche, which we can but respect. Where the child is in special difficulties, we can aid him, either by providing a more adequate, more secure and more stable environment, or by strengthening his ego through the special work of analysis. But by neither of these functions can we actually determine the lines upon which his individuality shall develop, and what his actual solution of conflict shall be. The more clearly we ourselves recognise this, the greater support we are likely to be to him. If, from the beginning, we respect not only his early efforts at practical independence, in the way Dr Montessori has taught us to respect these, but the individual genius of his expression in creative art, in imaginative play, in the special choice of individual skills and achievements, we give him a very real support towards the solution of his own difficulties. If we try to cramp and control him by our own notions of what he ought to be, we may close up the very channels which will bring him value and safety.

Here, then, is another profound reinforcement of the teaching of the best educators of our time, namely, that we need to respect the child's developing personality and to treat him as an individual, with personal rights, even whilst, at the same time, we recognise that other side of our educational responsibility, that need to help his control of the more crudely destructive impulses, and to train him to a settled routine in the fundamental activities of his daily life, as well as to those minimal levels of mutual consideration which make social relations possible.

The fourth general bearing of all the facts of child behaviour illustrated and examined here is that of the immense value to the young child of the companionship of his fellows. In our study of early egocentrism, and of group hostility and aggression, we saw how the children are carried on to real independence through discovering the value of other children as allies, against the fear both of real grown-ups and of the internal super-ego. I need not elaborate this point further here, except to bring it in relation to the child's deeper phantasy life. Through the co-operative expression of phantasy in dramatic play, the child is led out from his deepest rivalries and anxieties to the discovery of the delights of real satisfaction in social life. He is, moreover, carried from his earliest and deepest needs for sensual satisfaction in actual bodily contact, to the non-sensual satisfactions of ordered social life, and the sharing of interests and activities, upon which not only his social adaptation depends, but his sublimatory activities and real achievements also. The children can help each other in their play, by giving each other support against the dread of rivals, as well as by the common pursuit of non-sexual aims. Companionship in play, therefore, is from an early age one of the greatest needs of little children, whatever aspect of their developing life one is considering.[1]

In all these directions, then, the psycho-analytic study of young children serves to reinforce the established values of the best practice of modern educators. The value of play, play with companions, free imaginative play as well as play leading to ordered skill and knowledge, is enormously supported and confirmed by this deeper study of children's phantasies. The notion that children must not be interfered with at all, but left to work out their own salvation, without control or guidance, is, however, seen to be without firm basis. In some directions, the child cannot do without our guidance. He needs the help of external restraints in learning to control and deflect his own impulses, particularly the aggressive ones. On the other hand, he needs our *passive* help as educators in giving him opportunity for indirect expression in social activities and the mastering of skill.

There is a further significant general bearing of psycho-analytic studies upon the education of young children, namely, the re-valuation of standards of behaviour which it brings about. The evidence I have gathered here will help to establish the truth that infantile sexuality is not only a matter of symbolic interpretation and unconscious phantasy, but to a real extent of actual observable behaviour; and that amongst quite normal and healthy children. In my introductory chapter, I pointed out what a very great help it

---

[1] In *Health and Education in the Nursery* and the revised edition of *The Nursery Years* I considered in detail the reasons why the only or solitary child so often suffers from greater psychological difficulties than the child in a large family or nursery school.

would be to children and parents alike if it were widely understood that some amount of open sexual behaviour, such as masturbation, mutual display and examining of parts, and " rude " talk about the excretory processes, quite normally and generally occurs among children, in the early years. With many children it is kept quite secret and unobserved by grown-ups; with others, it comes out more into the open. Now, if parents finding this sort of behaviour realise that it is fairly common and ordinary, they are in a much better position to help than if they become terrified and think their children abnormal monsters. Where sexual behaviour is flagrant and persistent in children over five years of age, it is very likely that the children in question do need some special psychological help. But this is not true of occasional though secret sexual play of the same kind, which is quite ordinary and normal in the early years, and may occur with any child. Nor does it need any special attention on the part of the grown-ups. Little more may be required than a deflection of interest to other pursuits, a fuller opportunity for co-operative play in non-sexual directions.

I shall consider these particular issues presently as specific problems. For the moment, I am concerned to draw attention to the fact that the scientific study of children's behaviour and sexual development calls for some measure of modification of our own cultural super-ego. In the light of this knowledge, we ourselves need to re-adjust our standards of what is normal behaviour amongst children, and to build these upon objective reality rather than upon our own personal anxieties. Such a change in the cultural super-ego is actually taking place. Parents and educationists in general can tolerate a little more of the truth about children's sexual development than they could ten or twenty years ago. We are less likely than we were to think children abhorrent monsters when they masturbate; we are less likely than we were to over-value the too-good child, who never shows any sign of sexual interests or aggressive impulses. And this greater tolerance on our own part is likely to enable us to deal more wisely and patiently with the children's difficulties—quite apart from that question of the unwise attempt to understand their " complexes " in any direct personal way, with which I dealt in the last chapter.

I may now go on to consider some specific problems of the early education of children, and in particular those arising from the facts of their sexual development.

The problems I shall consider are those constantly put to me during the last few years, by mothers, nurses or nursery school teachers, problems that may arise any day in any nursery or nursery school. I shall include one or two (e.g. feeding and weaning) which belong in the first instance to the earliest days of infancy, and thus do not as such lie within the main scope of this volume. They have their reverberations in the nursery school period, however, and serve to emphasise my main thesis of the continuity of personal and social development; and they have practical bearings on the later work of the nursery school teacher.

1. Feeding and Weaning

It will be clear, both from the actual data I have brought together and from the interpretative theory, that the child's oral experiences are fraught with considerable consequences to his mental life.

A certain amount of frustration with regard to oral pleasures is quite inevitable. The child cannot, either at this or any other time of his life, be kept in a continual state of complete satisfaction. Even where his feeding times are regular and the supply of milk satisfactory he is bound to experience an interval of hunger and longing for love, between the periods of actual satisfaction. Such normal frustrations of desire are, however, the spur which carry his mental life on from the first primary identification with his mother and the helpless omnipotence of the suckling, to the first awareness of the external world, the first hold upon external reality, and the first organisation of the ego towards ordered responses. Through his hunger and his longing for love, he comes gradually to recognise the reality of the breast as an external object independent of himself, and, later on, to know his mother as a person, with all those manifold activities in which she serves him.

Where this normal and inevitable frustration is, however, enhanced by difficulties in feeding, whether this arises from an inadequate supply of milk, the necessity for bottle feeding, or a general bad management which leaves the child to long or irregular periods of helpless hunger and desire, serious effects upon the child's mental life will ensue. I have earlier referred to the established fact that the most serious disturbances in mental life are undoubtedly associated with severe deprivations in the suckling period. If the child is deprived of the normal satisfaction of nutritional impulses or of associated libidinal wishes in the oral period, it is doubtful whether his mental life ever entirely recovers. Psycho-analytic studies again, therefore, reinforce the wisdom of normal breast feeding in the early months (especially the first two or three months), and of a regular, settled feeding routine.

Even in the suckling stage, however, the human mind has some measure of resilience and adaptability. Most children can adapt themselves and their libidinal demands, even to the long intervals between feeding which nowadays have been set up as the standard by dieticians and physiologists, only provided these are regular and stable. There are children, it is true, who cannot accept these long intervals, just as there are individual children who from the outset are difficult feeders, this probably being the outcome of a constitutional enhancement of oral sadism and resulting anxieties. But in general, the ordinary infant can and does learn to adapt to a normal, ordered life of regular satisfaction.

It is, however, extremely important that the libidinal factors in the feeding situation should be recognised. Where, for example, the mother cannot feed her child satisfactorily at the breast, whether for physiological or psychological reasons, it is important that the bottle should be given in such a way as to minimise the libidinal loss to the child. The manner in which he is held while feeding from the bottle will, for example, make a great difference to his general satisfaction. It is not only food he requires, but also love.

It will, moreover, be clear that the crisis of weaning is an enormously important event in the child's love life, as well as in his physiological adaptation to diet. Fortunately, it has not escaped observation by ordinary doctors, mothers and nurses that a sudden or dramatic weaning has serious effects upon the child's behaviour. Ordinary sense, even without the deeper knowledge of what the weaning situation means to the child himself, has sufficed to build up general standards and methods which on the whole are satisfactory. The modern practice of accustoming the child to drink water from a spoon from his earliest weeks, so that this becomes already a part of the loving attention given to him, and the sensations and movements it involves become familiar in ample time for the weaning crisis, is very sound ; and the graduation of the change by introducing one or two artificial feeds at first, and then by degrees increasing the number, also makes the situation much easier for the child.

The age at which weaning occurs is, moreover, important. On the whole, it can be safely said that the later the better, and the third quarter of the first year is undoubtedly better than any earlier period. If the child is not weaned until, say, the seventh to the ninth months, he has enjoyed something like a normal satisfaction of his impulses towards the breast, and has so far developed in his perceptions of his mother and in the organisation of his sense of reality, that he can now understand other signs of her love. He is interested in other modes of relation with his mother, and can thus tolerate the withdrawal of the breast with much greater ease than he can at a time when to lose the breast means to lose love altogether. He can feel her love satisfyingly in her face and smile, and ways of response to his active play. She is now much more than a breast to him, and so he can feel secure that although the breast is withdrawn, she remains, and her love remains. It would appear that there is an optimal satisfaction of this (and all other) libidinal needs, which makes later development more secure. But this optimum will not be exactly the same for each child. There cannot be any formal rule about it. Children vary in the readiness with which they can accept weaning at any particular age, and their individual responses need to be watched, and the time and rate of the weaning graduated to their personal needs.

I have already referred to those frequent cases of children who are difficult to feed after weaning. This is probably due, or at any rate partly due, to the way the weaning has been handled ; but the exact cause cannot always be traced. There are children, too, who cannot tolerate the taking of hard food, even when the transition to the first soft foods after weaning has been successfully accomplished. This refusal to take hard food, and inability to bite and chew and swallow it, or the refusal to take any sort of meat course, is undoubtedly an outcome of the child's anxieties connected with biting. The opposite kind of difficulty occurs, too, in some children. Sometimes children will turn completely against any form of milk food, once they are weaned. It is as if they said to the mother, " If I can't have milk from your breast, then I won't have it at all." In this case, the weaning itself appears to have been felt as a *punishment* for previous sadistic wishes towards the breast.

On the whole, it is best to respect these minor idiosyncrasies arising from anxiety. It is unwise to force the child to eat the sort of food which he finds difficult, especially where it does not happen to be absolutely essential to a normal diet (for example, milk puddings). If we remember that these are not purely local and mechanical issues, but indications of deep undercurrents in the child's emotional life as a whole, we shall not so readily attempt to compel the child to follow our own oral patterns.

The more general difficulty about eating solid food will often pass away after the second year, especially in those children who do not eat alone, but have companions at the meal-table—for instance, children in large families or those who have their main meal at a nursery school. With children who are in general reluctant eaters, too, one of the best remedies is to arrange for the meal to be taken in company with other children. The child's anxieties about masticating, or other fears connected with food, are more easily resolved if he has the support of watching other children eat these things naturally and happily, and take pleasure in them. To stand over the child, as many mothers and nurses do, attempting to cajole or bribe or threaten him into eating food he does not want, invariably increases the difficulty. Some children, if they gain the extra libidinal satisfaction of this special attention on the mother's part, or the extra support against their own super-ego of the mother's command to eat, can then manage to chew and swallow the food required. But, as a rule, this is a situation that repeats itself. The child goes on needing this persuasion or command, and comes to tyrannise over his mother or nurse more and more fully with regard to meals. If he eats his meal in a nursery school, and is left to eat or not as he wishes, seeing other children enjoy their meals in the ordinary way, and with no one making any fuss or comment if he does not, he does seem to learn to master his anxiety; or perhaps the anxiety is itself actually lessened, since the child finds that other children, as small and weak as he, can do this thing forbidden by his inner mentor, and still be alive and safe and happy. Eating together with other children supports him against the feeling that it is a dangerous and a wicked thing. It has been found universally in nursery schools that most children who are difficult and reluctant feeders at home give little or no trouble at school, at any rate after the first few weeks of their nursery school life.

These are the deeper reasons which underlie the advice I am accustomed to give to mothers of such children, namely, not to attempt either to cajole or threaten the child, but leave him free to eat or not, as he will ; and if at all possible, to arrange for him to share his meals with other children, especially in a well-run nursery school.

2. THUMB-SUCKING

The problem of thumb-sucking occurs frequently, and I am constantly approached about it by mothers and nurses. The general attitude is that it should be stopped, either because it looks unpleasant, or because of the risk of spoiling the shape of the teeth and jaw, or making the thumb sore, or some other rationalisation of this kind.

The behaviourists have made many pronouncements, too, on this issue, taking the line that thumb-sucking ought to be stopped because it leads to "introversion".

The underlying reason for people's wish to interfere with the child's thumb-sucking is, however, undoubtedly the intuitive awareness of its sexual nature, and the feeling that the child ought not to be allowed to indulge in such pleasures.

All these views assume that thumb-sucking is as such a *cause* of later psychological events, and that if it can be prevented, these later events will not ensue. If, however, my general argument has been clear, my readers will be ready to see that thumb-sucking is not so much a cause as a symptom. It is an expression of an intense need for oral satisfaction, the thumb being a substitute for the mother's nipple, in the first instance. It is resorted to because it is always there for the child, and oral frustrations can thus be largely neutralised by the child himself. At any time after the earliest days, however, thumb-sucking is by no means a simple reinstatement of primary oral gratification, but also a re-assurance against the *inner* dread of punishment for biting and destructive impulses. If the child feels this strong and persistent need to get satisfaction from sucking, we can be quite sure that he is suffering from great anxiety connected with oral destructive impulses. That is why, when we forcibly deprive him of this gratification, we often throw him into a state of overwhelming, helpless exasperation, which must have a far more serious effect upon the mental life than the sucking itself.

The physical harm of thumb-sucking, either to mouth or thumb, is undoubtedly much exaggerated. It is probable that it rarely does any permanent harm. But the forcible deprivation of the thumb-sucking always does cause more serious psychological disturbance. Some children take to bed-wetting, some to later stammering, some to the habit of sucking their tongues (a habit much more likely to persist than the thumb-sucking itself, since it is not open to deflection by the growing manipulative skill of the hands, as thumb-sucking is; and in any case it is uglier to watch). Other children show a great increase of general guilt and anxiety, night terrors, and so on, as well as to more marked open aggression to other children and grown-ups. There can be little question that if quite gentle attempts to prevent the child's hands from being put into his mouth do not succeed, forcible methods, such as tying the child's hands down or putting on woollen mittens, or scoldings or punishments, are extremely inadvisable.

It is unusual for the habit to persist after four or five years of age, except in occasional moments of stress, or possibly when falling asleep. The normal self-regard of the child of five and six years of age will lead him to give up this habit, as he becomes able to substitute other gratifications and real achievement—even when it persists as late as this.

We touch here one of those points in which a great deal of the child psychology now being taught in academic text-books needs to be re-written. In recent years, there has been far too great an emphasis on the crude " habit " psychology, both in this and other regards. Thumb-sucking has been treated as a simple local reflex, of accidental, unknown origin, which must be mechanically interfered with, without any inquiry being made as to the origin of the first impulse towards the habit, or its meaning for the emotional life of the child. I have little doubt that forcible interferences with this and other natural gratifications which the child finds for himself have much to answer for in the way of later difficulties of behaviour and temperament, and a big contribution to mental hygiene would be made if we could persuade mothers and nurses generally not to interfere with thumb-sucking in children, at any rate by severe or forcible methods.

I might usefully add a note here about the allied problem of nail-biting.

I have accumulated a good deal of evidence showing the uselessness of negative methods of dealing with nail-biting, whether these take the form of scoldings, whippings, tying the hands up, putting bitter aloes or mustard on the nails. These methods almost invariably fail, and invariably cause misery and guilt in the child. Lately, however, I have had several cases reported in which nail-biting has been cured, and very easily cured, by treatment of the nails with olive oil.

It is clear that the physical effect on the nails of the olive oil itself must be an important factor. The oil makes the nails smooth and soft, with no jagged edges; the child has therefore less temptation to tear at them and bite the corners off. But it is the psychological value of the jagged corners that is important to the child, and it is the psychological service which the mother renders in putting on olive oil which chiefly helps the child. Nails are bitten because they are "bad" nails, because they want to scratch, because they are like biting teeth; and the more jagged and menacing they become by being bitten, the more they have to be bitten—to punish them and prevent them from scratching and biting other people. When they are softened by olive oil, they become good nails, loving nails, not jagged, dangerous nails, and the mother who puts on the olive oil is the helpful "good" mother, who turns them from bad nails into good, and thus helps the child not to have bad, scratching impulses. She demonstrates to the child, as it were, the possibility of their being good and loving nails, instead of bad, scratching and biting nails.

3. Cleanliness

The problem of training in control of bowel and bladder and general cleanliness occupies several years in the child's early life. With some children, it is not really settled until three-and-a-half or four, although with others it is solved in the second year. One of the commonest situations is for the child to respond easily and happily to training in regular habits during his first year, and then, in special circumstances, at any time during his second, or even the third year, to become dirty and uncontrolled again, either in occasional spasms or as a constant thing. The problem has then to be tackled afresh, almost as if no attention had been paid to it in the early days.

Training in cleanliness, moreover, not only covers a long period of time in the child's early life, but a wide area of his relation with mother and nurse. With many children, indeed, it is almost the chief element in the child's relation with mother and nurse. They have more contact about this than about anything else except feeding, and very often a disagreeable form of contact—especially if we include as well the question of training the child in clean and tidy ways of eating. The letters I have quoted illustrate some of the difficulties mothers experience with children, and the material quoted from the school shows some of the phantasies underlying these difficulties.

It is with regard to this question that the " habit " psychology of the text-books, upon which so many of the modern practices in infant training are based, can clearly be seen as inadequate, and in need of re-writing. Such a large number of infants nowadays have been " conditioned " to the regular use of the pot for both bowel and bladder, from the earliest weeks of life. If habit were the real key, we should without doubt find the majority of such children experiencing no later difficulty, remaining perfectly clean and regular in their evacuations from the first few months of life onwards, without any break. I have referred, however, to the frequency with which children in whom the habit of cleanliness has apparently been securely established in the first year, nevertheless break down and become sometimes extremely difficult in this regard, in their second or third year. In my paper, " Some Notes on the Incidence of Neurotic Difficulties in Young Children," I brought together a number of instances of this kind, and my own evidence is further confirmed by other observers.[1] " Habit " psychology, therefore, will not take us very far in understanding the child's problem with regard

[1] See, e.g., *Clinical Notes on Disorders of Childhood* by Dr D. W. Winnicott.

to cleanliness, nor in learning how best to educate him. The meaning of these processes for the child's instinctual life and for his unconscious phantasies has to be taken into account.

These breakdowns in regularity of cleanliness probably have a complicated origin. They may arise from the jealousies and rivalries with regard to the two parents or other children, which themselves spring from the normal course of the child's early psychological development, not later than the end of the first year. They may be the result of some specially strong stimulus, for example, waking in the night in the parents' room and hearing sounds of parental intercourse, observing signs of the mother's pregnancy, or the actual birth of a baby; and other similar occurrences. Miss Searl has suggested that such breakdowns in cleanliness, at any rate when they are sudden and violent and a difficult period ensues, often arise out of screaming fits, when the child has been left to scream to the point of exhaustion, without external help or comfort—for instance, when he has awakened in the night. This situation is so overwhelmingly terrifying to the child himself, because of the painful effect of the screaming upon his own body, that he comes to substitute the voiding of urine or faeces, the dirtying of his bed or his clothes, for the screaming attack upon his parents. The pain he suffers in himself from wetting and dirtying is so very much less than from screaming that these seem much safer ways of expressing anger, and of attempting to control the parents. We have here a link between the problem of training in cleanliness and that of how to deal with the child's screaming fits, which I shall be discussing shortly.

Even from the point of view of the mechanics of adjustment, the problem of learning to be clean is obviously much more complicated for the child than most people realise. He has first of all to learn to retain faeces and urine by contracting his sphincters, and not yielding to the impulse of voiding the moment it arises. The first lesson is " You must not " (urinate). Then, in the prescribed time and place, he has to learn to relax what he has just violently contracted, on immediate demand. Many children find they cannot do this. The importance of keeping the bad urine and faeces in seems to outweigh by far the importance of voiding them when told. They cannot obey this request. But having thus successfully withstood the demand of the mother or nurse at the required time and place, they then, a few moments later, relax control and soil their clothes or the floor. With many children this process goes on for months, or even years. Now, if we look at the unconscious meanings of excremental processes and products, as seen, for instance, in some of the remarks in the school records, it is easier to understand why the child so often behaves in this way. The primary wish to retain the faeces, for the sake of the greater erotic pleasure so obtained, would not, in itself, account for such obstinate defiance. In all these cases of great difficulty, one can be quite sure that this primary attitude has been overlaid by phantasies of the dangers of letting out bad, poisonous, attacking substances. The faeces have become identified with the bad wishes, bad thoughts, hostility and greed of the child. They represent dead things, which the child has produced from the good food his mother gave him, and instead of the good babies which his mother can produce. He is terrified of being discovered in possession of such bad substances, and it seems safer to defy his mother's request, by withholding the faeces and keeping control of them, than to yield them up at her demand. The question of control by another person is enormously important for these children. They are really terrified of allowing other persons to dictate to them about bodily processes. It becomes (in phantasy) a matter of life and death to remain in control of one's own body and one's own evacuations. In the analysis of adults, it becomes quite clear that in unconscious phantasy it really is death that is apprehended by the child, should he yield himself up and relax to the demands of the mother from the outside, and the pressure of the faeces from the inside. He must prove to himself, over and over again, that he can please himself and that *he* is in control. Having proved this, he can then relax and allow the sphincters to relax. And thus he soils his garments or the floor.

The precise details and precise colouring of these phantasies vary from individual to individual. Something on the general lines I have described will, however, always be found in the case of children who are difficult and stubborn in this matter.[1]

[1] See letter 6 on p. 131 as an example of excessive, probably psychotic, reactions.

Now, such phantasies are quite ordinary and common in a milder degree. Even where they are for periods fairly acute, however, the majority of children learn to deal with them successfully, as the sense of reality develops, and if, and in so far as, the real love they have for mother or nurse is not damaged by cruel or clumsy handling. These phantasies become repressed, and the anxieties attaching to them are diffused or deflected in various ways, so that the child presently is able to accept more or less regular habits of cleanliness, on more or less agreed social lines. But if I have succeeded in making these states of mind on the part of the child in the least degree convincing and intelligible to my readers, it will be readily understood that severe treatment, or clumsy nagging of the child, only serve to increase his anxieties and to make his problem more difficult. That this is true descriptively is proved every day in the nursery. I am constantly receiving evidence of it in letters from mothers and nurses, who assure me how they have scolded and whipped and punished and cajoled the child, all to no purpose. The reasons why these methods fail become clear as soon as one gains any inkling of the nature of the child's anxiety. The methods that succeed far more readily and surely are those of quiet encouragement, a relative unconcern at the child's dirtiness, and steady confidence that he will shortly be able to manage things for himself more successfully. That is to say, a method which avoids confirming the child's phantasies that he has done something really very dreadful in being dirty, or that the faeces themselves are really bad and dangerous things, which one ought not to have at all ; and which patiently shows him *how* to be clean ; in other words, that gives the child *skill* instead of increasing his fears.

The practical inconvenience to mother or nurse of failures in cleanliness is real, and need not be minimised. The mother need not pretend that she does not find them a nuisance. But most mothers and nurses do, in fact, go far beyond this in their response to the dirty child. Their own anxieties get the upper hand, and they do really feel that his dirtiness is deliberate malice or wickedness, and that he is *never* going to be clean. Where the mother does not react by such excessive worry and horror of the child, but treats the matter as simply one of real inconvenience, and shows the steady hope that the child will soon be able to give her the pleasure of his cleanliness, she can, in fact, help him to security far more readily. It is a help to the child if the mother's manner assumes that the act of voiding is in itself a good one, although this, again, must not be overdone. Another great help is, by sense and judgment in the practical arrangements of clothes, vessels, etc., to give the child the chance of managing all these things really for himself, instead of being at the continued behest of another person.

Another very important point is that of the actual standards of behaviour. Recent nursery fashions have tended to demand very high standards of cleanliness at an earlier and earlier period. Some mothers are extremely worried if the child is not perfectly clean within the first ten months or a year. This is much too early to expect regular cleanliness. It does occasionally happen, but is by no means necessarily a good augury for the child's later development, since it signifies too severe a ban upon excretory pleasures and too great an anxiety about the excretory substances, as bad and dangerous things. The prognosis of a happy and successful personal life is undoubtedly more favourable in the case of children who are at any rate moderately troublesome in, say, the third and fourth years, than in those who become excessively clean at an early age. The dangers of too high standards at too early an age lie in the excessive stimulation of the child's guilt and anxiety about bodily processes and products, and the connected wishes and hostilities " inside " his mind.

It should now be clear : (a) That too much attention should not be paid to attempting to set up regular habits in the early months, although it is valuable to do this in an unostentatious way. It is a good thing to give the child regular opportunities, but not a good thing to be disappointed, or angry, or reproachful if he does not conform, or to punish or scold later on, in the second and third years, if there are occasional or even frequent difficulties ; (b) the motives to which it is most helpful to appeal are those of the child's affection, and of his " growing up ". It is possible to convey to the child that it is desirable to give up urine and faeces in the chamber pot or lavatory at required times, without conveying to him the idea that it is very wicked not to do so, or that the excrements themselves are bad and dangerous stuff. It is an important general maxim to avoid such circumstances or such behaviour as appear to increase the child's fear and guilt about defaecatory processes, even if this means a long, patient waiting for the time when he can be clean ; (c) it is wise to respect the individual phobias which some children spontaneously develop, for example, fear of using the pot or the w.c.—sometimes a fear of falling down the drain, or of the terrifying rush of the water, or of the helpless position in sitting down on the chamber pot. If these phobias develop, it means there is great dread on the part of the child, probably connected with some unconscious hostile phantasy, and attempts to ignore this dread and force the child to conform serve but to increase his fears. It is not necessary for the mother to know the nature of the phantasy, but it is advantageous for her not to treat the child as merely " naughty " or obstinate, but to recognise that he *is* afraid, and to find some way round. One common mistake is to leave the child on an uncomfortable vessel, without proper support, so that he has reason to fear falling over. Another is to stand over the child, urging him, and not giving him a moment's respite. The situation which enables one child to evacuate easily and regularly will not, however, be the same as suits another, and wise mothers and nurses know how to discover the circumstances which help each child most, and to find such a technique as will put him at ease.

In the nursery school one very often meets instances of children who show themselves bitterly ashamed of any loss of control of bladder or bowel, as well as of children who show open scorn for any fellow who makes such a mistake. The good nursery school teacher understands that the best help, whether to the child who is at fault or the others who are contemptuous of his failing, is to show a cheerful sense of proportion, and take the attitude that this is just a temporary mistake, and that the child will soon be able to manage his affairs more successfully. She understands, too, that the child's confidence in himself is a very important factor in his success, and that helping him to gain actual skill, e.g. in unfastening of garments and other accessory processes, is far more valuable than merely urging him to be clean. She knows, too, that growing social confidence is a factor in the child's willingness to leave an entrancing game for the necessary purpose. Little children find it hard to

PROBLEMS AND CRISES OF DEVELOPMENT

leave their play occupation of the moment in order to obey the call of nature, partly because of their deficient sense of time and the fact that they live so much in the present moment, so that leaving their game feels like giving it up; partly because of the fear that other children may come in and take their place or their playthings. The child's growing sense of confidence in all these different directions, as well as his growing skill and perception of time, gradually enable him to control the voiding impulse until the appropriate moment. Mothers and nurses in the private nursery have yet much to learn from the trained and experienced nursery school teacher with regard to these positive methods of handling the training in cleanliness.

With regard to this whole question, practical wisdom can be summed up by saying that *it is a matter of technique rather than of morality.*

4. Screaming and Tantrums

Sufficient has already been said about the psychology of the screaming fit to make it clear that no one who understands the meaning of such a situation to the child can agree to the hard modern doctrine that a young child should be left to scream until he falls asleep, and that then he will " learn better ". Most upholders of this doctrine fail to distinguish between the inevitable wailing of the very small infant on the first hunger pangs, before he has adapted himself to the required rhythm of the feeding routine, and the screaming of the one- or two-year-old in the grip of deep emotional conflict and overwhelming anxieties. There is at present no reason to doubt that it is better, in the first few weeks, not to take the child up or nurse or dandle him at every cry that he gives, but to leave him to adjust his needs to the required routine of satisfactions. Most children brought up on these methods, without the old-fashioned nursing and rocking, do appear on the whole to thrive. But this is quite a different situation from that of the child of a year, eighteen months, or two years, who suddenly begins to wake in the night and cry for the reassuring voice or presence of the mother, and scream with terror if he does not get it; the child who begins to appear unable to fall asleep unless mother or nurse stays with him; or the child who falls into a violent tantrum when mildly thwarted in the day-time and then is put into a room alone and left to scream himself to exhaustion. These situations are liable to affect the whole course of the child's later development. It is in such moments that the child's worst phantasies of avenging dangers grip his mind. He has to deal with these by one method or another : whatever choice he makes will be fraught with consequences for his mental life.

Nowadays, a great many mothers, whose natural impulse would be to cherish and soothe the child who wakens in the night with terror, or calls her back after she has left him in bed, showing that he is unable to fall asleep without her comforting presence, have been persuaded into harsh, rigid treatment of the children on this mere theory that children " must not be spoilt " or allowed to tyrannise over adults, and that they should go on being left to scream " until they learn better ".[1] It is very necessary that this seriously mistaken doctrine should be challenged, and the grounds for its unwisdom made clear. Children who are in the grip of night terrors, or of any of the phobias described in the letters quoted in the body of the material, cannot master these acute anxieties without the help of mother's or nurse's presence. If they receive this help at the onset of the

[1] " I wonder if you would help me with my problem. I should think it is a fairly common one, but I should like to know how you would deal with it. My little girl (now aged one year four months) has been kept to a regular routine where the right thing was done cheerfully. She was such a good little thing, although by no means a placid child, that all my friends wanted their babies to be like her. She went to bed happily and was left alone to fall off to sleep, and she would peep round her cot to see one go out of the room. Suddenly at thirteen months she took to screaming when left in her cot. I had heard it said that if allowed to scream they would soon learn better. So for three nights we left her to scream, and she worked herself up to an almost hysterical condition. After this the very sight of her cot caused her to scream, and it was most distressing. Then we decided that we must prevent the screaming at all costs, so we sat with her until she went to sleep, which sometimes took over an hour, for often when nearly asleep she would open her eyes suspiciously to see if one was there. Next she started waking and screaming in the night, and I have often sat with her for two hours, while she watched to see that I did not leave her. She seemed to be afraid of falling asleep. This has gone on for three months during which time she has improved, in that she does not scream so violently. To-night for the first time, having told her to sing, I walked boldly out of the room and left her. She has now fallen asleep. I may say incidentally she has been cutting her back teeth during this period, but they cannot have been giving her much pain, as she has been so good in the daytime. I want you to criticise what I have done, so that were I faced with this problem with another child I should do the right thing. And what am I to do if she continues to wake in the night ? "

phobia, they very often get over the most acute difficulty fairly easily.[1] If they are left to struggle with it themselves, they are often reduced to a general state of dis-equilibrium.

The same thing applies to the defiant day-time screaming of those children who get into violent tantrums on being thwarted. Some mothers and nurses will not take the least pains to avoid unnecessary situations which throw the child into such violent tempers, and their way of treating the tantrums, when they arise, is either to whip and punish and scold, or to isolate the child. More understanding mothers realise that the child screaming in temper needs the help of a firm but soothing and gentle voice, and that whilst, on the one hand, it is unwise to let the child gain any advantage or power of control over the adult by means of his tantrums, it is, on the other, equally unwise to leave him entirely alone in his enormous stress of feeling and his struggle with inward terrors of attack. He needs the reassurance that his real mother is not going to eat him up or attack him; and this he can only gain by her real presence.

5. Sexual Behaviour

I have already made various incidental points about the wisest attitude with regard to open sexual behaviour amongst children, but must now gather these up more systematically.

I have spoken of the advantage to the educator of realising that such behaviour is not, in itself, unusual or abnormal, especially in the earlier years. But I have also pointed out that flagrant or defiant behaviour of this kind, for example, open and persistent masturbation, or open and apparently unashamed exhibition of sexual parts in public, does point to the fact that the child is suffering from very considerable mental stress, which he is seeking to allay by this daring and

[1] " You deal this week with a baby suddenly frightened of his bath, and as the problem frequently arises, I thought you might be interested to hear my experience. Colin recently took fright at the shadow of the sponge basket (hung in a different place), screamed and tried to get out. For two nights he screamed and would not get in, and I gave him a sponge down instead. Then an experienced mother gave me an idea; we bought a clay pipe and blew bubbles. It worked immediately. The first night, he stood up clutching me while I blew, but soon relaxed his hold in the excitement and let himself be washed standing up. The next night I made the bubbles bounce on the water, and he promptly sat down to catch them. The trouble was over. I am immensely grateful to the wise mother who suggested it, and pass on the tip for what it is worth."

defiant behaviour. If this is in any way marked or persistent, the child needs special psychological help, and the mother, nurse or teacher is wise to realise this and to consult either a child guidance clinic or a medical psycho-analyst. I need not, therefore, say more about such cases (undoubtedly exemplified in some of the letters quoted, e.g., pp. 137, 148).

Taking, then, the sexual behaviour of ordinary children, children who show no special persistence or defiance about it, but an ordinary measure of naïvety in, say, the third to the fifth years, and an ordinary degree of guilt and secrecy in the years over five, let us now consider how it is best to deal with this.

(a) *Masturbation*

In my theoretical discussion of the meaning of masturbation, I have already said enough to indicate the general lines I would advocate. Direct reproaches or prohibitions are undoubtedly unwise. If one remembers that masturbation is only a symptom of unconscious conflict with regard to the parents, and that even in its milder forms it very largely springs from anxiety connected with the primitive sadistic phantasies, one can then understand that a mere direct prohibition of the act itself is of very little help to the child. On the other hand, it is equally clear that the indirect influence of an environment which gives ample opportunities for sublimatory activities, and ample reassurance by real social experience with mild parents and the companionship of other children, is the best help against masturbatory activity. It is not only unwise to reproach or scold the child, but quite unnecessary. If the child has plenty of play materials and occupations suited to his age, if he has a satisfactory social life with other children, either in a large family or a nursery school, if his parents prove their goodness to him by showing him how to develop skills and arts and understanding, the need to get physical reassurance in his own body by masturbation will gradually pass away. The development of real skill and the experience of real social life are the best aid to the child's inner security; and with increasing inner security masturbation largely disappears.

(b) *Exhibitionism and Open Sexual Play*

This, too, is best dealt with by indirect methods. Straightforward but mild prohibitions, on the lines, " It's better not to do that ", " I shouldn't do that if I were you, come and do this," are more in place and more effective here than with masturbation. In these activities the child is turning to other people and their real responses for his needed reassurance, and this attitude is further on the line of development towards normal adult sexuality and social responses than masturbation is. Nevertheless, it is important that interferences should take the positive rather than the negative line : " Come and do this rather than that." Very often it is not necessary even to say " rather than that ". The child is quite aware that " come and do this " carries the implication " I shouldn't do that ". The indirect satisfactions gained through song and dance, dressing up, dramatic play and handicrafts, do for the majority of children come to serve as a sufficient reassurance against the anxieties that give rise to the naïve wish to display the body or the genital.

Active curiosity to see the genitals of other children and grown-ups can be largely deflected by the willingness of adults to answer questions and permit discussions about bodily processes, the origin of babies, etc. This I shall speak of under the next point.

Many detailed practical questions arise with regard to the social education of children in sexual and excretory matters. For example, when two or more quite little children want to go to the lavatory together, my own method is to avoid suggesting that the lavatory is a bad or dirty place, or that all visits in common must be prohibited, since such an attitude reinforces the child's primitive phantasies. I would, however, go with the children and concern myself, in a quiet, matter-of-fact way, with getting through the practical business sensibly and straightforwardly, not, however, prohibiting conversation, and not scolding for any naïve impulses of exhibitionism. The child's own development will presently lead him to show a certain awareness of guilt about such visits to the lavatory in common, and when this is apparent, I would quietly suggest that it was better to go singly, and to come back to these other games (or occupations) as soon as possible, rather than waste time playing in the lavatory. Such an attitude goes along with the training in independence, in managing garments, shutting and opening the door, pulling the plug, and so on, which I have already spoken of in considering training in cleanliness. With children over five, it is sometimes necessary, and sometimes wise, actually to request them to forgo such visits in common to the lavatory; but again without making a great fuss, or suggesting that there is anything wicked or morally dangerous in such happenings.

The frequent and defiant wish of the small boy to urinate in public, or secretly in a corner of the garden, instead of in the lavatory, is best met by a firm request; but again without punishments or severe reproaches. The impulse does not persist if it is met in this way. The grounds stated for the request should be purely practical and hygienic. If we say that it is a bad and wicked thing to do, we often increase the child's wish to do it, that is, to gain the reassurance of showing that he dares to do it. Ursula's desire to use her chamber in public (p. 201) would have been best met by a firm refusal on the ground that, from the point of view of hygiene, such things are best kept in the place assigned to them, as well as on the social ground that people in general prefer not to see these processes occurring and that she herself would, in the end, be happier if she kept them private. There is no need to indulge the child in these exhibitionistic tendencies, any more than there is need to treat her as a reprobate because she feels them.

(c) *Verbal Exhibitionism*

The question of how to deal with children's talk about excretory or genital matters is a rather more difficult one than that of dealing with actual behaviour. It is obviously easier to forbid or deflect actual sexual play than to forbid or deflect chanting or joking about these things. The children themselves have a sense of reality in this regard, and distinguish between words and deeds. Sometimes they distinguish this better than the grown-ups do, whose own anxieties about what children may *do* often lead them to treat their naïve remarks as severely as if they were actions. My own experience leads me to believe that it is helpful to the child if the grown-ups do not make this error in the earlier years. Naïve questions or jokes or the verbal exhibitionism of children between, say, three and five years, should not be treated as if they were actions. This channel of discharge in words should be left open to the children at a time when they are faced with the biggest struggles in their inner psychic life. Quite apart from actual analysis, I have reason to believe that a certain measure of freedom to joke naturally about bodily processes or even, as we saw in the *Records*, to play at having a lavatory or a " potty " in the make-believe house or ship, is helpful to little children. Children under five do need greater verbal freedom in these matters than it is useful for older children to have. Again, I would suggest that the best way of dealing with the children's wish to chant " Bim-bom-bee-wee thing " or their occasional, somewhat defiant references to excretory processes, is not to prohibit or reproach directly, but to allow the fact that the adult does not join in these particular activities to have its unostentatious effect, and to rely on the positive attraction of other interests. With the child over, say, four-and-a-half or five (I do not, however, mean to suggest any rigid age demarcation), who has attained a greater measure of emotional self-reliance and security of ego-development, one can make more definite requests that jokes or songs about these things should not be indulged in.

Children of over five are quite well aware that the general adult world does not condone such pleasantries on their part, and if they are left free, in any special place or atmosphere, to say what they like with adults present, they fail to understand why the adult in question thus indulges them. I am far from suggesting that we should totally forbid joking references to these things, or show marked disapproval. But it is a help to the child if we are on the side of a reasonable conformity to the general public standards in these matters ; otherwise, again, we become " bad " to the child and fail to support him against his own guilt. The risk of prohibiting all references to sexual or excretory affairs, whether serious or joking, is that it leaves the child to battle alone with his curiosities and ponderings about these matters, and gives his social relation with the educator a feeling of unreality. The child needs the support of our unafraidness in these difficulties, just as much as he needs our skill in imparting knowledge about the physical world or the realm of art and literature.

The part of the educator here, as elsewhere, should be to stand for sense and perspective. He has to avoid the snare of a priggishness that is out of touch with physiological realities, on the one hand, and the pitfall of a licence that is equally out of touch with social realities, on the other.

In the latency period, with children of over six or seven years of age, open excretory jokes or rhymes will always wear a defiant air, and very often the child who indulges in them in the presence of adults is quite obviously trying to provoke the adult into actual prohibition. The actual ground of request that the child should not indulge in these things should be that other people do not like it.

The situation is different with regard to serious questions or discussions of human biology. This serious discussion will often arise out of playful or joking remarks in young children, and it is one of the inescapable responsibilities of the educator of young children to understand how to deal with the child's questions about the origin of babies and the sexual relations of parents. I have stated what seem to me the most significant reasons for dealing honestly and capably with the child's curiosity about these matters in other writings, for example, *The Nursery Years* and need not elaborate them further here.

Summarily, there are two main reasons : One is the child's emotional need for the frank willingness of parents to give him information on these questions ; the other is the cultural importance of not closing the field of biological interests to the child's developing mind.

With regard to the first point, the child's satisfaction comes not so much by way of the actual information, but rather by the reassurance against his most primitive phantasies about the badness and danger of the genitals, of excretory processes and of parental intercourse, which he gains from the simple, frank acceptance and unafraidness of the adult. One of the biggest difficulties for the child in dealing with the secrecy of adults about sexual processes, and their reproval if he shows any interest in them, is the confirmation which such secrecy affords to the child's own feeling that these things are really bad and dangerous. If his own drive of curiosity to inquire into them is treated as a purely destructive thing, this further confirms his fears.

It has been said in recent years by some advocates of a frank honesty about sexual matters that if there is no covering up of sexual matters, and little children are given the information they ask for, such children cease to take any secret interest in sexual affairs and never joke or giggle in a furtive way about them. That view I believe to be much exaggerated, and my own experience, both with children in the Malting House School who had the fullest possible information about sexual matters both in man and animals, and children in private families who have been brought up on the same lines, has shown that this is not true in any absolute way. Such children are still capable of joking and giggling about either excretory or genital matters. It is, however, true that they do it very much less than children whose curiosity has never been satisfied. Their amusement is much less sly and furtive, and has a less anxious, or defiant, air. But it is fortunately not true that little children whose questions are answered necessarily become priggish about these common human affairs—unless they are brought up in a generally priggish atmosphere. They can retain their sense of humour, like most sensible and well-informed grown-ups do. But nevertheless, they feel much less need for *sotto voce* salacious remarks, or sly and furtive pryings.

With regard to the second point, there is little need, at this time of day, to emphasise the enormous importance of biological studies for human life. The economic and social relations of man to-day rest upon biological science. Agriculture, the breeding of animals, the conquest of disease, the maintenance of health, the science of infant welfare and the hygiene of childhood itself, these and many other fundamental aspects of human society are bound up with the progress of biological science.[1]

. . . . .

Regarding the whole problem of the education of little children in sexual matters, whether knowledge or behaviour, one very important thing has to be remembered, namely, that the development of a satisfactory emotional attitude towards sexual relations, marriage and parenthood depends far more upon the internal psychic development of the child, conditioned by his experiences in infancy and quite early childhood, than upon any direct teachings in later childhood and adolescence. Nevertheless, these earlier

[1] The detailed methods by which the biological interests of the children in the Malting House School were met and furthered have been described in the relevant chapters in *Intellectual Growth in Young Children*.

favourable situations having been secured, the attitude of educators in giving or withholding knowledge, and the manner of their approach to these problems, does exercise a considerable influence over the child's later growth. I have said enough to suggest that it is the educator's general *attitude* that matters, more than any detail of information or method.

Moreover, as regards methods of dealing with children's specific sexual behaviour, it can be said that no method will produce immediate results—except, that is to say, a bad method. Severe whippings or brutal treatment will undoubtedly check all sexual behaviour in very many children—although not in those whose conflicts are the greatest and who are, therefore, in most need of help.[1] The majority of children can be cowed or whipped into complete silence and complete conformity, but there is no need for me to say that such a result is entirely undesirable. The more positive methods of real education towards control and understanding and responsibility, and a happy emotional freedom, are inevitably bound to allow for the factor of time, and the child's own real individual growth towards those aims. One cannot expect to find in little children (or in adolescents) that just balance of feeling and action which constitutes satisfactory sexuality in adults. There is little doubt that it is better for the educator to err on the side of verbal freedom than on the side of silence and secrecy.

* * * * *

There are a number of practical points left over for discussion from the theoretical survey of the overt social relations of children, and these I must now briefly take up, in order to round off my statement of the educational bearings of this study of social and sexual development.

One general maxim with regard to the social education of young children is that the educator should act for the child, *where the child cannot act for himself*, whether because of the overpowering urge of his impulses, the overwhelming stress of his anxieties, his physical weakness and lack of skill, or his ignorance of physical and social realities. Where, however, the child can act for himself, the educator should stand aside.

[1] E.g. the child described in the letter on p. 137.

In social matters, the educator cannot teach the child, nor can he learn for him. All that he can do is to create such situations as will give the child opportunities to learn for himself. In this regard he has to control the social environment of the child as well as the physical, in order to make it possible for the child to learn. The child can, however, learn only by his own real experience, whether social or physical, and the educator must not stand between the child and his experience.

To take up some particular points:

(a) *Egocentrism.* In my theoretical discussion of the egocentric attitudes of the young child, I raised the practical question as to how far the grown-up should interfere with, for example, the domination of a group of younger children by an older or more influential child along the pattern of the latter's wishes. It seems to me that the answer to this is a question of the individual situation, each case being judged on its own merits. As long as the younger children appear happy whilst the leader arranges their play and assigns their functions, there seems no good ground for interfering. If, however, the younger children show that they are being intimidated, or reveal any signs of anxiety in the situation, even when the leader does in the end succeed in cajoling or bribing them into conformity, it is undoubtedly well for the educator to intervene and to make some new suggestion, which distributes functions differently. The domination of a group by a single child or minor group of children can easily become a form of real bullying, even though there is no physical hurt or teasing or harshness. The younger children do need the support of the adult against their tyrannical elders in these regards, but not to the point of the continual planning of their activities by the educator. It is best for the children to arrange their own make-believe play as freely as possible, whilst the educator has an eye to the need of the younger children, and does not hesitate to intervene when this seems to be called for.

(b) *Hostilities and Rivalries.* The problem of the children's active hostilities and aggression needs practical consideration.

The first hostilities on the part of the new-comer in a group soon pass away, except in the case of the more neurotic children. The best way of dealing with these first negative signs is by positive suggestion: " Won't you come and do this?" "Would you like to use this?" or even a positive suggestion of some fresh common activity for the group as a whole. Punishment or reproaches are quite out of place.

More continuous hostilities on the part of children who are not shy and anxious new-comers are also usually dealt with best by positive suggestions of change of occupation, either for the individual or the group. Actual bullyings and teasings have, however, to be stopped, with an even distribution of justice, and opportunity given for the indirect expressions of rivalry and hostility in various familiar games (such as "Nuts in May"). Laughter and humour are the best solvents for active hostility, especially when the children feel a justified confidence that the adult in charge will come to the aid of any really frightened or intimidated child.

It is not, however, helpful for the teacher to be always preaching the doctrine of co-operation, and to admit no ethical value in the motive of rivalry. It is one thing to condemn the wholly bad practice of using the motive of competition as a spur to intellectual effort (e.g., by moving children up and down in class, according to their achievements in arithmetic, etc.) and quite another to rule the motive of competition out altogether, as a spontaneous element in children's social relations. It is in games and sports that this motive has its place and value, not in activities of skill or understanding.

The hostility and aggression that in particular children spring from a feeling of inferiority gradually disappear as the child becomes more confident of his growing skill and independence. This was remarkably demonstrated by one or two of the children in the school, notably, as I have shown, by Cecil. Cecil was a particularly unskilful child when he came to the school. He could not wash his own hands, and would not even try. He cried bitterly when any of his bricks fell down, as they usually did. He screamed more often than he talked. From the beginning he was an extremely aggressive child. He could not pass behind another child without hitting him, whether with his hand, or anything he happened to have in his hand. Mere blind possessiveness was extremely strong in him. As, however, his helplessness grew gradually less, so did his hostility and aggression. His relations with the other children slowly improved, as his real physical and social skill grew, until, before the end of the first term, he played freely and co-operatively with the others, and could safely be left without any intervention.

Other children exemplified this in a less extreme way; and it can be taken as true in general that the need to be quarrelsome and domineering with other children disappears as achievement in personal skill and in social relations slowly develops.

(c) *Possessiveness*. The problem arises of children's quarrels over property, and the need to train them in co-operative sharing of common property, as well as in the willingness to lend and borrow private goods. I have shown the very great strength of the impulse of ownership in young children, and the complex psychological meanings which it has for them. It seems to me a cardinal point in the education of very young children not to press too hard at high standards of unselfishness.

First of all, we need to recognise the rights of the private owner and to respect the child's possessions, as we look to him to respect ours. It is better to lead the children towards mutual respect of ownership rights, than to ride roughshod across this impulse and insist upon their sharing everything. It not seldom happens that adults attempt to train children to a degree of disinterestedness which the adults in question are quite incapable of themselves. (I quote in a footnote a letter which illustrates the qualms which even an obviously sensible mother can have about respecting her little daughter's sense of ownership.)[1] I do not believe that it is a sound moral training for children to be made to live up to unreal standards of so-called unselfishness, and to be compelled to share things they wish to cherish even at the risk of having them broken.

---

[1] "Grace is not really a selfish child, but when she has any little friends to play with her, she often resents their touching her toys. This is, I think, because during the last few months her tea-set, sewing machine and other treasures, with which she played so carefully, have been broken by some of these visitors. She is careful with her possessions, but some of the other children have been most destructive. Grace is very distressed about this. She loves companionship and used to give the visitors a free hand with her toy box, but this unselfishness has brought its punishment. Nearly every time we have children here, something is broken. Grace is an only child and I do not want to spoil her or teach her not to share her toys, but I do sympathise with her when she comes to me in tears with a broken doll or torn book. There is no shop here where any skilled repairing can be done, or any toys bought. I have now suggested that the favourite toys should be put away before the children arrive. Do you think this is unwise?"

It is much better to be more matter-of-fact, and, whether in the nursery or in the home, to allow each child, in the first place, to have his own genuine possessions, over which he has an absolute right to ownership, but to have certain fundamental properties in common, such as general apparatus, furniture, swings, and so on. With these it is best to make sure that the children understand that they belong to everyone in common, and that their use is a question of reasonably " taking turns ". Any request by a child to another child to lend him a private possession should then be reasonably endorsed by the adult in charge, but not enforced if the owner is unwilling.

If we try to take the child too fast over this ground, we shall defeat our ends. All the life of the nursery school, the sharing of materials and carrying on of common pursuits, and even the dispassionateness of the teacher's attitude, helps to tone down the desire for ownership on its less useful sides. But it is not desirable, in a real world, to suggest that the sense of private possession is altogether and in itself undesirable or blameworthy.

. . . . .

In conclusion, I would like to emphasise once again what seems to me the essential outcome of this deeper understanding of the psychology of young children, namely, that the key lies in *an emphasis on technique rather than on morality*. We have seen how profound a drive towards morality the child has in his own nature. We have not to *create* this in him. What we have to do is to show him how to attain his moral ends in the real world. We have to give him the skill which makes possible an effective morality, and the psychological conditions which will foster his own seekings for such skill. In so far as he needs our help towards a change in his moral values, it is towards making him more tempered, more humane, more secure in a world of real values.

I have said that the educator cannot forgo her function as the super-ego. But I have emphasised at every point how, if she is to help the child to attain security in the real world of social relations, she must exercise that function, not for the purpose of prohibitions and punishments, but towards positive ends, opportunities and achievements. She must be on the side of reality and of the child's own activity.

APPENDIX I

The following is a story written (or, more accurately typed on his own typewriter) by Tommy two years after he left the Malting House School, viz. at the age of seven and a half.

Chapter 1   MY DOG AND MY LIFE
Once upon a time there was a man his name was Mr Watson he left home on a tuesday nirght to go to a freind that lived at Huntingdon and his friend had gon to Kedington for the day Mr. Watson had brought his dog with him and as nobody opend the door he made his dog bark. sudenly he herd a vvoice cry out the've gon to Kedington for the day
were are you
here of caouse you little fool
weres here
at kedington
oh Isee

it was a wireles

so I caute the bus to Kedington and it cost 9d and the bus conduktor got verry·cross and seid hay you dogs are not ulloud on our busses
oh well mines coming on
when I got there i found my freind waiting for me.   I seid hullow ? and then Kissed her.
but she did not kiss me.   she took out a pistle and killed me.
she was not seen.

Chapter 2 MrWatson was berrid
When the conduktor of the bus saw me lying ded he went to the poleis. The poleis seid well i-ll fech the gardenners to berry him.
so the gardenners came and heeps of peaple came to the funeral and he was berrid
his freind was found out by a datective.
But his wife wonderd why he did not come home.
when she saw a funerul letter saing her husband was killed by his sweethart at kedington.
Mrs. watson went to see her husbands sweet-hart hung.
when Mrs. Watson went to see her husbands sweethart hung she got killed to
then they thought of the nastyist way in wich they coud kill her and it was ti starve her in prison.

APPENDIX II

I am greatly indebted to Dr. I. Schapera of Capetown University for permission (obtained for me through the kindness of Professor C. G. Seligman) to include here the following notes on certain points in the behaviour of children among the Bakatla, a Bantu tribe. The questions are Professor Seligman's; the answers those of Dr. Schapera.

" (a) Have you observed any interest in the excreta, as indicated by the children making mud-pies, modelling clay balls, sausages, etc., collecting or hoarding objects (not food), difficulties in establishing bodily cleanliness ?

" (b) Have you observed the bigger children, i.e. more than three or four years old, biting, sucking, or chewing odds and ends ?

" (c) Destructiveness—have you observed children destroying things for no very valid reason except that they seemed to be enjoying doing so ?

" (d) Have you observed sexual interests between, let us say, six and eleven or twelve years of age, or is there a latent period at this time, as has been stated by some authorities for European children ?

" [Negative observations, where you are in a position to make them, are just as valuable as positive.]"

" (a) Small children when playing together occasionally make use of urine : (1) Small boys sometimes urinate on each other for fun, or when out at the gardens take old melons, make holes and urinate inside them, and then chase each other about, sprinkling the urine in the melons over their fellows. (2) Sometimes they heap up some earth, make a hollow on top of the heap with their elbow (pressing it down on the heap), then urinate in this hollow and thus harden it for a while, when it cakes ; then scoop away the hardened ground with their hand, and as long as it holds together use it as a receptacle for porridge—in fact they call it *maxo-pyana*, ' eating bowl '. . . . In addition small boys make oxen, men, etc., out of mud and play with them (this is very common), and they also have a game called *kama* which they play at the river : they make small cylinders of clay, about the length of a finger, and make a slight hollow at one end, then toss these into the water, the idea being to make them land in the water on their hollow end so that they give out a special sort of sound. The boys compete with each other to see who can achieve this effect most often. They also build little household enclosures in the streets and other open spaces out of mud and play about in them. I don't know of children collecting or hoarding objects, except for : (a) beads, which the poorer children collect one by one from their friends until they have enough for a necklace ; (b) I have sometimes seen children grubbing about in the refuse heaps in front of a trader's store for small tins, boxes, bits of glass, etc., which they use as toys. . . .

" So far as personal cleanliness is concerned, small children are taught from the beginning that they must not micturate or defaecate inside the household enclosure, and they are scolded whenever they do so or else smacked. There seems to be no difficulty in this connection, nor could my informants recall hearing of children who deliberately held back their faeces as long as they could. The only habit in this connection which I have heard commented upon is that of wetting the blankets during sleep at night. This is said to be difficult to cure, and appears to be common enough as a fault. The remedy is said to be to feed the child, without its knowledge in the first instance, with the flesh of a frog (mixed in its porridge) ; often it is told afterwards and warned that if it persists the experiment will be repeated. (By the way, when small children ask their mothers where babies come from they are told that the mother gets them from the well.)

" (b) No, in general ; there may be exceptional instances, but not enough to warrant comment about the children in general. You may, however, be interested in the following description of the weaning process, which I copy verbatim from my notes. Weaning is a gradual process : it generally starts when the mother's milk begins to fail, or when she becomes pregnant again. They start by keeping the child away from its mother for a longer time than formerly, e.g. she tells the children to take the baby and go to play some distance away, so that they don't get back too soon, and when the children come back the mother doesn't simply give it the breast but waits for it to say ' I want it ' ; often when it cries and wants to suck the mother lets it do so, but the nurse girl (the child who carries the baby about on her back) says to the child, ' How can you suck that stuff ! ' and spits with disgust ; then she points to the teat and says . . . ' You are sucking a worm ', and snatches it from the baby's mouth, squeezes out a little milk, and spits, saying, ' It's a worm, can't you see ? ' and adds . . . ' It is faeces ' (*mpepa*, a childish word for *maseps*, faeces). This sort of thing is kept up for about a fortnight—whenever the child sucks, its nurse says something like this to it, or simply snatches it away from the mother and runs away with it, and then when it cries she gives it porridge. Then at last the mother takes snuff or some other bitter substance and sprinkles it on the breast after squeezing out a little milk ; then the child sucks, finds it bitter, and cries, and its little nurse laughs at it and takes it away, saying, ' I told you so ', and as it cries she adds, ' Be quiet, you shouldn't suck any more ', and next time the child wants to suck they tell it that there is a worm on the breast, so she fears to suck, just sits by the mother's side and cries. They feed it with porridge, and then keep on like this until it no longer wishes to suck. . . .

" (c) I cannot speak definitely on this point, but am inclined to answer in the negative.

" (d) Briefly speaking, there is no latent period between the ages of six to twelve.[1] The small children of these ages, boys and girls, play together, and one of their games, called *mantlwane* (' little houses ') consists in erecting miniature household enclosures ; then they pair off, boys and girls, into couples and celebrate mock weddings, which end up with each couple going to its little enclosure and lying down together, and occasionally they both remove their loin-girdles and rub together their genitals, without of course achieving penetration. This game is played at night, when the parents can't see them. One of my informants, a young man, told me the other day that when he was a child of about nine or so his older brother, together with boys and girls of his age (i.e. thirteen to fifteen) used to get the smaller children at night, pair off the boys and girls, make the little boys lie on top of the girls, and then shout *e tsenye, e tsenye,* ' put it in, put it in ' (referring of course to the penis). This is definite enough, I think, as a sign that infantile sexuality is never latent !

" Lastly I send a couple of threats sometimes uttered by their parents against disobedient children. When, e.g., a small herdboy has allowed his cattle to go astray, his father may say to him . . . ' You have let your cattle stray, it must be your testicles making you like this, you want to be castrated, then perhaps you will listen, for when a bull goes about a lot it is castrated, or you want to have your penis removed or tied up, so that when it is sore you may think of your cattle, you thing with long swinging testicles.' And to girls they say . . . ' May your little vulva be sore, it

[1] I think there is probably some misunderstanding of the character of the latency period behind this negative statement, as will be seen by comparing my account of it in the text.—S. I.

wants to be pierced with a stick, if you don't listen I'll rub you with an irritant shrub.' "

For further evidence as to the sexuality of children in other cultural environments, reference should be made to :

B. MALINOWSKI, " The Sexual Life of Children ", Vol. I, Chap. III, *The Sexual Life of Savages*, Routledge (1929).

and

G. RÓHEIM, " Psycho-Analysis of Primitive Cultural Types ", *Int. J. of Psycho-Analysis*, Róheim Australasian Research Number, Vol. XIII, 1932.

APPENDIX III

The following spontaneous remarks of J.G., a boy aged 2;7, have been supplied to me whilst this volume is in proof. They are recorded in the notes which the boy's mother is keeping, and cover a period of one month. My own interpretation of the main theme which they illustrate is given in parenthesis:

"At bath-time he got his duck out of the stool and put it in the bath near the plug-hole, saying, ' Duck want wee. Duck wee in hole. Duck have penis.'[1] I asked him which was the duck's penis and he pointed to a place on its underside and said, ' Penis dere,' but there was nothing like a penis there." (Denial of castration anxiety.)

"After tea, when I went in the nursery, he got off his chair and rubbed it and said, ' Dry, dry.' Then he said, ' Motion in trousers—mammy clean you.' He had done a bit of loose motion. He looked rather anxious while he was rubbing the chair, and said, ' Dry ' almost as if he were asking a question." (Anxiety re loss of anal control, and reassurance by thought of helpful real mother.)

"When I went in at 3 p.m. to get him up from his rest, he said at once, ' Penis dry, botty dry, nappy dry, legs dry.' He looked rather anxious, so I guessed he was *not* dry. In fact he was in rather a mess from a loose motion. I just said, ' No, they're not dry, but I'll soon make them dry.' He said, ' Mammy wipe your botty.' " (Denial of reality, followed by reassurance of mother's actual willingness to help.)

"Said at night in bed, laughing and shouting : ' Anus in your mouth,' and repeated it a lot." (Identification of mouth and anus, food and faeces, for purposes of reassurance against anxiety connected with anal functions.)

"Said when he was on the lavatory : ' Hole in your botty—motion in dere.' His mother told him it was his anus. He said, ' Gergel touch anus—motion in anus.' " (Anxiety connected with anal functions, and the idea of being full of faeces inside.)

"Said this morning, ' Daddy has penis in his mouth.' (Nothing has been said to him to suggest this.)" (Identification of tongue and penis, based on oral phantasies.)

"Said to his mother, holding his own nose : ' Got nuvver penis.' His mother asked, ' Where ? ' He said, still holding his nose, ' Dere—penis dere.' " (Reassurance against castration anxiety.)

---

[1] The boy has been given the terms "penis" and "anus", instead of the usual nursery terms. Otherwise his upbringing in these respects is quite normal.

BIBLIOGRAPHY

ABRAHAM, KARL, *Selected Papers on Psycho-Analysis*, London, 1927: " Manifestations of the Female Castration Complex " (1921) ; " A Short Study of the Development of the Libido " (1924) ; " The Influence of Oral Erotism on Character-Formation " (1924) ; " Psycho-Analytic Studies on Character-Formation " (1925).

ANDRUS, R., *An Inventory of the Habits of Children from Two to Five Years of Age* (1928). Teachers' College, Columbia University.

BRIDGES, K., *Social and Emotional Development of the Pre-School Child*, Kegan Paul (1931).

BRIERLEY, MARJORIE, " Some Problems of Integration in Women ", *International Journal of Psycho-Analysis*, Vol. XIII, 1932.

BÜHLER, CHARLOTTE, " The Social Behaviour of the Child ", *Handbook of Child Psychology*, Clark University Press, 1931.

FERENCZI, SÁNDOR, *Contributions to Psycho-Analysis*, Boston, 1916: " Stages in the Development of a Sense of Reality " (1913).

" Attempt to Formulate a Genital Theory " (1922), *International Journal of Psycho-Analysis*, Vol. IV, 1923.

FREUD, SIGMUND, " Analysis of a Phobia in a Five-Year-Old Boy " (1909), *Collected Papers*, Vol. III, London, 1925.

" Instincts and their Vicissitudes " (1915), *Collected Papers*, Vol. IV, London, 1925.

Introductory Lectures on Psycho-Analysis (1918), London, 1920.

Hemmung, Symptom und Angst, Vienna (1926).

The Ego and the Id (1923), London, 1927.

" Some Psychological Consequences of the Anatomical Distinction between the Sexes " (1925), *International Journal of Psycho-Analysis*, Vol. VIII, 1927.

Civilization and its Discontents, London (1929).

" Female Sexuality ", *International Journal of Psycho-Analysis*, Vol. XIII, 1932.

GLOVER, EDWARD, "The Significance of the Mouth in Psycho-Analysis", *British Journal of Medical Psychology*, Vol. IV, 1924.

"Notes on Oral Character-Formation", *International Journal of Psycho-Analysis*, Vol. VI, 1925.

"Grades of Ego-Differentiation", *International Journal of Psycho-Analysis*, Vol. XI, 1930.

"Introduction to the Study of Psycho-Analytical Theory", *International Journal of Psycho-Analysis*, Vol. XI, 1930.

"Sublimation, Substitution and Social Anxiety", *International Journal of Psycho-Analysis*, Vol. XII, 1931.

"A Psycho-Analytic Approach to the Classification of Mental Disorders", *Journal of Mental Science*, October, 1932.

HORNEY, KAREN, "On the Genesis of the Castration Complex in Women" (1923), *International Journal of Psycho-Analysis*, Vol. V, 1924.

"The Flight from Womanhood", *International Journal of Psycho-Analysis*, Vol. VII, 1926.

ISAACS, SUSAN, "The Mental Hygiene of the Pre-School Child", *British Journal of Medical Psychology*, Vol. VIII, 1928.

"Privation and Guilt", *International Journal of Psycho-Analysis*, Vol. X, 1929.

Intellectual Growth in Young Children, Routledge (1930); Schocken (1966).

Health and Education in the Nursery (jointly with Dr. Victoria Bennett), Routledge (1931).

"Education of Children under Seven Years of Age", *British Journal of Educational Psychology*, Vol. I, 1931.

"A Brief Contribution to the Social Psychology of Young Children", *Journal de Psychologie*, 1931.

"Some Notes on the Incidence of Neurotic Difficulties in Young Children", *British Journal of Educational Psychology*, Vol. II, 1932.

The Children We Teach, University of London Press (1932); Schocken (1971).

The Nursery Years (revised and enlarged edition, 1932), Routledge; Schocken (1968).

JONES, ERNEST, " The Theory of Symbolism " (1916), *Papers on Psycho-Analysis*, London, 1923.

"The Origin and Structure of the Super-Ego", *International Journal of Psycho-Analysis*, Vol. VII, 1926.

"The Early Development of Female Sexuality", *International Journal of Psycho-Analysis*, Vol. VIII, 1927.

"Fear, Guilt and Hate", *International Journal of Psycho-Analysis*, Vol. X, 1929.

On the Nightmare, Hogarth Press (1931).

KLEIN, MELANIE, " The Development of a Child ", *International Journal of Psycho-Analysis*, Vol. IV, 1923.

" Infant Analysis " (1923), *International Journal of Psycho-Analysis*, Vol. VII, 1926.

" The Rôle of the School in the Libidinal Development of the Child " (1923), *International Journal of Psycho-Analysis*, Vol. V, 1924.

" Zur Genese des Tics ", *Internationale Zeitschrift für Psychoanalyse*, Bd. XI, 1925.

" The Psychological Principles of Infant Analysis " (1926), *International Journal of Psycho-Analysis*, Vol. VIII, 1927.

" Early Stages of the Oedipus Conflict " (1927), *International Journal of Psycho-Analysis*, Vol. IX, 1928.

" Personification in the Play of Children ", *International Journal of Psycho-Analysis*, Vol. X, 1929.

" Infantile Anxiety-Situations Reflected in a Work of Art and in the Creative Impulse ", *International Journal of Psycho-Analysis*, Vol. X, 1929.

" The Importance of Symbol-Formation in the Development of the Ego ", *International Journal of Psycho-Analysis*, Vol. XI, 1930.

" A Contribution to the Theory of Intellectual Inhibition ", *International Journal of Psycho-Analysis*, Vol. XII, 1931.

The Psycho-Analysis of Children, Hogarth Press (1932).

MALINOWSKI, B., " The Sexual Life of Children ", *The Sexual Life of Savages*, Vol. I, Chap. III, Routledge (1929).

PIAGET, JEAN, *The Language and Thought of the Child*, Kegan Paul (1926).

Judgment and Reasoning in the Child, Kegan Paul (1928).

The Moral Judgment of the Child, Kegan Paul (1932).

RASMUSSEN, V., *The Primary School*, Gyldendal.

RIVIERE, JOAN, "Womanliness as a Masquerade", *International Journal of Psycho-Analysis*, Vol. X, 1929.

RÓHEIM, GEZA, "Children of the Desert", "Psycho-Analysis of Primitive Cultural Types", *International Journal of Psycho-Analysis*, Róheim Australasian Research Number, Vol. XIII, 1932.

SCHMIDEBERG, MELITTA, "Psychotic Mechanisms in Cultural Development", *International Journal of Psycho-Analysis*, Vol. XI, 1930.
"A Contribution to the Psychology of Persecutory Ideas and Delusions", *International Journal of Psycho-Analysis*, Vol. XII, 1931.

SEARL, M. N., "A Paranoic Mechanism as Seen in the Analysis of a Child", Abstract in the *International Journal of Psycho-Analysis*, Vol. IX, 1928.
"The Flight to Reality", *International Journal of Psycho-Analysis*, Vol. X, 1929.
"Danger Situations of the Immature Ego", *International Journal of Psycho-Analysis*, Vol. X, 1929.
"The Rôles of Ego and Libido in Development", *International Journal of Psycho-Analysis*, Vol. XI, 1930.
"A Note on Depersonalization", *International Journal of Psycho-Analysis*, Vol. XIII, 1932.
"Some Contrasted Aspects of Psycho-Analysis and Education", *British Journal of Educational Psychology*, Vol. II, 1932.
"The Psychology of Screaming", *International Journal of Psycho-Analysis*, XIV, 1933.

SHARPE, ELLA F., "History as Phantasy", *International Journal of Psycho-Analysis*, Vol. VIII, 1929.
"Certain Aspects of Sublimations and Delusions", *International Journal of Psycho-Analysis*, Vol. XI, 1930.

STRACHEY, JAMES, "Some Unconscious Factors in Reading", *International Journal of Psycho-Analysis*, Vol. XI, 1930.
"The Function of the Precipitating Factor in the Aetiology of the Neuroses: A Historical Note", *International Journal of Psycho-Analysis*, Vol. XII, 1931.

"Symposium on Child-Analysis", *International Journal of Psycho-Analysis*, Vol. VIII, 1927.

VALENTINE, C. W., "The Innate Bases of Fear", *Journal of Genetic Psychology*, Vol. XXXVII, 1930.

WATSON, JOHN B., *Behavior: An Introduction to Comparative Psychology*, Henry Holt, New York (1914).
Psychology; from the Standpoint of a Behaviorist, J. B. Lippincott Company (1919).
"What the Nursery has to say about Instincts", *Psychologies of 1925*, Clark University, 1927.
Psychological Care of Infant and Child, Allen & Unwin, (1928).

WINNICOTT, D. W., *Clinical Notes on Disorders of Childhood*, Heinemann, 1931.

WOOLLEY, HELEN T., "Eating, Sleeping, and Elimination", *Handbook of Child Psychology*, Clark University Press, 1931.

ADDITIONS TO BIBLIOGRAPHY, 1944

FREUD, ANNA, *The Ego and the Mechanisms of Defence*, Hogarth Press, 1937.

GLOVER, EDWARD, "A Developmental Study of the Obsessional Neurosis", *International Journal of Psycho-Analysis*, Vol. XVI, 1935.

HEIMANN, PAULA, "A Contribution to the Problem of Sublimation and its Relation to Processes of Internalization", *International Journal of Psycho-Analysis*, Vol. XXIII, 1942.

ISAACS, SUSAN, "Bad Habits", *International Journal of Psycho-Analysis*, Vol. XVI, 1935.
"A Special Mechanism in a Schizoid Boy", *International Journal of Psycho-Analysis*, Vol. XX, 1939.
"Criteria for Interpretation", *International Journal of Psycho-Analysis*, Vol. XX, 1939.
"'Temper Tantrums' in Early Childhood in Their Relation to Internal Objects", *International Journal of Psycho-Analysis*, Vol. XXI, 1940.
"An Acute Psychotic Anxiety Occurring in a Boy of Four Years", *International Journal of Psycho-Analysis*, Vol. XXIV, 1943.

KLEIN, MELANIE, " A Contribution to the Psychogenesis of Manic-Depressive States ", *International Journal of Psycho-Analysis*, Vol. XVI, 1935.
  " Mourning and its Relation to Manic-Depressive States ", *International Journal of Psycho-Analysis*, Vol. XXI, 1940.
KLEIN, MELANIE, AND RIVIERE, JOAN, *Love, Hate and Reparation*, Psycho-analytical Epitomes, No. 2, Hogarth Press, 1937.
MIDDLEMORE, M., *The Nursing Couple*, Hamish Hamilton, 1941.
MURPHY, LOIS BARCLAY, *Social Behaviour and Child Personality*, Columbia University Press, 1937.
READ, HERBERT, *Education Through Art*, Faber and Faber, 1943.
RICKMAN, J., (Edited by) *On the Bringing-up of Children*, by Five Psycho-Analysts, Kegan Paul, 1936.
RIVIERE, JOAN, " Jealousy as a Mechanism of Defence ", *International Journal of Psycho-Analysis*, Vol. XIII, 1932.
  " On the Genesis of Psychical Conflict in Earliest Infancy ", *International Journal of Psycho-Analysis*, Vol. XVII, 1936.
  " A Contribution to the Analysis of the Negative Therapeutic Reaction ", *International Journal of Psycho-Analysis*, Vol. XVII, 1936.
SCHMIDEBERG, MELITTA, " The Play-Analysis of a Three-Year-Old Girl ", *International Journal of Psycho-Analysis*, Vol. XV, 1934.
SHARPE, ELLA F., " Similar and Divergent Unconscious Determinants underlying the Sublimations of Pure Art and Pure Science ", *International Journal of Psycho-Analysis*, Vol. XVI, 1935.
  Dream Analysis, Hogarth Press, 1937.
  " Psycho-Physical Problems Revealed in Language : An Examination of Metaphor ", *International Journal of Psycho-Analysis*, Vol. XXI, 1940.
  " Cautionary Tales ", *International Journal of Psycho-Analysis*, Vol. XXIV, 1943.
WINNICOTT, D. W., " The Observation of Infants in a Set Situation ", *International Journal of Psycho-Analysis*, Vol. XXII, 1941.

INDEX OF AUTHORS

Abraham, K., 301
Aichhorn, 405
Anderson, J. E., 4

Bernfeld, S., 405
Brainard, P., 7
Bridges, K., 5, 6, 10, 28, 41, 45, 46, 62-64, 72-3, 76-7, 92, 121, 154, 186-7, 231, 233, 235, 243, 255, 257, 268-9, 345, 349
Bühler, C., 5, 28, 147, 344
Dewey, J., 18, 19n.
Freud, Anna, 405
Freud, S., 17, 18, 207, 253n., 259, 269, 280, 284, 289, 320, 328, 363, 403, 404
Gesell, A., 5
Glover, E., 295
Hughes, R., 14n.
James, W., 225
Jones, E., 289, 354n.
Klein, M., 208, 210, 282n., 294, 360, 404, 405
Koehler, W., 7

Montessori, M., 427
Piaget, J., 11, 213
Rasmussen, V., 28, 121, 162-3, 354
Riviere, J., 289
Russell, B., 19n.

Schapera, I., 458-61
Schmideberg, M., 325n.
Searl, M. N., 208, 244, 245n., 285-88, 295n., 297n., 298, 299-302, 312n., 356n., 372, 397n., 406, 438
Staples, R., 7n.
Stern, W., 147

Valentine, C. W., 7

Watson, J. B., 7, 28, 154-5, 220
Winnicott, D. W., 437n.
Woolley, H. T., 17n., 28, 134, 153

INDEX OF SUBJECTS[1]

Adolescent, 395, 413, 415, 452
Aggression, 6, 13, 14, 24, 218, 235, 322, 410, 424 (see also under Displacement, Frustration, Guilt, Hostility, Inferiority, Moodiness, Possessiveness, Power, Rivalry, Sexuality, Superego, Superiority).
 active, 22, 232, 243, 260, 265, 276-7, 370, 454
 and anxiety, 14, 238, 243, 244-5, 247, 257, 269-70, 278, 286-8, 289, 312, 316, 317, 318, 322, 324, 325-6, 331-2, 368, 373, 374, 375, 382, 389, 407, 408, 409, 410, 417, 422, 423, 424, 431, 432, 433-4, 436, 438, 439, 440, 441, 442
 and real treatment, 14, 21-22, 218-9, 385-7, 422-3
 defensive, 218, 220, 358, 385, 408
 group, to adults, 244, 256-64, 268
 group, to other children, 21, 22, 227-8, 247-56, 366, 422-3, 453, 454
 individual, to adults, 229, 230, 257, 322, 366, 369, 386-7, 435
 individual, to other children, 218-37, 241-7, 248, 249, 251, 256, 366, 367, 377, 385-6, 393-4, 423, 435, 453, 454, 455
 individual, to parents, 256, 257, 286-8, 289-90, 292, 293, 294-5, 297n., 298, 301-2, 307n., 308, 316, 317, 318, 323, 324, 325, 331, 332, 343, 347, 348, 351, 352-3, 356, 357, 359, 361, 363, 364, 368, 369, 373, 377-8, 381-2, 391, 397, 407, 418, 420n., 423, 438
 make-believe, 227, 228, 230, 260

Aggression, make-believe and real, 226-8, 243-5
 modes of, 220
 normality of, 221, 231
 phantasies of, 228, 294-5, 373, 393, 407, 408, 423
 place in social development, 231-2, 257
 unconscious, 244-5
 use of term, 218n.
 verbal, 20, 227, 258, 260, 263, 265, 267, 329-30, 331, 332, 369
Aggressive wishes, fear of own, 228-9, 230, 237, 257, 269-70, 287, 306, 308, 310, 315, 316, 317, 318, 363, 364, 365, 373, 379, 382, 408, 422-3, 432, 438, 439, 440, 442
Agoraphobia, 297n.
Allyship of children against parents and other adults, 236, 259-64, 394-5, 427
Ambivalence, 12, 240, 250-1, 258, 259, 268, 277, 324, 389, 390, 391, 409-10
Ambivalent feelings, " splitting " of, 240, 246, 249, 250, 251-3, 256, 257-8, 319, 392-3, 393-4
Anal and urethral erotism, 283, 284, 322, 327-8, 329, 331, 333, 334, 439
 interests, 19, 280, 282-3, 328-9, 331, 334, 335, 429, 447-8, 449
 phantasies, (see under phantasy)
 sadism and aggression, 20, 221, 230, 265, 283, 302, 315, 322, 329, 330-1, 332, 333, 343, 373, 374, 438, 439
Anal masturbation, 368, 369
 phase, 292, 327-9, 330, 331, 332, 333, 373
Analyst, function of, 405, 406-12

[1] No reference to the *Records* chapter is included in the index.

INDEX OF SUBJECTS

Anger, 10, 15, 220, 238, 243, 249, 251, 256, 287, 288, 293, 302, 305, 309, 331, 373, 378, 407 (see also under Frustration)

Anxiety, 14, 208, 210, 211, 228n., 232, 236, 260, 286n., 289, 290, 296, 300, 301-2, 303, 307, 308, 311, 319, 326n., 334, 352, 353, 371, 389, 394, 398, 405, 407, 408, 424, 426, 428, 435, 438, 440, 441, 452 (see also under Aggression, Exhibitionism, Frustration, Guilt, Masturbation, Rivalry, Sexual aggression, Sexuality infantile, Super-ego)
attacks, 296-7, 310, 438, 443, 444, 445
mechanisms for dealing with (see Mechanisms; also under separate mechanisms)
unconscious, 247

Aphanisis, 354n., 356n.
Asocial behaviour, 417
Auto-erotism (see Masturbation)

Bargaining, 275-6
Bakatla children: infantile sexuality in, 458-61
Bed-wetting (see Incontinence)
Behaviouristic theory, 7, 229n., 434, 435-6
Birth: psychic significance of, 289
Biting (see Oral sadism)
Breast (see Oral satisfaction)
as love, 238, 273, 293, 321-2, 326, 432
British Psycho-Analytical Society, 405

Castration fear, 354-62
fear and aggression, 356-7
fear and bodily processes and accidents, 355-6
fear and masturbation, 347, 348
fear and real experience, 355, 359
Castration fear in boy, 343, 354, 356, 357, 358, 359, 360-2
fear in girl, 317, 343, 354-5, 357, 358, 359, 376, 378-9
Castration phantasies, 341, 354-62

Castration, threats of adults, 347n., 348, 355
Child Guidance Clinic, 446
Child study, comparison of methods, 4-8, 9-13, 16-19, 266
Cleanliness, 9
emotional factor in, 9, 16, 315, 318-9, 328, 330-1, 332, 333, 355-6, 373, 381, 382, 437-43
training in, 16, 318-9, 327, 436-43, 447-8
Cognitive activity and emotion, 7-8
and unconscious phantasy, 209-12, 395, 411
Companionship, value of, 217, 236, 260, 261, 263-4, 279, 394, 395, 396, 427-8, 433-4, 446
Comradeship, 388, 394, 395
"Conditioning," 7, 9, 437
Conflict, inner: psychic devices for dealing with (see Mechanisms; also under separate mechanisms)
Conscience (see Super-ego)
Constipation, 9, 333
Constructive activity, 21, 23, 257, 317, 349, 386, 395-6, 425, 446, 447
Co-operation, 11, 12, 13, 20, 21, 24, 236, 248, 253, 260, 261, 266-9, 271-2, 385, 388, 393, 454, 455
Co-operative activities, 214, 217, 266, 267, 276, 428, 429, 453, 454-5, 456
"Cosy Places," 280
significance of, 362-5, 376-7, 379-80
Creative activity, 23, 271, 335, 395, 410, 411, 426, 427, 446, 447,
Cruelty, 8, 228, 235, 265, 422

Day-dreaming, 312
Death wishes, 237, 258, 289, 297, 352-3
Defiance, 15, 237, 256, 257, 258, 260, 288, 307n., 310, 337, 366, 387, 411, 445-6, 448, 450, 451
Dependence on parents or other adults, 248, 257, 285, 286, 287, 288, 289, 290, 388, 390, 417

Destructiveness, 22, 237, 247, 257, 318, 387, 408, 411, 427
educational provision for, 410
Development schedules, 5, 8, 9
Difficulties in emotional development, 9, 10, 15-16, 257, 285, 30/n., 318-9, 417, 428n., 430-1, 432-4, 435-6, 437-46, 449-51
table of classification, 27-8
Difficulties of behaviour, 8, 16, 21, 22, 23, 218, 238-240, 257, 284, 307n., 318-9, 351, 353, 385-6, 411, 417-8, 418n., 419, 420n., 439, 453-4
Displacement, 230, 234, 245, 251-3, 254, 261, 264, 309, 322, 339, 392, 393, 394
Divided self, 228-9n., 371-2
Dreams, 229, 347n., 365, 377, 378, 381

Education and psycho-analysis, relation between, 13, 18-19, 403-13, 414-6, 428-9
Educational method, 14-15, 18-23, 254, 281, 417-29, 431-4, 435-6, 440-3, 444-56
Educator and understanding of child's deeper problems, 13-16, 412-3
Educator, function of, 269-70, 271-2, 405, 410, 411, 412, 413, 421, 422, 423, 424, 425-6, 427, 428, 446-7, 448, 449-50, 452, 453-4, 455-6
Ego, 228n.
  and unconscious phantasy, 295-7, 304-5, 306, 375
  and wish-self, relation between 285-90, 296-7, 298, 299-302, 309, 421, 425, 427
  danger-situations for, 285-6, 296, 297n., 299-302, 356n., 372-3, 418
Ego development, 210, 278, 296-7, 306, 309, 315, 327, 343, 375, 396-7, 398, 399, 409, 411, 421, 425, 427, 449
  and frustration, 288, 289-90, 430
Ego-ideal, 272, 405, 417
"Ego" parent and educator, 272, 286, 299, 300
Egocentrism, 248, 453
  and aggression, 216

Egocentrism and social development, 213-8, 249, 250, 253, 254, 388, 427
  and social play, 213-8
Egocentrism, types of behaviour constituting, 30, 213-7, 218
Egoism, 11, 231, 254
Emotional development, 9, 210, 254, 260-1, 280-320, 374, 375, 387-400, 417, 425, 435, 444, 449, 450, 451-2
Environment, effect of, 8, 235, 257, 269, 371, 384-7, 389, 390-1, 396-7, 453
  and emotional development, 235, 236, 257, 260-1, 325, 343, 348, 371, 385-6, 391-2, 393, 394, 395, 420-1, 424-5, 426, 427, 433-4, 446
  stable, need for, 417, 421, 427
Envy, 230, 238, 377, 378
Equation of babies with food and faeces, 353-4, 376, 380-1, 382
Erection, 293, 356
Erotogenic zones, 291-4, 326-7
Excremental processes and substances: significance of, 295, 318-9, 327-335, 337, 355-6, 358, 373, 374, 376, 380-2, 438, 439, 440, 441, 442, 450
Exhibitionism, 283, 355, 357n., 429, 446-8, 449
  and anxiety, 337, 338, 347n., 379, 382, 445-6, 447
  compulsive, 338, 379
  direct, 335, 336, 337, 338, 339
  sublimated forms of, 336, 337, 338
  verbal, 335, 337, 338, 339, 448-50, 451

Family play, 350-4
Father "bad," 285-6, 363, 364, 373, 385, 392
  "good," 274, 285-6, 363, 373, 385, 392, 407, 409
Fear, 7, 10, 22, 210, 243, 297n. (see also under Possessiveness)
  about food, 433-4
  of animals, 308, 324, 363, 364, 379
  of attack, 236, 306, 310, 385, 445

INDEX OF SUBJECTS

Fear, of " badness " of body, 331-2, 347, 376
of being given bad food, 332-3, 373, 407
of being starved, 370
of burning, 306, 310
of death, 370, 439
of desertion, 361, 418
of destruction, 240, 273, 310, 315, 316, 370, 409
of destruction of inside of body, 306, 317, 355, 357
of drowning, 306, 310, 370
of exclusion from love, 226, 233, 236, 238, 273, 370
of excremental processes and substances, 330, 331-2, 333, 334-5, 337, 355-6, 373, 381-2, 438, 439, 440, 441, 442, 450
of helplessness, 230, 236, 259-60, 274, 289, 290
of impotence, 356
of loss of love, 233, 236, 240, 316
of own aggressive wishes (see under Aggressive wishes)
of parents, 236, 240, 259, 260, 306, 310, 347, 352, 364, 398, 399, 418-9
of poisoning, 306, 373, 407
of retaliation, 243-4, 260, 287, 293, 305-6, 316, 347, 356, 357, 358-9, 360, 369, 406, 407, 408, 410, 418
of robbing, 273, 306, 316, 353
of super-ego, 306-7n., 372-3, 417, 421, 422, 424, 427
Feeding, 430-2
problems, 15, 292, 320, 325, 430-1, 432-4
Fighting impulse, 220, 286
Fixation, 284, 327, 343, 374, 418
Flatus, 322, 330-1
" Flight to phantasy," 312-6
to reality," 312-6, 320
Friendliness and identification (see Identification)
to adults, 233, 237, 266-72, 278
to other children, 223, 236, 248, 253, 266, 267, 272-9, 394, 395, 396, 397-8
Frigidity, 283
Frustration, 285-6, 292, 306n., 307n., 430 (see also under Ego-development and Super-ego)

Frustration and aggression, 220, 286-9, 293, 295, 301-2, 325, 333, 343, 356, 372-3, 389, 390, 391
and anger, 220, 225, 273, 286-7, 289, 301-2, 356, 356n., 373, 438
and anxiety, 211, 274, 289-1, 293, 300-2, 356, 356n., 391, 438.
and psychic death, 289, 356n
and sense of reality, 289-90, 430

Genetic theory, need for, 206-7
theory and classification of material, 24, 212, 280, 282-4
theory and psycho-analytic studies, 12-13, 17, 207-9, 210, 212, 225-6, 230, 238, 240, 244, 251-2, 257, 259, 270, 280, 282 et seq., 321, 325, 328, 342-3, 344-5, 352, 371, 372, 375, 400, 414, 416, 417, 422n., 425, 426-7, 428-9
Genital phase, 292-4, 326-7, 341-2, 356, 359, 374-5
Gifts: equated with mother's breast, 273
significance of, 226, 272-4, 351, 385, 407-8
Giving, 272-4
of services, 274, 276
" Good " and " bad," significance of, to child, 285-7
Grimacing, 10
Group psychology, 247-79, 388, 394
Guilt, 13, 228n.
and aggression, 12, 228-9, 230, 238, 247, 269-70, 276, 366, 368, 369, 372-3, 374, 417, 422-3, 424
and anxiety, 332, 367, 368, 369-70, 371, 417, 422
and destructiveness, 247, 367, 368, 369, 370
Guilt and excremental processes, 16, 333, 366, 367, 369, 373, 439, 440, 441, 442, 447
and real treatment, 270-1, 366, 370-1, 417, 418, 419, 421, 422-3, 435, 436, 440, 441, 442

INDEX OF SUBJECTS

Guilt and sexuality (see under Sexuality)
  and super-ego, 228, 270 (see also under Super-ego)
  and projection, 230, 253, 306, 332, 344, 366, 367, 368, 369, 370, 374
  unconscious, 247, 270

Hate, 24, 224, 243, 250, 254, 273, 286, 297, 298, 360, 379, 389, 410, 411
Herd behaviour, 388
Heterosexual preferences, 303
Homosexuality, 283, 303, 360
Hostility, 13, 22, 383 (see also under Inferiority, Moodiness, Possessiveness, Power, Rivalry, Superiority)
  group, to adults, 22, 256-64, 366
  group, to other children, 21-22, 233-4, 242, 247-56, 264-5, 366, 454
  group, to strangers and newcomers, 255-6
  group, to temporary scapegoat, 264-5
  group, to younger or inferior children, 263, 264-5, 422-3
  individual, to adults, 229, 237-41, 256-9, 267, 269-70, 275, 366, 385, 386
  individual, to other children, 218-28, 229, 230, 231-6, 243-7, 251, 266, 366, 385, 453-4
  unconscious, 251-2, 257, 354
Hypochondria, 296-7n.
Hysteria, 295, 296n.

Id (see Wish-self)
Identification, 297n., 305, 318, 405, 439
  and friendliness, 274, 275, 276, 278
  and power, 229-30, 235
  boy's with father, 303, 350, 352-3, 357, 360, 407
  feminine in boy, 303, 350-1, 353, 357, 359-62
  girl's with mother, 303, 350, 376, 377, 378, 382
  masculine in girl, 303, 350, 359, 376, 380
  of one's possessions with one's body, 226

Identification of parents with bodily processes and substances, 295, 330
  with animals, 244, 313, 315
  with father, 222, 274, 305
  with mother, 289, 305, 318, 430
  with parents, 229-30, 235, 236, 278
Impotence, 283, 343
Incontinence, 9, 314, 320, 355, 358, 391, 407, 418, 420, 435, 437, 438, 439, 440, 441, 442
Incorporation, 226, 304, 324, 356, 360, 372
Independence, 385-6, 426, 427
Individuality, 426-7
Infancy, central emotional conflict of, 240-1, 285-320, 388-90, 391, 392, 393, 394, 395-6, 397, 398, 422n.
Infant, psychological situation of, 285-320
Inferiority, 259
  and aggression, 245-7, 385-6, 454-5
  and hostility, 219, 220, 248, 454-5
Inhibition, 257, 294, 317, 373, 375, 416-7
  of sexual impulses, 17, 281, 321, 327, 336
Introjection, 228n., 270, 293, 295, 304-5, 306, 306-7n., 372, 389

Jealousy, 231, 233, 234, 235, 236, 237-9, 288, 377-8, 379, 388, 438
Justice, sense of, 223-4, 259

Latency period 12, 259, 310, 320, 389, 395, 397-9, 450
Leadership, 242, 248, 255, 264
  in play, 216, 217, 218, 453
  of adult, 267, 269-71
Libidinal development (see Sexual Development)
" Libido " parent, 300
London Clinic of Psycho-Analysis, 325n.
Loss, real, effect of, 9
Love, 24, 251, 254, 289, 292, 298, 302, 318, 326, 343, 348, 356, 357, 360, 364, 373, 417, 430, 431, 432

INDEX OF SUBJECTS

Love, adult's, effect on phantasy life, 236
and rivalry (see Rivalry)
dependence on parents' or other adults', 232-3, 257, 261, 273, 288, 289, 388, 430
deprivation of, felt as punishment, 226
in unconscious phantasy, 238, 272-3
loss of (see under Fear)
mother's, 238, 273, 293, 368, 423, 430, 431, 432
parents' to child, 235, 236, 308, 360
parents' and other adults', importance of, 11, 236, 269, 270, 271, 343, 348
to adults, 231, 237, 267-70, 271, 276, 328, 363, 392-3, 410, 422n., 440
to other children, 236, 242, 251, 253, 261, 266, 272, 277, 351, 363, 385
to parents, 235, 238, 240, 379, 407-8, 440
Loveworthiness, 226, 236, 273

Magic, 215, 273, 318, 328, 331, 340, 347, 348, 358, 380, 381, 396
Malting House School children, ages of, 28
description of, 20-23
educational method, 19-23, 281, 385-7, 422-3, 451
Mannerisms, 10
Masochism, 219
Masturbation, 10, 15, 17, 281, 293, 320, 345-50, 429, 445, 447
and aggression, 347, 348
and anxiety, 345, 346, 347, 348-9, 379, 445, 446
and group life, 345, 349-50, 446
and guilt, 10, 283, 349, 368, 369
attitude of adults to, 345-7, 348
compulsive, 345, 347n., 348, 369
in boy, 345, 347-8
in girl, 345
phantasies, 346, 347-8, 349
severe treatment of, 346, 348, 349, 355, 446

Masturbation, treatment of, 15, 346-7, 348, 349-50, 429, 446
Mechanisms, psychological, 207, 228n., 234, 235, 249, 250, 251-3, 254, 258, 261, 275, 278, 291, 303-20, 389, 400, 424
Melancholia, 270
Mental conflict, 12, 15, 207, 210, 228-9n., 269-70, 335. 346-7, 349, 350, 354, 360, 389-90, 393, 394, 396, 397, 413, 417, 421, 422, 424-5, 426-7, 443, 445-6, 448-9
hygiene, 16, 436
illness, 15, 284, 296-7, 371, 372-3, 417-8, 430-1, 443-4
Moodiness, 218
and aggression, 220, 243
and hostility, 219, 245, 247
" Moral imbecility," 373, 417
Morality, children's sense of, 4, 261, 366-75
Mother " bad," 285, 286, 307n., 318, 331-2, 373, 385, 392, " good," 285, 286, 307n., 318, 351, 363, 373, 385, 392, 409, 436

Nail biting, 10, 436
Naughtiness, notions about, 366-70, 374
Negativism, 231, 236
Nervous habits, 10
Neuroses in adults, 284, 312, 392n.
Neuroses in children, 211, 284, 307, 383, 453
Neurotic and normal individual, comparison of, 251-2, 284
New baby: reaction to, 233, 234-5, 237, 264, 314, 315, 376-8, 379, 380, 423, 438
Night terrors, 15, 22, 307n., 319-20, 435, 443, 444, 445
Norms of development, 425
Nose-picking, 10
Nursery school, 17, 235, 241, 260, 281, 349, 388, 390-2, 394-5, 421, 426, 433-4, 442-3, 446, 453-6
versus home education, 392n.
Nursery training, 16

Obsessional neurosis, 270, 295, 304n., 330, 381, 423

INDEX OF SUBJECTS

Obstinacy, 15, 307n., 310, 330, 333, 438-9, 442

Oedipus conflict, 237, 238, 256, 287-8, 297-303, 347-8, 351, 357, 358, 359-62, 376-7, 378-80, 381, 382, 438

Omnipotence, phantasies of, 228, 260, 274, 347-8, 361, 380, 381

Oral erotism, 211, 292, 293, 294-5, 321-2, 323, 324, 326, 327, 342, 356, 368, 369, 430, 431, 432, 434-6
- frustration, 288, 289, 292, 295, 301-2, 356, 359, 372, 391, 430-1
- phantasies, (see under Phantasy)
- phase, 292, 293, 294-5, 304, 307n., 316, 317, 318, 321-2, 323-4, 325, 326, 327, 356, 372, 373, 430-2
- sadism and aggression, 220, 221, 227, 229, 260, 287, 291, 292, 293, 294-5, 316, 317, 318, 322-4, 325, 326, 342-3, 356, 359, 373, 374, 391, 418, 431, 432-3, 434-5. 436
- satisfaction at breast: significance and importance of, 225, 238, 292, 293, 318, 327, 359, 374, 431-2

Oral-sucking attitude to penis, 360

Origin of babies (see Sexual curiosity and Sexual theories)

Ownership (see Possessiveness)

Paranoia, 306

Parental intercourse, child's interest in, 283, 341, 367-8, 377, 380,
- child's reaction to, 298-9, 301-2, 343, 438
- phantasies about, 209, 283, 299, 342-3, 344, 350, 352, 353, 360, 380-1, 382, 389, 411, 450

Parental relationship, child's reaction to, 17, 237-8, 240, 287-8, 297, 298-302
- relationship, sexual, child's intuitive awareness of, 298-9, 300-1

Parents, child's wish to control, 229-30, 260, 373, 380, 381, 438,
- child's wish to separate, 240, 256
- their real behaviour to child, 236, 300, 301, 307n., 385, 386, 389, 417-8, 420, 421, 423, 446

Patriotism, 252

Penis, equation with breast, 326-7, 360, 374
- girl's wish for, 354-5, 358, 359, 378
- significance of, for boy, 316-7, 347-8, 356, 357-8

Personification, 314, 350, 381

Phantasies about parental intercourse (see Parental Intercourse)
- of alliance, 263
- of burning, 306, 310
- of cutting, 306
- of destruction, 386
- of destruction of inside of body, 306, 317, 355, 357
- of drowning, 306, 310
- of poisoning, 306, 373
- of revenge, 244, 260, 287, 306, 308, 316, 356, 357, 360, 369-70, 373, 374, 379, 389, 393, 406, 407, 408
- of robbing, 227, 306

Phantasy, affecting social relations, 11, 207, 208, 236
- anal, 283, 295, 297, 299, 327, 328-35, 344, 353, 368, 373, 376, 380-2, 407, 438, 439-40, 441, 442, 447
- and reality, 296, 296-7n., 310-6, 361, 374, 375, 384-7, 389, 398-9, 406-9, 411
- confirmation of, by real experience, 296, 296-7n., 351, 355, 385, 417-8, 421, 440, 450
- fixed, 313, 315
- in play, 30, 213-8, 244, 305, 313, 324, 334-5, 357, 362-3, 364-5, 368, 369, 370, 376-7, 379-80, 406-7, 411, 425-6, 428, 449,
- genital, 293, 299, 326-7, 335, 341-2, 343-4, 347-8, 354-5, 356-9, 361, 374, 450

INDEX OF SUBJECTS

Phantasy, oral, 287, 291, 294-5, 299, 304, 306, 308, 322, 323-4, 325, 326, 327, 331, 342, 359, 360, 370, 373, 374, 407, 409, 418, 421, 433
   unconscious, 209, 210, 211-2, 304, 323, 324, 325-6, 328, 331-2, 342-3, 347, 350, 352, 366, 373, 380, 406, 408, 428, 438, 439, 442
   urethral, 283, 295, 299, 327, 328-35, 344, 352, 373, 381, 407, 438, 439, 440, 441, 442, 447
Phobias, 15, 235, 307n., 307-8, 310, 320, 324-5, 379, 442, 444, 445
Play, value of, 19n., 209-10, 425-6, 428, 429
   competitive, value of, 228, 254 393-4, 410, 454
   dramatic, value of, 210, 228, 324, 325, 334-5, 395, 425, 428, 447
   free, value of, 21, 210, 335, 426
   make-believe, 209, 213-8, 305, 316, 426, 427
   manipulative, 209, 425
   reality element in, 214
   solitary, 214, 362
Possessiveness, 219, 221, 222, 256, 264, 454-5
   and aggression, 219-20, 221-6
   and fear of being attacked, 226
   and fear of being robbed, 225
   and fear of helplessness, 225-6
   and feeling safe, 225-6
   and hostility, 219, 248
   and power, 219-20, 222, 225
   and rivalry, 220, 222-3, 224-5, 226
   arising from desire for breast, 225
   as social response, 224-5, 226
   forms of manifestation, 221-6
   stealing, 224
Potency, phantasies of, 273-4, 348, 352, 358
Power, 220
   and aggression, 220, 227-30, 236
   and hostility, 219, 248
   and identification (see Identification)
   and rivalry, 242

Power, phantasies of, 228, 229-30
Privation, 235, 240, 343, 431
   as frustration, 289
Projection, 12, 228-9n., 261, 305-8, 313-4, 352
   of aggression, 253, 261, 262, 263, 287, 308, 369
   of " bad " self, 253, 271, 305, 314, 363, 364, 367, 409
   of ego, 409
   of guilt, 230, 263, 308, 366, 367-8, 369
   of super-ego, 228-9n., 270-1, 305-6, 306-7n., 311, 324, 366 368, 369-70, 372-3, 390, 409, 417, 422-3
   of wish-self, 228-9n., 305, 314, 324, 332, 344, 363, 364-5, 366, 367, 368-9, 374, 386, 409
Protectiveness, 235, 236, 278
Psychic death, 289, 356n.
Psycho-analysis, 207-9, 210, 228n., 252, 259, 270, 281, 284, 294-5, 296, 304, 308, 310-11, 315, 317, 325, 333, 339, 341, 363, 385, 423, 439 (see also under Genetic theory)
   and education, relation between, 13, 18-19, 403-13, 414-6, 428-9
   child's need of, 15, 338, 349, 411, 417, 427, 446
   of adults, 405
   of children, description of process, 208, 405, 406-13
Psycho-analytic theory, outline of, 285-320
Psychological material, system of classification, 24-8
   trends, inter-relation of, 13, 24-7
Psychosis, 284, 291, 304-5, 306, 312, 439n.
Punishment, 15, 21, 386, 387, 417-9, 420, 421, 435, 436, 440, 441, 445, 448, 454
   corporal, 15, 20, 21, 218-9, 386, 387, 418-9, 420, 421, 436, 440, 445
   children's notions about, 366, 369-70, 373-4, 386
   phantasies of (see under Super-ego)

Rage (see Anger)
Rating scales, 5, 6, 8, 9
Real experience and social responses, 208, 236, 385-7
Reality, adaptation to, 290, 409, 411, 421, 425
  testing by, 244, 296-7, 310-11, 319, 326, 364, 379, 382, 393, 398-9, 417, 418, 445-6, 450
  sense of, 290, 394, 396, 398, 409, 432, 440
Reassurance, 273, 317, 332, 347, 348, 355, 361, 378, 380, 434, 443, 444, 445, 446, 447, 450
Regression of boy to feminine attitude, 360 et seq.
Relation, child's, to both parents, 11, 210, 235, 236, 237, 238, 239, 240-1, 252, 256, 259, 287-8, 289, 290, 291, 297-303, 306-7, 320, 324, 343, 347-8, 350, 352-3, 357, 358, 360-2, 363, 372-3, 376-83, 388-9, 391, 392, 394, 395, 397-8, 419, 420, 421, 438, 446, 450 (see also Oedipus conflict)
  to brothers and sisters, 233, 234-5, 236, 245, 264, 298, 376-8, 379-80, 390, 423
  to family, 8, 232-3, 297, 350, 351, 376-80
  to family, and later social responses, 11, 12, 207, 232-41, 245, 259, 264, 298, 387-400, 422n.
  to father, 303, 316, 360
  to mother, 7, 11, 235, 238, 240, 273, 285-9, 290, 292-3, 294-5, 298-302, 303, 307n., 316-8, 321-2, 325, 326, 332, 351, 356, 363-4, 379-80, 391-2, 418, 423, 430-2, 433, 436, 437, 439, 440, 441, 442, 443-5
Remorse, 276-8
Repression, 210, 228n., 235, 291, 295-6, 308, 309, 310, 317, 320, 321, 328, 391, 397, 404, 408, 410, 424, 440
Restitutive trends, 271, 276-8, 316-9, 348, 374-5, 407-8
  compulsive, 318
  educational provision for, 271, 319, 411
  in boy, 316-7, 318
  in girl, 317, 318, 319

Rivalry, 249, 298, 388, 393, 394, 454 (See also under Possessiveness and Power)
  and aggression, 220, 231, 232-42, 251, 264, 297, 301-2, 340, 347, 352-3, 357, 374, 377-8, 407, 410, 438
  and anxiety, 218, 233, 236, 238, 240, 279, 298, 300-1, 360, 377, 378, 379, 385, 428
  and hostility, 219, 231, 232-42, 245, 248, 254, 255, 256, 257-8, 269, 351, 359, 360, 393, 454
  and love, 11, 231, 232-240, 269-70, 376-8, 379-80
  with adults, 237-41, 256
  with other children, 11, 218, 231-6, 241-3, 245, 250, 254, 260, 261, 264, 278, 279, 393-4, 407, 428, 438

Sadism, 224, 243, 244, 252, 341, 342, 343, 352-3, 361, 389, 423
Schizophrenia, 312
Screaming, 286, 289, 368, 369, 391, 407
  fits, 320, 418, 438, 443-5
  fits and super-ego, 372, 418
  fits as psychic death, 356n.
Self-punishment, 235, 271, 370
Sexual aggression, 282, 341, 342, 343, 358, 361
  aggression and anxiety, 342, 356-7, 358-9, 364
  and social development, interrelation of, 237, 282, 384-400, 428, 446
  curiosity, 17, 19, 283, 339-41, 367-8, 378, 379, 380, 429, 447, 450, 451
  curiosity and anxiety, 339
  development, 259, 280-320, 343-4, 359, 374-5, 389, 397-8, 429, 447, 451-2
  development in boy, 303, 316-7, 326-7, 359-60, 374
  development in girl, 303, 317, 374
  development, inter-relation of stages in, 326-7, 335, 341-2, 356, 359, 360, 373, 374
  development, phylogenetic factors, 299, 302, 397n.

INDEX OF SUBJECTS

Sexual development, stages in, 17, 259, 284, 292-4, 302, 320, 389,
   education, 383, 447, 450-2
   perversion in adults, 283, 323, 327, 338
   play, 283, 320, 336-7, 341-2, 344, 429, 446-8, 449
   rivalry, 237-40, 241-3, 298-9, 301-2, 303, 316, 347, 348, 351, 353, 357, 359, 360-2, 376-7, 378, 379, 380, 438
   theories, 299, 326-7, 340, 350, 352, 353, 354, 376, 378, 380-2, 383
   wishes, 300-1, 302, 309, 320, 339, 341-2, 343, 344, 347, 351, 365, 388, 397
Sexuality, infantile, 12, 13, 17, 18, 212, 237, 280-320, 321, 364, 428, 429, 434, 435, 436, 445-52
   and aggression, 237, 238, 240, 287-8, 289-91, 292, 293, 294-5, 298, 301-2, 316, 322, 323, 324, 325, 340, 347, 348, 351, 352-3, 356-7, 358, 363-4, 369, 373, 389, 410, 434-5, 446
   and anxiety, 14, 211, 238, 240, 285-8, 289, 290, 291, 293, 296, 298, 300, 301-2, 303, 309, 316, 324, 344, 351, 354-62, 364, 376-80, 381-2, 383, 422, 424, 450, 451
   and group life, 281, 429
   and guilt, 12, 24, 283, 344, 351, 367-8, 369, 424, 435, 446, 447, 449, 450
   and mental conflict, 15
   attitude of adults to, 13-15, 336, 355, 404, 428-9, 434, 445-52
   in Bakatla children, 458-61
   normality of, 14, 428-9
   severe treatment of, 14, 15, 355, 435, 436, 452
   treatment of, 14-15, 281, 429, 434-5, 445-6, 447-51, 452
Skill, place in normal development, 245, 395-6, 425-6, 427, 435, 446, 454-5
   emotional factors in, 245, 385-6, 411
Sleep, mid-day, 7
   problems, of 7, 22, 443-5

Smacking (see Corporal punishment)
Social adaptation, 6, 22
Social and sexual development, inter-relation of, 237, 384-400, 428, 446
   anxiety, 218, 279
   development, 11, 12, 21-22, 231-2, 236, 249-55, 258-62, 263-4, 267-70, 271-9, 309, 316-8, 334, 387, 389-96, 397-400, 427-8, 453, 454-5, 456
   development and intellectual growth, 10-11, 20, 395, 396, 398, 399
   development and lessening of inner conflict, 392-6, 397-8, 399
   development beginnings of, 11
   development stages in, 11, 231, 232, 233, 235, 268-9, 387-8
   factor and behaviouristic theory, 6-7, 8, 9
   " instincts," 11, 12, 387
   responsibility, 12
   skill, 271, 274
   talent, 218
Sources of material, 27
Spitting, 19-20, 220-1, 322-3, 332, 352, 378
Stammering, 326n., 435
Stereotyped action, 211
Sublimation, 309, 328, 335, 349, 395-6, 421, 426, 428, 446, 447
Super-ego, 228-9n., 270, 273, 290n., 322, 386, 394, 405, 416-7, 419, 426
   adult as, 228-9, 386-7, 390, 422, 422n., 426
   adult as " bad," 271, 307n., 417-9
   adult as " good," 270-2, 306, 307n., 349, 390, 390n., 410, 412, 421, 423, 424, 427, 456
   and aggression, 417, 418, 422, 423
   and anxiety, 306-7n., 372-3, 417-8
   and ego, relation between, 278, 372-3, 374, 375, 417
   and frustration, 290, 306-7n., 372-3

Super-ego and real treatment, 270-1, 370-1, 416-9, 421-3
and wish-self, relation between 290, 306, 306-7n., 311, 369, 372-4, 389
origin of, 270, 290-1, 295, 304, 371-3, 374
projection of (see under Projection)
and punishment phantasies, 226, 260, 270-1, 278, 290-1, 293, 296, 305-6, 306-7n., 308, 310, 311, 316, 317, 324, 325, 330, 360, 366, 369, 370, 373, 374, 375, 385-6, 389, 399, 406, 407, 408, 409, 417, 418, 419, 421, 424, 434-5
Superiority and aggression, 246, 422-3
and hostility, 219
Suspicion, 236, 239, 279, 399
Symbol-formation, 210
Symbolic activity, 209, 210, 211, 212, 273-4, 342, 344, 359, 407-8, 409, 411, 428
Symbolism, 210, 274, 338-9, 340, 357, 358
Symptoms, 295, 296n., 304, 307n

"Taking turns," 222-3, 275, 276, 456
Talion law, 374, 418, 423
Tantrums, 15, 307n., 320, 443, 444, 445
Teething, 302
Thumb-sucking, 9, 10, 211, 320, 321, 322, 368, 369, 434-6
Togetherness, 217, 236, 249, 250, 253, 260, 276, 394
Transference, negative, 410, 413
positive, 409-10, 413
Truamatic experience, 289-90, 296-7n., 300-2, 311, 356n., 359, 372-3

Unconscious : danger of disturbing by unskilled persons, 412-3

Unconscious mental processes, 208, 240, 280, 281, 285n., 403, 406, 424, 426
mental processes and real behaviour, 208, 280, 281, 319-20, 340, 362, 385-6, 406, 407-8, 411, 417, 418, 421, 439
mental processes and social responses, 207-8, 236, 259, 385-7, 389-90
phantasy and real experience, 236, 278, 296-7n., 307n., 312, 315-6, 324-5, 343, 351, 359, 361, 384-7, 389, 405, 407, 418, 419, 421, 422n., 423, 424-5, 440, 442
Understanding, child's need of, 13
Unworthiness, feeling of, 319

Weaning, 431-2
emotional effect of, 292, 302, 325, 359, 430-3
Wish for a baby, boy's, 350-1, 353, 360
child's, 286n.
girl's, 237, 350, 351, 354, 376, 377, 378, 382
Wish to attack father's penis, 357
to possess father's penis in love, 357, 360
to enter mother's body, 363, 364
to rob mother's body, 294-5, 316-7, 353, 357, 378
Wish-self, 228-9n., 285, 286, 287, 288, 289, 290, 291-5, 298-9, 304, 310, 406, 407, 410, 424, 427, 434
and ego (see under Ego)
and super-ego (see under Super-ego)
projection of, (see under Projection)
super-ego and ego, relation between, 294, 372, 408, 409, 417